HARDCASTLE AND McCORMICK

A Complete Viewer's Guide to the Classic Eighties Action Series

HARDCASTLE AND McCORMICK

A Complete Viewer's Guide to the Classic Eighties Action Series

by Deb Ohlin,
Cheri deFonteny,
and Lynn Walker

BearManor Media
2009

Hardcastle and McCormick:
A Complete Viewer's Guide to the Classic Eighties Action Series
© 2009 Deb Ohlin, Cheri deFonteny, and Lynn Walker

For information, address:

BearManor Media
P. O. Box 71426
Albany, GA 31708

bearmanormedia.com

Published in the USA by BearManor Media

ISBN—1-59393-324-X

*This book is respectfully
dedicated to the memory of*

Brian Keith and Larry Hertzog

Acknowledgements

Many people offered their assistance in the production of this book, sharing their expertise, their time, and their memories. We are very grateful and this volume wouldn't be complete without the mention of them: Joan Abend, Brian Bell, Tom Blomquist, Joe Candrella, Stephen Cannell, Dick Clark, Gary Combs, Gil Combs, Bob Del Valle, David E. Dines, Mike Fennel, Suzanne Forgo, Terry Frazee, Patricia Harty, Patrick Hasburgh, Marilyn Hay, Heidi Jaeger, Angela Kaiser, Daniel Hugh Kelly, Karen Kish, Carole Manny, Chris Matheson, Carol Mendelsohn, Mac Patterson, Bob Quast, Patricia Rogler, Mario Sciortino, Steven Sears, Cynthia Shannon, Jim Sharp, Les Sheldon, Ari Starr, Jo Swerling, Thomas Szollosi, Liz Tucker, Scott Velvet, Richard Wiedner, and Susan Zodin.

But, of course, all the mistakes are ours. The most challenging thing in gathering the information offered here was identifying as many as possible of the people who appeared in the series as guest stars. Matching actors' names from the credits with photographs that were sometimes decades newer, and character names that occasionally changed from script to final production, meant that at times we just couldn't be absolutely certain. We apologize in advance for the ones that got away.

About the Authors

Like many people these days, the authors first met online. Though from different time zones and generations, they discovered they had one thing in common: they were all long-term fans of *Hardcastle and McCormick* with an insatiable passion for trivia. From that came this.

Table of Contents

Prologue
September 18, 1983

It was a Sunday, and temperatures in Los Angeles were expected to reach the nineties. Rainstorms were sweeping the Midwest. There was trouble in Lebanon, and Iraq and Iran were still at it. The Congressional Research Service had just released a study that said the U.S. remained dependent on foreign oil. Prices, currently at nearly thirty dollars a barrel, could rise to over one hundred if new problems arose in the Middle East.

The stock market had closed slightly up, with the Dow at just over 1200 on Friday. The Sunday paper featured ads for computers—a cool three thousand dollars (down from $4100) could set you up with an Apple IIe business package; it had 125k RAM with a monitor, printer and two disk drives. You could get a Sony slim-line Betamax video recorder marked down to only $649 and cable ready. Chicago had thirteen cable stations listed; New York City had fifteen.

If you already had a VCR (and only about five percent of American households did), you could have taped your evening's selections and headed out to see a movie. *Risky Business*, the summer's hit, was in first run, and the Stephen King horror film, *Cujo* (featuring a newcomer, Daniel Hugh Kelly) was still appearing in outlying theaters. You might even have cracked open a book; James Michener's *Poland* was at the top of the New York Times hardcover best seller list for fiction.

But if the rains had discouraged you, and you still hadn't popped for that Betamax, ABC was kicking off its new season ahead of the pack that night with the two-hour premier of a program called *Hardcastle and McCormick*. There was a three-quarter page ad in the major market TV listings: "Ex-Judge, Ex-Con, Ex-citement! Together they'll win the war on crime, if they don't kill each other first!" There'd been promo ads on the network all that week. One of them featured two guys leaning against a snappy red car, bantering about the premise of the show. It felt delightfully extemporaneous.

i

It started at nine p.m., Eastern Time, and was up against a rerun of *The Jeffersons* on CBS and a special called *The Best of Everything* on NBC. In Chicago and New York, PBS was offering part six of *The Flame Trees of Thika* against the second hour.

Those who turned to Stephen J. Cannell's latest offering got exactly what the advertising promised. There was action abounding in the two-hour presentation, as much as any regular watcher of Cannell's hit show, *The A-Team*, would have come to expect—six chase sequences and seven spectacular crashes.

There were also the two guys from the promo ads—veteran movie and TV star Brian Keith as the irascible Judge Milton C. Hardcastle, and rising young actor Daniel Hugh Kelly as ex-con "Skid" Mark McCormick. Even the reviewer for the New York Times, after calling the show "a tribute to every car chase opus ever made", was forced to admit that these guys had a chemistry that gave the show "an engaging edge".

And they were working with an interesting premise. One protagonist had sent the other to prison. Both were actually pretty nice guys, but, naturally, there were some hard feelings on the part of the ex-con, who believed he was innocent. Now he was stuck again, and the only one who could help him avenge a wrong was asking for an awful lot in return. Could he swallow his pride, and his anger, long enough to work with someone he thought was a few peanuts short of a full jar? And, worse yet, was he starting to like the guy?

By the end of the first two hours, the answer to both questions was an unqualified yes. As for the viewers, they seemed to like what they saw as well. The premier grabbed a 26.6 Nielsen rating (26.6 percent of all TV-owning households were tuned to it). By comparison, a sustained rating of 25.7 was enough to garner CBS' *Dallas* top ratings honors for the 1983-84 season, and current top series are lucky to achieve overall ratings in the middle teens.

To be blunt, though, we're not discussing a series that ever made it into the record books. However, it did do what many shows fail to do. In 1972, veteran producers William Link and Richard Levinson had floated a made-for-TV movie titled *The Judge and Jake Wyler*. Bette Davis was a judge turned P.I. and Doug McClure was her paroled ex-con assistant. It never sold as a series. In 1973, they tried again. It was rewritten and recast. This time it was called *Partners in Crime* and starred Lee Grant and Lou Antonio. There were still no buyers.

By contrast, *Hardcastle and McCormick* went on to a respectable run of three seasons and sixty-five episodes. Though it never acquired the critical acclaim of Cannell's earlier effort, *The Rockford Files,* the high lunch-box profile of some other Cannell properties, such as *The A-Team*, or the popularity of the later Cannell-Hasburgh collaboration, *21 Jump Street*, it carved out its own niche in popular culture and still, after twenty-five years, has a dedicated following.

So, if you will, return with us now to those thrilling days of yesteryear. If you own them all on DVD, or only half a dozen episodes on battered old VCR tapes, if you always wondered just how many times Milton C. Hardcastle said "Now you're cookin'!" or how many cop cars were toasted in the course of the series—this is the book for you.

Chapter 1
Two Guys and a Vehicle
How it all started and what it became

In the beginning, the vehicle was a script, a hundred and eleven pages from FADE IN to THE END. The first draft is dated February 16, 1983. It was titled *Hardcastle and McCormick* (pilot) by Patrick Hasburgh and Stephen J. Cannell. "Rolling Thunder" was penciled in at some later point, presumably after the five revisions and one addition of scenes, a process that took through late June of that year.

Patrick Hasburgh was a story editor and script writer who had gotten his start on Cannell's series *The Greatest American Hero* and gone on to write episodes for *The A-Team*, which had premiered in January, 1983. He had an idea for a show about a repo man. That evolved into an ex-race car driver. Driving was a major interest of Hasburgh's.

From Cannell came the idea that their unlikely hero would be in the custody of a judge. From Hasburgh there was the enduring notion that it was really a show about fathers and sons. The two of them produced a script which deftly executed the job of introducing two men—one an iconoclast who wore a parrot shirt and shorts under his judicial robes, the other a smart-talking scam artist who could fool anyone except the guy in the parrot shirt.

ABC signed on for the ride. All that was left was to find two actors who could bring the characters to life.

Brian Keith had the right balance of crustiness and concern to be Judge Milton C. Hardcastle. He could play the consummate fifties kind of guy, for whom actions speak louder than words. Hasburgh called him "a pro's pro". Persuading him to take on another series might have been a challenge. Even back in 1966, at the start of his most successful show, *Family Affair*, he was wary of the immense time commitments of series television. It may have helped that some of the main location shoots of this show would be at the Gull's Way Estate in Malibu, only a short walk from his own home in the Malibu Colony.

1

Finding someone to play the role of paroled car thief Mark McCormick was a more daunting task. Robert Carradine lasted a week—a good actor, but the chemistry wasn't there. The two creators met with Robert Blake, who'd worked with Cannell before on the series *Baretta*. Casting him would have involved major changes to the show's dynamics.

Daniel Hugh Kelly, a New York based actor who'd done everything from theater to daytime serial television, was in Northern California shooting his first movie (*Cujo*). During a break, while the dog sequences were being filmed, he headed down to Los Angeles. He remembers receiving a script for "Rolling Thunder" and liking it, but being told that someone was already cast.

When he returned to L.A. in January of 1983, with the intention of staying longer, he got word from his new West Coast talent representative that Cannell wanted to meet with him. He doesn't remember that first reading but according to Hasburgh "he drilled it." There was a further audition for the ABC

Daniel Hugh Kelly and Brian Keith in a publicity shot for the first season.

executives, and then a glass of champagne with Stephen, Patrick, and John Crosby (head of casting at ABC) in John's office.

With the production already having been underway, Kelly knew things might be a little awkward. He'd never met Brian Keith, though he was very familiar with his work. On the first morning, en route to the location, he made a decision, "I knew he wouldn't be pleased at having to re-shoot so many scenes, so I decided, during the long trip up the mountain, that I would quote him some of my favorite lines from a few of his movies. I remembered specifically a line he gave in *Nevada Smith* that all the kids in my neighborhood had liked: 'Don't ever make a threat, but don't ever walk away from one,' and it made us both laugh."

With the ice broken, they went on to shoot their first scene together. It was a chase sequence using a vintage Corvette, with Brian Keith behind the wheel. Again Kelly made a decision. "I decided to totally adlib much of the scene, thinking if they're going to replace people, I may as well have a lot of fun with this and go down with my own take on it. It made Brian somewhat angry, he got out of the car after the director yelled 'cut' and he was a little chagrined, but he quickly got over it. I believe the scene was kept intact in the pilot. Brian recognized what I was doing, and from then on, allowed me to the freedom to do it and would follow along. He was very, very good at it."

From this came a partnership that was clearly recognizable on the screen as rooted in something real. As Kelly put it, Brian Keith "was incredibly creative and very funny. We were adlibbing often, even during the first year."

Chris Matheson, who co-wrote "Never My Love" with Tom Szollosi, re-ferred to one of those changes in the script, this one from Brian Keith, in a scene where McCormick asks Hardcastle if he ever got over the loss of his father: "I forget the response we wrote. But Brian suggested a line that was one hell of a lot better, commenting about losing a loved one. He said about such losses: 'You don't get over it, you get used to it.'"

Kelly contributed his own unscripted moments. In "You Would Cry, Too, If It Happened to You" there was a memorable scene in which McCormick essentially trips over the Coyote and lands sprawling on the front hood. Kelly says, "That was totally adlibbed. It was a deliberate fall on my part (I had warned Brian I was going to do something before they called "action"). I did not know he was going to say, 'Who do you think you are, Errol Flynn?' It was the perfect line, very typical for him and the whole crew was laughing—everyone was on the floor. I dusted myself off and got back into the car. We would do that kind of a thing constantly. The next year—I think it was the second year—they had it in the opening credits. I remember later seeing a [Lawrence] Kasdan movie where one of the lead characters, playing a TV action star, did the same thing as part of the script, and I remember thinking, 'Ahh, old news, been there, done that'."

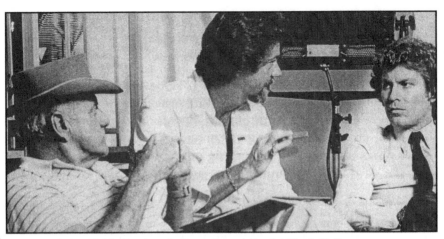

Brian Keith, Stephen J. Cannell, and Daniel Hugh Kelly on set.

Writers write, actors act, and characters come into existence. In the end, if it's properly done, the characters take on lives of their own. We know where they came from (as much as they're willing to tell us), how they got where they are, and where they want to go.

Hasburgh and Cannell created the chemistry Keith and Kelly transmuted to the screen. The results were two very unforgettable characters.

The Judge

Milton C. Hardcastle was raised in Arkansas, near the town of Clarence. He had a brother, Gerald C. Hardcastle, seven years his junior, and a sister, whose age and name are not known. There were also two aunts, May and Zora Hardcastle. The judge's sister had a daughter named Warren who followed in her uncle's footsteps, attending the same law school that he had.

Gerald, a possibly tainted source, described his older brother as having a preternatural interest in the law. His aunts also implied that he was a serious boy. He suffered from asthma and reportedly scheduled his holidays around tours of the circuit court. It wasn't all torts and writs for the young Hardcastle, though. He found time for skinny-dipping in the local swimming hole and at least once leaned on Gerald to produce a term paper for him.

He also played on a championship high school basketball team in Clarence, where he earned the nickname "Hooker" for his ace hook shot. Though his father was a sharecropper, Milton managed to graduate high school in 1939.

It is not known how or why he immigrated to southern California. He attended college there, majoring in history and political science. He continued playing basketball, now with the new nickname "Stumpy", for being the prover-bial immovable object. This time, though, when his team made the champion-ship playoffs their hopes were dashed by an unexpected defeat.

During WWII he served as a captain in the Sixth Army, which saw action in the South Pacific. Prior to his departure from Los Angeles, in 1943 he had a brief but intense relationship with an actress, Jane Bigelow. Due to a miscommunication, he missed his opportunity to propose marriage to her on the day he shipped out.

After his return from service, he found employment with the Los Angeles Police Department. While still a rookie cop, he met his future wife, Nancy. Her first words to him were "Move it or lose it", and his first gift to her was a parking ticket. They overcame that rocky start, however. Milt later proposed to her on Seagull Beach, at Gull's Way, an estate in Malibu that belonged to Nancy's family.

The property was bequeathed to the young couple and they set up housekeeping there. Though there were some uncertain moments in their early marriage, Milt Hardcastle was devoted to his wife, even going toe to toe with a mob boss, in 1953, to avenge an insult to her. About Nancy, we know that she loved gardening, and enjoyed having young people around.

Milton's police career advanced. He joined an elite unit of motorcycle cops colloquially known as the Georgia Street Motors. From there he left to attend law school. Though admittedly older than the average student, Hardcastle participated in student life, visiting a local hangout known as The Brass Rail, and contributing to the Law Review.

Little is known of his early law career except that it must have been successful. He made a spectacularly early transition to a judgeship. While serving on the bench, he was well respected by his former colleagues in the police department, some of whom were heard to call him by the mostly affectionate nickname "Hardcase" Hardcastle.

He and Nancy had a son. Almost nothing is known about this child, except that he died in the Vietnam War. After Nancy's death, in 1973, Judge Hardcastle was left alone, with only his housekeeper, Sarah Wicks, living with him at Gull's Way.

However, it wasn't a life of solitude. He had a wide range of friends, extending from the squad rooms of the LAPD, to street-wise informants like "Sid". He had a devotion to Dixieland jazz, and his own amateur band—The Jazzmasters and Courthouse Racketeers. There were poker buddies of several stripes, and the occasional trip out of town for a judges' convention. Fishing and pick-up games of basketball were also among his abiding interests.

The judge continued forging a respected judicial career that included "landmark decisions on such issues as child pornography". Most of his work on the bench, though, was the routine and the mundane. As Hardcastle himself put it, he mostly passed rulings on "cheap hoods".

On a fateful day in early 1981, one such routine case entered Hardcastle's docket—*The State of California v. Mark McCormick*. In a jury trial that featured the defendant's ex-girlfriend as a witness, Mr. McCormick stood accused of stealing a car which was registered in her name. With her paperwork in order, and his previous record apparently in disarray, the jury found him guilty. Hardcastle sentenced him to two years imprisonment.

All along, since Nancy's death, Hardcastle had been engaging in experiments in practical rehabilitation. It's not known how many ex-cons spent time at Gull's Way, but, as Sarah put it, they'd seen more than their share. The last of these temporary residents was a felon named J.J. Beal who, in the spring of 1983, lasted less than a day in Hardcastle's employment and then stole Hardcastle's vintage Corvette on the way out. The judge personally tracked him to New Orleans, where he was arrested, extradited back to California, and re-imprisoned.

Apparently undiscouraged by this failure, and approaching his own retirement, the judge took an interest in yet another of his former cases. Mark McCormick was released from San Quentin at about the same time that J.J. Beal was remanded to Strykersville Prison. Hardcastle stayed in touch with McCormick's parole officer, John Dalem, and kept tabs on his latest candidate's progress. Mr. McCormick perceived this as harassment.

Through another fateful series of events, Mark McCormick appeared one last time in Hardcastle's courtroom, on Milt's final day as a member of the judiciary. Exercising his own small piece of the "the discretionary power of judges", he enticed McCormick into a deal—the young man escaped trial for yet another felony, and instead was paroled into Hardcastle's custody indefinitely.

Judge Hardcastle liked Dixieland and big band tunes, hated country music (and most rock and roll). He enjoyed liver and onions. Pecan pie was his favorite dessert. He preferred paper files to computers but knew how to use the latter in a pinch. He thought all cars had spark plugs even though they didn't make 'em like they used to. He was a fan of the Celtics *and* the Lakers. He had a more than passing familiarity with the Saturday morning cartoons shows, and a deep respect for the ethos of the Lone Ranger. He loved John Wayne movies and owned an extensive collection of guns.

He didn't mind making a gentlemanly wager once in a while. He could find his way around a wine menu, but preferred beer with his poker games. He was loyal to his friends, sometimes to the point of blindness, but once he realized something wasn't on the up-and-up, he could never look the other way. He was (according to his best friend) a donkey, an Arkansas mule, and a stone cold, hay-bearing jackass. He was definitely all three of those things when it came to doing what was right.

The Ex-Con

Mark McCormick was a man of mystery. We don't even know if he had a middle name. It's possible his family couldn't afford one.

We do know that he was born to a woman named Donna McCormick in New Jersey in 1954. His father (who had more than enough names but apparently couldn't spare one for the birth certificate) was a lounge singer. It seems that Mark's very early years weren't unpleasant. Though he never got that puppy he wanted for Christmas, there were walks on the beach at Atlantic City.

All that abruptly changed on his fifth birthday. His father didn't return home on that day, or any of the days after. Left in dire straits, Donna McCormick moved to Hoboken with her only son. McCormick admitted to at least one period of depression and even contemplated suicide when he was fourteen. A conversation with a radio DJ that he greatly admired gave him some perspective on how much worse off he could be.

He graduated from vocational high with "a doctorate in auto shop". He had a juvenile record, and admitted he'd been stealing cars by the age of seventeen. He had a serious girlfriend, Cyndy Wenzek, but she fell for another guy. If you believe his resume, he worked as a skip tracer and in auto repossession in New Jersey.

He moved to Florida where he had further scrapes with the law in pursuit of a career in auto repossession. Eventually he came west to California, where in the late 1970s, he had a near brush with success in the form of a point lead in the Outlaw Trail dirt track racing series. The final race, and the series championship, went to his friend and competitor, E. J. Corlette. Mark's engine had "blown" when Corlette's handler spiked the tank with sugar.

Somehow, in the years after he came to California, he acquired a felony conviction. He was a familiar face in three state prisons there and admitted to being "a two-time loser".

In 1980 he was involved with a woman named Melinda Marshall. Viewpoints differ as to what happened next. Mark claimed he put the title to his Porsche in Melinda's name only to save money on the insurance. When they broke up, he took the car. She reported it stolen and he was arrested and charged with the theft.

He was convicted by a jury of his peers and sentenced to two years in prison by Judge Hardcastle. The length of the sentence is consistent with a second offense of felony theft in California. He served his term in San Quentin State Prison. During his time there he had a cellmate named Buddy Denton, and another, Teddy Hollins. He was apparently on good terms with both men.

During his incarceration, McCormick "played a lot of baseball". He also joined group therapy, Bible class, the choir, and even the book drive, all in an attempt to "get out of that dump". He was eventually discharged into the parole system in the spring of 1983, as is policy in California, where even those who have served their sentences have a mandatory period of supervision. He did not see eye to eye with his parole officer, but managed to fulfill the requirements of his parole for nearly six months.

On a fine late summer afternoon in 1983, Mark met with his old friend, car designer Flip Johnson. Flip offered him a chance to drive the vehicle he had developed. A day later, Flip was dead—a victim of his business partner, industrialist Martin Cody. Mark's ill-conceived attempt to repossess Flip's design for his daughter, Barb Johnson, landed him back in Hardcastle's courtroom.

There, on the eve of his retirement, Hardcastle offered Mark the chance to avoid returning to prison by joining forces with him in the pursuit of criminals who had taken advantage of the system. Mark turned him down. It was only after the judge added Martin Cody to the top of the list that McCormick reconsidered his position.

It looked to be a match doomed from the start. Mark McCormick was a believer in shortcuts and scams. He hated Dixieland and thought big band music was "hopelessly sterile". He liked country songs and rock and roll. He loathed liver and onions. He missed his racing days, hated doing yard work, and had a whole list of questionable skills that were best practiced quietly while wearing gloves.

He had a bad habit of making book, but mostly broke even. He was astonishingly unlucky with women but never stopped looking for Ms. Right. He didn't know steak tartare from a t-bone, and when he wore a tie he usually got mustard on it. He could also talk his way out of most situations, knew what a reversible error was, and could drive anything that had wheels. He was loyal to a fault, but once he knew something was fishy, no lock, door, fence, or security system could come between him and the truth. He was (according to his best friend) a facile liar. But that was usually a good thing.

The Judge and the Ex-con

Hardcastle installed his new associate in the gatehouse at Gull's Way. After they'd brought Flip Johnson's murderers to justice, Flip's daughter, Barbara, gave Mark the Coyote, her father's prototype car.

In addition to his duties around the estate, which ranged from hedge clipping to painting to truck repair, Mark played Tonto to Hardcastle's Lone Ranger. His approach to chores may have been lackadaisical, but he usually did these other duties diligently. Sometimes it was because the suspects annoyed him ("Man in a Glass House"), sometimes because they intrigued him ("The Black Widow"), and sometimes for no apparent reason at all ("Goin' Nowhere Fast"). He was usually warier than Hardcastle ("Killer B's", "Fat City"), but occasionally it was the judge who was the more suspicious ("Hotshoes").

Hardcastle had said from the start that the partnership would be strictly business. He wasn't looking for a buddy ("Rolling Thunder"), or a substitute for his son ("Man in a Glass House"). He said it would be six months before he trusted McCormick ("Goin' Nowhere Fast").

These were brave words, but not borne out by actions. He quickly learned to tolerate fairly flagrant parole violations ("The Crystal Duck") and was soon heard admitting that "That kid means something to me." ("The Black Widow").

McCormick returned the favor in kind. He offered an element of practical action to the methods of the sometimes hidebound ex-jurist, instructing him in the finer points of breaking and entering ("Man in a Glass House"), liberating him from a Caribbean prison against his will ("Flying Down to Rio"), and demonstrating a thorough understanding of Good Cop/Bad Cop theory ("Mr. Hardcastle Goes to Washington").

At the end of six months, more than mere trust had been achieved. Hardcastle gave up a chance at his life's dream, a seat on the Supreme Court, to hang onto his unusual custodial responsibilities ("Mr. Hardcastle Goes to Washington"). Mark swore, on what he supposed was Hardcastle's watery grave, that he would get the guys who killed him even if he ended up going back to prison for the rest of his life ("The Homecoming—Part 2"). It wasn't just a working partnership; they'd become friends.

A year's time—and Mark's thirtieth birthday—brought new wrinkles to the relationship. McCormick's search for his long-missing father, Sonny Daye, ended far short of his hoped-for dreams of a joyful reunion ("Ties My Father Sold Me"). His attempt to prove that he could get a real job resulted in a near-disastrous encounter with a murderous conman ("You and the Horse You Rode in On").

Hardcastle didn't get off scot-free, either. He learned the perils of fame ("Whatever Happened to Guts?") and spent Christmas in jail after being framed for a murder ("Hate the Picture, Love the Frame"). None of this discouraged him from the policy that "justice begins at home" ("Did You See the One That Got Away?"), though sometimes it began with his eccentric relatives ("It Coulda Been Worse, She Coulda Been a Welder", and "Hardcastle, Hardcastle, Hardcastle, and McCormick").

But despite the setbacks in their personal lives, the duo brought down a steady string of high-profile bad guys. Both mobsters and well-heeled political types fell to the snares of the Lone Ranger and Tonto.

As their second year together progressed, the peril increased. Mark's efforts to reenter the racing world brought him a victory, followed by an encounter with two sociopaths who deprived him of both his winnings and the Coyote, and left him for dead ("You Don't Hear the One That Gets You"). By this point, there was no question that he could lean on Hardcastle—that's what friends are for.

Not long after that, Mark's ill-starred attempt to give the judge a really special gift landed Hardcastle in the hospital, at death's door ("The Birthday Present"). McCormick was left to make a split-second moral decision of the irreversible kind. Not every adventure ended with a bit of light-hearted banter.

In the third year of their partnership, as Mark's parole was drawing to an end, neither man seemed inclined to talk about it. McCormick's continued presence seemed to be a given, whether along for the trip, and the crash ("She Ain't Deep but She Sure Runs Fast"), or off on his own, but ready to ride to the rescue ("The Career Breaker").

He seemed mostly resigned to being a sidekick: "the other guy", the one whose name was always gotten wrong in the news report. Hardcastle, on the other hand, was finally willing to admit that Mark was more than that.

Twice it was the proximity of death that ushered in these confessions ("She Ain't Deep but She Sure Runs Fast" and "Do Not Go Gentle"). Both times Mark was less than receptive. He feigned sleep or distracted the judge with an argument.

Overall though, in their third year together things seemed to be more relaxed, with less ransacking through the files, and more weekend jaunts. Never mind that the jaunts always ended in mayhem ("You're Sixteen, You're Beautiful, and You're His", "The Career Breaker" and "Mirage a Trois").

Through this, there was a feeling that the partnership was moving toward a more equal footing. Occasionally it even took the form of an outright competition ("Duet for Two Wind Instruments"). When Hardcastle had another run at political fame ("Hardcastle for Mayor"), there was no hint that Mark would be left at home, though the judge's campaign advisors saw the ex-con as a liability.

It took an outsider (their new housekeeper, the precognitive Millie Denton) to point out the obvious—that Mark was like a son to Hardcastle ("If You Could See What I See"). Her observation was met with a moment of strained silence from both men.

Of course Mark still had issues with his biological father, which came to a boil when Sonny Daye showed up trying to make amends by offering the deed to a nightclub ("McCormick's Bar and Grill"). The three-way partnership was a good measure of how equal things had become. Even though Hardcastle provided the seed money, it was McCormick's name that ended up over the door.

Sonny might come around once in a while, but the judge seemed to be there for keeps, even if Mark sometimes valued a hot date over his poker commitments ("Poker Night"). In his third year at Gull's Way, Mark fit right in, joking with the players and flirting with Hardcastle's fellow jurist, Mattie Groves, who flirted right back at him. He was far more an insider than his last-minute replacement, an assistant D.A. He was so much a part of the establishment that he knew, beyond a shadow of a doubt, which boot Hardcastle had stashed the rum in.

McCormick complained vociferously that they would go on like that forever, drinking Pinky Fizz and chasing bad guys ("When I Look Back On All the Things"). But of course it couldn't be. Mark's parole was up. An uneasiness had settled on both men, with each suspecting that he was imposing on the other by continuing the arrangement ("Chip Off the Ol' Milt").

There were other secrets being kept. Mark had been making veiled allusions to law school for months, without confessing that he'd actually started attending. Hardcastle had bought a repo business, intending it as a gift for McCormick, and perhaps as a bond that would hold things together a little while longer.

There was no need for such machinations. No path to self-improvement could ever run smoothly for Mark McCormick. It was only a matter of time before his new paralegal job fell prey to his finely-honed forensic curiosity.

And so things came back around to where they had started, under the hoop at Gull's Way, with Hardcastle offering to pay Mark's way through law school if he made twenty-one points first. Not exactly a bet, since Mark had nothing to lose. It wasn't even a long shot, though that's what Mark claimed he had been. This time it looked like a sure thing.

Chapter 2
The Episodes
Casts, summaries, trivia, and quotes

Running three full seasons, with sixty-seven hours of programming, *Hardcastle and McCormick* consisted of a two-hour pilot, sixty-three one-hour episodes, and one two-part episode ("The Homecoming"). Episodes ran roughly forty-eight minutes, including thirty seconds of teasers at the top, and about three to four minutes of opening and closing credits. That left just under forty-five minutes to cover four acts and an epilogue.

Beginning with the fourth regular episode ("The Black Widow") and running through the end of season one, the premise of the series (that retired judge Milton C. Hardcastle was going after two hundred bad guys who walked out of his courtroom on technicalities) was spelled out in an eighteen-second prologue that played between teasers and credits. It was initially accompanied by an establishing shot of a traditional courthouse. In midseason (with "Third Down and Twenty Years to Life"), the visuals in this prologue changed to a scene of Hardcastle, in robes, with Mark, in blue jacket and handcuffs, exiting a different courthouse.

In the trial run of this, Mark was snapping gum, and looking cheerfully insolent. The scene ends with Hardcastle removing the handcuffs. Two episodes later, with "Mr. Hardcastle Goes to Washington", a second version appeared. This time a still-cuffed Mark pulls a cigarette out of his pocket. Hardcastle snatches it away and tosses it down. Mark looks disgruntled. The cuffs get removed. There's a quick slap on the shoulder from Hardcastle, then Mark walks off, smiling cheekily. Of course, it's a mystery as to when any of this was supposed to have happened; it's the wrong clothes and the wrong time of day for "Rolling Thunder", but the prologue did a good job of catching up those who might have come late to the party, and the later variations were far more engaging than the courthouse alone.

Despite the emphasis on the premise, those two hundred unpunished criminals were fairly safe during the run of the show. If they'd kept at it steadily, it would have taken Mark and the judge about nine seasons to hack through the backlog. But though the guys stayed busy, they didn't get down to the file cabinets all that often. Even giving them points for getting *any* information whatsoever from the judge's old records during the course of an investigation, only eighteen of the sixty-five stories had anything to do with Hardcastle's old case files, and not all of those fell under the classification of "the ones who got away". In two episodes ("Third Down and Twenty Years to Life" and "The Game You Learn From Your Father") the judge pursued the truth regarding men he *had* sent to prison. In a third case ("Duet for Two Wind Instruments"), the bad guy went to prison for the wrong crime, as part of a ruse to avoid punishment for a more serious offense.

On the other hand, there were never two guys better at finding trouble than the judge and his stalwart assistant. Every vacation was fraught with danger ("The Homecoming", "She Ain't Deep but She Sure Runs Fast", "The Career Breaker", and "Mirage a Trois"), and even a simple trip to the car repair shop could have serious consequences ("Really Neat Cars and Guys with a Sense of Humor" and "One of the Girls from Accounting"). In addition to occasionally being the targets of vengeance ("Goin' Nowhere Fast" and "The Birthday Present"), random crime was also a major feature in their lives ("There Goes the Neighborhood", "You Don't See the One That Gets You", and "Poker Night").

But mostly it was an uncanny knack for getting involved that was the duo's downfall. Old friends in need came to McCormick with alarming regularity ("Crystal Duck", "Never My Love", "The Yankee Clipper", and "Strangle Hold") and neither guy could turn down a woman in distress, major or minor ("One of the Girls From Accounting", "Hate the Picture, Love the Frame", "You Don't Hear the One That Gets You"). Above all, they were hopelessly drawn to seeking out wrongs and righting them.

Throughout the series run, action, drama, and humor were on hand in varying proportions. The show's structure was usually that of an open mystery—one in which we know who committed (or intends to commit) the crime. Sometimes even our intrepid heroes knew right from the start, and it was only a matter of catching the bad guys in the act, or acquiring the evidence needed to get a conviction. Occasionally there was a relatively closed mystery ("Something's Going On On This Train", and to some degree "Duet for Two Wind Instruments") or an additional turncoat good guy in addition to the known villain.

Epilogues were most often humorous, and were frequently used to normalize the situation. "If You Could See What I See" is the classic example. Occasionally these closing scenes went for a touch of the absurd ("The Homecoming" and "She Ain't Deep but She Sure Runs Fast") or the whimsical ("Hate the Picture, Love the Frame" and "In the Eye of the Beholder"). Epilogues sometimes expanded on or emphasized the relationship between the two characters ("Mr. Hardcastle goes to Washington" and "The Career Breaker").

A few of the epilogues were pensive. "Ties My Father Sold Me" and "Strangle Hold" were shaded that way, both being used to show that McCormick's checkered past had its darker moments. But the archetypical example of a more serious coda is the concluding scene of "The Birthday Present". It was an unexpected exploration of the cost of even a justifiable homicide, and one of the dramatic high-water marks of the series.

In all three seasons, the closing credits played over reprises of scenes from the episode. Occasionally, especially in the later episodes, the scenes were so short as to be practically freeze-frames. Sometimes they were extended (or even completely different) from what had appeared in the episode. "Do Not Go Gentle" and "Conventional Warfare" are prime examples. Two episodes ended with still shots only ("In the Eye of the Beholder" and the series finale, "Chip Off the Ol' Milt"). Both those episodes broke the mold in other ways as well.

With that framework in mind, here is a more detailed look at each of the sixty-five episodes, with overviews of the casts, detailed summaries of the plots, context, trivia, and a selection of some of our favorite quotes.

Rolling Thunder – premiered September 18, 1983 (Pilot)

Written by	Patrick Hasburgh and Stephen J. Cannell
Directed by	Roger Young
Second unit director	M. James Arnett

Cast

Mary Jackson	Sarah Wicks
Faye Grant	Barbara Johnson
John Saxon	Martin Cody
Ed Lauter	Rick Vetromile
Michael Swan	John Dalem
Spencer Milligan	Johnny "Flip" Johnson
Harry Caesar	Sid the Bailiff
William Bryant	
James Canning	Steve Miller
Gerry Gibson	Willard Tolchin, Flip's lawyer
Rick Fitts	Tom Riley
Roy Jensen	
Kurt Grayson	

Cast Notes

Mary Jackson was 72 years old when she was cast as Hardcastle's indomitable and loyal housekeeper, Sarah Wicks. She began her career in the 1930s in summer stock. Her television appearances spanned five decades, beginning with the Philco Theater in 1952, but she is probably best remembered for her portrayal of Miss Emily Baldwin, on the long-running series *The Waltons*.

Faye Grant, who portrayed Barbara Johnson, came to this series from her previous role as Rhonda Blake on Cannell's *Greatest American Hero.* She also had a continuing part in the TV series *V.*

John Saxon was born Carmine Orrico in Brooklyn. He's worked widely and steadily in both TV and movie roles from the 1960s on. One of his most famous films is *Enter the Dragon,* in which he actually had top billing over Bruce Lee.

Michael Swan appeared as hardnosed parole officer John Dalem. He'd had roles in three other Cannell productions: *The Rockford Files, The A-Team,* and *Riptide,* and he appeared in the second season *Hardcastle and McCormick* episode "Ties My Father Sold Me".

Spencer Milligan, who (as Flip Johnson) was the first of many victims of roadway mayhem on this series, also had the role of Ranger Rick Marshall in the 1974 camp classic, *Land of the Lost.*

The Details

The scene opens at a beachside café in southern California. Mark McCormick and his old friend, Johnny "Flip" Johnson, are studying the plans of Flip's new car design, the Coyote. He's building it for Cody Automotive Industries and he wants Mark to race it.

McCormick is grateful. His dirt track racing career was cut short by a two-year prison sentence for auto theft. He's been out of San Quentin for less than six months.

In the middle of this happy reunion, Mark realizes he's late for a five o'clock meeting with his parole officer, John Dalem. Even with Johnson offering him a fast ride, he'll never make it on time and may have his parole revoked. But McCormick is resourceful. With a tape recorder he borrows from Flip, a "time at the tone" recording, and the aid of Dalem's charming secretary, he scams his parole officer into believing he's not late.

In the hallway outside Dalem's office, McCormick encounters Milton C. Hardcastle, the judge who sentenced him to prison. Mark angrily tells him to back off.

That night, Flip Johnson and his lawyer are summoned to an after-hours meeting with Martin Cody, head of Cody Industries. On the way there, two of Cody's minions run Johnson's car off the road, killing both men.

Mark gets the news the next morning while running practice laps at the track. He's devastated.

Johnson was more than his entry back into racing; he was also a close friend. At the funeral, he comforts Johnson's daughter, Barbara, who angrily confronts Martin Cody.

Mark and Barbara adjourn to the racetrack. She tells him that Cody had her father murdered in order to take control of the Coyote design. She asks Mark to get the prototype car back from Cody. Mark hesitates; if he's caught, he'll go back inside for a long time. He finally agrees.

He stages a late-night break-in at the Cody facility. He looks like he knows what he's doing and quickly locates the Coyote, but a high-speed chase ensues. When a pursuing cop car crashes, McCormick stops to help the driver. He finally makes his escape.

He is arrested the following morning. The officer he aided got a good look at him and was able to identify him. While he's being taken into custody, Mark's main concern is that he not get Judge Hardcastle again.

The fates aren't kind. Though Hardcastle is due to retire that Friday (he's already had his party and been given an honorary gold shield by his devoted friends in the LAPD) Mark lands in his courtroom. Things start badly and go downhill from there. Hardcastle hauls him back into his chambers. Mark vents; we hear the story of his first conviction—that he claims the car was his and was only put in his girlfriend's name for insurance purposes. Hardcastle didn't buy that defense the first time. For him, the law is the law.

But now he has a different offer for McCormick. He plans to track down two hundred bad guys who got off on technicalities in his courtroom. It's going to be his retirement project and he's looking for a right-hand man to help out. All Mark has to do is make restitution to Cody—the Coyote must go back. Mark says no, vehemently. He tells Hardcastle that Cody is a murderer.

Later that night, after Mark is back in his cell, Hardcastle confronts him again. He's dug up some information on Cody that seems to confirm Mark's suspicions that the man uses murder as a business tool. This time the offer is two hundred and one cases, with Flip's death as number one. He's made Mark an offer he can't refuse.

After a midnight release from the lock-up, a trip home in Hardcastle's ancient truck, his first glimpse of the man's estate, Gull's Way (it belonged to his deceased wife's family), and a meeting with his prickly but devoted housekeeper, Sarah—Mark finally gets to bed in the gatehouse. Only a few minutes pass before he's up again. Hardcastle shoots baskets every night and the hoop is right outside McCormick's new bedroom window.

If you can't beat 'em, join 'em. Mark and the judge play a rough and tumble game of basketball, and we see the beginnings of grudging respect.

It's a very late night, and the morning comes early. Cody sends two men to kidnap McCormick. He needs the car back quickly—there's an important showing for potential investors scheduled in Las Vegas. Hardcastle interrupts the abduction with a shotgun blast. After a brawl in the gatehouse, the kidnappers flee with Mark and the judge in pursuit.

With the small fish under arrest, they go after the big one. Mark reluctantly summons Barbara and the Coyote. They tow it to Las Vegas, where McCormick brazenly shows it to Cody's less than stalwart henchman, Rick Vetromile.

Under Hardcastle's supervision, Mark scams Vetromile *and* Cody, getting them to turn on each other. When the dust settles, Cody is under arrest and the Coyote is restored to Flip's daughter. She promptly gives it to McCormick. She says her father would have wanted him to have it.

But it's Friday afternoon again, and Mark is due in Los Angeles for another meeting with his parole officer at five p.m. sharp. He's got only three hours to make the Las Vegas to L.A. run.

Time to see what the Coyote can do.

The Context

Drama is created through conflict, and for a lighthearted action show, this one has a whole lot of conflict at its core. The writers spent a great deal of effort laying the foundation of the two characters. We can see they're likeable guys, though both are strong-minded. But at the bottom of it, one of them sent the other to prison for two years and it's an unstated fact that they can't *both* be right about what happened. Can Mark be more than a grudging servant to a person he holds responsible for ruining his life? Can Hardcastle admit that there might be some gray areas in the law? Are they going to get to be buddies, against their strongest instincts? By the end of the first episode, we're sure hoping so.

The Trivia

In the insert scene as Mark is hurrying to his parole meeting, we see he's wearing a digital watch. So what's the deal with thinking it's earlier than it is because his watch "stopped"?

The painting that takes the shotgun blast in the gatehouse is Pablo Picasso's *Petit Pierrot avec Fleurs* (a print, we hope).

To make the trip from Las Vegas to Los Angeles in three hours requires an average speed of just over ninety miles an hour.

Four police vehicles were crashed in the pilot—a harbinger for the nineteen total cop cars toasted in the three year run (with occasional repeats of more spectacular crashes).

Memorable Quotes

Hardcastle: Now don't get me wrong, McCormick. I'm not looking for us to be buddies. I just figure it takes one to catch one, and the research I did on you tells me you're my best candidate.

McCormick: And what if I say no?

Hardcastle: Then I put you back inside.

McCormick: See you in the morning, Hardcastle. (walking away)

Hardcastle: McCormick? You play…fairly decent basketball. (tosses ball to him)

McCormick: (smiling) Well, we can file that under who gives a damn, right? I'm taking this in with me. I don't wanna play anymore. Go to bed.

Man in a Glass House – premiered September 25, 1983

Written by	Stephen J. Cannell
Directed by	Guy Magar
Second unit director	Gary Combs

Cast

Mary Jackson	Sarah Wicks
Robert Hooks	Lieutenant Kelly Carlton
John Marley	Joseph Cadillac
Lance Hendriksen	Deseau
Frank Campanella	Nathaniel Reems
Pepper Martin	Davey
Len Lesser	Sammy Allo
Michael Hawkins	Father Atias

Kathryn Harlan	Bookstore Clerk
Chris Capen	Motorcycle Cop
Glen Morshower	Officer McAdams
Don Galliani	Louis Taggart
Tony O'Neill	Don
Mick Eldredge	Murphy
John Otrin	Officer Peters
Ronald Meszaros	Carl
Monica Romig	Little Girl
Eric D. Wallace	Keeney

Cast Notes

John Marley, veteran character actor, had over 150 movie and television credits. Most memorably he was the movie producer who woke up next to a horse's head in *The Godfather*. He was 76 when he appeared in this episode. He died in 1984.

Lance Hendriksen, the ruthless hit man Deseau, appeared in two episodes of *Hardcastle and McCormick*. He was also Josh Fulton in "Never My Love". He guest-starred on *The A-Team* and *Riptide*. He's perhaps best known as Frank Black in the series *Millenium*.

Robert Hooks was the first of Hardcastle's helpful cop-friends and semi-official departmental liaisons. Curiously, he even gets called "Frank" once in the script. Maybe even the Judge had trouble keeping all of his lieutenant buddies straight.

Frank Campanella played mobster Nathaniel Reems. Here's another familiar character actor. He had multiple roles in *The Rockford Files*. He got his start in television as Mook the Moon Man in the *Captain Video* series.

The Details

The story opens in the attractive greenhouse of an upscale California home. A distinguished, gray-haired man, Joe Cadillac, is tending his orchids. Davey (his factotum and bodyguard) enters, telling him it's time to go. They're off in, naturally, a gray Cadillac. Louis Taggart and his fellow mob minions intercept the Caddy, informing Joe he has an appointment. Taggart shoves a copy of a book at Cadillac. His picture is on the cover and it is titled *Without Sin*. Louie's obviously not happy.

In a bookstore Hardcastle picks up a copy of the same book, studies it for a moment, and summons Lieutenant Carlton. The blurb reads, "One man's struggle to achieve the American Dream…a heartwarming journey." The judge grumbles that they left out the stop at San Quentin. He finds there is an extensive listing after his name in the index, even his own chapter: "Black Hat on the Bench—Milton C. Hardcastle, Man Without Honor." Cadillac is no kinder in his description of the police.

Both men emerge from the bookstore, noses in their copies. They part ways, not even looking up.

The judge continues reading as he drives. Just as he discovers he's been called "an unprincipled liar who charges blindly into anything in his path" he rear-ends a police cruiser. Officer Peters recognizes him and tries to let him off, but Hardcastle insists on being written a ticket.

At the estate, McCormick indolently clips a shrub while lying

on the lawn, shirtless and with a glass of iced tea. He jumps up at the approach of the squad car. Seeing Hardcastle climbing out of the passenger side, he asks the officer what trouble the judge is in now. Hardcastle is not amused. He stomps into the house.

In the study, he's on the phone telling his lawyer he intends to sue Cadillac for libel. Mark walks in and picks up the book. He reads aloud from it as the judge hangs up. McCormick is enjoying the heck out of it until he discovers that the author is a powerful ex-mobster and Hardcastle intends to go after him. The man's file is already in the pile on his desk. Mark tries to demur. He takes a sudden interest in his unfinished chores, but Hardcastle's mind is made up. He figures Cadillac must be in possession of some good dirt on his fellow mobsters, or he wouldn't have felt safe writing about their criminal activities. Hardcastle is going after that evidence.

In an abandoned building in a remote location, Cadillac talks with fellow mobsters Nate Reems and Sammy Allo. They're angry, but Cadillac tells them if they try anything, he'll make sure the evidence he has on them goes straight to

the authorities. He departs, unmolested. A figure steps in through another doorway. It's Deseau. He looks cold and ruthless. He accepts his assignment: get the evidence and kill Cadillac.

At the estate, the judge and Mark head to the garage. Mark is told to go to Cadillac's neighborhood, observe his home, and take notes on who comes and goes. Hardcastle will be at Carlton's office. He tells Mark to call 911 if anything interesting happens. Mark climbs into the Coyote, and Hardcastle gets into the Corvette. Pulling out turns into an impromptu road race. Mark runs Hardcastle into the bushes.

Back in the greenhouse, Cadillac and Davey are uncovering boxes, intending to move the evidence to a safer location. Cadillac makes a quick phone call to a priest, Father Atia, who calls him "Pop". He tells his son there's some trouble and he may have to drop out of sight for a while.

Meanwhile, Mark parks on the street nearby. The Coyote immediately attracts a small swarm of neighborhood kids. He observes Davey carrying boxes out. Mark asks the kids where he can find a phone. He's directed to the neighbor's back yard where there's a poolside "porta-phone" and also a Doberman. Phone in hand and dog at his heels, Mark scales the fence. He tries repeatedly to call 911. He's put on hold and is now too far from the base unit to be heard. He gives up and takes off after the departing sedan.

He finally stops at a pay phone. Another crowd gathers. Again he's put on hold for 911. He attracts a cop's attention. The report is radioed in and the chase begins in earnest. Hardcastle and Carlton join in. Cadillac's car is run to ground, but the man knows his rights. Hardcastle can only find a slightly improbable cause for opening the trunk—Davey's gun permit expired a week earlier. Rather than risk losing all the evidence because of an illegal search, the car is sent to the police impound with its trunk still locked, until a proper ruling can be made.

Outside a small stucco church, Deseau and his accomplice snatch the unsuspecting Father Atia.

Back in the squad room of Carlton's police station, many cops are standing around, most with copies of Cadillac's book. Officer McAdams reads a vividly negative passage about a drunken Hardcastle. The man himself enters, along with Mark. McAdams reads on, unaware, until the judge is standing over him. Mark gets a gibe in, but one of the other officers thanks Hardcastle for being "the best damn judge in L.A. for thirty years". Mark looks mildly peeved when the accolade ends with a round of applause and a standing ovation.

Milt and Mark adjourn to Carlton's office where they learn that the ruling will come from Judge Hightower, a man who is both constitutionally indecisive *and* has tickets for an opera that evening. Hardcastle says it will take at least until morning.

On the way home, Mark asks him about one of the stories from the book. Hardcastle admits he duked it out with Cadillac back in 1953 in a park, after the man called him a liar and insulted his wife. He also admits some grudging respect for Cadillac—the man fought his own fight, fair and square. Mark wants to know who won. The judge says nobody wins something like that but where he came from, a man has to stand up for himself.

Cadillac and Davey are waiting for them, unarmed, at the Gull's Way gate. Cadillac wants to talk. Hardcastle lets them in. Sarah meets them on the front porch and lambastes Cadillac for what he wrote. Even Mark jumps in, insulting Davey and telling him to stay outside. He follows the other two men into the study and when

Cadillac objects, Hardcastle says, "He works with me; you can say anything in front of him that you'd say to me."

Cadillac asks for help. He reminds Hardcastle about his son who died in Vietnam. This is obviously news to Mark. Then Cadillac tells them both about his own son, how he shielded him, kept his existence secret, and that he is a priest. He tells them about the kidnapping, and that he must have the evidence from the trunk of the sedan by six a.m., or his son will die. He offers to turn himself in.

Hardcastle promises nothing except that he'll think about it. Cadillac leaves. Mark asks why the judge never mentioned having had a son. Hardcastle says he doesn't need sympathy and Mark isn't a substitute. Then he sends him out so he can think.

That night, at the back of the house, Hardcastle creeps down the steps. He opens the door to the darkened garage and is about to get into the Corvette when he is startled by McCormick's greeting. The lights come on and we see the younger man reclining on the Coyote. The judge makes excuses for being in the garage, but it's apparent that he was planning a little "midnight raid on the police impound". Mark offers his services and expertise.

It's midnight at the impound. Mark explains about guard dogs, and the two go over the fence. They find Cadillac's Cadillac. Hardcastle grouses about Mark still owning a set of lock picks. The trunk lock is hastily picked as the guard dogs charge over. The food Mark brought doesn't distract them and the two men hastily clamber into the Caddy. Mark hotwires it and then rams it up against the fence. They evade the dogs and escape with the boxes.

Early the next morning, the guys show up with the goods at Cadillac's house. The mobster is pleased but surprised. He asks how Hardcastle got the evidence. Mark tells all, in fulsome detail, emphasizing the felonious aspects of the night's escapade, much to the judge's displeasure. Hardcastle is reluctant to risk the evidence. Cadillac offers his word that he will turn himself in, even if the records are lost. The judge accepts that over Mark's objections. The deal with Deseau is set up.

At Indian Dunes, Cadillac, backed by Davey, confronts Deseau. The exchange is made with Hardcastle riding in on a dirt bike to present the papers. Deseau calls in his reinforcements, intending to kill all the witnesses. Hardcastle also has police backup. Deseau, seeing that he's been outmaneuvered, attempts to escape with the evidence in a Trans Am. Hardcastle and McCormick give chase. They corner Deseau and his men and, with Cadillac's assistance, take them down. Mark points out that Deseau's car is going up in smoke. They rescue the evidence in the nick of time.

In the epilogue, Mark and the judge are in the hallway outside Carlton's office, still in basic burglary black. Mark wants to know what they're doing there. Hardcastle informs him he intends to confess to the impound break-in. Mark is appalled. They argue, but Hardcastle is intent on going in, with or without McCormick. Mark is left standing in the hallway, ranting. His determination lasts for about ten seconds and ends with a heartfelt "*dammit*" before he heads into Carlton's office. He interrupts Hardcastle confessing to having picked the lock on the trunk and says he was the one who did it.

To both men's surprise, and Mark's relief, Carlton merely smiles and tells them to go home and get some sleep. Judge Hightower skipped the opera and was unusually decisive. The search warrant for Cadillac's trunk was issued the previous evening and therefore Hardcastle, still an officer of the court, had the right to search the vehicle. Going over the fence in order to get to it is chalked up to eccentricity. Though Hardcastle is still determined to accept responsibility (after all, it's the intent that counts), a vastly relieved McCormick drags him out of the office.

The Context

Without Sin, the title of the mobster's memoirs, seems a little cheeky considering that the subtitle reads: "Joe Cadillac's rise from immigrant to undisputed Czar of Crime", but when taken with the title of the episode, it's obviously a reference to John 8:7—"He who is without sin among you, let him be the first to throw a stone." Joe Cadillac can't really exonerate himself— he's guilty as sin—but he tries to spread the guilt around, even onto the criminal justice system. He's even hoping that his son, the priest, will somehow offset his lifetime of criminal behavior. It's only when that one good thing in his life is threatened that Cadillac is willing to take some responsibility for what he's done. He offers to turn himself in if it will keep his son from being killed.

The flip side of this attitude is Hardcastle, the ultimate advocate of personal responsibility. Having committed a burglary for the most noble of motives, he voluntarily confesses, and Mark, who is initially baffled, ends up following his lead.

The Trivia

In the script, Mark mentions that Cadillac used to "run the Mafia". This is changed to "the mob" in production. A reference by Cadillac to Jimmy Hoffa's death is changed to his "disappearance".

Oh, those eighties references—Mark goes hunting for the porta-phone to try to notify Hardcastle that Cadillac is on the move. Hardcastle had to tell him to call 911 (and even takes a moment to be sure he knew what 911 was for) in the previous scene. That number was set aside in the U.S. for contacting emergency services in 1968, but municipalities did not rush to convert to it. The running gag of Mark being put on hold is not so absurd. In 1996 in Los Angeles it was reported that about 180,000 calls went unanswered because of system crowding.

In the script, Hardcastle's son's death is originally placed in Korea and his wife's name is given as Betty.

Memorable Quotes

McCormick: I never knew you had a son.
Hardcastle: Lot about me you don't know, kid.
McCormick: Why didn't you tell me?
Hardcastle: My son's in my memory. I don't need sympathy from you to sweeten it up. You're not a substitute, if that's what you're thinking.

Hardcastle: (to Carlton) I picked the lock, the files were in the back of the car.
McCormick: (interrupting) He couldn't pick the lock on a motel door in Iowa. I picked the lock.
Hardcastle: There, now doesn't that feel good?
McCormick: (vehemently) No, it feels dumb.

The Crystal Duck – premiered October 2, 1983

Written by	Stephen Katz
Directed by	Bruce Kessler
Second unit director	Gary Combs

Cast

Joe Pantoliano	Teddy Hollins
Nicolas Coster	Thomas Quinlan
Allan Rich	Judge Gault
Herman Poppe	Mallory
Ji-Tu Cumbuka	Giles

Cast Notes

Joe Pantoliano had been working for a full decade before he appeared in *Hardcastle and McCormick*, though, arguably, his career was just taking off in 1983. At the time, he was likely most widely known as "Guido, the killer pimp" from the movie *Risky Business*, and had also just appeared in *Eddie and the Cruisers*. Since then, he has managed to work consistently in both film and television, with roles in such films as *Midnight Run*, *The Fugitive*, and *The Matrix*, as well as recurring roles on such series as *The Fanelli Boys*, *The Handler*, and *The Sopranos*.

Nicolas Coster is commonly known for his work in daytime television, including *The Secret Storm*, *Another World*, and *Santa Barbara*. He also had guest roles in three other Cannell productions: *The Rockford Files*, *Tenspeed and Brown Shoe*, and *Silk Stalkings*. And, along with Brian Keith, he also had a role in the television movie, *The Court-Martial of George Armstrong Custer*.

Allan Rich appeared in the television movie, *Chicago Story*, which went on to become a series starring Daniel Hugh Kelly. He and Brian Keith both appeared in the television movie *The Seekers*.

Robert Hooks, who appeared in the previous episode, "Man in a Glass House", as Lieutenant Kelly Carlton, also appeared in the opening scene in this episode, though he was uncredited.

The Details

The episode begins with a game of basketball in the park, though not one-on-one. Hardcastle, with a team in LAPD t-shirts—including Lieutenant Carlton—is taking on McCormick and a group of nameless friends not seen before or since. The judge cries foul to get the ball back, manhandles McCormick, then simply overrules Mark's objections and declares that the "good guys win", and offers to drive him home.

Meanwhile, parole officer Thomas Quinlan is waxing philosophic about the state of the modern world with his newest parolee, Teddy Hollins. Teddy's not sure

why Quinlan called him in on a weekend, but he assures the P.O. that he's a model citizen. Unfortunately, Quinlan knows Hollins has recently been associating with a convicted felon named Delgado, and he's not interested in hearing that it was a chance encounter at a diner. He uses that information as a lead-in to explain about a "special program" to help out in these kinds of situations, and sends Teddy downstairs to meet with some friends for the details.

Outside, Quinlan's friends are clear: a thousand dollars a week—cash or merchandise—and Teddy can stay out of prison. Teddy doesn't want to play along, but these guys are ex-cons, too, and of a more violent variety. A patrolling squad car shows up in time to save Hollins from any permanent damage, but he's not about to tell the cops what really went down. He claims it was a robbery and sends the officer off after the bad guys, then steals a convenient car to make his own getaway.

Back at the park, Mark and Milt are having a varied conversation. They're still bickering over the basketball game; Hardcastle tells McCormick he hears Mark's been eating enough for two people lately, and then they segue into footprints in the tomatoes. The judge is worried someone's been on the property. Mark seems hesitant, then explains that he's been weeding the garden. But even so, Hardcastle thinks they ought to get some guard dogs, just in case. McCormick's got a lot of reasons why that isn't a good idea—including a newly discovered allergy for Sarah.

Back at the estate, Hardcastle's shooting solo baskets as Teddy Hollins silently climbs the gate, sneaks past him toward the gatehouse, pulls a ladder from the bushes, and stealthily climbs through the window. Half-dressed, McCormick is frantically searching his bedroom. He isn't surprised to see Hollins enter through the open window; he is surprised to see the other man wearing the shoes he's looking for. As he finishes dressing, Mark tells Teddy that he's got to find another place to stay before they both end up in trouble: ex-cellmates shouldn't be rooming together. Hollins assures Mark he's working on it, except that he had to call in sick for his first day at work because he was going to be late. Mark gives Teddy his own watch and tells him not to be late any more.

As they talk about Teddy's latest grand idea—a pizzeria/Laundromat—they also discuss the relative sanity of an ex-convict living with a retired judge. McCormick offers a brief defense of Hardcastle, but soon finds himself switching to protecting the judge's belongings. Teddy's a high energy guy, and he's moving through the living room, meddling with everything, including an autographed basketball and an expensive crystal duck. Mark tells him to leave it all alone because everything is "worth a fortune".

Suddenly, with an uncharacteristic knock, Hardcastle arrives at the gatehouse, and Mark sends Teddy upstairs to hide under the bed. Milt wants McCormick to get himself in gear so they can get moving to a much anticipated poker game, and, in his excitement, he goes into great detail about where they'll be playing and with whom.

The poker game is at the Beverly Hills home of Judge Gault. Mark isn't fitting in too well with the uptight folks around the table—maybe because he's winning—and none of them are too happy that Hardcastle brought him along. But the party is soon broken up when a burglar smashes through the door demanding all their money and jewelry. Mark stares in stunned silence as he recognizes the watch on the masked gunman.

As soon as the intruder exits, Hardcastle grabs McCormick and charges out, giving chase in the Coyote. McCormick does his best to appear he's doing his best, while Hardcastle, in typical no-holds-barred mode, yells at him to pick up the pace. The thief finally eludes them with the help of an ill-timed semi truck backing up from a loading dock. The Coyote screeches to a stop with only inches to spare, and neither McCormick nor Hardcastle is pleased.

Returning to Gull's Way, Hardcastle complains that not only did the guy steal his badge, but he also cost him the best hand of cards he'd had all day. Mark tells him the full house wouldn't have been good enough; Judge Gault's was better. Hardcastle puts the pieces together, and after Mark admits he cheated "a little" at the cards, wants to know if he was also cheating during the recent chase. Mark talks fast, but it's clear his heart isn't really in keeping the secret. He finally confesses that he knows the intruder, and tells the judge that Teddy's been staying in the gatehouse. Mark tries to keep things in perspective; at least Hollins didn't take the Rubens. Just then, Sarah screams from across the lawn. He took the Rubens. He also took the duck, the autographed basketball, and just about everything else. After examining the empty gatehouse, the guys go see Teddy's parole officer.

At the Department of Corrections, Hardcastle tells McCormick that he looks like an accessory, at least on paper. Mark proclaims his innocence, but that's what they all say. Inside, Quinlan welcomes the judge warmly, but Hardcastle is all business. Quinlan says Hollins missed his last appointment. Mark spots a familiar crystal duck on Quinlan's desk. He takes the judge into the outer office and points out the unlikely coincidence. Mark insists that he knows Teddy. He's a flake, but he's still a friend. Something isn't right.

Meanwhile, in his private office, Quinlan is getting worried. He calls his goons and sends them after Hollins.

Arriving at Teddy's former address, Milt and Mark run into Quinlan's men. The goons pull guns. The judge and Mark dive for cover. Hardcastle returns fire, but the bad guys jump into a waiting car and tear off. One of their bullets has hit the tire of the Corvette.

Responding to "shots fired", a patrol car screams up, at first mistaking the gun-waving Hardcastle for the problem. Once they recognize him, the cops issue the APB he's requesting. Then they break the bad news. They've just received an arrest bulletin on McCormick. It's a robbery complaint, with the warrant issued by Judge Gault. Mark is taken into custody.

Hardcastle visits Gault again. He tries to convince his colleague to release McCormick, but Gault reminds him that Mark was already in Hardcastle's custody. Gault got the report on Hollins' fingerprints from the lab. He's certain that the two were in cahoots on the robbery. Hardcastle has until the arraignment to prove to him that McCormick wasn't involved.

In jail, Mark mingles with the other offenders, asking around about Quinlan. Finally, after a near disastrous run-in with an inmate named Waldo, he finds someone who tells him about Quinlan's off-the-books business with his parolees.

Back at Gull's Way, Hardcastle and Sarah are discussing McCormick when an alarm is triggered. Hardcastle heads for the gatehouse with a shotgun and finds Teddy sneaking around inside. After introductions, Milt tells him that McCormick's locked up on the robbery beef. Hollins is willing to do whatever it takes to get Mark out of jail, but won't admit to any problem with Quinlan.

The next day, McCormick returns home vindicated. He convinces Teddy that he can trust Hardcastle to get Quinlan. The first step in the plan is for Teddy to call his parole officer threatening to go to the papers and the authorities if he doesn't get "traveling money".

Quinlan sets up a meet at an old airport hangar. Teddy wears a wire with the good guys listening in—first to his fanciful ramblings, and then to the business with the parole officer and his goons. Quinlan tells Teddy he's become a complication. With Hollins in immediate jeopardy, the good guys converge on the hangar.

Teddy is rescued and Quinlan's goons are captured, but Quinlan jumps into his car and escapes onto the runway with the Coyote in pursuit. After a close call with a small aircraft and a leap over a dirt barricade, the Coyote lands in front of Quinlan's car. He's forced off course and onto another mound of dirt. His car flies through the air, rolls, and comes to a stop upside down.

Quinlan, unhurt, climbs out and flees into an old bus graveyard. Mark and Milt continue the chase on foot, splitting up. Quinlan gets the drop on McCormick, holding him at gunpoint. Hardcastle, with a well-aimed shot knocks the gun out of his hand. Mark follows up with a one-two punch and Quinlan's down for the count.

In the epilogue, out by the pool Milt is relaxing and Mark is skimming. Teddy's gone to a job interview in the judge's Corvette. McCormick says such kindness is a serious risk to the Hardcastle reputation, but Hollins returns, and the car is none the worse for wear. He's brought a basketball, and takes a moment to scribble a signature across it before he heads to the pool. The three discuss his new career as a busboy, then Teddy tosses the ball across the patio to Hardcastle. The judge is momentarily grateful—until he reads the inscription. Teddy, it seems, is not a basketball fan, and has confused Wilt Chamberlain with Richard.

The Context

As we've seen before, McCormick is very loyal guy. Here we have an examination of that loyalty in conflict. Hollins is his friend, and Hardcastle isn't supposed to be. Teddy reminds Mark that "it's us against them, and Hardcastle's a 'them'". But McCormick has his own set of principles, and he holds true to them. It's one thing to let an ex-cellmate stay in the gatehouse, against all conditions of parole, but it's quite another to conceal knowledge of real wrongdoing from Hardcastle.

Yet even though he sides with Hardcastle on that issue, he's still not willing to simply throw Teddy to the wolves. His belief in his friend is unwavering. He's certain there must be a good reason why Hollins apparently betrayed him.

This is also the first time we see the bad guy coming from the system that Hardcastle is devoted to. It certainly won't be the last.

The Trivia

When Teddy is in the gatehouse, he throws the crystal duck into the air, with McCormick rushing to catch it and prevent its destruction. This is almost certainly a tip of the hat to Pantoliano's film, *Risky Business*, which made much ado about keeping a crystal egg intact.

When Mark and Milt rush out of Gault's garage to chase after Teddy, the door he's just crashed through is whole and functional.

Maybe there's a hierarchy in the parole department, but Quinlan's office was much more upscale than John Dalem's.

Memorable Quotes

  McCormick: I got a crazy man staying with me.
  Hollins: Oh yeah?
  McCormick: You're a crazy man.
  Hollins: Well, I ain't the one that's living with no judge.
  McCormick: Hey, now wait a minute now; it's not too bad, really. Hardcastle's all right. He is. For a donkey, he's all right.

Hardcastle: Now why, why would he do this to me? I don't even know him.

McCormick: Well, it mighta been because I called you a donkey.

Hardcastle: You did?

McCormick: Yeah.

Hardcastle: Well, I thought we were gettin' along real good here.

McCormick: Well, we are, but, Judge, I can't tell one con that the judge who sent me up is, is a good friend of mine.

Hardcastle: Why not?

McCormick: Well, because.

Goin' Nowhere Fast – premiered October 9, 1983

Written by	Patrick Hasburgh
Directed by	Guy Magar
Second Unit/	
Stunt Coordinator	Gary Combs

Cast

Mary Jackson	Sarah Wicks
Robert Desiderio	J.J. Beal
Caren Kaye	Donna May McCabe
Eric Fleeks	Johnny Barton
Anthony Ponzini	Landers
John Touchstone	Warden McCabe
Will Nye	Sergeant Preston
Vincent Howard	Officer Bill
Stuart Nisbet	Guard on bus
Michael J. Cutt	
Don Dolan	
Big Yank	Escaped Prisoner #4279C
A.J. Freedman	The Guard
Jeffery Josephson	Barton

Cast Notes

Robert Desiderio also appeared as Stevie Ray in the episode "Angie's Choice" and made guest appearances on *Riptide* and *The A-Team*. He has done work on many soap operas including *Ryan's Hope*. His more recent credits include a recurring role as Jack Massarone on *The Sopranos*.

Caren Kaye played the hapless warden's wife who is seduced and abandoned by Beal. She has a Doctorate in Psychology and has retired from her acting career.

The Details

It's a quiet morning in Strykersville Prison. Armed guards patrol the perimeter; inmates pump iron in the yard or stand around, killing time. The work details are tidying up outside the warden's quarters.

Inside the warden's home it's a domestic scene. Donna McCabe, the warden's wife, is clad only in a towel. She's reading a movie magazine. A shirtless man is combing his hair and applying aftershave. He looks right at home here, but he isn't the warden. He's J.J. Beal, a trustee prisoner. Mrs. McCabe is infatuated with him. She begs him to take her away from Strykersville.

Moments later, a sedan careens out through the closed prison gate. Guards fire after it and two black and whites take off in hot pursuit. Out on a rural road, Beal, now armed with the warden's handgun, takes out one of the pursuing vehicles and rams the other into a spectacular rollover crash.

It's an unusually noisy morning at Gull's Way. Hardcastle is doing target practice with a .44 magnum. His six shots all miss. On a twenty dollar bet, Mark drills the center six times, using a one-handed firing stance.

Sarah comes out from the house and announces a phone call. After Hardcastle departs, she takes Mark down a peg with a list of chores. He gripes good-naturedly about Lincoln having freed the slaves.

Hardcastle takes his call at the poolside. It's from Beal. The two have history. Hardcastle told Beal he'd do "sixteen years, minimum". Beal crows about being out in six months and then hangs up.

Mark strolls over. Hardcastle, in an ominous mood, tells him to bring the car around. Mark doesn't catch on right away and continues to crack wise. Hardcastle repeats the request and strides off.

At the public phone, Donna May walks over to join Beal. She's starting to sound whiney. Another man pulls up, demanding access to the phone. Beal ruthlessly pulls a gun. He takes the man's car and flees with Donna.

Mark pulls up to the damaged front gate of the prison. Hardcastle gets a friendly greeting from a guard, who obviously also knows McCormick. His career path is commented on ("race car driver, to car thief, to chauffeur"). Mark gives as good as he gets. He and the judge stroll along the yard fence. Mark is greeted warmly by some inmates ("auto shop school ain't the same without you"). Hardcastle comments on his celebrity status.

Inside the warden's home, an investigation is underway. Mark gets a little prickly and Hardcastle tells him to sit down and stay out of the way. The warden says Beal was giving his wife French lessons. While they discuss the facts of the case and speculate on Donna's role—victim or accomplice—Mark helps himself to a photo of the woman, and sundry other bits of evidence. The warden insists that his wife could be fighting for her life.

In the stolen car, speeding down the interstate, Donna is all over Beal. He's not in a very romantic mood. She mentions her sister's place—a roadhouse near Riverside.

As they walk back to the Coyote, Hardcastle tells Mark that Beal is a criminal genius as well as irresistible to women. Mark's starting to wonder how the judge knows so much about this guy. Once they're in the car and away from the prison, Mark produces a stack of Las Vegas brochures he found on Donna's table. He figures that's their destination. Hardcastle questions his deductions but doesn't have anything better to offer.

A Strykersville Prison transport bus sits stalled alongside the highway. Beal and Donna pull up. He pulls out his gun and forces the guards to release their prisoners.

The Coyote is on the same road, 140 miles west of Vegas. The debate continues, with Mark insisting he has some insight into the criminal mind. Hardcastle, much to Mark's annoyance, touts Beal ("Harvard, class of '69"). Mark announces he got his doctorate in auto shop from Burgard High.

Back at the bus, the guards are locked in. Beal tells the prisoners to scatter. Two remain behind, asking Beal what his plans are. He says "maybe L.A." They throw in with him. As Beal and his new accomplices climb into the car, he spots a lone prisoner, still standing by the bus. He doesn't seem in any particular hurry to get away. Beal offers him a ride as well, but he says no, politely.

Beal heads for L.A. with an increasingly irritating Donna beside him. He tells her he never intended to go to Vegas.

The Coyote continues eastbound on the same road. Mark and the judge hear a radio report about the prison bus incident. One of the prisoners has already been recaptured but isn't saying anything. Mark casually asks the judge if he has a hundred dollars on him. He says he has an idea. He pulls over and asks the judge to drive. Hardcastle is suspicious. When he gets out to trade places, Mark pulls away without him, telling him to be at the city jail in a half-hour. He speeds off, soon attracting a

police escort and, after a lengthy break-neck chase on back roads, is finally cornered by a roadblock.

In a county jail, Mark is being locked up. His hangdog look lasts only as long as it takes for his jailer to walk away, then he turns and strikes up a conversation with the other prisoner in the cell. It's the man from the Strykersville bus.

Outside, Hardcastle is checking his watch, apparently following instructions and waiting for the allotted time to pass. He reaches for a handkerchief and unknowingly dislodges his wallet. It falls to the ground. Right on schedule he heads into the police station.

In the cell, Mark is getting nowhere fast. The other prisoner tells him he's an institutional guy. He doesn't do well on the outside and he's miffed that Beal messed things up for him. Mark tries to scam him with a story about knowing Beal from Attica. He's soon tripped up on the facts by a man who has more prison experience. It looks hopeless for getting any cooperation.

At the sergeant's desk, Hardcastle introduces himself and says he's there to post bail for McCormick. The desk man doesn't believe he's a judge and asks to see Hardcastle's secret decoder ring. It's downhill from there as the judge first discovers his wallet is missing, and then is found to be carrying a handgun. Now he loses his temper as well.

Hardcastle is escorted into the cell. He tells the guard to notify Judge Benson. Mark expresses disappointment that the judge couldn't follow a simple plan. In mid-recrimination, the guy on the other bunk rolls over. He's an old acquaintance of Hardcastle's and willingly tells him that Beal is headed to L.A.

Out on the highway, Beal evades another black and white. He's a hundred miles from L.A.

In Vegas, Hardcastle and his friend, Judge Benson, stroll out of the police station. Matters have been settled for now, but Hardcastle assures him he'll have Mark back to face his traffic violations. The violator screeches up to the curb in the Coyote. Benson has provided Hardcastle with some background information about Donna May, including her sister's address.

As the other judge departs, Mark corners Hardcastle. He wants to know if Beal was his prototype and why Hardcastle threw Beal back in prison. When he doesn't get an answer, he speculates that Hardcastle has to believe Beal is a genius, since he was outsmarted by him.

At the Hillside Café, Donna's sister's place, Beal and his accomplices are changing clothes and cars again.

In the Coyote, speeding down the highway, Hardcastle finally tells the story of J.J. Beal. It sounds a lot like the McCormick Plan, except that Beal fled Gull's Way in the 'Vette the first night after he arrived, robbed some filling stations, and had to be chased all the way to Louisiana. Mark chooses this moment to return Hardcastle's wallet, which he found on the steps of the police station. His mood is slightly damped when Hardcastle checks the contents.

When he says, with a note of disappointed sincerity, "You don't have to count it, Judge," Hardcastle stops and replies, "I know that," and stuffs it in his pocket.

Back at the café, Donna runs out, handing J.J. a wad of cash. She sees that Beal intends to take her brother-in-law's car. She objects. Beal tells her it's settled and that he's leaving her behind. She pleads with him. He insults her and leaves.

In the Coyote, Hardcastle shows Mark a picture of Beal. As they approach the café they see him and his accomplices taking off. Mark pursues. Beal leads him on a chase through traffic and finally peels off onto a side road. It's a dead end and he executes a 180-degree turn.

Now it's become a game of chicken, with both men in stationary cars. Beal charges toward him. Mark swerves at the last moment and ends up in the bushes. When Mark takes up the chase again, Beal guns his car off an impossibly high point and lands on the road below. Mark doesn't follow. He watches in puzzled admiration as Beal drives off.

All they have left as a lead is Donna May. At least Mark has a photo of her, though he catches some heat from Hardcastle about that, too.

Outside the café, Hardcastle says he won't get anywhere with Donna May. Mark insists that this is his area of expertise. They saunter inside. Donna is at the bar in the otherwise deserted establishment. Mark takes a stool next to her. Hardcastle grabs one further down. Things start out a little chilly and Hardcastle gives a running commentary of negative facial expressions. Mark finally gets Donna May's attention when he tells her he wrote a song "about a girl who looked just like you." He drops Barry Manilow's name into the conversation, but backs away from an outright lie. Hardcastle heads outside, leaving the other two talking.

Mark tells Donna that a song is just a story about someone's life. Donna says maybe she has a song for him.

In the Coyote, parked outside, Hardcastle is yawning. Mark finally comes out. Donna gave him the name of the man Beal intends to meet in L.A. It's Johnny Barton. Hardcastle sent him up for ten years.

In a small room, back in L.A., Barton reclines on a bed with a collection of weapons laid out alongside him. Beal calls from a phone in an alley. They plan to meet at dawn at Hardcastle's place.

The Coyote is driving west through the night. A radio news bulletin announces that Donna May has been taken into custody. Hardcastle called while Mark was talking to her.

Later that night, Beal and his new accomplices rob a liquor store.

The next morning, the Coyote is parked in front of a residential building. The judge is dozing. Mark is wide awake and sees Barton leaving. He's heading for a car and carrying something wrapped up that looks like guns. He drives away. Mark and the judge follow.

In the judge's study, Sarah is in nightclothes and sitting primly in a chair. Beal and his men occupy the room restlessly. Beal sits down behind the desk and threatens to "sic my boys on you". Sarah says she doesn't know where the judge is and tells Beal to take his feet off the desk.

As they follow Barton, Mark predicts he's heading for Gull's Way. Hardcastle doubts at first but eventually it becomes undeniable. They realize Sarah's there alone.

Barton arrives at the estate. Mark and the judge park further off and approach on foot. In the study Sarah gives Beal a lecture on ingratitude. He tells her he's going to kill the judge. Barton enters.

Outside, the judge and McCormick sneak in via the pool area and arm themselves from a stash Hardcastle keeps there. He says Mark might not be a genius but he was right about Beal's ultimate destination. They plan their attack and part company.

In the study, the accomplices are restive but Beal is determined to wait for Hardcastle. Outside, Mark climbs up to the balcony, while Hardcastle enters through the back door.

The study door bursts inward and Hardcastle appears, firing his shotgun at the ceiling. One man drops. Beal gets off a shot but misses. Mark comes in through the window and tackles Barton. Beal makes a break for it. Hardcastle sends Mark after him. Sarah looks unruffled and quietly pleased.

Outside, Mark pulls to a halt looking for Beal, then hears the Corvette's engine revving. He turns just in time to see it smash through the closed garage door. He leaps aside, then gets up, runs to the Coyote, and takes off in pursuit. Hardcastle follows along in the truck, a distant third. Mark catches up to Beal but is forced to drop back when Beal opens fire. The chase ends on a beachside parking lot with Beal doing another one-eighty turn when cornered. This time the game of chicken ends with Beal and the Corvette driven into the water. He flees on foot, firing as he goes, but his route from the beach takes him smack into Hardcastle, waiting on the path with a shotgun.

Mark comes up behind, sweating and out of breath. Hardcastle gets the glory.

In the epilogue, back at the estate, the bad guys are being hauled off by the police. Hardcastle pulls up in the truck. Beal, handcuffed, is with him. Mark is right behind climbing out of the Coyote. Sarah sternly asks Beal if he has any-

thing to say for himself. He casually asks who's been taking care of the estate. "It looks like a dump."

Mark seems peeved as Beal is led away. He again tries to shake the faith of Beal's admirers. Hardcastle concedes that Beal is only a little smarter than Mark. They finally settle down to a pulse check bet. Mark wins,

96 to 112, but Beal, handcuffed and in the back of the squad car, leans out and announces "94", and Hardcastle reaches to take back his twenty from McCormick.

The Context

You've got to wonder why Mark puts up with it. He spends most of this episode being put in his place by Hardcastle and Sarah (but then, she puts everyone in their place, even J.J., and he has a gun on her), while Beal gets all the accolades. Of course Mark gets in a few digs of his own, beating Hardcastle at target practice, and providing some pretty good insight as to why the judge has to elevate Beal to criminal genius status.

But the bottom line here is that Beal is only good at being bad, and even if Mark is only so-so at being good, that's the better way.

The Trivia

This episode has five chase scenes, with the destruction of three police vehicles. The final chase ends in Paradise Cove, a Malibu landmark and the site of Rockford's trailer home in *The Rockford Files*. It provided location shots for innumerable movies including *Gidget* and *Beach Blanket Bingo*.

Everybody at Strykersville Prison knows Mark—cons and staff alike. The implication seems to be that he spent some time there. When? Why? Just another one of those little continuity mysteries.

This is only the first of the *Dirty Harry* references in the series. Mark is back at it again, doing his Harry Callahan imitation, in the second season's "Undercover McCormick", and in "Angie's Choice", Hardcastle says Nicky saw "too many Dirty Harry movies". The original film had come out twelve years earlier, forging unbreakable associations with the .44 Magnum. December of '83 saw the release of the fourth in the series, *Sudden Impact*.

What's the Strykersville prison bus doing in Las Vegas' jurisdiction? Or did Freddie, the institutional guy, thumb a ride into Nevada?

Hardcastle winds up behind bars for the first, but not the last, time in the series. It happens twice more in season one ("Flying Down to Rio" and "Scared Stiff"), and six times altogether.

Mark persuades Donna that he's a songwriter (or at least wants to be one). A year later, in the episode "Pennies from a Dead Man's Eyes", a song he penned while in prison is set to music by a presumed dead western singer.

Memorable Quotes

Hardcastle: You feelin' lucky?

McCormick: Lucky enough to go for twenty.

Hardcastle: (reloading) Now, out of fairness I gotta tell you. The gun pulls a little to the left and low. (handing it over to McCormick, who assumes a one-hand firing stance) One hand? (he does a series of six rapid-fire double-takes as Mark drills a tight grouping on the target)

McCormick: (handing the gun back) No it doesn't.

Hardcastle: I owe you twenty.

McCormick: Trust me. *Trust* me, all right?

Hardcastle: It's gonna be six months before I trust you, McCormick.

McCormick: Come on, Judge, we're on the same side here.

The Black Widow – premiered October 16, 1983

Written by	Stephen J. Cannell
Directed by	Richard Compton
Second unit director	Gary Combs

Cast

Marta Dubois	Tina Grey
Robert Viharo	Jersey Joe Bieber
Richard Kuss	Capt. Don Filapiano
Robert Pastorelli	Adler
Frank Annese	
Arthur Burghardt	Lieutenant Stanton
Joe Horvath	

Cast Notes

Robert Viharo is another *A-Team* and *Riptide* alum. His most recent roles are in a series of indie films set in San Francisco and directed by Ron Nilsson.

Robert Pastorelli, who also had a guest turn on *The A-Team*, in his later career had ongoing roles on *Murphy Brown* and *Cracker*. He succumbed to an accidental overdose of heroin in 2004.

Arthur Burghardt also appeared in the episode "The Prince of Fat City".

The Details

It's night, and in the backseat of a limo near the docks, mobster Jersey Joe Beiber tells Mike the chauffeur to take his girlfriend, Tina Grey, home. He gets out to do business with some men on the dock. From Tina's viewpoint we can see that one of the men is bound. She tells Mike to stop somewhere for ice. Mike's upset. Apparently he and Tina have some action going on the side, but they both know that Beiber must not find out.

Out on the dock, Beiber is explaining his position to a defiant local mobster named Kelly. Beiber is horning in on the West Coast action and Kelly is in his way.

In the parked limo, with Mike out getting the ice, Tina makes a phone call. At the other end of the line is a rumpled, tired-looking cop named Don Filapiano, still in his office at this late hour. She gives him word that someone is "going swimming" at the docks. After she hangs up, he quickly checks the loaded chambers of his gun and gets up.

At the dock, Kelly has lost the argument. Beiber watches as he's shoved into the water, still bound.

It's a beautiful morning by the pool at Gull's Way. Mark, in his robe, announces that the water's cold. The water heater in the gatehouse is broken. He expands his complaints to include the hard bed and the cockroaches under the sink. Hardcastle hasn't got any patience with this litany. He's studying a file. Mark starts to whine about that, too, but when he gets a look at Tina Grey's file photo, he changes his tune.

Hardcastle explains that there has been a raft of deaths, all underworld types, and all associated with Ms. Grey. Mark volunteers to go point on a mission that Hardcastle was already planning to handle himself. The argument comes down to a bet. Whoever wins a one-on-one basketball game will get the undercover job.

A short while later, under the hoop by the gatehouse, what begins as just an intense game quickly descends to a no-holds-barred battle. As Mark tips the winning basket in, he does a header into the garden. It's all over but the moaning. He's won the chance to pursue Tina Grey.

Cleaned up and presumably bandaged, Mark and the judge arrive at a gallery, where it's opening day for an exhibit. The featured artist is one that Ms. Grey favors.

Inside the gallery, Mark ponders a ghastly thing with spikes sticking out of it. Ms. Grey's taste in art is no better than her taste in men, apparently. Mark gives a shrug of confused disbelief, turns and encounters Grey. She's studying a gray, splotchy piece. Mark compares it to a drop cloth he once used while working on a Pontiac in high school. It's not a great start, but he follows it up with some banter about modern art. He might be making some progress but Mike shows up. Tina walks off with him.

Hardcastle comes over, critiques Mark's effort, and is on the verge of showing him how it's done when a couple of Beiber's goons grab Tina and Mike and hustle them out. Mark and the judge go after them.

In the back seat of Beiber's limo, Joe threatens to kill Mike.

Outside the gallery, Mark runs to the Coyote as the limo pulls away. He takes off before Hardcastle catches up with him. The judge stomps and shouts. Another car pulls around the corner following the Coyote.

Inside that third car are two men in Beiber's employ. Adler gives his boss an update on the Coyote by phone while the other drives. Beiber tells them to deal with his pursuer. The sedan dwarfs Mark's car but he outmaneuvers them and they crash.

In Beiber's limo, now parked near the docks, Tina is still protesting her innocence. Mark arrives, and uses the gun Hardcastle left in the car to accost Beiber. He tells Tina to get in the Coyote and then shoots Beiber's tire. Beiber watches Mark make a clean (and flashy) get-away, and vows to kill him.

Back outside the art gallery again, Mark tries to get more information from Tina. She says he wouldn't understand. He tells her he's a rock concert promoter and lives on an estate in Santa Monica. He gives her his telephone number but she won't give him hers. She departs by cab.

Later that afternoon, Mark pulls up the drive at Gull's Way. Hardcastle is already on the porch, ranting. He says he's in charge and threatens to put Mark back in prison if he ever tries a stunt like that again. Mark says he's fine and thanks for asking. The argument moves into the study. Mark points out that he was doing the job he was supposed to do. Hardcastle says he's been a chump, and got no information at all.

Mark did get one thing, Beiber's license number. The judge is somewhat mollified. McCormick is also utterly convinced that Tina has nothing to do with anyone getting killed. He's infatuated.

Later that evening, in Beiber's dark and elegant home, Tina's busy selling Mike down the river, kindly and gently, of course. Beiber issues the order for Mike's death, then turns his attentions toward McCormick. Tina says he means nothing to her. Beiber assures her that the next guy who comes on to her will die, and that she's had her last warning, too. He kisses her aggressively.

The next day, at the police station, Mark, the judge, and Lieutenant Stanton are studying the information they've gotten about Joe Beiber. His record ends back in New Jersey a year earlier. Stanton summons Don Filapiano, the guy in charge of the Organized Crime Strike Force. Hardcastle punches Tina Grey's name into the computer.

Filapiano arrives and sees what Hardcastle is doing. He becomes angry. He wants Hardcastle to leave Joe Beiber and anything associated with him alone. He threatens to charge Hardcastle with obstructing justice. Mark wises-off with a Freud impersonation about the captain's insecurity. Hardcastle hauls him out of there.

Outside the station, Mark asks what the heck is biting Filapiano. Hardcastle doesn't go into specifics but intends to respect the man's badge and the authority that goes with it and back off from the case. Mark objects.

Back in the study, in the middle of the continuing argument, the phone rings. It's Tina, asking to see Mark. He says yes, against Hardcastle's better judgment. Milt still thinks she's setting McCormick up. His unhappiness only increases when he discovers Mark has told Tina that the estate is his.

Later that night, Tina arrives. The two guys in the maroon sedan followed her. They report back to Beiber.

In the dining room, Mark is all spiffed up and Tina is elegant in black. Mark rings a bell to summon Milt and the barely controlled farce begins. The sound of smashing crockery is heard from the kitchen. Mark excuses himself.

In the kitchen, Hardcastle is in white-coated servant's attire bringing a new meaning to the words "tossed salad". Mark can barely control his glee as he pushes Hardcastle's buttons.

Mark returns to the dining room and rings the bell again, twice. Hardcastle finally appears. Mark asks him to pour the wine. Hardcastle discovers that Mark has substituted an expensive bottle of Rothschild for the California white that he had put out earlier. Mark has to get dictatorial, but in the name of undercover solidarity the wine gets poured. Mark excuses his servant and turns to Tina. He tells her he knows who Joe Beiber is and offers to help her. She says Beiber will hurt any man who gets near her.

As Milton returns with the first course, Tina and Mark are on their feet. Tina says she's no longer hungry. "But you haven't even tasted the soup," Hardcastle wails. He's dismissed to the gatehouse—cold showers, cockroaches and all.

Later that night, beside the pool, Tina says Beiber has a safe. There might be some incriminating evidence in it. Mark volunteers to break in and look for it. They kiss.

Early the next morning, Mark escorts Tina out to her car. As he says goodbye, they're accosted by Beiber's men. Mark is forced to drive, with Manny holding a gun on him. Hardcastle, while carrying the garbage out, sees what is happening. He takes off after them in the Coyote. In a repeat of the earlier chase, a third car tails the Coyote. This time the duel ends in a flaming wreck for the maroon sedan. Hardcastle hauls out the driver in the nick of time, but by then has lost the trail of Mark and Tina's kidnappers.

At the police station, Hardcastle confronts Filapiano. There's bad blood between them going back to an incident twenty years earlier when the captain killed an unarmed boy. Hardcastle had to throw the case out, but has never forgotten it.

In the privacy of his office, Filapiano admits that he killed the boy, but says it's too late for Hardcastle to do anything about that. He also says Tina is his operative. She functions by setting up someone else to take the fall when she is close to making a case.

Mike was supposed to be the patsy but was killed too soon. Filapiano suggested that Tina use McCormick in place of Mike. Hardcastle says "That kid means something to me," and Filapiano smiles as he replies, "I was told he did." He says it's too late, both Tina and Mark are doomed. Hardcastle storms out of the office, grabs Lieutenant Stanton, and heads off to talk to the guy he pulled from the wrecked car.

In an empty storage building, Tina and Mark are in the custody of Beiber's men. When Beiber shows up, Tina launches herself at him, pleading her case. She says Mark was threatening to go to the cops with information about him and she only went to Gull's Way to find out what he had. Beiber has had enough. He tells his men to take the two out to the desert and kill them.

In the car, on the way to their execution, Tina asks Mark to back her story. He, like Beiber, is fed up with her.

At the police station, in the interrogation room Hardcastle plays good cop to Stanton's crazed bad cop. Adler cracks in record time. He tells them where Beiber buries the bodies.

The sedan arrives at the deserted quarry. The police cars, and Hardcastle in the Coyote, tear off from the station. In the race to beat the execution, the Coyote takes the lead while the squad cars fall behind.

At the quarry, one of Beiber's men tosses Mark a shovel and tells him to start digging. Mark refuses. As the judge and the cops speed to the site, the bad guys dig the graves. Tina makes a final plea to Manny, and he gives her the kiss-off.

Hardcastle squeals up in the Coyote, gun blazing. Mark slugs Manny. The rest of the heavies head for the sedan. Hardcastle chases them. The bad guys' car flips and crashes.

Back at the unused graves, Tina offers Mark a trip to Switzerland. He says "no thanks" and hands her over to the cops.

Hardcastle returns, challenging McCormick to another wager on their pulses. Mark says he can't; his heart stopped ten minutes earlier.

In the epilogue, it's mop-up time back in the police station. Joe Beiber is brought in shouting belligerently. Mark sits down next to Tina, despite her cold shoulder. She says she did it for the money. The guys from internal affairs show up. Hardcastle tells Filapiano that Tina will probably rat on him. Mark seconds the motion. Hardcastle hands the captain a picture of the boy he shot twenty years earlier and then he and Mark head for the door.

Walking out of the station with Hardcastle, Mark wants to know what the picture was all about. The judge explains who the kid was and what happened. McCormick gives him a long look and finally admits that he's not such a bad guy.

The Context

As Hardcastle eloquently puts it, "Hey, McCormick, you gotta uphold the law. You bend it just a little, try and look the other way just once, and you've got the beginnings of anarchy." Of course there's flagrant necessity, but there's no room in Hardcastle's rule book for general exemptions. The cops are just as bound by the law as the crooks are.

Meanwhile, in the fourth episode, we've got Hardcastle admitting that the guy who isn't supposed to be his buddy, and whom he wasn't planning on trusting for at least six months, means something to him—enough to bend the rules and do some creative interrogation, it appears, but not enough to call the exterminator and the plumber.

The Trivia

Tina Grey's favorite artist, Herman von Skoik, is an invention, but abstract impressionism really exists. The thing with the spikes sticking out of it may or may not qualify but, like McCormick, sometimes you can only shrug.

In the script, Beiber's favorite body disposal site is "out past Palmdale". In the final version it's "an old quarry, in Bronson Canyon." Bronson Canyon is located in Griffith Park and is, in fact, the result of an early twentieth century quarrying operation. It was a popular film location site, featured in both westerns and science fiction movies. The first Lone Ranger television episode was filmed there as well as the climactic scene in John Wayne's *The Searchers*.

In the script, Lieutenant Carlton was tagged to be the buddy cop of the week. He was replaced by Lieutenant Stanton in the final product. Filapiano was originally spelled "Filapeno".

Memorable Quotes

Hardcastle: (after the no holds barred basketball game) Next time ya wanna just put on the brass knuckles and forget about the ball?

McCormick: (on the ground and staying there) Can't take it, huh, Hardcastle?

Hardcastle: Well, ya gonna get up or can't ya make it?

McCormick: I can make it; I just don't wanna get up just yet. Sarah wanted me to weed this garden. I figured as long as I was down here I'd take care of it, ya know?

Hardcastle: You're really something. I sit here for two hours. I don't know if you're dead, or worse—

McCormick: What's worse than being dead?

Hardcastle: I dunno where you are. I dunno what's happening to you—

McCormick: Wait a minute, Judge…are you telling me you care about me?

Hardcastle: *No*, I don't care about you. How could I care about a guy who makes a contact and then winds up with nothin'?

The Boxer – premiered October 23, 1983

Written by	Patrick Hasburgh
Directed by	Tony Mordente
Second unit director	Gary Combs

Cast

Richard Lawson	Kid Calico
Hank Rolike	Jack Calico
Richard Romanus	Frankie Kane
Wynn Irwin	
Jack Andreozzi	Tony Barrows
Chick Hearn	Himself

Cast Notes

Richard Lawson, as up and coming boxer Kid Calico, had also costarred with Daniel Hugh Kelly the previous year in the short-lived TV drama *Chicago Story.* In addition to performing, he has also taught acting for over twenty-five years.

Richard Romanus played crooked fight manager Frankie Kane. He also had guest roles on Cannell productions: *Tenspeed and Brownshoe, The Rockford Files,* and *The A-Team.*

Chick Hearn, the well-known voice of the Los Angeles Lakers, announced 3338 consecutive games between 1965 and 2001. He also found time for over fifty TV and movie appearances, often, as in *Hardcastle and McCormick*, playing himself. He died in 2002, as the result of injuries sustained in a fall.

The Details

At Sparky Furgess' gym, a promising young middleweight known as "Kid" Calico spars in preparation for his next amateur bout. He's in contention for a spot on the U.S. Olympic team and has a shot at the gold in the upcoming L.A. Olympics.

In saunters Tony Barrows, a middle management hood for Frankie Kane. Kane wants a piece of Calico's action. The fighter is strongly encouraged to turn pro. Barrows mentions Calico's father, and says they haven't finished their negotiations yet.

The following morning, bright and early at Gull's Way, the eternal struggle for the sports section continues. McCormick's won this round by preemptive strike and is already partway through it when Hardcastle shows up at the gatehouse breakfast table. Mark points out an "ex-con does good" story on the front page: Kid Calico is fighting at the Auditorium that evening. Mark knew him back when they were both in San Quentin.

This sets off a series of boxing reminiscences. The guys are miles apart in their opinions, with Hardcastle defending the old school of standing up and punching the other guy's lights out, while Mark favors the scientific approach. Hardcastle remembers Calico's father, a fighter from the fifties. Mark suggests they attend the bout that evening and Hardcastle is willing.

Meanwhile, at Jack Calico's Ringside Café, we see Kid Calico's father, a man long past his prime, leading a quiet life surrounded by mementos of his earlier career. The café is closed. He's straightening things up. In stalks Barrow and Frankie Kane himself. They do some more strong encouraging, saying the Kid should sign a contract with Kane "or else". Jack says his son will keep his amateur status. The bad guys bust Jack and his place up, and then leave.

The Kid is doing his roadwork, with a flock of neighborhood kids happy to pace him. He looks like he's enjoying himself until he arrives back at the café and finds his injured father amid the petty destruction. His dad assures him it is nothing. He doesn't want it to distract him for the evening's bout.

That night at the Auditorium, Mark and the judge have ringside seats—Hardcastle sacrificed some Lakers tickets to get them in. They arrive just in time

for Calico's match-up. He scores a thorough victory over his opponent. Mark takes Hardcastle back to the dressing room to meet the Kid. The younger Calico greets him warmly, but when Hardcastle mentions how good his father was, Jack looks edgy.

Kane and Barrows barge in again, with Frankie acting like he owns the place, and the people in it, too. Kane again insists that the Kid is going pro. There's a bit of pushing. When Hardcastle starts to push back, Barrows half unholsters a weapon. Mark restrains the judge. The heavies depart after one more refusal from the Calicos. Jack and his son refuse Hardcastle's help as well.

That night we see something being tossed through the window of Jack's café. The place explodes in a fireball.

The next day, at the estate, Hardcastle shares the results of his research into Kane's past. He's a felon who changed his name. With his record he shouldn't be anywhere near the fight game.

The guys head over to Calico's café to share the news. They find the place in ruins and hear that Jack was taken to the hospital. They arrive there just as the Kid is helping his dad to check out. The two Calicos are also in mid-argument about what to do. The younger man wants to give in to Kane to protect his father. Jack won't hear of it.

Calico Sr. is still wary of help from anyone. Hardcastle sends the two younger men out and then persuades Jack to put his own past behind him—as the original Kid Calico, Jack fudged his amateur status and was ruled ineligible at the '52 Olympics. He later threw a fight for his crooked manager. Then Hardcastle offers the man what he wants most—a plan to get Kane off their backs and preserve his son's chance at the Olympic gold.

Hardcastle takes over as Kid Calico's manager, with the younger man signing a pro contract (they plan to later void it as having been signed under duress). The judge makes sure an announcement is made to the press. Then he takes Jack and

the Kid back to the estate. He's royally enjoying his foray into boxing management and delights in giving good old-fashioned advice. Mark and the Kid listen tolerantly. Jack approves.

After a morning of supervising the Gull's Way training camp, the two older men take off to get some equipment. They are waylaid by Barrow. Calico Sr. is kidnapped. His son is

advised to fight a prearranged professional bout that night, and take a dive
in the fifth round, or his father will
be killed. He insists on seeing his father before he'll fight. Mark and the
judge pick up the kidnapper's trail at
that meeting, and rescue Jack. Mark
gets Kid Calico's dad back to the auditorium in time for the Kid to turn
his bout around and score a win.

In the epilogue, the Kid has his amateur status back. Mark and the Judge are
at Sparky's gym, with the Calicos. They're still debating the merits of scientific
boxing versus slugging. Hardcastle volunteers to demonstrate the latter against
McCormick in the ring. Mark tries to demur and, when he finally has the gloves
on, looks like he's fighting *way* out of his weight class. He keeps moving, out of
reach, doing so much footwork that Hardcastle grumbles "Stand still so I can hit
ya!" The episode ends in a freeze frame with both men in mid-punch.

The Context

Patrick Hasburgh returns to the theme of fathers and sons, touched on also
in "Man in a Glass House". Calico Sr. knows he made a mistake. He has higher
hopes for his own son, just as Joe Cadillac said that his son might in some way
make up for his sins. And what about Hardcastle? When Jack Calico brings the
subject up, Hardcastle deftly changes it. He's not yet acknowledging that Mark
has any place in such an equation with him. After all, he's a very successful retired
judge, and his one and only son is dead. All he wants from McCormick is a good
day's gardening and no hogging the sports section in the morning.

The Trivia

With the 1984 Summer Olympics slated for Los Angeles and less than a year
away, this episode was highly topical. At 163 pounds, Kid Calico would have
fought in the light middleweight division. It turned out to be a good year to stay
an amateur boxer in the U.S.—nine out of the twelve possible golds went to
American fighters. The U.S.S.R. and the Eastern bloc countries had stayed home
in retaliation for the 1980 U.S. boycott. The light middleweight gold medal was
won by U.S. boxer Frank Tate.

In the epilogue, Sparky tests Hardcastle's fight knowledge by asking him who
was the top light heavyweight of all times. The judge shoots back "Billy Cobb". Sparky
looks at him approvingly. Cobb was the first light heavyweight to challenge for the
heavyweight title, going up against Joe Louis in 1941. Despite the thirty-pound difference, he was ahead in points until the thirteenth round. Then he changed his approach,
trying to go punch for punch with the heavyweight champ. He was counted out with

only two seconds remaining in the round. The two had a rematch after the war (both men had been in the service). The result was another knockout by Louis.

This episode was substantially changed from Hasburgh's first draft of August 19, 1983. That version had Howard Cosell, rather than Chick Hearn, as the sports commentator who receives the news of Calico signing with Hardcastle. Jack Calico stays in the hospital and is kidnapped from there, and Hardcastle is also kidnapped by Kane's men.

Memorable Quotes

McCormick: (watching Hardcastle shadowbox) Used to fight a little, huh?
Hardcastle: What does it look like?
McCormick: Looks like a guy trying to take his pants off over his head.

McCormick: Oh, yeah. It brings it all back, just the smell of these places, you know? I used to do a little boxing.
Hardcastle: You did, huh?
McCormick: (shadowboxing) What does it look like?
Hardcastle: It looks like you're trying to run underwater.

Once Again With Vigorish – premiered October 30, 1983

Written by	Patrick Hasburgh
Directed by	Arnold Laven
Second unit director	Gary Combs

Cast

Michael Callan	Frank Kelly
Tricia O'Neil	Pamela Peterson
Antonio Fargas	Jerry Blackmore
Claude Earl Jones	Jack Harlan Bickford
Bill Wiley	Godfrey
Laura Dowd	Julie Bickford
Madison Mason	Kelly's henchman
Daphne Maxwell	Tanya Gray, the reporter
William Long Jr.	

Cast Notes

Michael Callan, who played loan shark Frank Kelly, got his big break when he was cast as Riff, the leader of the Jets, in the original Broadway production of *West Side Story* (frequent Hardcastle and McCormick director Tony Mordente also got his start in that production).

Tricia O'Neil appeared with Brian Keith again the following year in the pilot episode of *Murder She Wrote,* "The Murder of Sherlock Holmes".

Antonio Fargas—assistant bad guy Jerry Blackmore—had a memorable run as the street-wise Huggy Bear on *Starsky and Hutch.*

Claude Earl Jones also began in the theater, appearing, by his estimate, in over 150 plays. He's a familiar face to TV viewers with nearly as many guest roles in that medium, including his turn as Lecerta on *Battlestar Galactica.* In recent years he has turned mainly to stage directing.

The Details

Hardcastle has waited seven years to see loan shark Frank Kelly take a fall for his illegal activities. He and McCormick are in court to hear Jack Bickford, the prosecution's star witness, give the testimony that will finally convict Kelly. Hardcastle's interest is personal; the man walked out of *his* courtroom, beating a murder rap.

In the lobby, before the session begins, Hardcastle encounters Pamela Peterson, the D.A. who is prosecuting the case. She seems a bit hostile, saying he doesn't need to check on her work. She is his former law clerk.

Bickford (sitting at the prosecutor's table) is summoned to the phone. The call is from his wife's kidnappers, who threaten to kill her if he testifies. Bickford takes the stand and, glancing at a very satisfied Frank Kelly, quietly claims no memory of anything he supposedly told the D.A. earlier.

Without his testimony, the case collapses. The charges against Kelly are once again dismissed.

Hardcastle and McCormick go to Bickford's home to find out what happened. They interrupt a kidnapping, give chase, and rescue Bickford after forcing the bad guys' sedan off the road. Bickford still won't help. He leaves town and the guys settle down at the estate to do some more research. Pamela ("Don't call me Pammy") Peterson makes an ill-considered statement in a TV interview. She says Kelly is dirty and she's going to get him.

A short while later she shows up at Gull's Way. Mark's in the main house shower (apparently they still haven't gotten that broken water heater fixed that was his chief gripe in "Black Widow") and has to do his butler activities in a towel. He leaves Pam and Milt alone. She tells the judge she's been suspended for her remarks in the interview. She finally breaks down and asks for his help. In

the middle of his gruff consolation ("There, there, don't leak all over the rug.") Mark walks back in, with a shirt on and everything. He mistakes it for an intimate moment.

Hardcastle sets him straight and the three plot to snare Kelly. This time they'll have a sure-fire witness—Mark McCormick. Pam arranges a meet for Mark with Kelly's right-hand man, Jerry Blackmore. Mark poses as an escaped con, looking for a loan to start up as an independent trucker. He's told to come back that afternoon.

Kelly bites, deciding to try Mark out on a stolen goods transport first. Mark gets word to Hardcastle and Pam, and the three rendezvous at a truck stop. There Mark shows them the falsified bills of lading and they know their case against Kelly is made. All they have to do is take the evidence in.

The Coyote, with Hardcastle driving and Peterson along, takes the lead. Mark follows in the truck. He soon realizes he's picked up two tails. Kelly's men know he's deviated from his assigned route. Two sedans bracket the truck.

Hardcastle does a one-eighty and is soon on their tail. Shots are fired, but Mark, though unarmed, has the bigger blunt object. He and Hardcastle tag-team one sedan and drive it off the road. The second one is still coming on. Its passenger coolly boards the truck at high speed, aiming a gun into the cab. Mark takes him out with a combination of brake-work and a good right elbow. His brake line, having lasted only long enough to save his life, now fails completely, landing the truck in a rough stop among roadside rubble.

Mark gets some stern remarks from the judge on his truck driving technique. Pam Peterson requests a warrant for Kelly's arrest. She's certain that her suspension will be rescinded.

Kelly's trial date arrives. The judge and his reliable witness arrive at the courthouse, Mark resplendent in tie and trousers. He even has on a vest for the occasion. It's testimony time and Pam Peterson is back in charge of the prosecution. In a daring move, Jerry Blackmore snatches Pamela in the hallway. Shouting and waving his gun in the crowded courtroom, he frees Kelly. They force the D.A. to accompany them, fleeing with her in a car. Mark and the judge, using that special parking pass that allows the Coyote to always be *right* in front of the courthouse, give chase. Another fence is destroyed for justice, the bad guys are cornered, and Pamela is saved.

In the epilogue, Mark and Milt are meeting Pam Peterson at a restaurant. It's a celebration lunch, but Hardcastle has something else to say. He's convinced that Pam and Mark are attracted to each other and wants them to know he won't stand in their way. Oddly, though, Mark had the same impression about Milt and Pam, and wants to make the same generous offer. Turns out they're both wrong. Pamela expresses astonishment that either of them is interested in her, and in walks a man she introduces as her fiancé.

The guys give each other mutually chagrined looks, then smile.

The Context

The subplot throughout this one is the potential Milt-Pam-Mark triangle, which is raised between most of the action scenes. Pam, we know, was Hardcastle's law clerk when she was "young" (the actress playing her was thirty-eight when this was filmed). She admits she had a thing for him and even went so far as to buy a negligee, but he either didn't pick up on the signals, or chose to ignore them. Now he's sending mixed signals (or at least different ones) to Mark and Pam. He tells her he might want to start where they left off, while telling Mark there was never anything between them.

The guys have a not very heated discussion about age and attractiveness in one lighthearted scene. Meanwhile Pam is definitely playing two ends against the middle, leaving maddening clues that imply to each man that she's attracted to the other.

Buddies don't let the woman break up their partnership. Both are willing to stand aside in the end, but Pamela has pulled one over on them, and maybe extracted a tiny bit of gentle revenge against her former boss.

Which brings us to the second theme—they do seem to be buddies now. Mark is a willing member of the team. His excuse is that he doesn't want to be the gardener forever (shades of ambition already?). He's studying the files; he even goes and pulls them when they're doing research. And instead of griping about the gatehouse plumbing, he just takes over one of the main house bathrooms, and then acts right at home answering the door in his towel. It's all a very far cry from three episodes earlier, when Hardcastle announced that it'd be six months before he trusted McCormick.

The Trivia

Mark climbs into the cab of his semi and immediately starts fooling with the citizen band radio, letting loose a string of hyper-twanged CB code. His first two tries go unanswered and the third one gets a low key and very cool response telling him that slang has been out of style since *Smokey and the Bandit*. There were three movies in that series, the first, in 1977, building on and feeding the CB craze. The third came out in 1983 and was a pale shadow of the original. No craze can last forever, but maybe it's a nod to the fact that Mark's been out of touch with popular culture for the past two years.

The restaurant where Pammy and the guys meet was the old Players Club located at 8225 W. Sunset Boulevard, founded by director/screen writer Preston Sturgis.

Memorable Quotes

Hardcastle: Listen, pay attention, will ya. This is your first day in court as a spectator, so look alive and you might learn something. And listen.

McCormick: What?

Hardcastle: Stand up when the judge comes in. Judges are very important people around here.

McCormick: Why?

Hardcastle: Now, I have something to say, here, and I'm glad that we're all together. Because what I want to say is that if, if you two have got a little thing going then that's very nice, because I like you both, and if you break her heart, I'll break your arm.

McCormick: If there's one thing I can't take, it's a grandstand play.

Hardcastle: *What?*

McCormick: Cool it, Hardcase. If the lady's crazy enough to be crazy about you, fine. I'll back off, all right? Thank you.

Pamela: Just a minute please. Could you just tell me what game we're playing so I know what cards to keep?

Hardcastle and McCormick in unison: You and him.

Pamela: What?

Glen: Hi, Pam, I'm sorry I'm late.

Pamela: Hi, Glen. Uh, Mark, and Milt, I would like you to meet Glen Munson. This is my fiancé. We're going to be married in June.

Killer B's – premiered November 6, 1983

Written by	Stephen Katz
Directed by	Ron Satlof

Cast

Buddy Ebsen	Himself
Tracy Scoggin	Crystal Dawn
Edward Winter	Eddie Sands
John Sanderford	Joe Kyle
Michael Collins	Phil Hoover

Cast Notes

Buddy Ebsen was best known, of course, as transplanted rural patriarch Jed Clampett from *The Beverly Hillbillies,* He went on to star in yet another successful series, *Barnaby Jones.* His final movie role was a cameo appearance in the movie remake of *The Beverly Hillbillies,* in which he *played* Barnaby Jones.

Tracey Scoggin also appeared in two episodes of *The A-Team* and went on to regular roles in *Dynasty, The Colbys, Lois and Clark,* and *Babylon 5.*

Edward Winter was a Cannell regular with guest roles on *Riptide, The A-Team,* and *The Greatest American Hero.* He also appeared twice on *Barnaby Jones.* He is perhaps best known as the officious Colonel Flagg from the TV series *M*A*S*H.*

The Details

B-minus movie producer Eddie Sands has come under Hardcastle's scrutiny. The judge suspects he's using his stable of movie stunt drivers to smuggle cocaine. Hardcastle has inflicted a film festival's worth of Sands' productions on McCormick in an attempt to figure out who's who in the operation.

The judge has a plan. He intends to infiltrate Sands' movie-making operation with the help of his friend Buddy Ebsen, who's been offered a role in a Sands production. Hardcastle will be his stunt double (no risk there; they hope to have Sands nabbed before the car stunts are to be filmed) and Mark will be the go-fer, with a chance to snag Sands' attention for a driving job.

The production commences and Mark meets Sands' girlfriend, Crystal Dawn, who has regular ingénue roles in his films. She's obviously not happy with her current boyfriend. She brings Mark home to her apartment. Eddie shows up. Mark gets no farther than the closet, where he is discovered. It looks like he may wind up in a pair of cement overshoes, but he hastily explains that his overture to Ms. Dawn was all a ruse to get Sands' attention. He offers his service as a driver.

Meanwhile, the judge has a lead on the auto shop where the stunt cars are

being serviced. He intends to check it out. Ebsen volunteers to go along. They discover a false tank in one of the cars. One of Sands' men arrives and they are shot at as they flee. Hardcastle, but not Ebsen, is recognized.

The next day a change in the production schedule is announced. The driving stunt has been moved up. Hardcastle gets strapped in while

a nervous McCormick tries to give him last-minute pointers about safe driving. It doesn't help; Sands' people have rigged the car with a charge. It flips and burns. Mark pulls the judge from the wreck while Ebsen extinguishes the flames.

Meanwhile, Crystal is hurt by Mark's apparent two-faced behavior. He tries to explain to her that it's all a plot to trap Sands. The question is, will Mark's resume pass muster with the boss? Turns out two years in San Quentin is the right qualification for an entry-level position in cocaine smuggling.

Mark is summoned to the auto shop. He insists on driving the Coyote. It's modified, and he and Hardcastle haul it down to Mexico. He picks up the load of drugs and heads north to his L.A. rendezvous, equipped with a walkie-talkie so the judge can keep in touch. Hardcastle is overhead in a CHP helicopter, acting as McCormick's wingman.

Unbeknownst to him, Mark has also been issued an escort by Sands. A three-way chase ensues. Sands' guy, in a muscle car, tries to run Mark off the road. Hardcastle, in the helicopter, takes him on. Gunfire is exchanged but it's Mark who forces the bad guy out at a turn.

McCormick proceeds to his appointment with Sands. He advises Hardcastle to give him five minutes to get inside, then bring in the cavalry. It's a long five minutes when Sands' men discover the walkie-talkie behind the seat of the Coyote. Bullets fly, Mark ducks. The bad guys attempt to flee but the reinforcements arrive at five minutes on the dot.

In the epilogue, Ebsen, Hardcastle, McCormick and Crystal Dawn are having a celebratory meal at a nice restaurant. Buddy is particularly pleased—neither Sands nor the movie will be released anytime in the foreseeable future. A friendly man leans over from another table. Ebsen reaches for a pen, anticipating an autograph request, but it's McCormick who is being recognized. Momentarily pleased to be a minor racing celebrity again, Mark's mood is quickly deflated when the guy announces that they were once in the same cellblock together.

Context

"Killer B's" is cheerfully self-referential—a television episode about a movie producer who is using movie-making as a cover for a criminal activity, which in turn borrows a plot from a movie (*Thunder Road*) that was purportedly based on a real event. It's dizzying.

The 1958 movie, produced by (and starring) Robert Mitchum, is a cult classic. Its plot, with a moonshine bootlegger smuggling his product in a hotrod car with a false tank, is the avowed source for the bad guys' scheme in this episode. Mitchum, in turn, supposedly based his story—false tank, decoy driver, flaming crash and all—on real events in the moonshine trade. Two more side notes: smugglers' efforts to evade the ATF have long been seen as the folk roots of NASCAR racing, and, yes, the Bruce Springsteen song "Thunder Road" was inspired by an ad poster for the Mitchum movie.

But, of course, the layers of reference don't end there. Here we have an actor playing himself, talking about his role as a detective (the very successful *Barnaby Jones*, 1973-1980) and wishing he could participate in some of Hardcastle's "real-life" crime-fighting activities. Credit both Ebsen and Keith (two old hands who had, amazingly, never before appeared on the screen together) for keeping straight faces as they thread through it all.

Trivia

During one getaway, Buddy Ebsen notes, with amazement, that the Corvette has no seatbelts.

Mark mentions he was a big fan of Ebsen's when he appeared in *Davy Crockett*. Ebsen played the loyal sidekick, George Russell, to Fess Parker's title character in six episodes that appeared as part of the Disney series in 1955. Parker and Ebsen made coon-skin caps a national craze for young boys, though Mark would have been only a year old during the first run.

In the epilogue, Mark thinks he's getting a bit of his own fifteen minutes of fame when a man shouts out his name and a hearty greeting. But, no, it's not someone recalling his glory days as a race driver; it's a fellow ex-con from Joliet Prison. When and why was Mark in Joliet? It's another continuity mystery.

Memorable Quotes

McCormick: This guy, Sands, has got more ex-cons working for him than a jail cell's got bars. I'm really surprised that a big-timer like Sands never came through your court.

Hardcastle: Well, you might call it a bad case of scheduling on the calendar. I've been watching his career and you can lay odds I'm gonna meet up with him.

McCormick: Yeah, now that's another thing. I mean, you didn't exactly keep a low profile in certain circles, if you know what I mean. What if someone recognizes you?

Hardcastle: Nothing for you to worry about.

McCormick: What do you mean, nothing for me to worry about? I'm the guy that's gonna be standing next to you.

McCormick: You never told me you knew Buddy Ebsen.

Hardcastle: There's a lot of things I never told you.

McCormick: You know what the cops'll do to me if they catch me sitting on a load of drugs. We're not talking about a traffic violation, here, Judge.

Hardcastle: Oh, I already told the cops; I told everybody. Now we're gonna pick you up as soon as you get across the border. You remember how to work that walkie talkie?

McCormick: Yeah, I think I can press a button, Judge.

The Prince of Fat City – premiered November13, 1983

Written by	Patrick Hasburgh
Directed by	Tony Mordente
Second unit director	Gary Combs

Cast

Stoney Jackson	Harold "Death Ray" Thomas
Victor Arnold	David Shelcroft
Reginald T. Dorsey	Bullet
Arthur Burghardt	Lieutenant Stanton
Rod Colbin	Judge Brant
Chuck Lindsly	Bruce Johnson

Cast Notes

Stoney Jackson was twenty-three and a veteran actor with four years of television and movie credits when he played the sixteen-year old ex-leader of the Hub City Cobras. He went on to star opposite Daniel Hugh Kelly again with the title role in the pilot episode of *The 100 Lives of Black Jack Savage*. He also appeared as a principal dancer in Michael Jackson's music video, *Beat It*.

Reginald T. Dorsey, who played Harold's gang rival, also had guest roles in *The A-Team* and *21 Jump Street*. He was raised in Texas and is from a family with three generations of cowboy experience. And in addition to a background in rodeo competition and his acting career, he is a poet and filmmaker.

Arthur Burghardt reprised his role as Lieutenant Stanton, who he also played in "The Black Widow". This time his name is in the script, as well.

Rod Colbin, in addition to having many stage and screen credits (which include a reading of Henry IV, Part 1, for the Royal Family and many other Shakespearean roles), is a cofounder of the Society of American Fight Directors. He is a champion fencer and taught fencing to James Dean.

The Details

The scene opens on a chase between two sedans. One is being driven by Judge Brant. He tries to evade Bruce Johnson, who corners him and runs him onto the shoulder. We hear that Johnson's boss is expecting a favor from Brant. He's expecting the judge to spring a particular juvenile delinquent. Brant assures him it's all taken care of, and the boy will be staying for a few days with Brant's former fellow jurist, Milton C. Hardcastle.

At the gatehouse, it looks like preparations are underway for a sleep-over. Mark's not too happy. He thinks kids are okay, but he doesn't want one whose nickname is Death Ray camping in the gatehouse. He starts rattling off potential psychiatric diagnoses for the boy. Hardcastle assures him the young man is really just Harold Eugene Thomas and, anyway, he's coming and that's that.

They go to the juvenile detention center to meet the newly-released delinquent. Things start out on a rough note and a little "tougher than thou" competition occurs between Mark and Harold, but, like the flip of a switch, when Harold gets outside he begins to ingratiate himself with Hardcastle, even complimenting the judge's ancient truck. Mark smells a scam artist. Hardcastle isn't completely taken in, but wants to give Harold the benefit of the doubt.

At the gatehouse, and on their own, Harold is much more abrasive with McCormick. He tells him he's capable of murder if someone gets in his way. As Harold gets more confrontational, McCormick holds his ground and tells the kid he's not letting a sixteen-year old gangster push him around.

Hardcastle arrives. It's dinnertime. Harold is gracious again. Mark tells him he's laying it on a little thick.

That evening, Hardcastle enters his study and finds McCormick reading a dust-jacketed tome entitled *The Maladjusted Child*. Hardcastle scoffs at Mark's concerns. He's decided to play a little one-on-one basketball with Harold to get things off on a better footing and maybe teach him some respect.

It's as physical a game as we've come to expect on the court at Gull's Way. When it's over, Hardcastle owes Harold fifty bucks. But after the judge walks away, Harold lets his façade drop a little; he obviously wasn't expecting that dirty a game from the old guy. Mark tells him he taught Hardcastle how to play gorilla basketball.

That night Harold is on the phone with a fellow gang member. He's told to come to an abandoned subway station. Mark overhears and tells him to stay put. Harold swings and connects with Mark's left eye. McCormick is down, but hits the alarm. Hardcastle comes on the double, but two other men have shown up as well

and are attempting to grab Harold. A fracas ensues. The judge grabs Harold. Mark goes after the fleeing intruders. All he gets is another punch to the face and a license plate number.

Morning at the estate, ice packs all around as Mark and the judge discuss who might want Harold and why. Mark tells him about the midnight phone call. Hardcastle confronts Harold who still won't say anything; he just gives a brief recital of his grim family history. He doesn't want any help from a do-gooder. Hardcastle sends him out to do chores. Mark's supposed to keep an eye on the kid (the one that isn't swelling shut) while the judge meets Lieutenant Stanton to track down the license Mark saw.

Out on the lawn, massacring the hedges, Harold finds out that it was Judge Brant who put Hardcastle up to this project. He's not pleased.

At the police station, Stanton gives Hardcastle the rundown on the owner of the intruder's car. It's a guy named Shelcroft who's suspected in a long list of criminal activities. Harold's file is plenty thick, too, and includes his most recent conviction for burgling a psychiatrist's home. Now the pieces start to fit. Tapes and patient records were stolen. Shelcroft and Brant were both patients.

Back at the estate, the Hub City Cobras—all five of them—show up at the estate. Bullet confronts Harold, demanding the tapes. Mark steps in. Bullet fires a gun. A momentary distraction allows Mark to get in a punch, but it's downhill from there with five against two. Mark is soon felled and Harold is taken.

In the subway hideout, Harold confronts his gang. Bullet wants the tapes. He intends to blackmail every one of the doctor's patients. Harold argues that they should only go after Shelcroft and Brant—the others are innocent.

When Harold is hauled out of the hideout to be "taken for a ride", Mark and the judge give chase in the Coyote. It's a brief but wild trip down the dry concrete bed of the Los Angeles River until the gang crashes. They run away, but Harold is again grabbed by Mark.

Back at the estate, Harold still won't tell where the tapes are, but he says he threw all but Shelcroft's and Brant's away. Hardcastle departs to see Brant. Mark challenges Harold to a game of one-on-one—betting the Coyote against the tapes. It's another ruthless game but it looks like Mark is holding his own.

Hardcastle confronts Brant. He's angry at being used. Brant explains how he got deeper and deeper into Shelcroft's dirty business. The judge gives Brant twenty-four hours to turn himself in.

Mark and Harold played to a hundred points and both look wiped out. As Hardcastle pulls up in the truck, Mark announces that he won and the tapes were the prize. He tells Hardcastle, on the side, that he thinks Harold needed an honorable way to give the tapes up, going against his word as a Cobra.

At Hardcastle's behest, Harold calls Shelcroft and offers to trade the tapes for fifty thousand dollars. Mark and Harold go off in the Coyote to retrieve the tapes. Hardcastle heads to Griffith Park to reconnoiter the spot where the trade will take place.

The Coyote is followed by the Cobras. Back at the hideout, Harold grabs the tapes and a gun he had stashed. When the gang shows up it looks touch and go for Harold's newfound loyalties, but he turns on Bullet and then escapes with McCormick. Once they are away, Harold gives Mark the gun and admits he's not "a shooter". It was all an act to make people back off.

It's out of the frying pan and into Griffith Park, where Shelcroft and his goons are waiting. Harold walks into the ambush and is attacked. Mark zips up in the Coyote. Hardcastle, arriving in the truck, takes down two more assailants. Only Shelcroft makes it back to the bad guy's sedan. Mark careens after him and, after a spectacular jump, runs him off the road.

In the epilogue, Harold shows up in the den, wearing Mark's sport coat and tie, asking if he looks like a chump. Hardcastle tells him after he does the last three months of his sentence, he should come back to Gull's Way. As they're walking Harold out to the car, he challenges them both to a game of basketball. The other two don't take much persuading, and it's every man for himself as Hardcastle takes the ball out for a game of three-man cutthroat.

The Context

As it's pointed out in the script, gangs can serve as substitute families. Harold traded one bad family situation for another, but now he's been brought into Hardcastle's family. "Didn't you ever wanna have a little brother?" the judge asks Mark, who's not too keen on the idea.

The evening basketball game is apparently a rite of passage for new arrivals at Gull's Way. The game serves as common ground for all three guys.

By halfway through the episode, we realize that Harold has some principles—the other gang members are far more ruthless. By the *end* of the episode, good heavens, he's borrowing Mark's clothes. In another week he would have been listening to his Bruce Springsteen albums.

The Trivia

The original script used the name of a well-known L.A. street gang. In the episode this is transformed into one of those multicultural TV gangs, the Hub City Cobras, complete with this hissing thing they do when they're all worked up. Hub City is the nickname of Compton, centrally located between Long Beach and Los Angeles.

The name of the blackmailed judge in this episode was changed from Bryon, in the script, to Brant in the filmed version.

The gang meeting place is the much graffitied (and often filmed) Toluca Substation, number 51, next to the west portal of the Belmont Tunnel. It was built in 1925 as part of the Pacific Electric Subway.

Mark admits to being a "joiner" in prison, everything up to and including the choir in an effort to improve his chances of getting out. Hardcastle confesses a weakness for Saturday morning cartoons.

Memorable Quotes

McCormick: I don't know this kid. For all I know, he would be a 16-year-old axe murderer.

Hardcastle: He's not gonna kill you with an axe. I don't think.

Hardcastle: Listen, McCormick, I told ya, he's smart. Now we might have to sand some of the rough edges off him, okay? But what he's going to do is learn that there are fundamental values that are important. Like for instance the value of a dollar. Good solid stuff.

McCormick: Oh, who're you kidding? What you mean is you're gonna have him trimming the hedges out behind the greenhouse for minimum wage.

Hardcastle: Well, he might trim a hedge or two, but look what he's gonna get in return. Good food, good company, an even break. Chance to kill you with an axe.

Hotshoes – premiered November 27, 1983

Written by	Patrick Hasburgh
Directed by	Richard Compton
Second unit director	Gary Combs

Cast

Terry Kiser	Larry Singer
Joe LaDue	Dennis Collins
Chip Lucia	Tom Peck
Howard Witt	Lieutenant Bill Jenkins
Crofton Hardester	

Cast Notes

Terry Kiser, as Larry Singer, is perhaps best known for his role as the not-quite-dead-enough Bernie Lomax in *Weekend at Bernie's.*

The Details

The episode opens at trackside. Denny Collins arrives, asking his pit crew chief how things are looking for the upcoming Trans Am races at Riverside. Winning will be a big boost for Denco Racing and he's sunk a lot of money into the effort. His chief assures him that everything is going great.

But the best-laid plans can't stand up to a high-speed crash. Just then, Davey, Denco's main driver, smashes into a wall. He ends up in the hospital, his leg in traction. He reaches for a phone.

At the estate, Mark is working under the hood of Hardcastle's old truck, with the judge offering unwanted advice. Sarah tells Mark he has a call. While he steps away to take it by the pool, Hardcastle picks up a wrench and fiddles with the engine.

Mark is overwhelmed as Davey offers him the Denco ride at Riverside. His unbridled happiness is short-lived, though, when he sees that with Hardcastle's assistance the truck has caught fire.

Back at the Denco Auto Parts warehouse, Larry Singer is supervising "inventory acquisition". Denco cuts down on overhead by running an auto-theft ring. Collins shows up and tells Larry that McCormick is replacing Davey.

But will he? At the Gull's Way breakfast table, Mark pleads his case to Hardcastle and Sarah. Driving a race car is like riding a bike (except, as Sarah points out, you can't fall off a bike at two hundred miles per hour). Both the judge and Sarah disapprove, but Hardcastle finally gives in.

It's practice day at the track. Mark's doing laps in a hot car, deeply in his

element. Milt's a fish out of water, wandering around giving unsolicited advice. During a break, they run into Collins' right-hand man, Larry. Hardcastle thinks he looks familiar.

Things are a little tense as Mark adjourns to his trailer. Hardcastle is astonished at how much money goes into sustaining a racing team. He wants to know where it comes from.

Mark begs him not to create any problems and assures him everything is on the up and up.

Somewhere in an upscale neighborhood, we see a Mercedes Benz being boosted in broad daylight. It's brought to the Denco warehouse where there are more stolen cars, all looking anonymous, draped in canvas.

Mark shows up for a pre-race get-together with Milt in tow. Things get tense again as Hardcastle continues to wonder where all the money comes from. Larry seems edgy, too.

Collins arrives in a stretch limo. Larry goes out to greet him. He says McCormick has been beating Davey's lap times but, better still, he has a criminal record and might be just the guy for their operation. He's not very happy about Mark's "leaner", though.

Inside, Mark is introduced to Collins, who repeats the leaner term when he sees Hardcastle. Mark hastily corrects him, saying that Milt is his manager.

As they leave the party Hardcastle asks what Collins meant with the comment. Mark is unwilling to tell him at first, but eventually breaks down and informs him that a leaner is someone who stands around, leaning on something, and yaps. That's one step below a go-fer, who at least fetches things.

Hardcastle sends Mark off to get some rest while he heads over to the local police department. He looks up an old buddy of his, Lieutenant Bill Jenkins, and asks for any records on Collins and the mysterious Larry.

Another car-boosting interlude—it's a Mercedes again, in broad daylight. This time the thieves are apprehended.

It's race day at Riverside. Mark is doing well in the qualifying laps but spins out and crashes. He's able to walk away (albeit stiffly) from the wreck, and there's another car ready for him to use in the race. In the trailer, Hardcastle brings him up to speed on his own investigation. Mark is aggravated that his big chance to get back into racing is turning into yet another one of Hardcastle's cases. The judge offers a consolation prize—as the inside man in the operation Mark can continue racing for Collins.

Mark's behind the wheel of the replacement car. Collins spots Hardcastle talking to Lieutenant Jenkins, who arrives with news of the car theft bust. The

two thieves work for Denco.

As soon as Jenkins leaves, Larry accosts Hardcastle and takes him to see Collins. They search his wallet and find both his honorary detective's shield and his superior court ID. Collins tells Larry to have McCormick's car rigged to crash.

The race commences with Mark soon in contention for first place, but when his sabotaged brakes fail, he spins out. It's not the fatal crash that was expected. He's out of the car in a moment and sees a sedan departing with Collins, Larry, Hardcastle, and the guy who rigged the race car.

Mark runs to the Coyote and gives chase. They soon attract two police vehicles. Hardcastle, sitting in the back seat of the sedan, turns around briefly, and smiles when he spots McCormick on their tail.

The sedan runs headlong into a road construction site and crashes. The bad guys are busted and Mark pulls a cranky Hardcastle out of the back seat. He's kvetching ("You mean you dragged me all the way out here and you didn't even win?").

In the epilogue, the judge and Mark are leaving the hotel. Mark says he's fine but his helmet is shot. Hardcastle offers him a slightly-used leather football helmet from his youth. Mark informs him that racing helmets are specialized equipment and very expensive. They take off, still talking about the vagaries of racing. Mark seems reconciled to having lost, but when he spots a police car in his rearview mirror, waving him over, he says, "Betcha twenty I can win this one."

He doesn't.

The Context

This episode throws Hardcastle into unfamiliar surroundings, after first making the point, in the GMC repair scene, that he knows next to nothing about cars. His self-appointed role as Mark's manager seems to annoy the heck out of the younger man, but annoyed or not, when Hardcastle is called a leaner (and doesn't even know he's being insulted) Mark jumps back in and asserts that he *is* his manager.

Of course, Hardcastle quickly gets back to familiar circumstances—bad guys and crimes to be thwarted. In the meantime, Mark's begging him to just let things be. But the judge can't help himself. He's got an instinct for bad guys, and though Mark protests vociferously, there's never any doubt that he'll back Hardcastle in his effort to get Denny Collins and his ring.

The Trivia

This is the last appearance of Sarah Wicks, Hardcastle's prickly housekeeper. It's also the last appearance of the judge's ancient GMC truck. The truck at least gets a brief moment of mourning from both guys ("She was a good old girl, McCormick." "Yeah, she was.") Sarah, on the other hand, disappears from the cast without comment or explanation.

This is the first (not counting the pilot) of four episodes that featured racing. Patrick Hasburgh wrote three of them. In two of the episodes ("Faster Heart" and "You Don't See the One That Gets You") Mark wins a race, in this one he is sabotaged, and in "Outlaw Champion" he races informally against a stock car champion and loses.

The address of the estate in this episode (as seen on the speeding ticket in the epilogue) is simply "Gull's Way, Santa Monica".

Also in the epilogue, Hardcastle admits he used to do a little informal racing up on Mulholland.

Memorable Quotes

McCormick: Driving a race car is like riding a bicycle. Once you learn, you never forget.

Sarah: Except you can't fall off a bicycle at two hundred miles an hour.

Hardcastle: Yeah, and you haven't been inside a race car since before you went up.

McCormick: And whose fault is that?

Hardcastle: Yours.

McCormick: Look, Judge, haven't you ever wanted something more than anything in the whole world? Something that you'll get one shot at and that's if you're lucky?

Hardcastle: Yeah, I always wanted to play center for the Celtics, but they wouldn't lower the baskets and I was too short.

Hardcastle: Look, Mark, go get yourself some rest. I'm just going to nose around…

McCormick: Wait a minute. When you call me "Mark", I get nervous. I told you this race is very important to me, Judge.

Hardcastle: Well, you're important to me, okay? Now get out of here.

Flying Down to Rio – premiered December 4, 1983

Written by	Stephen Katz
Directed by	Tony Mordente
Second unit director	Gary Combs

Cast

Alan Feinstein	Peter Avery
Bruce French	Howard Daner

Victor Mohica	Emilio Salazar
Julio Medina	Judge Ramirez
Gail Strickland	Agatha (Aggie) Wainwright

Cast Notes

Alan Feinstein has had a varied career, appearing on stage, screen, and television, including 100 different television productions, and 800 episodes of daytime drama, primarily *The Edge of Night*. He and a partner are currently running an acting studio in Los Angeles.

Bruce French had a small role in the film, *Star Trek: Insurrection*, in which Daniel Hugh Kelly also appeared. Bruce's Trek affiliation doesn't end there, however; he also appeared in episodes of *The Next Generation*, *Voyager*, and *Enterprise*.

The Details

The scene: a National Guard armory, but the guys loading up the crates of weapons aren't in uniform, unless you count the ski masks.

Outside, Hardcastle and McCormick wait in the Coyote, operating on a tip about Peter Avery, former CIA agent and current international arms dealer. They've brought along a small contingent of police officers, ready to make an arrest if the tip proves accurate. Peter Avery appears to have other ideas, though, and smashes his truck through the barricade, then lays down a barrage of cover fire, bursting the black and whites into flames and blocking the Coyote's pursuit.

Back at the gatehouse, Hardcastle breaks out the Avery file and explains his latest plan for capturing him, but Mark's not interested. Even with an island "vacation" as incentive, McCormick's not buying; he has no intention of tracking a lunatic CIA agent down to a banana republic. But Hardcastle has an offer McCormick can't refuse, and they're on their way.

Arriving at the hotel, Mark's immediately intrigued by a chance encounter with an attractive tourist, and his first plan is a visit to the pool; the judge's news

that he's gotten the location of Avery's company is of no concern. The tone changes, though, when Hardcastle breaks the news that Avery has arrived on the island and is staying in the very same hotel. They argue about the wisdom of going after the guy, but since the first thing Milt wants the kid to do is keep an eye on Avery down at the pool, Mark decides it might not be such a bad idea after all. And, even with a pretty girl to distract him, McCormick can't help but overhear Avery's plans for the evening.

When Hardcastle finally shows up poolside, they retreat to the shade for cool drinks and are joined by Aggie Wainwright, local air charter pilot and Lakers fan. Mark immediately launches a not-so-subtle cupid routine, but Avery's business partner shows up for his meeting. Aggie provides an ID for the guy—"Emilio Salazar. Not a nice man."—and Mark takes the opportunity to escape upstairs, leaving Milt and Aggie alone.

Meanwhile, in the Avery suite, business is progressing smoothly, and he promises to arrange delivery of the armory weapons.

Later, down in the lobby, McCormick's still singing Aggie's praises to the judge when they bump into Avery. The exchange between the men is superficially genial, with undertones of contained hostility. Avery tells his companion it's time for Hardcastle's vacation to come to an end.

Hardcastle and McCormick pay a visit to a local judge, Ramirez—seems Hardcastle really does know people everywhere—but Ramirez tells them there's nothing he can do about Avery, due to the corruption on the island. Even Mark doesn't understand that, but the judges agree it's not as easy as it ought to be to arrest the guilty. But when Hardcastle asks for information about Avery's business holdings, Ramirez agrees with McCormick that they should leave the island and forget about Avery. Hardcastle can't be convinced, however, and he plans a raid on Avery's warehouse.

Avery has developed a cautious streak of his own, and sends men to the warehouse to safeguard the crates, but he's too late; Milt and Mark have already gotten the proof they need in the form an automatic weapon and forged import documents.

The bad guys chase the good guys through the building and up to the roof, where the only choice for escape is a forty-foot jump down, and a quick hotwiring of

a convenient jeep. Hardcastle ensures their getaway down a jungle road with a barrage of automatic weapons fire, hitting one pursuing jeep and sending it flipping dramatically into the path of a second.

Taking stock back at the warehouse, Avery realizes they're missing an M-16 and all the incriminating paperwork. Salazar isn't happy, and wants Hardcastle taken out of the picture.

After a quick stop at the embassy, Mark and the judge go back to the hotel, ready to head for home. But between a basket of flowers compliments of Aggie, and Mark's teasing, Hardcastle is distracted enough to send the kid downstairs while he finishes packing. But the armed soldiers at his door with orders to search the room delay the plans. "Discovering" drugs in the nightstand, they immediately place Hardcastle under arrest. Passing McCormick in the lobby, the jurist fills him in and orders him to call the American embassy.

It's not the local version of the drunk tank Hardcastle is taken to to await justice, but an isolated prison filled with grim looking guards and grimmer residents.

Mark's back at Ramirez' office, making his case to the judge and Daner, an embassy official, but they insist that everything that can be done is being done. McCormick isn't convinced, and he's clear that he wants Hardcastle out of prison immediately.

That night, Hardcastle receives a visit in his cell. Avery explains that money can buy anything inside these walls, and advises the judge to return the missing papers. When Hardcastle refuses, Avery leaves behind a couple of friends to deliver a more stringent message.

The next morning, it's McCormick's turn to visit, and he's not happy with the judge's condition. He explains that Daner has the papers and has sent them to Washington, but he also says that they're going about things the wrong way. Hardcastle is sure "the law works any place", but McCormick plays his trump card: Hardcastle might know legal, but he's the go-to guy for prison breaks.

Mark's next stop is the Wainwright charter service. Aggie agrees that the embassy isn't going to be able to help Milt, and she's willing to go along with anything McCormick cooks up.

Back at the prison, Hardcastle is out for an exercise break when Aggie's helicopter comes sweeping over the mountain. The guards are about to signal the alarm, but McCormick's throwing money to the ground by the fistful, and everyone soon forgets their duty in order to  grab their share. Hardcastle is stunned and at first refuses to go along with the escape, but McCormick leaves the helicopter and forcibly pulls him into it so Aggie can fly them to safety.

Hardcastle shouts about accessories and dumb moves all the way back to the airfield. Even Aggie is on the receiving end, but that doesn't stop them from making a date for after the bad guys are rounded up. Ramirez is at the airfield, too, and explains that the escape is already widespread news; roadblocks have gone up all over the island. Undeterred, Hardcastle assures them he's got a plan.

Avery is back in his suite rearranging his own plans. He's trying to find the judge but not counting on anything, so the weapons delivery will have to be moved to that night. Salazar agrees and Avery takes off for his warehouse.

Gathered in Ramirez' office, the judge and McCormick are briefing Daner; they've got permission from the State Department to go after Avery. Bureaucrat to the end, Daner wants a precedent; Hardcastle assures him there will be one: "State of California v. Avery, '83".

Driving along an empty highway toward the airport, the guys are spotted by one of Avery's men. He reports to his boss and they make plans; Avery leaves the warehouse to join in the ambush. Once everyone's in place, the plan swings into action, beginning with McCormick's "hotshot driving".

The cars bump and swerve as Avery and his men try to take out the good guys—they even manage a small jump in the sedans—but shortly afterward they're down one bad guy as the henchman hits a fruit stand and flips. Avery isn't concerned and continues to give chase in his limo, pulling a handgun and opening fire.

But McCormick is on a mission: he's got to stay ahead of Avery long enough to reach the upcoming security checkpoint. Once there, waiting soldiers converge to arrest Avery and his driver. Smug as always, Avery smirks that Hardcastle has accomplished nothing since there's no extradition agreement with San Rio Blanco, but the judge takes great pleasure in explaining that they've just crossed the border into San Rafelo, which—as Mark points out—does honor extradition to the U.S.

The epilogue finds the guys at the airfield once again; it's time to say goodbye to Aggie. She's glad to hear everything worked out, but there's some hem-hawing around as it seems neither she nor Milt quite know what to say. But before he leaves, Hardcastle hands Aggie a plane ticket to LA, to be used should the Lakers ever make the playoffs.

The Context

It's an interesting look at the balance of power. McCormick's the cautious one, easily recognizing the inherent danger in trying to target a weapons dealer who happens to also have CIA training. But Hardcastle can't be deterred, and when he's tired of listening to objections he simply reminds the kid he could send him back to prison if he doesn't cooperate. McCormick's not thrilled with the ultimatum, but he naturally goes along—though not without a continuing litany of objections and a real show of refusing cooperation once they've reached San Rio. But it *is* mostly show, and it gets little response from Hardcastle—they both seem to understand the game.

But once Hardcastle is arrested, it's a different story. Now McCormick's not playing, and he intends to ensure the judge's safety, no matter what it takes. For his part, Hardcastle is adamant that the system has to be allowed to work, though McCormick ultimately defies him completely. Though reluctant at first, Hardcastle does eventually go along with the jailbreak, and one has to wonder how much of that is an honest realization that McCormick might be right, and how much it is a desire not to take the younger man down with him in a stubborn stand on principles.

Earlier in the season ("Man in a Glass House") we see the judge badger Mark into a confession that could've landed them both in hot water, with no apparent concern for the fact that McCormick's kettle would surely have been hotter. And even here, he's clearly not opposed to using his legal power to coerce cooperation. But when push comes to shove, he lets McCormick do things his own way, without repercussion, and Mark shows no sign of concern that Hardcastle might actually carry through on the threat to send him back up the river. So just who is in charge, anyway?

The Trivia

It likely goes without saying, but there is no such place as San Rio Blanco (or San Rafelo, either, for that matter), though there is a Rio Blanco located in San Marcos, Guatemala.

When the guys check in to their hotel room, the desk clerk tells them they've got a "lovely suite on the third floor". But when Hardcastle tries to check out later, they're in room 1008. Leaky shower in the first room, maybe?

Mark teases Milt about Aggie, even going so far as to say, "If I was ten or fifteen years older…", but if we use the performers' ages as a guideline, Aggie is only five years Mark's senior, and twenty-five Milt's junior.

California didn't quite make the 1983 deadline, but there was a People v. Avery in 2000. Nothing as exciting as illegal arms trading, though; simple burglary. (Though the case did make it as far as the state Supreme Court.)

Memorable Quotes

McCormick: Are you insane?

Hardcastle: We'll go deep sea fishing, and maybe we'll just nose around and check out the operation.

McCormick: The only deep sea fishing we're gonna do is when this guy tosses us into the ocean. What're you going to do if you do find out something? Call the LAPD? Judge, this is a banana republic down there; you don't have any power base.

Hardcastle: Come on. It's beautiful down there.

McCormick: Life is beautiful, and I plan on enjoying mine for a very long time. I'm not going to let you get us both killed.

Hardcastle: Okay, let me put it to you this way. You're in my judicial stay. Now, it's gonna be San Rio or San Quentin, okay?

Hardcastle: Put some suntan lotion on; you're whiter than a tree toad's tongue.

McCormick: I'm from Florida; I never burn.

McCormick: Whoa. Oh, no, no. Nah, you gotta be kidding me. They only do that in the movies. You don't really want to jump down there.

Hardcastle: It's only about forty feet.

McCormick: Well, that's thirty-eight too many. Besides, it's looks like a hundred, and I'm allergic to heights, Judge.

Hardcastle: Don't worry about it. The fall'll probably knock you out.

McCormick: This Lone Ranger stuff, I don't know.

Just Another Round of that Old Song –
premiered December 11, 1983

Written by	Patrick Hasburgh
Directed by	Allen Reisner
Second unit director	Gary Combs

Cast

Keenan Wynn	Henry Willard
Jack Ging	Joe Cagney
Larry Drake	Jesse Roberts
Lisa Rafel	The Waitress

Cast Notes

Keenan Wynn was a longstanding utility player in the studio era who went on to become one of the most recognizable character actors on television. In 1958 (the year Hardcastle supposedly sentenced Henry Willard to twenty-five years), he appeared in five episodes of *77 Sunset Strip* with Brian Keith.

Jack Ging played recurring roles on both *The A-Team* (General Fulbright) and *Riptide* (Lieutenant Ted Quinlan).

Larry Drake took home two Emmy awards for his convincing portrayal of Bennie Stulwitz, a developmentally delayed man, in the series *L.A. Law*.

Lisa Rafel plays the friendly server in the sandwich shop and the first of many people to tell Willard that Los Angeles has no subway. She also appears in the second season episode "Hate the Picture, Love the Frame" as Sergeant Ferguson. In recent years Ms. Rafel has set aside her acting career to become a "chantress, spiritual teacher and sound and energy healer".

The Details

Hardcastle's amateur Dixieland band is having a late night practice session in the study. It's about the one hundred and twentieth round of "When the Saints Go Marching In". Mark, not asleep in the gatehouse, has finally had enough. *He* goes marching  in, demands that they cease and desist, and stuffs a basketball in the tuba. It's war. The Jazzmasters take it from the top and Mark retreats to the gatehouse where he cranks up "In-A-Gadda-Da-Vida". The two men stalk out to confront each other. A cop shows up and tickets them both for disturbing the peace. Both stomp off, Hardcastle pocketing his ticket and Mark tearing his to bits and tossing it in the air.

Morning, and all is quiet except for the residual ringing in their ears. Hardcastle gets a call. It's an old cellmate of Henry Willard, a man who was sent to prison for an armored car robbery in 1958. Willard's been released but the money was never recovered. The caller thinks someone will lean on Henry to get it.

In a busy urban shopping district a white-haired man wanders, staring in bemusement. It's Willard. He asks a clerk in a sandwich shop for directions to the subway. She tells him L.A. doesn't have one. He's mystified. He has a map that shows the proposed route. She can't help him in his search, beyond telling him that she thinks the whole idea was canned.

He's out on the sidewalk, wandering again. A man, Jesse Roberts, is watching him. Roberts puts in a call to Joe Cagney. He thinks Willard doesn't know where he's going. Cagney still believes he does, and orders him to stick to Willard.

Breakfast at Gull's Way is accompanied by a lot of yawning. Hardcastle shows Willard's file to McCormick who is impressed with the guy's record—twenty bank robberies and only three arrests. He thinks that maybe crime does pay, at least in Willard's case, since the $750,000 is still missing and the statute of limitations is up. Hardcastle tells him that Willard still has a ten-year tail on his sentence. He's on parole and if he spends a dime he goes back inside. Besides, as the judge points out, it's not his money; he stole it. But mostly Hardcastle is worried. He thinks the old man will be attacked.

Willard, talking to his cat in a seedy residential hotel room, is trying to figure out where he stashed his loot. A lot has changed in twenty-five years. Roberts bursts into the room, gun drawn, demanding to know where the money is. Willard tries to explain his dilemma. Roberts drags him out.

Mark and the judge pull up just in time to foil the kidnapping, with the help of a well-placed elbow from Willard. Mark takes off after the attacker but loses him. He returns to find Hardcastle reintroducing himself to Willard, who can't believe he's the same guy who sentenced him ("You got old!"). They convince him to come back to Gull's Way with them.

They have to do a lot more convincing. Willard doesn't want to give the money back, and even if he did, he tells them he's not sure where he put it. On top of that, the guy who tried to grab him got his map.

Meanwhile, Cagney and Roberts are puzzling over the thirty-year-old street grids. The instructions are based on subway stations and L.A. has no subway. Cagney says he's already pulled every old map of the area in the city planning office and he adds that at least with Willard's map, they may have an idea where to start.

But Willard certainly doesn't. He's standing on a corner in downtown L.A. reminiscing about fountains and Esso filling stations and sorely trying Hardcastle's patience. While Cagney and Roberts follow the landmarks on Willard's map, Hardcastle and Willard decamp to the city planning agency to find a replacement map. They discover that Joe Cagney had checked out the same map twenty years earlier. Willard says he was the detective who arrested him.

Back at the estate, Hardcastle makes some calls and confirms that Joe Cagney recently took early retirement. The judge looks through Willard's sparse belongings and finds a playbill dated the day after the robbery. Willard can't remember seeing the play, but Hardcastle decides to take him down to the theater to see if it will shake something loose for him.

A visit to the outdoor theater doesn't jog much loose for Willard except for some fond memories of how crime used to be. There was more style and it wasn't just about the money. In the middle of this nostalgia, Cagney and Roberts arrive. Cagney grabs Willard and hustles him out. Roberts stays behind to deal with the guys, but Mark disarms him with a well-placed kick. He's left to guard Roberts while Hardcastle chases, and loses, Cagney and Willard.

Back at the theater, Roberts is under arrest. He's an ex-con who was also busted by Cagney and knew about Willard's money because he did time with him in San Quentin.

Now Mark and the Judge have the map they took off Roberts. Hardcastle tracks down a retired city planner and learns that construction was begun on the subway but most of it was bricked off. He and Mark go to the abandoned terminus, equipped with hardhats and flashlights, unaware that Cagney, with a handcuffed Willard, is tailing them.

They head down into the
tunnel, reaching the end of the line.
Cagney, with Willard in tow, follows them in. Mark finds a hollow
spot in the wall and Hardcastle
bashes it in with the bolt cutters
they brought along. On the other
side of the wall, the two men see a

fifties-era armored car. The back is unlocked. Inside they find Willard's loot.

Cagney closes in. He orders Mark to load the loot into his sedan. Willard
knocks the flashlight from Cagney's hand. In the sudden darkness, shots ring
out. Hardcastle is armed, too. Cagney flees; Mark chases. Cagney swerves to
miss a truck, smashes into a shack, and flips his car.

In the epilogue, the judge tells Mark there is a twenty-five thousand dollar
reward still being offered for the money he helped recover. Hardcastle intends to
give his share to Willard. Mark, initially unwilling, eventually succumbs to the
idea, while watching a very old Henry (alone in the world, except for his cat)
waiting for a bus.

It's night, and Mark's in bed, listening to the not-so-dulcet tones of the
Jazzmasters. He trudges over to the main house and asks Hardcastle if he knows
what time it is. The judge answers, with annoying sprightliness, "No, but if you
hum a few bars, we'll try and fake it." He hands McCormick a tambourine and,
finally beaten, the younger man joins in.

The Context

Mark's not quite up to speed with this right versus wrong thing. It's hard
to convince him that Willard hasn't somehow "earned" the money he stole by
doing the twenty-five years, but Willard himself is a pretty good object lesson
in the perils of a life of crime. He's old and alone, and people are trying to kill
him.

A recurring theme in this episode is Mark's amazement that Hardcastle
cares about the guy he sent up. The judge brushes it off, but eventually admits a
grudging fondness for Willard. He was a criminal who wasn't violent and had a
certain amount of style.

By the end of the episode McCormick is mostly convinced that crime, at
least in Willard's case, doesn't pay. Then, just as in "Man in a Glass House"
(another episode about a criminal grown old, and in trouble as a consequence of
his crimes), Hardcastle puts the moral screws to Mark. He's planning on giving
his reward money to Willard to help him get started again. Mark can do as he
pleases but it's obvious what Hardcastle wants. McCormick resists briefly, but
then gives in, just as he did when it came time to confess to the impound break
in. It's the right thing to do.

The Trivia

The Courthouse Racketeers and Jazzmasters play a banjo, a tuba, a trombone (Hardcastle), the drums, a trumpet, and a clarinet...all badly. Well, actually the clarinet sounded pretty good. In later episodes their repertoire expands and their performance skills improve. By what is possibly the oddest of coincidences, keyboardist and composer Paul Hardcastle works with a group of studio musicians known as The Jazzmasters. Though he was active as a musician in the early eighties, it might have still been a bit of insider humor before his album, "19", made the charts in 1985.

When the guys try to orient Willard, they are standing at the corner of Temple and Main. The sculpture the camera initially lights on is Joseph Young's *Triforum*, erected in 1975 at a cost of nearly one million dollars. It has been a source of controversy. In this episode it provides a delightfully ironic backdrop to Willard's comments about the fountain, complete with cherubs and harp, that he remembers being there before. The building across the street, visible behind Willard, is the United States District Court. They are standing on the corner directly east of the Los Angeles City Hall.

The abandoned terminus where Willard hid the loot is at the same location used for the gang hideout in "Prince of Fat City". This time they're in the tunnel just past the station. Before they go inside you can see Toluca Substation No. 51 right behind them.

Willard calls the judge "Hardcase" eight times in this episode—a record for any single show.

Memorable Quotes

Hardcastle: (when McCormick interrupts practice) What's the matter with you? Don't you like music?

McCormick: Music? I thought Burl Ives was in here beating on a tomcat with a bag of nails.

Willard: (seeing the Coyote) What is that, a leftover from Tom Corbett and the Space Cadets?

McCormick: Leftover from what?

Hardcastle: Commander Tom Corbett. A TV show in the fifties. You don't remember me, do you, Henry?

Willard: Should I?

Hardcastle: Sure.

McCormick: The name Hardcastle ring a bell?

Hardcastle: *Judge* Hardcastle?

McCormick: Eats peanuts, plays basketball?

Willard: *Hardcase* Hardcastle? I don't believe it, 'cause he was a young guy.

McCormick: What'd they do, Judge, baptize you with that nickname or what?

McCormick: (interrupting practice) Judge, do you know what time it is?
Hardcastle: No, but if you hum a few bars, maybe we can fake it! (rim-shot)

Third Down and Twenty Years to Life –
premiered January 1, 1984

Written by	Evan Lawrence
Directed by	Georg Stanford Brown
Second unit director	Gary Combs

Cast

Corinne Bohrer	Gina Longren
Gary Wahlberg	Bud Hinkley
Liberty Godshall	Susan Jean Leonard
James Karen	C. Calvin Moore
Robert O'Reilly	Fletcher
Lee Lucas	
Helen Martin	Mrs. Prufrock
Trevor Henley	

Cast Notes

James Karen's first television role was in a 1948 Philco Television Playhouse production of "A Christmas Carol". He also co-starred in the 1970 movie that did not destroy Arnold Schwartzenegger's acting career, *Hercules in New York*.

Robert O'Reilly appeared in a recurring role as Klingon Chancellor Gowron on *Star Trek: Deep Space 9*.

Helen Martin has a short but charming scene in this episode as the dotty Mrs. Prufrock. She was 74 at the time and continued her work in television until her death at age 91.

The Details

A college student, whose brother is in prison, gets a disturbing phone call. someone tells her to stop nosing around in the case or her brother will die.

Hardcastle has a guest lecturing gig at the college. He waxes prolix on the topic of evidence. The young lady who received the call is in the class. She's obviously hostile and challenges the judge with a hypothetical case in which a man is convicted for murder and sentenced to twenty years. The bell rings and Gina walks out, refusing to speak to him further.

The judge and Mark reconnoiter at the local hangout. Hardcastle is hoping to run into the angry young woman. She shows up as expected and they have another confrontation. Gina hasn't got much more than her faith in her brother's innocence while Hardcastle has opportunity, and method, in the form of the murder weapon with her brother's fingerprints on it. The motive is that Gina's brother, Kenny, was a second string quarterback who wanted the victim's starting position in the Rose Bowl game.

But this time when Gina stalks off, a man brandishing a gun forces her into a car. The guys chase him. He drives over barrier spikes, flattening his tires, then escapes on foot.

That night at Gull's Way, Mark discovers Hardcastle up late. He's reviewing the Longren file. The judge has found several witnesses the public defender didn't call. Chief among these is a purported eyewitness, Mrs. Prufrock.

The guys get Gina to take them to meet her. Mrs. Prufrock is a charmingly dotty lady who lives in a mostly cardboard shack and pours her "tea" out of a jug. Her version of the night of the murder involves a "car with eyes". She also has an invisible dog.

Hardcastle sends McCormick undercover as a student at the college. Hardcastle also talks to the coach, Bud Hinkley, and arranges for Mark to have a tryout with the football team. He tells him he's investigating the murder of their former quarterback. Hinkley is amenable, but as soon as Hardcastle leaves, he calls C. Calvin Moore to tell him there's trouble.

Hardcastle picks McCormick up after class. Before they can pull away from the curb, Gina's would-be kidnapper drives by, blasting the Coyote with a shotgun.

The next day, Mark takes a pummeling at football practice, but when he meets Hardcastle and Gina later on that day, he's got a load of team gossip. Susan Jean Leonard was Kenny's girlfriend. She was another no-show at the trial. Now she's moved back to town.

Moore and Hinkley are thinking about Susan, too ("She's been paid. She's been talked to."). Moore sends the shotgun-wielding kidnapper out to reminder her to keep quiet. Mark and the judge get there first. Susan, now with one kid and another on the way, is unhelpful, but a picture on the

mantel—her with the team—shows a van with a paint job that looks like Mrs. Prufrock's description of the third vehicle at the murder scene.

As they're leaving, an orange van with the football team logo passes by. The guys turn to follow, and interrupt yet another attempted kidnapping. Coyote chases van. Van crashes.

Back at Susan's home, she's now much more willing to cooperate. She says Dewey, the first string quarterback, had been shaving points for Mr. Moore, but refused to throw the Bowl game. By setting up Kenny and killing Dewey, Moore guaranteed a loss for the team.

The guys return to campus to confront Moore but find him dead—murdered in his office. While they're puzzling over who's left to have killed him, Hardcastle receives a call from Coach Hinkley, offering information about the murder. They go to the deserted football field, where Hinkley pulls a gun on them. Hardcastle had already summoned the police, but when they show up, Hinkley grabs Gina and flees in his car.

The guys and the cops pursue. Gina is pushed from the car, unhurt, and Hinkley, in headlong flight, crashes into a police car.

In the epilogue, there's a touch football game on the lawn at the estate. Gina and her brother are there. It's not all roses, though. Susan shows up. It turns out she and Kenny both kept quiet to protect one another. Too late now—her husband is waiting in the car.

The Context

Hardcastle goes out of his way to draw a line distinguishing college kids from guys like McCormick. It would be annoying, except that almost every time he brings it up, the college kids fail to perform as expected. This episode is reminiscent of "Goin' Nowhere Fast". But Mark is the guy who gets the key fact—from locker room gossip—that breaks the case open.

The Trivia

How long ago were the eighties? Mark's temporary fraternity, Sigma Epsilon Delta, seems to consist entirely of bookish types. A coed he's chatting up refers to them as "a bunch of hackers". He asks Hardcastle what that means and the judge, pondering briefly, tells him that a hacker is a guy who plays lousy golf.

This is the first of three episodes in which Hardcastle investigates a possible wrongful conviction among his cases. The other two are in the episodes "The

Game You Learn from Your Father" and "Duet for Two Wind Instruments". In two of the three, the convicted men were innocent. In both cases, they were framed.

Memorable Quotes

McCormick: What are you nervous for! Every time you're nervous, your nostrils flare. What are you nervous for?

Hardcastle: I'm not nervous! What are you doing in here anyway? Go on out there and get to hoeing—relate to the soil.

Professor: Well, Mr. McCormick. You seem to be attracting a lot of attention.

McCormick: Yeah, I guess, uh, well, I guess I'm a little older, you know? It's not exactly like I'm fresh out of high school, you know.

Professor: What have you been doing for the last few years?

McCormick: Time.

Whistler's Pride – premiered January 8, 1984

Written by	Stephen Katz
Directed by	Tony Mordente
Second unit director	Gary Combs

Cast

Anne Dusenberry	Casey O'Bannon
Kathryn Leigh Scott	Lenore Alcott
Timothy Scott	Brady
Peter MacLean	Tony Barlow
Ed Bernard	Lieutenant Bill Giles
Duke Stroud	
Richard Reicheg	
Shawn Campbell	Eddie Malone
Bryan O'Byrne	
Logan Clarke	Dorcette

Cast Notes

Kathryn Leigh Scott began her television career with a long-running stint on the gothic soap opera *Dark Shadows*.

The Details

The episode opens on a horse race—thoroughbreds thundering around the turn and across the finish line. Then we see the jockeys, dismounted and heading for the locker room. One of them is Eddie Malone. He's accosted by two shady characters who advise him to "stand up on his horse" in the upcoming Oak Royal race. He says he won't. They threaten

to injure his mount and then gut punch him to get their message across.

At the estate, Mark is mixing equal parts chores and complaining. In a maneuver that would have delighted Tom Sawyer, he suckers Hardcastle into a bet that involves him painting half the garage door. While paint is being slapped on, a certified letter arrives for the judge. It's from the lawyer of a man Hardcastle sentenced ("He was a pickpocket…he reformed and became a bookmaker."). Willie the Whistler has gone to his just reward, and Hardcastle has been named in his will.

At the reading of the will (attended by the judge, Mark, and six guys who look like mobsters) he hears that Willie left him a racehorse, Whistler's Pride. Mark comments that all he ever got from a dead relative was a bottle cap collection and a plaid sport coat.

Before he's even laid eyes on the horse, Hardcastle is planning the Whistler's racing career. Mark counsels him to try and maintain a little perspective. Arriving at the track where the Whistler is stabled, Hardcastle discovers that his new property is vertically challenged and has a reputation for being "a stone". They also meet Casey O'Bannon, a young woman who wants a chance at being a jockey and who is the Whistler's biggest fan.

From somewhere out in the Great Beyond, Willie the Whistler has had the last laugh. His bequest comes with a stack of unpaid bills. Hardcastle now needs $36,418 just to break even. O'Bannon advises that they enter the horse in the

Oak Royal to recoup the money.

In a limousine, racing stable owner Lenore Alcott is discussing the upcoming race with one of the men who threatened Eddie Malone. She has a half-million dollars riding on the outcome. Her two entries must win and place. He assures her everything is under control and he will be informed if anyone else tries to enter.

Back at the track, Hardcastle dispatches Mark to enter the Whistler in the race. Mark can't resist spinning a tale about "Hardcastle Farms" along with his request for an application. The man in the racetrack office tries unsuccessfully to discourage him, then makes a quick phone call the moment McCormick leaves.

Mark is waylaid and advised to scratch his horse from the race. The request is backed-up with a few well-aimed punches and Mark is left on the floor of a horse stall, where Hardcastle discovers him.

Here's something Hardcastle likes even better than horse racing: a chance to roust out some bad guys. He and McCormick go to see the race registrar. While Mark glowers, Hardcastle tells the man that if anything comes between the Whistler and his run in the Oak Royal, he'll call in the feds and talk to the racing commissioner.

They leave. The registrar makes another call, this time to Mrs. Alcott directly. He tells her she needn't worry about this particular entry; the horse can't win.

Casey O'Bannon is begging for a chance to ride the Whistler. Mark explains to her that they don't need the horse to win, only to look like a contender while working out, in order to force a move from the people who are rigging the race. They get Eddie Malone to agree to ride the horse in a timed lap. Mark rigs the track clock to run slow, and the Whistler comes off looking like a hot prospect.

Mrs. Alcott is watching. She instructs her minions to go to Gull's Way and get both the horse and the jockey. A midnight raid results in Eddie's arm broken, the Whistler horsenapped, and one of the intruders, a guy named Dorcette, nabbed and under arrest.

Hardcastle goes to Lieutenant Giles. He wants to interview Dorcette. They find the man being beaten by two other arrestees in the holding tank. He refuses to talk to anyone but his lawyer. They use his employment record to tie him to Alcott Farms, which has two horses entered in the race.

At her home, Mrs. Alcott is on the phone to Mr. Barlow. He's the money behind all these shenanigans. He makes veiled threats that the race must come out as planned.

The guys and Casey show up at Alcott's place. Alcott confronts them in the stable area and is about to throw them off her property when Casey whistles up the Whistler and Mark uses a well-placed elbow to start a brawl. As mayhem

erupts, Alcott escapes in the judge's truck. Hardcastle grabs a horse and goes after her. Mark gets some elemental satisfaction out of pounding a couple of Alcott's goons, and Casey rescues the Whistler.

When the dust settles, Hardcastle has rounded up Alcott, and Mark is temporarily under arrest with the rest of the brawlers. When the dust settles further, Hardcastle has the Whistler back at the estate. Casey is still begging to ride him in the Oak Royal. His plan is to scratch the horse, now that they think the bad guys are all rounded up.

At the police station one of Alcott's employees makes a phone call to Barlow, telling him what has happened. Barlow, in turn tells one of his men to "fix it".

At the estate, Hardcastle is speculating that Mrs. Alcott may not have been at the top of this criminal enterprise. He gets a call from Lieutenant Giles informing him that Dorcette is a known associate of a hood in Las Vegas named Tony Barlow. Hardcastle figures they will have to run the Whistler and win in order to foil Barlow's plans. Casey is more than willing, and appears to be the only one who has a chance of making the Whistler a contender.

At the weigh-in, Barlow's goons show up and threaten Casey. Mark and the judge take them out. Then they have the Whistler scratched. Mark steps in to slow down Tony Barlow in the betting line, and once his bet is made, the Whistler is unscratched. Barlow panics and, when confronted by the guys, flees. Mark goes after him. Barlow's car crashes after an unfortunate encounter with a road-watering vehicle.

In the epilogue, Mark is already figuring out how he'll spend his ten percent of the purse. Hardcastle reads off the list of fees involved and, when he's done, calculates that they are still $1800 short. Mark will have to work his part of the debt off by doing hedges.

The Context

This is possibly the weakest entry in the first season. It's not that we expect realism, but the viewer always hopes that not *too* many of the rules of logic will be bent or broken.

The set-up is entertaining, though. It's good fun to see Hardcastle get snookered by an old associate, with his expectations of a fiery steed lowered precipitously. But of course he turns the whole situation into another ride for the Lone Ranger, both metaphorically and with four hooves at a full-speed gallop. It's right and proper that the series have at least one classic horse chase.

The Trivia

The musical accompaniment to Hardcastle's ride is, of course, the "William Tell Overture", probably better known to old radio and TV fans as the theme from *The Lone Ranger*.

The first woman jockey to ride in a pari-mutuel race in the U.S. was Diane Crump, who began her career at Hialeah Racetrack in Florida in 1969, and went on to ride in the Kentucky Derby. But female jockeys remained a primarily East Coast phenomenon. A woman rider would have still been an unusual sight in California in the mid-eighties, particularly in the tough Southern California circuit.

This episode led the pack for Lone Ranger references, with five. It would not be equaled in that regard until season three's "Duet for Two Wind Instruments".

Memorable Quotes

Hardcastle: Oh, would you look at him, look at him! He's a mass of muscle. Look at the power in those haunches, do you see those legs? And chest size, do you see the size of that chest? I mean, big lungs! Oh, look at the flared nostrils on him, will you, huh? Oh, that's spirit! He wants to win. The horse is ready to *run. Run*!

Hardcastle: Excuse me, is that Whistler's Pride.
McCormick: Looks more like Whistler's Mother. Yes sir, Judge, flared nostrils, big chest, short legs.

Mr. Hardcastle Goes to Washington – premiered January 15, 1984

Written by	Patrick Hasburgh
Directed by	Arnold Laven
Second unit director	Gary Combs

Cast

Richard Herd	Arthur Huntly aka Lonnie Vanatta
James Whitmore, Jr.	Kenneth Boyer
Jack Rader	Detective Thomas
Alex Courtney	Charlie Watts
Linden Chiles	Doorman
Michael J. Aronin	
Frank A. Miller	

Cast Notes
Richard Herd plays the hiding-in-plain-sight murderer, Lonnie Vanatta. His extensive and ongoing career includes continuing roles on *Seaquest DSV* and *Star Trek: Voyager*. He also appears in the third season *Hardcastle and McCormick* episode "The Yankee Clipper". And yes, he too began his movie career in the epic *Hercules in New York*.

James Whitmore, Jr., in addition to having guest roles in this episode and "She Ain't Deep, but She Sure Runs Fast", also directed episodes of three Cannell series: *Riptide*, *21 Jump Street*, and *Wiseguy.*

The Details

It's dinner time at the estate and Mark's turn to cook. Macrobiotics is the culinary theme tonight. Hardcastle is unreceptive ("Haven't you got a pork chop in the icebox?"), but he's soon distracted by a news broadcast. The nominees for a Supreme Court vacancy are being announced. Mark chokes down his tofu while the judge comments disparagingly on the nominees.

When Hardcastle's name is added to the list Mark drops his fork and both men sit in shocked silence. A half beat later the phone rings. It's the *Washington Post*. Mark witnesses Hardcastle's instant transformation. He's gone from being his usual outspoken self, to someone who is determined not to offend.

In Washington, in a conference room of Huntley Press International, Arthur Huntley holds a staff meeting. He is taking reports on the nominees and making decisions on how to slant the coverage of the story. He sounds like a mover and shaker but when the staff is dismissed, it's Milton C. Hardcastle's photograph that he is contemplating with concern. Ken Boyer, who remained behind, tells him not to worry. Hardcastle was only nominated as a political favor to another judge and isn't a viable candidate.

Huntley is still worried. Hardcastle gave him a life sentence for murder twenty-five years ago. He escaped, changed his name, and restarted his life. He tells Boyer to have someone pay Hardcastle "a visit" when he gets to Washington.

Back at the estate, in the study Mark's all dressed up and giving a pep talk to the judge, who's ready to leave for Washington. It turns out Mark doesn't need a suit.

Hardcastle wants him to stay behind and look after things at Gull's Way. Mark is initially offended, but eventually appears to accept the decision. He gives the judge a little more sage advice and they shake hands. Hardcastle heads out the door to run the gauntlet of reporters camped on his front lawn.

Hardcastle's plane has barely cleared the runway before McCormick is on the phone, trying to buy a ticket to Washington. He can't afford it (not even without the movie and the dinner) but he does have enough cash to buy five tanks of gas, which is what he figures it'll take to get him there. He's off, suitcase in the passenger seat and a bunch of candy bars for sustenance.

When Hardcastle checks into his Washington hotel, Boyer points him out to two goons in his employ. He hands over an envelope of cash, telling them they'll get the rest when Hardcastle becomes "just another victim of the high D.C. crime problem".

Morning, and McCormick is straggling into the city, draining his last cup of coffee and looking just about done-in. Hardcastle is on the phone in his hotel room, wondering why no one's answering back at the estate. He goes out for his morning jog and encounters Boyer's goons, asking for directions.

Mark pulls up just in time to see the judge forced at gunpoint into a car. He takes off after them. In the back of the car, Boyer's goon, Miller, has his hands full with a cranky Hardcastle. He notices Mark, burning rubber right along behind them. Hardcastle glances back as well, and does a double-take at the last car he expected to see in Washington.

The chase gets heated. The sedan is finally forced up and over a series of parked cars, crashing to a halt. Mark and the judge tackle the two kidnappers and Mark even recovers Hardcastle's watch ("It's broken").

Back at Huntley's headquarters, the boss is not pleased at the screw-up. Now Hardcastle has gone from long shot to local hero. He tells an apologetic Boyer that now they will do this *his* way. His new plan is to make Hardcastle look dirty.

It's evening in the hotel room. Mark is listening in mild aggravation to the umpteenth news report lauding Hardcastle for single-handedly doing his bit to clean up the streets of D.C. They're going to a reception where the President will be making an appearance. As they step out of the hotel Mark has difficulty hailing a cab, but the doorman signals up a limousine.

At the reception reporters flock around one of the other nominees, Appellate Court Justice Maggie Williams. She's telling the reporters that lack of appellate experience isn't an *absolute* bar to being a Supreme Court Justice. Blackstone, another nominee, gets in on the shiv job with a few well-chosen remarks of his own.

Against Mark's advice, Hardcastle elbows into the discussion. When he's asked about a decision of his which was overturned by Williams, he fumbles. McCormick jumps in with a response worthy of a Washington press secretary. Afterwards Hardcastle gets a stern talking-to from Mark. He's got to stop trying to

be political. It's not his style and it leaves him tongue-tied. The judge agrees.

As the reception continues he's approached by a man named Watts, who claims to be an admirer. He poses for a picture with him. As the event winds down, two women that Boyer had smuggled in drape themselves on the guys as the flash bulbs pop again.

The morning headline in the Huntley paper is a smear job. The photos make the judge look like a womanizing booze-hound. A second piece shows him as cozy with crime figure Charlie Watts. Mark points out that it's only one newspaper. Kenneth Boyer's by-line is on both articles.

At the morning press conference we see a new Hardcastle. No more fumbling for the "right" thing to say. He speaks his mind and what he wants is to know why Boyer is spreading all this dirt about him. He and Mark head off to see the police.

Back at Huntley headquarters, Arthur Huntley thanks his right hand man graciously then, as soon as Boyer has left the room, makes a phone call arranging for his death.

It should come as no surprise that Hardcastle has a friend in the D.C. police department. Detective Thomas gives him the word that one of his two muggers is suspected to have been in Boyer's employ on a previous hit job. He provides Hardcastle with Boyer's home address.

The judge and Mark arrive to find the door open and Boyer dead on the floor. The police show up a moment later. Things look bad, but they convince Detective Thomas to let them go have a talk with the one loose string that's left—Charlie Watts.

Mark persuades the judge to try a little "good cop, bad Mark" on the guy who is their last hope for some answers. They accost Watts in his own home and Mark, with the help of a lamp (and looking like he forgot to take his medication), scares the truth out of him. After Watts tells them Huntley's former alias, the guys find the publisher's old photo in a mug shot book.

Hardcastle gets himself deputized so he can break the news to Huntley himself. The attempted arrest goes haywire when Huntley grabs his own secretary as a hostage and then flees in his car. The Coyote chases. Huntley's car crashes in an impressive 360-degree, lateral flying rollover.

In the epilogue, the press is clamoring for interviews. Mark fields the calls as Hardcastle packs to go home. Mark thinks he'll get the nomination; after all, the judge is a hero now. The phone rings again. Mark answers wearily. It's the President. Hardcastle takes the call. We hear that he sent a letter, withdrawing himself as a candidate for the Supreme Court.

Mark is stunned. He wants to know why. Hardcastle explains that he'd rather be chasing the bad guys and, besides, if he were in Washington who'd keep McCormick out of trouble? Anyway, he could never get used to wearing a tie.

The Context

It's said that victorious Roman generals riding in their triumphal processions always kept a guy in the chariot to whisper "all glory is fleeting". Hardcastle has McCormick to do the honors. This is the first of three episodes where he discovers that, in the words of his younger associate, "fame is an ugly drug". The other two episodes on this same theme are "Whatever Happened to Guts?" and "Hardcastle for Mayor". In all three, McCormick is portrayed as the guy with his feet mostly on the ground. Of course, Hardcastle stands ready to return the favor when Mark gets his occasional shot at the big time.

Although Hardcastle has his doubts about taking Mark to Washington (mostly because he's going to be scrutinized, and explaining his association with an ex-con might be awkward), when it comes to smear tactics, Huntley doesn't even bother to use Mark. By contrast, in the third season episode "Hardcastle for Mayor" Mark is seen as a liability by everyone but the judge. When a reporter raises the question, Hardcastle quickly and definitively disarms the issue.

The Trivia

McCormick takes the indirect route from L.A. to Washington, dipping south along U.S. Interstates 10 and 20. But even the most direct route would be a distance of 2689 miles. If we assume Hardcastle's plane left very early on day one, and Mark departed shortly thereafter (losing three hours to the time zones), in order to arrive the next day in time to foil the kidnapping, he would have had to have averaged something around 100 miles an hour.

At minute 14:45, as Mark is pulling up to the hotel, watch for the phantom second Coyote, parked on a flatbed tow truck in the background.

At the moment just before Hardcastle's kidnappers crash (18:06), a cluster of palm trees are visible in the background landscaping. More palms are seen in the final chase involving Arthur Huntley.

While twentieth-century U.S. Supreme Court Justices hail from a variety of sources, including one former president, the majority of them have federal appellate court experience. There is nothing in the U.S. Constitution, however, that dictates any qualifications for the office.

Memorable Quotes

Hardcastle: Sitting on the Supreme Court bench has been a dream of mine ever since I was in law school.

McCormick: And you don't want me to mess it up.

Hardcastle: Did I say that? I didn't say that. It's just that who's going to take care of this place if we're both out in D.C.? Come on now, there's a list of a lot of stuff that's got to be done, and, uh…

McCormick: Oh, I get it. I'm good enough to cut your front lawn, but when it comes to hobnobbing with the Washington elite, I'll be outclassed, right?

Hardcastle: No, it's just that there's a lot of chores to be done around here.

McCormick: I tell you what, Judge, I really didn't want to go anyway. No, I just thought maybe you could use a friend down there and, well, you know, so I asked. Excuse me, I'm sorry.

Hardcastle: Well, don't get sore.

McCormick: I'm not getting sore about it.

Hardcastle: These congressional guys are going to throw a lot of light on me. They move up real close, you know.

McCormick: And you don't want them looking too close at a judge who's hanging out with an ex-convict.

Hardcastle: Come on. Didn't you ever want anything so bad that you're afraid to even think about it because it might not happen? Every guy that's ever sat on a bench dreams about being on the Supreme Court. I got my chance. I got to give it my best shot.

McCormick: Alone?

Hardcastle: Well, you can understand that, can't you?

McCormick: Yeah, I understand. Hey, Judge. Just remember you get where you're going because of who you are; don't change, all right?

Hardcastle: What're you looking at?

McCormick: You were going to say no.

Hardcastle: Yeah, but he wasn't going to ask me anyway, so it's no big deal, right?

McCormick: Yes, it is. I mean, you didn't know that. Well, you really wanted this. What changed your mind?

Hardcastle: Well, I did. But, I got to thinking about it and I figured if I'm sitting on the Supreme Court bench, then I'm not going to be out chasing bad guys on the streets and a lot of them would get away. Besides, you wouldn't be in my judicial stay anymore and somebody's got to keep you out of trouble, right? (throws tie away) I couldn't get used to wearing one of these anyway.

McCormick: Incredible.

Hardcastle: Now you're cooking.

School for Scandal – premiered January 29, 1984

Written by	Tom Blomquist
Directed by	Tony Mordente
Second unit director	Gary Combs

Cast

Robert Culp	Arthur Farnell
Doug McClure	Detective Jeff "Jay" Hamilton
Randi Brooks	Trish
Charles Cooper	Terrence Harlow
Joe Restivo	Frankie

Cast Notes

Robert Culp is widely known for his role as Kelly Robinson in the 1960s series *I Spy*. Almost two decades later a new generation came to know him as Bill Maxwell, a very different kind of government agent, in Cannell's *The Greatest American Hero*. He also appeared with Brian Keith in the film *The Raiders*, as well as making a guest appearance on Keith's earlier series, *The Westerner*.

The Details

It's nighttime, and the guys are uncharacteristically in suits and ties as they enter a small-scale mansion. They're attending the retirement party of a good friend of Hardcastle's. McCormick isn't approaching the occasion with the restraint the judge would like. Inside, things don't go much better as Mark stocks up on the drinks and fingers all the finger foods. And all of this is before dinner.

No one is aware of the two black-clad figures slinking around outside. While the party guests enjoy their meal—and Mark continues to embarrass Milt—the intruders quietly break into the house and go about their business upstairs.

The after-dinner mingling is interrupted by a shriek when the hostess discovers the robbery. These are clearly guests of the Hardcastle ilk; the men all pull out concealed weapons and rush to assist.

Before the police have completed the initial crime scene processing, Hardcastle has pegged the culprit. A million dollar Monet was left hanging on the wall. That's enough for him to identify the *modus operandi* of Arthur Farnell, supposedly retired super-thief. Mark is skeptical.

Hardcastle floats his theory to the detective in charge (another old friend, of course), but Jay Hamilton is no more receptive than McCormick. Farnell's not only retired from the criminal life, he's also gone Hollywood. In addition to his book writing career and the talk show circuit, Farnell has a movie deal.

At the Beverly Hills Hotel, the burglars are being congratulated; they got out clean, and they left the Monet. There's a knock on the door. Farnell is expecting room service. Instead, it's Hardcastle.

Hardcastle and Farnell spend a few minutes catching up on old times. The judge accuses him of the burglary at the Richards home, giving notice that he's on the case. Farnell denies any involvement. As a farewell comment, Hardcastle tells him he shouldn't have left the Van Gogh, and in a glaring display of arrogance, Farnell comments that it was a Monet.

At Gull's Way the next day, Hardcastle has McCormick studying up on Farnell. Mark still isn't convinced Hardcastle's got the right man, but the judge won't back down. When the police scanner announces another robbery in progress nearby, they rush out in response. A vehicle is leaving the drive just as they pull up. They pursue in the Coyote. Mark runs the bad guys off the road and the car flips down a ravine. The burglars—a well-dressed young man and woman—are pulled from the wreckage and turned over to the arriving police.

Back at the gatehouse, Hardcastle gets word from Hamilton. The kids they arrested claim to have graduated from a crime school. McCormick's still amused by the whole idea. When Hardcastle bristles, Mark demands to know the real reason the judge is so keen on tagging Farnell. Hardcastle tells him that Farnell appeared in his court twenty years earlier. He gave him a lenient sentence and the young thief was paroled after six months. After that, to Hardcastle's chagrin, he embarked on a lifetime of high-profile crime. Now the judge wants to finally nail him.

Nighttime again, outside a swanky restaurant, and Hardcastle's trying to put his plan into action. Mark's still arguing. He says Farnell is never going to fall for the yuppie makeover the judge has put him through. As soon as he leaves the truck, Mark switches to his *own* M.O. Posing as a valet, he steals Farnell's car, handing over a claim ticket with a ransom note written on the back.

The next day, at Gull's Way Hardcastle's still fuming about Mark's stunt with the car. McCormick's certain it's the only way to reach Farnell. As they argue, the phone rings.

Mark shows up poolside at Farnell's hotel to return the car as agreed. Introducing himself as Mark Benchley, he lays on a dose of flattery, asking Farnell to mentor him in the finer points of the second-story business. Farnell seems mildly impressed with "Benchley", but doesn't commit.

Mark thinks he's blown the gig, but he's not so disappointed that he doesn't stop to hit on Farnell's companion, the lovely Trish. She gently rebukes him, but sets up a meeting with him for later that morning. He eagerly keeps the appointment, but this is no date. Trish blindfolds Mark and drives him to their destination.

In what looks like a darkened living room, a team of burglars practices their skills. They're closely observed by a dozen people, including McCormick and Trish. This is Arthur Farnell's classroom. When Mark makes a smart comment to Trish and challenges one of Farnell's ideas, Arthur instructs him to "steal" the Corvette that's on hand as a teaching aid. "Benchley's" obvious expertise arouses Farnell's suspicions. He tells his right-hand man, Jackson, to run a check on his prints and "put Trish on him".

Later that night, Hardcastle drives McCormick to another meeting with Trish. Mark's trying to play it off as more of the rigors of undercover work, but he clearly hopes he's headed for a date. His protestation that it's all strictly business backfires when Hardcastle insists he wear a wire.

Meanwhile, Farnell's getting his report on his new pupil. Apparently Jackson has contacts at the parole board. McCormick's cover has been completely blown. Arthur orders the school shut down and puts in a call to Trish.

Over drinks, Trish flirts with Mark and compliments his criminal aptitude. She suggests a trip to her place. On the way out the door, Mark ditches his wire.

It doesn't take him long to realize he should've kept it. In a limousine, Farnell holds him at gunpoint and asks for a favor. There's a car he wants stolen.

McCormick tries to refuse, but relents when Farnell threatens to kill Trish.

In basic black, Mark scales the fence at the auto dealership and enters the showroom from the roof. He seems back in his element as he approaches the Excalibur. Quick thinking saves him as some people pass by the display window; then he gets to work. He outwits the on-site security guards, but isn't aware that there's a camera snapping his picture as he slips into the car and speeds away.

The next morning, on a golf course, a guy named Frankie is delivering a report to his boss. He's already got McCormick's rap sheet. Frankie's boss, Terrence "Terrible Terry" Harlow, is furious. He smuggles heroin into the country in special-order cars. Mark has messed up his operation. Harlow wants him killed.

Later that morning, as Hardcastle and McCormick leave for the police station, Mark patiently explains again why he's had to steal two different cars in the course of twenty-four hours. Hardcastle doesn't think much of his reasoning, and he certainly doesn't think Trish was in any danger. He's convinced she works for Farnell and it was all just part of the job.

Frankie had them staked out, and now gives chase. McCormick leads him through twists and turns until they finally blow past a stationed patrol car. The officer joins in the pursuit. When the Corvette whips around, Frankie is trapped between the two cars. Frankie is taken away by the cops. Hardcastle finally tells McCormick whose car he stole, and why Harlow has people out to kill him. McCormick realizes Farnell set him up.

Back at the estate, Hardcastle has Mark call Farnell and offer to sell him the Excalibur for twenty thousand dollars; otherwise, he's going to tell Harlow who was the real mastermind behind the theft of his car—and the drugs. Mark arranges to meet him in a cemetery in one hour.

Next up is Terrible Terry. This time, Mark's more reluctant. Against his better judgment, he throws in a few insults to get Harlow's attention. Then he offers to sell him back his car, and his dope. Same time, same place for the meeting.

Mark's at Hollywood's All Saints Cemetery as agreed. He looks nervous, but he's all business once the players start arriving. Farnell's first, and—to Mark's surprise—Trish is with him. Artie still thinks he's in control as he slips into the Excalibur and tells Mark to drive. Harlow moves in and cuts them off. McCormick introduces them, telling Harlow that he stole the car for Farnell.

Just as the two sides are about to attack, the cops move in. Shots are exchanged, bad guys scatter, squad cars screech into place, and everyone gets rounded up except Farnell, who makes his escape in an unattended cop car. McCormick careens after him in the Coyote. It's a short chase before McCormick forces Farnell's car off the road and into a flip.

Arriving back at the cemetery in Mark's custody, Farnell looks disheveled but not much the worse for wear. He's still convinced he won't be convicted.

Hardcastle points out that McCormick's testimony ought to pretty much seal the deal. Artie tells Mark that he's wasting a "considerable gift". Hardcastle tells Farnell that McCormick has a flaw that separates him from the other criminals, though he won't tell McCormick what that flaw might be.

The Context

The partnership continues to evolve. Hardcastle clearly wants to be the boss, but McCormick argues about almost everything he says, and it's mostly taken in stride. Even when he starts doing things his own way—including the theft of a couple of cars—there are no consequences, not even any threats of incarceration, just a couple of pointed comments. Though it's clear the judge was taken in by Farnell decades earlier, he doesn't seem concerned that McCormick might be the next felon to make a fool of him.

McCormick, for his part, is comfortable enough to do what he thinks needs doing—including stealing a couple of cars—with no fear of repercussion. The judge doesn't even blink when Mark works Farnell on the phone, telling him in his most convincing style that he's been scamming Hardcastle for the past eight months.

Of course, by the epilogue we find out why. Hardcastle knows McCormick has integrity, even if he won't admit it to Mark.

The Trivia

The car McCormick stole for Farnell was a 1983 Excalibur Series IV Phaeton; only 107 of them were produced that year. The Excalibur was last produced in 1989.

When Hardcastle asks Farnell if his hotel is $300 a day, Artie doesn't know (though surely it's on the back of the door). Based on current suite pricing at the Beverly Hills Hotel and adjusted for inflation, his manager was probably shelling out at least $475 a night. And they say crime doesn't pay.

Joe Restivo was one of the original owners of Vitello's Restaurant in Studio City, the site where Robert Blake shared his last meal with wife Bonny Lee Bakley. The restaurant has since been sold to other owners.

When Mark is driven to the secret crime school location, Hardcastle is following in the truck, yet there's no indication they make any move to make an arrest or seize evidence there.

Memorable Quotes

> **Hardcastle**: That was a finger bowl.
> **McCormick**: I committed a fox pass.
> **Hardcastle**: Faux pas.

Farnell: You know you are wasting a considerable gift, my boy, on this one. (gestures at Hardcastle)

Hardcastle: There's a little problem there, Artie. You see, the kid's got a flaw, kinda sets him apart from somebody like you.

Farnell: What is that?

Hardcastle: (whispering to Farnell) He's got integrity.

McCormick: What'd you say? What'd you say? What flaw do I have?

Hardcastle: I'll tell you when you're old enough.

The Georgia Street Motors – premiered February 5, 1984

Written by	Shel Willens
Directed by	Joseph Manduke
Second unit director	Gary Combs

Cast

Efrem Zimbalist, Jr.	Emmett Parnell
Andrew Duggan	Roy Stern
Dana Elcar	Frank Cadigan
Danny Goldman	Dwayne Morton
Jake Dengel	Joe Fingers
Stack Pierce	Prison Guard
Beau Starr	George Morgan
Curt Lowens	
David Sage	

Cast Notes

Efrem Zimbalist, Jr. also appeared with Brian Keith in the television series *77 Sunset Strip* and the 1958 film *Violent Road.*

Dana Elcar was probably best known for his continuing role as Pete Thornton in the series *MacGyver*. When he became blind due to glaucoma his disorder was written into the series. During the last years of his career he played several other roles that involved characters who were blind. Mr. Elcar died in 2005.

Andrew Duggan was a television mainstay across five decades until his death in 1988. He had the role of John Walton in the movie that preceded the series.

Danny Goldman, who played brainy bean counter, Dwayne Morton, is now mainly involved in the casting end of the business as the head of Dan Goldman and Associates.

The Details

It's night in the city. A man walking down a dark alley is followed by two men on motorcycles. They look like cops and we hear them confront the man, telling him to halt. A moment later, two shots ring out. The man lies dead and the two others cruise off, into the anonymous darkness.

Daytime at the estate, and two men struggle for supremacy. McCormick's watching a classic *film noir*; the judge just wants to see the news. After missing a grab for the remote, Hardcastle pulls a second one out of the drawer. It's dueling channel changers for a moment until the news flashes on a familiar face and a "man bites dog" story—embezzler Dwayne Morton, sentenced by Hardcastle, is refusing to accept his parole. He wants to stay in his cell at San Quentin. Just then the cable fails.

Hardcastle's curiosity is piqued. He's decided to drag a reluctant McCormick back to his old stomping grounds. He intends to ask Morton what's up.

In Judge Emmet Parnell's chambers, a first-time offender gets his fifteen-year sentence confirmed. As soon as the miscreant is taken away, two of Parnell's judicial colleagues, Roy Stern and Frank Cadigan, step in. Parnell hosts a quick slide show. The subject is a soon-to-be ex-con named George Morgan. He was convicted of killing two cops. Parnell originally sentenced him to death; now he's getting out.

At San Quentin, George Morgan, a hard-looking man, is being walked through the facility by a guard. He's wearing street clothes.

Mark and the judge arrive. Mark looks very reluctant. They pass Morgan on his way out through the visitor's area. Hardcastle is waved through to cell-block A, but Mark isn't allowed in. He's not very disappointed.

Hardcastle confronts Dwayne Morton in his cell. At first, Morton tries to explain the advantages of prison life, but eventually his nervousness seeps through. Hardcastle observes he's been collecting obituaries—all from ex-cons. Morton finally breaks down and reveals the statistical anomaly he has discovered. Recently, the survival rate of parolees has plummeted.

Back outside, Hardcastle explains Morton's findings to McCormick. Mark can't believe there'd be anyone tough enough to take on the men in question.

Back in the city, George Morgan is leaving the train station. Parnell and his judicial posse are stalking him. Morgan eludes them in a stolen taxi but, after a high-speed chase, he's killed when his vehicle is struck by a train.

Back at the estate, having heard this latest twist to the tale, Mark is a believer. He thinks there are vigilantes at work, and he guesses it's probably cops.

Hardcastle does a little nosing around. As Mark expected, he gets nothing from the police. The judge does some speculating of his own. The ex-cons who have died prematurely were all sentenced by one of three men. He knows them all, having spent time with them in the LAPD in a unit called the Georgia Street Motors. Mark is impressed. This was a tough bunch who were known for crossing the line. Hardcastle says he got out before any of that started.

Another day, another vigilante hit. Roy Stern takes out Sammy Johns with a blast from a shotgun.

Mark is washing windows and waxing admiring over Hardcastle's days as a motorcycle cop. Hardcastle admits it was fun, but he suspects these same guys of being murderers. He's got a plan to win their confidence.

At a restaurant, an old hangout he hasn't been to in a while, Hardcastle looks like he's nursing both a beer and a grudge. Parnell is sitting across the room, watching him. Mark stalks in and shouts Hardcastle's name, then gets in his face, demanding to know why the judge is sending him back to prison. A push leads to a punch and soon they're brawling. Mark is grabbed by two other patrons who look like off-duty cops. Hardcastle waves them out as McCormick shouts threats. Parnell, having observed it all, gets up and makes a phone call.

Leaving the bar, Hardcastle is followed by two guys on motorcycles and then approached by Parnell. He goes to Parnell's place and they discuss "the McCormick problem".

The next day, at the estate, while a satellite dish (with a few important modifications) is being connected, Mark complains about Hardcastle's plan. He's not happy to be the next intended victim of the Georgia Street Vigilantes.

That evening, he and Hardcastle go to a swanky French restaurant. Mark is at least happy about the quality of his last meal. Hardcastle is not impressed. Mark is less pleased when he discovers he can't have his steak tartare well done. Hardcastle finally spies the object of his trip to *Chez Petite*, a reformed pickpocket named "Joe Fingers". As a condition of his parole, and at Hardcastle's recommendation, Joe can't leave his home without a pair of cotton gloves on. When he takes them off, he's the best there is.

The next day, Mark's still fretting about the set-up. Joe Fingers will have to get Roy Stern's gun, substituting one with blanks. Mark rightfully wonders if this is such a fool-proof plan. Hardcastle is confident. Mark takes him to "see a man about some wheels".

Hardcastle next appears, fully rigged as a motorcycle cop, tooling up to the

same hangout where Mark confronted him before. The other three bikes are already parked there. Fingers is inside. When he sees the judge walk in, he removes his gloves. Hardcastle meets his old compatriots and they rise to leave. Joe Fingers also gets up and collides with Stern. There's some action with the gun, but Stern quickly

begins to manhandle the little thief. Stern is pulled off by Hardcastle. Joe staggers away. The four ex-cops depart.

Mark comes out of his new lodgings and climbs into the Coyote. The posse is watching him from their bikes, nearby. They're on his tail a moment later. He spots them, does a hairpin turn and leads them on a chase, but he's finally run into something faster and more maneuverable than the Coyote. They corner him at a dead-end, on a deserted rural road.

As Hardcastle expected, it's Roy Stern whose gun is drawn first. Mark tries persuasion, but the judge tells him this is "a preemptive strike". Mark continues to argue and Hardcastle lands a quick punch that appears to knock him off his feet. Mark struggles back up, looking worried. Stern hands Hardcastle the gun and tells him to do the honors. He shoots once, appearing to draw blood. Mark emotes like crazy, clutching his reddening arm and shouting that the bullets are real. Looking grimly implacable, the judge fires five more rounds.

It's night and we see the Coyote coming through the gate at Gull's Way. In the gatehouse it's apparent that Hardcastle has been waiting, maybe even pacing. When Mark strolls in (looking "bloody" and a little bruised), the judge asks him where he's been. Out getting burgers, it appears. Getting gunned down made him hungry. It's obvious that Hardcastle was concerned, but he states his worries on the most practical level. If something had happened to McCormick, they wouldn't have been able to put this sting together. The next step is going to be "a haunting".

In a steam bath that night, Roy and Frank are sweating. Roy thinks they let Hardcastle back in too easily. He doesn't trust him. The door to the room opens and in walks a silent McCormick, shrouded in sheet and steam. As soon as he's gotten Roy's attention, he hauls out of there. He piles into the truck and Hardcastle peels away.

At an emergency meeting of the three vigilantes, Roy insists he saw McCormick and says Hardcastle is running some kind of scam on them. They decide to pay him a visit.

The next morning we see all three riding up the Gull's Way drive, in full motor-cop regalia. The confrontation takes place in the study, with a very live McCormick backing Hardcastle up, and a two-camera system in place that's beaming it all to the nearest police station. In the middle of the discussion, Roy pulls a gun. Mark holds off the other two while Hardcastle disarms Roy and dukes it out with him, eventually getting the upper hand.

In the epilogue, the guys enjoy the fruits of their new satellite television system. Hardcastle ambles into the study, bearing snacks. Mark is watching a baseball game. The judge extols the virtues of the system ("A hundred and fifty stations…baseball, soccer"). He asks who's winning—the Giants, he's told. Hardcastle squints at the screen. Mark informs him it's the *Tokyo* Giants. The judge asks for a change of venue. Mark hits the remote and takes them to a news station. It's in Japanese, too.

The Context

Hardcastle and McCormick had encountered some flack in pre-release for its premise of hunting down the ones that didn't get punished in court. Was this going to be a show about vigilantism? The producers qualified the objectives early on—he was only going to tangle with guys who committed *further* crimes, or who had somehow escaped prosecution altogether. This episode draws a line in the sand and shows that Hardcastle stands well on the side of proper procedure and due process. He'll even go after the guys who are wearing the home team uniform if they're not following the rules.

In fact, in five of the seventeen episodes thus far, it was the good guys who turned out to be bad guys, with the guilty parties fairly evenly distributed between cops, judges, and parole officers. Eventually sheriffs and mayors would be added to the list. Through it all, as Roy Stern pointed out, Hardcastle holds the line. He may be slightly slower to suspect the white hats than Mark is, but once he's got an inkling, he doesn't let his loyalties stand in his way.

The Trivia

In the script, the classic movie that Mark is trying to watch is Humphrey Bogart's *The Maltese Falcon*, and it's evident that he's got the dialog memorized. It's a logical choice for a McCormick favorite, with its double-crossing female lead who gets one trusting man killed. In the final production, that's swapped for a more obscure film, probably with fewer copyright entanglements.

The New Jersey grapefruit fly, subject of reports on both American and Japanese news reports, is obviously a spoof of the Mediterranean fruit fly that was found in the San Francisco area in 1982. A massive and controversial program was instituted to eradicate this pest.

Hardcastle's trick of transmitting a video signal to the police station as he lures the vigilantes into a confession sounds fairly improbable, but in 1986 a Florida satellite dish salesman who called himself "Captain Midnight", was able to successfully block HBO's feed and overlay his own protest message about the newly instituted fees that were damaging his dish business.

And note those other eighties touches—the big satellite dish and the shoebox-sized security cameras.

Memorable Quotes

Hardcastle: You wanna take a little ride?
McCormick: A ride to San Quentin? Can't we just go to the zoo?
Hardcastle: That's where we are going.
McCormick: Aw, come on.
Hardcastle: Come on, come on, come on. I'll let you ride up front, with me.

Hardcastle: They're not gonna bust you up. They're just gonna kill you.
McCormick: You know, I'm getting kinda tired of being the duck in this partnership. When I finally get out of your probation, the only job I'm gonna be qualified for is that of a target in a penny arcade.
Hardcastle: I'll give you a good reference, too.

The Homecoming (parts 1&2) – premiered March 5 and 11, 1984

Written by	Patrick Hasburgh
Directed by	Bruce Kessler
Second unit director	Gary Combs

Cast

Cathy Lee Crosby	Christy Miller
Stephen Elliott	Bill "Punky" Paxton
David Graf	Deputy Steve Bellows
John Ireland	Bucky Miller
Cameron Mitchell	Tom "Stinky" Broadmore
Robert Moberly	
Mitchell Ryan	John "Stretch" Carter
Byron Webster	Judge Stuber
John Amos	Albie Meadows
Rosalind Cash	Connie Meadows
Treva Frazee	

Cast Notes

Cathy Lee Crosby is likely most famous for being one of the hosts of ABC's *That's Incredible!* In her younger years, she was a professional tennis player, playing at Wimbledon in 1964.

John Amos, perhaps best known as the father on the sitcom *Good Times* and the adult Kunta Kinte in *Roots*, has also been a social worker, professional football player, and Golden Gloves boxing champ.

Cameron Mitchell appeared in hundreds of productions on stage, screen and television, but may be best remembered as Buck Cannon from *The High Chaparral.* He also had a part in the television mini-series *How the West Was Won*, along with Stephen Elliott and Brian Keith.

The Details

We open in Clarence, Arkansas, a typically quaint small town. Outside City Hall, Mayor Tom Broadmore is delivering bad news to his friend, Punky Paxton: "Judge Stuber wouldn't overturn". That means Bucky Miller gets to keep his farm and no freeway will come 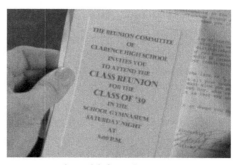 through town. On cue, Bucky shows up to join his old friends in conversation. Even with their disagreement over the town's future, they all agree they'll be at the upcoming high school reunion.

Back in Malibu, Judge Hardcastle is also looking forward to the class reunion. He's reminiscing about neat nicknames and the year the basketball team went all the way to the state championship. Besides past glories, Hardcastle's also being recognized as the "significant alumnus of 1939". Mark isn't impressed with any of it, but he still wants to go along. Hardcastle thinks a dose of small town Americana is just what the kid needs.

That night in Clarence, there's an explosion outside Bucky Miller's farmhouse.

Driving to Arkansas, Hardcastle fills McCormick in on the details of the small-town lifestyle, including the Miss Amber Waves pageant. Mark gets a big kick out of making fun of the Norman Rockwell routine. But once they're in Clarence, even McCormick seems touched by the affection the town has for Milt.

Tom and Punky meet again that afternoon, joined by the sheriff. They decide Bucky must be forced to sell his farm. That evening though, at the reunion, everything seems mostly genial as old friends are reunited. Later, over a game of basketball, Bucky tells Hardcastle and McCormick about his falling out with the others and mentions the explosion that subsequently destroyed his barn. Hardcastle thinks Miller is misreading things. He believes Clarence is the same good town it's always been. The next morning, a police vehicle forces Bucky Miller's pickup off the road. It plunges into a ravine. Miller's body is retrieved from the wreck while Hardcastle judges the Miss Amber Waves contest.

Christy Miller, Buck's daughter, arrives in Clarence and takes up residence at the family farm. Punky Paxton worries that she intends to stay and there will have to be another "accident". Tom and Stretch are sure she'll sell. But when Paxton approaches her after the funeral, she makes it clear that she's going to keep the farm.

Meanwhile, McCormick broaches the idea to Hardcastle that Buck's death might not've been just an accident. The judge refuses to accept that anyone in Clarence would resort to murder over a freeway, but he begins to reconsider after Christy is terrorized with a hanging effigy left on her porch. The judge's concerns are casually dismissed by Mayor Broadmore. Hardcastle decides to start asking a few questions of his own.

The questions don't get them very far. Everyone they talk to maintains no one cared one way or the other whether the freeway came through. They do hear the rumor that there are some sealed real estate bids on undeveloped land. Punky Paxton, who's also the county recorder, stonewalls when Milt asks to see the bids. Hardcastle threatens to get a warrant from Judge Stuber and bring in the state authorities for further investigation.

By the time Hardcastle arrives at Stuber's office, there's been another convenient death. Sheriff Carter blames it on a heart attack, but Hardcastle's now convinced there have been two murders in town.

Later that night, McCormick in-sists that the only way to know who's behind everything is to find out whose names are on the bids; Hardcastle warns him not to go on any evidence gathering missions. Mark agrees, but only until bedtime, when he sneaks out of the hotel and over to Paxton's office. He finds the information, but only just manages to stash the evidence in the bushes before he's arrested.

Hardcastle retrieves the papers the next morning and discovers that the people with a motive to kill Bucky were Paxton, Sheriff Carter, and Mayor Broadmore. He confronts the mayor, intending to get McCormick out of jail. Instead, he finds himself held at gunpoint. He's taken away to go "swimming in the reservoir".

Christy Miller observes the abduction. She heads directly to the jail to see McCormick. Mark stages a jail break, and he and Christy go after Hardcastle.

They arrive at the reservoir in time to see Hardcastle knocked unconscious behind the wheel of a police cruiser. Still too far off to prevent it, they watch as the car is pushed into the water with Hardcastle still inside. The mayor and sheriff run them off, but McCormick and Christy lose them in the Coyote. After eluding their pursuers, the two return to the reservoir. McCormick dives repeatedly, desperate to find Hardcastle. Christy finally convinces him the judge couldn't possibly be alive and drags him back to shore.

Back in town, Mayor Broadmore spins the story that Hardcastle was killed while trying to flee when approached in connection with Bucky's death. Mark's also a suspected murderer, who now has Christy Miller as his hostage.

While the manhunt is getting underway, Christy leads McCormick to an old abandoned cabin in the woods. They hide out there for the night, sharing the grief of losses suffered, and finding some comfort in each other's company.

That same night, at Albie Meadows' farmhouse, there's an unexpected knock on the door. Albie cautiously opens up. A disheveled and weakened Hardcastle collapses into his arms and exclaims, "They're trying to kill me!"

Albie and his wife, Connie, tend to Hardcastle and hide him overnight, but the morning paper's headline causes them concern. Milt does his best to convince his old friends that the story's not true, but ultimately resorts to calling in old family markers. When the posse arrives, Milt waits safely inside while Albie sends them on their way. After they're gone, Albie throws in with Hardcastle completely and they set off together to try and find McCormick.

Back in the cabin, McCormick's got a plan to retrieve the evidence after nightfall and take it to the state police. Meanwhile, the manhunt continues. The Coyote is discovered and the searchers are closing in.

Milt and Albie are nearby, too. They reach the cabin just in time to overhear McCormick reminiscing about some of Hardcastle's more colorful personality traits. Mark is stunned and overjoyed when the judge steps into view, returned from the dead. Mark quickly tells him about the plan, and assures him that no one could possibly know he and Christy are at the cabin. While Albie and Christy try to convince the guys that their best bet is to trust the townsfolk of Clarence, the hunting party shows up, demanding that McCormick surrender. Of course Broadmore and Carter have no intentions of letting him be taken alive.

McCormick escapes under a barrage of fire. Returning quickly in Albie's truck he smashes through the cabin wall. The other three pile in, with Hardcastle hidden from sight. The plan works. The truck flies through the front wall, and makes it safely into the woods. Broadmore and his men are left in the dust, unaware that Hardcastle is alive.

But the truck is identified, leading Carter and Broadmore directly back to the Meadows farm. They're still a step behind Hardcastle and McCormick, though; the guys have left Albie and Connie tied up in the house so the cops will never know Meadows helped the fugitives escape.

Hardcastle, McCormick, and Christy spend the night knocking on doors in Clarence, trying to find someone who will help them get to the state police. They are repeatedly turned away. One of the citizens calls the mayor and tells him Hardcastle's still at large.

The next morning, the manhunt intensifies as Broadmore stirs up the people of Clarence, making them believe that Hardcastle was the one willing to kill to make a profit off the new freeway. Meanwhile, Hardcastle—in disguise—manages to get the land deeds back from Paxton. McCormick commandeers a vehicle, and the chase is on. The bad guys are lured out of town and straight to the waiting barricade of state police.

The epilogue finds all the bad guys safely behind bars in their own jail; Christy making plans to return to Clarence full time to help make it the town it used to be; and Mark is finally convinced of the virtues of small-town life, with just a little help from Wally and the Beav.

The Context

With this episode following directly after "Georgia Street Motors", one has to start wondering if Hardcastle has any old friends that haven't become sociopathic murderers. It won't be the last time in the series that we'll see long-time friends and acquaintances disappoint both Hardcastle and McCormick, only to contrast with the ever-present reality that they never let each other down.

Hasburgh returns to the father and son theme. In the brief time that McCormick believes Hardcastle to be dead, there is a clear correlation drawn between the grief he feels and Christy's grief over the death of her father, with Mark memorably vowing to get the men who killed Hardcastle even if it means spending the rest of his life in prison.

The Trivia

The song heard in the secondary title sequence, "Wings of My Heart", is sung by Joey Scarbury, who would go on to perform the second season theme song, "Back to Back". He also performed the main theme for Cannell's earlier production, *The Greatest American Hero*.

Jerry Mathers was thirty-six when he performed this tongue-in-cheek cameo as his most famous character, over twenty years after the final *Leave it to Beaver* episode was broadcast.

In later episodes we will learn about Hardcastle's aunts, brother, and sister, but there was no family to greet him in Clarence.

When retrieving the evidence McCormick had hidden, Hardcastle mumbles that the kid is the "best safe cracker in twelve states". Of course he hasn't met Mark's father yet.

Hardcastle calls in his markers with Albie by reminding him that his father had given Albie's dad a tractor ("It was only an old Diamond Reo…"). Ransom E. Olds established the REO Motor Car Company in 1904. The Diamond T Company was founded by C.A. Tilt in 1905 and began producing trucks in 1911. The two didn't merge until 1967 and their product line consisted of heavy duty tractor rigs for hauling trailers and for construction, not farm implements. Diamond *Rio*, the country music group, was founded in 1984, but originally known as the Grizzly River Boys, and didn't take the name Diamond Rio until 1985. Their first album was released in 1991.

With the exception of the pilot, this is the only two-hour episode produced for the series.

Memorable Quotes

Sheriff Carter: (explaining Judge Stuber's death) Look, I know you guys are friends, but these things happen. People die.

Hardcastle: Well, around here, they seem to die just at the right time. I mean, you know, it's like when you go duck-hunting. You see one, it don't mean much. But you see two, there's probably a flock nearby.

McCormick: I say we go to the state police with what we've got now.

Hardcastle: No, if you're gonna hunt deer out of season, you gotta put down a salt lick to scare up the buck.

McCormick: Great. Here comes Mr. Greenjeans again.

Hardcastle: And then, you don't pull the trigger 'til you see the buck so the rest of the herd doesn't know which way to run.

Hardcastle: Did anybody see you come out here?

McCormick: Hey, Kemo Sabe, this is Tonto you're talking to. Good scout leave no trail for Long Knives. Don't you worry.

Hardcastle: Very nice to see that my near brush with the Great Hunting Grounds in the Sky didn't put a crimp in that fat mouth of yours.

Hardcastle: (on their hideout being discovered) Good work, Tonto.

McCormick: Listen, I'm from Jersey. It's all sneakers and concrete. What do I know about leaving trails?

Did You See the One That Got Away? – Premiered March 18, 1984

Written by	Lawrence Hertzog
Directed by	Ron Satlof
Second unit director	Gary Combs

Cast

Dennis Franz	Tony Boutros
James Wainwright	Lionel Ryan
Victoria Young	Rose Carlucci
Sam Scarber	the computer man
Gene Dynarski	Eric Goodburn
Stephen Liska	
Richard Fullerton	
Mike Genovese	Gurner
Sandra Kronemeyer	Goodburn's sister

Cast Notes

Dennis Franz later played Lieutenant Norman Buntz on *Hill Street Blues* and went on to fame with a twelve-year run as Andy Sipowicz on *NYPD Blue*. He had a second guest spot on *Hardcastle and McCormick* in "There Goes the Neighborhood". He had previously co-starred with Daniel Hugh Kelly in the 1982 series *Chicago Story*.

Victoria Young, Brian Keith's wife, appeared three times during the run of the show. Twice she played the overworked but helpful Rose Carlucci. She also appeared in the final episode, "Chip Off the Ol' Milt", as the dance instructor at Sunset Acres.

The Details

At Boutros Trucking Industries the boss, Tony Boutros, (a plaid shirt and gold chain kind of guy) is giving his most trusted employees, Tommy and Eddie, a pep talk. Half a ton of brown heroin is being shipped in on his trucks on Friday. He spills the details in his instructions. Outside, a non-descript man in overalls is using an electronic device to listen in. Another employee notices something's up. The eavesdropper pockets the tape and escapes in a truck.

Six a.m. in a Glendale television studio—Hardcastle is appearing on a show called *Let's Talk Law*. Mark's there for moral support and to tell him not to smile so much. When Hardcastle worries about how he looks, Mark assures him that no one will see the program. It broadcasts at the crack of dawn on channel 82, one of those stations you need a coat hanger on the back of the television to pick up.

After it's all over, they head for home. When Hardcastle pulls up to a stop light he looks over and sees a familiar but unexpected face in the vehicle alongside his. It's the man with the tape and his name is Eric Goodburn. Goodburn takes off. Hardcastle chases, but loses him at a railroad crossing.

He explains to McCormick that he sentenced the man to life without parole for killing a cop. Back at the estate, Hardcastle is frustrated in his efforts to find out why Goodburn is out. In fact, he can't even find any evidence that Goodburn was ever in. It's starting to look like Eric Goodburn was a figment of Hardcastle's imagination.

They finally pay a visit to the Los Angeles County Hall of Records and the file room lair of Rose Carlucci. She runs a computer search on Goodburn. It draws a blank at her end, but sets off alarms in the FBI's computer system. Two agents are dispatched to look into the "security breach".

The guys leave the Hall of Records still with no evidence that Goodburn ever existed. Mark advocates a little fishing trip and Hardcastle mutters. As they drive away, the FBI agents follow. Pursuers become pursued as Mark executes a one-eighty. The agents flee and Mark loses them.

The next stop is police headquarters. Mark is left standing in the lobby while Hardcastle visits one of his lieutenant cronies. When he emerges, a few minutes later, he still has no evidence that Goodburn ever existed, but he's determined to keep looking.

At FBI headquarters, a conference is being held. The subject is Goodburn, one of their most reliable electronic surveillance men. He's disappeared, along with the tape that will nail Tony Boutros' operation. The agents can't figure out what's triggered Hardcastle's sudden interest.

Meanwhile, Goodburn himself calls his FBI handler. He's getting nervous

with both Boutros and Hardcastle breathing down his neck. He says he'll call back later.

At the Hall of Records, Rosie's hit pay dirt. She's found a paper file on Eric Goodburn. There's an address for his sister.

Meanwhile, Boutros takes the abandoned electronics equipment to an expert who identifies it as Goodburn's work. The technician knew Eric and remembers his sister very well.

Hardcastle gets to the sister's place first. It's the apartment where Goodburn made the call to the FBI. His sister is there but she says she hasn't seen him in a while.

An anxious Goodburn returns in a taxi. He gets out and notices he's been tailed. Panicky, he tries the locked door of a car, then spots the Coyote and slides in behind the wheel. No key and no escape, but he hastily shoves the tape into the tape player. Tommy and Eddie pull up next to him.

Mark and the judge emerge from the house, hear shots fired, and interrupt the attackers. The gunmen flee, leaving Eric dead in the Coyote.

Very early the next morning, at Boutros' headquarters the television is on, tuned to one of the "coat hanger stations". Boutros asks his men what happened. They still don't have the tape but they got a good look at the guys who interrupted them. Just then the picture on the TV changes to the interview that Hardcastle taped the morning before.

Mark and the judge are watching the same program. Hardcastle talks about "the power of the tube". He says a half-hour of TV exposure and half the town will want to know who he is.

Maybe not *half*, but Tommy and Eddie arrive soon after. Picking the lock on the Gull's Way gate, they break in and head for the Coyote. They are interrupted again and this time captured.

Hardcastle has Rosie run the two men's names and discovers they're both truck drivers with petty records. He asks Rosie how hard it would be to remove someone from the computer files completely. She demonstrates, using his own file on her computer. Hardcastle says it couldn't have been a couple of punks like Tommy and Eddie who did that for Goodburn. As he and Mark leave, he reminds her to restore his file. Just as she turns to do it, her phone rings.

Milt and Mark arrive back at the estate and find two more men searching the Coyote. Charging in, fists flying, they inflict some damage before they realize that these guys are from the FBI. The agents are forced to explain that Goodburn was never in prison because he was recruited by the government. They refuse to say what they were searching for. Mark is incensed. He tells them to show him their search warrant and when they cannot, demands that they leave. Hardcastle backs him up. It's the law and he's right.

After the agents leave, Mark and the judge head out in the Coyote. Mark intends to take it to the garage so he can strip it, looking for the evidence. They're being followed. It's Boutros himself this time. While they're driving, Mark hits the tape player. After a moment of polka music, they hear Boutros outlining his drug smuggling plans. Shortly after, they're surrounded by Boutros' men and forced out of the Coyote.

They and the tape are taken to Boutros' office. The drug kingpin is understandably confused. He wants to know why Hardcastle had his office bugged. He doesn't believe the explanation and he tells his men to take them out and "bury them" along with the tape.

As the guys are escorted away, Mark causes a distraction and the two get the jump on their captors and escape in the Coyote. The FBI, which had been watching Boutros, scrambles units to follow the Coyote. Boutros does the same, siccing his already rolling trucks to hunt them down. They evade a trucker adversary, but lose the FBI tail at the same time.

As Tony hurries to the scene, three more of his truckers catch up with the Coyote. A dangerous game of cat and mouse ensues. Mark finally resorts to tucking the Coyote under one of the eighteen-wheelers, pacing it. From there they spot Boutros coming from the opposite direction. Mark scoots out, hairpin turns, and pursues. Boutros goes off the road, flips and crashes. He is taken into custody by the arriving police, and the tape is handed over to the FBI.

That night, at the estate, Hardcastle stomps into the gatehouse, demanding to know what McCormick did with the paper. Mark's in the shower, but not for long. The water stops flowing. The utilities fail in rapid succession and from the darkness we heard the two men utter in unison, "*Rosie*".

The Context

With its frequently updated "time and location" tags, typed in eighties computer tech style, this episode has an Orwellian feel. There are unseen forces out there, manipulating events in our lives. In this case it's the FBI, distorting the system to get the services of a tech wizard, but the system itself is portrayed as being somehow both pervasive and powerful, yet easily manipulated and hardly foolproof.

Into this mixed message walks Milton C. Hardcastle, with his mantra "law begins at home". It's all about personal responsibility. Everyone has the same rights and obligations under the law. Eric Goodburn, convicted murderer, ought not to have slipped out between the cracks, and Mark has the right to stand up to a couple of federal agents who aren't following the rules.

The judge, and now Mark, too, take that personal responsibility to the extreme, refusing to let the FBI search the Coyote, preferring to look for the evidence themselves, even though they don't even know what they're looking for. It's a matter of principle.

The Trivia

In the preview clip, the "under the moving eighteen-wheeler" stunt is accompanied by Hardcastle's casually uttered "always the easy way" remark. In the episode he far more appropriately hollers, "What are you, *nuts*?"

Mark never gets his "two cheeseburgers, fries, and a vanilla milkshake" from the clown at the fast food place. Modern drive-thru service, with its endless potential for miscommunication, originated in the early seventies.

Memorable Quotes

Hardcastle: (at a television interview) Hey, McCormick, how'm I doing?
McCormick: Great. You haven't said anything yet.
Hardcastle: I said "thank you". What do you think? You think "thanks" would be better?
McCormick: Let's face it, Judge. You're not exactly a man of few words.

Hardcastle: You're not sitting in front of the camera. You think I look fat? They say television puts thirty pounds on you, you know.
McCormick: It makes you look jolly.
Hardcastle: That stinks, McCormick! Who's gonna listen to a jolly judge?

McCormick: Do you have a court order to search that Coyote?
FBI Agent: There wasn't time.
McCormick: Well, I'm gonna give you guys some time. You got two minutes to get outta here. But before you go, listen to this. The law is for everybody, you understand? Not just for bad guys, and it begins right here at home. You guys go get that court order and I'll *think* about letting you search the car.
Hardcastle: The kid's right.
FBI Agent: (to other agent) Let's go.
Hardcastle: McCormick, there's hope for you yet.

Really Neat Cars and Guys with a Sense of Humor
– premiered March 25, 1984

Written by	Lawrence Hertzog
Directed by	Ron Satlof
Second unit director	Gary Combs

Cast

Patrick Collins	Howard Kaye
Marilyn Jones	Cheryl Dirksen
Alexa Hamilton	Debra
Peter Iacangelo	Masters
John Carter	Paul Danton
Jim McMullan	the groom
Fil Formicola	
Clare Peck	

Cast Notes

Patrick Collins, here seen as hapless Howard, appeared as comedian Denny Frye in the episode "What's So Funny?"

Marilyn Jones also played crazed fan Kay Barrett in the episode "Whatever Happened to Guts?"

Jim McMullan, the dashingly handsome (and doomed) groom, also appeared in the episode "Hardcastle, Hardcastle, Hardcastle, and McCormick" as Larry Satin.

John Carter also played Nolan Ashley in the episode 'Whatever Happened to Guts?'

The Details

It's night, and a newly-married man carries his bride across the threshold of their beautifully appointed home. They seem very much in love. They retire to the bedroom. He empties his pockets, tossing down a matchbook that bears a logo and the word 'Doubles'. He's waiting for her in bed. She emerges from the bathroom, lovely in ivory satin. As he admires her, she levels a silenced gun and shoots him.

It's morning at the estate and Mark is getting his auto insurance cancelled for the third time in eight months. It's a small matter of fourteen more bullet holes. The adjuster points out that it's "just like the last time". Mark is grim about the prospects of finding anyone else who will take on his business but Hardcastle soon comes up with a guy who doesn't ask too many questions.

It's off to the body shop for Mark. Howard Kaye, the repairman, says it'll take a couple of days. He apologizes for putting a crimp in Mark's weekend plans and segues into a discussion of cars like the Coyote and their attractiveness to women. He admits to owning a Studebaker himself. Mark tries to steer him back to business. Howard finds out who Mark's new insurance company is and balks—their adjusters wear shoulder holsters. Mark promises to sic the judge on them if there's any hassle. Howard finally agrees to do the work. Mark asks him for a loaner car.

It's Mark's turn to see the effect a Studebaker has on women. He's reduced to driving Howard's burnt-orange model.

It's night time at the body shop, and Howard is overdosing in 'Stud Musk'. He reviews a file folder. It's his date for the evening—Cheryl Dirksen. He heads out the door and climbs into the Coyote. With much varooming he arrives at his destination, mentally preparing himself for the introductions. But as he approaches the door, it slams open, with Cheryl shouting, "They're trying to kill me" as she rushes out.

She grabs his wrist and drags him along. They climb in the Coyote and flee just as two men come out of the house, firing after them. It's the beginning of a perfect evening.

The two heavies report to their boss, Paul Danton. He says Dirksen is blackmailing him. He wants her. The men saw the license of the Coyote. Danton says if they can't find Cheryl, he wants the man who drives that car.

On Monday, Mark and the judge pick up the Coyote. While they're out, Danton's goons search the house. They're departing in a hurry when the Coyote pulls up to the drive. Mark takes off after them but all he gets is four more bullet holes in his quarter panel. The bad guys escape.

Another trip to Howard's to drop off the car. On the way home, Mark dismisses the break-in as an attempted burglary, but later that day the heavies return, this time accosting Mark and asking him questions he can't answer. They start to rough him up, but Hardcastle steps out of the house with a shotgun and a bad attitude. The bad guys are disarmed and arrested.

Hardcastle wants to know what Mark's been up to. Mark denies everything. Heck, he didn't even have a car over the weekend. Howard did, though.

One more trip back to the body shop, this time to demand some answers. Howard tells them of his night of romance after he saved Cheryl's life. He doesn't believe she could be involved in anything shady.

In his elegant study, Paul Danton is contemplating the blackmail photos—he and Cheryl caught in a passionate kiss. He hastily hides the evidence in a locked drawer as his wife walks in.

Howard, Mark, and the judge head to Cheryl's house, which had also been ransacked. They encounter Eileen Weller, who claims to be Cheryl's roommate and appears equally puzzled by what has happened.

The three guys adjourn to a restaurant. Howard is still pleading Cheryl's case. He wants to go to the dating service and get to the bottom of things. Mark says they have to do it right.

It's daytime, outside the Doubles main office. A stretch limo pulls up and Mark steps out, decked out as well-to-do single guy, 'Elliot Wimbleton'. He makes a video, laying on his eligibility with a trowel. Now it's his turn to shop and while in the waiting area he mentions Cheryl Dirksen. Danton overhears. It's Hardcastle's turn up at bat. He's 'Nick Van Norden'.

Mark goes back out to the limo and climbs in. Paul Danton squeals by in his car and lets loose a shotgun blast that takes out the rear window and puts eleven holes in the door. Amazingly, Mark is unharmed.

Back at the estate, while Mark waits eagerly for the first nibbles, Hardcastle gets a call from the police identifying Danton's car. They head off to his address, only to find the police already there. He's been murdered. The blackmail pictures are found in his desk.

Mark and the judge have to take the news to Howard. He's angry, and doesn't believe that Cheryl had anything to do with it. On the way home, Mark, half persuaded himself, tries to convince the judge to keep an open mind.

It's evening, back at the estate. Mark has one contact from the dating service. Hardcastle's sorting through a pile of them. They were going to just sit back and let the police handle it from here out, but Hardcastle has always favored a more hands-on style of criminal justice.

Mark goes off to meet his one and only—the statuesque Tina. Hardcastle stays home for an encounter with Debra, the murdering bride from the opening scene. The evening gets off to a fine start, then he asks casually if she knows Cheryl. Debra says no, but when he steps away to get another bottle of wine, she sneaks into the study and snoops, discovering he is not who he says he is. She makes a phone call to the woman who claimed to be Cheryl's roommate and tells her they have troubles.

The evening proceeds and Hardcastle, in bed, is waiting patiently for Debra to join him. He is not quite as trusting as he appears. When she comes out of the bathroom and levels a gun at him, he throws back the bedcovers and reveals...a shotgun.

Back at the Doubles office, Eileen is looking at Howard's file. At gunpoint, she forces Cheryl to call Howard and tell him to come to the Starlight Motel.

Mark returns home, entering warily. No one is in sight downstairs. He's appalled at Hardcastle's apparent good fortune. Upstairs, Hardcastle has everything under control, with his would-be assassin having already given him the low-down on the scams that Doubles is running.

Howard rushes to the aid of Cheryl at the motel. He's captured and, in turn, Eileen forces him to call Mark. The trap is set at Howard's garage, with Cheryl and Howard tied up, and the guys, unsuspecting, on the way.

When they arrive at the shop, bullets fly, with the Studebaker being the first victim. While windows shatter overhead, Howard and Cheryl rediscover true love. After a barrage of gunfire, Eileen and her henchman take off, with the guys in pursuit. Their sedan careens off course in a tunnel and comes to a crashing halt.

Back at the shop, the star-struck lovers have been freed. It's obvious that they're crazy about each other. They head off to an all-night Chinese place, Howard, Cheryl, the Studebaker, and a Neil Diamond tape. It's chemistry.

In the epilogue, Hardcastle enters the study where Mark is watching his 'Nick Van Norden' tape. It starts out low-key and, as McCormick puts it, 'kinda sweet', but the secret of his success soon becomes apparent. Van Norden claimed to have a sideline in the movie business and was offering a well-upholstered casting couch. Mark was clearly outclassed in the scam department…this time.

The Context

This was Hertzog's second outing for this series and an episode which emphasized humor alongside the action. There's a sense of many action show conventions being turned upside down. Here's what would be going on between the chase scenes—the Coyote getting patched up repeatedly, "three coats of paint, the good stuff", and the hassle of dealing with unsympathetic insurance adjusters.

Howard is the antithesis of an action hero, and as far as you can imagine from a romantic lead, but he gets many of the good lines and is allowed to tell his story. And he really is a romantic, holding out for the power of instantaneous love and defending Cheryl's innocence.

At the same time, there's an undercurrent here that shows up from time to time in the series. Men compete for women, lying and cheating if necessary and judging the quality of the prize mostly by looks. Women do the same right back at 'em, and the Studebaker Effect is rampant. Some women will take your car and land you in prison, but the really vicious ones will just shoot you on your wedding night. It's enough to make a guy want to take up fly fishing permanently.

The Trivia

The self-help book Howard is studying is 'authored' by Lawrence Hertzog (and it's the same style dust-jacket as 'The Maladjusted Child' from "Prince of Fat City"). Stephen J. Cannell originated the idea in his series *Tenspeed and Brownshoe*, in which his name and picture appeared weekly on the dust jackets of the hardboiled detective novels that were the protagonist's favorite reading material.

Howard's car is a 1950 Studebaker Champion.

We see a close-up of Hardcastle's undergraduate diploma on the wall of the study. It's from the 'University of California'—a bachelor of arts with majors in political science and history, awarded September 7th, 1943.

Memorable Quotes

Insurance Agent: Personally, it's terrific to know that someone's willing to go out there and do their part to clean up the streets. But as a representative of Corbin Casualty and Life, I'm afraid I have to cancel your insurance. Keep up the good work.

McCormick: Not again.

Hardcastle: Don't worry about it. We'll get somebody else to pick us up.

McCormick: Who's gonna pick us up? This is our third insurance company in eight months. Nobody's gonna pick us up. Oh, I know, it comes with the territory, right? It's all routine. *Everybody's* car gets shot up. I'm telling you, the next insurance form I fill out, I'm telling them my name is Jimmy Olsen and I work with a guy in a cape.

Howard: Guy like you, car like this…I bet you get the kind of girl who thinks the car is *really neat*.

McCormick: Yeah, I've had my moments, Howard.

Howard: I never get girls like that. I love girls who say 'really neat'. Ooh, yeah. I don't know what it is, you know? Girls and cars, cars and girls.

McCormick: Girls and cars.

Howard: I have a Studebaker. You ever see the effect a Studebaker has on a girl?

McCormick: Can't say that I have.

Howard: Right! Because there isn't any!

Howard: You guys don't need car insurance. You need life insurance.

Hardcastle: Yeah, well, it's been kind of an unusual week.

McCormick: Now, how can you say that? I look upon it as just another busy day in the life of Milton C. Hardcastle, searcher of injustice, sitting duck.

Howard: (searching through the destruction at Cheryl's house) Oh, my God.

McCormick: What?

Howard: This is Cheryl's umbrella. (holds up the paper umbrella almost reverently) They put it in her Singapore Sling at Mona's Luau. She wouldn't let the waitress take it back. She loved this umbrella. She wouldn't have left it here.

Howard: Okay, now what, we go to the dating service and pick up some clues?

McCormick: Howard, this isn't a Raymond Chandler novel. Now, there are guys out there with forty-two-inch necks, they drink cheap red wine, use paper napkins, and they like killing people, all right?

Howard: Then, I'll do it myself.

Hardcastle: The cops are looking into it.

Howard: Boy, you guys are real romantic, you know that? When's the last time you had a date?

McCormick: Saturday. Hardcastle bought me a pizza after we went through some mug books.

McCormick: (looking at his lone response as the judge flips through multiple inquiries) I can't believe it. What did you say on your tape?

Hardcastle: I told you. I just gave them the basic, honest, straightforward Hardcastle picture, that's all.

McCormick: You threatened them with prison?

Hardcastle: The secret is maturity. Now, you gain a little self-confidence, smooth your rough edges off, you're a good-looking kid. You—well, on the other hand, a lot of women don't like kids. They like men.

McCormick: (after a pause) All right, knock it off.

Hardcastle: I didn't say anything.

McCormick: You didn't have to. I could hear you gloating all the way over here.

Scared Stiff – premiered April 1, 1984

Written by	Tom Blomquist
Directed by	Tony Mordente
Second unit director	Gary Combs

Cast

Red West	Paul Connors
Tim Robbins	Johnson
Alan Fudge	Warden Porter
Michael MacRae	George Kyle
John St. Elwood	Lieutenant Barger
Dermott Douns (Downs)	Tyrone
Daryl Anderson	Ernie Delrosa
James Avery	Convict #031701
Carl Strand	
Ron Max	
Mark Giardino	

Cast Notes

Red West was a regular in Cannell's *Black Sheep Squadron*.

Tim Robbins' prison "career" didn't end with *Hardcastle and McCormick*. He went on to star ten years later in the award winning prison film *The Shawshank Redemption*. He also won an Oscar for his role in *Mystic River*.

Alan Fudge has over 145 television and movie credits, spanning four decades, most recently including a recurring role as Lou Dalton on *7th Heaven*.

James Avery played the father, Phillip Banks, in *Fresh Prince of Bel Air*. He's another very productive actor, in productions ranging from *Anthony and Cleopatra*, to the voice of Shredder in *Teenage Mutant Ninja Turtles*.

The Details

A man lies dead on the floor of an office while his murderer does a quick ransacking, intending to make it look like a robbery. He's unknowingly triggered an alarm. When he returns to the car where his accomplice awaits, a police cruiser arrives, running lights and sirens. The killer and his driver flee. They fire back on their pursuers with a shotgun. The police car crashes and the men in the other car escape.

The same vehicle approaches the gates to Clarkville Prison. The driver appears to be alone. He is greeted as Captain Freedman and waved through. He pulls up in a secluded spot and lets the other man out of the trunk. He's a prisoner named Johnson, and he makes veiled threats to his guard as he's escorted back to his cell. He wants to be paid off for what he's done.

Six thirty-five in the gatehouse—Hardcastle is doing his darnedest to roust out a reluctant McCormick. He doesn't want them to be late picking up their charges at juvenile hall. They have an appointment at Clarkville prison. Hardcastle calls his intervention "Scared Stiff".

Mark is driving the bus. He's got a mixed lot of miscreants in the back and it's a free-for-all. Hardcastle is acting pretty tolerant, though he disarms one playful switchblade-wielding young person without missing a beat.

At the prison, Johnson's body is being carted out of his cell. Captain Freedman is supervising the clean-up. The Warden doesn't really want to know what happened—just get things tidied up as quickly as possible.

Freedman strolls past the prison cells and across the yard. The atmosphere is tense and threatening on both sides, with the guards finally forming a cordon against the inmates in the yard.

Into this setting comes the school-bus. Mark is joking sharply with his load of smart-ass juvies. Hardcastle lets him say his bit but then tells him, *sotto voce*, to knock off the humor; the place is supposed to be scary. Mark assures him that it is. The kids are boasting that the place isn't so tough. A prisoner being escorted in chains spots Hardcastle and lunges for him. He's dragged off by the guards.

The tour begins on a slightly more sober note when they see an ambulance pulling away. The Warden tells them one of the inmates was a probable suicide.

Inside the prison laundry, two prisoners have gotten guns. George Kyle wants to take Hardcastle. Paul Connors says they'll do things according to the plan.

Captain Freedman takes the guests on a stultifying tour of the main cell-block. In an aside, Mark says something's up. He's getting "weird vibes". Hardcastle scoffs; the only thing that's up just then is that Mark is apparently everyone's favorite former bookie in this joint.

The meeting between the kids and the prisoners is very effective. Paul Connors and his fellow convicts are plenty scary. Afterwards, as prisoners and visitors are walking to the dining hall, guns are pulled. Connors has Hardcastle at gunpoint. In the dimly lit hallways a coordinated uprising has started.

Hardcastle, McCormick, and the kids are under Connors' control. Mark tries to intervene when Kyle threatens the judge, but it's Connors who keeps things calm. The judge asks him to let Mark and the juvies go. Connors sends the kids out, but tells Mark he has plans for him.

In the yard, hostages are being taken. Outside the gate, reinforcements arrive.

Connors and his crew have occupied the Warden's office. Hardcastle is now in prison denims. Mark is ordered to take the prisoners' list of demands out to the authorities. Connors wants an independent panel to investigate corruption at Clarkville. He says Captain Freedman uses cons to do hits for the mob.

Mark makes the long walk across the yard, under the scrutiny of both prisoners and guards. He presents the demands to Warden Porter just outside the gate. Porter refuses to negotiate. McCormick insists that they speak to the governor, but the word comes down, even from there, that there will be no negotiations until the hostages are released. Captain Freedman is among the missing.

It's night now. Mark, having exhausted the possibilities, goes back inside. The prisoners who escort him debate whether he's sold out or is simply running a scam. Mark makes it back to Connors' outpost. He and Hardcastle try to get him to release the hostages.

It's apparent that discipline among the prisoners is breaking down. A group is heading up there to "get Hardcastle". Connors and his men take the judge and McCormick to Cell Block A. Along the way, Mark and Kyle foil an assassination attempt against Hardcastle. Connors still has his own men under control.

Mark and the judge are briefly parked in a cell. To Hardcastle's annoyance, Mark nervously cuts loose with a verse of "Jailhouse Rock". Connors returns, moving them along again.

Out at the gate, the Warden encourages Lieutenant Barger, the man in charge of the state police team, to attack the prison. Barger refuses. The Warden moves on to his own, smaller group of guards. He tells them they can't afford to wait, and that once they're inside everyone who knows about Freedman's activities must die.

The guards charge in. The state police quickly follow. It's chaos, with gunfire in the darkness.

Inside, loyalties shift rapidly. Kyle goes looking for Hardcastle. Connors already moved him. Kyle grabs another guard, Thompson, then encounters Connors and *his* two prisoners. When Kyle tells him his plan for using his hostage to escape, the guard panics. He offers to show them where Freedman is.

They all descend into the bowels of the prison, where Freedman's body is hanging from a pipe. Thompson says the warden had him killed. Elsewhere in the prison, the uprising is coming under control. In the sub-basement, Kyle and Connors are still debating whether to surrender. Kyle fights Connors and wins.

The guard, Thompson, finds the Warden and tells him. The Warden again says they must die.

Kyle and another prisoner take Mark and the judge and escape in a car. They burst through the gate in a barrage of gunfire and roar off, followed by the

police. They evade their pursuers but run out of gas.

The hunt intensifies, with *four* prisoners reported as escaped. The warden and the lieutenant issue orders to "shoot to kill". Men and dogs scour the early morning countryside.

Mark and the judge, linked by a set of wrist shackles, are being marched along train tracks by their nervous captors. Hardcastle throws a punch and Mark joins in. Kyle is down but not disarmed. He fires after them as they escape. They're forced to jump off a railroad trestle bridge into the river.

The hunt continues, but now Hardcastle and McCormick are on a dusty road in the middle of nowhere, looking every bit like a couple of desperate escaped prisoners. The warden's men are close on their trail.

Mark and the judge, in an example of grace under pressure, can't seem to get the hang of the "chained at the wrist" concept. They finally stumble upon salvation in the form of a rural gas station with a telephone booth. No luck though—the phone is out of order. They encounter a citizen with a bolt action rifle and a not unreasonably suspicious nature. They confiscate his truck and his toolbox, and head for the Warden's home, where they capture him in the act of fleeing.

In the epilogue, Mark's back in Clarkville, on the basketball court in the yard. He and four prison buddies are counting their money, waiting for Hardcastle and Connors to arrive with their side. The bets are already made, but Hardcastle suckers them into doubling the wager before revealing the rest of his pick-up team—three guys who look like they average seven feet each.

The Context

We can add prison wardens and guards to the list of good guys gone bad on this series and, once again, Hardcastle is willing to listen to accusations made against the system.

Mark is, as usual, not happy about returning to one of his old haunts (and there are so *many* of them). He jokes and bluffs his way through the encounter, almost like the kids, but is perfectly willing to admit to Hardcastle that he's scared. When the knives come out, though, McCormick steps between the judge and his would-be assailants twice. And then, after the futile attempt at negotiations, when the Warden tells him he doesn't have to go back inside, he says "Yeah, I do," and strides through the gate. There's no hesitation and no doubt.

The Trivia

For reasons which seem obscure, Mark has a framed photo of Hardcastle on his desk in the gatehouse. It gets whacked by his vehemently tossed boot.

The "Scared Straight" program—an effort to expose juveniles at risk of criminal conviction to the harsh realities of prison life—began in New Jersey in 1976 and was the subject of the 1979 Emmy-winning documentary by the same title. Though over 50,000 youths went through the program over almost twenty-five years, it remained controversial, and was phased out in that state in 2000.

When they arrive at Clarkville, Tyrone asks Mark if he did two years at this prison and Mark assures him it was indeed two "very long years", while casting an accusatory look in Hardcastle's direction—more continuity issues. We're up to four prisons mentioned in season one: San Quentin, Strykersville, Joliet, and now Clarkville. At least this Warden remembers his name.

In the perennial fashion of a good fieldtrip chaperone, Mark does a quiet head count of the juvies after they are moved by their captors.

At minute 36, it's a repeat of the escape from Strykersville ("Goin' Nowhere Fast") as the sedan heads down the sloped drive and makes a sharp right followed by a series of black and whites in pursuit.

At minute 39:13, the wrist shackle is suddenly missing between the two guys, then it's back again in the next scene.

Memorable Quotes

McCormick: Yes, yes, little girls. We would like to welcome you to our fantasy tour of Terminal Island. Now, on our right is Felon's World, an incredible array of losers and father-stabbers. And, of course, on our left is our famous exhibit of first-degree murderers and lunatics. Now we ask that you don't touch—they are all very real—and we'll be able to mingle with our new-found friends right after we have lunch in the Pirates' Galley.

Hardcastle: You want to knock off the funny stuff, McCormick? This place is supposed to scare them.

McCormick: Well, it scared the spit out of me.

Hardcastle: Were you making book while you were in here?

McCormick: Judge, book-making's illegal, you know that.

Hardcastle: So's picking flowers in the park.

McCormick: So I took a bet once, big deal. Twice.

Inmate: You running a play-off pool this year, Skid?

McCormick: Three times maximum.
Hardcastle: How about the Lakers tonight?
McCormick: Lakers are favored by four. I'm giving six and overtime's a push.
Hardcastle: Right.

Outlaw Champion – premiered September 23, 1984

Written by	Patrick Hasburgh
Directed by	Leo Penn
Second unit director	Gary Combs

Cast

Larry Wilcox	E.J. Corlette
Ray Girardin	Martin Grayson
Jonathan Banks	Bill Rogers
John Hancock	Mike Delaney

Cast Notes

Larry Wilcox rode a motorcycle for five years as Officer Jon Baker in the TV series *CHiPS*.

Jonathan Banks, best all-purpose *Hardcastle and McCormick* villain, also appeared in "The Birthday Present" and "She Ain't Deep but She Sure Runs Fast". In addition, he played the Emmy nominated role of Frank McPike in the series *Wiseguy*.

The Details

Up on Mulholland Drive, a young man in a yellow street-rod waits for his opponent to show up for a grudge match. The man arrives. He's at least ten years older and looks grimly determined. They're off, and it's a twisting, turning battle of wits in which neither man takes a commanding lead at first. In the end, though, the younger man makes a mistake. He and his car plummet off a cliff in what looks like a fatal crash.

The older man stops and sees the results of the crash, on the slope far below the road. He appears horrified, but flees when he hears the sirens of the approaching police.

Morning, poolside at the estate, and Mark is reading, out loud, yet another article about racing champ E.J. Corlette while Hardcastle complains about the coffee. Hardcastle points out that Corlette has the big racing career and all the endorsements to go with it. He asks if this is going to end with Mark saying he knew the guy "back when".

Mark says he did, and not only that, but they ran fender to fender plenty of times. The judge seems doubtful. Mark asks him if he wants proof, and a wager is on.

In the parking lot of a strip mall, a cardboard cut-out of E.J. Corlette is standing in for the champ at a meet and greet session. People are milling around. A limo pulls up, disgorging an angry corporate handler named Bill Rogers. He finds E.J. sitting in his trailer. Rogers shows him the morning's paper. The victim from the drag race is in critical condition and he wants to know if Corlette had anything to do with it.

E.J. thinks he's lost his stuff. He can't win real races anymore so he went up on Mulholland to try and get his confidence back. He didn't find it there. Rogers warns him that Corlette Enterprises is a lot more than just him and his racing. There's money at stake and he can't quit now. E.J. walks out on the man, still angry.

Mark and the judge show up at E.J.'s extravagant home. Hardcastle still thinks Mark is exaggerating about how well he and Corlette knew each other and at first it looks like he's right. E.J. stares at him blankly and doesn't seem to be making any connections at the mention of Mark's name.

On that awkward moment we go to the offices of Corlette Enterprises, where an executive type named Grayson is questioning Rogers about Corlette's unreliability: drunk driving, an affair with an underage girl, and now a suspicion of drag racing. Grayson isn't happy with his company spokesman. He suggests that maybe it's time to "retire" Corlette via a racing accident—something sudden and heroic.

Back at Corlette's, the guys are now reminiscing. E.J. says Mark was a good driver who had some bad breaks. E.J. just wants to hold on to a little something from the old days. He says those were better times. Mark can't believe that E.J., the guy who has everything, isn't happy.

A limo pulls up the drive. Corlette says he has to do some business. Mark and the judge start to leave. They encounter Rogers getting out of the car. *He* recognizes Mark immediately. We find out that E.J. only beat Mark for the '78 Outlaw Trail Championship in the last lap of the last race, when Mark's engine blew. Rogers raises the subject of prison. Hardcastle speaks up firmly in Mark's defense. Rogers walks away.

On the way home, Mark thanks Hardcastle for sticking up for him. The judge brushes it off. He wants to know why Mark never mentioned his near-win on the Outlaw Trail. Mark says he doesn't like to think about it. It was a bad bit of luck for him. It was that racing series, and Bill Rogers' bank roll, that propelled E.J. to the top. Mark still wants to know who the heck Bill Rogers really is and where all the money came from.

E.J. is listening to the broadcast detailing the condition of the drag racer. Police are looking for a red sports car, but its driver hasn't been identified. Rogers comes down the stairs with E.J.'s suitcases, all packed. There's a new store opening to attend in New York. E.J. refuses to go. He confesses to the drag racing incident and blames himself for the accident because the other guy was an amateur. He swings on Rogers, who turns out to be fast and ruthless.

Rogers clues E.J. in. Corlette Enterprises was started with mob money. Rogers says the Outlaw Trail Championship was the first fix he did for Corlette, by sabotaging McCormick's engine. E.J. is shaken.

At the estate that night, Hardcastle is immersed in a file but won't talk about it. Mark gets a call from E.J. inviting him to come up to Saugus. He doesn't say why he wants to meet.

Mark meets him at a deserted race track. They race. It's nip and tuck until Mark hits a bale of straw and spins out. Both guys seem pretty pleased with themselves and they retire to a bar for some beer and nostalgia. Corlette's memories aren't so fond. He thinks he's caused at least one accident on the track. Now he confesses the drag racing incident to Mark as well.

McCormick is appalled. Corlette is upset and angry. He stomps off and Mark follows.

The next morning Mark returns home. He tells Hardcastle where he was and what he was doing. He also divulges what E.J. told him and that he spent the night trying to convince him to turn himself in. Hardcastle says that could get sticky. He's dug up information about Rogers and his mob links.

Mr. Grayson is in his office, smooth talking E.J. over the phone, trying to convince him not to confess. E.J. hangs up on him. Grayson tells Rogers to arrange an accident for Corlette up on Mulholland.

Mark and the judge are driving to E.J.'s place. Mark is explaining how he used to be jealous. Corlette got "his" life. Hardcastle tells him everyone feels that way sometimes but after all that consoling advice, he reminds Mark that E.J.

blew his fenders off the night before.

They arrive at E.J.'s just in time to see a sedan pulling out. Two of Grayson's goons have kidnapped E.J. They pursue and run the sedan off the road, rescuing Corlette.

At the police station, E.J. makes a full confession about the Mulholland incident. He is released into Hardcastle's supervision. Back at the estate, Mark gives E.J. a lecture on the importance of living up to expectations when you've become a hero. They persuade him to help them trap Grayson and Rogers.

E.J. calls Grayson and threatens him with exposure if he doesn't hand over a million dollars. He says he'll meet him up on Mulholland.

At the meet, Grayson and Rogers confront E.J. and Rogers pulls a gun. The Coyote roars up. Shots are fired. Rogers is wounded. Grayson grabs Corlette and forces him into a sedan. They take off with Corlette at gunpoint and behind the wheel. Mark and Hardcastle pursue and outmaneuver him. Corlette's vehicle flips and crashes.

In the epilogue, Mark and the judge are in the study with Mark reading from his racing scrapbook. Hardcastle just wants to watch the news. There's a knock at the door. It's E.J. He says he got six month's probation with no driving for two years. He plans to buy and restore an old racetrack so there will be a safer place for kids to race.

He reaches into his satchel and pulls out the Outlaw Trail trophy. He explains that Rogers sabotaged McCormick's car and so the trophy is rightly Mark's.

The trophy goes on the mantel. Mark stands next to it, posing proudly, while Hardcastle beams and takes a "picture".

The Context

At the start of season two, and with his first episode since "The Homecoming", Patrick Hasburgh returns to the racing theme. It's another look into Mark's past and a very interesting one. Even the "World Champ" admits Mark had the right stuff, and we find out by the end that it took more than just a twist of fate to keep him out of the winner's circle.

Hardcastle, initially skeptical of Mark's claims, eventually seems to accept them fully, and even wonders why the guy never mentioned it before. He also comes to Mark's defense. As usual, Mark and Milt squabble, but stand united when anyone else steps in.

The main theme here again appears to be personal responsibility. E.J. has done some despicable things and let his handlers buy off his troubles, but he still has to live with the consequences. Eventually it proves too much for him. He's angry with himself and everybody else.

Bill Rogers is an interesting character, given a very deft interpretation by Jonathan Banks. He's ruthless, and will do what needs to be done in the end, but he also seems to treat Corlette almost as a protégé. He defends him to Grayson, and handles E.J. as if he were a recalcitrant teenager—lots of nagging, occasional shouting. It's only when Corlette makes the mistake of swinging on him that we discover Rogers is a very fast and physically scary guy. There is even some visible regret at the moment when Grayson tells him they have to do Corlette in. It's almost as if Hasburgh is writing the Hardcastle/McCormick relationship in a minor key.

The Trivia

Corlette's car is a Cobra. There were only about 1000 made during the original production run. They had a V8 engine on an English sports car chassis and were considered hard to handle.

Riverside, where Corlette was reported as racing, was also the scene of Mark's return to the sport in "Hotshoes".

Memorable Quotes

Hardcastle: You went out and ran against him last night, didn't you?
McCormick: Yeah, I did. I guess he wanted to see if he still had it.
Hardcastle: You wanted to see if you still had it, too.
McCormick: (nods)
Hardcastle: Well? Well, have you still got it?
McCormick: Yeah.

Hardcastle: There's a little part in all of us that wants our friends to fail. It's not that we don't want them to do well. But if they get too famous, we feel like we're being left behind, so...
McCormick: Where do you come up with this stuff?
Hardcastle: Watching guys like you fall on your face all their lives.
McCormick: Oh, thanks a lot.
Hardcastle: Don't mention it. (pause) So, E.J. blew your doors off last night, huh?
McCormick: He beat me by a heartbeat.
Hardcastle: He won.
McCormick: By a fender. Big deal.
Hardcastle: He beat you fair and square.
McCormick: Thanks a lot! You're a real pal, you know that?

Ties My Father Sold Me – premiered September 30, 1984

Written by	Patrick Hasburgh
Directed by	Ron Satlof
Second unit director	Gary Combs

Cast

Steve Lawrence	Sonny Daye
Alex Rocco	Tommy Sales
Michael DeLano	Jace Trimmer
Michael Swan	Tony Rothman
John Brandon	Boner
Carole Tru Foster	
Barbara Keegan	the waitress
Frank Pesce	Mike, the valet at the Chancellor
Nicky Blair	the maitre d'
Chanelle Lea	Kitty Comfort

Cast Notes

Steve Lawrence, along with his wife of over fifty years, Eydie Gorme, has been a Las Vegas headliner and Broadway star. He has won both a Grammy (for "We Got Us") and two Emmy awards.

Michael Swan appeared as McCormick's parole officer, John Dalem, in "Rolling Thunder".

Frank Pesce was the first winner of New York's Empire State Lottery, back in 1976. He took home six million dollars, plus change, and eventually wrote a movie about his life and that experience (*29th Street*). Anthoney LaPaglia played him in the film, while he played the role of his real-life older brother, Vito.

Nicky Blair was a real life Hollywood restaurateur who, in addition to a multitude of other character parts, also played waiters or maitre d's in seven other productions.

The Details

It's evening at the estate and Hardcastle is slaving over a hot grill, flipping the burgers. Upstairs in the gatehouse, Mark is sorting through newspaper clippings. The headlines look unrelated and meaningless—some bad breaks for a couple of petty criminals named Knight and Thompson. The phone rings. It's a call from a P.I. named Bailey. He tells Mark the investigation has hit a wall. He can't find anything more recent than ten years ago on "this guy". Mark thanks him.

Hardcastle shouts that the burgers are ready and, getting no response, comes in. Mark scrambles to hide what appears to be a large file. Mark takes a pass on dinner. He says he has something to do but won't say what.

It's after dark, and we see McCormick in basic black, breaking into a government records building. He lets himself in through the roof and heads for a room with a computer. A guard discovers the break-in and summons help. Mark proceeds to a file cabinet and takes a list of aliases. Pursued by two security guards, he escapes.

It's seven a.m. and Mark wanders into the gatehouse, still studying the stolen folder. Hardcastle is waiting and asks where he's been. Mark apologizes. He explains that the day before was his birthday. Hardcastle already knew. Mark tells the judge there's someone he needs to find. He hands him what he found that night. Looking the list over, Hardcastle asks, "Who the hell is Sonny Daye?"

In Atlantic City, at a second-rate lounge, a tacky, illuminated sign bears that very name. Inside, a ruffle-shirted lounge lizard performs to a smoky, half-empty room. Two mobsters watch from a back table. They're going to ask Sonny for a favor.

Outside a cab pulls up. Mark and the judge step out with Hardcastle grousing, still not sure why he's been dragged to "Meyer Lansky's home town". They go into the lounge room. Mark still hasn't explained what's up but he's oddly subdued as they catch the end of Daye's stand-up shtick.

Afterward McCormick drags Hardcastle backstage to Sonny's dressing room. Daye offers him an autographed picture. Mark asks him about his previous aliases. Sonny becomes evasive, then worried and puzzled. Hardcastle doesn't know what's up, either. All becomes clear when Mark finally asks Sonny if he used to live with a woman named Donna McCormick. Sonny doesn't try to deny it, and that makes him Mark's father.

It's an awkward reunion, with Sonny in turns doubting and effusive. Mark is hostile, slowly revealing the residual pain that Sonny's desertion caused. Hardcastle tries to smooth things over. Sonny finally invites them to dinner the next evening.

In the morning, on the Atlantic City boardwalk, Mark apologizes to Hardcastle for dragging him into this. The judge tells him to give Sonny a chance, whether he deserves it or not.

Sonny is summoned to a meeting with mob kingpin Tommy Sales. Sales wants him to break into a federal judge's office and recover some tapes. Sonny demurs but Sales is leaning hard.

The following evening, at a fancy restaurant, Daye squires an attractive bimbo named Kitty. It's obviously an uncomfortable meal for Mark. Hardcastle once again tries to keeps the conversation moving, but it's an uphill battle and it looks like Mark has thrown in the towel.

The bill arrives and Sonny tries to sign for it. He is initially refused credit, but then one of Sales' henchmen steps in, takes care of the bill, and tells him he needs to give Mr. Sales the right answer. Things get threatening. Mark stands up. The hood flashes a gun, tucked inside his jacket. Sonny leaves with him.

A moment later, Mark and the judge follow. They attack Sales' goons and prevent Daye's kidnapping. Back at their hotel, Hardcastle questions Sonny, who admits he was a safecracker and has done time. The judge gets a reluctant Sonny to agree to testify against Sales.

Mark talks to Sonny again. He still can't get a straight answer about why he left, but Daye asks him if he wants to move to Jersey once the problem with Sales is settled. Mark says no—he's already got all the help he needs.

Hardcastle is going to take Sonny to the police. Mark stays behind. He has some things to think about. Thinking soon turns to running, as Sales' men pursue and capture him. Sales makes a call to Hardcastle, telling him that if Sonny doesn't cooperate, Mark will die.

Sonny is nervous, and it looks like he'd rather just leave town. It's Hardcastle who decides that the burglary is justified in order to save McCormick's life. He leans on Sonny and "persuades" him to lend his expertise.

It's nighttime at the federal courthouse. Sonny is deft, but an alarm system has been triggered. While Sonny tackles the safe, Hardcastle says, in Latin, "necessity overrules the law". Moments later the police show up and the judge and Sonny are caught in the act.

At Sales' office the next morning, a call comes in. It's Sonny and he says he has the tapes. He offers to meet at a drive-in. After he hangs up, Sales tells McCormick he intends to kill him and his dad.

At the drive-in, Hardcastle makes the exchange. Sales' men open fire, but McCormick makes it to the car. A wild chase results in Sales' capture.

In the epilogue, it's the next night in Atlantic City. Mark's mood is ebullient. He's wearing a tacky tie that is a gift from his dad. He's bugging Hardcastle to tell him how Sonny convinced the judge to break the law. Hardcastle keeps his mouth shut, except for one brief remark about the receipt for the tie. Mark gently accuses him of being jealous.

They go into the lounge. It's empty. Mark asks one of the waitresses what gives. She tells him Sonny left suddenly for a gig up in Boston. When she finds out he's Daye's son, she says, "Too bad", and hands him a letter. It's vaguely apologetic and not much comfort. Sonny is Sonny and he doesn't hang around.

Hardcastle's still there, though. He ushers a slightly stunned Mark out of the room, and, to the quiet strains of "Strangers in the Night", offers to take him to a ball game.

The Context

Hasburgh again tackles the issue of fathers and sons. We didn't know anything about Mark's up till now. He didn't either, apparently, and it left a huge hole in his life. The guy he finds definitely won't fill it. Hardcastle is standing by, obviously big enough. He's already pretty much doing the job—he travels all the way to Atlantic City without asking for an explanation, leans on Sonny to break the law to save Mark, and then picks up the pieces when Sonny ducks. But Hardcastle never admits to being anything more than a friend, even when Mark hints that the dad job is available

The Trivia

There's no Chancellor Hotel in Atlantic City, but there is an establishment by that name in Los Angeles—at 3191 W. 7th Street. In the script it was The Rondeau Hotel.

There are palm trees in the background as Mark tries to elude Sales' goons in what is purportedly Atlantic City.

All government buildings look alike. The hallway outside the judge's office in N.J. is identical to the one outside the records office in L.A.

The deserted drive-in theater where the exchange is to take place is advertising "*The Tenth Level*—Now in Its 15th Smash Week". A little-known made-for-TV movie from 1975, *The Tenth Level* starred William Shatner as a Stanley Milgram-like psychologist who experimented with people's willingness to hurt others. It was directed by Charles Dubin, who also directed an episode of *The Rockford Files*. The drive-in doesn't appear in the script.

The bill for the reunion dinner comes to $208.11. Apparently Kitty only had a chef's salad (you have to watch your weight if you're going to climb a fifty-foot feather every night in the Hallelujah Hot Time Revue).

Memorable Quotes

Hardcastle: Why didn't you tell me it was gonna be so swanky. I could've worn the bullet-proof vest with the French cuffs.

McCormick: Gimme a break.

Hardcastle: You drag me halfway across the country, I'm supposed to give you a break?

McCormick: Friends are supposed to do favors for friends without asking questions.

Hardcastle: I lend you ten bucks, it's a favor. Help you rotate your tires on your car, that's a favor. Sit up on a plane all day long to come to Meyer Lansky's home town, that qualifies me for sainthood.

McCormick: Relax, they're not making square halos yet.

Sonny: Now, look, you two probably aren't crazy about me for a lot of reasons; that's okay. Like, like, I did some time.

McCormick: I know. So did I. But I'm not working for some hood.

Sonny: Look, you could be a little impressed by the fact that a big guy like Tommy Sales needs a favor from your old man.

McCormick: Impressed wasn't the word I had in mind, Sonny.

Sonny: You would've been impressed, years ago. I was the best damn safecracker that bad money could buy.

Hardcastle: I thought just baldness was hereditary.

You Would Cry, Too, If It Happened To You
– premiered October 7, 1984

Written by	Lawrence Hertzog
Directed by	Tony Mordente
Second unit director	Gary Combs

Cast

Paul Gleason	Jack Fish
Andrew Rubin	Mickey Noonan
Debi Richter	Kimmy
Victoria Young	Rose Carlucci

Marc Adams	Eddie Dyson
Paul Willson	the janitor
Betty McGuire	woman at the party with the flower in her hair
Bill Handy	
Mickey Jones	
Chester Grimes	Biker Guy
Nicholas Mele	
Garry Goodrow	Sid, the informant
Vinny Argiro	Nell
Chad Block	the bum

Cast Notes

Paul Gleason often played buttoned-down types like Jack Fish. Perhaps his most famous role was as principle Vernon in the 1985 movie *The Breakfast Club.*

Debi Richter, who played Kimmy, the girl who couldn't leave Hardcastle's t-shirts alone, was Miss California, 1975.

Victoria Young, Brian Keith's wife, made a second appearance as Rose Carlucci.

The Details

It's nighttime, in the computer room of a bank. Jack Fish researches Milton C. Hardcastle, only to find he's the original Boy Scout. He's looking for a hook to take this guy down. All he finds is an upcoming trip to Hawaii.

The next morning, at the estate, Mark helps Hardcastle with his packing. The parrot shirt has gone missing, the cabby is waiting, and lots of last minute advice is being given to McCormick, including the final admonition, "Don't do anything stupid."

And then he's gone. Mark has a whole glorious week as an independent adult. In a loving homage to the movie *Risky Business,* the newly unsupervised

 McCormick throws open the doors to the den and enters—in robe and with boom-box—dancing. He makes himself utterly comfortable in Hardcastle's desk chair and can't help conducting a little drawer exploration.

He's soon wearing the Yankees hat and pounding the gavel, doing his best imitation of Hardcase dispensing justice. In mid-parody, he remembers his instructions to lock up the files. He conscientiously grabs the keys and gets up to do it.

In the middle of that chore, the phone rings. It's an old ex-con buddy, Mickey. They shoot the breeze and Mark winds up agreeing to host a poker game for Sunday afternoon.

Sunday, and the motorcycle gang is pulling in the drive. They're joining the hundred or so people already there. The study is packed and there's some hard partying going on. A horrified McCormick enters the study, trying unsuccessfully to restore order. He finally finds Mickey and his buddies out in the gatehouse, actually playing poker. As he's threatening them, the phone rings. It's Hardcastle, at LAX, home two days early and looking for a ride.

Mark tells Mickey he has two hours to get the estate back to order. He heads out, intending to take the scenic route in the hope that things will be able to pass for normal by the time he gets the judge home.

Mark tries to make pleasant conversation on the circuitous drive back. The judge didn't have much fun in Hawaii ("Nostalgia can become pretty ugly."). All he wants to do is get back to the peace and quiet of his own home.

Mark drives through the gates with trepidation. All looks tidy and calm from the outside though. Too calm—when they enter the house, they discover it's been stripped bare, every stick of furniture, every piece of paper, and the judge's file cabinets, along with their contents.

Mickey and Eddie are in a storage building, sitting on a load of antique furniture. They already had a pre-buyer for the file cabinets. They're getting twenty thousand for those alone.

Mark is doing his best to make amends. He takes Hardcastle to Mickey's old apartment. The guy's on the lam. It doesn't help matters that practically everyone they run into, from now until the epilogue, remembers how great "Mark's" party was. Nostalgia *can* be ugly.

Mark's contrite; Hardcastle is angry. He says it's a good thing he left backup copies of his files with Rosie in the Hall of Records. Unfortunately, we soon discover that Rosie's not infallible. The files were deleted.

Meanwhile, the originals have just changed hands again, being loaded onto the back of a truck and hauled away.

But Mickey and Eddie still have an antique sale to run. They've taken out an advertisement. Hardcastle spots it in the paper. The line about "antique law diplomas" is the dead give-away. He and Mark show up at the sale. Mickey and Eddie bolt. After a chase, they smash through a barricade and plummet off the end of a raised bridge. When they're finally hauled out and returned to the scene of the sale, Mickey wants to be read his rights.

Of course, that only works when it's the police who are in charge. Hardcastle quickly convinces them that he isn't playing by those rules right now. Eddie forks over the number of the trucking company that picked up the files.

While Mark moves the furniture back in, Hardcastle tries to get a warrant to search the trucking company. Mark is convinced that delay will be fatal for the files. While Hardcastle pursues the legal alternatives, he puts on a black turtleneck and braves the hounds of hell to get a look at the company's records.

He returns home, slightly chewed on, with an address of a California bank. He and the judge visit the facility, gradually working their way up to janitor, who remembers the files being delivered. They finally find the cabinets, stripped bare, their contents reduced to excelsior by a shredding machine.

Mark and the judge work their contacts. A guy named Sid brings a hot tip. There's going to be a sale of the files the next morning. He gives them the address. They show up. There's a line of bad guys out the door and they catch Fish doing business inside. He and his accomplice bolt. The guys follow. This time the flashy red Coyote is intercepted by the police, while Fish escapes in his gray sedan.

In the delay, while Hardcastle recruits the cops to his side, Fish makes it back to his bank office. He's one keystroke away from deleting the last remaining copy of Hardcastle's files when the judge arrives. As Fish lowers his finger, intending to do the deed, the computer screen goes blank. Mark's pulled the plug on his operation.

In the epilogue, Mark's in the study, reprinting paper files from Fish's disk and grousing about how much easier it would be to just leave them on the computer. Hardcastle likes file cabinets and he's the boss.

Mark does see one advantage to being a filing clerk. He's going to take this opportunity to clear his own file from the records. Too late even for that. Hardcastle printed that one up first.

The Context

Hertzog continues to be the go-to guy for humor and pop culture references. His titles most often come from old rock songs, while his scripts have a
light touch. In this one, Mark's ex-con buddies treat the whole escapade as a
game and whine because Mark "told" on them. There's never a sense that Mark's
in serious trouble with Hardcastle, and the whole crime is so over the top that it
crosses into absurdity.

The Trivia

According to Jack Fish's records, Hardcastle's last moving violation was a
speeding ticket on Dec. 24, 1948. Rear-ending the squad car in "Man in a Glass
House" must've been expunged from his record. Also, according to the screen
Fish is looking at, Hardcastle's flight to Hawaii is taking place on Nov. 12,
1983, and he is due to return home on the nineteenth, a Saturday.

Judges are party animals, too. There are three mentions of riotous happen-
ings at judges' conventions in the series: in "Ties My Father Sold Me" as having
been the year before in Atlantic City, in this episode it's Hawaii, and in the third
season, we witness it first-hand in Palm Springs.

Hardcastle's left hand desk drawer contains a bottle of Excedrin in addition
to his Yankees cap. Too bad it gets stolen.

At 40:28 into the episode, hustling after the bad guys, McCormick jumps up
onto the rear deck of the Coyote, trips and sprawls onto the front hood. Hardcastle
mutters "What are you, Errol Flynn?" This stunt and comment aren't in the script.

Finding Kimmy and a man in Hardcastle's bed, Mark shrieks that it's only
previously been occupied by "*Wigmore on Evidence* and the judge"—referring to
John Henry Wigmore's seminal treatise on the rules of evidence, first published
in 1904. Mark seems to be picking up the legal lingo already.

Need a cabbie? Call Bob Goldstein, who did the honors in both this
episode and in "Ties My Father Sold Me".

Memorable Quotes

McCormick: So how was your trip?

Hardcastle: Well, let me put it this way. It got so I was looking forward to
coming home and seeing you. Does that give you a hint?

McCormick: Got to see all your old buddies. That should've been fun, huh?

Hardcastle: Reunions are weird, kiddo. They make people want to reminisce, see? Nostalgia can become pretty ugly.

McCormick: Boy, that sounds great.

Hardcastle: We're talking grown men, here, McCormick. Sixty-five years
old, wearing little grass skirts, going boom-boom-boom-badoom-badoom.

McCormick: You name it. Whatever you want, you got it. I'll work for free for the next ten years, on the house, okay? I'll paint, I'll do the hedges, I'll straighten up.

Hardcastle: There's nothing left to straighten up.

McCormick: I'll re-do the floors, then. All right, let's have it. What do you want, huh? You wanna sue me? You wanna sentence me to life imprisonment? Electrocute me? Whatever makes you happy, Judge, *whatever* makes you happy, only I can't make it not happen. Didn't you ever make a mistake?

Hardcastle: You mean other than leaving you alone for a coupla days?

D-Day – premiered October 14, 1984

Written by	Lawrence Hertzog
Directed by	Bruce Kessler
Second unit director	Gary Combs

Cast

Trish Van Devere	Diedre Drylinger
Greg Mullavey	Ira Trattner
David Opatoshu	Gus Rossman
Jonathan Goldsmith	Arnie Hoffs
Bill Marcus	Ralph Bilsky, Didi's landlord
David Kagen	Steve (killed in the restaurant bathroom)
Wally Dalton	Poolman assassin with baseball cap
Lomax Study	Rossman's butler

Cast Notes

Trish Van Devere was formerly married to George C. Scott and appeared in several films with him. She began her television career in the mid-1960s with roles on the soap operas *One Life to Live* and *Search for Tomorrow*.

Greg Mullavey played Mary Hartman's husband, Tom, on the series *Mary Hartman, Mary Hartman*.

Jonathan Goldsmith also played the murderous lawyer, Wendell Price, in the episode "If You Could See What I See".

Bill Marcus also played John Mareno, the D.A. in the TV series *Beauty and the Beast*

David Kagen is currently the director of a film acting school in North Hollywood.

The Details

Hardcastle is a man with a mission. He wants the place straightened up before his sister-in-law, Didi Drylinger, arrives for dinner. A brief inspection of the gatehouse shows that there's still a lot to be done. Mark suggests that maybe Didi has changed; after all, Hardcastle's avoided her successfully for ten years.

Out in front of a nice restaurant, a frumpily dressed woman in sunglasses has a trash-filled shopping cart. She is apparently tailing a man. She makes notes on her tape recorder, then she reminds herself to bring a bottle of wine "to Milton's", so she won't wind up drinking beer.

She notices a sale sign on a shop across the street. She crosses, continuing her monologue into the tape recorder, half shopping notes, half pep-talk, preparing herself for the ordeal ahead at Hardcastle's house.

Meanwhile, back in the restaurant, there's a meeting in the men's room between the man she was tailing, and a drug dealer. When the dealer gets greedy, the other man has him shot. He calmly exits the restaurant and departs, unnoticed by the woman, who is now thinking self-improvement.

Dinnertime at the estate, and we see Didi in her natural state, totally put together and cheerful, no trace of the morning's bag lady left. She comes bearing a gift of dishtowels and advice about micronutrients. Over dinner, out on the patio, she discusses her program of self-discovery since the death of her husband, Harry. She tells them she's taking a course in police procedure and they listen to her surveillance notes.

Hardcastle is concerned. He warns her about invasion of privacy issues. The conversation gets a little cool, though Didi remains smilingly polite. She knows they never got along, but part of why she's taking this course is an attempt to understand him. It looks like Hardcastle would prefer to be misunderstood.

It's daytime, at the gate of police impound lot number 12 where a truck full of narcotics is being moved. Two men in police uniform stop it, stealing the drugs at gunpoint. We see that one of the thieves is the man who was being tailed. He's Ira Trattner. In the next scene, a classroom at night, he's teaching Didi's police procedures class. He's an ex-cop who's written popular books about the police.

After class, Didi tells Ira that she's been following him. She won't tell him when, or for how long. She coyly says he'll find out next week when she hands in her class project.

At the estate the next day, Mark and the judge climb into the Coyote. Hardcastle intends to return Didi's tape recorder. He even has flowers, though he says it's not an apology.

Meanwhile, someone is ransacking Didi's apartment. The guys arrive and meet Didi in front of the building. The man flees as they enter. They chase, but lose him.

Didi moves to the estate for safety, bringing her dog and her late husband's shoe trees. Hardcastle asks her who might have had reason to search her place. The list is long. Didi has been using her newly-discovered investigatory skills on many of her neighbors.

Tratter and his former police partner, Arnie Hoffs, have a meeting with Gus Rossman, a big drug buyer. The deal will go down in two days on Rossman's boat. After Rossman leaves, Arnie worries that Ira's student may know too much about what's going on. They agree that they have to get the tapes she's made.

The judge and Mark check out some of Didi's suspicions. Her apartment manager, Mr. Bilsky, is their first target. They see the complicated phone lines running into his building. Hardcastle suspects a bookie operation.

Returning home, the judge intends to hide out in the gatehouse. There's no escaping Didi's efficiency, though. Even Mark's inner sanctum has now been cleaned and flower-bedecked.

Ira and Arnie make another try for Didi's apartment but find the place swarming with cops. They're busting Mr. Bilsky for making book.

That night after class, Ira is on the verge of pulling a gun on Didi when Milt walks in to pick her up. Didi makes a few more worryingly cryptic comments about her surveillance project, and they depart. Ira calls Arnie. He tells them now they have Hardcastle on their backs. He intends to eliminate that threat before the drug deal goes down.

Ira and Arnie take their troubles to Rossman who offers to take care of Hardcastle for them.

The judge continues to review Didi's tapes. Her list of suspicious characters includes the Girl Scouts and the mail carrier. They've nearly concluded that the only guilty party was Mr. Bilsky, when two fake pool men arrive to change the filters and let loose a couple of shotgun blasts. Mark knocks one assassin into the water, and the other crashes his truck into a closing gate.

Didi decides to leave. She thinks she's dangerous to be around. She won't listen to Mark's assurances that this is business as usual at Gull's Way. Hardcastle sends him out, then he and Didi have a heart-to-heart talk. He wants her to stay.

Back at his apartment, Arnie packs hastily. Ira shows up, just as he's heading out the door. He thinks Arnie's double-crossed him and pulls a gun.

There's one last person on Didi's list. The judge and Mark go see Lieutenant Delaney, to get some background on Ira Trattner. He's a very popular guy in the department. There's nothing dirty in his file, but Delaney suggests they go visit Arnie Hoffs.

They do, and find him dead in his apartment. Now Delaney wants everything else they've got. He also tells them the shotgun-wielding assassins have been connected to Gus Rossman.

Hardcastle heads home to question Didi. She can't believe Ira's up to anything but she does recognize Rossman from her surveillance. Hardcastle intends to question Rossman. Mark gets dragged along. Didi, who's worried about what she's started, waits until they've left, and then goes to Trattner's house. He pulls a gun on her.

Meanwhile, the judge and Mark arrive at Rossman's elegant estate. The soon to be unemployed house-man tells them where his boss is.

At the marina, on Rossman's boat, Mark and Hardcastle show up mid drug deal. They find Rossman, Trattner, and Didi, who suddenly lets loose with a couple of martial arts moves and converts a hostage situation to something a little more lively. Trattner escapes in a power boat, pursued in another by the guys. Mark leaps across at high speed and takes Trattner overboard just before the boat runs smack through a shed.

In the epilogue, Hardcastle thinks all engine problems have something to do with the points. Didi's still looking for an apartment and she's threatening the guys with steamed vegetables and brown rice. Even Didi's dog prefers pizza.

The Context

Eventually we'll meet five members of Hardcastle's family. Four of them have a definite interest in criminal justice, the other (Gerald, his younger brother) is a ne'er-do-well compulsive gambler.

But the one thing they all have in common is that they seem to accept (and even like) McCormick. Didi, who's apparently never seen him before, gives him a peck on the cheek and says "I'm safe. I'm family." Warren (Hardcastle's niece) went to an all-night drive-in with him. Aunts May and Zora make him cookies. Gerald uses him as a buffer between himself and his brother. No one even looks squinty for a moment at the ex-con living on the estate, and McCormick seems equally comfortable around them, often more so than Hardcastle is. It's probably fair to say that Mark gets along better with Hardcastle's family than Hardcastle does.

The Trivia

The exteriors for the "Saint Monet Restaurant", where the hit goes down in the first act, were shot at 1323 Montana Avenue in Santa Monica—nearly across the street from the Aero Theater.

Didi was apparently intended to be a returning character. There were scenes for her in the episode "Outlaw Champion", which was slated to appear later in the schedule. It became the season opener, and her part was eliminated.

Memorable Quotes

Didi: I took a course entitled "Everything that Happens is Me". Well, I learned more in six months than I learned in a lifetime.
Hardcastle: Well, most of what happens around here is McCormick.

Hardcastle: (comforting Didi) I don't want you to go.
Didi: I thought you hated ironed underwear.
Hardcastle: It took me five years to break your sister of that habit. I just want 'em...just roll 'em up and stick them in a drawer by the socks, okay?
Didi: How did you do it, Milt? I mean, after Nancy died. How did you keep it from falling apart?
Hardcastle: I didn't. But, I had work to do, and there's always somebody around the house, underneath my feet, keeping me busy.
Didi: He's a nice kid, Milt.
Hardcastle: Oh, he's okay.

Never My Love – premiered October 28, 1984

Written by	Thomas Szollosi and
	Richard Christian Matheson
Directed by	Bruce Kessler
Second unit director	Gary Combs

Cast

Molly Cheek	Cyndy Wenzek
Peter White	Senator Evan Crocker
Lance Henriksen	Josh Fulton
Raymond Singer	Jerry Miles
John Hancock	Lieutenant Delaney
Harvey Vernon	Captain Anthony Switzer
Robert Denison	
Seth Jaffe	
E. Hampton Beagle	Louis
Larry McCormick	the reporter

Cast Notes

Lance Henriksen was also the ruthless hit man in "Man in a Glass House". He played the role of Frank Black in the series *Millennium.*

Molly Cheek returned as Diane Templeton in the episode "Games People Play". She played the role of Nancy Bancroft in *It's Gary Shandling's Show.*

Larry McCormick had a thirty-year career as a reporter and anchorman at KTLA-TV in Los Angeles. In over forty appearances as an actor in both TV and movies, he often portrayed newscasters, including in the pilot episode of *Murder She Wrote,* "The Murder of Sherlock Holmes", which also featured Brian Keith.

The Details

At a mausoleum, a small group is gathered for a funeral. Mark and the judge are among the mourners. While the dark-suited generic funeral-conductor drones on about how Cyndy would want them all to move on, Mark is remembering a night twelve years earlier, when the now-deceased woman broke up with him. She left him for a guy named Clayton Pasternak.

As the service concludes, Hardcastle tells him he'll be waiting outside. Mark mentions he sent her flowers every year on her birthday, even from prison, but she never contacted him.

Two other mourners are departing. Jerry Miles comments quietly to Senator Crocker that a funeral is a helluva way to get rid of an eyewitness.

A week and a half later, at the estate, Mark is moping around, helping Hardcastle prepare for a Halloween costume party. In the middle of listening to the RSVPs on the answering machine, they hear someone claim-

ing to be a very much still alive Cyndy. Mark is sure it's her voice. Hardcastle is doubtful about it all. He says he'll look into it and tells Mark not to do anything stupid in the meantime.

Mark goes to Josh Fulton, the director of the facility where Cyndy was purportedly interred, and demands to see her death certificate. Fulton tells him he has no rights in the matter. After Mark leaves, still determined, Fulton calls Jerry, the man we saw at the funeral. He tells him there's a problem. Now Jerry is confronted by his boss, Senator Crocker, and one of Crocker's other handlers, Stan. Jerry was supposed to have had Cyndy killed. She witnessed a fatal drunk driving incident involving the senator. They tell Jerry he messed up by only faking the girl's death. Stan and Jerry argue about the necessity of more deaths. Jerry resigns but before he can make it official, Stan terminates him with extreme prejudice.

Back at the estate, the decorating and the debate go on. Mark is arguing for an exhumation. Hardcastle, still doubting, tells him he needs a better reason than a phone call from beyond the grave. Mark stalks out.

It's nighttime at the cemetery. Mark climbs over the fence and picks the lock on the mausoleum door. He slips inside. He's been followed.

He locates Cyndy's crypt, pries it open, and pulls the casket out. Just as he lifts the lid and leans over to peer in, a hand descends on his shoulder.

After he starts breathing again, Mark shows Hardcastle the empty casket. The judge quickly assembles the pieces. Cyndy's crypt is surrounded by names that are familiar to him—mob figures who have purportedly also gone to their just rewards.

While Hardcastle explains the possible uses of a body laundry, Stan and company arrive. Mark and the judge flee, pursued by bad guys in two sedans. Mark takes evasive maneuvers and the two other cars crash headlong.

Returning home, they find the missing woman waiting for them in Hardcastle's study.

The next morning, Cyndy and Mark have taken up as though twelve years had never elapsed. Mark's not surprised to find out that Clayton Pasternack, the guy Cyndy left him for, dumped *her* for a Greek translator. Hardcastle finds them bickering in the study. He interrupts and makes Cyndy tell them the whole story of the crime she witnessed. She says Crocker was drunk when he ran a man down.

In Crocker's office, the senator is being prepped to deal with the press about the same incident—it was an accident; the man ran in front of his car. He's also prepared to mention the disappearance of his campaign manager, Jerry Miles.

At the estate, Cyndy and the guys hear the broadcast. She's frightened about Jerry's disappearance. They agree Fulton must've been part of this. Hardcastle goes back to police headquarters do some more digging in their files. He instructs McCormick to stay put.

Fulton shows up at Crocker's office, whining about being an accessory to Jerry's murder. He prefers empty caskets to full ones. Stan sends him away.

Hardcastle leans on yet another police buddy, asking him to run more names through the computer. He's persuasive, as usual.

Mark doesn't take instruction well. He and Cyndy brave a stormy night to break back into the mausoleum. They're followed, this time by one of Stan's men. After a continuation of their discussion about their relationship, they finally get back to business. They discover Jerry's body in the holding morgue but are cornered there by Stan, Fulton, and company.

Hardcastle arrives back at the estate to find the party underway but no McCormick.

Cyndy and Mark are forced into a box in the crematorium. Stan and Crocker depart for a press conference and Fulton is left to do the dispatching. As the box is pushed toward the oven, Hardcastle arrives with reinforcements. Mark and Cyndy are freed, and take off with Hardcastle in pursuit of Crocker.

While Crocker answers questions from the reporters, Cyndy makes a surprise appearance. With Mark and the judge behind her, she announces that she's seen Jerry

Miles' body and that he was murdered. As the police move in, Stan slips out the door. Mark goes after him, tackling him in the stairwell.

In the epilogue, back at the estate the party is rolling. Mark tells Cyndy he's done being angry. Just then the phone rings. It's for Cyndy. It's Clayton Pasternack.

The Context

You almost have to feel sorry for the really bad guys in this episode. Stan's just trying to do a professional job of it—in this case, dispose of witnesses properly. He's got his hands full, surrounded by incompetence. First it's Jerry, trying to spare Cyndy's life, then it's Fulton, leaving Jerry's body lying around, when he has a perfectly good crematorium right down the hall.

Meanwhile, Mark's taste in women remains relentlessly questionable. This one dumped him, ignored him for twelve years, and then only lets him know she's not dead ten days after the funeral, and still he's there for her when she needs him.

The Trivia

The back story in this one raises more questions. What was Mark doing in an anthropology class back in 1972? Isn't this the guy who got his "doctorate in auto shop" ("Goin' Nowhere Fast")?

"Never My Love", Mark and Cyndy's song, was written by Don and Dick Addrisi and went to number two on the charts as performed by The Association in 1967.

The mausoleum which is *not* Cyndy's final resting place (called J.H. Fulton and Son's Mortuary in the episode) is located in what was then the Hollywood Memorial Park at 6000 Santa Monica Boulevard. Founded in 1900, it has been refurbished and under new management since 1998. It's now known as Hollywood Forever and, in true Hollywood fashion, late night open air film screenings are shown there, projected against the marble wall of a mausoleum. Visitors may visit the graves of Rudolph Valentino, Clark Gable, and many other celebrities.

Memorable Quotes

McCormick: With all the holidays in the world to choose from, how come you picked the runt of the litter, huh?

Hardcastle: Ah, runts are in the eye of the beholder. I like Halloween.

McCormick: You would. No presents. No turkey, no tree, not even any chocolate hearts. Just a bunch of big orange gourds you cut faces into. How much this party cost you, anyway? Six or seven bucks?

McCormick: There cannot be no laws broken if there's no body. There's no body, there's no illegal exhumation. Look. Look, I was right. There's no Cyndy. She's alive. You know what that means? It means she's alive!

Hardcastle: No Cyndy, huh?

McCormick: You're a little slow, but you're sincere, Judge. That's what I like about you.

Whatever Happened to Guts? – premiered November 4, 1984

Written by	Richard Christian Matheson and Thomas Szollosi
Directed by	Michael Hiatt
Second unit director	Gary Combs

Cast

Marilyn Jones	Kay Barrett/Stephanie Gary
Patricia Harty	Elaine Camp
Bill Morey	Judge Dremmond
John Carter	Nolan Ashley
John Hancock	Lieutenant Delaney
Jim McKrell	the announcer

Cast Notes

Marilyn Jones also had a role in "Really Neat Cars and Guys with a Sense of Humor".

Patricia Harty is the wife of *Hardcastle and McCormick* producer Les Sheldon. She also played the role of Jeannine Alexander in the penultimate *Hardcastle and McCormick* episode, "The Day the Music Died".

John Carter also played Paul Danton in "Really Neat Cars and Guys With a Sense of Humor".

Jim McKrell was a game show host in the 1970s, including a four year stint on *Celebrity Sweepstakes*. He had a guest role on *The A-Team,* in a script written by Cannell and Hasburgh, in which he played an airline pilot named Larry Hertzog.

The Details

The camera pans over a collection of dolls and some family photographs and fixes on one of an intense young girl and her dignified father. That same person, now a young woman, is watching TV with rapt attention. News anchor Nolan Ashley is the object of her attention.

Late that night, in his office at the studio, Nolan slips on his sport coat and takes a sip of whiskey. The door behind him opens. It's the young woman. He greets her as "Kay", and thanks her for her letters. There was a gift, too, a silver music box in the shape of a piano.

They leave together in her car. She asks him if he's nervous about his wife finding out. She offers him a drink from a hip flask.

She takes him to a deserted spot under the highway. He's drunk and makes a move toward her. Her demeanor changes, from seductive to angry. She calls him "Daddy" and berates him. Nolan is bemused but not yet worried as he watches her climb back into her car. A moment later he's running for his life, as she chases him down and kills him.

It's daytime at the same station. Mark and Milt are in the audience for a taping of *You Be the Judge.* It's one of those reality court shows, and Hardcastle is appalled that anyone watches such dreck. He wants to leave, but Mark says they can't. The TV judge is a friend of Hardcastle's and they've agreed to meet him for lunch. During a commercial break, the old friend, Dremmond, is self-deprecating about the show and says he'll meet them at a swank Malibu restaurant.

On the way to the rendezvous, Mark speculates about what Dremmond wants from Hardcastle. It's not long before they find out. He asks Milt to take over his TV show—keep the bench warm while Dremmond is having his gallbladder out.

Hardcastle is at first astonished. He says he's not the type. Dremmond mentions that the show grossed twenty-five million dollars the previous year. He certainly has Mark's attention. McCormick is all for the career move.

In the office of psychiatrist Stephanie Gary, we hear Kay saying her relationship with Nolan didn't work out. She's still looking for Mr. Right.

In the studio, it's almost show time for Hardcastle's debut as a TV judge. His last minute instructions to McCormick include a request to start a fist fight in the audience if things aren't going well in front of the cameras.

No need for fisticuffs; the judge may be unpolished, but he's quickly in his element, dispensing popular justice in a no-nonsense way. He even coins a popular saying—"Whatever happened to guts?"—before the first commercial break.

Kay is watching the debut as well. She seems to like what she sees.

A few days later, back at the estate, Mark carries in the mail. He may need a wheelbarrow soon. He also reads the review from Variety. Hardcastle feigns disinterest, but stops pumping iron long enough to get the gist of it. He's now a hot property.

Kay is in Dr. Gary's office again. She's struck by the new TV judge and determined to meet him. As if being a murderous psychopath wasn't enough, we now discover that she's also floridly delusional. Though she's playing the role of patient, calmly discussing her situation with her psychiatrist, there is no one else in the room.

The next day, the judge has to run the gauntlet of press and fans just to get into the studio. Elaine Camp tells him the ratings are going through the roof. Hardcastle is still nonchalant about the whole thing, though very interested in exact numbers. Mark offers him his services. Any position will do, especially if it's manager.

The judge sits down to get his make-up applied. Kay has slipped in and has a makeup box. She tells Hardcastle he reminds her of her father. She fishes a straight razor out of the box but is interrupted by Elaine and Mark. She rushes off.

The judge and Mark stop for burgers on the way home. The attractive carhop recognizes Hardcastle. He has a photograph handy to autograph. Mark is appalled.

At the station, Elaine is working late. Another member of the staff comes in with a package addressed to Hardcastle. They discuss the number of new affiliates who are picking the show up. The man leaves. Elaine is alone in the office. She opens the package and finds a music box. She listens to it for a moment, then goes into the former office of the murdered anchorman. She finds an identical one on his desk.

Disturbed by her discovery, she makes her way through the deserted building. Despite a startling encounter with a janitor, Elaine gets safely to her car. As she heads for home, another car, following close behind her, looms in the rearview mirror. It finally turns aside. Elaine lets out a sigh of relief, and then Kay, knife in hand, grabs her from over the back of her seat.

The next day, in a studio executive's office, Hardcastle is being propositioned about his future plans. The honchos think he's too big for *You Be the Judge*. The new idea is a show that would turn real divorces into entertainment. Mark and Milt are both appalled. The judge says no.

As they're getting up to leave, Lieutenant Delaney calls, summoning them to the scene of Elaine's murder. Kay watches from a short ways off.

Back at the studio, Mark picks the lock on Elaine's desk. They find the two music boxes.

That night at Gull's Way, the guys contemplate the dark side of fame. Mark says he wants Hardcastle to get out while he can. He's given up his own aspirations to be a manager; he says the work they do chasing bad guys is more important. Hardcastle looks pleased.

The next morning, a crisply-suited and businesslike Dr. Stephanie Gary calls at the estate. She's asking Hardcastle to help with a patient of hers, a young woman with a father fixation. She offers to take him to her. Hardcastle reluctantly agrees.

Shortly after they depart, Lieutenant Delaney arrives with the news that the fingerprints on the music boxes belong to Stephanie Gary. Mark and the police head out in pursuit.

In Gary's car, Hardcastle and the psychiatrist talk about fame and the attraction that famous people have for others. Dr. Gary puts on some music. It's a band arrangement of the music box tune. Hardcastle looks puzzled. Dr. Gary pulls into the same place where she murdered Nolan Ashley. Hardcastle tries to calm her as she starts to berate him. She sprays him with mace. He is temporarily blinded, but escapes from the car and eludes her first few attempts to run him down.

The police arrive, with the Coyote keeping pace. One squad car crashes but Mark runs Gary's car into a parked pick-up. A moment later, Hardcastle emerges from the back of the truck, not too much the worse for his brush with fame.

In the epilogue, Dremmond is back on his feet and the guys take him out to lunch. He thanks them for resurrecting his show—it's going to syndicate for ninety-six million. As they wave good-bye to Dremmond outside the restaurant, Mark teases the judge about how he went just a bit Hollywood. As Hardcastle's denying it, three older ladies accost him. Mark is shoved to the side, as Milt cheerfully poses for pictures with part of his geriatric fan base.

The Context

This is Hardcastle's second appointment with destiny; the first was in "Mr. Hardcastle Goes to Washington". Of course becoming a TV judge isn't quite the same as having a run at the Supreme Court. In some ways it's higher profile. Mark is, as always, eager to grab the coattails of popularity, but once again he's the first guy to get some perspective—maybe because it's Hardcastle's turn at fame again.

When the series turns its perspective on Hollywood, the results are always interesting. There's running commentary on the ratings, audience shares, and sponsors of the show-within-the show. Everyone is scrambling to make the most of their unexpected runaway hit, and nobody, of course, can explain exactly why it took off. From Dremmond's attitude in the first lunch scene, there may be a slight suspicion that he picked Milt precisely *because* he wasn't a show-biz type, and therefore was not likely to steal his thunder.

In the end, though, Milt and Mark both agree that there are more important things than TV success. Hardcastle looks willing to settle for only fifteen minutes of fame.

The Trivia

"Bulldog" Dremmond is a nod to Bulldog Drummond, a British fictional character created by H.C. McNeile in 1920. Drummond was an ex-Army Captain turned private investigator.

The music box tune favored by "Kay" for her victims is "My Heart Belongs to Daddy", written by Cole Porter in 1938.

When the police and Mark are searching for Gray's car, the dispatcher summons all available units to "the Del Amo Underpass, San Diego Freeway". Del Amo street crosses over 405 (The San Diego Freeway) at a point about 40 miles (by road) from Malibu.

Twice in this episode, the guys and Judge Dremmond have lunch at the Beau Rivage Restaurant—it's located at 26025 Pacific Coast Highway and opened in 1982. It advertises "a Riviera shores ambiance on the Pacific." (In the epilogue, as they get up from the table, Mark makes an extra contribution to the tip.)

The proposed show that so horrified the guys became a reality a year later when *Divorce Court* premiered (there was actually an earlier version that ran in the fifties and sixties). The "presiding judge" of that show—William Keene—came to fame as the judge in the Charles Manson trial. The earlier version of this show used actors. In 1999 the show was reincarnated using the actual couples involved in real divorces.

Memorable Quotes

Hardcastle: I'm not through here! You can do your commercial later. (to defendant) Listen, pal, this is a little old lady who saved up for fifteen years to make a dream come true. And you let her get all the way out to Hawaii, knowing full well what would happen—

Defendant: But that really wasn't what—

Hardcastle: Quit interrupting!

Defendant: But, Your Honor—

Hardcastle: Quiet! (slams gavel) I'm sick of "buts". Everybody's sick of "buts". Whatever happened to *guts*, anyway?

McCormick: Fame has a way of working on a guy, Judge, no matter what you think. So if you're thinking about hanging around the show biz routine for a long time…well, I'm not in the mood for that and I want you to reconsider.

Hardcastle: I thought you wanted to be my announcer and all that.

McCormick: I did. That's just it.

Hardcastle: Meaning if you can't, I can't.

McCormick: No, meaning your overnight fame made *me* forget what's important, if only for a while, and I don't want that to happen to you. The work you and I do is important—I mean, those files, chasing the bad guys down, dropping 'em through the slot. That's what's important, not just some dumb TV show. (pause) Aren't you going to say anything?

You and the Horse You Rode in On
– premiered November 18, 1984

Written and directed by	Patrick Hasburgh
Second unit director	Gary Combs

Cast

Ray Buktenica	David Waverly
Steve Levitt	Peter Trigg
Shawn Southwick	the receptionist
Michael Ensign	Waverly's all-purpose heavy
John Hancock	Lieutenant Delaney
Brett Johnson	Tommy, the kid at the Rose Bowl

Cast Notes

Shawn Southwick is talk show host Larry King's wife.

Michael Ensign has over 140 TV and movie credits, including the role of Lieutenant Northacker on the 1980 movie *Raise the Titanic* and Benjamin Guggenheim in the 1997 blockbuster, *Titanic*. He spent three years as a member of the Royal Shakespeare Company.

Brett Johnson was the voice of Charlie Brown in two TV specials.

The Details

On an otherwise ordinary morn-ing, an executive type climbs into his Cadillac and leaves home. He is fol-lowed by another car. The driver crowds him, then rams the side of his car and fires a shot at it, forcing him off a cliff to his death.

In his corporate office, David Waverly gets the news that the man has been taken care of. He tells his second in command that he needs a replacement by next week. This time he wants someone who won't get nervous and run to the police. He wants someone who's mature and suave, someone who has a fast rap, and has some dirt in his past that can be used as leverage if needed.

Meanwhile, it's free Nerf football night at the Rose Bowl, though Hardcastle has to pay six dollars for theirs, since the kid *he's* with is over twelve. Mark's bedecked with football souvenirs more suitable for someone one-third his age. He's annoyed and embarrassed.

In the Gull's Way dining room that evening, the argument continues. Mark accuses the judge of treating him like a punk teenager. He wants to move out on his own. Hardcastle says it's a tough world. It turns into a shouting match, with the judge telling him if he doesn't like it he can leave. He doesn't, and so he does.

In the montage that follows, we see an initially cheerful, brushed, and sport-coated McCormick gradually lowering both his expectations and his sartorial standards as the day passes. Meanwhile, back at the estate, Hardcastle waits for an admission of defeat that doesn't come.

Mark lands in Waverly's waiting room. He's psyching himself up for what may be his last chance, while inside his headquarters, Waverly and his right hand man, Peter Trigg, discuss McCormick's "special" qualifications. Trigg says he's the right man for the job. Waverly points out that they had to kill the last man Trigg recommended.

An unusually nervous McCormick is summoned into the luxurious office. He's apologetic and self-effacing. Waverly congratulates him. He's got the job as Regional Director of Waverly Water Filters. Even after the spiel from his new boss Mark is doubtful, but Waverly is a master of persuasion, and he soon has McCormick on his team at a salary of "five grand a week".

Back at the estate, Hardcastle finally gets his phone call. It's Mark, calling from the car phone of his Mercedes convertible. He invites Hardcastle to lunch. They meet at a fancy French restaurant. Mark's dressed to the nines in suit and silk tie. Things start out rocky, but in the middle of what's shaping up to be another argument, Mark thanks the judge for giving him the proper foundation. Still, despite all the humble gratitude, Mark can't help flashing his accessories. Hardcastle wants to know what kind of job allowed him to buy a three thousand dollar watch.

Mark finally shows him his business card. All becomes clear for the judge. He explains that David Waverly is a well-known bunko artist and perpetrator of pyramid sales scams. Mark angrily defends Waverly.

At the Waverly warehouse, David and Peter discuss their sales protégé. Mark has only done one seminar, but already he's brought in seventy-six new sheep to be sheared.

Back at the French restaurant, Hardcastle is laying out the particulars of Mark's new job with uncanny accuracy. The dispute escalates; he calls Mark a shill. McCormick stomps out.

At the convention center, it's another presentation for prospective Waverly franchise buyers. Mark seems to have lost his boundless enthusiasm. Waverly won't let him deviate from the program, though.

Meanwhile, Hardcastle is visiting Lieutenant Delaney. There's no current dirt on Waverly, but Hardcastle intends to get it.

Back at David Waverly's office, Mark is getting feisty. He demands to see one of the filters. Waverly delays, but eventually produces the prototype "dash nine" model. Mark is not impressed. It's a coffee filter in a plastic tube. The

discussion goes downhill from there, until Mark finally tenders his resignation by dropping his watch and car keys into a fish tank and walking out the door.

Next up in the Waverly office is Hardcastle, who takes one look at the dash nine model and pronounces it "a hamster feeder". He spots Mark's watch in the fish tank. Waverly threatens to call security on him. The judge tells him he made a mistake when he put the hustle on Mark. Waverly assures him that McCormick's already quit. The judge isn't surprised to hear it but tells Waverly that he'll still get him investigated for fraud.

After Hardcastle leaves, Waverly puts in a call to his goon. On his way home, the judge is waylaid and kidnapped.

Mark shows up at the estate and finds three newspapers on the front steps. The judge isn't there and the answering machine plays back two days worth of his own messages telling Hardcastle he wants to come home. The phone rings. It's David Waverly. Mark angrily tells him he's not coming back. Waverly tells him to reconsider. If he doesn't return, Hardcastle will be killed.

Mark goes to Waverly's office. He apologizes to the judge, tries to punch Waverly's lights out, and finally agrees to make another presentation. Waverly takes him at gunpoint to the convention center. Lieutenant Delaney and the cops close in on the rest of Waverly's goons, who are still holding Hardcastle in another vehicle.

At the sales seminar, Mark is dutifully giving the spiel when Hardcastle and Delaney walk in from the back of the auditorium. Changing his tune in mid-line, Mark starts to tell the crowd exactly what David Waverly has been up to.

Waverly makes a run for it. Mark chases him on foot, then in the Coyote, until Waverly's car does a rollover smash through a truck. Mark has him subdued when Hardcastle and Delaney arrive moments later. He wants to know how the cavalry got there in time to rescue Hardcastle. Delaney tells him that the judge was wearing a wire right from the start.

In the epilogue, it's mail call at the estate and Mark is the recipient of a stack of bills from his short tenure as a young executive. His expense account went up in smoke along with Waverly's company. The judge lectures Mark on the fine points of contract law and then gives him a raise in his allowance that will allow him to break even on the bills in about nine or ten years. Then he hands him the hose and tells him to wash the truck. As they part company he tosses Waverly's line back at McCormick: "There's no respect in the world today for water."

None for judges, either, it appears. Mark lets him have it with the hose.

The Context

This episode returns to Hasburgh's integral theme of fathers and sons. This time Mark's having a bad outbreak of delayed adolescent rebellion.

It appears that Hardcastle holds all the cards in this one. He was absolutely right about Mark's job prospects and even had the lowdown on David Waverly right from the start. But there are a couple of nice moments that give things some balance. When Mark thinks he's landed his dream job, he doesn't use it as an opportunity for unbridled crowing. Instead he takes the opportunity to thank Hardcastle, which shows that maturity isn't really about having a fancy watch and a Mercedes.

And even though he's loath to admit that Hardcastle is right, once his eyes have been opened to the possibility of fraud, Mark uses his own judgment and starts asking Waverly the tough questions. When he doesn't like the answers, he quits. He's mature enough to call up Hardcastle (twice) and admit he was wrong, and then, most important of all, when the hammer comes down he goes back to bail his friend out. It's all a performance well worthy of a handshake and a "Welcome home, sport" from Hardcastle in the end.

The Trivia

The music video that's on the TV when Hardcastle stomps in with dinner is "The Hero Takes a Fall" being performed by The Bangles. It premiered on their first album, *All Over the Place* in 1984.

The unemployment montage is set to "Get a Job", the 1958 hit by Richard Lewis, performed by The Silhouettes.

Memorable Quotes

McCormick: I'm an adult. I'm a grown man. I can even get into an X-rated movie without showing any proof.
Hardcastle: Yeah, you're right. I'm sorry.
McCormick: Okay.
Hardcastle: Wait a minute. Wait a minute.
McCormick: What? What is it?
Hardcastle: You've got mustard all over your face.
McCormick: Well, that's okay. Don't! (makes protesting noises)
Hardcastle: What?
McCormick: I don't care if I've got mustard on my face.
Hardcastle: Here. (offers napkin)

McCormick: Don't, you're embarrassing me. Knock it off.

Hardcastle: Go around with mustard all over your face! I don't care either!

McCormick: Give me that. (takes napkin, wipes face) Okay?

Hardcastle: Good. Sorry if I embarrassed you.

McCormick: Ah, that's okay. Listen, I tell you what, why don't you let me drive us home, okay? That way, you can relax.

Hardcastle: Nah, there's a lot of post-game traffic, kid. Could be tricky. I better do it.

Hardcastle: Well, you're looking pretty good, kid. Fancy suit, silk tie, French cuffs.

McCormick: How do I really look though?

Hardcastle: You look like a pimp.

Waverly: Know what you're doing? Know what you're doing? You're making a big mistake.

Hardcastle: No, you made a mistake. You made a mistake when you pulled McCormick into this and made a shill out of him, see? Now, that was wrong, 'cause he's a friend of mine. You might even say he's my best friend. And nobody gets to put the hustle on my best friend, see?

Waverly: Okay, all right. Look, just relax. McCormick quit.

Hardcastle: I figured he would.

One of the Girls from Accounting – premiered November 25, 1984

Written by	Stephen J. Cannell
Directed by	Bruce Kessler
Second unit director	Gary Combs

Cast

Bonnie Urseth	Kathy Kasternack
Edmund Gilbert	Captain Lanark
Marc Alaimo	Captain Medwick
Robert Dryer	Rod Anvilinosa
Kelbe Nugent	Madge
David Gautreaux	
Charlie Dell	"Stoney" Firestone
John Hancock	Lieutenant Delaney
Stan Haze	Smith
Patrick Stack	Police Officer

(Note: in the closing credits Haze is listed as playing Smith. IMDb credits Dryer as Anvilinosa. In close watching of the episode, it appears that Stan Haze is being addressed as Tremaine Lane and David Gatreaux is being called Anvilinosa.)

Cast Notes

Kelbe Nugent, Kathy's drop-dead gorgeous roommate, also appeared in *The A-Team, Riptide,* and *Stingray*

Charlie Dell is a very busy character actor who's portrayed a career's worth of doctors, professors, and ministers. He deserved to be a guy called "Stoney" just this once.

The Details

Mark's doing the straightening up while Hardcastle works on his income tax forms. He looks over the judge's shoulder and discovers he's being claimed as a deduction, under the classification of "ward". Won't work, he says. Blatantly fraudulent. You can't claim an employee as a deduction.

While commenting on the nuances of the tax code, he's also bemoaning his break-up the night before with Alicia. He thinks dating has become superficial. Alicia told him he wasn't good-looking enough for her. He says even his sign is wretched—"Cancer with Virgo rising". He wants to meet Ms. Right (or even *Mrs.* Right).

As he contemplates just who that might be, in a government office a bookish woman with bottle-bottom glasses is bringing an accounting error to the attention of her boss…again. Ten policemen who are retired or otherwise off the force are still getting paychecks. He impatiently tells her he'll look into it. As soon as she steps out, he makes a phone call.

The clerk, Kathy Kasternack, is clocking out for the day. She tells her friend that there's no commitment anymore. All she ever meets are shallow disco guys. As she parts from her friend and steps into an alley, she is dogged by two scary-looking guys in a postal truck.

They accelerate and she flees, losing her glasses in the process and then stumbling blindly into a parking structure and smack into McCormick. She shrieks, then tells him someone was trying to kill her.

The rogue postal truck is nowhere in sight but Mark offers to give her an escort. He sounds doubtful of her story and his condescension aggravates her.

Fortunately for Kathy's credibility, as Mark is walking her to the dry cleaners, the guys in the truck come back for another pass. This time shots are fired. McCormick and Kathy duck into another parking lot, playing cat and mouse

with their pursuers. Mark tries to boost some wheels. He sets off an alarm. They are cornered, but he bluffs his way out of the dimly-lit situation by pointing his shoe and talking tough.

Mark takes Kathy to a diner. He calls the police and then Hardcastle. Captain Medwick shows up first. On hearing his name, Kathy realizes he's one of the ten officers she was telling her supervisor about. Things quickly turn ugly and Medwick tells them they're both under arrest. They bolt.

Another alley, another crazed pursuit. This round, it's a water department vehicle. Hardcastle arrives in the nick of time. They scramble into his truck and are off.

In a barrack-like building, Medwick musters his men and tells them they're moving out. The botched hit on Kathy has made things too hot for them. One of his men complains that the investigation they were in the middle of will have to be scrubbed.

Back at the estate, Hardcastle tries to reach the police commissioner. While waiting to hear back from him, Kathy explains that she is a payroll clerk and is studying to be an accountant. Mark poses the issue of his status as employee versus ward. Kathy comes down on his side of the tax argument.

She's also able to list, from memory, the ten men whose names are incorrectly still on the police payroll. She asks Mark to take to her back to her office to retrieve a spare pair of glasses. At her desk she discovers that her records for the ten men are gone. She suspects her boss, Mr. Firestone, took the papers.

She asks Mark exactly what it is that he does for a living. He hesitates, but doesn't lie outright.

At the police department, Captain Lanark gets a radio message from his undercover unit. Medwick is unhappy and it looks like he and his guys aren't taking orders from their commanding officer anymore.

It's morning at the Gull's Way breakfast table, and Hardcastle has just finished working the phone. He's hunting down information on the ten men. He tells Kathy to call in sick to work. She discovers Mr. Firestone didn't come in either.

They go to Firestone's house and find him dead, asphyxiated in his garage after a blow to the head. But Firestone woke up long enough to write the word "Toystore" on his windshield.

The cops arrive. Mike Delaney hears Kathy's story but doesn't believe there are cops behind the incidents. He thinks Mark's smitten and the whole conspiracy theory is just speculation.

Mark *is* smitten. Kathy thinks she's not his type, being deficient in the cobalt blue eyes department. He assures her that he's not looking for that any more. Besides wondering about their mutual compatibility, Kathy is worried that people are dying because she wouldn't let go of an "accounting error".

Back at the estate, reports are coming in. Hardcastle now knows that everyone on Kathy's list worked at one time for a cop named Lanark. Mark says they have to keep going on this. He talks about how different Kathy is from his usual dates and that he can't even think of what to say when he's around her. Hardcastle recollects the first thing his future wife ever said to him—"Move it or lose it"—and how important she was to him. He offers to help Mark figure out what's going on with the list.

They visit Captain Lanark. He's initially friendly, but unhelpful. He denies knowing any unit named "Toystore" and says he barely remembers the men on the list.

After they leave, Lanark makes radio contact with Medwick again. He tells him about Hardcastle. Lanark goes to a prearranged meeting place—a lonely spot near the river after dark. His former undercover squad forces him into a van and drives off.

At the estate, it's dinnertime. Being smitten extends to food appreciation. Mark can find no fault with Kathy's stew, even the lumpy, chewy, cat-like bits. The three discuss what a deeply undercover cop unit might be up to. In mid-discussion, Delaney calls. Lanark has gone missing at the riverside rendezvous. His car and the radio have been found. Delaney has been listening in on some Toystore activity, but can't figure out where they are or what they're doing. Hardcastle wheedles temporary possession of the radio from him, and ten minutes to look around Lanark's office. They both know going through the official channels will take weeks.

A quick search of Lanark's office uncovers a map of potential Toystore hangouts. One hot prospect is a condemned neighborhood near the airport. The guys and Kathy go there, still listening to the radio messages that indicate the group is doing a surveillance operation. They enter the deserted neighborhood and find one house with signs of occupation. It's Toystore's base of operations and there's a heavy stockpile of weaponry. They also find Lanark, beaten and handcuffed in a storeroom.

As he tells them about his rogue unit, they realize the men have returned and are aware of their intrusion. The gun cabinet is at hand. Mark and Hardcastle arm themselves. Kathy gets a shotgun. The judge puts out a radio call for police

back-up. The rogue unit attacks and is held off. A police helicopter circles overhead and Medwick's men fire at it. Mark and the judge use a rocket launcher to destroy one of the attacker's cars. The police arrive in force, scattering the bad guys.

Mark sees one of the men bolt for the back yard and takes off after him. Hardcastle tackles Medwick and hands him over to the cops. Mark catches up with his fleeing suspect but loses in hand-to-hand combat. As he's down, and about to be stabbed by his opponent, a shotgun blast strikes the knife-wielding man. Kathy lowers her shouldered weapon, obviously distraught.

In the epilogue, Mark is asking for advice—wear the tie, or not? He's taking Kathy out for dinner and a concert. Hardcastle tells him to take it slow, this one is special. Mark agrees. After he leaves, the judge looks over at a picture of his wife, and says he knows he should stay out of it, but he likes the kid.

Mark shows up at Kathy's door, daisies in hand. Her roommate—Madge of the cobalt blue eyes—sees them off, remarking enviously that "some girls have all the luck."

The Context

Cannell seems to delight in standing plot conventions on their heads. In this case, the standard routine—mousy woman takes off glasses, shakes hair loose, and becomes a stunningly attractive *femme fatale*—is pointedly reversed. Kathy starts out with her glasses off, and all it makes her is blind. She gets them back on eventually. Her hair never comes down, and Mark, against his own inclinations and track record, falls hard for a woman who liked him before she knew what he looked like.

The classic "take the glasses off" scene is even worked into the plot a second time, but Mark's motivation isn't to transform Kathy, but to change how he appears to her. He sees himself as flawed, external appearances aside, but he wants her to like him for what he *is*, not for what he looks like.

Other conventions also bite the dust in this episode. Kathy is the one who saves Mark with a well-aimed blast from the shotgun and, despite having perfect justification, still takes it hard. It's some interesting foreshadowing for the ending of one of Cannell's later episodes, "The Birthday Present", in which Mark faces the same split-second decision and, having made the same choice, is equally distraught.

Kathy, of course, will never be seen again, and Mark will soon return to his appreciation of externalities, but she was an interesting experiment in character development.

The Trivia

In the opening scene, the camera pans over a collection of photographs (shades of the opening of "Whatever Happened to Guts?"). It's Mark and a series of very attractive women. The music is Julio Iglesias' "To All the Girls I've Loved Before".

According to the income tax form Hardcastle is filling out, he's over 65, and Mark has been in residence at Gull's Way for twenty-four months.

In the den, act one, Mark snatches up a single sheet of the income tax form, then is holding a whole sheaf of papers, then is putting the single sheet down again. Income tax forms are like that, though.

According to Mark, his *monthly* allowance from Hardcastle is $168.50.

The meet-cute/attempted assassination scene was filmed in a garage in the vicinity of Third and Traction Streets, southeast of downtown Los Angeles.

Mark's weapon in the Toystore hideout appears to be a Vietnam-era M-16-A1— an assault rifle patterned on the ArmaLite Ar-15. He's firing in semi-automatic mode. It has been estimated that there are about 70,000 legal AR-15s in California alone.

For someone uninterested in astrological signs, McCormick seems to have several of them. Here, he's a Cancer (birthday June 22-July 22), but in season three ("She Ain't Deep but She Sure Runs Fast"), he'll claim to be a Pisces (February 19-March 20). But this season's earlier episode set during his birthday, "Ties My Father Sold Me", would put him squarely as a Libra (September 23-October 23).

Memorable Quotes

Kathy: So, tell me, what do you look like when you're not being a fuzzy blur?
McCormick: Ah, most people tell me I look like Paul Newman. And, just to get this awkward moment behind us, I'm a Cancer with Virgo rising.
Kathy: You know, I have never understood why people pay any attention to that stuff.
McCormick: I'm beginning to like you, Kathy Kasternack.
Kathy: I had to find a sucker eventually.

McCormick: Huh, what do you think? She's kind of different.
Hardcastle: What?
McCormick: She's different. She's not a ravishing blonde dingbat, you know? She's gonna take a CPA exam in June. I like that. Shows the girl's got direction. You know what? She doesn't care what my birth sign is either. She thinks that's silly.
Hardcastle: What're you *doing*, McCormick?
McCormick: I don't know. I've just never met a girl who liked me even before she knew what I look like.
Hardcastle: She's in for a terrible shock.
McCormick: I hope she likes what she sees.
Hardcastle: Well, I like her, if that's your question.

McCormick: Yeah. That was the question. You do?
Hardcastle: Yeah.
McCormick: Yeah? Yeah?
Hardcastle: Yeah. Yeah. Yeah.

Hardcastle: They got a twelve-gauge?
McCormick: They've got a bazooka. I'll take that.
Kathy: I'll take the side by side with the outside hammers.

It Coulda Been Worse, She Coulda Been a Welder
– premiered December 2, 1984

Written by	Lawrence Hertzog
Directed by	Tony Mordente
Second unit director	Gary Combs

Cast

Maylo McCaslin	Warren Wyngate
Joe Dorsey	Calvin Moreland
Val Avery	Willie Lerner
Arthur Taxier	Billy
Gary Allen	
Michael Dan Wagner	Steve
Eileen Seeley	Ellen, the girl who didn't date teachers
Richard Fullerton	Broadmore
Duncan Ross	Dean Whitmore
Judith Searle	Shelley, the dean's secretary
Bunny Summers	Ruth
John Hancock	Lieutenant Delaney
Fred D. Scott	Allison

Cast Notes

Maylo McCaslin also had guest roles on *The A-Team* and *Riptide*. She had a recurring role on *Santa Barbara*.

Arthur Taxier also appeared as George Delgado in the episode "Conventional Warfare".

Richard Fullerton also appeared in the episode "Did You See the One That Got Away?"

Judith Searle has authored several books, including *The Literary Enneagram: Characters from the Inside Out*.

The Details

Hardcastle's niece, Warren Wyngate, is suing her college to prevent the demolition of The Brass Rail, a local student pub, to make room for the Calvin Moreland Library. Hardcastle's stuck in a meeting of the college board, where Dean Whitmore is gnashing his teeth over the problem. Mark's sitting in the anteroom, bored to tears. He practices his scamming technique on a cute coed, only to find he's now old enough to pass for a teacher.

Hardcastle promises the board he'll have a talk with Warren. The dean swears them all to secrecy.

But the word is out. Even Mark knows what's up and he says Warren's winning. As they walk across campus they encounter Calvin Moreland himself. He's a judge and he's currently presiding over a high-profile murder trial. He seems relaxed and pleasant. Again Hardcastle promises to straighten things out with his niece.

Elsewhere, two men are rifling through the contents of a car. They're looking for a 1942 University of Illinois yearbook.

Meanwhile, Mark and the judge are driving to see Warren. Hardcastle warns Mark off his niece. Mark apparently went out with her one time about six months earlier. The judge doesn't want Mark involved with her—she's a hardworking law student.

She's also a dancer at The Brass Rail, where the guys find her with not just her nose to the bump and grindstone. Her uncle is annoyed. He tries to discourage her efforts to block the library. She says she's already deposed Calvin Moreland, and he's such a stick in the mud that he can't even remember his old college hangouts.

It's not a stretch for Hardcastle to remember, though. He is linked through eternity (or at least until the injunction is lifted) with somebody named "Ruth"—their names are both carved into a table top at The Brass Rail. In the middle of all this reluctant nostalgia, Warren informs him she'll be deposing him the following day.

Outside, Warren discovers her car has been vandalized. Her books and papers are strewn on the ground. Hardcastle asks her if there could be anyone with a vendetta against her. Even she can't believe it has anything to do with the board—that's not their style.

Hardcastle gives her a ride home. He soon regrets it. Warren announces that her moot court case will be *State of California v. Mark McCormick*, and she's found a lot of holes in it.

As they pull up in front of Warren's apartment, two men run out. They knock Warren aside and flee in a sedan. The guys give chase in the truck. The intruders sustain a rollover crash. One escapes and the other is captured.

Back at Warren's apartment, it's impossible to tell whether anything's been taken. Mark volunteers to stay behind and help her straighten up. Hardcastle departs with a quick warning and a scowl. Once alone, Warren scoffs at her uncle's concerns. Mark's too old for her and, besides, he's "the guy who works around the house". Mark tries to stamp a slightly higher skill level on his job description but it's no use. When Warren does start coming on to him, he's too worried about what "Uncle Miltie" will do to actually enjoy himself.

Uncle Miltie is down at the police department, getting the low-down on the guy who broke into Warren's apartment. He's got a name, and a potential employer—Willie Lerner. Hardcastle knows Lerner's been linked to Rick Benti, the guy whose murder trial is currently in front of Calvin Moreland. They suspect Warren may have unknowingly uncovered some dirt that Benti intends to use against Moreland.

Back at The Brass Rail for the night show, and Mark is having trouble keeping eye contact with the judge while Warren is onstage. Afterwards, the judge asks her what she knows about Lerner. Aside from the fact that he kills people, her answer is nothing.

Lerner has what he sent his guys after—the 1942 yearbook. But he thinks Warren brought Hardcastle into this because she knows something. He tells his goons to take care of both of them.

At the neighborhood law clinic, waiting to be deposed, Hardcastle does not feel he is among friends. Warren is confrontational during his deposition, and uses the occasion as a soapbox. Afterwards she asks him for a ride home. She also mentions that she figured out one item that's missing from her apartment. It's the yearbook from Moreland's old university, part of her research for his deposition. She'd never bothered to look at it.

The guys can't make anything out of the theft. A moment later a car is on their tail. They're run off the road, and only a couple of blasts from Hardcastle's shotgun are enough to discourage their attackers.

They go to see Moreland, who claims to have no idea what Lerner could have been after. Warren is convinced he's lying. Back at the estate, in the study, she rags relentlessly at the judge and, after he walks out, continues on with Mark. He asks her if it's a Hardcastle thing, this annoying quality they both share. She backs down slightly.

They go off to see the yearbook man—a mousey, bald guy who's been collecting other people's memories for forty-two years. He provides her with a second copy of Calvin Moreland's yearbook and they discover, beyond a shadow of a doubt, that the man sitting on the bench for Rick Benti's trial is not the Calvin Moreland who graduated from the U of I.

Meanwhile, the man who would be Moreland pays a visit to Willie Lerner. He says if Lerner doesn't stop Hardcastle's investigation, Benti will go to prison. Lerner says he's done all he can to protect "Moreland's" secret. After the judge leaves, Lerner makes a phone call and dispatches one of his men to the courthouse.

In his chambers, "Moreland'" confesses all to Hardcastle. The real Moreland died shortly after graduating law school. The ersatz Moreland appropriated his university transcripts and then sat for the bar. Lerner found out and has been blackmailing him for judicial favors for the past ten years. In the hallway, before the trial can reconvene, the faux-judge tells the press he's going to declare a mistrial. Mark spots Lerner standing nearby and a moment later a hit man pulls a gun. Mark's well-thrown hat spoils his aim, and after a tussle he disarms him.

He and Hardcastle dash off after Lerner. Mark pauses momentarily to pull a parking ticket off the windshield of the Coyote, and then the chase is on. After a heated pursuit, Lerner's sedan is abruptly turned into a convertible when it encounters a loaded forklift.

In the epilogue, because we haven't seen Warren dance enough, she does another routine. After that, Hardcastle gives her the good news; the university has suspended plans to build the new law library. But it's Warren who produces the cherry for the top of the sundae—she's hunted up Hardcastle's old college flame. It's the enigmatic Ruth, larger than life and *very* glad to see her old heart-throb.

The Context

Warren definitely has one thing in common with her uncle; she's mastered the art of being both right and annoying. According to the script, this branch of the family tree belongs to Hardcastle's sister, and the apple fell straight down. But as irritating as Warren is (both guys just up and walk away from her at one point, as she's ranting), it's apparent that she and Mark hit it off at one point. He didn't get home from their first date until seven in the morning. It doesn't look like there'll be another, though. He already has to put up with one Hardcastle in his life; two is probably more than anyone should be expected to tolerate.

Is there a theme in this one? (Besides the importance of dance to personal development, that is.) Well, as "Moreland" finds out, no matter where you go, or what you do, the guy you look at in the mirror every morning is always going to be you.

The Trivia

The title, of course, is a reference to the movie *Flashdance*, in which the protagonist did have a day job as a welder.

The establishing shot of Ye Olde College Campus is a shortened sequence from the titles of "Third Down and Twenty Years to Life". The music is an academic version of "Back to Back".

Warren does her first dance routine to the Pointer Sisters' hit "Jump for My Love" which went to number three on the charts in 1984 and won the group a Grammy in 1985. The second routine is to Huey Lewis' "Heart of Rock and Roll", which was part of the 1983 album, *Sports*. Her third routine is to Rod Stewart's "Young Turks", which was released in 1981 and made it to number five in the U.S.

Memorable Quotes

Chairman: The ringleader of this whole affair is a young man called Warren Wyngate. And I want to get the creep.

Hardcastle: Ah, John, Warren Wyngate's not a "he".

Chairman: What's that, Milt?

Hardcastle: Warren's a girl.

Broadman: Warren? Are you sure, Milt?

Hardcastle: I'm reasonably sure, yeah. She was named after Earl Warren, Supreme Court.

Allison: I wonder whose brilliant idea that was.

Hardcastle: Ah, it was kind of my idea. Warren's my niece.

Warren: Well, I've been over it with the lawyers. I'm deposing you tomorrow at ten-thirty. Be there.

Hardcastle: Warren, Warren…

Warren: And don't let the big brown eyes fool you. I'm a killer.

McCormick: Chip off the old block.

McCormick: Maybe you ought to lighten up a little bit on Uncle Milt, huh?

Warren: Lighten up? Lighten up! Look who's talking. I've had dinner with you guys, remember?

Hate the Picture, Love the Frame – premiered December 9, 1984

Written by	Erica Byrne
Directed by	Dennis Donnelly
Second unit director	Gary Combs

Cast

Ed Bernard	Lieutenant Bill Giles
Jon Cedar	Cherney
Fil Formicola	Granger
Michael Gregory	Joey
Mady Kaplan	Ashley Austin
Lisa Rafel	Sergeant Ferguson
Mike Moroff	Roncoe
David K. Johnson	Jerry
Russ McGinn	Pete Bishop
Larry Williams	Kid with wreaths
Dr. Joyce Brothers	herself

Cast Notes

Jon Cedar also appeared on *The Rockford Files* and *The Greatest American Hero*.

Fil Formicola appeared in "Really Neat Cars and Guys with a Sense of Humor".

Lisa Rafel appeared in "Just Another Round of that Old Song".

Larry Williams began his acting career at the age of seven, retired from that to attend college on a baseball scholarship, then went to work for William Morris. He now has his own company, Williams Talent Agency.

The Details

At the docks, a few days before Christmas, a deal is going down—large amounts of cash for a truckload of assault rifles. Hardcastle and McCormick are observing. Once the money changes hands, they signal the cops. After a short chase, two men are captured.

Hardcastle is aggravated. They've busted up four sales in two weeks, but they aren't any closer to the top. Mark suggests they take a break for the holidays. All he gets is a scowl.

In a fancy high-rise office, Martin Cherney is berating Granger, his right hand man. Hardcastle is costing him business. Granger suggests they back off for a little while. Cherney does more than scowl. The boss says they'll get Hardcastle thrown inside and let his own system take care of him for them.

He summons his girlfriend, Ashley, who wants nothing more than to go away with Cherney for the weekend. He tells her first she'll need to do a little favor for him.

Mark convinces Hardcastle to go halves on a Christmas tree, but the judge's mind is really elsewhere. He's still working on the gun running case. After loading the tree into the truck, Mark goes off to get some tinsel. Hardcastle, left alone, is approached by Ashley, who asks him for help reading the small print on the bus route. She plants a kiss on him as one of Cherney's henchmen snaps away with a telephoto camera.

Nighttime at the estate and Mark decorates the tree while Hardcastle considers Granger. He's still looking at a minnow. Mark heads out to get some more holiday necessities. Cherney's henchman is watching from a car near the gate. Ashley's there with him. He tells her to call Hardcastle.

He's putting Mark's present under the tree when the phone rings. Ashley tells him to meet her at the water reclamation plant in a half-hour if he wants more information about the gun running. He goes, but finds no one there.

He and McCormick arrive home at nearly the same time. Mark's loaded down with purchases. Hardcastle, belatedly remembering that he left Mark's gift out, tries to sidetrack him, but Mark, his curiosity piqued, plows ahead. Both men are in for a surprise—Ashley's lying dead on the floor of the study.

The police come; the body is taken away. Lieutenant Giles listens to Hardcastle's story and goes off to look into things.

In the gatehouse, Mark finds Hardcastle watching a program about holiday depression. He does his best to distract him.

Lieutenant Giles returns the next morning with further evidence (the photographs and some checks made out to Ashley from Hardcastle). He also has an arrest warrant. The judge is handcuffed and taken away. Mark protests in disbelief.

Mark finds him in the Los Angeles County Jail instead of the local lock-up, which was overcrowded with holiday drunks. Hardcastle defends the system. Unfortunately, half of the system is out of town for the holiday and there is no one except Mark to arrange for Hardcastle's bail.

Mark goes to Giles, trying to get the file on Granger. Giles can't hand anything over to him, but tells his men to pick Granger up for questioning.

In the jail yard, a guy named Ronco closes in on Hardcastle with a knife. He's intercepted by another inmate who then tells the judge he has plans for him.

It's evening, and a very depressed McCormick is making the rounds of bail bondsmen. At his last stop he's accosted by an elf, but no one wants to touch a judge who's being charged with murder. A guy like that will never stick around for the trial.

Back at the police station, Granger has been questioned and released. He goes directly to Cherney, who's annoyed that Hardcastle can still pull investigatory strings despite being in jail. He tells Granger to find someone on the inside who can eliminate him.

It's visiting hours at the jail. Mark runs into Tommy, a guard he knows. He asks how Hardcastle is doing. "Sharkbait," Tommy replies. Mark goes to the visiting area. Hardcastle doesn't show. Mark panics. He finds Tommy again, who takes him to the prison library. There he finds the judge finishing up a law clinic session. As the last consultation is concluded, Hardcastle's rescuer from the day before smiles and thanks him.

Mark has gone from worried to miffed. Hardcastle seems to be handling himself just fine. When he asks Mark what he's accomplished on the outside, there's a lot of shuffling. Hardcastle has had more luck. He's seen the Granger file and now has a new suspect—Martin Cherney. He's a gun-running mobster from the Midwest and Hardcastle recognized him from a picture in Granger's file.

But despite those developments, with McCormick not having any luck raising bond it's beginning to look a lot like Christmas behind bars. Hardcastle tells Mark to save him some eggnog.

It's nighttime again in the prison yard. Hardcastle's shooting baskets when another inmate strolls up. A knife is flashed. Hardcastle blocks with the basketball and bolts, hiding in the jail kitchen. He grapples with the assassin, disarms him, and then clips him in the jaw with a fire extinguisher. The guards arrive too late to be of assistance.

Out on the street, Mark leaves yet another bail bond office, most likely the last one on the list. It's late and dark. A streetwise kid selling Christmas wreaths approaches him. On an impulse, Mark buys the whole stock and hands them out to passers-by.

Back at the jail, in the community area, Hardcastle gets the word from one of the other prisoners that the attempt on his life was paid for by someone on the outside. The inmate says he won't last long in jail.

It's almost time for lights out. The prisoners are returning to their quarters. Hardcastle finds a wreath on the wall of his cell with a card, signed by Mark.

In the study, sitting at the judge's desk, where he's been all night, Mark appears to have come to a decision. He goes out. It's daylight. He climbs into

the Coyote and roars off. We see him next at a car lot, deep in negotiations.

At the jail, back in the community room, Hardcastle sits, staring morosely. His spirits brighten considerably when Mark is escorted in by the guard. Bail has been raised. As he's being processed out, Hardcastle asks Mark how he did it. The answer is short and not very informative, but the real explanation becomes obvious as they step outside and he sees Mark's substitute wheels, a rusted-out Volkswagen.

In Cherney's office, an attractive raven-haired woman claims to have Ashley's diary. She's offering it to Cherney for ten thousand dollars. He counter-offers with fifty thousand if she will assist him.

A page from the diary is delivered to Hardcastle and the woman makes a call, offering to sell him the rest. Cherney is standing by as she hangs up. He applauds her performance.

Mark and the judge show up at the warehouse where the deal is to be made. Cherney and Granger are watching from afar. After the guys enter, Granger triggers an explosive device. Cherney departs with the woman. They go to her bank. She produces a diary from her safe deposit box but it is blank.

Cherney returns to the dock, where his latest shipment of guns is being loaded. He tells Granger to deal with the woman. She pulls a gun, announcing she's a police officer. She's quickly disarmed. As the Coyote and cops roar up, Cherney and his men flee. They don't get far before their sedan flips and crashes.

Back at the scene of the gun deal, Hardcastle thanks the woman, Sergeant Ferguson, for getting taped evidence on Cherney. One of the officers wheels up a bow-bedecked motorcycle and asks Hardcastle where it should go. The judge says he'll take charge of it. As Mark stands there admiring it, Hardcastle points out that there's a card attached. It's addressed to Mark, from "Santa" (and it reminds him to wear a helmet).

In the epilogue, the guys are home and the case is wrapped up. Mark invites Hardcastle into the study for a belated Christmas dinner. There's a caterer's bill to go with it. Mark spent all his money on Christmas wreaths. But he did manage to have enough left over to buy *one* special gift. Hardcastle unwraps the package and we see a group photo. It's the judge and all the guys from the cellblock. How could you not love that picture?

The Context

Hardcastle's faith in the system is darn near unshakable, even when the system turns on him and he winds up behind bars. He also proves remarkably adaptable to life on the inside, though it's hard to imagine that his foray into running a prison law clinic was entirely uncoerced.

Mark doesn't always believe in the system, but he believes in Hardcastle. Even as the evidence piles up under the tree, it's just a question of keeping the man out of trouble (and preferably out of jail) until they can figure out who rigged the frame.

It's another look at the system gone wrong, with individual effort and personal loyalty being the only things that can set it back on track. Even though Mark eventually comes through with the bail money, without Hardcastle's dogged determination, his contacts, and his extensive knowledge of the underworld (not to mention some quick work with a fire extinguisher) Cherney's plan to get him out of the way would have succeeded.

The Trivia

It's the third of Hardcastle's five trips to the pokey and the second of three times he's framed (also the second of three times Mark springs him, and the only time he uses legal means to do so).

Memorable Quotes

McCormick: Ah, come on, Judge, you've gotta be kidding me, right? Now, I mean, what kind of presents can you fit under a twelve-inch tree?

Hardcastle: Presents? Don't get carried away here.

McCormick: You musta been a heck of a kid. What'd you do anyway? Bang your gavel and find your parents in contempt?

McCormick: Why didn't you want me to come into the house?

Hardcastle: I told you that already.

McCormick: I know, I know. Because the present was under the tree. At least, it was supposed to be there, you know…

Hardcastle: What do you mean, it was supposed to be under the tree? It was under the tree. I told you. Whoever killed that girl took your present.

McCormick: No, no, I believe you. I believe you on that.

Hardcastle: Okay, okay. I'm sorry. If it had happened to you, I'd be asking the same questions.

McCormick: No. Will you stop it?

Hardcastle: Well, what else did you want to know?

McCormick: What'd you get me?

Pennies from a Dead Man's Eyes – premiered Dec. 31, 1984

Written by	Marianne Clarkson
Directed by	Tony Mordente
Second unit director	Gary Combs

Cast

Larry Gatlin	Sam Jones/Jesse Wingo
Steven Keats	Bruno
Joan Sweeny	Teresa Lynn
Norman Alden	Deacon Mobley
John Hancock	Lieutenant Delaney
Hugh Gillen	
Gary Lee Davis	
Gary Goodrow	the driver

Cast Notes

Larry Gatlin, country songwriter and performer, also appeared as a country singer in an episode of *Simon and Simon*. His stage career included the title role in the Tony Award winning musical *The Will Rogers Follies*.

Norman Alden also appeared with Brian Keith as a guest star in a first season episode of *Family Affair*. In the movie *Back to the Future*, he played the coffee shop owner who couldn't give Marty McFly a Tab because he hadn't ordered anything yet.

Gary Goodrow, who was Sid, the informant, in "You Would Cry Too, If It Happened to You" makes a brief appearance here as the truck driver who gives the guys a lift after they escape their own fiery crash.

The Details

It's amateur night at the Country Palace, and the Jazzmasters are putting their hearts into it. It's the wrong audience, though. After their performance,

Hardcastle joins McCormick at the bar and consoles himself with a beer.

Outside a stretch limo pulls up. It belongs to Jadestone Records. Two men step out, one a slick, dark-suited guy named Bruno, the other, Deacon Mobley, is in a white suit, cowboy hat and a string tie. They've come to hear one act in particular.

Inside, the steel saw performance is finishing up. Next on the list is a

guy named Sam Jones and he's clearly in a class apart from the other performers. As Hardcastle starts to leave, Mark stands, listening raptly. The two guys from the limo are pretty engrossed, too.

Mark tells the judge he's heard the guy before, and it was on a record. "Sam Jones" finishes to great applause and steps down from the stage. The two guys in suits depart. Deacon Mobley insists that the man inside is Jesse Wingo, a person who died years earlier in a car crash. He was Jesse's manager for ten years, and he's owned the rights to his music since the man's supposed death. His new business partner is concerned. Jadestone Records is republishing Wingo's songs. He thinks they may need to make Wingo's death more permanent.

Back in the Country Palace, Mark and the judge sit down with Sam and his girlfriend, Teresa Lynn. Mark asks Jones if he's ever been recorded. Sam denies it. Mark's trying to remember a song that he thought he'd heard Jones sing. When he recalls the word "statues", Sam gets nervous and leaves.

Mark follows him out and apologizes. He'd already figured out that Sam spent some time behind bars. The two men end up at the waterside. Sam tells a story of manslaughter, and spending seven years in prison. Teresa Lynn doesn't know about all of that, though, and Sam doesn't want to tell her.

The next day, at Jadestone Records, Bruno tells Mobley that Jesse Wingo must die. It's the only way they can keep the rights to the album that is about to be released. Mobley says Jesse's not stupid and they can convince him to stay dead.

It's morning at Gull's Way, too, and Mark is going through his stack of old albums, still looking for the elusive recording. Hardcastle shows up to insult country music. He finds a scrap of paper with a poem on it. It's a country music lyric and it's Mark's. Hardcastle reads it out loud and with sarcasm. Mark mostly ignores him, continuing his search. He finds an album by Jesse Wingo and he's convinced he's nailed his man.

At Sam's gas station, a couple of heavies show up to give Jesse his warning. They pummel him and depart. Teresa Lynn witnesses it. He finally tells her about the time he's done in prison. She already had a suspicion.

At Jadestone, Bruno insists they'll have to finish Jesse off. Mobley chickens out.

Mark is still certain that Wingo and Jones are one and the same. Hardcastle has done a little research of his own. He says Wingo died in a fiery car wreck after getting out of prison. They attend Sam Jones' Saturday performance at the Country Palace. Hardcastle is finally convinced that it's Jesse Wingo's voice.

They confront Sam, who admits he's Jesse, and he faked his own death. They offer him help. Jesse tells them about Deacon Mobley. On the way home from the performance, he also explains to them how his "death" happened and why he started singing again. In the middle of this conversation a car rams them from behind, and then forces them off the road. The three guys barely escape before the truck plummets over a cliff, exploding in a fireball.

They hitch a ride in the back of another truck. Despite the danger, Jesse still refuses to go to the police. He asks for one more day to think it over. After they part ways with Jesse, Hardcastle heads for the police.

Back home at his gas station, Jesse asks Teresa Lynn if she'll leave with him.

At the police department, Lieutenant Delaney pulls the records on Mobley. He asks Hardcastle what's going on. The judge is trying to give Jesse his one day. He won't give Delaney the details yet.

While Teresa Lynn is loading her things into the car, Mobley calls Jesse. He says he wants to help and asks to meet with him. When Jesse doesn't accept, Mobley includes a threat to Teresa Lynn.

Jesse goes to Mobley's house and finds him dead. The murderer shoots at him as well. Hardcastle and McCormick pull up. Jesse tells them what happened and they take off after the killer. The chase ends in a rollover crash and an assistant bad guy under arrest.

Delaney again asks for information. Hardcastle still asks for more time. The lieutenant points out the convenience of Hardcastle having a whole police department at his service. Hardcastle can't argue with that. It is pretty handy.

The guys head over to Jadestone records, where Bruno unwisely opens fire as soon as they show up. A brawl ensues. Bruno wings Wingo and takes off in a car, with the Coyote close behind. The chase ends in, hard to believe, a rollover crash.

In the epilogue, Jesse, Teresa Lynn, and the guys are back at the Country Palace. Jesse is giving up the music biz. When the amateur show begins, he goes onstage one last time as Sam Jones and performs the song Mark wrote in prison. Then the episode ends, just as it opened, with a reprise performance by those indomitable cross-over favorites, the Jazzmasters.

The Context

There are many episodes in this series that deal with fame and the human desire for public recognition. This one starts with the Jazzmasters, playing in an awkward venue at Mark's suggestion that they need "some public exposure". It ends with Mark's utter delight at seeing his own verses transformed into a song and given a public performance by a professional musician.

But in-between we meet a guy who had fame and saw it turn into infamy. All he wants is to bury the man he was and start over again—safely anonymous. He won't even tell the woman he loves who he was. Still, the desire to perform is there, and though he knows it endangers his life, Sam Jones can't resist stepping back into Jesse Wingo's shoes one night a week.

This is yet another case whose source is Mark. Hardcastle doesn't even believe there's a problem at first, and if there is it's none of their business (though Mark makes the very valid point that *most* of what they deal with is none of their business). Yet Hardcastle is at least willing to discuss things, and there's never a question of him not lending a hand. The pattern was there all along—eleven of the thirty-two episodes thus far (including the first) have begun as "Mark's problems". It's a partnership.

The Trivia

This is the second appearance of Hardcastle's Dixieland band, The Jazzmasters (they debuted in "Just Another Round of That Old Song"). They've finally learned more than one song and in the opening scene we hear them belting out "The Tiger Rag", a tune that was first recorded in 1917.

Larry Gatlin performs three of his own songs in this episode, "Pennies from a Dead Man's Eyes", "Statues Without Hearts", and "Broken Lady".

Apparently McCormick missed his calling. "Mark's" song, "Broken Lady", won a Grammy in 1976.

Hardcastle says he can play the trombone like "Jack Teagarden"—Teagarden was an influential and innovative jazz and blues trombonist whose career began in 1920 and ended with his death in 1964. He is buried in Forest Lawn Cemetery.

Memorable Quotes

Hardcastle: Hey, we get enough heartaches and grits last night? Turn that down!

McCormick: Howdy, Judge.

Hardcastle: Howdy? What happened to "groovy" and "right on"? It's eight o'clock in the morning. You ought to be looking at your cartoons.

McCormick: You ought to be listening to some country and western music. Give it half a chance, it'll grow on you. It's pure American poetry.

Hardcastle: It's pure American noise.

Sam: I did seven years in the state prison.
Teresa Lynn: I thought so.
Sam: What?
Teresa Lynn: Well, every morning you walk outside, look up at the sky, kick up the dirt. Most people just brush their teeth.

There Goes the Neighborhood – premiered January 7, 1985

Written by	Lawrence Hertzog
Directed by	Ron Satlof
Second unit director	Gary Combs

Cast

Dennis Franz	Joe Hayes
Kenneth Kimmins	Hal Rogers
Jed Allan	Laughton
Frank McCarthy	Koznoff
Joan Freeman	Adell Rogers
Tony Longo	Tim
Kai Wulff	the kidnapper
Jimmy F. Skaggs	Eric
Lesley Woods	Mary, refreshment and artillery committee
William Wintersole	Barker
Martin West	Arthur
Ricky Supiran	Danny, the kid in the grocery store
Carol Culver	Kim, Danny's mom
Joe Lewin	Mel, in favor of Robert's Rules of Order
Ken Hill	This week's pool man
John Hancock	Lieutenant Delaney

Cast Notes

Dennis Franz made his first *Hardcastle and McCormick* appearance in "Did You See the One that Got Away".

Kenneth Kimmins had a recurring role as Howard Burleigh in *Coach* and as Dr. Klein in *Lois & Clark*.

Ricky Supiran, the kid in the grocery store, is the younger brother of Jerry Supiran, who played the son on the series *Small Wonder*.

Joan Freeman is married to Bruce Kessler, who directed seven episodes of

Hardcastle and McCormick. She also co-stared with Elvis Presley in the 1964 movie *Roustabout.*

The Details

Even the Lone Ranger needs groceries, but after a late night trip to the market, the judge and Mark run into trouble on their own front porch. Accosted by home invaders, they're forced inside at gunpoint, robbed, and left tied up on the floor of the study.

The next morning they tell Lieutenant Delaney what happened. Delaney says their area's been hit hard lately. He advises them to start a watch group.

Mark's worried. He thinks it's a bad idea to let untrained civilians run around playing cops. Hardcastle says his neighborhood is more sensible than that.

The first meeting of the neighborhood watch is gathering. Mark meets Joe Hayes, who got rich off auto wax and carries an M-16. He also meets Hal Rogers and his wife, two people who seem very calm and sensible. As Hardcastle calls the meeting to order, the first business is electing a captain. The judge is the logical choice, but a neighbor, who is still angry at him for cutting down a tree, nominates Mark McCormick for the position. In an overwhelming show of support (and with appreciation for his extensive previous experience with criminal matters) Mark is swept into office.

Meanwhile, elsewhere, the two home invaders are also summoned to a meeting. They are being paid by a mysterious man who tells them to continue what they are doing. One of the burglars asks why they're being paid to rob houses. He's told nothing.

The man who paid them gets back in his limo and returns to the Soviet Embassy.

The watch is on patrol. Milt and Hal cruise the neighborhood. They find Mary, who also runs the refreshments committee, on her porch with a weapon at the ready. Hardcastle unloads her shotgun and they proceed on. He takes the opportunity to get to know Hal a little better. Hal works at a plant that designs military equipment. He comments pensively that it's nice to be out on patrol, where things are more straightforward.

Nearby, the home invaders are on the prowl again. This time they trip an alarm. Hardcastle and Hal pull up, are fired upon, and give chase. Careening through the dark, the burglars' sedan finally crashes, rolls, and starts to burn. They are pulled out of the wreckage by the judge and Hal.

The next morning, Mark objects to the judge's plan to disband the watch. He says it can prevent further crime. Hardcastle says Mark's just disappointed that his reign as watch captain has been cut short.

At the embassy, two men dis-
cuss the arrest. The robberies were being committed to disguise another
crime. The burglars will be taken care
of, and the move against Hal Rogers
will proceed as planned.

At the Rogers' house, Hal's wife
insists he must talk to someone. He
says he's not ready. He gave military
secrets away as a matter of conscience, to even the playing field, but now things
have gone wrong and an unfunded program has left the U.S. vulnerable. He
doesn't want to hand over anything more to the Soviets.

At the station, the judge wants to ask the suspects some questions. Too
late—both men are found dead in their holding cell. On the way home, Mark
again suggests that the watch not be disbanded. This time Hardcastle agrees,
though he says Mark's not admitting his real motivation.

That night it's Mark's turn to patrol. He's studying the *Block Captain's
Guide* while his partner, Joe, locks and loads. Joe expresses doubts about Mark's
commitment. As they drive by the Rogers' house, Joe spots something. He and
Mark get out to investigate.

They spot two intruders. Joe opens fire, but when they move in to appre-
hend the burglars, the tables are turned. Mark and Joe are efficiently disarmed
and their attackers escape.

Later that night in the Gull's Way study, a stiff and sorely embarrassed
Mark tries to explain that they weren't "regular guys". Hardcastle's not listening.

The next morning, at the police station, Delaney informs Hardcastle that
the two men in the holding cell died of a lethal germ warfare virus. They con-
tracted it before they were arrested.

At the embassy, one of the professional burglars is reporting to his boss.
They still don't have the papers that Rogers is hiding. The new plan is to get
Rogers himself.

Down on the beach, at the estate, Mark is pensively studying the water.
Hardcastle arrives and, in a roundabout way, admits he was wrong about the
situation.

That night it's Hardcastle's and Hal Rogers' turn to patrol again. Mark
volunteers to tag along. The judge tells him not to worry. After Hardcastle
departs, Mark calls up Joe Hayes for help. He intends to watch the watch.

Hardcastle and Rogers pull over to assist a stranded motorist. It's a trap.
The judge is attacked and Hal is grabbed. Mark and Joe arrive. Shots are exchanged but the kidnappers escape with their quarry. Another car pulls up and
the guys, still in full fight mode, quickly get the upper hand on the new assailants.

Unfortunately, it's the FBI. An interrogation session follows, with lie detectors. It reveals that while both men are clueless about Hal Rogers, they certainly have strong opinions about each other. Finally convinced that they're mostly innocent bystanders this time, the feds release the judge and Mark. They are given strict instructions to say nothing to anyone.

Back at the estate, the guys find Joe in their driveway, telling them he followed Hal's kidnappers to a landing strip up near Saugus. Mark thinks they should stay out of it, but Hardcastle sees the international superspys as just a couple more people who need arresting. He and Mark take off for Saugus. They arrive just as the plane is taxiing down the runway.

Mark runs interference. Hardcastle shoots something vital, and the plane crashes on take-off. Hal is saved and the bad guys are apprehended. And where are the cops when you need them? Moments later, at Joe Hayes' command, a swarm of black helicopters and unmarked sedans descend on the location. Operation Neighbors is a wrap.

In the epilogue, out by the pool, Mark is reading a greatly truncated version of the week's events in the morning paper. He gives full vent to his paranoia, going all the way back to a fifth grade math test he really thought he should have passed. At first, Hardcastle downplays everything. But apparently paranoia is even more contagious than germ warfare. When an innocuous-looking substitute pool guy shows up a moment later—armed only with an algae brush—it's the judge who clams up and heads for the house.

The Context

We hardly ever get to meet Hardcastle's neighbors. You have to wonder what they'd have thought about the goings-on at Gull's Way. Apparently they're mostly eccentric enough not to notice.

While Hardcastle seems to have a good working relationship with the local police, the FBI is another matter. This is the second time the guys have butted heads with the feds. Just as in "Did You See the One that Got Away?", there's a feeling here of forces beyond our control—that the federal government does as it pleases and manipulates things in ways we don't understand. This is the opposite of the self-reliant Hardcastle ethos. On top of that, the feds treat the guys as crazed amateurs, a completely different attitude from the friendly lieutenants of the LAPD. In the interrogations scene, the federal agent even asks Hardcastle if he thinks he's the Lone Ranger.

Precisely. He's the *Lone* Ranger, not another suited-up member of the Texas Rangers. Even as informal an organization as the neighborhood watch cramps his style.

The other theme of this episode is the familiar one of fame, this time in a minor key. It's only the captaincy of the neighborhood watch, but Mark gets the nod and Hardcastle doesn't. Worse still, the judge thought he'd be the uncontested choice, and Mark wasn't even trying. Still, Hardcastle overcomes his skewed perspective on the situation and even eventually apologizes for being pig-headed.

The Trivia

In the opening scene we hear a grocery store version of "Back to Back" playing over the P.A. system.

Joe Hayes has the same style of M-16-A1 that we saw Mark wielding in "Just Another Girl from Accounting".

Embassies are placed in the capitols of foreign nations. All other big cities get consulates.

Serratia marcescens, the pathogen that purportedly killed the two men in the holding cell, is a gram negative bacteria, not a virus. It was long thought to be harmless and, because of the easily detectable pink color when it grows in colonies, was sometimes used in experiments on bacterial dispersal. It is now known that *S. marcescens* can cause infections, but it is not an agent of biological warfare.

The FBI in Los Angeles currently occupies nine floors of the federal building at 11000 Wilshire Boulevard. A new structure is in the works. It only took up floors fourteen through seventeen in the *Hardcastle and McCormick* era. The same exterior shot was used in "Did You See the One that Got Away?"

An episode of *The A-Team* with the same title, also featuring a subplot involving a neighborhood watch group, premiered in December of 1985. In it, Hannibal is elected captain of the watch by popular acclaim, to replace a macho but incompetent guy named Joe.

Memorable Quotes

Danny: Can we get a bag of Chocolate Chippies?
Mother: Not now, Danny.
Danny: Pleeease?
Mother: Danny, they're full of sugar. When we get home, I'll give you some fruit.
Danny: I hate fruit. I want Chocolate Chippies.
Hardcastle: (to McCormick) Get a couple of bags of Chocolate Chippies.

McCormick: There's a lotta bad people out there, Judge.
Hardcastle: There's a lotta *wrong* people. You know why they're so wrong? Because they always think they're right.
McCormick: What brought all this on?

Hardcastle: Well…I'm sorry. (pause) Your dinner's on the stove. Don't let it get cold. Go eat it or I'm gonna throw it out.

Too Rich and Too Thin – premiered January 14, 1985

Written by	Thomas Szollosi, Richard Christian Matheson, and Ross Thomas
Directed by	Michael J. Kane
Second unit director	Gary Combs

Cast

Kenneth Mars	Burt Schneider
David Spielberg	Ronald Litkin
Tracy Brooks Swope	Susan Miller
Sam Jones	Grant Miller
Peggy McKay	Dr. Coley
Philip Baker Hall	Jack Marsh
Lynda Day George	"Mrs. Burt Schneider"

Cast Notes

Kenneth Mars reappeared in the third season episode "Brother, Can You Spare a Crime?" as Milt's younger brother, Gerald Hardcastle. Mars also costarred with Brian Keith in a 1972 made-for-TV move titled *Second Chance*.

Peggy McKay plays the role of Caroline Brady on *Days of Our Lives*

Lynda Day George had the role of Lisa Casey in the series *Mission: Impossible*.

The Details

At Watersong, an upscale and elegant "fat farm", we see that someone's breakfast grapefruit is being adulterated with an injection from a medicine vial. It's served as part of Tyler Peebles' well-balanced breakfast. A few minutes later, he goes for a jog and collapses, dead by the roadside.

At the estate, Mark and the judge are swapping stories about dead people from the morning paper. Hardcastle stumbles across his friend Peebles' obituary.

At Tyler's funeral, Hardcastle delivers a touching eulogy. A young woman in black leaves almost before he's done. It's Peebles' widow. She was formerly his broker and recently his fourth wife. Hardcastle wonders why Peebles' law partner, Jack Marsh, isn't at the funeral. He gets an even bigger surprise when he catches Mrs. Peebles in the back of a limo, in a lip lock with a man named Rafferty.

On the way home from the funeral, Hardcastle speculates with McCormick about the situation. Mark says that with a ten-million-dollar inheritance, Mrs. Peebles won't stay lonely for long. Hardcastle makes a detour to Peebles' law firm.

They find Jack Marsh packing up his things. He's been forced out of the firm by Mrs. Peebles and Rafferty, her new "business" partner. Marsh is bitter.

The guys visit Dr. Ann Coley, Peebles' physician. She tells them Peebles' visit to Watersong wasn't on her recommendation; it was a birthday present from his wife. She also tells them of another patient of hers who went to Watersong at his wife's insistence. He also died of a "massive coronary" while there.

Back at the estate, the judge hangs up the phone. Delaney has come through with some interesting information. An old acquaintance of Hardcastle's, Ronald Litkin, a physician who did work for the mob, now owns Watersong. Back in the day, Litkin was known as "Doctor Death".

Mark asks when they'll be leaving. Hardcastle informs him that at five thousand dollars a week, it'll be a solo undercover assignment. Mark bets him five hundred that he can get a job at Watersong ten minutes after he walks in the door.

He forges his resume, jumps in the Coyote, and heads out. He schmoozes Susan Miller, supposed daughter of Doctor Death, telling her that he's interested in the franchise potential of the establishment. He wants to learn everything about the place.

That afternoon, a large, uncouth man named Burt Schneider is checked in to Watersong by his wife. In Dr. Litkin's office, Mrs. Schneider says she still wants her husband killed, per their agreement. She gives him one hundred thousand in cash and then departs.

The next arrival is Milton Hardcastle, who is greeted by Watersong's newest hire, P.E. instructor Mark McCormick. The judge is rooming with Schneider. He also has a meeting with his old nemesis, Doctor Death, who knows he's snooping.

Litkin tells his son-in-law, Grant, that this time they will arrange a car accident for both Schneider and Hardcastle. He also wants McCormick to put some pressure on them.

Grant delivers the message to McCormick in mid-workout. Mark, in turn, tells Hardcastle that Schneider is a potential victim. Schneider is already making plans to go over the wall for pizza and beer later on.

That night, on the way back from the pizza joint with Schneider, Hardcastle thinks they've picked up a tail. A car has been following them. Susan and Grant are out there, too, with a semi-truck cab which they use to run Hardcastle's car off the road. Burt is thrown free. Hardcastle gets out just before the vehicle goes over a cliff.

Schneider is picked up by the car that was following them, driven by "Mrs. Schneider". They are in the middle of their own investigation of Watersong and already know what Hardcastle and McCormick are up to. She tells him to be careful, then drops him off to finish the walk back to Watersong. Hardcastle encounters him, confronts him, and finds out he's a P.I. from New York. The two conspire to bring their combined forces to bear on Litkin.

The next day, Schneider's partner picks the lock on Litkin's office. Mark calls Litkin to let him know someone is snooping around in there. Litkin and Grant trap both "Mr. and Mrs. Schneider". Mark and the judge are waiting outside. When the group emerges, with the Schneiders at gunpoint, Mark steps in, creating a distraction. In the scuffle that follows, Schneider is shot, Susan is captured, and Grant and Litkin escape in a car.

The race is on, with Litkin trying to get to his helicopter. Shots are exchanged, and Litkin's sedan does a slow-motion rollover to the accompaniment of baroque music. The Watersong emergency flight-to-avoid-arrest helicopter is disabled by a shotgun blast from Hardcastle, and the bad guys are all rounded up.

In the two-part epilogue, the guys find Jack Marsh at Tyler Peebles' grave site, toasting his old friend and bringing him up-to-date on the doings at the law firm that he is again a member of. Then, back at the estate, the Jazzmasters host their own farewell to Peebles, former saxophone player, with a final rousing rendition of "When the Saints Go Marching In".

The Context

With its team-written script, two sets of investigators, and double-barreled epilogue, this one has a lot of duality to its structure. Cannell had used guest appearances to launch characters previously—witness the evolution of Richie Brockelman, originally spun out of an appearance in *The Rockford Files*. Is it possible that the "Schneiders" were being primed for a series of their own? But Lynda Day George, at the time this episode was being filmed, had recently experienced the sudden and unexpected death of her husband, Christopher George. After twenty-five very prolific years in television, this was one of her last guest roles.

The Trivia

The 115-year-old man whose obituary McCormick quotes hails from Elizabeth, New Jersey, Daniel Hugh Kelly's home town.

Mark's forged resume states that he played "striker" for the Los Lobos Polo team in Buenos Aires in 1980, was a ski instructor in Gstaad, Switzerland in the winter of '80-81, and played third base for the (Osaka) Giants in 1982. Oh, and he was a formula one professional driver as well. His academic credentials included a degree from Yale with a major in philosophy and a minor in "pre-Columbian art".

This episode marks the return of the season one theme song and opening credits. It also débuted a new Cannell Productions clip—he has a new typewriter and a more casual outfit.

Memorable Quotes

Hardcastle: You met Doctor Litkin yet?
McCormick: No, just his daughter. She's the one who hired me.
Hardcastle: What kind of lies did you tell her?
McCormick: That my last employer was wonderfully generous and I loved working for him.

Hardcastle: Well, if you didn't come here to get in shape, what did you come for?
Burt: Well, first of all, of course, I had to sell my wife on the thought that the whole thing was her idea. Like I told you, I'm a salesman.
Hardcastle: Yeah. Why a *fitness* farm?
Burt: The cupcakes, baby. The pretty, young, walking, talking, oh-so-fit little cupcakes.

What's So Funny? – premiered January 21, 1985

Written by	Patrick Hasburgh
Directed by	Tony Mordente
Second unit director	Gary Combs

Cast

Joey Bishop	Boots Dikeman
Jan Murray	Leo Dikeman
James Sutorius	Sonny Austin

Mary-Margaret Humes	Pamela Bayer
John Aprea	
Patrick Collins	Denny Frye
J. Bill Jones	
Ed Bernard	Lieutenant Bill Giles
Bobby Kelton	Chick Miles
Howie Gold	Comedian

Cast Notes

Patrick Collins was the lonely auto body man in "Really Neat Cars and Guys with a Sense of Humor".

Joey Bishop got his start in vaudeville. His stage comedy, variety show appearances, and acting career spanned seven decades. At the time of his death in 2007, he was the last surviving member of Frank Sinatra's Rat Pack.

Jan Murray, like Bishop, had a long career in stand-up comedy and emceeing. He was a semi-regular in the center square of the '70s TV game show *Hollywood Squares*. He died in 2006.

Mary-Margaret Humes got her first big break in the movies when Mel Brooks saw a billboard ad she had taken out and cast her as Miriam in his *History of the World: Part I*.

The Details

Pamela Bayer has a thing for comedians; she also has a mobster boyfriend, Sonny Austin. Leo Dikeman sets her up with a yet another fresh young comic, Denny Frye, then informs Sonny's people about the situation.

Sonny is a guy with anger management issues. He goes to a hotel room and finds evidence that Pamela has bestowed her favors on Frye. Unlike Frye's three predecessors, who he had beaten up, Austin decides this rival has to die.

Meanwhile, at the estate, Hardcastle has received an invitation from Frye, who wants him to catch his act. Hardcastle previously sentenced him to ten years for bank robbery. Mark figures Frye intends to ridicule the judge.

Mark's right. Frye's humor is heavy-handed and he's even wearing Hardcastle trademarks, the Yankees cap and sweats. In his dressing room, after the show, Frye tells the judge that he's got a spot on the *Merv*

Griffin Show, performing the same piece. He wants Hardcastle to sign a release. Against his better judgment (and at Mark's urging), the judge agrees. An overjoyed Frye invites them to meet him in one hour for a champagne celebration.

Arriving at his hotel, they find his door unlocked, his phone off the hook, and a suicide note in his typewriter. He's on the roof, and a crowd of onlookers is gathered below. Hardcastle races upstairs but it's already too late. Frye plummets to his death.

Lieutenant Giles arrives. Mark and the judge doubt that Frye was suicidal. Giles tells them the man had been diagnosed as bipolar. He's going to close the case unless someone gets him more evidence.

The next morning, Pamela gets the news of Frye's death from the morning newspaper. She takes off, tailed by Sonny's men, who are worried that she'll go to the cops. Sonny, informed in Las Vegas by phone, tells them to pick her up.

At the comedy club where Frye was appearing, the guys talk to Boots Dikeman, Leo's competitor and former partner. Boots tells them that Frye is only the most recent of his comics to encounter violence. He suspects Leo is at the bottom of it. He tells them the other three, who survived their attacks, ended up working at Leo's club.

The guys visit Leo's place and catch an act by Chick Miles. When they try to get some information from him after the show, Miles clams up. Mark notices a framed photo of Pamela in Miles' dressing room. It's identical to one he saw on the desk in Frye's room. He also has a gold charm similar to one that Frye had.

When Leo Dikeman interrupts the conversation, Mark uses the distraction to slip Miles' charm into his pocket. Hardcastle confronts Leo, who denies everything. After the guys leave, Leo assures Miles that Frye's death was a suicide.

On their way home, Hardcastle speculates on the missing link between all the comics. Mark produces the borrowed charm. It's inscribed with the name "Pamela" and is in a box with the jeweler's name and address. A trip to the jeweler garners them Pamela's address. They visit her house, where one of Sonny's henchmen answers the door and tries to brush them off.

The judge pushes his way in, and the bad guy draws a gun. There's a tussle and the henchmen flee. Mark pursues. The chase ends with the bad guys escaping on foot after a roll-over crash.

In Las Vegas, the henchmen tell Sonny what happened. They also tell him he's being manipulated by Leo Dikeman. He throws them out and then heads for L.A.

Back at the estate, Pamela explains all. She tried to break up with Sonny; she even moved to L.A. to get away from him. She likes comedians and a friend of hers would introduce her to the ones she thought were cute. Hardcastle guesses that the friend was Leo. He's right.

Hardcastle notifies Giles, who gets a warrant for Leo's place. They're too late again. They find Dikeman in his office, dead.

Back at the estate, Hardcastle plots. What they need to draw Sonny out is another comic who'll let Pamela bat her eyes at him. Mark will have to do. He gets some coaching from Boots Dikeman and debuts that evening to a stone-cold audience. He lasts long enough for Sonny to spot Pamela watching his performance.

Outside in the Coyote after the show, he gets a sympathy kiss from Pamela. This is also observed by Sonny. He tails them. It turns into a chase. Mark leads him into a police roadblock, where Sonny crashes and is captured.

In the epilogue, back at the comedy club, Mark's off the hook, but he's also off the radar for Pamela. She only has eyes for the new comedian up on the stage.

The Context

It's a variation on "The Black Widow", only this time the woman isn't intentionally dangerous. She just has the same kind of psycho mobster ex-boyfriend who loses all perspective over a woman.

Competence is another recurring theme in the series, although in this case it's a lack of competence. Mark is a fish out of water up on the stage at the comedy club. He bombs badly. Of course comedic success is not what he's trying to accomplish, and moments later he's perfectly competent as a professional driver eluding a man consumed by road rage. But the *level* of his incompetence is a bit baffling, given his usual rapid-fire smart mouth (not to mention his lounge-lizard parentage). It all goes to illustrate a point—comedy is *way* harder than drama.

The Trivia

Bobby Kelton and Howie Gold are both stand up comedians. Kelton has made over twenty appearances on *The Tonight Show*. Gold appeared in *The Los Angeles Comedy Competition*, hosted by Jay Leno.

Memorable Quotes

McCormick: This Denny Frye is supposed to be a funny guy, huh?
Hardcastle: Yeah, he had me cracking up when I was sending him up for ten years for bank robbery.
McCormick: Sounds hysterical.
Hardcastle: Yeah, he was very funny. 'Course he couldn't make a living at it, so he started holding up banks.
McCormick: What'd he use, a squirt gun?
Hardcastle: He probably would've, if he'd thought of it.

Hardcastle: You know, you might amount to something yet, McCormick.
McCormick: Don't get sentimental, Judge. It doesn't become you.

Hardcastle, Hardcastle, Hardcastle, and McCormick
– premiered February 4, 1985

Written by	Lawrence Hertzog
Directed by	Kim Manners
Second unit director	Gary Combs

Cast

Mary Martin	Zora Hardcastle
Mildred Natwick	May Hardcastle
Joe Santos	Lieutenant Frank Harper
Jim McMullen	Larry Satin
Wolf Muser	the assassin
Loyita Chapel	Lisa Ryan
Treva Frazee	the waitress

Cast Notes

Mary Martin was seventy-one when she played Milt's inveterately curious Aunt Zora. She was probably best known as a star on Broadway, her roles including the lead in *Peter Pan,* and nurse Nellie Forbush in *South Pacific.* She made few appearances in guest roles on television and this was her last. She died in 1990.

Mildred Natwick was seventy-nine when she appeared as Aunt May. It was a role that was very evocative of her performance as Gwendolyn Snoop Nicholson in the 1973 series *The Snoop Sisters.* She died in 1994.

Joe Santos made his first appearance as Lieutenant Frank Harper in this episode, bringing much the same beleaguered sensibilities to the role that he em-

C-2
11

9503 000783936

000783969503

Sell your books at
sellbackyourBook.com!
Go to sellbackyourBook.com
and get an instant price quote.
We even pay the shipping - see
what your old books are worth
today!

ployed as Police Detective Dennis Becker in *The Rockford Files.*

Jim McMullen also played the doomed groom in "Really Neat Cars and Guys with a Sense of Humor".

The Details

Aunts May and Zora are leaving after a one-month visit at the estate. Hardcastle seems to be a mite impatient that they not miss their flight. While waiting in the airport snack shop, May and Zora overhear two men in a suspicious conversation. It sounds as if a murder is being plotted. When the two men leave, the aunts follow them. They take pictures of the men and their car.

The aunts find Milt and tell him they can't leave until they get to the bottom of it. A man's life is at stake. Hardcastle is equally insistent that he is not investigating anything and they should get on their plane. It is clearly a test of indomitable wills.

Hardcastle loses. Back at the estate, the aunts sip tea and explain what they heard. It's a little vague. Hardcastle points out that this is the thirteenth plot they've discovered in the past month and none of the others amounted to anything. He refuses to check into the license plate number.

Mark does the checking. He gets the owner's address. He and the aunts drive there. They see the car in question parked in the driveway. No one answers their knock on the door, but it swings open and May walks in, hoping they're not "too late".

Mark soon finds he's lost control. The aunts are inside, snooping avidly. They discover it's the home of Tom Ryan, a mystery writer. Much to everyone's astonishment, there actually is a body floating in the pool. They hear someone pulling out in a hurry. Mark loads the aunts into the truck and gives chase.

The aunts handle the wild, careening ride with great aplomb, aside from an occasional insightful comment ("You're driving on the wrong side of the road, Mark.") but eventually the truck becomes airborne and lands hard enough to put it out of commission. The mysterious stranger escapes.

On the lawn of the late Tom Ryan's house, Mark pleads his case to the judge. It's not going too well. The aunts move in for reinforcement. The discussion is interrupted by Lieutenant Harper. He says it looks like a heart attack—the man's bottle of heart medicine was at hand—but he admits the alternative might be a very clever murder.

Meanwhile, the murderer makes a phone call to Larry Satin, the man who hired him. He explains the slight wrinkle in their careful arrangements. He had to abandon Tom Ryan's car. Satin says he'll pick it up. Satin hangs up the phone and tells his lovely companion that everything is mostly going as planned.

At the estate, the guys and the aunts study the photos May took at the airport. As Mark points out, the pictures don't prove anything. On the other hand, someone ran from the scene of a heart attack. Zora and May appeal to Milt's reputation for tenacity. The aunts wax nostalgic, Hardcastle grumps, and Mark suggests they look up Tom Ryan's publisher, to see if he knows anything.

The four visit the publisher's office. It's a small, elegantly gothic building. Larry Satin, the head of the company, is the man who hired Ryan's murderer. The aunts recognize him from the airport. They confront him. He says the plot they overheard was merely a discussion about an upcoming book. Once again it looks like the aunts have been victims of their overactive imaginations.

On the way home, Hardcastle grouses while Mark again points out that the whole thing looks mighty fishy. Hardcastle hangs a sharp right and heads for the police station. He wants to see the coroner's report. He thinks Satin's lying, too.

Satin and the murderer meet at a gas station. Satin tells him what happened and advises him to take care of the Hardcastles and McCormick.

In the kitchen at Gull's Way, Zora and May are baking their way through their anxiety while they wait for Milt to finish studying the coroner's report. When he finally arrives, he says he's made an important discovery. No drugs of any kind were found in Ryan, not even digitalis, the one he was supposed to be taking.

Baking is forgotten as the four investigators head back to Ryan's house. Hardcastle leads them into the backyard, where he studies the pool and its

electric-powered retractable cover. He's interrupted by a woman who says she is Tom Ryan's widow. She's the woman who was with Larry Satin.

Back at Lieutenant Harper's office, the case is discussed. They were told by Mrs. Ryan that the pool cover was never used, yet there was water on top of it when

Hardcastle pushed the "on" button, and it had rained the morning that Ryan's body was found. Harper still needs a suspect and a motive.

Satin meets with Mrs. Ryan. He tells her he loves her. She's upset that now they need to have four more people killed. She takes Satin to pick up Tom's abandoned car. The aunts and the guys are waiting to tail them. They follow the guilty couple to a parking lot. Satin parts from Ryan's wife and climbs into Ryan's car. When he turns the key in the ignition, the car explodes in flames.

Back at Tom Ryan's former home, his widow nervously confesses. She doesn't know the name of the man Satin hired to kill her husband but she knows he is a professional. Harper arrests the woman and tells the guys and the aunts to go home, lock the door, and play a long game of Scrabble ™.

Back at the estate, the baking frenzy continues. May and Zora convince Hardcastle that they'll be fine by themselves. (They'll still have a couple of guys out front in a squad car to bake for.)

The judge and Mark head back to the publishing house. Hardcastle is convinced that the murderer will make an attempt to get his manuscript back. Mark picks the lock while they're watched by someone already inside.

Once in, they're fired upon from the upper floor. Hardcastle exchanges shots with the murderer, while Mark charges up the stairs and tackles him. He gains the upper hand briefly, but is knocked over the railing. As Mark dangles from the balustrade, with the murderer taking aim, Hardcastle kills the assailant with a single shot.

Out in front of the publishing house, as the body is being carted away, Mark asks the judge if he's okay. Hardcastle say he wasn't the one who came close to being killed. Mark says he's talking about Hardcastle's pride, since he was wrong and the aunts were right. The judge is heading into another lecture on what will happen once May and Zora are gone when the ladies themselves show up and again take Mark's side. But it's only a matter of time, now that the case is

closed. Soon he won't have them around to protect him from the wrath of Hardcastle.

In the epilogue, the aunts are finally departing, this time by cab. There are promises of cranberry bread and Christmas visits. Mark loads the luggage in the trunk. As the vehicle pulls out, Hardcastle looks around for his absent assistant. Mark's waving from the trunk of the cab, where he stowed away.

The Context

More Hardcastle kin, and again they seem to get along better with Mark than with Milt. The aunts treat him like a member of the family and at one point Mark comments that he's not responsible for their behavior; he's just adopted.

Another interesting theme presents itself in the dénouement. In order to save Mark's life, Hardcastle, with an implacable expression and a steady aim, fires a single shot and dispatches the murderer. There's an element of foreshadowing here for another Cannell episode which would appear four weeks later. In "The Birthday Present", the tables are turned, and Mark is the one who must fire the gun, killing the person who shot Hardcastle and is about to shoot another man. Mark's reaction is very different, far from the judge's stern and unshakable confidence. It's an interesting contrast in character; both are good men, but each in his own way.

The Trivia

The title evokes a line from the Marx Brothers movie *Animal Crackers,* in which Captain Spaulding sends a letter to his lawyers, the firm of "Hungerdunger, Hungerdunger, Hungerdunger, and McCormick".

We learn from Zora and May that Milt had asthma as a kid and that he wanted to grow up to be a cowboy "rounding up all the bad guys".

The guys are driving a rented Black 1952 Studebaker Champion. Mark's reference to the Cruise-O-Matic transmission is merely metaphorical. The Cruise-O-Matic was only available in Ford models.

A whole slew of other Hardcastle relatives are mentioned as being back in Arkansas (Aunt Sylvia and Uncle Dan, Gret, Paul and the eight kids), but apparently none of them live in the judge's hometown of Clarence.

Memorable Quotes

McCormick: That's against the law! It's breaking and entering!
Zora: Nothing's broken; it's just entering. Milton'll find a loophole.

Hardcastle: Now, I think it would be a real good idea if you'd just wait for us, okay?
May: Give us a break, Milton. This one's ours.
McCormick: They're your aunts. I just got here by adoption.

Zora: This is what we do when we're on edge. We bake.
May: It's very good therapy. You and Milton ought to try it.
McCormick: Aunt May, if we were to bake every time the Judge got a little tense, we'd be able to open up a twenty-four hour doughnut stand.

The Long Ago Girl – premiered February 11, 1985

Written by	Stephen J. Cannell
Directed by	Richard A. Colla
Second unit director	Gary Combs

Cast

Anne Lloyd Francis	Jane Bigelow
Lou Felder	Chip Meadows
Ed Bernard	Lieutenant Bill Giles
Russell Arms	Doris' Husband
Bob Madrid	
Mike Tulley	Young Hardcastle (flashback sequence)
Amy Stock	Young Jane (flashback sequence)
Susan Madigan	Andra Mason
Freddie Dawson	Paramedic
Jack Scalici	Man in the train station

Cast Notes

Anne Lloyd Francis and Brian Keith both appeared as uncredited extras in the 1948 film *Portrait of Jennie* and she played the wife of Brian Keith's character in the 1984 pilot for *Murder She Wrote*, "The Murder of Sherlock Holmes". She would have been only thirteen in 1943.

Russell Arms had a five-year run as a singer on *Your Hit Parade* from 1952-57.

Amy Stock, who played Jane in the flashback sequences, got her start as a winner on the second season of Ed McMahon's *Star Search.*

The Details

High on an icy cliff-face, two men work the slope. A piton fails and a man plunges, screaming, to his death.

In a placid stream, Mark and the judge practice the genteel art of trout fishing, except Mark is far from genteel. He's having all the luck with his "lube rack metric motor lure". They stop to eat breakfast and Mark's kidding continues as Hardcastle tunes the radio to *The Benny Goodman Hour.* A news bulletin cuts in—hotelier Chip Meadows has died in a mountain climbing accident. His

body has not yet been recovered. As the station switches back to music, Hardcastle falls silent and wanders away from the campfire.

It takes Mark a moment to notice his routine is falling on deaf ears. He follows Hardcastle down to the stream and asks him if he knew Meadows. Hardcastle says he didn't. Mark is momentarily relieved, having envisioned an undercover stint as a bellhop. His worries aren't over yet, though. Hardcastle has lost interest in fishing. They pack up and head for home.

While Mark tries to lift his obviously pensive mood, Hardcastle is lost in a memory of something that happened four decades earlier. Mark might as well be talking to himself as they arrive back at the estate, less than five hours after they left to go fishing. Hardcastle is still contemplating another trip—one that began in L.A.'s Union Station when he was an officer in WWII.

Mark drops the judge's fishing creel on the desk. He complains about the sudden change of plans and mood. Hardcastle says he's not offering an explanation, but finally lets slip that he had a near-miss in the romance department forty years earlier. It was with actress Jane Bigelow, who became Mrs. Chip Meadows.

It's the day of the funeral, and the judge is dressed in a dignified suit. Mark is giving him some feedback on the whole notion of showing up at an ex-girlfriend's husband's last rites. In a word, it's tacky.

Hardcastle finally agrees. He says she left him standing in the train station with a ring in his pocket, but that's all over and he's been perfectly happy without her. He takes his tie off, resolved not to attend the funeral.

A short while later, Hardcastle departs in the truck without a word of explanation. Mark, who's been trimming a hedge, watches him leave, then tosses down his clippers, climbs in the Coyote, and goes after him.

The judge arrives at the Meadows' home, observed from a distance by McCormick. Hardcastle hesitates, then rings the doorbell of a house that looks deserted. No answer, but he notices signs of forced entry. He pulls out his gun and opens the door. Inside, he startles an intruder, who shoots him.

Mark, hearing the gunfire, rushes in, finding Hardcastle wounded in the left arm. The burglar is gone. Hardcastle sics Mark on him. He gets outside barely in time to catch a glimpse of the car speeding away. He fires a few parting shots at it.

Back inside, Hardcastle tries to explain why he came there. Mark sees a painting of Jane up on the wall. She was a stunner.

The cops and paramedics arrive. Lieutenant Giles is just as puzzled as Mark. The
judge decides maybe he'd rather go to the hospital than try to explain himself again when
Jane Bigelow gets home from the funeral. Mark
is flustered—the whole thing is out of character for the Hardcastle he knows.

Hardcastle is still dwelling on what happened back in '43. Later in the war, Jane did a
USO tour and got engaged. He received the
news from a radio broadcast and only saw her
up on the stage one more time after that.

In the middle of this reverie an older but still recognizable Jane walks into
his dimly-lit hospital room. She tells him she parked across the road from Gull's
Way for an hour the day of his wife's funeral. She wants to know why he stood
her up at the Pacific Electric Station back in '43. He tells her he was waiting for
her the whole time at Union Station, until he had to leave on his train.

When they've recovered a bit from the cosmic joke, Jane tells him how
important he was to her, though they'd only known each other for six weeks. She
also loved Chip Meadows, but it wasn't the same.

It's nighttime, back at the estate, and Hardcastle gets out of a cab, his arm
still in a sling. He finds Mark in the gatehouse, nuzzling a coed from his eigh-
teenth-century literature class. She departs. Hardcastle says he went "out the window" at the hospital and then explains to an unenthusiastic McCormick the only
thing the police have reported stolen from Jane's house is last year's tax records.

Over Mark's objections, Hardcastle begins to lay out the foundations for
an investigation. He even has a lead on the parking sticker that Mark saw on the
burglar's bumper—he saw the same symbol on the masthead of a newspaper.
McCormick questions his motives—trying to impress Jane. He explains the
whole mix-up at the railroad station. He's not sure if the situation calls for
violins or a rim-shot, but he's determined to find out what's going on now.

Mark watches the old pro go to work. Hardcastle's phone call to the newspaper office (and a quick scam) produces the name of the car's owner—Bob
Gleason. A moment later, and still over Mark's objections, they're heading out to
see him.

At Gleason's place they find his bullet-ridden car ("Lousy pattern, McCormick.")
and the man himself, dead but still warm, inside the house. They hear a car pulling
away. Chasing it, they force it to the side of the road. The driver is a distraught Jane
Bigelow. She claims she didn't kill Gleason.

The next morning, at the lock-up, Jane tells Milt that Gleason was going
to write an article accusing Chip Meadows of embezzlement. She went to talk to
him, but he was already dead.

Back at the estate, Hardcastle is thinking out loud in the study. Half of it is about the case; the other half is memories of how well he and Jane understood each other. Mark puts up with it. What Hardcastle suspects is that Meadows had a partner in crime. What he needs are Gleason's notes, but he doesn't want Mark to get any notions about breaking into Gleason's office.

Mark says he wouldn't risk a ten-year sentence for a forty-year-old romance. He says he's never even seen a Jane Bigelow film. No problem there; Hardcastle has them all on videotape. He pops one in the player and is soon remembering the first time he saw the same film—in the middle of an air raid.

It's been a long day. He falls asleep while watching the movie.

Mark engages in some risk-taking behavior involving a black turtleneck and his lock picks. He gets into the newspaper building, locates Gleason's office, and searches it, taking the Meadows file. As he leaves, he's followed. Shots are fired at the Coyote, but Mark evades pursuit. The man left frustrated in his wake is a very angry Chip Meadows.

The next morning, poolside at the estate, Mark is innocently reading the paper. Hardcastle informs him he's putting up bail for Jane. The judge picks up the front section of paper and finds Gleason's notes tucked in among the pages. Mark claims no knowledge of how they got there. Hardcastle reads about the break-in in the paper. He's unhappy, but grateful.

They head for the Coyote, which has a bullet hole in the windshield. Mark gets some psychic energy off the car, having not himself officially been anywhere near the newspaper office. With considerable effort, he's able to vibe up a partial plate for the attacker's vehicle.

At the police station, Hardcastle arranges Jane's bail. He takes her to a quiet place on a pier and shows her Gleason's notes. It looks like Chip faked his death, killing another man in the process. Then he returned and killed Gleason as well.

Hardcastle accuses Jane of complicity in the plot, to see how she will react. She is incensed and he believes her. At Mark's coaching he even offers her a hug.

Jane finally believes Chip is guilty, and alive. She recognizes Mark's description of the car from the night before. It's the one they use at their place up in Arrowhead. The guys and Jane go there. The car is in the garage and Meadows emerges from the house. He fires shots, then tries to escape in the car. After colliding with the truck in the driveway, he runs to a dock and flees in a small boat. Mark pursues in another craft. Hardcastle chases in the truck, then intercepts him, jumping into Chip's boat from a foot bridge. When Mark catches up, Hardcastle has everything under control.

In the epilogue, Milt and Jane are finally at Union Station together. This time she's the one who's leaving—going to visit her sister until she has to testify at Chip's trial. Hardcastle hopes maybe they can get to know each other again, once everything is settled.

The Context

You can count on Cannell episodes for a good serving of back story. This one is intriguing: Hardcastle as a dashing young army captain, involved in a whirlwind six-week romance with a movie star, left standing in Union Station with the ring in his pocket. The smallest error is compounded by the maelstrom of war, and the two are parted, not to meet again for forty years. As Mark points out, life turns on small moments—a decision here, a choice there—but there's once again the sense of fate, and forces outside of us, controlling our lives.

In the face of this we have the Hardcastle system of applied personal involvement. Against Mark's steady voice of prudence, he forges ahead. Not that McCormick is much better at standing back and letting the proper authorities manage things. Whether it's risk-taking for its own sake or, more likely, as the consequences of deep-seated loyalty, Mark can't let a perfectly good piece of evidence lie untouched in a drawer just because it's in a locked building.

Once again, when presented with evidence of dubious provenance, Hardcastle takes the practical approach. This time Mark is careful to preserve his implausible deniability, but by now they've come to an unspoken understanding. Hardcastle has to say no beforehand, but when the "evidence elf" leaves something useful on the breakfast table, you don't question your luck and you don't call the cops.

The Trivia

In the flashback sequences, Hardcastle's uniform bears the patch of the Sixth Army. This force was activated in January of 1943 under the command of General Walter Krueger. Their WWII campaigns included Rabaul, New Guinea, Leyte, Luzon, and Mindoro. Their motto was "Born of War" and their patch was a six-pointed star bearing a red "A". The Sixth Army was deactivated in 1994.

Los Angeles' Union Station opened in May of 1939. Located at 800 N. Alameda Street, it still serves over a million passengers a year, both inter-city train and metropolitan transit. Jane was purportedly waiting at the Pacific Electric Station. Pacific Electric managed a system of light rail that served Los Angeles and nearby regions. The building which served as one of its main terminals was at Sixth and Main. It was last used for that purpose in 1961. There was also a subway terminal at 417 Hill Street. It opened in 1925, and was connected by a tunnel to the Toluca Substation seen in "Prince of Fat City". That part of the system ceased operating in 1955.

Hardcastle notes the bullet hole in the windshield of the Coyote but Mark disavows that he was anywhere but in Andra Mason's arms the night before. Luckily, the Coyote "tells" him what happened. Mark swears it's possible; he's seen cars talk on TV. It's a sly reference to the Sunday night competition on NBC that season, *Knight Rider*, with its sentient and talkative vehicle, KITT, voiced by William Daniels.

Daniel Hugh Kelly is reportedly an avid fisherman.

Memorable Quotes

Hardcastle: What've you got on there? A red snap lure or a blue steelhead?

McCormick: I've got the lube rack metric motor lure—hairpins taped to a lug nut.

Jane: You want to hear something strange? When your wife died, I drove all the way over to your house. I parked across the street and I sat there for a whole hour. I couldn't go to the funeral, I didn't even know her...and besides, Chip wouldn't have understood. I knew I couldn't call you, and yet, somehow, I knew I had to be there. She was your wife, but I was your long-ago girl.

Jane: Bob Gleason's notes. How did you get these?

Hardcastle: Well, I've got this elf that breaks into offices and gets me things.

You Don't Hear the One That Gets You
– premiered February 18, 1985

Written by	Lawrence Hertzog
Directed by	Tony Mordente
Second unit director	Gary Combs

Cast

Wings Hauser	Arvin Lee Potter
Karlene Crockett	Melissa Kantwell
Billy Drago	the state trooper
Christopher Roland	Deputy Dan Johnson
Sonny Landham	Sheriff Billy Blackstone
Emily Banks	the art teacher
Billy Gratton	
Stanley Brock	
Gary Lee Davis	
Jody Lee Olhava	the bank teller
Terrence Beasor	the bank guard

Cast Notes

Wings Hauser, playing the creepily unhinged Arvin Lee, also had recurring roles in *China Beach, Roseanne,* and *Beverly Hills 90210.*

Karlene Crockett had a recurring role as Muriel Gillis in *Dallas.*

Billy Drago, who has a brief, but intense role as a state trooper who looked pretty happy to take Billy Blackstone down, had the over-the-top evil role of John Bly in *The Adventures of Brisco County, Jr.* and played Frank Nitti in the 1987 movie *The Untouchables.* Part of his ancestry is Apache.

The Details

Out on the highway in Arizona a man drives. He and his companion, a soft-voiced young woman, discuss their plans: Mexico, their dream house, a sewing room and a color TV console with a stereo built right in. In the next town he pulls over, dons dark glasses, enters a bank, and brutally shoots the guard before robbing the teller. Back out in the car, with alarms going off behind them, the woman puts down the magazine she was reading, and does the getaway driving.

At a racetrack, Hardcastle offers McCormick last minute advice before the start of the Arizona Modifieds. Some of it, as usual, involves carburetors. Mark takes it all with a good-natured grain of salt. He's already set a track record in the preliminary heats and he thinks his loaner ride is fast enough that he may have a chance at the twenty thousand in prize money.

Meanwhile, Arvin Lee, the bank robber, and his accomplice, Melissa Kantwell, arrive in time to see the race. His plan is to rob and kill whoever wins the twenty grand.

It's Mark's race right from the start. With Melissa cheering him on, and Hardcastle barely able to watch, he crosses the finish line in first place. In the winner's circle for a change, Mark revels in his victory and accepts a smiling "you did all right" from the judge.

Out in the parking lot, as they climb into the Coyote for the trip home, Mark is observed. Melissa eggs on Arvin Lee with her admiration for "the boy that wins the race".

Mark has the twenty thou-sand dollars in his pocket and is chattering happily about what he could do—the sky's the limit. He might even get back into racing on the main circuit. He could afford his own place. It takes a moment for Hardcastle's less than whole-hearted response to register with the younger man, but then he sobers, just slightly.

They spot Melissa lying on the ground along the side of the road. Arvin Lee flags them down and tells them she's in labor. Melissa emotes. The guys are clueless but willing to do what they can. A moment later, Arvin Lee pulls a gun on them.

It's night, and they've been taken to a deserted spot. Mark asks Arvin Lee what else he wants. He's got the money; it makes sense to just take off. It looks like Arvin Lee is on the verge of listening to his advice, but Melissa stirs things up by coming on to Mark.

As Arvin Lee is about to shoot the guys, Mark scams him into believing the Coyote has a hidden fuel cut-off switch. Moving toward the car, Mark lunges at Arvin Lee. He and Hardcastle disarm him, but Melissa shoots McCormick. The judge and Mark run. Arvin Lee and Melissa climb into their truck and pursue. They get stuck in a gully. Giving up the chase, they take the Coyote and depart.

The guys are left behind, with Mark injured and now unconscious.

Morning, in a small hotel in Silver City, and Mark is getting patched up by the local doctor, who advises no strenuous activities. Hardcastle wants him to catch a bus home. Mark's in no mood for rational advice. He wants the people who stole his car and his money. He's counting on Hardcastle to back him up, including the part where he may need help staying on his feet.

At the sheriff's office they hear that their robber couple has also hit a string of banks. Sheriff Blackstone, who appears to have troubles of his own, is in Phoenix trying to run ID on the pair. The deputy sets up a session with a make-shift police artist (a grade school art teacher) who produces a sketch of Melissa.

Both the artist and the deputy recognize the subject. She's Sheriff Blackstone's wayward wife.

In a rural house, Melissa and Arvin Lee hide out. She flirts intensely with him. This is an ongoing issue. Arvin Lee won't accept her advances until they're settled in Mexico. Melissa mocks him. He finally decides they have enough money to leave right away, but it's not the fifty thousand they'd agreed on. She wants more. Arvin Lee agrees to one more bank job.

Sheriff Blackstone returns to Silver City. He's already heard the news about Melissa and he's angry, but Hardcastle is certain about the ID. The three men retreat to a coffee shop and Blackstone tells them about Arvin Lee. Blackstone complains about the state and federal authorities, but Hardcastle advises him to have the roads south to Mexico watched by the state troopers.

Elsewhere, Arvin Lee pulls off another bank heist, and Melissa uses the Coyote to elude the police. They pull into an abandoned gas station. In the flush

of excitement, Arvin Lee grabs
Melissa and kisses her. She's
amused, but he stumbles away,
looking stricken.

Back in the sheriff's office,
the wheels are in motion to prevent the violent pair from escaping to Mexico. Mark points out
one small road on the map.
Blackstone says it's not possible to
watch every spot. He looks un-
happy as he takes out a shotgun and starts to load it. Mark is obviously just
about done in.

To the melancholy strains of "I'll Fly Away", we see the judge walking
McCormick back to the hotel. Hardcastle points toward a bed. Mark lies down
but it doesn't last. Hardcastle is asleep in a chair, but Mark's bed is empty. Back
at the office, Blackstone loads another weapon, while out on the highway the
state troopers keep watch.

In their hideout, where the same song is playing, Melissa has had enough.
Arvin Lee turns it off and approaches her. He's still dwelling on the afternoon's
events. He's bolder, more forward. Now it's Melissa's turn to be coy. Arvin Lee
finally settles for discussing their plan. They're going to take the back road across
the mountains and into Mexico.

It's morning, back at the hotel. Mark returns and Hardcastle asks him where
he went. He's borrowed a car and intends to plug the one hole they spotted in
Blackstone's plan. He tells Hardcastle he can't just sit around and do nothing.

Arvin Lee and Melissa are in the Coyote. He is increasingly determined to
consummate their relationship. She says she wants it to be special. He sends her into
a dress store to get a nice dress while he goes to trade the Coyote in on a less flashy
vehicle. As soon as he leaves, she makes a call. She says Arvin Lee is starting to crack
and she may need help handling him soon.

Hardcastle is driving the car Mark borrowed. They spot the Coyote, parked in
a used car lot. Mark breaks the news to Friendly Harry, the dealer—it's hot and it's
his. With the Coyote recovered, the two head south to watch the mountain road.

It's night at Melissa and Arvin Lee's hideout, and a sheriff's car pulls up.
Blackstone gets out, looking grim. He goes to the barn where Arvin Lee is sleeping.
Arvin Lee awakens, but doesn't seem alarmed. Blackstone shoots him dead where he
lies. Melissa comes out of the house, encountering Blackstone. She throws herself
into his arms and asks him where he's been.

Daytime, and Mark's looking more upbeat, making plans again for what
he'll do with the money when he gets it back. They spot a burned-out car in
front of an isolated house. They pull in. The place seems deserted, but Mark

finds Arvin Lee's body in the barn. On closer inspection they realize that the burnt car is Blackstone's. They summon the state police. While evidence is being gathered, a radio call comes in. The suspects have been spotted in a nearby motel.

It's a stand-off. With the state police surrounding them, Billy Blackstone starts shooting from his motel room while Melissa gathers the cash into a bag. A barrage of return fire is followed by a teargas canister. Billy makes a run for the car, tossing the money into it, but then goes down in a hail of bullets. The car is struck, too, and a gas can in the front seat catches fire. Can, car and money are all aflame.

Melissa surrenders. Standing amid the wreckage, she claims that she wasn't responsible; she was forced into everything. Mark watches silently as his one big break goes up in smoke.

In the epilogue, the guys are in a café. In the background is a news broadcast detailing the events. Mark looks reconciled. They walk out to the Coyote and head for home.

The Context

We see less humor and more intensity here than is usual with Hertzog offerings. There's a sense of inevitable doom to this story that's outside the usual spectrum for *Hardcastle and McCormick*.

There are several themes revisited here—Mark's competence as a race driver alongside Hardcastle's utter unfamiliarity with both the sport and the workings of modern engines in general. But he's supportive and happy to see Mark win.

Mark is clearly just as inclined as the judge to take personal action against injustice, especially when the injustice happens to him. He feels entitled to call in his markers with Hardcastle, just as with the trip to Atlantic City. That's what friends are for. Hardcastle disapproves, but backs him up. Beyond their friendship, it would be hypocrisy to forbid him to actively pursue Arvin Lee and Melissa.

And once again, in this episode, we have a near brush with good fortune for McCormick, that ends with him back at square one. Just as in "Hotshoes" and "You and the Horse You Rode in On", the prize is always snatched away at the last moment. Of course series television isn't about change. We don't want Mark to go out and get his own place and make a down-payment on a muffler shop. And it happens routinely to Hardcastle as well, though usually it is he who turns down the reward in order to maintain the status quo.

The Trivia

The original script had Melissa Kantwell as Blackstone's stepdaughter, and some of the dialogue (along with the age disparity and the difference in their last names) still seems to reflect that. The third season episode "The Career Breaker" would re-explore the crooked sheriff theme, this time with a daughter as the accomplice.

The bank in the first robbery bears a sign that says "Silver City Federal Savings and Loan". Later on, Mark and Milt end up at the Silver City Hotel, suggesting that Arvin Lee boldly robbed the bank in the small town where he attended high school.

"You Don't Hear the One That Gets You" was recorded by Juice Newton on her 1984 album, *Can't Wait All Night*. At minute 17:39 the title of the episode is seen, scrawled on a board covering a broken window of the sheriff's office.

"I'll Fly Away" was written by Alfred Brumley in 1929. It remains a perennial favorite gospel song and was also used as the title for a NBC television series in 1991 and in the soundtrack for the movie *Oh Brother, Where Art Thou?*

Memorable Quotes

Hardcastle: You check the carbs? How are the carbs?

McCormick: It's fuel-injected, Judge. But thanks for the thought. Listen, uh, Tony's kept this thing up pretty good. We could have a shot at the race.

Hardcastle: Remember, you're not gonna be able to let off coming out of four, so you gotta hold the line in eight or nine and you'll be okay.

McCormick: "Hold the line", "coming out of four". Where'd you pick that up?

Hardcastle: What? You think I don't know anything about racing?

McCormick: Not unless it's got four legs and eats oats.

McCormick: Those two excuses for human beings have twenty grand that belongs to me and, worse than that, they've got my car. Now, you wanna go to the terminal and suck in bus fumes, you be my guest. I'm gonna find them.

Hardcastle: And what're you gonna do when you keel over after two blocks?

McCormick: You're gonna pick me up. That's what friends are for, right?

Melissa: Don't shoot! He was crazy. He was crazy. (to McCormick) You know. You know. Tell them. Tell them they made me do it. Tell them. They had guns. I was just trying to get away. You were there. Tell them! I'm just a girl.

The Birthday Present – premiered February 25, 1985

Written by	Stephen J. Cannell
Directed by	Tony Mordente
Second unit director	Gary Combs

Cast

Jonathan Banks	Weed Randall
Stephen Shortridge	Sandy Knight
Steve Sandor	Jerry Lee Barth
Vincent Schiavelli	Fix Henderson
Angel Tompkins	Sybil Monroe
Vernon Weddle	Doctor Marsh
Lesa Lee	Colleen
Chino 'Fats' Williams	the bartender
Frank Lauren	the bailiff
Bruce Tuthill	the motel manager

Cast Notes

Jonathan Banks, who had three opportunities to do bad guys on this series, topped them all as the psychotically vengeful Weed Randall. He does evil so well.

Stephen Shortridge is also a painter.

Vincent Schiavelli was an immensely recognizable character actor who had over one hundred and fifty TV and film credits. He died in 2005.

The Details

Out in the gatehouse, Hardcastle is trying to get a reluctant McCormick to put on a jacket and tie for their once a month dinner with Sandy Knight. He's the public affairs spokesman for the LAPD. His father, who was killed in the line of duty when Sandy was just a kid, was a good friend of Hardcastle's.

There's nothing about Knight that doesn't rub McCormick the wrong way. Sandy is successful, poised, perfect, and everything that Mark isn't. Hardcastle makes a final plea for Mark to just get along with the guy. The judge's birthday is right around the corner and this is all he wants.

Sandy arrives, bottle of wine in hand. As usual, he's perfectly coiffed and his teeth practically sparkle. He says he's tired of being on TV all the time but he takes a pass on Hardcastle's offer to put in a word about getting him back on the street.

After dinner, Mark and Sandy share the cleaning-up chores. Mark can't even meet Sandy's standards for dish rinsing, but Knight has a proposition for him. A vicious killer, Weed Randall, is due to be released after serving a fifteen-year sentence for murder. Hardcastle was the judge on the case. Sandy wants Mark to get Randall's file from Hardcastle's collection. He intends to look for evidence that Randall had his lawyer murdered during his last trial.

Mark understands first-hand how crazy Randall is; he knew him in prison. He also knows how much Hardcastle wants to see the man stay behind bars. He agrees to help Sandy.

In San Quentin, a barely-hinged Weed Randall calls an old friend, Jerry Lee Barth. He talks about how many people he has a score to settle with. On the wall of his cell, among the other clippings, a photo of Milton C. Hardcastle occupies a prominent position.

Back in L.A., Mark makes a late night visit to Sandy's bachelor pad to deliver the Randall files. He encounters the Sandy Knight lifestyle, which consists of a stream of lovely stewardess-types who only blame themselves for the complications they cause him when their visits with him overlap. Sandy is shocked to hear that Mark had to break into Hardcastle's files to get what they needed. Mark explains to him that they are different. He doesn't have Sandy's apparently charmed life.

Though there's nothing in the file that looks helpful, Mark has some insider information. He knows Pop Witherspoon, the guy who worked the prison telephone switchboard. He figures Weed made a call to Barth to order the hit on his lawyer.

They decide to visit San Quentin. Sandy returns to the gatehouse. The next morning, Hardcastle is astonished to see the two men voluntarily spending time together as Mark and Sandy head out in the Coyote.

In the infirmary at San Quentin, an ailing Witherspooon makes a deathbed statement that Randall arranged his lawyer's murder. The interview is overheard by an orderly, who notifies Randall.

On the way home from the prison, Mark and Sandy are tailed and fired upon. Mark eludes them, but on arriving back at the estate they hear more shots. Sandy and Mark go charging into the yard and find the judge laying down a tight grouping on a target with his hand gun.

Mark and Sandy offer him Witherspoon's testimony on tape and wish him an early happy birthday. Hardcastle is delighted. Sandy launches into an analysis of who did what to get the information. Mark is annoyed. He doesn't want any credit if it includes the bit where he broke into the judge's files.

The judge calls the D.A. and sets the wheels in motion. Sandy offers to move in with Mark while they get the evidence that will connect Jerry Lee Barth to the murder. Hardcastle overhears the plan and is pleased.

That evening, Mark and Sandy are coming to terms with Mark's interior decorating scheme at the gatehouse when Hardcastle bursts in. He's been pulled out of retirement to hear the Randall case. The authorities don't want Witherspoon to die before the trial can take place.

Outside, Jerry Lee Barth and an accomplice are planning an attack on the estate. Weed's girlfriend, Sybil, makes a call to draw Hardcastle to the window. Mark, in the garage, hears the phone and steps around to the front yard. He spots Barth aiming a gun, and tosses a wrench at him. Aim spoiled and victim alerted, the bad guys take off. Hardcastle emerges from the house, fires at them, then heads for the garage. Mark, wrenchless, stumbles after him.

The Coyote is in pieces, but Sandy is already rolling in his sports car. Hardcastle is running after, gun in hand. Mark doesn't have time to arm himself with anything more lethal than a bronze statue of blind justice.

He's the last one to arrive. After a heated gun battle, Sandy and the judge have cornered Jerry Lee Barth. The case against Weed Randall is complete.

Back in San Quentin, Weed talks to Fix Henderson. He arranges for a gun to be smuggled to him at the courthouse. His incentive program involves a sharpened spoon and a threat to kill Henderson if he doesn't come through with the weapon.

The next morning, back in L.A., Hardcastle is ready for Randall's pre-trial hearing. The setting is a tackily temporary courtroom in the Sutter Annex. His chambers are out back in a trailer. Mark cracks wise, but after the judge goes inside he admits to Sandy that he does that when he's upset. The two men exchange a few gibes.

Inside, Randall stays seated when Hardcastle arrives. When he's asked to enter a plea, he goes off on a rant. As his ravings escalate, he reaches for a revolver hidden in a hollowed-out book. He fires, striking the judge. Mark and Sandy rush to Hardcastle's side while Weed escapes in the panic.

Hardcastle has a chest wound. He's barely conscious and sinking fast. Sandy is convinced he's dying. Mark angrily denies it.

At the hospital, Sandy and Mark wait for news. Sandy berates himself for not having prevented the attack. He recalls his father's murder and insists they have to do something. A somber Mark says all they can do is wait and pray, but Sandy is already channeling his inner homicidal vigilante.

The surgeon comes out. He gives Hardcastle's gun to Mark, reportedly at Hardcastle's instructions before he went to surgery. He tells them the judge is in critical condition and shouldn't have survived even this long. He doesn't hold out much hope. Sandy stalks off. Mark is told he won't be able to see Hardcastle for at least twenty-four hours.

Mark finds Sandy outside and tells him he has an idea of how to track Randall. But he insists that they must do it legally—that's what Hardcastle taught him. Sandy is furious. He won't give Mark a ride, and says the wrong man got the judge's gun.

Sandy tears out of the lot. McCormick appropriates a late model Corvette convertible and heads out on his own.

Sandy goes to Sybil's old hangout, The See Thru Bar, where he accosts the bartender out in the alley. The man is an associate of Weed's. Shoved around by Sandy, and threatened with a gun, he tells him that Weed is up the coast at a place called the Sun Spot Motel. Sandy kidnaps him.

Meanwhile, Mark's made the drive up to San Quentin, where he confronts Fix Henderson, the only guy he knows who could have gotten Weed a gun. Mark promises Henderson that if Hardcastle dies, he'll nail him as an accomplice. Even through the grill in the visitor's room, Mark looks like a viable threat. Henderson tells him Weed's hiding out at a motel on the coast. That and a description of Sybil's car are all he has.

Sandy pulls in at the Sun Spot Motel. Weed observes him from a room. Sybil's there, too. Weed sends her out to distract Sandy, then gets the drop on him from behind. Mark pulls in, screeching to a halt as Weed pushes Sandy into his path. Sandy turns, attacks Weed, and is shot.

It's a stand-off, with Weed drawing down on the injured officer and Mark pointing Hardcastle's gun at him. Weed ignores Mark's threat and moves to fire.

Mark is forced to shoot him. While the ambulances are summoned, Mark goes to Weed's side. Randall, gasping, tells him he reminds him of a guy he knew in prison—"Mark, he was a real funny guy."

Kneeling next to a man he has killed, with the sound of approaching sirens, Mark says, "Oh, God, what happens next?"

In the epilogue, Hardcastle is awake in his hospital room. Mark is visiting. The judge knows about Sandy's downfall. Mark expresses some sympathy for the soon to be ex-cop.

He sits down next to the judge's bed. Hardcastle tells him he was a long shot, but he "has what it takes". Mark makes a shaky attempt at humor but it doesn't hold. He's clearly upset. He finally describes the act of taking a life—the only time he's ever had to do so. He feels diminished by it. Hardcastle is reassuring. Sandy would have died if Mark hadn't killed Randall. Sudden life and death decisions are what cops sometimes have to make. Though Mark says he's not a cop, Hardcastle tells him he's a "damn good friend".

The Context

Again Cannell comes through with an episode that stakes out new emotional ground for the characters, though it starts in familiar territory, with Mark trying not to bite his tongue too hard while holding his peace around Sandy Knight. This "perfect guy" brings to mind Lance White, the equally perfect private eye who was Rockford's *bete noire* from time to time. McCormick, like Rockford, is a mere mortal. Also like Rockford, Mark's not too keen on using a gun.

But this episode takes a sharp turn for the serious and Sandy diverges just as sharply from his prototype. Though superficially perfect, he's fatally flawed. Sandy never really understood the Hardcastle ethos. He resorts to vengeance when he feels his cause justifies it.

Mark, by contrast, is the obviously flawed long-shot. But underneath his rough exterior, he's the better man by far. When it comes to taking a human life, Mark's morality is stricter than Hardcastle's. The act, even when absolutely necessary, costs him more. We don't expect to see this kind of emotional consequence in an action show as yet another convention is turned upside down.

The Trivia

Sandy says Weed's lawyer was murdered halfway through his trial, yet he was caught arranging the murder by the telephone operator at San Quentin.

The book in which Weed Randall's gun was hidden is a volume of *Corpus*

Juris Secundum, an encyclopedic review of topics in American law, available with frequent updates since 1936.

The exterior shot of the medical facility is St. Vincent's Hospital. It was founded in 1856 as the St. Vincent Infirmary. In 1974 it became St. Vincent Medical Center. When Mark exits the building toward the parking lot, the sign reads "St. Mary's".

The Sun Spot Motel, constructed in 1938, is located across the Pacific Coast Highway from Will Rogers State Park.

Memorable Quotes

McCormick: They should've given him a better courtroom. This stinks.
Sandy: You were cracking a lot of jokes for a guy who thinks it stinks.
McCormick: You see, Sandy, you don't understand me at all. When I get upset, I turn a little smart mouth. It's a character flaw, but I'm working on it.
Sandy: I like it that you can evaluate yourself, Mark.
McCormick: You do? Want me to evaluate you?
Sandy: Not especially.

Hardcastle: You know something, kid, you were a long shot. I gotta tell you, there were times when I didn't think you were gonna make it. But, you got what it takes, you're okay.
McCormick: What kinda medication they got you on, man? You're starting to sound sappy.
Hardcastle: Just shut up, because I don't say this stuff a lot. You made all the right choices, and I'm proud of you.

McCormick: I'm not a cop.
Hardcastle: I know that. But, you're a damn good friend, and that's the best present ever 'cause it lasts.

Surprise on Seagull Beach – premiered March 4, 1985

Written by	Patrick Hasburgh
Directed by	Michael O'Herlihy
Second unit director	Gary Combs

Cast

William Windom	James Maxwell
John Dehner	Guenther Rieseman
Stanley Kamel	Zimmerman

Ken Stovitz	Razz
Michael Cornelison	
Erik Holland	
George Skaff	
Eddie Quillan	
Ed Bernard	Lieutenant Giles
Wendy Smith	
Darcy DeMoss	
Gary Morgan	
Peter Brocco	
Joe Praml	
Micheal J. Aronin	

Cast Notes

William Windom was a regular on the series *Murder She Wrote* as Doc Hazlitt. He also won an Emmy for his portrayal of James Thurber in *My World and Welcome to It*.

John Dehner had over two hundred and seventy screen and television credits, including a recurring role as Burgundy Smith opposite Brian Keith in his 1960 series *The Westerner*.

Stanley Kamel was most recently cast as an unflappable psychiatrist on the series *Monk*.

The Details

In Paris at a shop where WWII memorabilia is sold, a gray-haired customer studies a map of the California coastline. It has "Seagull Beach" prominently marked on it.

Back in Malibu, a disgruntled Hardcastle is heading down the path to that very same beach, with Mark alongside advocating that he exercise a little diplomacy. But diplomacy is in short supply as he encounters a crowd of surfer kids. Razz—their de facto leader—and the judge face off. The town council has not yet voted on whether Seagull Beach is to be declared public. Hardcastle details Mark to make sure the kids leave and don't come back.

The beach is also being observed from afar. Two men, Riese and Zimmerman, discuss the upcoming town council meeting. They have their own reasons for wanting the beach opened to the public and are arranging support for Razz. A map is being searched for and Riese's grandfather, a former Nazi named Rieseman, is involved in the plot. There's something out there that he is very eager to find.

In Paris, the man buys the map and departs the shop. He's also being observed, and a call is placed back to Malibu. James Maxwell is told that the map is in the hands of an ex-Nazi war criminal. Maxwell says he will take care of it.

On the beach, Mark is spinning a tale of ninety-foot waves and surfer's promises to the two young things who still grace a blanket there. He's pretty much got their attention, too, until Hardcastle interrupts, critiquing his story.

The map buyer arrives at LAX. He is followed from the airport parking lot by Maxwell, who chases him and runs him off a deserted dirt road. The man's suitcase is thrown clear of the lethal wreck. Maxwell finds the map.

At the town council meeting, Razz makes a tempered, rational plea for public access to Seagull Beach. The audience includes a large number of his supporters. Hardcastle's rebuttal is less polished, and offered up to boos from the same crowd.

The men who were watching the beach, Razz's silent backers, are now observing the meeting. Zimmerman informs Riese about the crash and the theft of the map. An unknown player is involved.

The next morning, at the estate, Mark tries to bring some perspective to Hardcastle's loss of the town council vote. The judge hasn't given in yet. He gets a phone call from a friendly colleague. He's got a temporary restraining order against the council's ruling.

Reisemen, the Nazi, arrives from Argentina, looking determined and accompanied by henchmen.

On the beach, Mark and the judge watch the surfers trudge away. Hardcastle doesn't look all that pleased with himself. Mark tells him the kids have a right to the beach. Hardcastle tries to explain. He comes down there sometimes, by himself, to think things through. He finally admits the place is special to him because it is where he proposed to his wife.

Mark asks him what Nancy would want. Hardcastle says she loved kids and liked having them around. He tells Mark to keep the surfers off the beach for just a little longer; he needs time to get used to the idea of giving their place away.

At his beachside shop, John Maxwell is studying the stolen map, calculating a location on Seagull Beach. Down the beach in question, Mark is standing guard—and keeping his beer cold. Maxwell is watching. He tells his accomplice that he'll kill anyone who comes between him and the gold that was buried on that beach fifty years ago.

That night, Maxwell digs on the beach and finds the gold. The next morning Razz discovers a series of deep holes dug in the sand. Mark arrives to warn him off yet again. Rieseman's goons are there as well, armed with a sub-machine gun. Mark and Razz are kidnapped.

A short while later, Hardcastle comes down to the deserted beach. He finds the holes, Razz's surfboard, and a handful of bullet casings. He takes the casings to Lieutenant Giles. He wants them checked by the lab. Mark's been missing for three hours. Giles gets a report that the casings are from a type of weapon associated with the elite Nazi units.

Back at the Nazi hideout, Razz gets whacked for a smart remark about his Volkswagen. Rieseman arrives, picks up an electric cattle prod, and the real questioning begins.

Back at the beach, Hardcastle is also doing some questioning. One of the surfers remembers a story he heard from an old-timer about treasure buried on the beach. Hardcastle seeks out the old man, a beach concessionaire. He hears the whole tale. Nazis purportedly left gold buried on the beach before the war to fund a local subversive movement. The man recollects that James Maxwell was in the civil defense then, and among the group that scared off the intruders.

Hardcastle visits Maxwell next, who says he's never even heard of Seagull Beach. The judge says he's lying and promises to keep an eye on him. He puts in a call to Giles and asks him to run a check on Maxwell.

Back at the Nazi hideout, the interrogation is about to begin again. It's Razz's turn, but Mark interrupts. He tells them that "Hardcastle's got it", whatever the heck it is.

At the estate, Maxwell shows up, ringing the bell and pulling a gun when the judge opens the door.

Back at the police department, Giles is receiving a lengthy report on Maxwell. He served a stint with Civil Defense, had a history of arrests for gun running, and trespassed on Seagull beach back in the forties.

In the study at Gull's Way, Maxwell wants to know who

Hardcastle has talked to. The judge just wants to know what Maxwell did with McCormick. As the discussion continues, a van pulls up. Razz and McCormick are in the back. Rieseman's men jump out.

The phone rings in the study—Giles doesn't get through because Maxwell pulls the jack.

Rieseman's guys burst into the study, followed by Rieseman and Mark. There are introductions all around, with Hardcastle realizing that Rieseman and Maxwell are probably old acquaintances.

Giles has moved his men into position. When Rieseman, his men, and their prisoners depart, the police follow discreetly.

At Maxwell's shop, Riesemen gloats over the gold. It will be used to restart the Reich.

Outside, Giles' men are closing in. They fire teargas. Hardcastle is used as a hostage as Rieseman and his men take the gold and escape to a boat on the beach.

Mark pursues in a second boat. Hardcastle attacks his captors. Their boat careens out of control toward a yacht. Everyone jumps just before the fiery crash. Mark pulls Hardcastle out of the water, but Rieseman becomes a victim of his own greed, pulled down, along with Zimmerman, by the weight of the gold bars he is carrying.

In the epilogue, Mark and the judge are discussing the outcome of the case as they fill in the holes on the beach. Mark confesses he's the one who sent Rieseman to Hardcastle. The judge lets him know, in surfer-speak, that he did okay. Razz and the gang pitch in on the shoveling detail, and Hardcastle extends the hospitality of Seagull Beach to the whole crowd.

The Context

We get some insight here into Hardcastle's personal life—his devotion to the memory of his wife and his desire to preserve a place, at least for a little while longer, that he once shared with her. Hardcastle knows he's being selfish, and even if he hadn't gotten it all figured out for himself, Mark's there to point things out to him.

Greed is the theme here—Hardcastle's unwillingness to share a place that's special to him, which he eventually overcomes, and Maxwell and Rieseman's lust for the gold, pure and simple. The judge is quick to observe that even though the two men are from opposite sides, they have everything in common. Their relentless greed lands one of them in jail and pulls the other to the bottom of the harbor.

The Trivia

The Nazis apparently used U.S. navigation maps.

Seagull Beach is located at 36 degrees 2 minutes 2 seconds north, 118 degrees 36 minutes 6 seconds west.

Mark's tale of surfing the big one back in 1968 (when he would have been fourteen) includes a made-up Hawaiian term for a killer wave. In the script it's "mookaihawa" which gets extended to "mookahaiwi ha na na" in the final production. Neither version can be found in Andrew's Dictionary of the Hawaiian Language, but "moka" means something which is torn up and "mokuhia" means "to drown", so maybe Mark wasn't a totally spun dude on this one.

Hardcastle and the bad guys shop for their brown and blue coffee mugs at the same store.

Cat Stevens' "Miles from Nowhere" was also used for a musical interlude in an episode of *The A-Team*, "Alive at Five", and in the *Hardcastle and McCormick* episode, "She Ain't Deep but She Sure Runs Fast".

Zimmerman calls his weapon a "Schmeisser"—Hugo Schmeisser was an innovative German weapons designer who produced the models from which the MP-40 was adapted, and also created the Sturgewehr 44, one of the first assault rifles. There's nothing exceptional about the ammo, though. The MP-40 uses a 9mm parabellum round which was first introduced by Luger in 1902 and is still, with variations, very commonly used today.

Memorable Quotes

Razz: Hey, look. This is a roust, okay? I mean, like, we're ready to go outside right now and, like, cowabunga, you know? I mean, me, Donnie, and Wigger are pumped to carve some tasty sets, okay? And you want to make us go all the way down to Newport and, like, ride the foam. I'm sorry, but that's fully spun, okay?

Hardcastle: What, were you get dropped on your head when you were a kid or what?

Hardcastle: What the hell is that? What're you doing? (pulls a six-pack from the surf)

McCormick: It's beer fish.

Hardcastle: McCormick.

McCormick: Well, listen, it gets hot out here guarding the beach like this. Just trying to keep it cold.

Hardcastle: I don't know. Some people get to hang out with John Wayne, Clint Eastwood, Babe Ruth. What do I get? Jethro Bodine.

McCormick: You would have figured it out in a day or two. I just couldn't afford to wait that long, that's all.

Hardcastle: What if I didn't figure it out?

McCormick: But you did. You see, I know you better than you do.

Hardcastle: Don't flatter yourself. Listen, I might be a fully spun dude, but I didn't expect you to hair out on me. I mean, I know that you were fully pumped up and ready to bail because that Kraut was a bad dude. However, seeing how sketchy the deal was, it was kind of a wheeze to see you get biffed by the Nazis.

Undercover McCormick – premiered March 11, 1985

Written by	Marianne Clarkson
Directed by	Les Sheldon
Second unit director	Gary Combs

Cast

David Ackroyd	Eddie Dawson
James Cromwell	Jake Fellows
John Calvin	Peeples
Raymond St. Jacques	Rod Frazier
Keith Charles	Commissioner Emhart
Dennis Farina	Ed Coley
Joe Santos	Frank Harper
Ted Sorel	
Steve Gagnon	
Lew Saunders	Officer Nicholls
Tom Simmons	
Ricardo Lopez	Officer Menendez
Tommy Lamey	the burglar
Hector Mercado	
Bernadette Williams	waitress
Kimberly Foster	woman at the party

Cast Notes

David Ackroyd also appeared with Brian Keith in the 1980 movie *The Mountain Men.*

James Cromwell has had recurring roles in the television series *24* and *Six Feet Under*, but is perhaps best known for his Oscar-nominated role as the laconic farmer in the movie *Babe.*

Raymond St. Jacques made over 300 guest star appearances on television. He had the recurring role of Simon Blake in the 1965 season of *Rawhide*. He died of cancer in 1990.

Dennis Farina, who was Detective Fontana in the series *Law and Order*, as well as playing dozens of other cop roles, spent years as a real police officer in Chicago before he turned to acting.

The Details

It's an ordinary morning for Joe Aramajian, except that it's the last of his life. He's pulled over by a squad car, apparently for speeding. Officer Fellows runs his plate and name for warrants, while his partner, Eddie Dawson, shoots the man in cold blood, then plants a gun on the victim and tosses packages of cocaine into his trunk. The hit concluded, Fellows calls it in as a justified shooting.

At the Studio City Theater, Mark and the judge are emerging from the Ingmar Bergman Film Festival. Mark quotes his latest love interest, Valerie the film major. Hardcastle is not impressed by the existential symbolism but at least they got some popcorn out of it.

They head for home in the truck with Hardcastle at the wheel. In what feels like an eerie echo of the opening scene, a patrol car pulls them over.

The officer, Rafael Menendez, is the son of an old friend of Hardcastle's. He accuses his fellow officers of murdering Aramajian, but won't say anything more until he can talk to the police commissioner. He pleads with the judge to arrange a meeting for the next day at the polo grounds.

Hardcastle passes the request along to an unhappy Lieutenant Harper, who reminds him that the police commissioner and the judge have a long-standing feud. Years ago Hardcastle insulted him in open court and threw him out of the witness box.

Commissioner Emhart hasn't forgotten. He's going to give the rookie cop ten minutes to explain himself. Menendez doesn't use any of them. They find

him dead at the meeting place.

In his office, Commissioner Emhart tries to get to the bottom of it. He orders Harper to set up an undercover operation. While Frank and the commissioner quibble over the details, the judge already has his eye on his preferred candidate for the man on the inside.

Mark, initially leery, seems to take to the proposition with nervous enthusiasm. He'll be William Thomas

O'Reilly, late of Jersey City and newly hired by the local police. The records supporting his cover story are on their way to New Jersey and he's on his way to his first night shift.

But first there's some hazing. He ends up in a locker at the precinct house. After a briefly rocky start, there are introductions, and his first patrol with Menendez's old partner, Officer Peeples. The night quickly turns interesting as they're radioed to a darkened building where Mark gets the drop on an intruder and disarms him.

Things seem to be going all right, but just after they leave the station, at the end of the shift, Peeples pulls a gun on McCormick and forces him to drive to a warehouse. It looks like an interrogation. Dawson, Fellows, and Peeples appear dead serious. The mood only holds for a moment—it's just a set-up for the welcome to a raucous after-hours cop party.

There's an impromptu indoor shooting range, and Mark doesn't do much for his cover story, missing cans at close range. He's taken aside a little while later by Fellows (already one and a half sheets to the wind), who advises him of "the rules". "Keep your mouth shut no matter what you see" is the main one. He passes him cash in an envelope. Mark refuses it.

In the morning, at the estate, a hung-over Mark discusses the situation with Hardcastle. They're still not sure what the cops are up to.

What they're up to is murder for hire. Dawson and Peeples meet with drug lord Rod Frazier. He gives them instructions to kill his old partner, Ed Coley, who's about to turn state's evidence.

Back at the estate, Hardcastle has ID'd the gun that was used to kill Aramajian. It was evidence taken from a crime committed seven years ago and ought to have been melted down.

That night, before his shift, Mark is confronted by Fellows, who is the weak link in the hit squad. He also knows, from contacts back in New Jersey, that Mark is a fake. But he's been drinking and McCormick quickly gets the upper hand.

Fellows breaks down and says he can't take it anymore and wants to make a deal. He tells Mark something big is about to happen, but he can't provide details; the other two don't trust him anymore. Mark takes what he has to the police commissioner but it's not enough information.

The next night, Dawson confronts Fellows. His distrust is increasing. Mark and Peeples arrived in a dark alley just in time to hear a shot go off. Dawson has murdered Fellows, but he used the gun that Mark handled two nights earlier when he took it off the burglar. It was a set-up all along. Dawson and Peeples tell Mark he needs to cooperate; all he has to do is make a phone call.

The next morning, at the estate, Hardcastle offers to let Mark drop the undercover job. Mark wants to continue; he feels he owes that much to Fellows. The judge says he'll be nearby to receive the information about the hit as soon as Mark has it.

Later that night, Mark, Dawson, and Peeples are at a diner. Hardcastle has tailed them, and is occupying a spot a few seats down at the counter. Mark finally gets a time and place for the hit and surreptitiously writes the information on a napkin. Dawson casually picks the napkin up to wipe his glasses, but the ruse is not discovered.

As soon as the three leave, Hardcastle grabs the napkin, notifies Frank, and then heads over to Ed Coley's house to warn him. Coley is understandably aggravated and unconvinced. Moments later the hit men/cops arrive, with Mark along for the ride. Bursting in through the front door, Dawson and Peeples encounter Hardcastle. They tussle with Mark and the judge, then retreat to their squad car and flee. The guys pursue in the truck, with Harper's reinforcements joining the chase.

The bad guys are cornered. Dawson is shot by the police and Mark takes down Peeples. With the two in Frank's custody, Hardcastle tells Mark he'd make a pretty good cop. McCormick shrugs and says it's not his style—too dull.

In the epilogue, Mark, Frank and Milt are riding in the back seat of a limo, on their way meet the police commissioner for a public ceremony. Harper tells Hardcastle that the commissioner has never forgiven him. He's right, Emhart

can barely swallow his bile long enough to get through the award ceremony. Mark gets his medal and Hardcastle gets short shrift. When Emhart finally mutters a quick and sullen "thank you" to the judge, Hardcastle—beaming at the photographers—smilingly reminds the man that he's *still* a jackass.

The Context

Here's another bunch of bad cops. Along with "D-Day", "One of the Girls from Accounting", and the sheriff in "You Don't Hear the One that Gets You", that's four times in this season.

More interesting, though, is that it's another example of Hardcastle not playing well with authority. He's friends with practically every patrol officer in the city, and has at least five lieutenants who do his investigatory bidding, but the police commissioner hates his guts.

And here we have Mark, only two episodes after his encounter with Weed Randall—when he swore he wasn't a cop—doing his Dirty Harry routine and treating the whole outing as though it's a lark.

All that bluster doesn't hold up long, though. There's an increasing air of menace—dark, claustrophobically narrow alleys and a sense of deep suspicion even among the co-conspirators. In the end, as always, the only one Mark can trust to watch his back is Hardcastle.

The Trivia

Les Sheldon remembers making his directorial debut with the scene outside the movie theater ("Day One, 7:10 a.m."). The Bergman film that is the subject of Mark and Milt's analysis is *Wild Strawberries*. Nearly every thing in the episode, from the lighting angles, to the slightly out of date elements of the police uniforms, to the location choices, was intended to invoke the *film noir* tradition.

"Steve from Hollywood" and the radio call-in show announcer were both wrong. The origin of the word "posh" has never been proven, and there's no evidence to indicate it ever meant "Port Out, Starboard Home", particularly not in trans-Atlantic crossings.

The cops party hearty to the Talking Heads' 1983 release "Burning Down the House", which reached number nine on the U.S. charts.

After proving himself capable of laying down a tight grouping in the season one episode "Goin' Nowhere Fast", McCormick is now incapable of hitting beer cans at less than ten paces.

As he heads into the building to work his second shift, McCormick is whistling the theme music from *Dragnet*.

At 6'7", James Cromwell spends significant parts of this episode sitting down, so as not to tower over nearly everyone else. When Fellows confronts McCormick in the alley, Cromwell and Kelly appear to be the same height.

The city seal, shown on the squad cars and the lectern at the press conference, bears a passing resemblance to that of the City of Los Angeles, but on closer examination is completely generic.

The city of Los Angeles actually presents a Medal of *Valor* (not *honor*) as its highest honor, but only to members of the police department, not civilians.

Memorable Quotes

Hardcastle: You cut open an eggplant and a rat comes out. What's that? Come on, you didn't understand any of it.

McCormick: Well, I didn't understand all of it, but most of it I did.

Hardcastle: Okay, what'd it mean when that guy's eyeball fell out and rolled along the floor, whir, whir, whir?

McCormick: That meant you gotta watch where you step in life, you know? You can't expect to be seeing everything. If you don't hold on to what you got, it'll roll away from you. That's what it meant. (shrugs and laughs)

Hardcastle: Are you okay?
McCormick: Yeah, you?
Hardcastle: You wouldn't make a bad cop.
McCormick: Nah, not my style. Too dull.

The Game You Learn from Your Father
– premiered March 18, 1985

Written by	Patrick Hasburgh
Directed by	Kim Manners
Second unit director	Gary Combs

Cast

Tim Thomerson	Duke McQuire
Jeff MacKay	Nick Farrell
Sandy Ward	Donald Farrell
Ray Girardin	Coach Harmson
Ken Swofford	Chuck Foster
Ron Cey	Himself
John Dennis Johnson	Billy Bauer
Ted Dawson	

Cast Notes

Tim Thomerson began his career in entertainment as a stand-up comic, but left that behind for over 175 movie and television appearances, including the role of Gene/Jean in the 1977 TV series *Quark*.

Jeff MacKay was a great utility player with recurring roles on *Black Sheep Squadron, Magnum, P.I.,* and a regular role on *Tales of the Gold Monkey*. He passed away in 2008.

Ken Swofford is another peripatetic character actor. He's had guest or recurring roles on 62 television series, playing eleven different characters on *Gunsmoke* and five on *The Rockford Files*.

Ron Cey played for the L.A. Dodgers from 1971 to 1982, helping lead them to victory in the 1981 World Series. In 1985 he was with the Chicago Cubs. He played himself in the 1990 Columbo movie, *Uneasy Lies the Crown*, and also had a role in the movie *Q*.

The Details

A ragged, worn-out man sticks up a convenience store at gunpoint. He doesn't even make it out the door with his ill-gotten gains before he's shot in the back by the clerk.

In the emergency room, Billy Bauer, the gravely wounded robber, demands to see Hardcastle. As he lies

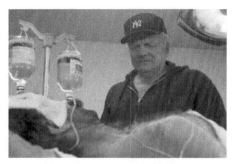

dying, refusing any treatment, he tells the judge that he committed a murder ten years ago for which his friend, Duke McQuire, was convicted. He was given twenty-five grand to set McQuire up. He dies before Hardcastle can find out who paid him.

Back at the estate, it's three in the morning and Hardcastle is still poring over the files. He was the judge on the case; it was his responsibility. Mark tells him it wasn't his fault. He reminds him that it was the jury that convicted McQuire. Hardcastle's not buying it.

McQuire is released from San Quentin. Running the gauntlet of reporters, he says he wants to ask the people involved in his conviction how he can get ten years of his life back. His baseball career was over before it could even begin. Hardcastle is watching the news interview in the study. Mark comes in and turns off the TV. He tries to distract the judge. Hardcastle tells him how good McQuire's prospects were. He wonders how much that loss is worth.

In a bar, McQuire is watching a newscast. A hot young college prospect, with a record not as good as his own was, is being offered a big bucks contract with a major league team. McQuire's release is mentioned in passing by the anchorwoman. The barkeep comments, barely remembering that there was a Duke McQuire and getting his name wrong.

Out on the grounds at the estate, Mark accuses Hardcastle of trying to channel his guilt into yard work. It's not helping McQuire a bit. Duke arrives in mid-discussion, pulls a gun on them and demands to know who framed him for murder. Hardcastle says Billy Bauer never had a chance to tell him. McQuire is still

threatening. Mark takes him down with a garden rake and a solid kick. Hardcastle discovers the man's gun wasn't loaded.

At a training session of the California Stars, pitcher Nick Farrell is observed by Coach Harmson. He's not throwing his A game. His dad nags Harmson to make Nick a starter. Harmson reminds Don Farrell that

he is an assistant pitching coach in name only. He warns him to stay away from the players; he's only on the staff because he's part of the package with his son and Nick's pitching may not rate any special favors right now.

After the practice, Nick's dad is pushy and demanding to his son. He advises him not to have any contact with his old pal, McQuire. Nick insists they're still friends and they're not kids anymore. He wants to see him. His dad adds a layer of guilt and treats his son like an eleven-year-old. Nick finally gives in, just as he must have done a thousand times before.

Back at the estate, the empty gun has been put aside. McQuire is conferencing with the guys in the study. He thinks he's washed up. No major league team will consider him. Hardcastle says Chuck Foster, the owner of the California Stars, is an old pal of his. Mark says that won't be enough. He's convinced McQuire will need an angle to catch the attention of the media.

Hardcastle's old pal Foster barely remembers him at first. Even after his memory's been jogged, he's still reluctant to give McQuire a tryout.

Meanwhile, Mark's working the phone, spreading the word that there'll be a media-worthy event that afternoon at the park. Ron Cey, former Dodger, is doing an autograph session. Mark shows up challenging Cey to a three-pitch duel against McQuire, with five thousand dollars to go to charity if Cey isn't struck out. Three pitches later, McQuire is back on the big league radar screen.

At home, Don Farrell watches his son's old pitching nemesis on a news clip. In his office, Chuck Foster catches the story, too, and invites McQuire for a tryout.

At the field, Don Farrell is hostile when McQuire arrives, but Nick is still friendly. The session goes well for McQuire but afterwards the police show up in the locker room. They're acting on an anonymous tip and have found drugs in McQuire's gym bag. The police are about to take McQuire into custody when Hardcastle tells them the bag is his—their arrests will have to include an ex-superior court judge. The police take a pass on what looks like a clumsy frame.

At the estate that night, the guys try to figure out who might have wanted to destroy McQuire's chances. They figure the only way to draw the suspect out is for McQuire to keep pushing for a spot on the Stars' roster.

The workouts go well and McQuire is signed to the team. That night, someone rigs a bomb to his car. Mark spots the device and the three of them barely escape before the explosion.

The next morning, Hardcastle's further digging bears fruit. He discovers Don Farrell sold his home for twenty-five thousand dollars a short while before Billy Bauer was hired, for that same amount, to frame McQuire.

They go to Don Farrell with the information. He says nothing. That night, at the baseball field, Don confronts his son, Nick. He gave him the twenty-five thousand "no questions asked" because Nick had told him he'd gotten a girl in trouble. Now Don knows the truth and he's furious. He says Farrells don't have to cheat to win. Nick is angry too. He spent years trying to meet his father's expectations and did what he thought he had to do to keep  from losing to McQuire. Don finally tells Nick "I have no son". Nick begs for another chance as his father walks away.

The next morning, Nick's a no-show at the first pre-season game. In the locker room, his father tells McQuire the truth about who hired Bauer. The game must go on. When the Stars are in trouble in the seventh, the coach puts McQuire in. Up in the stands, Nick Farrell is climbing to the roof, carrying a sniper rifle in a duffle bag. He opens fire, hitting Duke in the left shoulder. Mark goes after him on foot through the terrified crowd, out into the parking lot, and then by car until the erratic Farrell has a rollover collision. As he's arrested, Nick babbles about his Little League baseball prowess. He's crossed the line into madness.

In the epilogue, McQuire is signing autographs at the local park. The guys arrive, informing him he still has a two-year contract with the Stars as a player/coach. While they stand there, pondering his new chance, they can't help over-hearing a man. He's raging at his young son as he stands at home plate, not meeting his father's expectations.

The Context

This is the second episode where a wrongly-convicted athlete has lost a pro career. In "Third Down and Twenty Years to Life", it was football; in this one, Duke McQuire's career as a major league pitcher has been severely truncated. A pitcher's prime is early twenties to early thirties, but Duke is thirty-five and lacks the pitching education and fitness that a minor league season or two would have provided.

McQuire's future has been almost destroyed by a lapse in Hardcastle's be-loved system. Just as in "Third Down", we see that Hardcastle stays up late at night when he discovers a man has been wrongly convicted in his courtroom. By contrast, Hardcastle never exhibits any remorse about McCormick's conviction and, stranger still, it's Mark who offers comfort here with the reminder that the jury convicts, a judge merely sentences.

The other theme Hasburgh returns to in this episode is fathers and sons. This time it's a relationship taken to extremes; the overbearing father discovers too late that his demands have created a monster.

The Trivia

The odd spelling of Duke McQuire's last name recalls that of an actual athlete, who was in the public spotlight in 1984, playing for the U.S. Olympic team – Mark McGwire.

The Stars, and their uniforms, were also used in a second season episode of *The Greatest American Hero* titled "The Two-Hundred-Mile-an-Hour Fastball". Hardcastle is occasionally seen wearing a California Stars baseball cap in season three episodes.

"The Game Goes On" (heard during the three-pitch hustle) was written for that previous episode and sung by Joey Scarbury. John Fogerty's 1985 hit "Centerfield" is heard during the practice montage.

District Attorney Peterson is mentioned by Duke. Could this be Pammy Peterson from "Once Again with Vigorish"?

Duke was a first-round draft choice right out of college, yet is thirty-five after ten years in prison.

The script shows that Dodger Stadium had been Hasburgh's first choice, but Blair Field in Long Beach was used. It's a semi-pro facility.

Former Dodger Ron Cey appears as himself. His old teammate, Rick Monday, is credited but nowhere to be seen. The foundation Cey is appearing on behalf of in the episode is "Jacopson". Two charities he supports in real life are Florence Crittenden Services and Pacific Lodge Youth Services.

Bill Bauer is the bad guy whose confession sets Duke free. The name is used for an appealing conman in another Hasburgh episode, "The Yankee Clipper".

The players Duke lists as being former teammates are members of the *Hardcastle and McCormick* production staff: Hertzog, Swerling, Sheldon. In the club's locker room, the names "Weyman" (unit production manager), "Scott" (first assistant director), "Good" (camera operator), and of course "D. Kelly", are emblazoned on the player's lockers.

Memorable Quotes

> McCormick: Judge, it wasn't your fault. Try and understand that.
> Hardcastle: He had a sinker you couldn't hit with a canoe paddle.
> McCormick: Judge, you…
> Hardcastle: How much you figure ten years of a life like that is worth?
> McCormick: I don't know.
> Hardcastle: Everything. Everything he never got a chance to do.

Farrell: My God! You used that money to pay Bill Bauer to frame Duke for murder! My God, what kind of a son did I raise?

Nick: Dad…

Farrell: The Farrells don't have to cheat.

Nick: Dad, please…

Farrell: Why? Why? Why humiliate me like this?

Nick: (laughs angrily) You don't know, do you? You really don't know. Okay, Dad, okay, that's what I did. You wanna know why? Because finishing in second place was never good enough for you! *Winning* was always important; it was *everything*. Finishing second was losing.

Nick: I just wanted to make the majors for my dad. We're a team. I'm a pitcher. I won five straight games my first year in Little League. Did you read about me? Ask my dad. He said I was the best, the best damn ten-year-old in the state. I even had a curve. My dad taught me to throw a curve. We're a good team. I'm his boy. I'm much better than Duke McQuire. I've got heart. Ask my dad.

Angie's Choice – premiered April 1, 1985

Written by	Richard Christian Matheson and Thomas Szollosi
Directed by	Bruce Kessler
Second unit director	Gary Combs

Cast

Lynne Topping	Angela "Angie" Bloom,
Robert Desiderio	Stevie Ray
Bobby Jacoby	Nicky Bloom
Beau Starr	Scully
Robert Thaler	
Anne Marie McEvoy	Lindsey Bloom
Barbara Cason	Dolores
John Hancock	Lieutenant Delaney

Cast Notes

Lynne Topping and her husband, James Farrell, produce plays with their theater company, The Main Street Players.

Robert Desiderio played J.J. Beal in the episode "Goin' Nowhere Fast".

Beau Starr also appeared in the episodes "The Georgia Street Motors", and "Round up the Old Gang". He appeared with Brian Keith in the pilot episode of

Murder She Wrote. He also played Lieutenant Welsh in the series *Due South.*

Bobby Jacoby is still acting, but since age twenty has been credited as Robert Jayne. He played the role of Melvin Plug in the *Tremors* movies.

Anne Marie McEvoy appeared in the 1984 Stephen King movie *Children of the Corn.*

The Details

Angie Bloom makes a phone call to the police department from her apartment, offering information about the murder of a man named Chen. While her call is being routed, two henchmen arrive, spotting her car in the garage. One reports to his boss, Stevie Ray, who tells him to kill the woman.

Inside the apartment, the woman's young son, Nicky, spots the hit men watching the building. Angie hangs up on the police and hustles her two kids out to her car. She fires a gun at the two men and then escapes.

It's a dark and stormy night. A cab pulls up to the gate at Gull's Way. Nicky and his younger sister, Lindsey, get out. He tells her they'll have to be tough.

In the house, Mark and the judge are sitting down to a ham dinner (with cloves) and comparing childhood poverty stories. The doorbell rings. Mark finds the two kids. Lindsey promptly inquires if either of the guys is her father. Nicky cops an attitude and presents a note that reads, "Please take care of my children". It's not signed and the kids won't provide any more information.

The power flickers, Lindsey screams. Aid and ham are provided. Hardcastle, trying to notify the cops, finds the phone is dead. Nicky hands them a second envelope. There's no further information, all it contains is four hundred dollars.

In his high-rise office, Stevie Ray is hearing the bad news from his lawyer. He's out of delaying tactics and his case goes to trial in five days. Angie could finish him if she testifies. Grabbing the kids might work as leverage against that happening, but Ray says it's the last resort.

Back at the estate, the phone's still out and the roads are a mess. The kids will have to be put up for the night. Nicky's tough act takes a hit when his little sister asks him for a bedtime story. After the guests are tucked in, Mark gives the judge a stern lecture on setting limits with children.

At Angie's abandoned apartment, Stevie Ray and his henchmen search for clues to the kids' whereabouts. They find nothing. Ray tells them to stake out the night school Angie attends.

The next morning, at the police station, a social worker makes no progress at getting a last name from the children. She says they'll have to go to foster care. Mark argues that they'd be better temporary guardians and Hardcastle agrees. Strings are pulled.

Meanwhile, an anxious Angie is on the run. She tries to call the estate but gets no answer. Ray's henchman, Scully, gets a lead on the cabbie who dropped off the kids. Hardcastle takes Nicky out for a walk and a man to man conversation about trust. Nicky gives him a fake name for his mom.

The cabbie tells Stevie Ray where he took the kids. He mentions Hardcastle's name. Ray is increasingly desperate. He decides the kids must be grabbed.

Back at the estate, Nicky is palming cards and winning against McCormick at poker. He also brags about lying to Hardcastle. Mark takes him out on the porch and tells him where his bad attitude is going to land him. Hardcastle comes out with a match on the alias for Angie Bloom. He knows her and he says she's rehabilitated herself. He has an idea where she might be.

The judge and Mark head out, following that lead. They spot a strange car as they're leaving. It's not long before their suspicions cause them to turn around. Back at the estate they interrupt a kidnapping. They chase the fleeing bad guy, who is captured after a rollover crash.

A squad car is stationed at the estate and the guys set out again to find Angie. They visit Dolores, a good friend of Hardcastle's and a former madam. She was also a friend of Angie's and they find the missing mom hiding out there. Angie gets a hug and a ride back to the estate.

The next morning, at the poolside, Mark lectures Hardcastle on sensitivity. Angie joins them. She tells them about her ex-boyfriend, Ray, and the murder she witnessed. She agrees to testify.

The squad car coming to pick her up for the hearing is hijacked. Scully and his accomplice arrive at the estate disguised as cops. They take Angie to Ray.

News of the deception gets back to Hardcastle when the real cops are found in the trunk of an abandoned car. He and Mark head for Ray's office where they tussle with two of Ray's goons. They find out where his yacht is moored.

When the Coyote arrives at the marina parking lot, Ray is forced to flee in his limo, with Angie still a hostage. A chase ensues, with two crashed squad cars and the limo eventually cornered. Angie is rescued.

In the epilogue, Angie tells them she plans to move to Tacoma. Nicky can't quite choke out a thank you, but offers to help them out the next time they're in a bind. Milt and Mark find a crayon drawing of themselves taped on the fridge.

The Context

Brian Keith had a great track record in shows costarring kids, particularly *Family Affair*. For Hardcastle and McCormick, this is a classic fish out of water tale, with the kids knocking on the front door, interrupting the Lone Ranger and Tonto in the middle of dinner in which they're playing a round of "poorer than thou".

But somehow this one winds up on some fans' less-loved list. Nicky's relentless tough-guy attitude is the issue often cited, but another problem is the unexpected character shift that Hardcastle seems to take. It's interesting to see him soften up around the kids, but would he make repeated excuses for Nicky's boorish behavior and, horrors, offer to write a book report for Nicky's mom? One too many cloves in the ham, we think.

On the other hand, it's interesting to hear McCormick, the man who is a bit casual around rules, advocating a firm hand with children. There might be a tacit hint there that he doesn't mind his more structured life with Hardcastle.

The Trivia

Judy Collin's autobiographical song "Born to the Breed" is heard in this episode.

A mystery sedan is parked in the Gull's Way drive when the faux-cops arrive to pick up Angie.

The entrance of the underground parking structure of Stevie Ray's building is the same one used for the Washington headquarters of Huntley Press in "Mr. Hardcastle Goes to Washington".

In the final chase, Ray's limo loses its left rear hubcap twice.

Memorable Quotes

Hardcastle: When I was a kid, we didn't have this much food in a month.

McCormick: Now, don't tell me, you're going to give me that rap about how much poorer than me you were as a kid.

Hardcastle: No, no. Not "poorer". "More poor". "Poorer" is poor English. (laughs)

McCormick: Well, we couldn't even afford proper English in our house. That's how poor we were.

Hardcastle: Well, at least you had a house. You ever see a sharecropper's shack in Arkansas, huh?

McCormick: You put cloves on this ham, didn't you? You put cloves on everything.

Hardcastle: Cloves? Everybody likes cloves.
McCormick: Yeah? Cloves are for guys in tights.
Hardcastle: Tights? What?
McCormick: Tights.

Nicky: I can't stand cloves. (looks at McCormick) You made this, didn't you?

She Ain't Deep but She Sure Runs Fast
– premiered September 23, 1985

Written by	Patrick Hasburgh
Directed by	Tony Mordente
Second unit director	Gary Combs

Cast

Jonathan Banks	Taylor Walsh
James Whitmore, Jr.	Travis Baker
Pat Corley	Buzz Bird
Lee de Broux	Jay Staller
Richard Lineback	Clyde Jewkes
Terry Bradshaw	Lester Smith

Cast Notes

Jonathan Banks is back again as Taylor Walsh (after his memorable performance in the second season episode, "The Birthday Present"). You can't keep a good villain down.

James Whitmore, Jr. is also back, and has a long, nearly solo performance in this episode. Travis Baker's character is developed almost without dialog, and never comes face to face with Hardcastle or McCormick.

Pat Corley, an oft-seen character actor, also had the recurring role of Phil on the show *Murphy Brown*. He died in 2006.

Terry Bradshaw, quarterback for the Pittsburgh Steelers and twice Superbowl MVP, retired from football in 1983. He also appeared with Brian Keith in the 1978 film *Hooper*.

The Details

Tooling along in the truck, on a backwoods road in Oregon, Hardcastle rhapsodizes about the call of the wild. Mark would rather listen to Creedence Clearwater Revival and is resentful that the judge has substituted two weeks in the mountains for their planned vacation in Hawaii. Hardcastle is adamant, though.

This is the last expedition that his old flying buddy, Buzz Bird, is making before he retires, and the judge intends to share it.

Meanwhile, in the back country, Taylor Walsh is on the hunt. He's not the only danger in the mountains. A grizzly bear is tearing into the ill-planned camp of two city slickers who have more equipment than sense. The arrival of Walsh looks like a godsend. He faces down the bear and chases it off.

When the two campers, Lester and Travis, try to thank Walsh, things get ugly. They claim they're there for hiking and photography, but Walsh finds their rifles and the bighorn sheep they illegally shot. He smashes one of their weapons and holds the other one on the two men. He commands Travis to run. As soon as he's out of sight of the camp, Travis hears a single shot echoing from the camp.

At a small rural airport, the judge and Mark catch a first glimpse of Buzz Bird's plane struggling in for a landing. The man himself is not much better off, wheezing and coughing with a cigarette dangling from his lips. With the guys on board, Buzz nurses his plane back into the sky and barely makes it over the tree line.

Off in the woods, Travis is running for his life. Walsh methodically stalks him.

Up in the rickety plane, Buzz tells them he's going to put them down in an area that's "three hundred miles up from nowhere". Mark says he's always wanted to go there.

Travis finds a river just as Walsh finds him. He panics and staggers away, but is soon cornered between Walsh and his friend, Clyde. Travis begs for his life. Walsh tells him to use what he's learned so far, and commands him to start running again.

Back in the plane, they're well past nowhere when Buzz starts to gasp. He's no longer controlling the flight. Neither is Hardcastle, though he gives it a try. The plane slams into the woods below.

The guys are merely stiff and banged up, but Buzz was most likely dead before they hit the ground. They bury him next to the plane wreck and then consider their options. It looks like a two hundred and fifty mile trek south to Myrtle Creek and Mark isn't dressed for the conditions. Six hours of hiking takes them only a few miles. It's evening and bad weather is closing in.

At the scene of the crash, Walsh and his two companions discover Buzz's grave. Clyde says they have nothing against the survivors, but Walsh now insists that anyone who trespasses in the back country is their sworn enemy.

It's night, and the rain pours down. Mark and the judge have found a cave and built a small fire. It's just enough to cook the equally small fish that Hardcastle caught. Mark wants to pass on his half because it's still staring at him. Truth is,

neither one of them has much of an
appetite. Hardcastle apologizes for
getting them into the situation. He
tells McCormick that one of them
might have to bury the other. Mark
asks if Hardcastle has any regrets.
There are two, but the judge doesn't
say what they are.

Mark says he has a ton of
them—not ever being really in love,
not having a son. He says if he dies up there nobody will know he ever existed.
Hardcastle tells him no one ever thinks their footprints are deep enough but
Mark says his are the shallower by far. In ten years, when their bodies are finally
found, Hardcastle will at least be mentioned by name in the news stories, while
he'll be merely "the other man".

The judge slips into a soliloquy. He says he's made mistakes, and took
credit for things like having McCormick placed in his custody, when really his
motivation was mostly to keep himself from retiring alone and fading into
oblivion. He finally admits that he might have been trying to get his son back.
His heartfelt musings end on a snore from Mark.

In the morning, they find their way down to a roiling river. Mark's attempt to cross ends in near disaster. Hardcastle fishes him out about a hundred
yards downstream.

Meanwhile, Travis, who spent the night treed by a grizzly, had has an
epiphany. He uses a sharp rock to cut down a sapling and fashions it into a
weapon.

Mark and the judge plod on. They discover the abandoned camp and
Lester's body. The truck is missing a distributor cap but they find an inflatable
raft. As Walsh and his men draw nearer,
they ready the raft and launch it. Their
shaky progress through the first set of
rapids is observed by their pursuers.

Meanwhile Travis is rapidly learn-
ing the art of survival. He's making his
way down the same river, with only a
couple of logs for floatation.

Walsh's men take to the water in
their own raft, opening fire on the judge
and Mark and winging their boat. The
guys are forced to abandon it and make
for the shore. They are cornered. They're
taken back to Walsh's camp and treated

to a first-class rant about the purity of the land. Walsh says even nature photographers must die. Hardcastle calls it like he sees it; Walsh and company are nothing but pirates.

As Clyde is about to dispatch them, Travis arrives, and lets loose an arrow from his rough-hewn bow. Clyde falls dead. A second shot wounds Walsh's other man. Walsh uses his M-16 to kill Travis. McCormick and the judge bolt into the woods.

Walsh tends the wound of his sole surviving follower, Jay. He insists on taking time to bury Clyde, and his dead but now ennobled enemy, Travis. He can't be reasoned with.

Mark and the judge put some distance between them and Walsh, but know he'll be back after them by morning. Mark suggests they turn the tables and hunt Walsh instead.

Morning finds Walsh and Jay following a carefully laid trail with Hardcastle staying a little ways ahead. Mark is elsewhere, digging a hole. At the critical moment, Hardcastle reveals himself, and leads the two men in a headlong chase that ends with them falling into a camouflaged pit.

Mark snatches up their gun. Hardcastle is hefting a lethal-sized rock and looks like he intends to use it. Mark persuades him to put it down even though the alternative—taking the men back to civilization to face justice—seems impossible.

In the epilogue, McCormick and the judge limp into the town of Myrtle Creek looking like a couple of mountain men. They hand their two prisoners over to the sheriff and head to the café. Mark mentions the admission the judge made up in the mountains that first night; he was only pretending to have been asleep. Hardcastle says there aren't any witnesses and he'll never confess to it…but next year they're going to Hawaii.

The Context

At the start of a new season, Hasburgh carves out new territory for Hardcastle in the old theme of fathers and sons. This time around, with two years invested in the relationship, and under considerable duress, the judge admits that just maybe he intended all along that Mark would be more than a fast gun and a yard man. There's even a hint of an admission that he was looking for someone to help fill the spot left by his dead son.

Mark also makes a confession. The highest thing on his list of regrets is not having had a permanent relationship and a chance to have had a son of his own.

A second issue arises, almost lost in the aftermath of the endless chase and all that running through the jungle. When the trap is sprung, and the bad guys are disarmed, Hardcastle's first impulse is to pound them into the ground. He's got a rock ready and everything. In the moment of crisis, it's McCormick who hangs on to the thin veneer of civilization and persuades him to make a try at doing things according to the law. Maybe Hardcastle's frequent insistence that we're only one broken rule away from anarchy is really a reflection of his own shallowly-buried instincts.

The Trivia

Carole Manny, our aircraft consultant, noted that although Buzz Bird tells the guys he cannibalized parts of his aircraft (a Cessna) from an assortment of other manufacturers' aircraft, his chariot is a 1968 Cessna 206, and nothing else. It's a six-passenger, fixed-gear (non-retractable) aircraft powered by a 6-cylinder Continental IO 520-series engine, which was rated for between 285-310 horse-power. It has a three-blade propeller in the airport scene, but in the crash scene (when the aircraft is seen plowing toward the camera after it hits the ground) a two-bladed prop is visible, so they clearly inserted a stunt double aircraft

When McCormick yells, "Pull it up!" and then "Not *that* far up!" the stall horn can be heard in the background.

Creedence Clearwater Revival's hit, "Run Through the Jungle" gets major playing time here. Cat Stevens' "Miles from Nowhere" (previously used in "Surprise on Seagull Beach") has a reprise.

The fur hats and full beards that the guys sport in the epilogue look like a wink and a nod to Brian Keith's role in the 1980 movie, *The Mountain Men*. Danny Kelly says as soon as he saw Brian's get-up with full beard he wanted the same for his character.

Do not try this at home: two things that can't be done on the spur of the moment (and with no prior skills) are making a useful bow and arrows, and tanning animal skins.

Memorable Quotes

Hardcastle: Okay, I can understand how a guy that's never been outside of the wilds of Jersey City is gonna be a little intimidated and overwhelmed by an expedition that's this ambitious. That's okay.

McCormick: You know, you're starting to sound like Sir Edmund Hillary.

Hardcastle: Hillary? That Limey couldn't dig a latrine alongside of Daniel Boone and Jedediah Smith.

McCormick: My bet is he's got it all over Hardcastle and McCormick like a pup tent.

Hardcastle: (offering fish) There ya go. Eat half of that.

McCormick: Ah, okay, Judge, you caught it. You eat it.

Hardcastle: You eat half of that or I'm gonna throw it out.

McCormick: That would be a smart move. That way, we'll both starve.

Hardcastle: There's two ways we can do this and one of them's gonna hurt you.

McCormick: Could you maybe close its eyes?

Hardcastle: Eat it! (after McCormick takes a bite) There you go. Good?

McCormick: You used a little too much lemon in the du jour sauce.

Hardcastle: Like the deal with having you put in my custody. Listen, I didn't do that for you. I did that for me. I had all that legal stuff on my side and all that judicial hoo-ha that made it look like I was gonna redeem a kid who was in trouble and give him another chance. Or maybe I had it wired just so that I could have somebody around so I wouldn't have to retire all by myself and be alone and disappear. Could be I was trying to get my son back. I just wanted to make sure somebody was there to see the wind didn't blow my tracks out of the sand.

Faster Heart – premiered September 30, 1985

Written by	Patrick Hasburgh
Directed by	Charles Picerni
Second unit director	Gary Combs

Cast

Barbara Horan	Kiki Cutter
John Sanderford	Sammy "Sidewinder" O'Connell
Judd Omen	Jake Thomas
Robert Sampson	Hal Jenkins
Peter Van Norden	
Bob Delegall	Dr. Tanner
Paul Picerni	
James Crittendon	Roberts
Linda Hoy	the day nurse
Ronald Meszaros	Lawrence Fedders, banker
Michael Cunningham	Taggert
Virgil Roberson	Robbins
Dour Mears	the mechanic
Rita Grauer	Nurse Parkins

Cast Notes

Barbara Horan was also featured in a 1985 movie *The Malibu Bikini Shop*.

John Sanderford had a recurring part as Frank Ryan in the series *Ryan's Hope*, a role earlier portrayed by Daniel Hugh Kelly.

Robert Sampson had minor roles in two early movies that featured Brian Keith, *5 Against the House* (1955) and *The Bamboo Prison* (1954).

The Details

Mark has dragged an unwilling Hardcastle out to the Orange County raceway. The purported reason was to meet Sammy O'Connell (another racing champ of his acquaintance, this time in the top fuel category). But when the two come face to face in Sammy's pit, they exchange insults and very nearly come to blows.

Hardcastle can't quite figure it all out, until Mark says he brought him along to keep him from pounding "Sidewinder" O'Connell's lights out. He says the guy stole his girl and married her.

The woman in question is Kiki Cutter, also a drag racing champion. The next race up is a head to head competition for the quarter-mile championship between O'Connell and his wife. In mid-race, Kiki's car careens out of control, slams into a side barrier, and disintegrates.

At the hospital, Mark rushes in. When he hears that only family can visit, he claims to be Kiki's husband. It's a shaky cover story with Sammy standing right down the hall. The two men confront each other again. Sammy announces that Kiki isn't expected to live. He stalks away. The doctor amends that to "the next twenty-four hours are critical". She has swelling on the brain. All that can be done is to watch and wait.

Mark sends Hardcastle home. He finds a doctor's coat, a pair of glasses, and a stethoscope, then returns to the ward during the night shift, and scams the nurse. He gets into Kiki's room. He tells the unconscious woman that he thinks he's forgiven her for what she did to him. Then he settles in for some watching and waiting.

He dozes off in a corner. Another man in a doctor's coat enters holding a syringe. Surprised by Mark, he drops it and runs from the room. Mark tackles him in the parking lot. They brawl. The man pulls a gun. He escapes to his car and attempts to run Mark down. Mark is unharmed, but the attacker's car crashes into another and loses its front license.

Back at the estate, Mark gives the details to Hardcastle. There's not much to go on but at least he got more than a partial plate. Mark thinks Kiki's crash was not an accident. Hardcastle says they don't have proof yet and warns Mark against further unauthorized evidence-gathering.

Mark, as usual, doesn't listen. That night he goes to O'Connell's workshop, scamming his way past the front gate as a pizza delivery guy. Inside, he finds evidence that Kiki's car was sabotaged. Midway through Mark's black bag job, the guard becomes suspicious and pulls an alarm. Mark eludes the security forces and races off into the night with the suspicious parts.

It's early morning at the estate and Hardcastle is waiting in the study. Mark's basic black ensemble and box of cold pizza are a dead match for the *modus operandi* described in the morning paper. He gets a serious chastisement from the judge, followed by an inquiry: did he come home with anything useful?

Mark shows him the nearly sawn-through tie rod that led to Kiki's crash. Mark suspects Sammy. Hardcastle suspects the motives behind his accusation. He tells Mark that the hospital called; Kiki is out of danger and will be released soon. He also tracked down the car that belongs to the lost plate. It's the property of an insurance broker.

Mark convinces the judge to let him bring Kiki back to the estate. At the hospital, Kiki is up and about, and still thinks her accident was an accident. Mark shows her the tie-rod and tells her the lab report shows the mysterious syringe contained cyanide.

At O'Connell's office, Jake, the midnight assassin, is renegotiating his contract. He's still willing to go after Kiki if the price is right. It's going to cost Sammy fifty thousand more.

Back at the estate, Kiki still doesn't believe Sammy is at the bottom of it. She explains that they were on the verge of a divorce. She says it was to be an amicable split with an even division of property. Hardcastle asks her if she knows Hal Jenkins, the insurance broker who owned the car that tried to run Mark down. The name means nothing to her.

Hardcastle goes off to make some arrangements by phone. Mark retreats to the poolside to brood. Kiki seeks him out there. They discuss what happened seven years earlier. Kiki lied to Mark, telling him she was pregnant and that he was the father. When he asked her to marry him, she parlayed his request into a matching one from Sammy, and then opted to marry him instead. It was a matter of furthering her career. Sammy was the hotter driver that season.

Just as she and Mark are about to kiss and possibly make up, Hardcastle arrives. He's checked into Jenkins, who looks legit, but he wants to ask him about the car in person.

The judge, Mark, and Kiki pay a visit to Jenkins' office. He claims to know nothing about how his car got into the hands of the would-be assassin. The three are barely out of his office before Jenkins is on the phone to Jake.

That night, at the estate, Jake sneaks onto the property, armed with a silenced handgun. Mark and Kiki are in the gatehouse. She's still not convinced that Sammy wants her dead. Mark offers her the bed, and says he'll take the couch. Kiki offers to share the bed. Mark initially declines.

In the main house, the judge spots the intruder closing in on the gatehouse. He grabs a gun and heads over there.

In the gatehouse, despite his earlier resolve, Mark is just about to kiss and do more than make up with Kiki. Hardcastle arrives. He motions Mark into the bed and withdraws into the shadows. As Jake enters, Hardcastle orders him to freeze. He doesn't. Bullets fly, Mark lunges, Jake escapes, and Mark follows.

Out on the driveway he catches up with his quarry. Jake turns and has him in his sights, but Hardcastle has caught up as well, and kills Jake with a single shot. At close range, and unmasked, the judge identifies Kiki's would-be killer as a known hit man.

The next day, a besuited Mark drops in on a lunch between Sammy and a couple of sports reporters. Sammy is saying there's nothing wrong between him and Kiki. Mark begs to differ. He drops barely veiled accusations that Sammy wants his wife dead.

While Mark and Sammy are trading insults, Hardcastle is exercising a search warrant for Jenkins' office. He finds Sammy O'Connell's name on one of the insurance broker's files. Jenkins is taken in for questioning.

Hardcastle picks up Mark outside the restaurant. Mark comments that somehow Sammy can still make him feel like a loser.

The judge shows him the O'Connell file and when they make the rounds of the list of addresses contained in it, they find a series of burnt out buildings. Hardcastle figures Jake was torching buildings for Jenkins and then the insurance payoffs were being laundered through O'Connell's racing operation. The divorce proceedings would have brought the income discrepancies to light, so Kiki had to die.

Hardcastle thinks they have enough to arrest O'Connell. Mark asks him to hold off for one more day. He wants a chance to challenge Sammy on the track. The judge agrees, though he has a few second thoughts when he finds out that

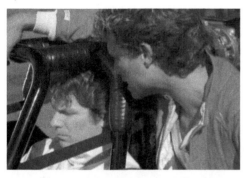

backing McCormick in a grudge match will cost him seventy-five thousand dollars.

After a quick visit to Hardcastle's banker, who is dubious, the car is rented and Kiki brings her influence to bear on the race promoters. The match is arranged. Sammy's not happy. He threatens Mark in the pit before the race. The strain is too much for Hardcastle, who goes off to sit in his truck and listen to the Dodgers. But it's all over a quarter-mile later, and Mark has finally defeated his nemesis.

Back in the pits, Hardcastle and the authorities arrive. O'Connell is arrested.

In the epilogue, it's morning at the estate and the judge finds Mark at the poolside. Hardcastle inquires as to the state of his love life. It's all over. He and Kiki are a thing of the past, McCormick proclaims solemnly. Scam in progress. Hardcastle has just enough time to extend his sympathies before Ms. Cutter comes out wearing a cheerful smile, one of Mark's shirts, and not much else.

The Context

Here's another dangerous, untrustworthy woman. Even though Kiki is the victim this time around, it's hard not to figure she made her own bed, as she used both Mark and Sammy to further her career. And Mark, despite saying repeatedly that he's not risking having his heart broken by her again, forgives all and barely hesitates before taking her up on an offer to renew their acquaintance.

For the second time, Hardcastle shoots and kills someone who is about to shoot McCormick. Once again it's done methodically and with no apparent second thoughts.

The Trivia

Glenn Frey's "The Heat is On" is used for both the opening drag racing montage, and for Mark's evasion of the security guys after his raid on O'Connell's garage. It went to number two on the charts and was featured in the movie *Beverly Hills Cop*.

You can pretty much figure Kiki was going to make it through her devastating accident with no brain damage because that was a real brand of racing helmet—Simpsons—that was prominently displayed in all the close up scenes.

Unlike Kathy Kasternack's glasses in "One of the Girls from Accounting", Mark's are the real bottle-bottom deal, appropriate for a myopic guy.

Season one Coyote footage is used for the getaway from O'Connell's garage.

When Jake comes in through the upstairs window of the gatehouse, we see an acoustic guitar propped up in the corner of the room, maybe for composing those country western ballads?

Ray Preston, the owner of Mark's loaner car, is a sprint racing champion who is still active.

The subject of champion women drag racers should bring to mind the indomitable Shirley Muldowney, whose first husband, Jack, was a fellow competitor. Muldowney was the subject of the 1983 movie *Heart Like a Wheel*, and was seriously injured in a crash in 1984. It was three years before she returned to racing.

Memorable Quotes

O'Connell: Hey, Skid, how about I say hello to the wife for you? Sure Kiki'd love to hear from you.

McCormick: Nah, she thinks about me enough. But you know that, don'tcha?

Kiki: Would you try to get past that male ego of yours?

McCormick: This has nothing to do with male ego. I am three times the man, the driver, and the lover that Sammy O'Connell ever hoped to be. It's got nothing to do with male ego!

Hardcastle: Come on, huh? (raises eyebrows)

McCormick: What's with you?

Hardcastle: Hey, man to man, huh...huh?

McCormick: Do you want some juice?

Hardcastle: When I was a kid, at least you had to ask them to marry you first. Well, things change...okay, I understand. Where's Kiki? She doesn't have to be embarrassed. I can understand.

McCormick: Judge, Kiki went home at ten o'clock last night.

Hardcastle: C'mon, I'm a modern guy here, huh? Huh?

McCormick: Well, sorry to disappoint Modern Guy...but, I never laid a glove on her.

Hardcastle: I thought she was the love of your life?

McCormick: The key word there is 'was'.

Hardcastle: So, that's it?

McCormick: That's it.

Hardcastle: Well, that the way she goes, huh? You save a girl's life and she just takes off down the road on you.

McCormick and Hardcastle: (in unison) Well...

The Yankee Clipper – premiered October 7, 1985

Written by	Patrick Hasburgh
Directed by	Sigmund Neufeld, Jr.
Second unit director	Gary Combs

Cast

Charles Rocket	Bill Bauer
Richard Herd	Colonel Joe Bartz
Joe Regalbuto	Peter Trigg
David Paymer	Patrick Burke
Vincent Guastaferro	Jack Steffan
Bennett Ohta	
Dana Lee	
Albert Leong	
Charles Parks	
Paul Eiding	
Arsenio "Sonny" Trinidad	

Cast Notes

Charles Rocket was a featured player in the 1980 season of *Saturday Night Live*. He lost that spot after uttering a word which violated network standards on the broadcast of Feb. 21, 1985. He died in 2005.

Richard Herd also played Arthur Huntley in the episode "Mr. Hardcastle Goes to Washington".

Joe Regalbuto had a supporting role in the series *Murphy Brown,* as Frank Fontana.

The Details

In the crowded back streets of Ho Chi Minh City, a tall westerner in ragged clothes taps his way using a white cane. He is observed by another man as he arrives at his destination. In an upstairs room he sheds his disguise of blindness and greets an old friend who calls him the Yankee Clipper. He gives the man fifty thousand American dollars. They talk lightly about the American's funeral plans.

As he departs, the man in the street follows him. The American hails a taxi and climbs in. The man who followed him tosses a grenade beneath the vehicle. It explodes.

Back at the estate, Hardcastle is entertaining an old friend, Colonel Joe Bartz, who is trying to convince him to make a speech at a fundraising dinner. Mark brings the refreshments and banters with the two for a while. Out front, a mail carrier arrives. It's a special delivery letter to Mark from the State Department. He opens it.

Back by the pool, the Colonel continues his campaign. It's not just a speech that Hardcastle is being solicited for. Bartz is raising money for a veterans' library, and he wants to put Hardcastle's name on it. The judge is reluctant.

Mark returns, looking depressed. The letter was notification of the death of Bill Bauer. Mark says he and Bill were best friends. Bauer had been MIA since 1975. Mark asks Bartz if he knew him—he was a lieutenant in the same regiment Bartz was with. The colonel says no, but offers his sympathy.

At dockside, Mark and a Marine honor guard receive Bauer's casket. The funeral is sparsely attended—three other men who were old school friends of both Mark and Bauer show up. Colonel Bartz is also there to pay his respects. Mark delivers the eulogy.

That evening the four young men, along with Bartz and Hardcastle, are gathered in the study at the estate. Patrick Burke is a TV producer who was going to be a playwright. He's touting his latest big hit. Jack Steffan is a slightly tipsy loan manager, who waxes nostalgic to blue collar guy, Peter Trigg. Mark seems to be the most withdrawn of the bunch. He sits, distractedly working through his recollections of Bauer.

Later that night, in the cemetery, a mysterious figure is digging at the gravesite. Mark, coming to pay his respects one last time, interrupts him. Mark tackles the intruder, only to discover it's Bill Bauer.

His anger turns to puzzlement—Bauer's been injured—and from there back to relief and astonishment. Bauer tells him there's sixteen million dollars in the coffin.

Mark gets worried. The two retire to a coffee shop and Bauer explains how he was left behind in Viet Nam during the evacuation while he was following orders to destroy millions in U.S. paper money.

Mark points out that the money's not his. Bauer says it doesn't belong to anyone else. He assumes Mark will go along with this but Mark informs him that things have changed.

The next morning, back at the estate, the three old friends are hanging out in the gatehouse when Mark returns,

announcing that Bauer is still alive. He's met with concerned disbelief, until Bauer enters a moment later.

Mark leaves Bauer with the others and takes his troubles to Hardcastle. When they return to the gatehouse, Bauer has already taken off. Jack, the nervous loan officer, is clearing out. Pat Burke is already on the phone to somebody, setting up a deal to make a movie from Bauer's story. Pete Trigg is ranting about political injustice. None of them know where Bauer went.

Burke can't hang around either. He's off to pitch his idea to the network. Pete's left behind to wait for developments. Mark and Hardcastle head back to the cemetery where they find Bauer watching a masked man dig up his grave. When Mark calls out to Bauer, the mystery man levels a gun and fires. Bauer goes down and appears dead. The intruder rushes away with a bag he retrieved from the grave. The guys chase after him but he flees in a van. Mark and the judge return to the spot where Bauer had been lying but find no sign of a body.

They return to the estate. In the study, Hardcastle makes phone calls. Bauer still hasn't been found. Peter Trigg, the only other one of Bauer's old *compadres* who's stuck around, rants about governmental conspiracies. When the judge calls Bauer a thief, Trigg says he's Robin Hood. Mark interrupts them both and says he's just worried about the guy and wants to find him. Trigg bows out. He says he has to head home; he has a family of his own to worry about.

Trigg departs in a cab. Mark and the judge head for the gatehouse where they find Bauer waiting for them. Bauer jokes and shows them his bullet-proof vest. Mark is understandably angry. Hardcastle starts to dial Bartz, to request some MPs. On hearing the colonel's name, Bauer says he was the one who assigned him to the money-burning detail and they were in on the scam together.

Now Mark sees a conspiracy. He says it's no coincidence that Bartz showed up with the library deal for Hardcastle just as Bauer was about to come home.

They go to Bartz's place and find him dead, wearing the mask they saw on the man who fled the cemetery with Bauer's loot. Hearing a vehicle pulling away, Mark rushes out and sees someone getting away in a van from the "Shanghai Noodle Factory". He's fired at. Hardcastle rushes out, too, but the murderer is gone.

When they go back inside, Bauer is also missing. A moment later they hear the Judge's truck peeling out.

Vehicle-less, they look up the Noodle Factory's address in a nearby phone booth. Hardcastle wants to call the police. Mark can't; Bauer is still his friend. Against Hardcastle's better judgment, they hitch a ride to the place. Mark is certain that Bauer will be there, too.

The factory looks deserted, but once they're inside, the guys are set upon by a group of men. It's a short fight and they're quickly overpowered. Peter Trigg is leading the attackers, along with the man who pitched the hand grenade back in Ho Chi Minh City.

Out front, Bauer is decked out as a health inspector. He scams his way in and then pulls a gun when an employee protests.

In the back, Trigg explains all. He's the one who arranged for Bauer to come home. He's in cahoots with an international band of 'freedom fighters'. He intends to use Bauer's ill-gotten gains for "the revolution".

Bill's not down with the plan. He bursts into the back room drawing on Trigg, who fires back. The brawl recommences. Trigg goes out the door. He careens away in the van. Mark pursues, clinging to the roof of the vehicle. Trigg tries to shake him and finally pulls a gun. Mark hangs on, disarms him, and eventually forces him to crash.

In the epilogue, back at the estate Mark is being chastised by a police lieutenant for not reporting Bauer's activities earlier. He passes it off as more Lone Rangering by the judge. Hardcastle appears, too late to hear himself catching the blame. He tells the police that Bauer's in the gatehouse. Alone. Mark, hearing this, hustles over there. Bauer's split, but he left a note saying he'll leave the Coyote somewhere convenient.

And the closing scene is Bauer, out on the open road, hotly pursued by a string of squad cars but still looking serenely confident.

The Context

Hasburgh is far from kind to his own profession, represented by his namesake, Patrick Burke. Here's a character who wanted to write plays, and now clears six hundred thousand a year producing a TV show about a neurosurgeon who fights crime in his spare time. No, you can't always get what you want, but it's nice to get a forty share.

As Burke said, it's all about male bonding this season, and we've got Mark's old buddies showing up out of nowhere. The most charming of the lot by far is Bauer himself. He's a scoundrel, to be sure, but a pleasantly insouciant one. Mark—a pretty good scam artist himself—looks like, well, Richie Cunningham next to his old pal Bill.

The slightly seamy Burke immediately sees a hit movie in Bauer's story; the Yankee Clipper is the perfect antihero. But Mark's moved past anti-heroism. As much as he likes Bauer and is reluctant to turn him in, right from the start he recognizes that the man is engaging in criminal behavior and he refuses to cooperate. And through it all—as Mark's old friends walk away, one by one—it's Hardcastle who stands by him, offering his usual gruff comfort, and finally agreeing to go after Bauer without involving the cops.

The Trivia

Yet another address for the estate appears in this episode. Bill Bauer sends his letter to Mark at "1 Gull's Way Road, Malibu, California"—no zip code.

Bauer tells his friend that in his next life, McCormick will be coming back as Richie Cunningham, a reference to the straight-arrow lead character of the sitcom *Happy Days* (or maybe an even slyer reference to the actor who portrayed Richie—Ron Howard—who went on to launch his directorial career with the movie *Grand Theft Auto*).

We only get a quick glimpse of the grenade in the opening sequence, but it appears to be an M67. Developed in the Vietnam era, it's a spherical fragmentation type with a kill radius of five meters and a four to five second fuse.

Mark says his draft classification was II-P (i.e., he was ineligible because he was in prison). In Vietnam era the "Class II" deferments were for essential occupations, agricultural workers, and students. There was no II-P.

Hardcastle wears his California Stars baseball cap again in this episode.

The arrival of Bauer's coffin is accompanied by Bob Seger's classic 1978 song "Still the Same", a slam-dunk perfect set of lyrics for Bauer and McCormick's relationship as it unfolds in this episode. The Rolling Stones' 1969 release, "You Can't Always Get What You Want", overlies the last part of the funeral scene.

Bauer, giving a précis of Mark's recent life, says Hardcastle retired from the Superior court in 1982. Oops. Well, the guy's been out of the loop.

The bad guys hang out at "The Shanghai Noodle Factory—since 1867". It's not from quite that far back, but Steve Winwood's group, Traffic, was founded in 1967, and "The Shanghai Noodle Factory" was their 1969 tribute to people with "impossible schemes" as "tiny cogs in one big machine". We are left to wonder if it's referencing Bauer, his friends, or the producer who's starting his third season of a pedal-to-the-metal weekly action show.

Memorable Quotes

Hardcastle: McCormick tells me you do that TV show, that what, what is it—'Doc-Star'?
Burke: 'Med-Star'.

Hardcastle: Yeah, 'Med-Star'.

Burke: Eight o'clock, seven central, channel three.

Hardcastle: Yeah, that's the one where the guy's that brain surgeon; then he goes out and catches bank robbers, you know, when he's not cutting people's heads open.

Burke: Thirty share. Top show for women eighteen to forty and men over fifty-five. Mark tells me you're a fan.

Hardcastle: Yeah, gee, tell me something. Why would a guy want to do that, though? I mean, most doctors I know only play golf.

Burke: You see, the scalpel is just a metaphor for a fast gun, Milt.

Hardcastle: Mmm.

Burke: Male bonding is the theme this season, Milt.

Hardcastle: Male bonding?

Burke: Yeah, I hope you'll watch the show. You're gonna love it.

Bauer: I'm the only one who knows about it.

McCormick: And me.

Bauer: I always thought that meant the same thing.

McCormick: It doesn't. I've changed, Bill.

Bauer: The only thing people can change is their clothes, man.

McCormick: Well, you haven't met my tailor.

Something's Going On On This Train
– premiered October 14, 1985

Written by	Lawrence Hertzog
Directed by	Tony Mordente
Second unit director	Gary Combs

Cast

Eugene Roche	Joe Murphy
Joseph Hacker	Carl Sharples/Charlie Carlson
P.J. Soles	Ellen Styner
Nancy Parsons	Elizabeth Foster
Ray Birk	Bill the steward
Richard Schaal	Bud
David Wiley	
Fred Tucker	the waiter
Linda Stewart	the ticket taker

Cast Notes

Eugene Roche had the recurring role of Luther Gillis on the series *Magnum, P.I.*, and over a hundred and twenty-five other guest or recurring roles. He died in 2004.

Nancy Parsons is another familiar character actress. She is probably best known for her role as Beulah Balbricker in the *Porky's* movies. She died in 2001.

P.J. Soles has several horror movies to her credit, including parts in *Carrie* and *Halloween*. She also starred with Bill Murray in the 1981 comedy *Stripes*.

Ray Birk, more often credited as Raye Birk, had recurring roles *The Wonder Years, Silk Stalkings,* and *Coach*.

The Details

In a darkened room, the black-gloved hand of fate addresses letters. One of them is to Milton C. Hardcastle. Fate appears to be a little cranky about something.

Morning, at the estate, and Mark's on the kitchen phone, getting the details of a blind date he's arranging with a girl named Tawny. The details agree with him. All he has to do is get the judge to the train on time.

In the study, Hardcastle explains that it's not just any old train to Chicago. This is the Casper Arrow, and he's been included on a list of distinguished jurists for a trip which will mark the train's fiftieth anniversary.

At the station, Mark and the judge board the train and look for his compartment. They encounter Joe Murphy, a coach. The steward announces five minutes till departure. Mark bids Hardcastle farewell, after receiving a few sage words of advice ("Take care of the house, no parties"), then makes an ill-timed visit to the facilities.

Moments before the train is to pull out, Mark realizes the door to the bathroom is stuck, with him on the inside. Hardcastle discovers an ominous message written in red lipstick on the mirror in his compartment: "Judge not, lest ye be judged."

Underway, the other passengers are gathered in a lounge car. Joe Murphy is telling a sports tale. Elizabeth Foster, Ellen Styner, and Carl Sharples are bored. Hardcastle walks in. Elizabeth is obviously pleased to see a new face. Confusion arises as it becomes apparent that the passengers all have invitations for different events. Elizabeth is there for a singles trip. Ellen is hoping for a mixer with movie industry types. Joe expected a gathering of sports fans. Carl says he's on board for a real estate event.

A boorish man named Bud walks in. Elizabeth departs, to look for the steward. Bud puts the moves on an unreceptive Ellen.

Elizabeth stops at the toilet, opening the door just as Mark finishes dismantling the inner part of the mechanism. She looks disapprovingly at his handiwork as he eases by her.

Hardcastle and the other guests confront the steward, who can't give them any answers. He tells them that the Casper Arrow hasn't been in operation for nineteen years. This train was specially chartered and he doesn't know by whom. The steward leaves them to discuss things. Hardcastle suspects it is some sort of promotion and is unconcerned. They're on a train; what can go wrong?

Mark walks in, smiles nervously at a startled Hardcastle, and takes a seat.

Evening, in the compartment, and Mark is trying to explain that it was really just an accident. Hardcastle asks him if he wrote the note on the mirror as well. He didn't. The judge is unexpectedly mild-mannered about McCormick's predicament. Mark is suspicious of all this good-natured tolerance. Hardcastle finally admits that he's glad Mark's along, because something is very wrong.

Elsewhere on the train, a black-gloved hand injects an item from the pastry tray with the contents of a syringe.

In the dining car, the seven passengers are finishing their meal. The dessert tray is presented. Mark takes two items, and is about to bite into a possibly fatal éclair, when Bud collapses to the floor. He's dead.

The judge, Mark, Joe, and the steward take the body back to the luggage car. Hardcastle sends the steward forward to have the engineer notify the police at their next stop. Bud's éclair smelled like almonds, and the judge suspects cyanide poisoning. Joe's panicky. Mark warns Hardcastle that the rest are liable to react badly to the news as well. Hardcastle insists they won't.

In the lounge car, accusations fly thick and fast. Elizabeth has McCormick pegged as the killer. Ellen suspects the undeniably odd steward. The real estate guy doesn't trust Hardcastle, and Joe wishes Bud had hung around longer so he could be a suspect.

The steward returns from the engineer. The radio has been tampered with. They won't arrive at the next station until the following day.

Morning, in Hardcastle's compartment, and Mark is climbing down from the top bunk. He's headed for the toilet. He refuses the judge's offer to escort him. An unknown assailant clobbers him in the hallway. He's dragged to the door and tossed off the train.

Dumped on a deserted slope, as the train recedes into the distance, Mark contemplates the ignominy of his second failed trip to the can in under twenty-four hours. He continues on with a few choice comments about the vagaries of his life as Tonto, but, by the end, he just wants to know how he can get back on that train.

On the Casper Arrow, Hardcastle is looking for his missing sidekick. A thorough search of the train reveals no clues as to what happened to him. The train finally pulls into the first stop—the station of Claremont. It's abandoned and the phone doesn't work. The engineer informs the passengers that they are two hundred miles off the main line and won't rejoin it for another seven hundred miles. He advises them that the fastest way to find help will be to get back on the train and keep going.

Out in the middle of nowhere, Mark comes across the camp of some tough-looking bikers. He pulls out all the stops, announcing he's a police officer and launching himself into a litany of all the violations on their bikes while surreptitiously collecting the ignition keys from all but one vehicle. A little sand tossed in the leader's face and he's off on the remaining bike, leaving the gang behind.

Back on the train, Hardcastle is collecting information from the other passengers, trying to figure out what's going on. Carl doesn't think it's going to help, but the judge says he refuses to just sit by when his friend is missing. After going over everyone's life histories, he has them search each others' cabins.

Meanwhile, Mark has finally encountered a police officer. Unfortunately his story of trains and murders sounds wildly improbably and he lost his wallet back at the biker's camp. Oh, and the bike he's on has a lot of structural violations.

The compartment search continues. Elizabeth Foster investigates Hardcastle's luggage with what appears to be slightly different motivations. Ellen encounters the steward, who tells her, sadly, that he is aware of her comments about him.

The train enters a tunnel, plunging everyone into darkness. When it emerges, Elizabeth is missing from the group. They find her in a compartment, dead.

Back on the road, the officer has decided to take McCormick in for questioning. On the spur of the moment, Mark distracts him and then steals his car. He catches up with the train, puts the squad car on cruise control, and steers it alongside the train while he climbs out. After he jumps onto the train, the abandoned squad car drifts into the trees, crashes, rolls, and bursts into flames.

Hardcastle, Joe, and Carl enter the lounge car where Mark is standing at the bar. He tells the judge he may need him to pull a couple of strings for him.

That night, Carl reads a note he's received from Hardcastle. It says he knows what happened in Van Nuys. In another compartment, Joe is reading a note as well.

Mark doesn't think the ruse will work, but Hardcastle tells him that's the only connection he's found—in 1970 everyone in the group was in the vicinity of Van Nuys. Mark doesn't have any better ideas, except that he's definitely not taking any more solo trips to the john. While they're out, a mysterious figure enters the compartment and deposits a scorpion under Hardcastle's covers.

It's morning, and Mark hears a knock on the compartment door. Joe's there, saying that the plan is for all of them to sit together in the lounge until they arrive in Lincoln. Mark turns and shouts at the judge, who doesn't respond.

A short while later, Hardcastle's been removed to the makeshift morgue. Mark is tearing his compartment apart, under the disapproving gaze of Joe and Carl. He tells them that Hardcastle had figured out what was going on and he must have written his conclusions down somewhere. It's soon apparent though, that there's nothing to be found. Joe tells him to do what he likes, but no one is to leave their compartments until they reach the station.

In the morgue car, someone approaches the most recently added body. Pulling back the sheet, he begins to search Hardcastle's pockets. The judge grasps the man's wrist. It's Carl. He says he was just looking for evidence. The others arrive. Hardcastle makes him hand over his wallet. He finds a picture of Ellen in it.

Carl has stepped back and now has a gun pointed at them all. He's raving about how they tried to destroy him. His name is Charlie Carlson. Ellen dumped him, he never made the team with Joe, and Hardcastle sentenced him to five years for armed robbery.

Joe charges him, but Charlie breaks free, slugs him, and slips out of the car, heading toward the engine. Mark goes after him, ducking the occasional bullet. The train is approaching the station in Lincoln. Charlie reaches the engineer and knocks him out. Mark arrives, and they struggle over the controls. He disarms and overpowers Charlie just in time to pull the brake and stop the train.

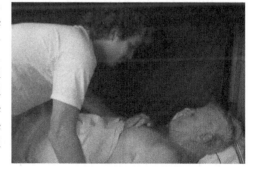

In the epilogue, the survivors of the last run of the Casper Arrow disembark and say their goodbyes. Ellen is assisted by Bill, the steward. She then reminds him he promised her a cold beer and "the best corned beef in Lincoln". They walk off together. Mark points out that if this were the movies, *he'd* have gotten the girl.

He suggests they fly home rather than wait for the next train. Just then a group of unhappy state police officers arrive, including the one who lost his car. Mark pivots, and encounters an even snarlier bunch of bikers. He gives the judge a pat on the shoulder, tells him he'll see him in three days, and bolts.

The Context

It's hard to say which guy has worse luck here. As Mark points out, it's always poisoned pastries when Hardcastle goes on vacation, but that's fairly ironic coming from a guy who can't even safely navigate a round trip to the bathroom.

There's lots of that kind of self-reflection in this episode. Mark longs for Sundays spent hanging out at Lumber World. He wishes this was a movie so *he'd* get the girl. And despite the fact that there is a higher than average body count in this one, the whole thing is played light.

But there are also a few moments here that touch on the human condition (besides Mark's soliloquy on a more ordinary life). Elizabeth came with expectations of finding friendship, or even love. Her attraction to Hardcastle seems amusing at first, but her scene in his compartment cuts to the heart of her loneliness and reveals the depth of her longing. And then a few moments later she's dead.

Bill, the steward, has no expectations at all. He's even mostly given up on being treated like a human being by the passengers. He makes one last effort to explain himself and against all expectations, he gets the girl.

The Trivia

There's a bathroom in the compartment, so what's with the trips down the hall?

When Hardcastle is found apparently dead he is shirtless. Later, in the morgue, he is wearing a shirt.

Memorable Quotes

Joe: Are you saying that someone popped this guy with a poisoned éclair? I thought his ticker stopped.

McCormick: Forget it, Joe. You're dealing with Calamity Milt here. We don't mess with headaches, indigestion, sprained ankles. You travel with Hardcastle you get poisoned pastries.

Joe: Well, we've gotta do something about this. I mean, I was looking forward to those Eggs Benedict tomorrow morning.

Carl: You're still worried about McCormick?
Hardcastle: It's a habit.

Joe (on Hardcastle's supposed death): You think you're the first guy that ever lost a friend? You were a team and, well, things happen. Hardcastle was just traded to a better league.
McCormick: What're you talking about? This isn't football, Joe. Someone *did* this and they're gonna do it again. What do you want me to do? Sit around and wait to get "traded"?

The Career Breaker – premiered October 28, 1985

Written by	Stephen J. Cannell
Directed by	Kim Manners
Second unit director	Gary Combs

Cast

Matt Clark	Sheriff Dale Cutler
Benjamin Slack	Dr. Grant Smith
Faith Ford	Tina Cutler
Randall "Tex" Cobb	Dennis "Corky" Conklyn
Bruce Wright	Lonnie Nichols
Rance Howard	Shaun Edwards
Kathryn Daley	Peg Foster
Mark Burke	

Cast Notes

Faith Ford was twenty-one when this episode was broadcast. She went on to have regular roles in *Murphy Brown*, *The Norm Show*, and *Faith and Hope*.

Randall "Tex" Cobb began his career as a professional boxer, but was best known for a brutal loss to Larry Holmes in 1982. His acting career has tended toward heavies. He graduated *magna cum laude* from Temple University in January of 2008.

Rance Howard (father of actor/director Ron Howard) has been an extraordinarily prolific character actor for over fifty years.

The Details

Welcome to Canary Creek, California, a small mountain town with an annual trout fishing competition. The judge is heading out from his motel room for a pleasant day on the river. He encounters Sheriff Cutler, who heard the judge was asking about an old plane wreck up in the creek. Cutler says the plane crashed a few years back and belonged to a local chicken farmer.

Out on the river, mild-mannered Dr. Smith is accosted by a local tough named Corky Conklyn who harasses him and steals a fish he caught. When Smith tries to take a stand, Corky gut punches him. Then Conklyn climbs in his truck, and drives away. Hardcastle pulls up just as he's leaving. He witnessed the whole thing from his spot on the other side of the river.

Smith doesn't want any trouble, but Hardcastle convinces him that he should press charges. They take their story to the sheriff, who believes them, but tells Smith to stay out of Corky's way until they can get the man in custody. A newly-emboldened Smith says he's not hiding anymore.

A short while later, the two men are unwinding at the local tavern when Corky walks in. He brags about his catch and Hardcastle asks him if it's the fish he stole from Smith. Corky gets feisty, but he's brought a knife to a gun fight and he's soon looking out from behind bars in the jail house.

Somewhere down in Mendocino County, Mark is swapping stories with two old friends. Hardcastle calls to announce he's lost the contest. Mark accepts an invitation to meet him up in Canary Creek the next morning.

After he hangs up, the judge finds an attractive and scantily-dressed girl in his bathroom. She calmly tells him she's about to frame him and then starts screaming. She runs out of the motel room as one of the sheriff's deputies pulls up. As the man arrests Hardcastle, he informs him that the girl is Tina Cutler, the sheriff's sixteen-year-old daughter.

Hardcastle ends up in the cell next to Corky's, who he suspects is the mastermind behind Tina's performance. The sheriff is summoned. With barely-controlled anger he tells his deputy to draw up the paperwork. He says he'll take Hardcastle to Twin Creeks in the morning for arraignment. Hardcastle's attempts to explain what really happened only anger the man further.

Mark and his two friends arrive at Canary Creek the next morning. Mark gets the news. As they're driving down to the jail, they encounter the sheriff heading the opposite way with his prisoner. Mark U-turns and follows them.

Hardcastle, handcuffed in the sheriff's cruiser, is still unsuccessfully trying to persuade Cutler that his daughter is mixed up with Corky. The sheriff, increasingly irate, pulls off the road and hauls him out of the car. He unfastens the handcuffs and tells Hardcastle to take off. The judge correctly surmises that he will be shot "trying to escape". He refuses to move. Cutler starts shooting. Mark arrives, interrupting the attempted murder.

Hardcastle gets back into the sheriff's car, after telling Mark to call the tenth district judge and let him know what's going on. Sheriff Cutler tells them to be on their way.

Mark's friends drop him off back at the Canary Creek Motel. He tells them to get lost and forget they even brought him there.

That evening, Mark visits a drugstore and gathers supplies. Returning to the motel room, he constructs an awkward-looking plaster cast for his right arm.

In the morning, he's out on the street, looking dirty, drunk, and disorderly. The deputy sheriff hauls him off to jail, where he proves at least as good at dissembling as Tina Cutler. He takes up residence in the cell next to the judge's and, while producing an endless stream of verbal distraction, strings a wire between the light socket and the bars of the cell.

Next the deputy is summoned to witness a full-blown attack of delirium tremens. When he goes to unlock the cell he gets an electrical shock, then finds himself staring at a gun when Mark smashes the cast that concealed it. Mark trades places with the deputy, frees a reluctant Hardcastle, and shorts out the radio system.

The sheriff returns to find his headquarters in chaos and his communications system down. He sets off in pursuit of the two escaped men, contacting the highway patrol and attempting to block the roads.

As they evade the local authorities in the patrol car Mark has stolen, a bemused

Hardcastle ponders the change in fortune that can happen in just two short days. They stop at a remote general store where the TV is on and they are the topic of the news. The clerk recognizes Hardcastle from the newscast photo and Mark's arguably suspicious behavior. They add the clerk's desk phone to their order and depart hastily. Hardcastle bewails his lost career ("forty years, right down the drain").

Off the road, the two sit, eating peanut butter and crackers and listening to the police scanner as the manhunt gets organized. The judge asks Mark why he staged the jail break and, besides that, what made him so sure he was busting out an innocent man? Mark reminds him about Vonna Westerlake, who was a free spirit girlfriend of McCormick's. Mark still hasn't forgiven Hardcastle for telling her to put some clothes on.

With that character reference to cheer him, Hardcastle goes back to pondering the Corky Conklyn angle. He's beginning to wonder why the sheriff would run such a risk to shoot him. A piece is missing. Mark asks him what else he talked to the sheriff about. Hardcastle remembers the plane wreck, and the name of the farmer who was said to have owned it.

The guys hike over to Shaun Edwards' chicken farm. Mark takes charge of the scam, claiming to be from the F.A.A. and wanting to close out the paperwork on the old crash. Edwards says he never owned a plane and doesn't know what they're talking about.

A search helicopter passes over. Things are getting hot. Hardcastle says he wants to have another look at the plane wreck. It's only a couple miles away. Mark starts to protest, then changes tacks, telling him he needs to get a drink of water first. Just water, he promises; there'll be no stolen cars.

A moment later he bursts through the shed door in an ancient but serviceable truck—at least technically not a car. They listen to the transistor radio they find inside and discover they are rapidly acquiring a more extensive list of charges.

Back in town, Sheriff Cutler is taking the afternoon off from the search. He's in his living room telling his daughter that he's going to dismantle the plane and haul it away. Tina is barely listening, more caught up in what she'll do with her portion of the loot. She's considering a career in Hollywood.

A short while later, Mark and the judge hear activity as they close in on the crash site. The sheriff and his deputy are out there, cutting the wreck into manageable pieces. Hardcastle figures the plane was used to smuggle drugs and Cutler has possession of them, too. He intends to follow the conspirators when they leave. He sends Mark to "borrow" a car.

The last of the pieces is stowed on a truck. Mark still hasn't returned with any transportation. Hardcastle starts out on foot to track the sheriff. He's losing ground when Mark finally pulls up on an ancient motorcycle with sidecar. The judge climbs aboard and they're off.

The sheriff has arrived at his destination—a large storage shed where a deal is about to go down between him and a drug lord. Mark and the judge get in close enough to hear that the deal may be going sour. Hardcastle tells McCormick to take a nearby tractor and knock down the wall with it. After a bit of grumbling, he does. The bad guys are pinned against the far wall but Sheriff Cutler escapes. Hardcastle shoots out the tire of his car; it flips and crashes. Hardcastle pulls the sheriff out. A few moments later the vehicle explodes in flames, taking the "borrowed" motorcycle with it.

In the epilogue, back at the Canary Creek Motel, the judge and Mark are catching the news. Hardcastle has been exonerated after a full confession from Tina Cutler. The reporter dwells glowingly on the judge's illustrious career but, to Mark's frustration, gets his accomplice's name wrong.

As they finish packing, Hardcastle alternates between a lecture on the importance of relying on the system, and a clumsy attempt at thanking Mark for saving his life. He finally backs out the door—and out of his argument—with a hastily uttered "You did all right…I appreciate it, much obliged." The door closes before he can hear Mark's reply, "For you, anytime."

The Context

There's a very nice subplot in the first part of this episode, with Hardcastle witnessing a crime and then behaving in a completely Hardcastlelike way. We get to see the contrast between what is normal behavior for him, and the far more common (and prudent) trouble avoidance that most of us engage in. Dr. Smith is right, Corky is dangerous and unpredictable, and it isn't worth fighting him for a fish, even a fish worth ten grand.

But in the proximity of Hardcastle, principles take hold, and once they're firmly rooted there's no turning back. Dr. Smith comes away from the encounter feeling better about himself—that he stood up for something this one time. He has a new sense of self-worth.

The other theme here is partnership. Hardcastle told Smith he'd back him up, and if Smith had been alone in the bar, he would have been a goner. When things go wrong later on, it's Hardcastle's turn to need back-up. Mark doesn't hesitate. He doesn't even need to be asked. He's witnessed personally just how high the stakes have gotten. Hardcastle talks nobly about the system, but he's always the first guy to jump in and deal with problems himself. Mark does exactly the same thing, only he has a different toolbox.

Hardcastle grumbles vociferously about Mark's techniques, but he adjusts to life on the lam pretty quickly for a formerly respected jurist. Once he's got a plot to unravel, and the chase is on, it's just a question of how fast Mark can borrow a car.

The Trivia

Mark plots a jailbreak to the tune of Bill Withers' "Lean on Me" which went to number one on the charts in the summer of 1972.

Edwards says his chickens have the highly contagious "myogravia toxicity". No such disorder exists. Mark's sage medical advice is to give them a couple of aspirin, and, in the immortal words of Harry Nilsson, "Put de lime in de coconut and drink 'em both up".

Memorable Quotes

Hardcastle: Ah, you're making a big mistake, kid.
McCormick: You think so, huh, Judge? Well, big mistakes have always been my specialty.

Hardcastle: Don't steal a car.
McCormick: I wouldn't steal a car. I'm rehabilitated.

Hardcastle: I thought you weren't gonna steal a car.
McCormick: It's a truck!

Hardcastle: You're gonna borrow something for us to ride in.
McCormick: You mean *steal*?
Hardcastle: Who said that? Stealing is when you don't intend to give it back and we're gonna give it back.

Do Not Go Gentle – premiered November 4, 1985

Written by	Patrick Hasburgh
Directed by	Bruce Kessler
Second unit director	Gary Combs

Cast

Allan Arbus	Dr. Charles Friedman
Sam Freed	Barry Jackson
Joe Santos	Frank Harper
Rand Holland	
David Selburg	Ned Phillips, mobile phone salesman
Gary Eimiller	Pirate #1
Stephen Meadows	Pirate#2 (calls Hardcastle "pops")
Ronald Meszaros	Lawrence Fedders, banker
Jack Axelrod	Mel

Cast Notes

Allan Arbus has often been cast as a physician in his TV guest appearances. Most memorably he had the recurring role of psychiatrist Sidney Freedman on the series *M*A*S*H*.

Gary Eimiller also had role in Patrick Hasburgh's movie *Aspen Extreme*.

Ronald Meszaros returns as Hardcastle's beleaguered banker, Lawrence Fedders. Last time, in "Faster Heart", it was the seventy-five thousand dollar withdrawal for a race car ("I hope it's a fast one."). This time it's a cool million for a yacht.

The Details

It's morning at the estate, and a grouchy Hardcastle is leaving for his annual physical. Of course he has to take a certain amount of good-natured gibing from McCormick, but he's eventually underway for a day of walking on treadmills and getting poked for blood.

That evening Mark gets a call from him. He's staying overnight at the hospital. He says nothing's wrong, just a few more tests. After he hangs up, Mark looks worried.

It's morning, and the judge is sitting in Dr. Charlie Friedman's office. The two have known each other a long time, but that doesn't make it any easier for Friedman to break the news. Hardcastle's blood tests indicate that he has a terminal illness with only six months left to live.

Later that day, Mark finds the judge down on the beach, lighting up a pipe. Hardcastle tells him everything went fine. He shows him how to skip stones on the water and then wanders off, leaving McCormick staring in concerned confusion.

At dinner, Mark is increasingly puzzled. Hardcastle is perfectly pleasant, even about being served corned beef and cabbage—not his favorite. He's been staring at a plastic rose. He refuses to rise to minor goading from McCormick, who finally decides it's a plot by the judge to get even with him for not spreading the peat moss—he's being tortured with kindness. Hardcastle ignores all of these ramblings, too, but he is paying attention to a story on the news. Later that evening, Mark overhears Hardcastle in the study, phoning a local hospital and offering to anonymously pay the bills of the burn victim who was the subject of the newscast.

The next morning, Mark visits Dr. Friedman at the hospital. He thinks Hardcastle's cracking up. Friedman assures him that the judge is not having a nervous breakdown. Mark asks him what *is* wrong with his friend. Friedman tells him to ask Hardcastle. Mark says he'll never get the story from the judge; he's old-school and would take personal information to his grave.

It was intended as a casual remark, but Friedman's solemn expression, and his repeated admonitions to ask the judge, leave Mark standing stunned in the hospital hallway.

He returns to the estate. It's pandemonium there, with contractors out working on the grounds. A mobile phone salesman accosts Mark as he arrives. The judge has purchased three units. Mark pushes him aside and heads into the house.

Hardcastle's in the study, surrounded by new electronic equipment. He babbles about the tennis court he's having installed and reads from the brochure of the elaborate stereo system. Mark looks stern. He says he spoke to Dr. Friedman. Hardcastle's demeanor changes abruptly. He turns away. Mark asks him what's going on. The judge responds euphemistically at first but, at Mark's further prodding, finally admits that he is dying.

A few nights later, they're seated in a fancy restaurant. Hardcastle appears to be relishing it. Mark looks unhappy and uncomfortable. He obviously has no appetite and he finally admits he feels like he's coming apart. Hardcastle, on the other hand, seems perfectly together. He can even admit he's dying. He describes it as seeing the finish line at the end of a long race. He adds that it won't hurt for him to do a few good deeds and be a nicer person.

He also tells McCormick that he has a legacy—a monetary one—and that he intends to leave it to him. Mark is incensed. He refuses to even discuss Hardcastle's bequest. He angrily attacks the judge's placid acceptance of his fate. He wants the old Hardcastle back. He asks him to fight to stay alive. He says they can pack six years of life into six months but he won't stay and watch the judge give up.

The judge's carefully arranged façade collapses under this onslaught. He admits he's scared.

It's morning at the marina. Hardcastle has just handed over a bank draft to Barry Jackson for the purchase of a handsome yacht, *The Fury*. It's fitted out and ready to make sail. Mark looks pleased. After they leave the office, Barry makes a call. He says to the man on the other end that if they do things right, no one will ever realize the boat left the dock.

On board *The Fury*, Captain Hardcastle and First Mate McCormick settle into a sailing montage. The judge looks like a new man. He regales Mark with tales of the horse latitudes and the doldrums as they plan their eighteen-day voyage to Tahiti.

Meanwhile, a fast powerboat is stalking them on its sonar. It's Barry's pirates, out to recapture *The Fury*. As they close with Hardcastle's boat, the judge greets them warmly. Mark is sent below for beers. The visitors board, along with their M-16.

Mark and Hardcastle are set adrift in a raft as the pirates sail off in the yacht. Hardcastle has accepted his loss and chastises McCormick for fighting back. The judge is also reconciled to rowing back to shore.

Sixty-three hours later, in the study at the estate, Hardcastle is pondering why the construction people have stopped work on his tennis court. He's otherwise still unruffled by all the downturns of the past few days. Mark notices a blinking light on the answering machine. It's Dr. Friedman's office requesting Hardcastle to contact them.

Hardcastle visits Friedman again. The doctor tells him there was a mix-up in the blood work. He has no fatal blood disorder. Hardcastle doesn't pause to rejoice; he barrels out of the building and climbs into the waiting Coyote. He grouchily tells Mark he's going to live another fifty years. Mark has very little time for rejoicing, either, as the judge hollers at him to get them to the police station. He wants the guys who stole his boat.

In Frank Harper's office, the lieutenant outlines all the steps he's taken since the judge filed his theft report the day before. Hardcastle isn't satisfied. Frank suggests he and Mark check out some of the marinas.

They spend the next two days, walking the docks and staring at boats (well, not *just* boats—there are a few lithesome women in bikinis, too). Hardcastle finally spots his yacht, edging into a slip. He sends Mark to call Frank while he confronts the boat's current occupants.

Harper arrives to find Hardcastle demanding arrests. Harper tries to explain that the boat belongs to Senator Delaplant, and the guy Hardcastle is waving his gun at is a senatorial aide. The senator himself appears from down below. The judge tells him he voted for him and compliments his taste in yachts.

A cranky Hardcastle pursues his one remaining lead, Barry Jackson. He finds the man's former office is now a bait shop. No one there has heard of Jackson. Hardcastle calls his banker, attempting to stop payment on the check. He is advised the money is already "in escrow" for payment at the Newport branch that afternoon.

The judge and Mark have the bank branch staked out. Jackson arrives. Hardcastle follows him in while Mark keeps watch on the man's driver. Inside, Frank is under-cover as a bank officer. Jackson flees after tussling with both Frank and the judge.

He's halted on the front steps. Mark blocks his accomplices with the truck, but one escapes on foot toward a handy marina. Mark chases. It's jet skis this time, and Mark finally gets close enough to tackle the guy. He hauls him in to a boat launch ramp and the waiting police.

In the epilogue, Mark has mastered the art of stone skipping, but the judge crabs that the peat moss still hasn't gotten spread. He's cancelled the tennis court, the stereo and the mobile phones are going back, and Mark's pretty sure he's glad Hardcastle isn't dying.

The Context

Hardcastle has relatives—a niece, a sister we never meet, a sister-in-law, two aunts, and an annoying brother who we'll soon see. Yet when the hammer comes down, Mark's the one who functions as next-of-kin. Both his concern, and Hardcastle's decision to leave his legacy to him, are actions consistent with a father-son relationship.

Once again, as in "She Ain't Deep but She Sure Runs Fast", it takes the threat of death to underline the situation, but this time it's not a middle-of-the-night impromptu bit of self-analysis, muttered out loud, but a bold-faced state-ment made over a plate of hot roast duck salad.

The crime is relatively secondary here; it doesn't even start to occur until about halfway through the episode and there are essentially *no* car chases, though Mark pulls up far enough to stop the pirates' getaway car from eluding the police, and there's a bit of jet ski action almost as an afterthought.

The Trivia

The title, of course, is from the Dylan Thomas poem. Its final verse runs:

"And you, my father, there on the sad height,
Curse, bless me now with your fierce tears, I pray.
Do not go gentle into that good night.
Rage, rage against the dying of the light."

According to Dr. Friedman's calculations, Hardcastle is sixty-four in this episode. He would therefore have retired at about sixty-two. Of course Friedman got the blood test results wrong, too.

The Fury sets sail to the Beach Boys version of the folk song "The Sloop John B." which was released in 1966 and topped at number three on the charts.

The song Hardcastle sings right before the pirates arrive is "Strike Up the Band, Here Comes a Sailor", written by Andrew Sterling and Charles Ward, and published in 1900. It contains the immortal lyrics, "*Strike up the band, here comes a sailor, Cash in his hand, just off a whaler, Stand in a row, don't let him go, Jack's a cinch but every inch a sailor.*"

Marina Del Rey is featured in the "searching for the boat" montage.

Newport Beach, where the money is sent, is about eighteen miles south of Long Beach, roughly sixty miles south of Malibu. It's also the location to which Hardcastle wanted the surfers to decamp in "Surprise on Seagull Beach".

Memorable Quotes

McCormick: It's about Milton Hardcastle, doctor.
Friedman: Oh, I thought I recognized the name. He told me about you.
McCormick: Yeah, well, he's…he's my best friend. And, I'm really worried about him.
Friedman: Oh?
McCormick: Yeah, I think he's cracking up.
Friedman: Why do you think that?
McCormick: Because he's being very nice.

Hardcastle: Oh, you're getting a big kick out of this, aren't you?
McCormick: What I'm getting a kick out of is poking a hole in another cliché.
Hardcastle: What cliché?
McCormick: That dying can change a guy, Judge. Losing money, maybe. Dying? Nah.

Games People Play – premiered November 11, 1985

Teleplay by	Carol Mendelsohn and Larry Forrester
Story by	Tony Michelman and Scott J. Schneid
Directed by	Peter Kiwitt

Cast

Bill Macy	Art Healy
Herbert Edelman	Harry Baxter
Tom Kennedy	Bryce Benson
Molly Cheek	Diane Templeton
Joseph Brutsman	J. Walter Ruxton
Joe Santos	Frank Harper
Robert Schuch	
Rob Monroe	the stage manager
Jean Vander Pyl	Agnes O'Toole

Cast Notes

Bill Macy is best known for his role as the husband of the title character in the series *Maude*.

Herbert Edelman had recurring roles on *Murder, She Wrote* (Lieutenant Artie Gelber), and *The Golden Girls* (Stan Zbornak). He died in 1996.

Tom Kennedy was a ubiquitous game show host with credits that include *Password, The Price is Right,* and *Name That Tune.*

Molly Cheek played McCormick's ex-girlfriend in the episode "Never My Love".

Joseph Brutsman had a recurring role on the series *Scarecrow and Mrs. King* as Efraim Beaman.

Jean Vander Pyl provided the voices for Wilma and Pebbles on the Hanna-Barbera cartoon show *The Flinstones.*

The Details

Art Healy and Harry Baxter, veteran game show producers, are on the carpet in front of J. Walter Ruxton, a TV executive who's young enough to be their grandson. They have four minutes to save their show, *Trivia Master*, which is currently the lowest-rated game show nationally. Harry wings it, proposing that they raise the prize to one million dollars. Ruxton bites.

Outside the office, Healy points out to his partner that they don't have a million to give away. Baxter reminds him that even when things are left to chance,

people rarely win the big prizes on their shows, and he has no intention of leaving things to chance this time. All they need now is a loser.

Back at the estate, there's at least one person who's a fan of *Trivia Master*. Mark arrives just as Agnes O'Toole is about to go for the big prize and Hardcastle is glued to the set. Mark says anybody could do it—you even get to pick your own topic on that show. Hardcastle points out you have to be bubbly. Mark has twenty dollars that says he can bubble and answer questions about racing at the same time.

Not long after, Mark is being interviewed by Diane Templeton who works for the show. Harry likes what he sees. He's already got a nickname for McCormick—The San Quentin Kid. Art isn't convinced.

McCormick collects on his twenty-dollar bet, but he has high hopes for more than that. He wants to win the whole ball of wax on the new *One Million Dollar Trivia Master*. Hardcastle counsels him to quit if he gets even one answer right.

Back at the office, Art is packing his things. Harry explains to him that the fix is in for McCormick. At the estate, a phony utility man is planting a bug in the study.

It's almost show time at the TV studio. Hardcastle still thinks Mark should quit as soon as he's won anything at all. As the lights come up, host Bryce Benson takes the stage. A wooden and nervous Mark is soon brought out to join him. In the player's circle, Mark nails the first question. Out in the audience, Hardcastle is signaling his earlier intentions. Mark ignores him. He perseveres, and makes it successfully to the end of round one—with ten thousand dollars won. When Benson asks him if he'll return for the next round, risking everything he's won so far, it's Hardcastle who's shouting "Go for it!" from the audience.

It's morning at the Gull's Way poolside a few days later. Mark is reading his reviews out loud from a TV fan magazine. Hardcastle looks frowningly on the whole thing. Mark tells him this time he's not stopping short. He's going to go all the way, even if he loses everything. Hardcastle pulls out a book of racing statistics and starts to quiz him.

In Harry and Art's office, the two men listen to a tape made using the bugs at the estate. Art's still fretting. They've fired their research company. He wants to know what Diane Templeton will think when she finds out they're writing their own questions. Harry says he'll take care of it if she causes a problem.

Unbeknownst to the two, Diane enters the outer office. She overhears Mark's and Hardcastle's voices on the tape. As she turns to leave, she knocks over an award. Harry hurries to the door and sees her departing.

On the stage of the game show, Mark's now survived eight and a half rounds and won eighty-five thousand dollars. As the bonus question is asked, Hardcastle looks down at his notes—it's another one he quizzed Mark on at home.

Walking to the car after the show, Mark has definitely achieved bubbly. He's talking about his future in television, or maybe it's not too late to go back to school since he's such a whiz at studying. Hardcastle tells him maybe it's not that he knows all the answers, but more like he somehow knows all the right questions.

Diane Templeton has suspicions of her own. She takes her concerns to Bryce Benson. She talks about F.C.C. regulations. He tells her she's watching too many detective shows and says he'll talk to the guys and see what's going on. Harry overhears her thanking Bryce for looking into things.

Back at the estate, Hardcastle's made some phone calls. He tells Mark that Baxter and Healy are up against the wall, with only one game show still on the air and no chance of having a million dollars in capital. Mark's unconvinced.

That night, at the station, Diane is doing some investigating of her own. She finds a tape of Hardcastle quizzing Mark. She puts it in an envelope and writes Mark's name on it.

She is observed as she leaves via a deserted sound stage. Someone arranges an accident, spilling water and then adding a live electrical wire. Diane is killed.

The next morning, Lieutenant Harper goes over the details at the scene. It looks like an accident. Milt expresses some doubts about the show. Franks asks him if his real worry is that Mark is getting too independent.

Back at the estate, Mark is attacking a hedge with unusual vigor. Hardcastle broaches the subject of breakfast. McCormick's not in the mood. He's convinced Diane's death was no accident. He says he picked a lousy time to try and go all the way on something. Hardcastle points out there's still one thing they can accomplish.

Back at their office, Art Healy has piled the tapes in a metal waste bin and sets them on fire. He has the final question written down and his only hope is that it will stump McCormick.

On the stage, it's the last regular round. Mark is forging ahead. Hardcastle takes advantage of the distraction and sneaks back to the offices. He's intercepted by a security guard who bewails people's disrespect for law and order and "do not enter" signs. As soon as the guard leaves, Hardcastle sneaks in again. In Diane's office, he finds the envelope with Mark's name on it. He plays the tape— it's Mark giving him a hard time between questions back at the estate. He returns to his seat just in time to hear Mark correctly answer the final question of round ten and win the right to return for the final million-dollar question round.

Backstage, Healy accuses Baxter of murdering Diane. Baxter denies it. Bryce Benson intrudes on the argument, taking credit for Diane's murder. Benson's confession turns into a rant against cop shows and sitcoms. "We need more game shows," he announces, as he tells the other two that they're all on the same team.

Back at the estate, Hardcastle has gathered up all the bugs and played the tape for McCormick. Harper calls. He wants Mark to show up at the station for the final taping so Baxter and Healy won't panic and bolt.

Healy and Baxter are already past panicking. They're heading out the door when Harper and Hardcastle arrive, ready to arrest them for the murder. They put the blame on Benson.

Down on the soundstage, it's show time. Mark is ushered out and Benson asks him if he's ready to go for the one million. As the police are moving in, Mark tells him it's all over.

Benson tries to keep up appearances. He launches into an upbeat defense of game shows as the audience and crew gradually realize that something is very wrong. Facing only stony silence, Benson turns and runs.

Hardcastle gives the high sign and Mark—looking a little put-upon—takes off, chasing Benson. He catches up with him on the catwalk. They struggle. Benson pulls out a gun and fires. Mark throws a final punch that sends Benson stumbling back through a railing and down to the stage far below.

As the loose ends are tidied up, Frank takes charge of the envelope containing the final million-dollar question before Mark can open it. Mark acquiesces, saying he understands completely. It's evidence. He gives Frank a hearty and distracting handshake. After the other two have walked off, he opens the purloined envelope and, with a mixture of delight and regret, realizes this time he would have made it all the way.

In the epilogue, back at the estate piles of consolation prizes are being unloaded in front of the gatehouse—a video camera, camping equipment, fruit pies, and, of course, a year's supply of fabric softener. Mark's in a generous mood. Milt gets the puppy chow, and a puppy to help him eat it.

The Context

It's another episode about show business, with some sideward comments about all those nasty detective shows that are such a bad influence. And poor Harry and Art, having to kowtow to a TV executive who's barely old enough to shave. They beg for just a little more time to find their audience. He gives them four minutes. TV is like that.

There are some wonderful moments of self-reference here, with Mark wondering if he can parlay his game show success into a series (*"McCormick...and Hardcastle"*) and then even throwing out a casual comment about going to law school—intentional foreshadowing or just a coincidence?

Meanwhile, it's one more near-miss at success for McCormick. This is the fourth one, and just as in the three previous occasions ("Hotshoes", "You and the Horse You Rode in On", and "You Don't Hear the One That Gets You") he's brought low by a criminal enterprise. As usual, Hardcastle has had to step in and point out that something is not quite right about the set-up, but this time even Harper thinks the guy is a little quick to smell a rat. More foreshadowing—Harper wonders what the judge is going to do when Mark finally moves on.

The final, unrigged question, and Mark's pressing need to see it, is an interesting sidelight into the character. He impulsively steals it back, while simultaneously talking about the importance of legal procedure. It's not worth a nickel to him anymore, but he really just has to find out if he would have gotten it right. No one will ever know but him.

The Trivia

KCED is a college radio station in Centralia, Washington.

The quiz show scandals of 1958 involved several programs, the best known of which was *The $64,000 Question*. This was a progressive prize contest in which a single contestant answered questions in their stated area of expertise (Dr. Joyce Brothers had a phenomenal run, in 1955, on the subject of boxing). The contestants staked everything on each successive question but could claim their money and quit at any level.

Only two months after this episode aired, a syndicated game show titled *The $1,000,000 Chance of a Lifetime* premiered. It lasted only nine months. The "one million" in prize money was a twenty-five year annuity. The first show to offer a cash prize of that magnitude was *Who Wants to Be a Millionaire?* which had its first top prize winner in November of 1999.

In this episode, McCormick's allowance is up to $130 a week.

This episode has no car chases, indeed, no vehicular chases of any sort whatsoever.

Memorable Quotes

Hardcastle: Listen, forget about it because even if you did know all the answers, you're not the right type.

McCormick: What do you mean, I'm not the right type?

Hardcastle: You're not bubbly, McCormick. You're a lot of things, but bubbly is not one of them.

McCormick: I've got twenty bucks that says I can bubble like champagne.

McCormick: Maybe they'll give me my own show—*McCormick*. Huh? Don't worry, you can co-star. A crusty old curmudgeon judge and a kid from San Quentin go out and round up the bad guys every week, huh?

Hardcastle: Great idea.

McCormick: I never knew studying could be so much fun. If I had, I woulda, I woulda went to law school. Heck, I'm still young. Maybe I'll still go.

Hardcastle: Mm-hmm.

McCormick: Mark McCormick, Esquire. *Judge* Mark McCormick.

Strangle Hold – premiered November 18, 1985

Written by	Marianne Clarkson
Directed by	Michael Switzer
Second unit director	Gary Combs

Cast

Tom Bower	Marty Torrance
Ernie Sabella	Clyde Whitley
Kit Fredericks	Kate Murphy
Dar Langlois	Denise
Deborah Rennard	Lucy
John Considine	Eric
Joe Santos	Lieutenant Frank Harper
Sharon Barr	Nancy Mack
Faith Minton	The Butterfly/Ms. Tallafero
Charli Haynes	Ferocious Fritzi
Debi Pelletier	Killer Tomato
Deanna Booher	Queen Kong

Cast Notes

Tom Bower is a member of the Board of Directors of SAG and has over 125 movie and television credits.

Kit Fredericks also had a minor role in a 1985 episode of *The A-Team* ("Blood, Sweat and Cheers") that costarred Wings Hauser (who also starred in "You Don't Hear the One That Gets You") and Stuart Whitman (who appeared in "Round Up the Old Gang")

Dar Langlois was "Dar the Star" on the short-lived 1989 TV program *RollerGames*.

Deborah Rennard played J.R. Ewing's secretary in the series *Dallas*. She is the wife of Oscar winning writer/producer/director Paul Haggis.

Faith Minton is an actress and stuntwoman who was also cast as a wrestler on an episode of *Roseanne*. She's 6'1" tall and played a Klingon warrioress in an episode of *Star Trek: The Next Generation*.

The Details

At the Sixth Street Gym, Marty Torrance and his henchman, Clyde, look over the prospects. He manages female wrestlers. One of his girls, Kate Murphy, asks to speak to him. In his back office, she tells him she's worried. It's been three weeks since Marty sent her friend, Penny, off to Rome for a modeling job and she hasn't been heard from since. Marty offers vague reassurances, trying to brush her off. When Kate stands her ground, insisting on a phone number for Penny, she's given the bum's rush.

At the estate, Mark's on his back, under the kitchen sink, doing an emergency sockectomy. The phone rings. He hustles to pick it up when Hardcastle tells him it's someone asking for "Wheels". Kate's on the other end of the line. She tells Mark she may be in a little trouble but, of course, she doesn't want to tell him about it over the phone. She asks him to meet her that night at the auditorium.

After he hangs up, Mark tells Hardcastle about her, particularly about how she never caught any breaks. Hardcastle tells him to go have a good time. Mark leans on him to come along. He thinks Kate might be in some sort of trouble, and it's the sidekick's turn to ask for a favor. The judge succumbs to a heavy dose of guilt.

That evening, in the locker room of the auditorium, Katy's in costume. Marty enters, offers more reassurances about the missing Penny, and tells Kate they'll call her from his office after the match. He has the team doctor give her "a vitamin shot".

In the balcony, Mark is puzzling over the venue. What's Kate doing at a women's wrestling show? They ask

around and a six-foot-tall butterfly gives them directions to the locker room.

It's a happy reunion for Mark and Katy, but he says she doesn't need to be doing this. She's a dancer. She could have asked him for help. Katy is fiercely independent, though, and would rather wrestle than take a handout. She tells them about her missing friend, but then says she was probably worried for nothing.

The guys stick around for the match. It's Katy versus the butterfly they met earlier. Down in the ring, Katy's in a clinch and looking a little sickly. Her opponent quietly asks her if she's okay and they agree on their next move. Katy takes a hard fall and doesn't get up.

As the ref checks her, Mark's on his feet and enters the ring. The butterfly is sobbing and begging her to get up. Kate is dead.

In the aftermath of the death, Frank Harper is investigating. He says the preliminary evidence points to heart failure. Mark is adamant. There was nothing wrong with Kate's heart and she said she was in trouble. Hardcastle asks about Marty Torrance. He has a record of petty crime. Frank still isn't buying that it was a murder, but says he'll look into it.

The next morning, at the estate, Hardcastle finds Mark tearing into his files looking for information about Torrance. He's distraught. Hardcastle tells him he has to get all that out of his system before he can start looking for answers about what happened. He also says he's willing to listen if Mark wants to talk. They go for a walk on the beach, with Mark explaining who Katy was—determined, optimistic, indomitable, and kind.

Later that day, at the police station, Frank tells them that Katy's death was the result of adrenalin. He says they still can't prove that it was administered to her. Mark becomes increasingly angry and finally walks out. Frank warns Milt to keep him under control.

Mark's waiting outside the station. He apologizes for going off on Frank. Hardcastle thinks they ought to start their own investigation with Marty Tor-

rance, but he wants to put someone on the inside. Mark can't pass the physical but Hardcastle has another prospect.

They go to a small-time night club and meet a chanteuse, Lucy Parmiter, who's an old friend of Hardcastle's. She's willing to help out and she's found a friend who'll pitch in as well.

In Marty Torrance's office, he's getting chewed out by an upper echelon bad guy named Eric. Penny is

dead and Marty still owes Eric's overseas customers ten girls. Torrance offers what he has on hand. Eric insists on better quality material.

Mark and Milt bring Lucy and her friend Denise to the auditorium for a show. They watch Nancy Mack defeat Ferocious Fritzie, after which Nancy issues a general challenge to the crowd. Denise, who's been watching intently, takes her up on it, and pins her in under twenty seconds.

Back in the locker room, after the impromptu match, Nancy is pushed around by her ex-boyfriend, Marty. He tells her she has one more match and she'll be taking the fall in that one.

A short while later, Hardcastle and his entourage, led by a leather-jacketed and sunglasses-wearing McCormick, confront Torrance in his office. The judge is "John Milton" and Mark's his bodyguard. The girls are his and he calls them "White Lightning and Sweet Lucy". He wants matches. Torrance reluctantly agrees. After Team Hardcastle leaves, Eric tells Torrance he wants Lucy.

In the back of his limo, Marty plots with a worried Clyde. If they don't get Lucy, Eric will kill them.

Poolside, at the estate, Lucy tells the guys that she has a date with Marty. He's taking her to a fancy restaurant.

That night, Marty wines and dines Lucy. She tells him she wants to be a singer and an actress. She's wrestling just to make a living. He talks about his clubs, and says they're mostly overseas. She excuses herself and goes to make a promised phone call to Hardcastle. One of Marty's henchmen interrupts her before she can finish dialing.

Back at the auditorium, Lucy has failed to show for her first match. The guys and Denise haven't been able to find her.

At Torrance's place, Lucy's getting an injection to keep her quiet for the plane ride.

At the Sixth Street Gym, Mark, Denise, and the judge search Torrance's office. Denise tells them the locker room gossip about Marty wanting Nancy Mack out. They find her in the locker room at the auditorium, drinking hard. She tells them Marty's a bum and he sells girls. She gives them the address of his beach house in Malibu.

They go there. It's deserted, but they find an empty syringe. They also find a notepad with traces of writing from the previous page—it says "Forest Mill, gate eight".

At the Forest Mill Airport, Eric and Marty have a drugged Lucy in a wheelchair. They're wheeling her out to the plane when Mark intercepts. He's briefly delayed by a couple of Marty's girls, but Denise helps him out and he's freed to tackle Marty and then Eric.

In an unusually somber epilogue, it's early morning at the estate. Mark stands at the edge of the lawn, looking out to sea. Hardcastle comes outside, asking him if he's okay. He's not; he's still thinking about Kate. He tells the judge how he met her. She showed up one day at San Quentin asking if there was anyone who needed a visitor. He says no one visited him in prison, and the day she appeared had been the day he thought he'd finally crack. Hardcastle gives him a pat on the shoulder and leaves him, still staring at the water.

The Context

Ex-girlfriends abound in the Hardcastle and McCormick universe, though it's not clear if Katy really fits the mold. But she can't be just his "best friend"; that was Flip Johnson, or Bill Bauer—or maybe Hardcastle himself. Anyway, it doesn't seem to be so much a romantic entanglement as an intermittent mutual support system. As it is, with McCormick not even three years out after a two-year sentence, and only having had six months on his own before falling in with Hardcastle, there hardly seems to have been enough time for as much back story as Mark is claiming. We have to give the writer and actors credit; they do their best to put some depth in the relationship. Even the supporting players (particularly Faith Minton's Butterfly) help to raise it above the "Katie we hardly knew ye" level.

There are some interesting and likable women in this one. Foremost is Kate herself, who'll do any work, as long as it's honest, in order to preserve her independence, and the Butterfly, who looks like someone you wouldn't want to run into in a dark alley, but who grieves touchingly for Katy's death. Then there's Denise, who takes to hand-to-hand combat like a duck to water.

Mark has a regrettable attack of antique civility when he's attacked by two women and refuses to fight back. Good thing he has Denise as back-up.

The Trivia

At 8:58 into the episode, while Mark is arguing with the judge, at the estate, about whose turn it is to be the Cisco Kid, someone is seen walking in the background, just to Daniel Hugh Kelly's left.

Epinephrine (aka adrenalin) raises the heart rate and increases oxygen demand for the heart muscle. Administered epinephrine is difficult, if not impossible, to distinguish from the body's own production of adrenalin, and concentrations in tissue measured postmortem are too variable to be useful as forensic evidence.

Lucy sings "I've Got a Crush on You", a George and Ira Gershwin song which was featured in the 1928 Broadway musical *Treasure Girl* and again, in 1930, in *Strike Up the Band*.

This is another car chase-free episode; in fact, the Coyote doesn't even get driven in this one.

Memorable Quotes

McCormick: I think she's in trouble, Judge.

Hardcastle: Oh, listen, I've been hearing you banging on the pipe for two hours, getting your scrungy old sock out of my sink, I've got a headache that's probably the worst headache I've ever had in my life, okay? So, just go find your old girlfriend. Do me a favor.

McCormick: Oh, I get it. I get it. When the Cisco Kid wants to ride, it's saddle-up on the double. But when Pancho's got a problem, Cisco wants to sit home and read E. Harold What's-his-name.

Hardcastle: E. Howard Payne! Okay? I just don't want to get dragged around like I'm a fifth wheel.

McCormick: What if she's really in trouble? Now, look, I've helped plenty of your pals.

Hardcastle: Who?

McCormick: I have. Now, look, I thought this was a friendship. I thought we did things for each other. But hey—I guess I was wrong, huh? Now that I know the rules, hey. I just thought that every once in a while, it'd be nice if you played Pancho and I got to play Cisco.

McCormick: You know how I met her?

Hardcastle: Huh-uh.

McCormick: She came to San Quentin.

Hardcastle: Yeah?

McCormick: Yeah, she used to come around and ask who might need a visitor. And she'd visit them.

Hardcastle: Nice lady.

McCormick: One day I woke up and thought, "This is it, McCormick. This is the day you crack." And then I was told there was a visitor for me. I couldn't believe it. I couldn't figure it out. Nobody ever came to see me. Not even my family.

Hardcastle: It was her.

McCormick: Yeah.

You're Sixteen, You're Beautiful, and You're His
– premiered November 25, 1985

Written by	Lawrence Hertzog
Directed by	Kim Manners

Cast

Gary Bayer	Ed Whitman
Jonna Lee	Melissa Whitman
Dean Devlin	Victor Hernandez
Rebecca Street	Marge Whitman
Jeff Austin	Brent Boston
Reni Santoni	Sergeant John Thomas
Earl Bullock	Rick Fuller
Jay Varela	
Mike Robello	
Chip Heller	Dave Winston
Lisa Wilcox	Sara
Erica Zeitlin	Betty
Leslie Bega	Luisa Montega
Christie Clark	Erin Whitman

Cast Notes

Gary Bayer, in addition to being a familiar character actor, is a founding board member of the New Harmony Project, an effort to support scriptwriting that promotes the "positive values of life".

Dean Devlin writes and produces movies. His credits include *Stargate* and *Independence Day*.

Leslie Bega went on to a starring role in the series *Head of the Class*, and more recently as Tony Soprano's girlfriend, Valentina, in *The Sopranos*. As a vocalist, she has performed at Lincoln Center.

Christie Clark, playing the younger Whitman daughter, also began a long-running role as Carrie Brady on the series *Days of Our Lives* beginning in 1986. She left that program in 2006.

The Details

A group of men approach a crossing point on the U.S./Mexican border under cover of darkness. They cut the fence and slip through while the guard is in his station, listening to the radio. One of the men stumbles. The guard is alerted. Warning shots are fired as the men pile into a trailer and escape.

In a high school auditorium in the southern California town of Asuza, the Miss Sixteen competition is underway. At the judge's table, respected former jurist Milton C. Hardcastle is currently the victim of a very long rendition of "I'm a Yankee Doodle Dandy", accompanied by baton twirling. Mark's in the back of the auditorium, rolling his eyes.

After the applause dies down, Ed Whitman, this year's Grand Marshall and a heckuva RV salesman, corners Milt and asks him what he thinks of the performances. He also extends an invitation to dinner at his home. Ed wants to share just how blessed he's feeling.

Out in the desert, the truck and trailer arrive at a desolate ranch building.

Back in the auditorium, Hardcastle asks Mark how he's holding up in the face of this onslaught of amateur talent. Mark draws a line in the sand at tap dancing to *Romeo and Juliet*. But the best is yet to come; Ed Whitman's daughter, Melissa, is about to do her monologue, "Growing Up".

Back to the desert, where one of the immigrants wants to know when they'll be taken to Asuza. The men who picked them up at the border aren't giving him any answers. Things get ugly. Shots are fired and an immigrant is killed.

In the auditorium, Melissa's monologue has reached cheerleading, the pinnacle of accomplishment, and day one of the talent competition is drawing to a close. Ed rounds up Milt and Mark, ready to take them home to dinner. Melissa begs off. She says she's going for pizza with the girls.

A little later, in the dressing room as the other girls are leaving, she tells *them* she's going home to dinner. In the now empty auditorium, she meets her boyfriend, Victor. He tells her he wasn't able to find his uncle, who was supposed to cross the border tonight. He's worried. Melissa offers to go back out with him to wait for the man.

At the Whitman home, it's macaroni and cheese night. Ed says he's not keen on "foreign food". The doorbell rings and Ed's wife, Marge, answers it. Ed goes to the family room to talk to his new visitors. It's the two men who killed the immigrant. They've come to tell their boss about the trouble.

The next day, there's a photo op at Whitman's RV lot. The girls pose like pros and the flash attachments are popping. Two of the contestants admire the Coyote. They're a little young for Mark's tastes but not too young to take him down a peg—one comments that they thought he was another contestant's dad.

Mark's disconcerted, and a short while later tells Hardcastle he's not sure what he's doing there, tagging along. He even thinks he likes it better when they're getting shot at.

He should be more careful what he wishes for. Just then Melissa steps up,

asking the judge if she can speak to him privately. Mark strolls away to contemplate the latest improvements in recreational vehicles. Melissa asks Hardcastle if he knows about the trafficking in illegal immigrants.

Meanwhile, her father is discussing a downturn in the same trade. His work contract for the last batch fell through; that's why they were abandoned in the desert. His two henchmen suggest shutting down the business for a while. Ed gives them a pep talk.

Outside, Hardcastle tells Melissa that people are supposed to play by the rules. She argues that Victor and his family had nothing. They had to make their own rules. Hardcastle agrees to look into the disappearance of Victor's uncle but insists that he's going to deal with things by the book.

At the car wash where he works, Victor is surprised by the arrival of his uncle. The judge and Mark arrive. Mark persuades Victor to talk to Hardcastle and he tells them about Antonio Morales, the lawyer who takes the immigrants' money in exchange for jobs and papers.

They visit him. At first Morales denies everything, but Victor tells him about the murder, and then calls him a coward. Morales finally confesses that he collects the money and leaves it where he is told. He says everything else happens by phone.

After they leave the lawyer's office, Mark tells Victor they will need evidence from his uncle. Victor says he will talk to him.

Later that day, at the Whitman home, midway through a showing of their vacation slides Victor arrives. In the back room, he tells Hardcastle that his uncle is waiting at the carwash and has agreed to talk to him. Ed overhears on the intercom system.

The judge and Mark accompany Victor to the car wash. They find his uncle there, murdered. The police arrive. Sergeant Thomas says they don't have much to work with and the immigrants will all be too afraid to talk.

After Thomas departs, Mark asks Victor how much it costs to come over. Hardcastle knows what he's planning and says it's a long shot, but Mark points out that those are the judge's specialty.

At the day's competition, in a back room, Ed talks to his henchmen again. He's getting nervous as the body count rises. He tells the two to deal with Hardcastle.

As the talent show continues, Mark slips out of the auditorium. He goes to pick up the necessary money and then passes it to Morales to set up a crossing.

Later, at the police station, Sergeant Thomas tells them that the original murder victim has been discovered. They inform him that the pick-up is scheduled for six a.m. at the border crossing. It's out of his jurisdiction. He wishes them luck.

At the RV lot, Ed meets with his men again. He wants to know if everything is settled. He receives assurances. Morales is there as well. He tells them the matter will be taken care of "first thing in the morning".

At dawn, Mark and the judge are hiding near the border crossing. No one else has shown up. Mark says things have to be bad for people to be willing to take the risk of coming across illegally, worse even than prison. He thanks Hardcastle. When the judge asks what he means, Mark changes the subject.

A moment later a truck arrives. Hardcastle brandishes a gun and the bad guys fire back. The border guard comes out and is shot. While the judge lays down cover, Mark sneaks around behind the two henchmen with a very big stick, and takes them both out. Hardcastle calls Thomas. The sergeant tells them their two prisoners work for Ed Whitman.

Mark and the judge arrive back in town. The judge sends Mark to keep an eye on Ed while he goes to talk to the police. Mark enters the auditorium. Ed spots him and slowly loses his composure. When Hardcastle and Sergeant Thomas enter through another door, Ed panics and tries to escape. Mark corners him backstage. While he is being placed under arrest, Ed tells his daughter to go out and win the pageant.

In the epilogue, the Miss Sixteen crown goes to Sara Jane. Off in the wings, Mark critiques the results. He says it's obvious that Kristy had loads more talent, and he really liked what Sonja did with the piecrusts.

The Context

This series really isn't about the big issues. For one thing, there aren't any easy answers, certainly not any that everyone in the potential viewing audience would agree on. Just as "Prince of Fat City" wasn't about the source roots of violence among disaffected youth, and "The Yankee Clipper" wasn't about the war in Vietnam, in the end, this one isn't about national policy toward controlling population movement across its borders. We'd be in a pickle if it came down to that, because Victor, an awfully likeable character, has broken the law. So has his uncle. And Hardcastle goes on record as saying (as we'd expect) that he does things by the book. While that may or may not be true, we'd have a real quandary here if the focus wasn't quickly shifted to the far more heinous crime of murder.

Hertzog is still the go-to guy for humor, so a fairly tight focus is kept on the pageant, and the Whitman family. It's a nice light satire, done somewhat more sharply in the script where Marge's idea of haute cuisine is franks in the mac and cheese, and Ed's xenophobia is given freer rein.

And there's no doubt that Ed is the bad guy in this episode. His minions pull the triggers, but he pulls the strings. He's not bad in the same mode as Weed Randall, slathering and ranting. Instead, like the guys back in Clarence, Arkansas, he's a publicly respectable man who has let greed lure him into violence.

The Trivia

The title is a twist on Richard and Robert Sherman's song, "You're Sixteen, You're Beautiful, and You're Mine" which went to number one on the charts in 1960 with Johnny Burnette, and again in 1974 when sung by Ringo Starr.

Mark's reference to packing a suitcase as one of the talent entries brings to mind that same skill demonstrated by a contestant in the 1975 beauty pageant comedy film, *Smile*.

Los Lobos' 1984 release, "Will the Wolf Survive", is used for the montage that follows the photo session.

The final performance in the talent competition is a lovely rendition of Randy Newman's 1966 song "I Think It's going to Rain Today" sung by Leslie Bega. Must be the long version; Mark gets to the bank, makes a substantial withdrawal, and returns, all in the course of the song.

In the original script, in the fourth act the henchmen get the drop on the guys at the border crossing. Mark and the judge are locked in the trailer and sent careening down a mountain road. Mark climbs out the front window, and into the cab of the truck, stopping it at cliff's edge. All in all, it's an expensive-sounding action sequence.

Memorable Quotes

Ed: I'm blessed, Milt. I am a blessed man. Why the good Lord picked me out and said "Bless this man", I don't know. Great family, great kids, great wife, business is great.

Hardcastle: That's great, Ed.

Hardcastle: (to McCormick) Hey, if you're thinking what I think you're thinking, it's a real long shot.

McCormick: Oh, that's your specialty. Milton Hardcastle, long shots since 1932; and they usually pay off.

Victor: You guys must be good friends. You talk and understand each other while no one else knows what's going on.

McCormick: In the joint, people used to talk about breaking out all the time. You didn't talk about girls, you talked about jumping the wall, getting outside.

Hardcastle: Hardly any of them do it.

McCormick: That's what I mean. Most of it is just talk. It's not worth the risk. But these people actually do it. They take the risk. I guess it gets pretty bad sometimes.

Hardcastle: Yep.

McCormick: Thanks, Judge.

Mirage a Trois – premiered December 2, 1985

Written by	Marianne Clarkson
Directed by	Sidney Hayers
Second unit director	Gary Combs

Cast

Michael Ansara	Sheik Abdullah Casir
Lycia Naff	Aleeya (Ali) Casir
Grant Aleksander	Biff Anderson
Ari Barak	Hassan Casir
Kavi Raz	Rabin Casir
Bruce French	Jack Stall
John Shearin	George Peck
Barry Sattels	
Ben Rawnsley	

Cast Notes

Michael Ansara was born in Syria. He portrayed Kang in the original *Star Trek*, and also *Deep Space Nine* and *Voyager.*

Lycia Naff had a three-year run as a dancer on the series *Fame*. Though she's stayed active in stage work and commercials, she's also pursued a career as a journalist.

Grant Aleksander also played Phillip Spaulding on the series *The Guiding Light.* He's recently directed episodes of *As the World Turns.*

Kavi Raz has recently been involved in writing, producing, and directing independent films. His movie, *The Gold Bracelet*, has won multiple film festival awards and is scheduled for release in 2008. He was frequently cast as a doctor, including an ongoing role as Vijay Kochar in the series *St. Elsewhere.*

John Shearin is the Director of the School of Theater and Dance at East Carolina Unversity.

The Details

In a darkened governmental office, three agents are discussing relations between the small but oil-rich country of Cassim, and the U.S. It all boils down to how the nation's absolute ruler, Sheikh Casir, is feeling at the moment. Right now he's in a bad mood because his youngest daughter, in the U.S. since she was four, has taken up with an unknown American guy. The agents have a mission: find the guy and squash the romance.

Meanwhile, at the Casir mansion, the sheikh and his daughter are having it out. He wants to know who the guy is; she wants to go shopping. Ali is a state of the art Valley Girl. She takes off in her VW convertible. Sheikh Casir sends Ali's two brothers, Hassan and Rabin, to follow her and find out who she's seeing.

Ali doesn't head for Rodeo Drive this time. Her destination is the docks. She's taking a trip to Catalina Island.

So is McCormick. Nine bucks is all he can afford for a getaway weekend but he's delighted to have a break from crime-fighting. Hardcastle drops him off at the dock with instructions to be back by Monday.

Ali is rendezvousing with her beau, Biff Anderson. He's a Princeton man; what's not to like? He's got the rock in his pocket and he's ready to propose. But Ali is sure her dad has someone tailing her, so she tells Biff to keep his distance until they're on the island.

On board the boat, Mark makes a fatal error, assisting the over-burdened Ali with her pile of luggage and introducing himself. From there it's downhill. Ali attaches herself to him, limpet-like, for the duration of the cruise, divulging her life story and her recent difficulties. All efforts to evade her are unsuccessful. From afar, they are observed by the Casir brothers and the two American agents.

They disembark at the island. Mark, now carrying all of Ali's baggage, finally bids her farewell. She impulsively gives him a good-bye kiss. Biff, the agents, and the brothers are all watching intently. Moments later Mark is firmly escorted onto another boat by the two agents.

He's taken back to L.A. and questioned, but he's eventually released when Hardcastle shows up to vouch for him. They won't tell him what it's all about and they send a man to follow him.

Outside the State Department offices, Mark is still muttering about his misfortune. He wants to make sure the record is straight: the girl kissed *him*, not the other way around. As they pull out, the Casir brothers are tailing them. Hardcastle notices, and then tests his assumption. The tail turns into a high

speed chase on a back road. A third
car intervenes and cuts off Hardcastle's
truck. The brothers tear away.

Biff Anderson emerges from the
interloping car and challenges Mark to
fisticuffs. The Princeton man gets two
punches in while Mark tries to explain.
Finally fed up, the guy who learned to
box in a different part of New Jersey
slugs Biff and scores a knock-down.

In their car, the Casir brothers discuss their dilemma. They're in the middle
of a big drug deal, using money they stole from their father. They can't afford to
have the sheikh pull up stakes and leave the U.S. now. They decide that Ali's
boyfriend must die.

Back at the scene of the fight, Biff is apologizing. He says he wants to
marry Ali. Mark encourages him in his plans and bids him farewell.

There's a wrinkle back at the Casir mansion. The sheikh tells Ali that she
must marry McCormick. She tries to explain about Biff, but no one is listening.

In another part of the house, the brothers meet with their buyer. He
insists that the deal must go down soon. They agree to hand over the heroin in
two days.

The brothers drive to Gull's Way that night and sneak in through the back
door. Mark is attacked in the kitchen. Hardcastle, hearing the commotion,
comes downstairs with a gun. The brothers run off.

Hardcastle calls in a partial plate to the police the next morning. Mark is
pacing. Ali and Biff arrive, distraught. Ali tells them about the impending forced
marriage. Mark is initially doubting, then horrified. Hardcastle thinks the sheikh is
just misunderstood. Mark says Hardcastle is the right guy to straighten things out.

Later, at the Casir home, the sheikh cordially entertains Hardcastle, who
tries to explain the situation. It's no use. Casir says he has already announced the
name of the groom so it must be McCormick. He bids a hasty good-bye to a
flustered Hardcastle.

Upstairs, the Casir brothers are transferring the heroin to a suitcase. Outside, Biff is approaching. He intends to elope with his beloved.

In the garden, the drug deal goes awry. The brothers and their buyer argue.
The buyer wants the price cut in half. Ali has joined Biff nearby. In mid-smooch,
she overhears. She is spotted eavesdropping. The deal collapses. The brothers
pursue her and finally return her to her room. They threaten to kill Biff if she
refuses to marry as arranged.

Back at the estate, Hardcastle is trying to convince Mark that Casir's
approach isn't all that unreasonable. Biff arrives in a tizzy, telling them what
Hassan and Rabin are up to.

Mark and the judge take their information to the State Department agents. They're told that the two have diplomatic immunity. Mark is also advised to go ahead with the marriage so that Casir will remain happy. Hardcastle is starting to like the notion, too. Much to Mark's horror, he has a plan.

The following day, at the Casir mansion, Mark's dressed as a groom and is in a state of high panic. Outside, everything's in place for the ceremony and the drug deal. Biff's in attendance, too. He spots the buyer and heads inside to tell the judge.

The ceremony is soon underway. Hardcastle is the presiding judge and Mark looks worried; he *knows* what kind of sentences this guy hands down. Off to the side, the brothers are sitting next to their buyer. As the rites grind on—and just before Hardcastle can finish pronouncing them man and wife—the exchange is made.

Chaos erupts as the judge, Casir, and Mark set off after the miscreants. Ali rushes into Biff's arms. The wedding cake is doomed, but the bad guys are all captured red-handed with the money and drugs…and Mark is still not quite married.

In the epilogue, at the airport, the sheikh is departing for his homeland. He bids a fond farewell to Biff and Ali and tells her to marry whom she pleases. As Mark and Hardcastle walk away, Ali runs up to them and says it's all over between her and Biff. She now feels a cosmic connection to Mark. He takes her aside and tells her it would never work—he steals cars and hangs out with the Green Lantern. She gets a peck on the forehead and a definite good-bye.

Out in front of the terminal, Biff is waiting, ready for another round of fisticuffs.

As the frame freezes, a postscript informs us that Aleeya is currently married to a thirty-five year old television producer, and lives in Sherman Oaks. Biff returned to Teaneck, New Jersey and the plumbing supplies business, and Mark still hangs out at Gull's Way with the Green Lantern.

The Context

1986 was a long time ago, and nowhere in the series does that seem more apparent than in this cheerfully innocent episode. We see Ali kneeling before her father, and hear the threat of a lifetime in prison, but the whole situation is played lightly and for laughs. All cross-cultural difficulties vanish, as if by fiat, by the end.

This is one in a series of episodes in which Mark, as an innocent bystander, encounters trouble in the form of a ditz. Teddy Hollins was the first, in "The Crystal Duck", followed by Howard Kaye in "Really Neat Cars and Guys with a Sense of Humor". Now it's Ali, a woman, but still in the classic pattern. Mark's a nice guy to whom bad things happen regularly.

Hardcastle encounters someone who believes in rules even more firmly than he does. The sheikh makes the judge look flexible. In a moment that almost gets lost in the rest of Sheikh Casir's hurried argument for the wedding, he observes that Hardcastle thinks of Mark as a son. Interestingly, Hardcastle doesn't deny it. He just says he doesn't want that to get back to McCormick.

The Trivia

In the opening slide show, three of the four pictures of Ali are taken from the show itself, including one where she's standing by the main house at Gull's Way.

The song played during Ali's interesting drive to the docks is "Girls Like Me", which was released by Bonnie Hayes and the Wild Combo in 1982 and was also used in the opening credits for the 1983 movie, *Valley Girl.*

Gamma Phi Delta, Biff's fraternity, is currently a sorority. In 1988, a Christian fraternity was formed with that name.

There were two boats in the wharf shots; one was the Long Beach Empress, which plies the channel, and the other was the Catalina King, which is a tender for cruise ships. Catalina ferries leave from the dock in San Pedro and the passage now costs $41 for an adult, round-trip.

The State Department offices are apparently located in the Los Angeles City Hall.

Why does Hardcastle wait until the next morning to phone in the license of the Casir brothers' car? Though it doesn't matter. He reports it as "2-B-E-X, something, 5." The car was parked at right angles to him and the plate was entirely different.

After the phone call, Hardcastle is reading William Burrough's 1981 novel *Cities of the Red Night.*

Memorable Quotes

McCormick: Look at this. Our first port of call is called Port of Call. I like that. That's classy.

Hardcastle: If it's so classy, how come it only costs nine bucks?

McCormick: Well, with the money you pay me, it's lucky I can afford that.

McCormick: Oh, here we go. Another lecture on "How We Hit on Girls in the 1940s".

Hardcastle: We didn't "hit on girls". We courted young ladies.

McCormick: "We courted young ladies"? Let me ask you—

Hardcastle: We talked to them, brought them flowers and watermelons—

McCormick: Do you remember the first time you ever met your wife?

Hardcastle: Yeah.

McCormick: Before you even talked to her?

Hardcastle: Yeah.

McCormick: What'd you see first, her brilliant mind or her sweet soul? It took you six months to figure out that she was pretty?

Hardcastle: Saw that right away.

McCormick: There you go.

Hardcastle: Whaddaya mean, there you go?

McCormick: There you go. You got to know your wife because you liked the way she looked. Right? Huh? You liked the way she looked. It wasn't her personality, her sensible shoes – something about her caught your eye.

Hardcastle: Okay, it was her ears.

McCormick: What?

Hardcastle: Her ears. It was all I could see. She had her back to me. It was at a church picnic and I could just see these little pink ears. You happy?

Conventional Warfare – premiered December 9, 1985

Written by   Steven L. Sears and Burt Pearl
Directed by   Sigmund Neufeld, Jr.

Cast

Tim O'Connor	Bucky O'Neil
Ray Reinhardt	Don Ferris
Jason Bernard	Arnie Sandoval
Anthony Ponzini	Sid Storm
Gerry Gibson	Howard Penny
Dan Lauria	Lieutenant Adkins
Arthur Taxier	George Delgado
Richard Brestoff	Freddie Dylan
Stan Sells	

Anthony De Longis	Dave
Judy Kain	the hotel desk clerk
Mark Fargo	
Angela Aames	the girl by the pool
Victor Rogers	the maitre d'
Tom McGreevy	Ray Ashton

Cast Notes

Tim O'Connor played Elliot Carson on the popular series *Peyton Place* and Dr. Elias Huer in *Buck Rogers in the 25th Century.*

Gerry Gibson also appeared in the pilot, "Rolling Thunder".

Anthony Ponzini played Landers in the episode "Goin' Nowhere Fast".

Dan Lauria had the role of Jack Arnold in the series *The Wonder Years.*

The Details

In a Palms Springs hotel room a man with an automatic weapon receives a phone call. He's told to deliver the weapon to a room at the Adobe Palms Hotel. It will be used in a hit on two mobsters, Don Ferris and Sid Storm. The man has everything packed up and ready to go in a suitcase.

At the estate, Hardcastle practices his acceptance speech while Mark packs his suitcase. He's been listening to it all week and he points out that so far the judge has only been *nominated* for the lifetime achievement award. But he can't fault Hardcastle's eagerness to go to this year's judges' convention.

On the drive to Palm Springs, Hardcastle mentions his hot competition for the award—Bucky O'Neill. Even Mark has heard about one of O'Neill's cases, but Hardcastle says the guy didn't work very hard—he took lots of vacations to Tahiti.

They park the truck at the Adobe Palms Hotel and make it past the greeting committee, complete with water balloons. In the front lobby, Mark finally spots some more distinguished-looking judicial types. Hardcastle tells him they are mobsters. Don Ferris and Sid Storm stop by to say hello. Hardcastle and Sid exchange a word or two. They are tense and barely civil. Don is somewhat more cordial.

Outside the hotel, the man with the gun has arrived. He has his delivery orders: room 279.

In the hotel manager's office, George Delgado is getting chewed out by Sid Storm for booking the mobsters and the judges for the same week. George promises he'll keep the judges happy and out of Sid's way.

A moment later, one of the judges isn't happy. At the check-in desk, Hardcastle wants the room he reserved—279. He's not about to accept any substitutes. George, coming upon the problem, promises to arrange things while the judge has a drink by the pool.

As they step outside, Mark wants to know what the big deal was. Hardcastle admits to a superstition; 279 is the closest thing to his lucky number that he could get.

Out front, the hit man is the next one to arrive. His instructions are to check into room 279.

Meanwhile, back by the pool, Hardcastle is talking seminars while Mark admires the female scenery. They encounter Bucky O'Neill and Hardcastle professes to be uninterested in the outcome of the competition. After Bucky moves on, Mark tells the judge he has nothing to worry about. O'Neill is too tan. He looks like a presenter and presenters never win anything.

In two separate locations, the mobsters and the jurists are meeting to discuss matters. Judge Howard Penny and mob boss Don Ferris tell their respective audiences to be tolerant of the opposing team.

In the middle of a nearly sleepless night, with lots of judicial tomfoolery for background noise, there's a knock on the door of room 279. Mark, stuck with the rollaway bed, is also saddled with door-answering duties. He's tired enough not to ask any questions when a mysterious man hands him a suitcase and tells him he has until Saturday to get the job done.

Mark puts the case aside, figuring it's just more hijinks. Hardcastle is curious, though. He opens it and finds bundles of cash, pictures of Don and Sid, and a high-powered rifle.

Visiting the check-in desk again, Hardcastle discovers that his room had been reserved for a man named Louis Oliver. The judge forks over some cash to get his phone number and address. He and Mark leave, carrying the suitcase and unaware that they're being followed.

As they head to the police with their evidence, Mark wants to know why the judge is so intent on finding out what's going on. Hardcastle convinces him that it's just concern that the death of Ferris might trigger a bloodbath. A moment later, the truck is trapped and run off the road by the tail and another car. The suitcase is taken by their attackers.

Minus his evidence, Hardcastle presents the story to Lieutenant Adkins of the Palms Springs P.D. Adkins thinks it's another practical joke—last year there was a fake homicide. It takes a stern talking-to and the threat of a court order to get him moving.

Back at the hotel, Hardcastle tries to arrange a meeting with Ferris. He's turned down. Mark is perplexed when the judge decides to go to the restaurant where the mobsters are lunching and force a meeting. He demands to know what Hardcastle's stake in this is.

The judge finally admits that he has some history with Don Ferris. Years ago, when he was a cop, he got into a fight with some of Ferris' colleagues. It was Ferris who pulled the guys off him.

Arriving at the restaurant, their initial reception is chilly, but Ferris invites them to his table and Hardcastle tells his story. Sid is also there and doesn't believe the judge would be doing anything to save Ferris. He insists that if there is a problem, it should be taken care of by "the family". As he stands to leave, he's killed by a rifle shot through the window of the restaurant.

A short while later, as the police process the crime scene, Lieutenant Adkins advises Hardcastle to leave police matters to the police. After they leave the restaurant, Mark asks the judge if he intends to follow that advice; after all, the victim was a mobster. Hardcastle says a murder is a murder even if you don't happen to like the victim.

Returning to their hotel room, the guys find Ferris and his men waiting for them. Ferris has his research man, Freddie, along. Mark's very willing to share what he knows about the weapon and the delivery. Freddie quickly narrows the field of potential hit men to one—Louis Orlando. His last known residence was Tahiti.

The guys do a little research of their own. In the convention headquarters room, the judge and Mark search for O'Neill's file. Hardcastle suspects a connection between O'Neill and the assassin. They've both spent time in Tahiti. Of

course his suspicions have nothing to do with O'Neill being his main competitor for an award.

They are interrupted as they find the file. Arnie, one of the other judges, comes in. He thinks Milt is scoping out the competition. Arnie goes down to the poolside where O'Neill is romancing a Miss Jurisprudence contestant. He mentions having just seen Hardcastle in the file room.

Back upstairs, Hardcastle is noticing an interesting pattern in O'Neill's record. He was the presiding judge in several cases in which Storm or Ferris were parties and his rulings favored them. Unbeknownst to the guys, O'Neill has sneaked up outside the door. He overhears their conversation.

Late that night, in Louis Orlando's hotel room, a knock is heard. An envelope is slipped under the door. It contains a photo of Hardcastle. Orlando mutters to himself that he'll do this one for free. He puts the envelope in his dresser drawer.

At the awards dinner the next evening, O'Neill greets Hardcastle warmly as the guys go to take their seats at the back table. Bucky moves on, heading for the dais. Mark asks the judge how the police investigation of O'Neill is going. Slowly, it appears.

In Ferris' room, Freddie tells his boss they've located Orlando's room. Ferris and his men saddle up.

Orlando isn't there, though. He's making his way up to the projection room that overlooks the banquet hall.

At the banquet, Mark wonders why Hardcastle didn't take his concerns about O'Neill to the committee. Hardcastle says they're just suspicions. That's not how the system is supposed to work.

Up in Orlando's room, Ferris' men have no such compunctions. They conduct a search. Freddie discovers Hardcastle's photo in the drawer.

In the banquet hall, Arnie invites Hardcastle to sit at the head table. The judge is pleasantly surprised, until he realizes he's being tapped as a presenter. As the ceremony gets underway, in the projection booth Orlando is assembling his rifle.

Ferris' men arrive and firmly escort McCormick into the hallway. Ferris tells him about their find. He's trying to even up the score with the judge, and is taking measures to protect him. Mark goes back into the banquet, now on the lookout. He notices shadowy movements up in the projection booth and dashes out. With Ferris' men following, he heads upstairs.

Orlando has Hardcastle in his sights as Mark bursts into the room and tries to stop him. Mark isn't up to the hit man's standards and ends up on the floor. Orlando single-mindedly returns to the business at hand, again taking aim. A shot is fired. Orlando slumps to the floor, dead from a bullet fired by Ferris.

Hearing the shot and seeing his plot fail, O'Neill panics and flees. Hardcastle pursues him to the poolside. O'Neill grabs a waitress and holds her at gunpoint. She demonstrates some good footwork, douses him with a drink, and breaks free. Hardcastle knocks O'Neill into the pool and subdues him.

In the epilogue, Hardcastle finally gets to give an acceptance speech—except that he's receiving the very lovely combination gavel and stiletto at a banquet hosted by Ferris and the gang.

The Context

Hardcastle has an unusual relationship with members of the underworld. There seems to be a grudging respect between him and old-time criminals. He can't be bought, but he plays by the book. We saw a little of this in "Man in a Glass House". Though Joe Cadillac was hardly respectful in his memoirs, when he was in a bind he sought out Hardcastle. With Don Ferris, there's the wary mutual honor accorded to an honorable enemy—one who fights fair and by the rules.

The rules are a major theme here. Hardcastle believes in them, as always, and tries to apply them equally to everyone. O'Neill isn't guilty until proven so, and people can't get away with murder just because their victims are criminals.

As for judges' conventions—two years retired and Hardcastle is still hanging out at them. But unlike the aborted trip to Hawaii in the second season episode "You Would Cry, Too, If It Happened to You", this time Mark is dragged along. Hardcastle is talking about getting some of that fine judicial reasoning to rub off on the man who increasingly appears to be his protégé. He's even encouraging him to attend the seminars. It seems like yet more intimation that Mark has a future in the law, only this time the nudges are coming from Hardcastle's direction.

The Trivia

Hardcastle's martial arts top makes another appearance. He also wore it in "Faster Hearts" and in the epilogue of "Strangle Hold".

In this final version, Mark and the judge are just left standing there after the gun is stolen back. A remark is dubbed in that they're lucky no one wants them dead. By contrast, in the closing credits we see them in a mine or a cave—their escape involved explosives. In the script they dove into an aqueduct and got away while shots were fired at them.

Memorable Quotes

Hardcastle: (oratorically) Being a recipient of such an award is not the real honor. The real honor and satisfaction comes from knowing that you, my – no – comes from the, comes from the *knowledge* that you, my contemporaries – no, my *peers*, my peers – comes from knowing that – I can't say acknowledged because I just said knowledge – comes from the – from *knowing* that you, my contemporaries, from knowing that you, my peers, have acknowledged my past accomplishments. For what they are worth. (to McCormick) How does that sound?

McCormick: Sounds about the same as it has every day for the past week. Rehearsed.

Hardcastle: You like the part about the 'past accomplishments'?

McCormick: Judge, I *am* one of your past accomplishments.

McCormick: Well, now, he's nothing to worry about. He's too tan. Don't worry about him. Strictly a presenter.

Hardcastle: Oh, I don't know.

McCormick: No, trust me, Judge. The guy's gonna be asked to present an award. You know how that is. It's like winning Miss Congeniality. It's the kiss of death. You never win anything.

Penny: (on the dais) Milt, I'm really glad you could come up.

Hardcastle: Ah, well, if you fellas really want me up here, I'm not gonna turn it down.

Penny: Terrific. Now, listen. You'll be presenting the William Jennings Bryan Award.

Hardcastle: That's…that's why you wanted me up here? To be a presenter?

Penny: Absolutely. It's a real honor, too, you know.

Duet for Two Wind Instruments – premiered December 16, 1985

Written by	Lawrence Hertzog
Directed by	Robert Bralver
Second unit director	Gary Combs

Cast

Cotter Smith	Randy Hopke
Laurie Prange	Val Mickaelian
Joe Santos	Frank Harper
Louise Caire Clark	Kristin
Jeff Donnell	Mrs. Hopke
Samantha Harper	secretary
KT Sullivan	Beth Purvis
Peggy Walton Walker	the diamond exchange manager
Garry Goodrow	the motel clerk
Lauren Woodland	the kid
Jeff Tyler	the attendant
Ernie Holmes	the prison guard
Craig Berenson	Andy

Cast Notes

Cotter Smith played Tony Vincenzo in the 2005 remake of the series *Nightstalker.*

Louise Caire Clark played Maggie Scott in the Disney series *Five Mile Creek.*

Jeff Donnell was born Jean Marie Donnell and took her nickname from the character in the cartoon strip *Mutt and Jeff.* She also played Aunt May Parker in the 1977 TV series *The Amazing Spiderman* and had the role of Stella Field for eight years on *General Hospital.*

KT Sullivan (no periods, please) is a Broadway performer, comedienne and cabaret singer who claims Boggy Depot, Oklahoma as her birthplace.

Garry Goodrow makes his third appearance in the series, the other episodes being "You Would Cry, Too, if It Happened to You" and "Pennies from a Dead Man's Eyes".

Ernie Holmes was a defensive tackle for the Pittsburgh Steelers from 1972-77 and played in the 1976 Superbowl.

Craig Berenson was the producer for the 2006 movie *Snakes on a Plane.* He also had the role of Paul Carey in the 1980 classic *Airplane!*

The Details

In San Quentin, Randolph Hopke is being released after serving two years of a four-year sentence for the brutal beating of his girlfriend, Valerie. The California Supreme Court has ruled that his lawyer was incompetent at the time of his trial. From all appearances, Hopke has been a model prisoner. Milton C. Hardcastle was the presiding judge in the original trial.

Back at the estate, Hardcastle is being interviewed for a TV program. The question of Hopke's case is raised. The judge hems and haws a bit. Mark, hovering in the background, is left out of the interview. His job is to go fetch tea.

Hardcastle discusses his post-retirement activities. Mark is mentioned in passing. His fifteen minutes of fame is reduced to about twenty-two seconds at the end of the interview. He doesn't take it too well.

After the reporter leaves, the two guys have heated words about the Hopke case. Hardcastle says the man was guilty, and his lawyer wasn't senile at the time of the trial. Mark says he knew Hopke in prison. He's the guy who helped him learn the ropes and stay alive. He doesn't believe Hopke had a fair trial.

Hardcastle decides to investigate the case and prove Hopke's guilt. Mark says he'll prove Hopke's innocence.

Both men set out on their missions. Hardcastle goes to the café where Valerie works. He tells her he'd like to have a word with her about Hopke. Mark goes straight to Hopke's mother's house, and finds Randy, who greets him warmly.

Back at the café, Valerie says she's still afraid of Hopke. She doesn't believe he's changed. She says he's vicious.

At the Hopke family home, Mark tells Randy he wants to go over the case with a fine-toothed comb, to prove his innocence once and for all and prevent any attempt to retry him. Randy turns suddenly cool.

At the café, Hardcastle tells Valerie that her statement could help him get a retrial for Hopke. She wants no part of it.

Mark is continuing to encourage Hopke to let him help prove his

innocence. Randy goes from cool to hot. He finally slugs McCormick and tells him to stay out of his life.

The next morning, a subdued and sore McCormick is out in the yard planting begonias. He does his best to look chipper as Hardcastle approaches. Mark says he's willing to drop the whole matter. The judge senses weakness and is in no mood to call it quits. Mark gets riled again.

McCormick goes back to his attempt to prove Hopke's innocence. He visits a toy store, encounters a spoiled brat, and acquires a model kit for an F-14. From there it's a trip to Hopke's former employer, Alfac Industries. Mark uses a decal from the model kit to create a fake Air Force ID and then passes himself off as an intelligence officer. He asks the receptionist for Hopke's employment file as part of a background security check. He finds that the Reverend Hardcastle has gotten there just before him. Mark intercepts the file Hardcastle already requested and makes off with it.

Beth, a secretary who overheard the whole exchange, calls Hopke and tells him two men are after his file. He describes McCormick to her and gets a tentative yes on his ID.

The judge catches up with Mark in the parking lot of Alfac, and demands the file. Mark informs him that according to what's in it, Hopke was installing a security system at the time he was purportedly attacking Val. Despite Hardcastle's

threats to end their partnership, Mark hangs on to the file and takes off in the Coyote.

The judge pursues. Mark eludes him after a brief chase. Hardcastle stops at a payphone and drops a dime. He asks Frank Harper to put out an APB on McCormick. Frank jokingly tries to find out why but Hardcastle is tightlipped and adamant.

A patrol officer spots the Coyote parked outside a diamond exchange. He radios the location in.

Inside, Mark is still in full scam mode. He asks the manager about Hopke's work on their security system. She tells him that the exchange was robbed of a quarter million dollars worth of diamonds shortly after the installation. The owner of the exchange was killed. She also says if Hopke hadn't been otherwise occupied with beating his girlfriend at the time, he would have been her prime suspect in the robbery.

Emerging from the exchange, Mark is observed by Hopke, who tails him. The tail quickly becomes a chase on a narrow, winding road. The two cars encounter Hardcastle's truck, coming head-on. After the near collision, Hardcastle does a 180-degree turn and follows them, firing shots at Hopke's car. Mark careens off the road. Hardcastle pulls over, and Hopke escapes.

Mark is furious at the judge's interference. Hardcastle says he was only trying to help and wonders why Hopke is trying to run his would-be benefactor off a cliff.

A few hours later, Mark and the Coyote return to the estate by tow truck. Hardcastle is in the study with Harper. They're discussing the physical impossibility of Hopke having been involved in the diamond exchange murder. McCormick enters. He's fuming. Frank bids them a hasty goodbye as Mark complains vociferously about Hardcastle's ego and his penchant for interfering.

It's not long, though, before Mark is admitting that the judge is right this time. Hardcastle just as quickly confesses that he was at least partly wrong. They both suspect that Hopke may have been behind the diamond exchange robbery and murder. Hardcastle wants to investigate further. Mark tries to bow out, but the judge says the Lone Ranger doesn't ride alone. He wants Mark to saddle up, too.

At the motel where Val was attacked, Hardcastle interviews the clerk. The man confirms the trouble started at ten-thirty a.m. that day. He knows Val's watch was broken during the attack and it stopped at that time. Hardcastle takes his information to McCormick, who's across the street at a gas station, talking to a pump jockey. The kid was there that day, too. Mark says that he puts the time at eleven forty-five. He was particularly attentive to Hopke's arrival because he was interested in the car Hopke was driving.

Mark suggests that maybe only Val was in the room at ten-thirty. She could have been in cahoots with Hopke all along. Mark and the judge make another stop at the toy store. Mark visits Valerie at the café, flashing his newly acquired detective shield and telling her the case is being reopened.

He leaves. He and the judge wait outside. Val departs in a hurry a short while later. They follow. As they're tailing her, Mark admits he was dead wrong about Hopke's innocence but Hardcastle points out he sent the man up on the wrong charges. The judge is angry about having been used by the two.

At Val's apartment, she and Randy are locked in a kiss. It looks like two years of unrequited passion, but Randy breaks it off and harangues her. She swears she's said nothing to anyone about their plan. He grabs her hastily packed suitcase and they depart.

Mark and the judge tail the two fugitives to the bus terminal. They catch Hopke in the middle of removing the diamonds from a storage locker. Hopke pulls a gun and then commandeers an empty bus from in front of the station. Mark takes another one and sets out in pursuit. It's a moderately high-speed chase as the two buses lurch around corners and scatter pedestrians in their path. Mark finally sideswipes Hopke's vehicle, sending him plunging down into a ravine. The police arrive to take custody of the two.

Arriving back at the terminal with their slightly scuffed bus, Mark pulls up by a group of patiently waiting passengers. He and Hardcastle exit the bus nonchalantly. The judge calls Mark "Kemo Sabe" and tells him he did all right.

In the epilogue, back at the estate the guys are battling it out under the hoop when a TV crew pulls up. Mark sighingly says he's outta there; it's glory time again and he'll step aside. The judge assures him it's not going to be like that. He encourages Mark to take over with the interviewer. As Mark prepares to enjoy his new role as Gull's Way spokesperson, the interviewer informs him that four more of Hardcastle's cases have been overturned. For once, Mark is delighted to be able to defer to the judge.

The Context

It's the third time we see Hardcastle considering a case that he may not have adjudicated correctly. In "Third Down and Twenty Years to Life" and "The Game You Learn from Your Father" the defendants were ultimately proven innocent. Hardcastle felt guilty about his role in their convictions, and Mark tried to be supportive. This time out, the judge is convinced he got it right and Mark, who's already ticked off at the man, sets out to prove him wrong.

The theme is partnership. There are frequent references to the Lone Ranger and Tonto in this episode, with the implication that Mark's not too happy about always being the sidekick. This point was raised earlier in the episode "Strangle

Hold", when Mark used the Cisco Kid and Pancho as his example. He wanted to be Cisco once in a while. Hardcastle went along with it that time.

As the show progressed through the three seasons, there was a steady increase in the percentage of episodes where the problem being tackled originated with Mark. There were five such situations in season one, seven in season two, and ten, or nearly half, in the final season. The relationship was evolving into a more equal partnership. This time Mark stalks off to do his own investigation without much regard for the fact that he is technically in Hardcastle's custody, and the judge's threats seem mostly perfunctory curmudgeonliness. When Hardcastle finally asks for an APB, Frank questions his motivations, and acquiesces to his demand only reluctantly.

When Mark returns home after the crash (and, of course, he *does* return because it *is* home) Harper refers to him as the prodigal son. In the end both Mark and the judge are half-right, and both are willing to admit they were half-wrong.

The Trivia

If Hopke only served two years and twelve days in prison, and Mark's been out since the spring of 1983, how did they know each other in San Quentin? For that matter, how did Hardcastle convict Hopke? He's been retired for over two years.

Here's to equal rights whining; the little boy in the toy store is a very young actress, Lauren Woodland, who was eight at the time of the filming. She graduated *magna cum laude* from USC and went on to play Brittany Hodges in *The Young and the Restless*.

Hopke rented a storage locker in the bus terminal for two *years*?

As the two buses round the first turn at the start of the chase, a black cat darts across in front of them.

Memorable Quotes

Hardcastle: We'd just like you to get some iced tea, okay? I'd help you but I'm tied up here.

McCormick: (to interviewer) These Lone Ranger guys are really amazing, aren't they? I mean, they just go out there and saddle up all alone, grabbing bad guys unassisted and taking credit for it.

Hardcastle: You wanna get the tea?

McCormick: You got it, Kemo Sabe.

Hardcastle: I got what you got.

McCormick: Do you really? You know, the only thing you have is the biggest damned ego I have ever had the misfortune to come across.

Harper: Yeah, I tell you what. Listen, you guys fill out the complaint between you and then you come down to the station when you're ready.

Hardcastle: You look who's talking about ego. You wouldn't even let me pull you out of that hole you were in.

McCormick: Well, I wouldn't have been in that hole if you didn't fly in there—

Harper: Listen, don't bother. I know my way out.

McCormick: —with six-guns blazing, trying to save the day!

Hardcastle: I wasn't trying to save the day!

McCormick: Oh, come on, who're you—

Harper: Anything you need down at the station, I'll be there. Take care!

McCormick: You think he did the murder at the diamond exchange?

Hardcastle: I think we oughta find out.

McCormick: Nah, you go ahead and do it. I don't want to. It's your case.

Hardcastle: Get your coat, Tonto.

McCormick: Nah, I don't—

Hardcastle: The Lone Ranger doesn't want to ride alone. Come on, saddle up. Get 'em up, Scout.

If You Could See What I See – premiered January 4, 1986

Written by	Carol Mendelsohn
Directed by	Kim Manners
Second unit director	Gil Combs

Cast

Rosemary Clooney	Millie Denton
Jonathan Goldsmith	Wendell Price
Teresa Ganzel	Loni Summers
Lyle Waggoner	Dex Falcon
Joe Santos	Frank Harper
Sandy Joseph	the waiter

Cast Notes

Rosemary Clooney was an enduring performer whose singing career began in the 1940s. She is perhaps best remembered for the role of Betty Haynes in the movie *White Christmas*. She also played Madame X in two episodes of the series *ER* which also starred her nephew, George Clooney. According to *Hardcastle and McCormick* producer, Les Sheldon, Carol Mendelsohn wrote this part specifically for Ms. Clooney.

Jonathan Goldsmith was also bad cop Arnie Hoffs in the episode "D-Day."

Lyle Waggoner was announcer and performer on *The Carol Burnett Show*. He also played Major Steve Trevor on the series *Wonder Woman*.

Teresa Ganzel was one of the Mighty Carson Art Players on *The Tonight Show*.

The Details

A woman sits alone in a room, assailed by visions that seem meaningless but full of portent—one of the images is of Mark, struggling with a man and being shot. She sees his body tumbling down a hill. She leans forward, appearing distraught. Her vision concludes with the image of Hardcastle, standing solemnly by a casket.

But all that appears to be in the future. For now Hardcastle's biggest concern is that he can't find any orange juice. Mark's not interested. He has too many housekeeping chores. He's tired of all the housework and is determined to hire a maid. He's even willing to pay for it himself.

Meanwhile the woman, Millie Denton, sees the beginning of her vision yet again. She sits by the phone. Of course it rings. It's Mark. Her deceased husband was Mark's old cellmate. He's heard that she's a housekeeper who's looking for work. He offers her a job. While they're talking, she again flashes on visions of him being shot. She agrees to come to Gull's Way. As she hangs up, the visions become more intense.

The next morning, Hardcastle is indeed standing solemnly by a casket. It's the funeral of an old colleague, Charlie Clarkson. The eulogy is short and pithy. The deceased was a lawyer who was not much liked. After the ceremony Hardcastle strolls away with Frank Harper. Another lawyer, Wendell Price, approaches. He mentions the last time he saw Hardcastle. It was at a trial in which Price's client was convicted of attempting to strangle his ex-wife. Harper comments on Price's current status as divorce attorney to the stars.

After Price departs, Hardcastle says the guy is "a crumb". Then he asks Frank why *he's* at the funeral. It's official police business. Clarkson and his secretary were murdered. Hardcastle asks Frank to keep him informed about any developments.

Back at the estate, Mark's cleaning frenzy continues. The doorbell rings. It's Millie. She is assailed by another bout of the visions when she first sees Mark. Sitting down in the study a few moments later, she passes off her momentary weakness as the result of the long bus ride over.

While Mark chats with Millie, Hardcastle is searching for his keys. He and Mark have an appointment with Frank Harper. Millie reaches deep between the sofa cushions and extracts the missing keys. Mark is delighted. He hires her on the spot.

At the station, the guys encounter actress Loni Summers leaving Frank's office. Hardcastle asks Frank what gives. Frank says Loni received a phone call from Clarkson the night he died. Charlie told her he had information that would help her get a good settlement in her divorce from her husband, Dex Falcon. He asked her to meet him in his office the next day.

Hardcastle asks Frank how soon he can get a warrant to search Clarkson's office. Frank and Mark both want to know why the judge is so intent on finding out what happened to Clarkson.

Hardcastle explains that Charlie once did him a favor. Years earlier, he and his wife, Nancy, had gone through a rough patch. She had gone to Clarkson seeking advice about a divorce. He'd told her to stick it out.

Frank says getting the warrant will take time and until then there's nothing else he can do. The judge says that fortunately doesn't apply to him.

Hardcastle arranges to assume Charlie's law practice. As he arrives at the office, Millie, back at the estate, experiences another small vision—it's a fish, floating dead in a tank. In Charlie's waiting room, the aquarium that figures in Millie's vision already contains the piscine corpse.

That night, at the estate, the guys are finishing dinner. Millie's cooking is top-notch. She's even made the judge's favorite dessert. She says that was just a lucky guess. Hardcastle heads for the den. Mark offers to lend Millie a hand with the dishes.

In the kitchen, Millie tells Mark that his life is in danger. Mark jokingly says that's not news. Millie tries to get him to take the threat seriously. She tells him that she has had visions since she was a child. She's been isolated all of her life because of it. Mark turns and drops a plate, which shatters. It's another component of Millie's vision. In the minor confusion that follows, the subject is pushed aside, but Millie still appears troubled.

The next morning, Mark mentions Millie's predictions as the guys head out to continue the investigation. The judge scoffs.

At Charlie's old office, they interview Loni Summers. She tells them that she gave Charlie a number she found written on a piece of paper on Dex Falcon's nightstand. The guys speculate that it may have been a secret bank account. Loni explains that Dex never had as much money as he should have because he gave generous gifts to his friends. She shows them the diamond bracelet he just gave her the day before. The divorce is now off.

At a restaurant, Dex is telling Price that he can't put up with Loni for another night. Wendell tells him it's necessary, at least until Hardcastle is off their backs. They're worried that if Hardcastle represents Loni in the divorce, he'll discover Dex's ten million dollar off-shore account in the Grand Caymans.

The judge and Mark arrive at the restaurant and invite themselves to Falcon's table. Hardcastle congratulates Dex on his reuniting with Loni. Mark mentions the bracelet. Falcon jokes. Hardcastle raises suspicions about a secret bank account. Price insists that it's all just Hollywood rumors. He invites the guys to the reconciliation party he's hosting for Dex and Loni the following evening. As they rise to leave, a waitress turns and a glass of champagne is spilled—it's another part of Millie's vision.

That evening, in the study, Millie brings Mark a sweater and answers Hardcastle's questions before he finishes asking them. With all the minor domestic business settled, the judge heads for bed, leaving Mark with the gun-cleaning chores. As Mark gathers up his supplies to head back to the gatehouse, Millie has another vision of Hardcastle's gun discharging and a light fixture breaking. She appears troubled, but when Mark asks her if there is something wrong, she says no.

A short while later, Mark is in the gatehouse reloading the newly cleaned revolver. A shot discharges and strikes the fixture, just as Millie foresaw.

The next morning, in the gatehouse, Mark and the judge are inspecting the damage—a table lamp and a hole in the wall. Mark is increasingly nervous. He thinks Millie's anxious look the night before was indicative of precognition. He's worried about her other prediction. Hardcastle doesn't believe any of it.

Later that day, they hit pay dirt. Their sources reveal Falcon's secret Cayman Island bank account. Hardcastle decides to attend Price's party.

That evening, in the study, Hardcastle is ready to go. Mark is still shirtless; Millie is ironing his. She enters with it. She tells the judge he shouldn't keep a glass award so close to the edge of his desk, then tells Mark he oughtn't attend the party. He jokingly informs her the judge will have him home before curfew, but Millie is serious. She describes her vision which ends with Mark's death.

Hardcastle grumbles. She asks him if he wants to lose another son. Hardcastle says he's going and Mark is free to do as he pleases. Then he leaves. Millie again pleads with Mark not to go, but he tells her the judge is counting on him. He heads out the door.

They arrive at Wendell Price's elaborate home. The party is underway. The judge tells Mark that Harper will be there in an hour with a search warrant. He intends to get a jump on things and instructs Mark to have a look around the lower level. The two split up.

Wendell Price wends his way through the party. He's looking for Dex. He finds him necking with an attractive woman in the den. Unfortunately, Loni is right behind him and also spots her husband in the compromising situation. She stalks off.

Price steps in, dismisses Dex's current paramour, and informs him that Hardcastle has Harper working on a search warrant. He insists that they must get rid of the judge and his sidekick. He tells Dex to meet him in the pool house in ten minutes.

A short while later, Mark is approached by a server who tells him that Judge Hardcastle asked him to meet him in the pool house. As he walks outside, the lights and images are those that Millie foretold. Mark apparently wasn't listening. He proceeds to the rendezvous.

Back in the party, Hardcastle also receives a message from the same waiter. He's told Mark wants him out in the pool house. As he heads out, he's intercepted by Loni, who is upset. She wants a divorce *now*.

McCormick finds Price and Falcon waiting for him. He struggles with them and Price shoots him.

Hardcastle, having been delayed by Loni, finds the pool house empty. There's a small puddle of blood on the floor.

On a darkened stretch of twisting road, a car stops. Wendell Price gets out. He drags an unconscious McCormick from the trunk and pitches him down into a wooded ravine.

Back at Price's home, the police are arriving. Hardcastle confronts Dex Falcon, asking him where McCormick is. Dex jokes and Hardcastle slugs him. Harper has to pull him off.

Out in the pool house, Harper studies the blood. He adds Mark's name to the APB list. He tells Hardcastle that they found Clarkson's files in Price's office. The judge is incensed and determined to question Dex further. Harper stops him. He tells him to go home and see if Mark returned there. He says he'll call if they find anything.

In the woods, Mark is lying where he fell, with only the barest movement of his left hand to indicate he is not yet dead.

Back at the estate, Hardcastle finds no signs of anyone. Standing near his desk and reaching for the phone, he bumps the glass award. It falls and shatters. He stares at it a moment, then hangs up the phone and heads for Millie's room. She's gone, but left a note with her address on it.

He goes to her home and finds her still up, sitting in her rocker. She's adamant that Mark is dead. She rewitnessed the events of her visions as they were happening that evening. Hardcastle is equally adamant that McCormick is only missing. Though she's convinced it's futile, he drafts her to help in the search.

As they drive, and Millie protests, Wendell Price searches Gull's Way and finds her note. He heads back to the area where he dumped Mark.

As dawn breaks, Millie suddenly becomes more hopeful. She gets a new set of vibes off of one of McCormick's cassette tapes and becomes convinced that he is nearby. Price, waiting in ambush, pursues them. They attract police attention and Price is stopped by a roadblock. Harper already has Falcon under arrest.

The judge doesn't stay. He heads back the way he came, with Millie at last recognizing the spot from her vision.

He parks and gets out. From the edge of the road he sees Mark lying at the bottom of the slope. As Millie watches from above, he hurries down. Mark, looking battered, mutters "What took you so long?"

In the epilogue, out by the pool Mark's recuperating while Millie fusses over him just a bit. Hardcastle tells him things will be different after she leaves. Millie confirms that she's going to live with her sister. Mark protests—she can't leave him alone with the judge; he's *vicious*.

Over Hardcastle's objections, Millie tells Mark that the judge fretted while Mark was in surgery, and sat with him afterwards. She whispers something else to him that looks suspiciously like "He loves you." Hardcastle wants to know what the big secret is. Mark, of course, isn't telling.

The Context

The psychic subplot is handy, allowing for the threat of death to be raised right at the start of the episode and kept on the front burner throughout. Millie's recurrent visions come true in bits and pieces—though not always in the obvious way, as we see with Clarkson's casket slipped in among the other references.

Millie's abilities don't seem limited to predicting death. She's also pretty quick on the uptake when it comes to emotional issues. She points out Mark's joking as a cover for his affections, and seems to not only pick up on the relationship between the judge and Mark, but also knows this is the judge's *second* chance at having a son.

The whole idea of psychic abilities always has the element of inevitability to it. As Hardcastle points out, we've got free will. But psychics must all be Cassandras, because if we listened to them, and took steps to avoid our fate, then how could they foresee that which never comes to pass?

The underlying theme here is loyalty. As the threat is revealed, only one of the two concerned parties believes. Hardcastle isn't buying any of it. Mark, who seems much more convinced by Millie's strange powers, still won't back down from his commitment to the judge.

The payoff, of course, is that Hardcastle—hardheaded and practical-minded—is the one with the greatest faith. He refuses to believe that Millie's vision is *true* and persists until he finds his friend, still alive.

The Trivia

Carol Mendelsohn remembers Les Sheldon suggesting Clooney for the guest role of Millie Denton. "They were friends. Years later, I had the good fortune to have dinner with Rosemary. And, while I never introduced myself to her during the episode, we had a long talk about the show and her character, and how much she enjoyed the experience."

The latest address of the estate is, according to Mark, 101 Pacific Coast Highway, Malibu.

Mark's litany of hazards he's risked in the service of the Lone Ranger now includes being thrown off a train, a reference to the episode "Something's Going On On This Train".

Memorable Quotes

Hardcastle: Look at this place. Hey, we got no groceries. There's laundry piled up all over the place. You haven't vacuumed in two weeks.

McCormick: Do you have any idea how tired I am of having dishpan hands? Not only am I doing the dishes, but I'm also polishing silverware. I'm washing the garage. I'm even cleaning your dirty socks.

Hardcastle: Well, that's too bad, McCormick, because you're stuck doin' it.

McCormick: That's where you're wrong. I'm not stuck with doin' it. I'm gonna hire a maid.

Hardcastle: She doesn't know what's gonna happen. Nobody knows what's gonna happen. You can't predict the future. You got free will.

McCormick: Well, I am exercising my free will, and I'm getting off this case.

Hardcastle: No, you don't exercise any free will in my cases. You do what I tell you to do.

McCormick: Judge, you know, why, I must be some kind of psychic 'cause I knew you were going to say that.

Millie: Mark's dead.

Hardcastle: No, he's not dead. He's missing. Do you know where he is?

Millie: He wouldn't listen to me. You wouldn't listen to me. And now he's dead.

Hardcastle: No, you listen, he's not dead, you hear, and you're gonna help me find him. Come on.

Hardcastle for Mayor – premiered January 13, 1986

Written by	Alan Cassidy
Directed by	Kim Manners
Second unit director	Gary Combs

Cast

J.A. Preston	Vic Dutton
Andy Romano	Charlie Sykes
Richard Anderson	J.J. Norcross
Alvy Moore	Birdy Fletcher
Edward Bell	Jack Mann
Diana Douglas	Frances
Stacy Keach, Sr.	Kemp
Richard Kuss	Lou
Tom Dahlgren	Herb Austin
Greta Shipman	Stephanie Baxter
James Williams	Pierpont

Cast Notes

Richard Anderson was Oscar Goldman in the series *The Six Million Dollar Man* and *The Bionic Woman*.

J.A. Preston played the recurring role of Ozzie Cleveland in *Hill Street Blues*. He was Judge Randolph in the movie *A Few Good Men*.

Andy Romano also had a recurring role on *Hill Street Blues* as Inspector Aiello. He appeared with J.A. Preston in several episodes of that series.

Diana Douglas is Michael Douglas' mother.

Stacy Keach, Sr. was the producer and director of the radio and TV classic *Tales of the Texas Rangers*. In addition to six decades of TV guest and semi-regular appearances, he was the spokesman for Birdseye vegetables, appearing as the company founder Clarence Birdseye.

Richard Kuss also played Captain Don Filapiano in the episode "The Black Widow".

The Details

High up in the corporate headquarters of Norcross Industries, a cabal discusses the upcoming elections for mayor. They've decided their candidate, Jack Mann, can't beat the incumbent, Gilmore. What they need is a three-man race to siphon off some of Gilmore's votes.

Lunchtime, at the estate, at least it is for Mark. He's chowing down on take-out from Taco Tilly's. Hardcastle is headed for a more refined repast. He has an invitation to dine with J.J. Norcross at a country club. Mark suspects Norcross wants a parking ticket fixed.

He doesn't. On the veranda at the club, Norcross offers Hardcastle a shot at the mayor's office. The judge is at first astonished, but gradually warms to the idea. He tells Norcross he'll think about it.

Back at the estate, Mark is equally astonished. He says politics is the art of compromise (also the art of not telling the truth and not keeping promises). That's not Hardcastle's style. The judge asks why it has to be that way, but he also says he probably won't run.

Not very much later, at Hardcastle campaign headquarters, the copy machine is hammering away and the staff is on board. The judge looks less undecided as he meets his campaign manager, Charlie Sykes, and his media adviser, Vic Dutton. While Dutton takes Mark aside and informs him he is a political

liability, Hardcastle is swept into the thick of the process. He's handed a speech and sent to a press conference at city hall.

The scripted speech is the first casualty. Hardcastle crumples it up and proceeds with his own responses. One of the reporters asks him what's the deal with him, a strong law and order candidate, having an ex-con staying

with him. The judge says McCormick's paid his debt and is his friend. Mark, in the audience, looks pleased.

Inside, at a meeting of the city council, Herb Austin argues with Park Commissioner Jack Mann. The meeting is adjourned without a vote. Returning to his office, Austin is wished a happy birthday by his secretary, Frances. There are presents piled here and there, and she leaves to make some final arrangements for his surprise party. A moment later, yet another box is delivered. As the judge and Mark enter the building, intending to visit Austin, an explosion engulfs the man's office.

At Austin's funeral, reporters accost Hardcastle, who isn't very politic about his intentions to find out who killed the councilman. He seeks out Frances and asks her what Herb was working on. She mentions the parks bill. He asks to see Herb's papers. She tells him the office is sealed.

That night, Mark puts in an after-hours appearance at the city hall, posing as a plant specialist. He sneaks into Herb's boarded-up office and locates the file. The security guard gets curious. Mark has to climb out of the window and hang from the sill to escape detection.

The next morning, at the estate, Mark sits at Hardcastle's desk studying the map he acquired on his midnight spree, while taking heat from the judge about how he got it. The map shows prospective locations for a new park. One site, Pinewood, has a question mark next to it. Mark suggests they visit it and see what's up.

Before they can act on that idea, Hardcastle's campaign managers arrive. He's scheduled for a video op. The man of the people makes a brief speech from his yard with the ocean view. The managers want more but he finally breaks away.

On the way to check out Pinewood, Hardcastle says the campaign isn't going to his head. Mark's not so sure.

The entrance to Pinewood is gated and locked, with a guard dog and a grumpy caretaker to look after things. Before they're turned away, Hardcastle notices the tire tracks of heavy trucks inside the gate. As soon as they've left, the caretaker, Fletcher, puts in a call to Jack Mann.

That night, the judge and Mark stake out the place. They see a tanker truck approach the gate. Fletcher lets it in. Mark cuts through the fence and they follow the truck to a pond. A load of foul-smelling chemicals is being pumped into the water. Fletcher's guard dog takes alarm and chases Mark and the judge back to their truck. Fletcher shoots at them as they pull away.

The next morning, Hardcastle takes his suspicions to the police. He's told that Fletcher is in the hospital, recovering from a beating. Fletcher says Hardcastle and McCormick attacked him when he caught them doing illegal dumping. They visit Fletcher and tell him he's looking at accessory to murder charges. Fletcher clams up, but Hardcastle leaves him a phone number in case he comes to his senses.

The guys head back to the TV studio. Hardcastle is scheduled to appear in a debate with the other candidates, but the one he really wants to talk to is Jack Mann. He confronts him in the trailer where Mann is putting on his make-up for the broadcast. Hardcastle says he knows why Mann killed Austin. Mann is incensed. He threatens to sue Hardcastle if he goes public with his accusations.

Mann leaves. He goes straight to the top man in the conspiracy—J.J. Norcross—and tells him Hardcastle is out of control. Norcross promises it will be taken care of.

Back at the studio, in his trailer dressing room, Hardcastle assures Mark that everything is going as planned. He's sure Mann went to his boss and a move will be made against them very soon. Mark tells him to be careful if any packages arrive. The campaign managers show up. In the middle of their critique of his suit and tie, the judge gets a call from Fletcher. He wants the judge to meet him at Pinewood, alone.

The managers are aggravated. Hardcastle shags them off. Mark doesn't like the "alone" part. He gets invited along.

As Hardcastle is announced as a no-show at the debate, he's driving up to Pinewood. Mark's down on the floorboards, staying out of sight. Norcross is waiting with his man and Fletcher up at Pinewood. After Fletcher assures him that Hardcastle is on the way, he is shot and killed.

The judge drops Mark off a short way up the road then heads in. Entering Fletcher's cabin, he finds Norcross and the gunman waiting for him. Mark scales the fence and approaches. He sees Hardcastle coming out of the cabin at gunpoint. Mark tells them to stop. Hardcastle jumps Norcross' henchman, while Norcross and Mark exchange shots.

While Hardcastle brawls with the henchman, Norcross flees in a car. Attempting to run Mark down, he crashes into another vehicle. Both bad guys are soon subdued.

In the epilogue, back at Hardcastle for Mayor Headquarters, his campaign manager is disappointed that the judge wouldn't let them use the Norcross and Mann arrests as part of his campaign. Hardcastle has lost the election. It's concession speech time.

The Context

It's Hardcastle's second shot at high office and what a difference two years make. In "Mr. Hardcastle goes to Washington", the judge saw Mark as a political liability. Now he's willing to stand up in front of a mike and tell the reporters that not only is Mark reformed, but he's also a friend and he's proud of him.

As usual, Mark is in charge of keeping Hardcastle's feet on the ground. Curiously, though, he is not in charge of sticking a pin in the judge's balloon. The judge may be perpetually suspicious of McCormick's turns at good fortune, but Mark accepts Hardcastle's opportunities as being perfectly legit.

The Trivia

In the black and white "Happy Days Are Here Again" montage, we see clips from "Whatever Happened to Guts?" and "Mr. Hardcastle Goes to Washington". There's also newsreel footage of Roosevelt, Truman, Eisenhower, and Nixon.

What town is Hardcastle running for mayor of? Gull's Way has been variously established as being located in Santa Monica (first season) but more often Malibu. Malibu was an unincorporated part of Los Angeles County until 1991. It is now the City of Malibu, with a population of 12,575. Mark and the judge walk through the lobby of Los Angeles' City Hall on their way to see Herb Austin.

Looks like a real pair of eyeglass lenses on Daniel Hugh Kelly again for Mark's city hall break-in disguise. It's a different pair than he wore in "Faster Heart".

Memorable Quotes

Hardcastle: I have *not* been primping.
McCormick: What do you call standing in your room, trying on every jacket in your closet along with every shirt and tie you own?
Hardcastle: I call it none of your business.

Dutton: Judge, it's all wrong. The tie's going to make a glare, the suit's no longer in style. If only you'd trust me. I do know a little about politics, you know.
Hardcastle: Listen, give this a little thought, will ya? I know you're trying to do your job, but if I get elected or don't get elected because of the tie, then there's gotta be something wrong, huh? It's just a thought.

Hardcastle: I do hope that I did make a difference, and in my own way, I did my small part...to serve democracy. And that's a privilege. And, I guess, that's all I got to say, except to thank everybody who worked for me and voted for me and listened to me. Thank you. So long. (to McCormick) Come on, kid, I'll buy you a hot dog.

When I Look Back On All the Things
– premiered February 3, 1986

Written by	Lawrence Hertzog
Directed by	Steven Beers
Second unit director	Gary Combs

Cast

Jeanetta Arnette	Melinda Marshall
Vincent Baggetta	Ricky Gennarro
Paul Carr	Ted Rubin
Fred McCarren	Richard Wall
Dick Bakalyan	Paul Perry
Alan Cassidy	the mechanic
Tracy Ryan	the blonde
Heidi Banks	the brunette
Bryan Douglas Hatton	the second cop
R. J. Adams	the first cop

Cast Notes

Jeanetta Arnette is probably best known for her role as Bernadette Meara in the series *Head of the Class*.

Vincent Baggetta also co-starred with Daniel Hugh Kelly in the 1982 series *Chicago Story*.

Paul Carr played Lieutenant Kelso in the premiere episode of *Star Trek*, "Where No Man Has Gone Before" and was the first crewmember of the Enterprise to die in the line of duty—thus becoming an inspiration to red shirts for years to come.

Fred McCarren was a graduate of Ringling Brothers and Barnum & Bailey's Clown College.

Dick Bakalyan also appeared with Brian Keith in the 1957 teleplay, "Dino", which was broadcast as an episode of the TV series *Studio One*.

The Details

After a discouraging day that includes a wordless rejection by one woman, and plenty of words from another, Mark has a sudden attack of adulthood. He tells Hardcastle he wants to get a grown-up car. He pines for a desk, a Rolodex, and a vehicle that you don't have to "climb into".

Hardcastle offers him a cookie and a can of Pinkie Fizz. He also reminds him that he doesn't have the wherewithal for the monthly payments for a grown-up car. Mark is dispatched to the market to buy steaks for dinner and the judge holds out scant hope that he can even do *that* without getting sidetracked into trouble.

Mark is sidetracked, but only into an upscale car dealership, where the allure of real leather gets him as far as the salesman's office and a computer credit check. There he discovers he's already eighteen thousand dollars in arrears.

He and Hardcastle visit the credit records company and are told that his debt is owed to the Riverview Land Company. Mark adamantly denies ever signing on any dotted lines, though Hardcastle points out that he is a connoisseur of the free giveaway.

Meanwhile, in the offices of the land company, Ted Rubin is reviewing the sale in question with his right-hand man, Ricky Gennarro. McCormick purportedly bought six units from another salesperson, allowing her to win a car which was offered as an incentive prize. Now that the loan has defaulted, Gennarro hopes to reclaim the prize, but first he has to find the woman who won it.

Mark and the judge continue their discussion on the way to the developer's office, with the judge still suspecting McCormick was snookered into something. When they arrive, they are shown the contract. Mark doesn't recognize the signature he supposedly made, but there is another name on the contract that's familiar. It's his ex-girlfriend, Melinda Marshall, the woman whose testimony landed him in prison for car theft.

At Melinda's apartment, Ricky is trying to explain the rules of the game to her. He wants the keys to the prize car. Melinda finally agrees, but then slips out a back door and speeds off in the new Caddy. She collides head-on with the Coyote.

It's a touching reunion. Actually it's more than touching; there's quite a bit of front-end damage on Mark's side.

Back at the estate, Mark tries to get an explanation from Melinda. It isn't easy. This is a woman who has trouble seeing the difference between living in Bel Air with a dermatologist and two years in San Quentin.

Meanwhile, Ricky, who followed them to the estate, now returns to his boss to report. He's again advised to get the car back. Rubin is getting ready to shut his operation down.

Night, back at the estate, and Mark is outside looking pensive. Melinda joins him. The discussion turns to the Porsche that Mark went to prison for. Melinda remembers distinctly that the love-struck McCormick gave her the car in a fit of devotion. In his version, a lovelorn Melinda volunteered to have her name on the Porsche's papers in an attempt to win his affection.

It's morning in the kitchen and the argument staggers on. Outside, Ricky and an accomplice trip the alarms on their way through the gate. Hardcastle rushes out to the front steps. There's an exchange of gunfire that ends with the Coyote taking most of the hits and the two would-be car thieves escaping.

Later that day, at the body shop, Mark, Melinda, and the judge watch the Caddy get stripped down in a search for whatever is attracting the thieves. Hardcastle questions Melinda. He recognizes the name of her boss.

Back at the estate, Hardcastle pulls his file on Ted Rubin. Melinda gives a positive ID based on a very general description. Mark expresses some doubts and then they're back at it. Hardcastle wanders into the argument and Mark expands his doubts to include the judicial system. This leads to another set of highly skewed recollections—Mark's and the judge's—of McCormick's trial. The debate ends when Mark spots a tow truck hauling the Caddy away.

Scrambling off in pursuit, Mark and the judge climb into the battered Coyote, now held together with swaths of duct tape. By the time they catch up with the tow truck, they've acquired a coterie of squad cars determined to halt them. When they're finally sidelined, with four flats, they discover the guy in the tow truck is an FBI agent.

At Bureau headquarters, Mark and the judge are only briefly questioned. After that, they and the Caddy are inexplicably released.

Back at the estate Hardcastle points out that they're now under surveillance. Why else would a hot dog truck be parked just outside the gate? He and Mark continue to search the car and finally discover valuable postage stamps hidden in the roof liner. Hardcastle theorizes that this is how Ted Rubin moves his ill-gotten gains around.

As he's explaining, a sedan pulls up. Rubin and his men pile out, demanding the stamps. The FBI's hot dog wagon commandos join the fray and a full-fledged gun battle ensues. The bad guys surrender. Ricky is the sole holdout and Mark disarms him with a wheel cover from the Caddy.

The Coyote seems to have survived this encounter with only minor additional damage until an FBI agent tosses down a cigarette, igniting a trickle of gas which then triggers an all-consuming explosion.

In the epilogue, the guys say good-bye to Melinda at FBI head-quarters. She's off to Miami to testify in the case against Rubin. She offers them the use of the Caddy while she's gone. On the way home, Mark finally gets to ride in a grown-up car. But it's Hardcastle who's doing the driving when they're pulled over by a

motorcycle cop. Melinda Marshall reported the car stolen that morning and now the judge is under arrest.

The Context

The oft-discussed incident that landed McCormick in Hardcastle's court the first time is here examined with the Hertzog slant toward humor. The viewpoints are taken to such extremes that we are in no danger of believing any of them, but that means the essential question of who was right remains unanswered. Well, mostly so. Melinda behaves so irresponsibly that she confirms Mark's judgment (and the viewer's inclination) that she falsely accused him. Exactly what happened in the courtroom is left to our imaginations. Neither of the witnesses is portrayed as reliable.

It's probably better to leave it so. Any closer look at the situation would upset the tenuous balance required to make both characters equally likable. Hardcastle can't be wrong, and Mark can't be guilty. The immovable object and the irresistible force exist in the same universe.

There's another major recurring theme here as Mark continues to look for adulthood. He's looking for it in the wrong places and for the wrong reasons, but the search continues. All previous attachments are sacrificed on the altar of that ambition—at least this week anyway. The Coyote is just a car and Mark wants to trade up. That surprising turn of events, along with the extreme nature of the flashbacks, push the whole episode decidedly in the direction of a humorous fantasy.

The Trivia

In the heat of an argument, Mark mentions that Melinda's testimony landed him in Vacaville, adding yet another prison (if he wasn't speaking metaphorically) to McCormick's string of slammers. The ones previously mentioned by name include Joliet, Strykersville, Clarkville, and San Quentin.

Alan Cassidy, associate producer and writer for the series, has a cameo role as the body shop guy.

The Coyote, destroyed in stages in this episode, will make its official come-back five episodes later, at the end of "In the Eye of the Beholder", but it's seen briefly in the background of the epilogue of "McCormick's Bar and Grill" and mentioned as being outside and intact in "Poker Night".

Memorable Quotes

Hardcastle: What do you mean, a grown-up car?

McCormick: Well, something you don't have to climb through the roof to get into, you know? Something mature. Something sophisticated. Something… not *red*.

Hardcastle: What, are you going through a post-adolescent mid-life crisis here?

McCormick: No, Judge, I…I'm thirty-two years old. I don't even have a job.

Hardcastle: What? I don't pay you?

McCormick: You give me an allowance if I do my chores. I feel like John Boy.

McCormick: So you figured, what the heck, I'll burn McCormick. Worked before. Hah!

Melinda: That's always going to be there, isn't it? You're never going to let that go.

McCormick: Melinda, I went to *prison*! Jail, el slammer! I spent two years of my life with my back against the wall, playing hall tag with guys named Crusher! You were in Bel Air!

Melinda: Maybe, Mark. But you didn't know Gaylen. You don't know what dermatologists are like. It was like a prison to me.

Brother Can You Spare a Crime? – premiered February 10, 1986

Written by	Donald Ross
Directed by	James Conway

Cast

Kenneth Mars	Gerald Hardcastle
Robert Picardo	Manny
Claudette Nevins	Judge Sheila Mooney
Andrew Masset	Lionel Eagle
Leslie Bevis	Tori Van Zandt
Phil Rubenstein	Horace Munson
Clare Nono	Reporter
Wanda Richert	the defense attorney
Eric Fleeks	
Patrick Wright	
S. Marc Jordan	the tout
Charles Walker	

Cast Notes

Kenneth Mars also had a role as a P.I. in the episode "Too Rich and Too Thin".

Robert Picardo was the holographic doctor on the series *Star Trek: Voyager*.

Claudette Nevins had a minor role in the movie *Star Trek: Insurrection*, which also featured Daniel Hugh Kelly.

Andrew Masset also had a guest role in *Second Noah*, a 1996 series that starred Daniel Hugh Kelly

Clare Nono was cast as a reporter in the movie *Cujo* which starred Daniel Hugh Kelly.

Eric Fleeks appeared in the episode "Goin' Nowhere Fast" as J.J. Beal's accomplice, Johnny Barton.

The Details

It's race day at a track in Florida and the ponies finally come in for Gerald Hardcastle, who's just broken his unlucky streak with a $1152 win. As he chats with a tout, two men approach, looking unfriendly. And they're off, with Gerald in the lead by a couple of lengths, after hesitating only long enough to place one last quick bet with his knowledgeable friend.

It's a close race, and the two heavies finally catch up with him at the gate. He's hustled into a limo to meet with Manny, who wants the hundred thousand Gerald owes him, or else. Manny tells Gerald it's time to put the touch on his rich brother in California.

At the estate, Hardcastle quizzes Mark about the phone call he got from Gerald. All Mark can tell him is that the man is on the way there from the airport. He's astonished that Hardcastle never even mentioned that he had a brother, and further surprised that the judge hasn't seen him in ten years. Hardcastle looks edgily wary. He wants to know what his brother said he wanted.

With a honk of the horn, a cab pulls up. Out steps an effusive Gerry who embraces Milt warmly. The judge asks him what brings him to California. Gerald dodges the question. Mark barely needs an introduction. Gerald's already heard all about him from Aunt May and Aunt Zora.

Mark brings iced tea out to the yard and listens to Gerry give a monetary assessment of the estate. The judge is a no-show. Mark heads back into the house and finds him brooding in the kitchen. Mark lifts his hopes momentarily by telling him that Gerry said he's only staying for a few days. He finally convinces Hardcastle to go outside and be nice.

Nice isn't on the agenda. The judge finally loses it and demands to know what Gerry is up to. Gerald is indignant at his suspicions. Milt complains about all the times he's had to pay off Gerald's bookies, but mostly he's bitter that Gerald didn't even show up for his law school graduation. Gerald has some gripes, too. He says Milt never needed anyone. He announces that coming for a visit was a mistake and he'll go to a hotel.

The judge backs down, insisting that he stay at the estate. He even offers to take Gerry out to a basketball game, though the last time they were at a game together, Milt was playing and Gerry asked him to throw it in order to win some bets. Hardcastle thinks his brother hasn't changed. He pleads with him to just behave, especially tonight. He's having someone special over to dinner, Sheila Mooney, the presiding judge in a big murder trial—the Van Zandt case.

Even Gerald's heard of that one. He says people are betting on the outcome. He suddenly seems very interested. He even suggests that inside information could be profitable. Hardcastle scowls and his brother backs off. Hardcastle asks him one more time if he's in any trouble. Gerry says no, crossing his heart and everything.

That evening, it's dinner for four. Gerry only has eyes for Judge Mooney as he plies her for information about the case. Mark interrupts with a brief lecture on the inviolability of the judicial system. Mooney gives him a gold star for effort and deportment. The phone rings and Mark goes to answer it.

Gerry pursues her opinion on what will be the outcome of the trial and Mooney caves, telling them that it will probably be over in the morning—the Van Zandt woman has no defense. Mark returns, telling Gerry the call is for him.

It's Manny, who's arrived in town to oversee his investment. He tells Gerry to meet him outside in five minutes.

By the fountain, he threatens Gerry, who then offers him the Van Zandt information. He tells him it's a sure thing. Manny agrees to bet on the trial's outcome, promising to kill Gerry if it's wrong.

The next morning, Gerry, Milt, and Mark, at Gerry's insistence, have front row seats at the trial. The defense has called a surprise witness, P.I. Horace Munson, who says he was hired by the murder victim, Harlan Eagle, to follow the accused woman, who was his fiancé. Munson gives Trish Van Zandt a carefully noted and photographed alibi for the day of the murder.

That afternoon, back at the estate, Gerald hastily packs while making reservations for a flight to Mexico. Down in the study, Mark and the judge watch the newscast announcing the outcome of the trial. Van Zandt has gone free. Hardcastle is still suspicious about the very convenient surprise witness. In the meantime, the judge has dug out an old family photo album that he wants to show Gerald. Mark mentions that Gerry's been acting odd since they left the trial. Milt says it can't be his fault; he's been following Mark's advice and being nice to his brother.

Mark goes to get Gerald and discovers him heading for the door, suitcase in hand. There's a brief, tense scene in the hallway, with the judge throwing in the towel. Gerald walks out. A moment later they hear noises from outside. Manny and his guys are there. Gerry's been pushed down, guns are being pointed, and Manny tells the judge that his brother now owes two hundred thousand. He gets in his limo and departs.

Back in the study, Hardcastle is irate after hearing about the bet on the trial. Mark leaves them to sort things out. Gerald tells Milt that he has impossible standards. The judge retorts that they aren't impossible for McCormick but Gerry never even tried. Gerald says he's leaving for Mexico, so that Manny will follow him and be out of Milt's hair.

Mark returns as Gerry walks out. He agrees that the judge can't just pay off Gerry's debts, but he entices him with the notion that they might help Gerry *and* serve justice by proving Van Zandt really did commit murder. Hardcastle bites. He insists that Gerry can't leave yet.

The three guys visit Judge Mooney. They get a look at Munson's journal, which is a suspiciously homogenous document. They also get an address on Munson.

At his office, Horace Munson is in conference with Trish Van Zandt and the murder victim's brother and business partner, Lionel Eagle. He's demanding another fifty thousand dollars for perjuring himself.

Mark, Milt, and Gerry enter Munson's building. The judge and his brother are still bickering. They find Munson's office untidy and unattended. They search it. Mark finally finds the original notebook from Munson's surveillance of Van Zandt. It doesn't exonerate her.

At Eagle Brothers' corporate headquarters, Van Zandt assures Lionel that their troubles are over now that Munson is dead. Lionel, pondering a portrait of his dead brother, says he was never good enough for Harlan. Trish tells him to get rid of the painting. It's not that easy.

Back at Munson's office, Hardcastle has run a check on a license plate Munson jotted down from the murder scene. It belonged to Lionel Eagle. As they head out the door, Gerry notices a closet door ajar. He opens it and finds Munson's body inside.

A short while later, Hardcastle is in Lionel's office, claiming to be Munson's partner, Mr. Milton. He also claims to know what Munson knew about the murder. He tells Lionel to meet him at the Eagle Brothers store on Pico later that night.

Out in front of the building, Gerry frets while Mark is reassuring. The Lone Ranger always rides solo and Tonto never lets him get too far out of sight. While they discuss Milt management, Manny's limo pulls up. The henchmen grab Gerry and slug Mark. As Milt emerges from the building, Manny tells him it's two hundred grand or else. Hardcastle agrees to the deal and tells them to come to the same store location at nine p.m.

That night, at the rendezvous, Mark and a cop monitor Hardcastle's wire as he waits for his company. Lionel Eagle parks his car, Manny pulls up moments later. An unexpected third vehicle makes a run at the judge. It's Trish, who smashes up a couple of cars, but fails to fell Hardcastle. The officer summons assistance, while Mark uses the truck to block Trish's escape. Lionel bolts into the store, getting off one shot at a pursuing Hardcastle.

Gerry knocks Manny's henchmen aside and goes to his brother's aid. Mark isn't far behind. Gerry hollers a warning to Milt, who ducks another bullet from Lionel. Manny's goons catch up with the Hardcastles and a pitched brawl follows. Mark arrives and Hardcastle sends him after Lionel. He catches up with the man at the back of the store and takes him down. Hardcastle captures Manny, and the police arrive to take the bad guys away. As the dust settles, Gerry wonders how a guy could want to kill his own brother.

In the epilogue, Gerry is sharing the finer points of pari-mutuel betting with Mark in the study while he waits for the taxi to arrive. Hardcastle intervenes. Gerald is supposed to be going cold turkey and he's not allowed to corrupt McCormick. The cab is finally there. Milt gets a one-way hug from his brother, who then departs.

Hardcastle heaves a sigh and says he thinks this time maybe Gerry is going to get his life turned around. Mark winces. He says Gerry bet him Milt would say that. Mark's out twenty bucks.

The Context

It's parallel tales playing out, involving two sets of brothers. One is a tragedy and the other is a comedy.

The last of the Hardcastle relatives puts in a visit and once again it's Mark who's advocating just getting along. Of course he doesn't know Gerry, but even after he does, he's in favor of peace and brotherhood. Of course Mark is astonished when the judge announces that he'll try to follow the advice.

Gerald Hardcastle is the perfect antithesis of Milt—an unreliable rascal who doesn't give a whit for the rules—just the sort of person who would drive an orderly, rule-abiding mind crazy. Curiously, the judge, who always accuses Mark of playing fast and loose with the law, puts him in a separate category from Gerry. Mark has standards; he most often breaks the rules for the greater good, not just to save his own skin or turn a profit.

Mark's explanation of Lone Ranger and Tonto operating procedures (that he lets Hardcastle think he's riding solo but doesn't let him get too far out of sight) is a very nice commentary on how far the relationship has come. The sidekick is really a partner who's willing to keep up pretenses for the sake of his friend. He even admits (in front of Hardcastle) that he's given the notion of law school some thought.

The Trivia

The stock footage outside the stands in the opening sequence is from Hialeah Race Track in Florida. Famed for its resident flamingos, Hialeah has been out of the racing biz since 2001.

Gerald Hardcastle's middle initial is also "C".

Mark says he's an only child.

The judge is sporting his California Stars baseball cap again.

Hardcastle says he graduated law school at age forty-two. If so, he would have graduated in about 1960.

The Coyote, destroyed in the preceding episode, is seen in the driveway here, intact, in one establishing shot.

Shockingly, law and order Milt admits that he paid his brother to write a paper on the Magna Carta for him in high school.

This is the second time Hardcastle adopts the name of Mr. Milton for a scam. The other time was in "Strangle Hold".

Memorable Quotes

McCormick: I asked you whether there were any more at home like you—any sisters or *brothers*?

Hardcastle: Okay, I guess it's because I never thought of Gerald as a brother—he was more like a vagrant that had the room next to mine.

Gerald: You know what your problem is?

Hardcastle: Yes! I'm looking at it.

Gerald: You have standards—standards that nobody but you can live up to!

Hardcastle: McCormick can cut it! You never even tried.

Gerald: I don't want any help from you!

Hardcastle: Shut up! You're my brother and you're going to get help from me whether you want it or not!

McCormick: Now you're cooking.

Round Up the Old Gang – premiered February 16, 1986

| Written by | Stephen Katz |
| Directed by | Tony Mordente |

Cast

Abby Dalton	Fran Hendrix
Stuart Whitman	Teddy Hendrix
Peter Mark Richman	Roy Barlow
Beau Starr	Jensen
Sam Scarber	Farrell
John Crawford	Charlie
Robert Rockwell	Jerry
Joe Santos	Frank Harper
Virginia Peters	Dede
Kate Williamson	the secretary
Clint Carmichael	the security guard

Cast Notes

Abby Dalton was Julia Cumson on the long running series *Falcon Crest*.

Stuart Whitman's TV career spans five decades, beginning with a recurring role in the 1956 series *Highway Patrol*. He is credited with guest or regular roles in over sixty series including the ongoing part of Marshall Jim Crown in *Cimarron Strip*.

Beau Starr also appeared in the episodes "Angie's Choice" and "The Georgia Street Motors". He's also credited as a policeman in the pilot episode of *Murder She Wrote*, which featured Brian Keith as the murder victim.

Robert Rockwell played biology teacher Mr. Boynton, the love interest for *Our Miss Brooks*. He was also Jor-El, Superman's father, in the 1952 series. He died in 2003.

Kate Williamson is the wife of Al Ruscio, who played bailiff Charlie Masaryk in the episode "Poker Night".

The Details

The judge has received a summons from the L.A. County Fire Department. There's a five hundred dollar fine and orders to clean out the junk in the

garage. Mark has visions of a garage sale and big bucks rolling in, though neither man seems very eager to part with his own stuff. As they peruse their castoffs, Hardcastle uncovers a dusty trophy. It belonged to an old college teammate of his, Teddy Hendrix. The judge puzzles out how the switch must've occurred. Mark is surprised to hear that Hardcastle played ball with a famous former professional.

At dinner that night ("pasta a la McCormick"), Hardcastle waxes nostalgic about Teddy's days on the court. Now he makes commercials for a sports magazine. The judge decides to look Teddy up and return the trophy in person.

The next day, at his office, Teddy is unhappy. He tells Roy Barlow's henchmen, Jensen and Farrell, that he won't do commercials for Barlow anymore. He wants out and if they give him trouble, he'll take what he knows to the D.A. Jensen issues an unspecified threat. Hendrix summons his security guards to usher the two out.

The judge and Mark are heading over to see Hendrix. Hardcastle comments on how the man always had everything—great career, wonderful wife, the perfect life. He's looking forward to reliving old times with him.

They arrive at the office only to be told that Teddy has just left. Down in the parking garage, Teddy is being confronted by Jensen and Farrell. The judge and Mark interrupt the kidnapping, Teddy runs off while the guys duke it out with the henchmen. Mark has some problems with his, and in the confusion the bad guys escape.

Hardcastle taps Frank for an ID on the license plate of the fleeing kidnappers. It's registered to *Sports Action Magazine*—the people for whom Teddy works.

The judge and Mark head to Teddy's home. His wife Fran is there. She greets Milt warmly. They tell her about the attempted kidnapping. She says she doesn't know of any trouble he's in, but that he'd said he wouldn't do the ads anymore. She hints that he might be drinking. The phone rings. It's Teddy. Fran tells him Hardcastle is there. Teddy asks to speak to him and then tells him everything is okay. The judge tells Teddy he's having a get-together for the old team the following night. Teddy agrees to come.

Mark and Milt depart. Mark wants to know when the judge arranged the party. He hadn't, yet, but wanted to be sure Teddy came over.

Teddy was watching from his car, parked near the house. As soon as the guys have left, he heads inside. He takes a gun out of a hiding place in the closet but offers Fran reassurances.

The next day, Teddy enters his office and finds Roy Barlow sitting at his desk with henchmen in attendance. Barlow makes threats. Teddy pulls his gun. Barlow is unconcerned until Teddy puts a bullet through a vase. He backs off and Teddy leaves. An embarrassed Barlow angrily tells his men to make Teddy's death look like an accident.

That night, at the estate, Hardcastle's old teammates regale the judge and Mark with tales of basketball glory. There were elbows, and unfortunate nicknames. Teddy still hasn't shown and Hardcastle is getting concerned.

A sedan pulls up the drive and Teddy gets out. At the door, Hardcastle greets him. Ted seems jovial. Fran isn't along. It soon becomes obvious that he is slightly pickled. Hardcastle ushers him out of the party.

Out front, Jensen and Farrell have followed him. Jensen sees Hardcastle's name on the mailbox and puts that together with the rescue in the garage. They suspect that Teddy is inside telling all.

Teddy is in the kitchen, drink-ing coffee. Hardcastle wants to know why he's taken up boozing. He says he doesn't like himself anymore. He confesses that he threw the state cham-pionship game years ago. The judge is disbelieving at first, but Hendrix as-sures him it was only the first of many mistakes. He also steered young play-ers to Barlow for inclusion in his on-
going game-rigging activities. He plans to tell all to the authorities in the morning. He rises to leave but is obviously still drunk. Hardcastle insists he stay at the estate.

Out on the patio the next morning, Mark presents Hardcastle with Teddy's good-bye note. He sneaked out during the night, after deciding he must go it alone. The guys intend to find him.

Jensen and Farrell are already on Teddy's tail. They are planning a fatal mugging for the man.

Hardcastle calls Teddy's office. His secretary tells them the place was ran-sacked. She also says he has a weekly session coaching underprivileged kids at a local church. Hardcastle and Mark take off in the truck.

On a basketball court, next to a church, Hendrix coaches the teens. Jensen and Farrell are watching. Farrell says he'll knife Hendrix. Jensen will keep watch.

A moment later Mark and the judge pull up and get out, just as Farrell makes a move on Teddy. Hardcastle shouts a warning. Farrell misses his stab and flees. Mark chases after. Jensen is there with the car. He and Farrell get away.

Milt sends Mark with Hendrix to keep the appointment with the D.A., while he heads over to see Frank about some warrants. In Frank's office he gets the low-down on Barlow and his goons. While he's there, he gets a call from Fran. She's worried and she says she has something to show him.

Hardcastle goes to Fran's house. Barlow and Jensen are waiting inside in ambush. As Fran distracts him, Hardcastle is slugged from behind.

Fran, Barlow, and Jensen take Hardcastle up to a remote spot in the hills where Farrell is already waiting. Barlow places a phone call to the D.A.'s office, where Hendrix is in the waiting room. He threatens to kill Fran and Hardcastle if he doesn't show in an hour. Fran plays along with the ruse. Hendrix agrees to come.

As they leave the D.A.'s office, Teddy explains to Mark what's happening. Mark says they'll need some help.

A short while later, two of Hardcastle's old teammates are driving a station wagon, wearing hardhats and looking like engineering types. Mark and Hendrix are hunkered down in the back, out of sight. Barlow is not alarmed by their approach. He tells Jensen to get rid of them. Jensen steps too close and is taken down by an unexpected door maneuver. Mark and Hendrix pile out of the back and join the fray. Hardcastle slugs Farrell and Mark finishes subduing him.

Hendrix is winged by a shot from Barlow. Hardcastle connects on a few good punches with Barlow before Hendrix, still on his feet, moves in. It's all over, and Fran is left standing there, looking guilty.

In the epilogue, Hardcastle and Hendrix are out on the side lawn, pondering the misfortunes of love. It looks like Fran will be going to prison. Hendrix is set to testify against Barlow's operation. As he says good-bye, Hendrix thanks Hardcastle again for being one person who can be relied on.

Out back, at the garage sale, Mark revels in his sales skills. He presents the judge with the grand total, which is thus far $432.16. He's already calculating his ten percent fee. Hardcastle points out that there's still the fire department summons to pay, and ten percent of that will be fifty dollars. He's willing to accept Mark's check.

The Context

It's another look at Hardcastle's sports past, and another old friend who proves a disappointment, though the judge seems to take it in stride. Hendrix, in a state of inebriation, makes a very interesting comment about Milt. He points out that the man wouldn't recognize a bad apple if it fell out of the tree and hit him on the head.

The observation is not without merit. It isn't that Hardcastle is naïve; he knows there's plenty of bad in the world and is quick enough to spot wrong-doing. But it seems as though he has a blind spot when it comes to his friends. Just as in Clarence, when he was reluctant to see the flaws in his childhood companions, with Hendrix he was oblivious to the possibility of wrong-doing.

This episode is a nearly perfect inverse of "Outlaw Champion", with Milt's and Mark's roles reversed. There's even a point where Hardcastle comments on Hendrix's perfect life, just as Mark did about E.J. Corlette.

But this doesn't have the punch of the other episode because the judge had success enough of his own. Nor does Mark ever doubt that Hendrix and Hardcastle were buddies, even when Teddy stands the judge up at their first appointment. And while Hendrix may have lost the championship game for the old gang, it was just a game, not Hardcastle's intended career.

The epilogue is more-or-less a repeat of the twist at the end of "Whistler's Pride" where Mark, expecting to share the prize, also gets to share the much larger expenses.

The Trivia

The baseball cap that Mark knocks the dust off, and then dons, has a N.J. State Police patch on it.

On the table full of junk outside the garage is one of the hats from Hardcastle's mayoral campaign (a boater with a red, white and blue band). It's also the style worn by the Jazzmasters in their public performances.

Memorable Quotes

Charlie: And poor old Stumpy here had to, he had to help Teddy off the court—and he gave him oxygen, for five minutes or so. Yeah. He even, he had a couple of whiffs—oh, I remember that.

McCormick: "Stumpy"?

Charlie: Like in tree stump.

Jerry: Big, hard, stuck in the ground. Old Stumpy here'd set a pick and the guys would bounce off him like they ran into six feet of solid oak.

Hardcastle: Well, they don't call me "Stumpy" any more. It's, ah, it got kinda embarrassing.

McCormick: Oh, I think it's kinda cute.

Charlie: Hey, you want to talk about elbows? This guy was an artist. You should've seen the elbows this guy'd throw.

McCormick: Oh, I have.

Jerry: Oh, I can see the headline now—"Retired Stockbroker Shot in Shootout". And underneath—"Wife Refuses to Visit Him in Hospital Claiming He's Crazy". Didn't anyone ever tell Hardcastle he's retired? Man his age should be sitting around the pool taking in the sun.

McCormick: Tell him that.

McCormick's Bar and Grill – premiered February 24, 1986

Written by	Jeff Ray
Directed by	James S. Giritlian

Cast

Steve Lawrence	Sonny Daye
Michael Callan	Doyle Madison
Sam Anderson	Teddy Peters
Denny Miller	Blake
Joe Santos	Frank Harper
Teddy Wilson	Les the delivery guy
William Gallo	Billy the valet
Mike Finneran	Marty
George Parrish	the cop

Cast Notes

Steve Lawrence returns as Mark's wayward father, Sonny Daye, last seen in the second season episode "Ties My Father Sold Me".

Michael Callan also played Frank Kelly in "Once Again with Vigorish".

Sam Anderson plays the role of Bernard Naylor on the series *Lost*.

Denny Miller appeared with Brian Keith in an episode of *Wagon Train*. He had a recurring role as Duke Shannon on that series.

The Details

In the poker room of the Lady Luck Casino, two men face off over a hand of cards. On one side (holding a full house, queens over twos) is Sonny Daye. On the other side (with three of a kind) is Teddy Vestro. The cards are revealed. Teddy, already slick with sweat, is now twitching with nerves as he watches the last of his chips join the heap in front of Sonny. They've been at it since the afternoon before and Sonny wants to call it a night but Teddy insists on one last try. He's tapped out except for a deed to a club in the Valley. He offers it against all of Sonny's chips, for one cut of the deck. Sonny succumbs to the drama of the moment. A deck is produced and shuffled. Daye cuts it to reveal…an unbeatable ace of spades.

With winnings and deed in hand, Daye strolls out of the club. He tips the valet a twenty-five dollar chip and climbs into his Cadillac convertible. Driving through the night, he's heading for Malibu.

At Gull's Way, there's the sound of quietly breaking glass. Sonny slips in through the patio door of the gatehouse, a shadowy figure in a dark room. A newly awakened McCormick creeps down the stairs toward the intruder and gets the jump on him. He hits the light, and almost hits his father, recognizing him in mid-swing.

In the office of Doyle Madison, Teddy isn't so lucky. He's up against the wall. Doyle gave him the club property and told him to hold onto it. He only gave Teddy that job as a favor to Teddy's father. Doyle tells Teddy to get the deed back or else.

It's breakfast time in the kitchen at the estate. Sonny can't seem to understand why Mark's upset. He says he didn't come sooner because he was waiting until he had something that would make Mark less embarrassed about him. The argument snarls on, with Sonny finally admitting that as a man gets older he dwells more on the mistakes he's made. Hardcastle encourages Mark to accept what's starting to sound like an apology.

Mark's not in the mood for forgiveness. When Sonny tosses down the deed ("a gift"), he regards it with suspicion and hands it over to Hardcastle for further inspection. The judge isn't too confident about the gesture, either, but he thinks they should check it out. He also points out that he's the only one at the table with any money and much chance at getting a liquor license. He offers his contribution in exchange for a fifty percent share.

It looks like it'll be fifty percent of nothing. The guys go out to inspect their new investment and find a boarded up and derelict spot formerly known as the Ooh-La-La Club. The inside is even worse. Hardcastle manages to prod Mark into thanking Sonny ("It's the thought that counts.") then rushes off to see if he can halt the filing of the deed.

Sonny sits at the dusty, broken-down counter and tells Mark he'd always thought about working at a business with his son. Then he segues into the hope that they can get Hardcastle to go for an even split between the three of them, giving him and Mark controlling interest. Mark squashes that, saying the judge is his friend.

Hardcastle returns from his futile attempt to halt the wheels of bureaucracy. The deed has been filed and the joint is officially theirs.

A moment later, Teddy walks in. He offers fifty thousand to buy the place back. Sonny says no. The offers go higher, with Sonny looking pained. When Teddy reaches seventy-five thousand, Sonny seems to waver, walking outside with him. Mark looks disappointed but unsurprised.

Outside, the deal climbs to one hundred thousand, with Teddy ready to hand it over in cash right there. Sonny tells him to put his money away, and then goes back inside, scoffing at the idea that he could be bought. Teddy goes to a public phone, calls Doyle, and tells him he's failed. Doyle angrily says from now on they'll take care of it his way.

Back at the estate, Hardcastle and Sonny are alone in the study. The judge asks Sonny what gives. Sonny says everything's fine. He says he doesn't want to get in the way of Mark and Hardcastle's friendship. The judge points out that Sonny has gone years without even seeing Mark. He wants to know why the sudden and generous gift. Sonny doesn't give a very straight answer, only that the notion of leaving Mark a legacy occurred to him about two days ago. Hardcastle asks him if he can trust him about the bar and grill. Sonny says yes.

The two join Mark out on the patio. They discuss what they're going to call the place. Each has a suggestion. It looks like Hardcastle, as the banker, may have the deciding vote. Either that or it'll be an Irish singles bar with peanut shells on the floor and velvet on the walls.

They go to work (at least two of them do), and the Ooh La La Club is reborn as a mostly Irish pub. Meanwhile, across town, Doyle hires an arsonist.

The sign is delivered. The banker finds he's been outmaneuvered. It's "McCormick's Bar and Grill". As they discuss this development, an arsonist is at work in the alley. A squad car pulls up. The cop chats with Hardcastle. He also spots the guy in the alley, who takes his explosive device and skedaddles.

That evening, everything is done and the guys take a moment to enjoy their handiwork. Mark says it doesn't matter if they don't make any money; it's the effort that counts. He thanks them both. He and the judge leave. Sonny decides to stay behind. He wants a little more time to soak up the atmosphere.

Mark, almost out to the truck, turns back to get his jacket and overhears Sonny doing a pensive version of his lounge routine. Mark hastily retrieves his coat and excuses himself. Sonny delays him for a moment, and offers a half-hearted explanation of why he abandoned Mark and his mother. It was nothing intentional, more like an episode of absentminded neglect. He excuses himself as bad father material. Mark tells him that his mother kept Sonny's picture in her wallet. He used to take it out and look at it. The guy in the picture had a nice smile. Sonny agrees; he had that.

Mark goes back out to the truck, looking more reconciled. He's had his explanation, such as it is, for what Sonny did.

After they depart, Doyle and his men arrive. Doyle insults Sonny and then sics his men on him.

In the morning, at the estate, Mark tells the judge that Sonny hasn't returned yet. Mark is convinced he's run out on him again. He's working up to a good rant on the subject when they hear someone at the front door. It's a much-battered Sonny. After Mark's sent off to get the first aid kit, Sonny admits it was another attempt to buy the bar back. He doesn't want Mark to be involved and he refuses to make a police report.

Hardcastle goes to Frank who questions the wisdom of letting Mark go into business with Sonny. The judge has to admit that he's also in on the partnership. He tries to haul the conversation back to Teddy Vestro. Frank explains that Teddy

is the son of a crime boss and now works for Doyle Madison, who is a high level hit man for the mob. His victims disappear and are never found again.

Back at the bar, Sonny gets a call from Teddy, who's panicking. He says there's a price on his head and he's on the run. He tells Sonny he's coming over.

The judge and Mark walk in. Hardcastle wants information about Teddy. A moment later the man himself appears in the doorway. He barely has time to say he needs help, when he's killed by a drive-by shooter.

After the coroner's wagon leaves, Harper questions Sonny. The story of how he got the bar comes out. The guys ponder why Doyle put the deed in Teddy's name and why he wants the place back so badly. They conduct a thorough search of the premises. Hardcastle finds a false wall. Behind it are stacked twelve coffin-sized boxes.

More coroner's wagons depart. Frank quickly has the first body ID'd. They've found the missing mobster burial ground. They contemplate how to connect it back to Doyle. Hardcastle suggests a trap. Sonny calls Doyle and tells him what he's found. He asks for a half a million as pay-off. He tells Doyle to meet him at the bar in two hours.

It's opening night at the bar and grill. Sonny belts out a tune to a crowded house. A bunch of Doyle's heavies come in. Sonny wraps up the set. He strolls over to the counter, where Frank and Milt are sitting, and Mark is fetching cases of soda. Doyle enters and Sonny joins him at a back table. Doyle puts a briefcase on the table. He opens it, pulling out a gun. Harper draws, as do some of Doyle's men and most of the customers, who are all cops.

Doyle grabs Sonny and uses him as a hostage to escape. Mark, out back with yet another case of soda, shouts a warning to Sonny, distracting Doyle with a thrown can and then jumping him. The police screech up as Mark finishes pummeling Doyle. Sonny, looking astonished by his rescue, hugs a now equally astonished Mark.

In the epilogue, back at the estate the guys and Sonny discuss the fallout. The police have impounded the bar and Doyle Madison is under arrest. They walk Sonny out to his car. He's off again and he can't even promise that he'll be sending any postcards. He does have a parting gift for each of the guys. As Sonny drives off, they unwrap their matching peach t-shirts, emblazoned with Sonny's picture and, beneath it, "Have a Sonny Daye".

The Context

It's a nice bit of closure (at least as much closure as one could expect from a guy like Sonny) and a pleasure to see these three guys play off each other. The script has Mark calling Sonny "Dad" fairly often. In the filmed version, it happens only once, and only after some nudging from Hardcastle, in the middle of a thank you. It's a moment any parent can relate to, trying to get your kid to be polite to an annoying friend or relative, and a bit of irony that it's the judge who's filling that role for

McCormick, while his biological father stands by and receives the title.

Even a self-absorbed guy like Sonny comments that Hardcastle is like a father to Mark. Of course Mark brushes it off, amending it to "like a friend." And we hear from Frank that Hardcastle has talked about Sonny a lot since coming back from Atlantic City. Presumably he'd have had to talk to *somebody* about it. Presumably also he would have been a lot less circumspect without Mark around.

A major theme in this one is Hardcastle's cautious encouragement of Sonny's and Mark's relationship. To some degree it's a reversal of their roles in "Brother, Can You Spare a Crime?", though an abandoning father is in another league from a disappointing brother.

The Trivia

The script was pared down substantially. A particularly good sequence had Sonny leaving the card table and being gradually shorn of his winnings by a gauntlet of creditors between the table and his car, ending with the valet parking guy, who took his last $100 for two weeks parking and a tip.

Sonny heads for Malibu to the tune of "Father and Son", from Yusaf Islam's (then Cat Stevens) 1971 triple platinum album, *Tea for the Tillerman.*

In the Sonny and Mark montage we hear Steve Lawrence sing "I'll Be Seeing You". The tune is by Sammy Fain, the lyrics by Irving Kahal, and it was published in 1938. Much of the footage is from "Ties My Father Sold Me", but one clip is actually from further along in this episode. It's a sort of precognitive montage.

In the epilogue, Sonny mentions the site of Dillinger's demise at the hands of the FBI. The Biograph Theater, built in 1914, still stands at 2433 N. Lincoln Avenue in Chicago. It was designated a historic landmark in 2001.

Memorable Quotes

Sonny: We're more like a biological coincidence than a father and son. Maybe the judge here is more of a father than me.

McCormick: What he's like is more like a friend.

Sonny: Well, what do you want me to say, I'm proud of it? Well, I'm not. Look, Mark, the older a guy gets, the more he starts thinking about the mistakes he made, that's all.

Hardcastle: Listen to him, willya? He's trying to apologize. Pay him some attention, come on.

Sonny: I never meant to leave. I mean…I mean, I really didn't mean to walk out on you and your mother. It just, just happened. Got on a plane one day to do a club date and I just never looked back. I don't regret it, though. I mean, I wouldn't have been any good for you.

McCormick: She used to keep this picture of you in her wallet. I used to pull it out and stare at it…and think, this was my father, this's my old man. Got a nice smile.

Sonny: Yeah, sorry, kid. I got a nice smile.

Poker Night – premiered March 3, 1986

Written by	Marianne Clarkson
Directed by	Michael Kane

Cast

Gregg Henry	Tommy Kitchens
Marlyn Mason	Judge Mattie Groves
Paul Drake	Crazy Horse
Al Ruscio	Charlie Masaryk
Lou Richards	Freddie Bumgarner
Glen Withrow	Joey Britton
Jill Hill	Debbie Pledger
Joe Santos	Frank Harper

Cast Notes

Gregg Henry played the double-crossing best friend in the Mel Gibson movie *Payback*.

Marlyn Mason was devoted secretary Nikki Bell on the series *Longstreet*. She also had recurring roles in both *Ben Casey* and *Dr. Kildare*. She co-starred in the 1969 Elvis Presley film *The Trouble with Girls*.

Al Ruscio's movie and television career spans fifty years with two movies currently in post production, *Winged Creatures* and *Goy.*

Lou Richards is often cast as DJs or announcers. He started out as a radio announcer in Lubbock, Texas, and later in Honolulu where he had his first on-screen part in *Hawaii Five-0*.

The Details

It's late afternoon at the gatehouse. Mark is trying on ties. Hardcastle enters looking mighty peeved. He retrieves the bottle of 151 proof El Papagayo rum that Mark purloined. Tonight is poker night at Gull's Way and Hardcastle intends to present it to Charlie Masaryk, who's celebrating his twenty-fifth anniversary as a bailiff. Mark, on the other hand, has pulled out of the poker engagement. He has a hot date with a woman he met in an elevator that afternoon and he's already heard she likes daiquiris.

Meanwhile, elsewhere in town, three men are robbing a liquor store. They shoot the owner and flee.

In the den, the regular players are setting up. In addition to Charlie, there's Frank Harper and Judge Mattie Groves. When Milt steps out, Mattie tells Frank that she's snagged Freddie Bumgarner from the D.A.'s office as a last minute replacement for Mark. Frank tells her this might not sit too well with Milt. He's not a big fan of Freddie's.

Frank heads off to the bathroom, where he hangs his holster and service revolver on a hook inside the door. Hardcastle returns with chips. Charlie tries to tell a joke that Mattie says he's told too many times before. She begs him to stop and gives him his anniversary present. It's an engraved pair of handcuffs. The judge asks who the replacement player is going to be. Mattie and Charlie stall but it's no use; the doorbell rings and Hardcastle goes to answer it.

Freddie Bumgarner, a vision in buttoned-down obsequiousness, greets him. He's delighted to be there. Hardcastle smiles through gritted teeth. Freddie, who volunteered to bring the beer, has substituted a nice dry white wine. Hardcastle assures Mattie, *sotto voce*, that he will get even with her for this.

Hardcastle excuses himself. Mark arrives. He and Mattie flirt outrageously like old friends. He greets Charlie and Freddie.

Hardcastle is upstairs, hiding the rum somewhere he considers McCormick-proof. It ends up in a boot in the closet. He's muttering the whole time.

There's a honk outside. It's Mark's date. He bids everyone a hasty farewell and is off.

Hardcastle returns. The phone rings just as the game is about to commence. It's for Frank. After a brief conversation, he returns to the table looking grim. He's received news of the store robbery. The owner is dead. The conversation at the table turns to law and order, and the ruthlessness of modern criminals.

Freddie makes a long and fulsome toast. Mattie tells him to sit down and play. He sits, and then asks them to go over the rules of the game for him. It's a very slow hand as Freddie contem-plates his options. The doorbell rings. Hardcastle, feeling grumpy and ex-pecting McCormick, growlingly opens it. He's confronted by three armed men.

The leader of the trio, Tommy Kitchens, is a soft-spoken blond man in a sweater and tweed coat. He could pass for a high school teacher except for the assault rifle he's carrying. He tells the judge and his guests that if they cooperate they'll survive. The

second gunman is Crazy Horse, a wild-eyed, aggressive guy who moves into the room and surveys the hostages with a grin of anticipation. The third is a kid named Joey, who holds his gun nervously and looks and acts like he's about sixteen, though he's twenty-eight.

Tommy dispatches his men to disconnect the phones and search the house. He smashes the lock on Hardcastle's gun rack. The other two return after some general pillaging.

Joey is excited. He's seen the "race car" and wants to take it. He talks about how many cops are after them. Tommy tells him to be quiet.

Crazy Horse fiddles with the radio, and finds a news report about the robbery. The newscaster gives the names of the three murderers and the details of their criminal careers. Crazy Horse revels in their notoriety, while Kitchens looks worried. Hardcastle points out that there'll be a house-to-house search. They're trapped. Kitchens becomes angry. Crazy Horse laughs until Charlie points out that he's a punk criminal who murdered a man for two hundred dollars.

Crazy Horse moves to hit Charlie. Mattie protests. He insults and threatens her. She slaps him. Kitchens warns Crazy Horse to settle down and when that fails, physically intervenes, shoving him away from Mattie, then pushing him down and kicking him. Kitchens then turns to Mattie, who looks shaken. He moves her to the chair behind the desk, speaking solicitously.

He addresses the group again, very calm and in charge, telling them they're all going to wait until the roadblocks are gone. Crazy Horse is still on the floor.

Joey approaches Hardcastle and asks him about the Coyote. The judge says he owns it. Joey is disbelieving. Hardcastle says he hires the guys who drive it. Joey talks naively about his aspirations to be a driver. Hardcastle encourages him, then asks him if he shot the liquor store owner. Joey says no. Kitchens tells Joey to shut up.

Crazy Horse is back on his feet, and now harasses Freddie, demanding his tie, ring, and watch. At a nod from Hardcastle, Freddie hands them over. Frank asks to use the bathroom. Kitchens sends a reluctant Crazy Horse to keep guard. After Crazy Horse leaves the room, Hardcastle and Mattie try the collegial approach with Kitchens. He promises Mattie he will protect her.

In the bathroom, Frank discovers his gun is gone. Crazy Horse already found it and now has it out and is pointing it at him. He shoots Frank.

A few moments later, Crazy Horse is telling Kitchens that Frank went for his gun. He shows him Frank's badge. Hardcastle tries to tend to Frank, who is lying on the bathroom floor, shot in the abdomen. Kitchens gives Hardcastle permission to move Frank to a bedroom.

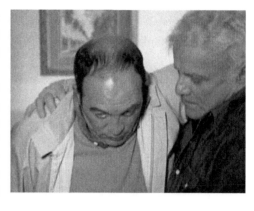

Back in the study, Kitchens has Joey retrieve wallets. Upstairs, Hardcastle settles Frank in the main bedroom. When he and Crazy Horse return to the study, Kitchens tells Crazy Horse who they've taken hostage. Crazy Horse says he'll enjoy killing a judge.

The hostages whisper among themselves. Mattie wants another try at reasoning with Kitchens. Crazy Horse tries to intervene, but Kitchens is still in charge. He lets Mattie talk.

Out in the gatehouse, Mark and his date, Debbie, have returned to spend the rest of a romantic evening. He's got the lights dimmed and the mood music on. He mixes her a daiquiri and pours himself a glass of wine. He proposes a toast to two people in the night. Debbie ratchets down the romance a notch or two.

Back in the study, Joey's twitchy. Hardcastle plays on his fears and reminds Kitchens and Crazy Horse that they haven't got all night.

In the gatehouse, Debbie waxes enthusiastic on the subject of daiquiris.

Things are getting tense in the study. Crazy Horse threatens Hardcastle. Kitchens tries to rein him in. Crazy Horse shifts his aim to Kitchens, who cautiously backs off, putting his own gun down. Mattie sees her chance and lunges for it, but Kitchens is too fast and intercepts her. He's now wound tight in a silent rage. Crazy Horse reveals that it was Kitchens who shot the store owner—he isn't someone you want to get mad at you. Kitchens tells the other two to line the hostages up.

Back in the gatehouse they're out of rum. What's a good host to do?

In the den, a radio news bulletin announces that the police are focusing their search. Kitchen tells the others they're leaving. Joey is sent outside to check the truck. Hardcastle is ordered to open the safe.

Mark sneaks in the back door, looking for the bottle. He searches the kitchen in vain. He creeps by the closed door of the study and slips upstairs. In Hardcastle's darkened room, he heads straight for the closet, and directly to the correct boot.

Turning to go, he hears a groan and sees Frank, who tells him they have a situation.

Downstairs, Kitchens cleans out the safe.

Upstairs, Frank gives Mark the lowdown. McCormick says they need a diversion. He heads into the bathroom to rustle one up.

Joey comes into the study, announcing that the truck is loaded with supplies. He realizes Kitchens intends to shoot the hostages. He objects. Kitchens tells him to go check Harper.

In the bedroom, Mark hands Harper something made from a cardboard tube and bathroom supplies. He tells him he's to light it and toss it down the stairs at the proper moment. They hear someone approaching. Mark kills the light. Joey enters. Mark punches him out. Frank suggests Mark call the police from the gatehouse. Mark says that won't work. His phone service has been shut off. Mark helps Frank out of bed, then heads for the window.

In the study, Kitchens intends to shoot Hardcastle first. Freddie steps forward and offers himself instead. Mark is just outside the front window. Debbie's at the door, looking for companionship.

Crazy Horse rushes into the hallway. Harper staggers onto the second floor landing and tosses a flaming object. Crazy Horse lets off some badly aimed shots. Mark crashes through the study window. Hardcastle tackles Crazy Horse, Mattie and Freddie jump Kitchens. Mark and the judge rescue Frank from the smoking hallway. The bad guys are all subdued.

In the epilogue, it's poker night again, two weeks later. Frank's nearly recovered. The Papagayo is flowing, and so is a tribute to Freddie from Hardcastle, who apologizes for having been not very nice to him in the past. Debbie also thinks Freddie's pretty interesting, much to Mark's chagrin. Freddie tries to give a speech. Mattie shuts him down.

It's time to deal. Debbie, who says she played a little in college, takes charge of the deck. She shuffles like a Las Vegas pro.

The Context

This is a non-traditional episode that's unusually taut and suspenseful. Though only Frank is a recurring character, Hardcastle's guests feel like old friends with a lot of shared history. Mark, ducking out at the last minute for his date, still seems to fit right in when he says his farewells. With the thunder rumbling outside, and the sudden arrival of bad guys in the night, things get increasingly claustrophobic.

The recurring theme here is that people aren't what they seem. Tommy Kitchens, calmly reassuring, is a thinly-veneered psychopath. Freddie Bumgarner, socially inept, has a stubbornly courageous streak. Innocent Debbie Pledger can probably drink El Papagayo straight shots and still deal from the bottom of the deck (and while Mark is conducting a "liquor is quicker" campaign, one gets the impression that the lady is engineering her own seduction).

The Trivia

151 proof rum is 75.5 percent alcohol and is also called *over-proofed*. It is usually used in cocktails not, as is done in the epilogue here, drunk straight. By itself, or when floated on other liquids, it can be ignited. Papagayo in Spanish means parrot, or one who talks excessively.

The only vehicle seen in this episode is a car in the establishing shot outside the liquor store.

Glenn Miller's 1939 hit "In the Mood" is heard as background music at the outset of the poker gathering. It was also the first song played on the jukebox in "McCormick's Bar and Grill".

Memorable Quotes

Hardcastle: Charlie and I go *way* back, a long way. We put Goosey McGowan in the pen together.

McCormick: Look, Judge, I would love to stand here and reminisce with you about criminals with nursery rhyme names, but I have a date. What do you think? Think I should I wear a tie?

Hardcastle: You can wear a dress for all I care.

McCormick: There's my girl.

Mattie: Hello, handsome. (they dance and kiss)

McCormick: How are you?

Mattie: Okay. I hear you got a hot date tonight.

McCormick: Yeah, but I'd dump her in a minute if I thought I had a chance with you.

Mattie: Oh, oh, that curly hair and those blue eyes. If I was only twenty years younger.

McCormick: If I was only four years older.

Harper: Did we get 'em?

Hardcastle: Yeah, we got 'em.

Frank: The house is on fire, huh?

McCormick: Nah. We just smoked them out.

In the Eye of the Beholder – premiered March 17, 1986

Written and directed by	Daniel Hugh Kelly
Second unit director	Gary Combs

Cast

David Rappaport	Cluracan
Leo Rossi	Marvin
Walter Olkewicz	Conyo
Fran Ryan	Mrs. Vassah
Steve Levitt	Ivan
James E. Moriarty	Benny
David A. Kimball	
Michael Mertz	
Peter Risch	Cluracan's shorter cousin
Chuck Schneider	the weapons salesman

Cast Notes

David Rappaport had the role of Randall in the movie *Time Bandits* and the lead in the 1986 series *The Wizard.* He was a British actor who had been, early in his career, a professional drummer and a school teacher. He was 3'11" tall. He died in 1990.

James E. Moriarty also appeared with Daniel Hugh Kelly in the 1987 film *Someone to Watch Over Me.*

Leo Rossi and **Walter Olkewicz** also costarred in the 1984 series *Partners in Crime*

Fran Ryan costarred with **David Rappaport** in *The Wizard.*

Steve Levitt played the role of assistant bad guy Peter Trigg in the episode "You and the Horse You Rode in On".

The Details

It is another dark and stormy night. In the study, Hardcastle is watching a basketball game while Mark studies a book on Celtic legends that he found in the judge's library. He wants to talk about leprechauns. Hardcastle isn't interested. He's more concerned about McCormick getting the place spruced up in time for the *Ladies Garden Monthly* "Best Home in Southern California" contest. Mark doesn't get it. Gull's Way already took the prize once before, ten years earlier.

Mark is mildly irate. He says he hasn't been paid for all the sprucing up he's been doing the past few weeks and his car is languishing in the shop since being blown up by the FBI. His insurance policy doesn't cover Green Hornet-related damage. Hardcastle moves closer to the TV, ignoring him. Mark returns to the subject of leprechauns and the rewards of capturing one. He could use the cash.

Hardcastle impatiently tosses him out. He wants him up bright and early to get on with the preparations.

Out on the highway, the door of a moving truck opens and a group of colorfully dressed little men leap out.

In the gatehouse, Mark is still delving into Celtic myth. His reading is interrupted by noises from the yard. He douses the light and listens closely to whispering voices. He is drawn to the window and sees the little men carrying a chest. Rubbing his eyes and rechecking his primary source material, he notices a striking resemblance between the intruders and ...*leprechauns*!

Scurrying to the main house, he tries to explain what he's seen to Hardcastle. The judge is irate, too. He tells him it's the result of weird books, peanut butter, and pizza right before bed. Mark, undeterred, grabs a fire poker and heads outside. Striding across the grounds, he comes upon the spot where he saw the little men. They're gone, but a hole's been dug and a chest is lying at the bottom of it. Opening it, he sees a hoard of gold coins. A moment later, he's struck unconscious.

It's morning. The storm is past...sort of. Hardcastle is still irate. Mark's not up and at it, nor is he in the gatehouse. He's out in the garden, staggering to his feet and claiming he was knocked out the night before while looking at a chest full of gold. Now there's no hole, no chest, no gold, and no leprechauns. Hardcastle hands him some paint and a brush and tells him to get to work.

In the office tent of a two-bit circus, Marvin's henchmen inform him that his star act has absconded. He's very irate. What's worse is that the missing act took off with the down payment he'd received for his promise to deliver them to Circus Maximus.

In the body shop, Benny the mechanic is also irate. Mark's just told him he can't pay for the repair of the Coyote. The car is lying in pieces and Benny says it'll stay that way until Mark comes up with the scratch.

Marvin, increasingly irate, chews out his staff of henchmen and strongly advises them to retrace the route of the previous night and find the missing act. He says it shouldn't be too hard; they're very short.

Mark is back at the estate, beating the bushes. He's unhappy, verging on irate, because he had to walk home from the body shop. Hardcastle hands him his mail—a letter notifying him his insurance is about to be cancelled for nonpayment. The judge also hands him a paint can and brush (again).

In a wood-paneled consulate office, an official listens impatiently to his three henchmen. They'd been following the circus caravan in order to locate and "termi-

nate" the little men. They, too, have misplaced their quarry. Their exceedingly irate boss instructs them to locate the missing former citizens and kill them.

Back at the estate, while preparing to paint statues, Mark notices a diminutive footprint in the dirt between the highway and the yard. With renewed determination, he heads for the garage and gathers up supplies. While he sets up booby traps all over the estate, the two sets of henchmen continue to search.

At the body shop, the Russian consulate car pulls out in a hurry as Marvin's men arrive. Benny mutters as he does his full service routine for the new arrivals. He's tired of everyone talking about little people.

In the gatehouse, Mark settles down, butterfly net and baseball bat at hand, with his booby traps all wired to a central alarm.

Meanwhile Benny is getting beat up by Marvin's men. He finally tells them what he told the guys in the consulate car—a man from an estate up the road mentioned seeing the little people.

Back at the estate, Hardcastle receives a call from Mrs. Vassah of *Ladies Garden Monthly*. He says everything is ready for the inspection tour. The call ends abruptly. It sounds like she's irate.

Afterwards, he steps outside to survey his domain and trips one of Mark's traps. McCormick, at the other end of the line, is jarred awake and dragged (by something considerably heavier than a leprechaun) smack into a wall. Pulling himself together, and armed with net and bat, he sallies forth. Hardcastle is plenty irate, so much so that he doesn't notice the second booby trap behind him. He's hoisted in the air.

The next morning, Mark has a black eye and Hardcastle, for reasons of plot furtherance, is paying off Benny. The mechanic is past irate, he's flat out angry. He says the doctor's bill will follow. He tells them about the various henchmen who've been hanging around since Mark mentioned the pixies. He also says the Coyote will be ready in about two months.

Walking away from the auto shop, Mark is even more convinced that there are leprechauns afoot. Hardcastle figures there's a more prosaic explanation and wants to go to the police. Mark pleads for a chance for the two of them to figure this out on their own.

That night, the guys are done up in camo, hiding in the bushes. Mark spots something moving. It's an irate skunk. Hardcastle gets hit.

Back at the consulate, the official informs his henchmen that the estate has been entered in an imperialist land contest. Meanwhile, at a local gun shop, Marvin and his lackeys are loading up on firepower. They intend to strike before the Russian agents can get to Gull's Way.

At the estate, Mark and the judge are still hunkered down in the dark. Mark is prattling on about leprechaun lore. Hardcastle is grumbling. Off in the distance, through the underbrush, they suddenly spy flames. Creeping closer, they see a group of little men playing music near a campfire. Chaos breaks loose as Mark trips over one of his booby traps and stumbles into the camp.

As the little guys scatter, Hardcastle scoops one up. Mark tells him to hold on while he threatens ("Tell us where the gold is or you've cobbled your last shoe!"). The rest of the little men return and their leader, Cluracan, asks the judge to put his cousin down. Hardcastle complies. Cluracan says they are defectors from an Eastern European country. The gold belongs to them and was stolen by the circus manager who locked them up like animals. He promises that he and his family will still be there in the morning. McCormick doesn't believe a word of it but Hardcastle hauls him away and leaves the little people in peace.

The next day, Hardcastle apologizes to Frank for dragging him all the way out to the estate—the camp is deserted. Mark rushes up, carrying his book and arguing that they were lied to by leprechauns.

The barbarians—ahem, *ladies*—are at the gate. There are three of them, looking very determined but not at all well-shaved. Mark warily lets them in. Meanwhile Marvin and his men scale the side fence, carrying their weapons.

Over on the lawn, by the refreshment table, Frank tells the judge he'll check into the missing little people. He asks him if this isn't the same contest that his wife won ten years earlier. As the judge hurries off to see to the ladies, Frank muses that this is also the anniversary of Nancy Hardcastle's death.

The front gate bell rings again and Mark encounters three more lady judges, almost as scary as the previous set. He lets them in. Back at the refreshment table, now stripped clean by one of the counterfeit judges, Hardcastle approaches the second trio. As Mrs. Vassah expounds on this year's theme ("order"), the faux-judges and Marvin's men encounter each other. Small arms fire is heard. A rocket launcher is deployed. A swift downward spiral of order ensues. Frank is hit, as are several statues. Marvin's men get the upper hand and quickly have everyone at gunpoint.

From the trees, Cluracan's men swing into action. They scatter, distract, and ambush most of the bad guys. Mark takes off after Cluracan himself and chases him straight into the clutches of Marvin. The circus owner tells Mark to back off. He's not giving up one of only three people in the world who can do "a triple".

As Mark tries to fit this into the facts as he sees them, Marvin steps back, and trips a booby trap. Mark ducks. Marvin gets a tire to the nose and is knocked out. Cluracan is about to run, but halts at a look from McCormick. His accent shifts from Romany to Irish and he asks Mark what he wants. Mark says he thought he knew, but now he figures he has enough—a friend who'll stay up all night and help him look for leprechauns. He's decided he has no right to chase after someone else's gold.

He deliberately turns his back and when he looks over his shoulder, a moment later, Cluracan and his men are gone.

In the epilogue, Hardcastle's in the study, using a skunk smell cure. Mark is on the sofa, waking up and moaning about Benny taking two months to fix his car. Hardcastle informs him he's been out cold since the fight, knocked down (along with Marvin) by one of his booby traps. He also explains who the various henchmen were, and that one set had diplomatic immunity and the other was bailed out by mobsters from New Jersey. The gypsy acrobats have disappeared.

Mark tries to relate his version. Hardcastle's not buying. Mark throws in the towel. Hardcastle tells him he should take up realism. A rainbow, such as the one currently visible through the front window, does not lead to a pot of gold. He points at the rainbow in question. Both men stare. It leads down to a perfectly restored Coyote and an immaculate yard.

The Context

And now for something completely different—two parts comedy and one part fantasy, this one is unique among the episodes. The characters are taken to humorous extremes. Hardcastle fanatically watches the game, with his Lakers jacket on and the Celtics pennant on the mantelpiece, and rags at McCormick incessantly about the yard work. Mark quests after pixies with single-minded determination and grumbles at Hardcastle, also incessantly, about not getting paid. *Everybody* is irate in this one, except Frank, who gets shot (two weeks in a row!).

But in the end the message is the same. It's about friendship, and even in the midst of mayhem and mythology, that remains a constant.

The Trivia

Chuck Schneider, who ran lines with Brian and Danny, read the script and wanted to know what really happened in the ending—did the leprechauns fix the car, or what? Danny Kelly said, "I'd kinda like to leave that up to the audience." And Chuck replied, "Well, I think that's what you should call it, 'In the Eye of the Beholder'," which became the title of the episode.

In his rant on the subject of authenticity, Marvin mentions the "unicorn fiasco" of the previous year. Though not exactly a fiasco, in 1985 the Ringling Brothers and Barnum & Bailey Circus did feature the "original genuine unicorn". It was all three of those things, but was also an angora goat named Lancelot, who had been surgically altered so that he grew a single central horn using a process (U.S. Unicorn Patent 44279685) developed by Timothy Zell. The last of the nine unicorns he created died in 2005.

Leo Rossi took over the role of Marvin on short notice after original cast member, Tim Phillips, sustained an injury while the episode was being shot.

The tune being played by the little people at the campfire is "Planxty John O'Connor" composed by the blind Irish harpist, Turlough O'Carolan. This recording is by The Chieftains.

On the morning of the judging, Frank muses to himself that Hardcastle's wife won the contest ten years previously and died "five years ago, to this day" (spring of 1981). In the pilot episode Hardcastle said his wife had died ten years earlier, or in 1973.

This episode premiered on (of course) St. Patrick's Day.

Memorable Quotes

McCormick: What is the big deal about winning "Best Home of Southern California"? You already won it once, already.

Hardcastle: That was ten years ago. Never mind why I want to win it again. That's none of your business.

Cluracan: Like most men, they are not satisfied with what they have, although that is already too much. But, you know this, Judge Hardcastle. You have seen it with your own eyes. You have seen it firsthand.

McCormick: How do you know his name?

Cluracan: It is printed on his mailbox.

McCormick: You know, if you'd asked me that yesterday, the answer would've been easy. But I think I've got everything I want, thanks.

Cluracan: Oh, do you now?

McCormick: Yeah. I got a friend who'd do anything for me, including staying up all night looking for a pack of pixies. That's gotta be worth more than all the gold in the world.

Cluracan: That's true. That's true.

The Day the Music Died – premiered March 31, 1986

Written by	Tom Blomquist
Directed by	Charles Picerni

Cast

Louis Giambalvo	Nick Damion
Patricia Harty	Jeannine Alexander
Daniel Davis	Joey Kello
Michael David Lally	Warren Rutledge
Georgann Johnson	Kate Bell
Joe Santos	Frank Harper
Marc Solver	
Ted White	
Courtenay McWhinney	the cashier

Cast Notes

Louis Giambalvo had recurring roles portraying Phil Harbert on *Knots Landing* and Rob Nelson on *Hill Street Blues.*

Patricia Harty also appeared in "Whatever Happened to Guts". She's the wife of producer Les Sheldon.

Daniel Davis, a native of Arkansas, played the British butler, Niles, on the series *The Nanny.* He also played a holographic Moriarty in two episodes of *Star Trek: The Next Generation.*

Georgann Johnson had a recurring role as Marge Bellows on the 1952 series *Mr. Peepers.* She also played a guest role as the evil Princess Arura on the series *Captain Video and His Video Rangers.*

The Details

Hardcastle is in the study, holding a practice session with the Jazzmasters, when Mark calls. He's supposed to be home already; instead he's in Las Vegas. Hardcastle wants to know the girl's name. It's Brenda, but Mark promises he's leaving soon.

On the road at night, out in the desert, Mark hears a familiar voice on the radio. It's Nick Damion, broadcasting from Lost Springs, Arizona. Mark's an old fan. He pulls out the map and finds the town. It's only a half an hour away. On an impulse, he heads for it.

It's a tiny station in a desolate spot, and the man in the broadcast booth is calling himself Joe Cross. Mark insists he recognizes the voice and the phrases. He's certain the guy is Nick Damion, the Midnight Prince of Rock and Roll, who broadcast out of New York in the mid-sixties. Joe Cross denies it all. Mark hesitates, then apologizes for his error and leaves, casting one look back at the man who says he's nobody famous.

In the morning, back at the estate, Hardcastle doesn't have much sympathy for Mark's story. Mark tries to explain that Damion was a hero to him. In the end, he gives up. It's just something personal. The judge is more interested in getting some help setting up for the company he's expecting. The organizing committee for the new music museum is arriving soon. Mark can't quite get his mind off the Nick Damion mystery, though.

Later that morning, the committee is in session. Kate reads off the tentative schedule, while casting some significant glances in Milt's direction. Sidney mentions the first nominee in the rock category, Danny Phillips, who's being honored posthumously. A presenter hasn't been found yet. At the mention of this, Mark excitedly interjects, suggesting Nick Damion. Sidney is all for it. Damion was an early promoter of Phillips' songs. Joey Kello says it's impossible; Damion dropped out of sight fifteen years earlier.

Mark relates the story of his encounter with the man he thinks is

Damion. Kate becomes enthusiastic, too. The resurfacing of a DJ legend after so many years would be a publicity coup. Kello is still discouraging, but Mark says he and Hardcastle don't mind a little trip out to Lost Springs.

Later that day, in the office of his record company, Kello is angry. He discusses the situation with his partner, Warren Rutledge. Warren thinks Nick will stay out of sight, the way he's supposed to. Kello wants a little more insurance.

In Lost Springs, at the radio station, the guys talk to the station's manager, Jeannine Alexander. She tells them Joe left town for a vacation. Mark floats his theory about who Cross really is. Jeannine shoots it down. She says she hired Cross herself, mostly out of sympathy.

She takes them down to the local café for some coffee. She applauds the choice of Danny Phillips for the hall of fame. Mark remembers where he was when he heard the news that Phillips had died. Hardcastle finally says they should get going. Mark asks the woman at the cash register if she knows where Cross is staying. It's at a motel near the outskirts of town. Mark suggests to Hardcastle that they stay there, too. Jeannine offers them a room at her place but Mark can't be dissuaded. He's still hoping to find Damion.

Later that night, outside the motel, Jeannine talks to some men in a sedan. She tells them she's worried about Joe and says he's "strung out". The men head to his room.

In another room at the motel, Hardcastle grumbles about the state of the place. Mark says he's going out to see if Damion is around.

He's there, and the two men Jeannine talked to are with him. They're searching his room.

Mark lets himself into the motel clerk's office, and goes through the registration cards.

In "Joe's" room, one of the men has found something. The two men haul him outside.

Mark, hearing the noise, steps out of the office and sees the man being hustled into the sedan. He intervenes, throwing a punch at one of the captors. A short fight later, Hardcastle arrives. Mark says it looked like a kidnapping. The man he slugged flashes a badge. Mark and Joe Cross are both under arrest.

In the local lock-up, Mark's holding a one-sided conversation. Joe just wants to be left alone. Mark tells him that when he was a kid, Nick Damion kept him up all night. Mark hid a radio under his pillow so he could listen to him. Mark tells him Nick saved his life. Cross finally admits he once was Damion, but he isn't anymore.

In the morning, Hardcastle springs Mark, who still wants to help Nick. Hardcastle says the guy needs a couple years in drug rehab. Mark insists that what Damion really needs is his self-respect back. He wants him to present that award. He tells the judge that when he was fourteen he was very depressed. One particularly desperate night, he called up Nick Damion at the radio station. Nick talked to him for two and a half hours and convinced Mark that he was better off than he'd realized. Now that Damion is down, he feels like he owes him the same favor. He asks Hardcastle to help him get Nick out of jail.

Back in L.A., Kello and Rutledge discuss the fallout. Nick's now been released into Hardcastle's custody. Kello doesn't trust Nick and wants to finish him off for good. Damion knows Kello killed Danny Phillips. Rutledge says he can convince Nick to leave town again.

At the gatehouse, Hardcastle is laying down the law to Damion. He's got to stay clean and he has to show up for the ceremony at the museum. Nick asks to call Jeannine, to let her know he's okay.

The guys step out. Nick makes the call and tells Jeannine where he is. She says it's dangerous for him to be in L.A. He says Danny gave him a tape he made of his last telephone conversation with Joey Kello. On it, the two talked about payola and Danny wanting out. Kello threatened to kill Phillips. Nick still has the recording and just needs a couple of days to get his head straight. She tells him she's coming to L.A.

That evening, in the study, Nick asks Mark what he said that time he talked with him on the phone. Mark tells him. He says he was "real close" to the edge. Nick says he's been there, too. He says he was paid to push Danny Phillips' records. He also says he killed him.

The next day, at the police station, Frank Harper tells Mark and the judge the coroner's report indicated that Phillips' death was the result of an accidental car crash. He also says Damion's been in a lot of small town jails, working his way to the bottom. Mark springs to Nick's defense. The judge is more interested in who was paying him. From the station's records, it looks like Kello's company had the most airtime on Nick's show.

They leave Frank's office. Mark thinks Phillips objected to the payola and Kello had him killed. He still doesn't believe Nick could have murdered anyone. Hardcastle isn't sure there even *was* a murder but he still has pieces to put together.

On a boardwalk, overlooking the harbor, Rutledge meets with Damion. He tells him Kello wants him dead. He says he's been the one protecting Nick all these years. Nick talks about Phillips' talent and his death. Rutledge finally hands Nick an envelope that contains money. He makes one final plea for Nick to leave.

The judge and Mark go to the music museum's offices. They ask Kate for the file on Kello Records. In it they find a newspaper photo of Jeannine with Joey Kello at Madison Square Garden.

In Kello's office, Jeannine tells him that Nick has evidence on a tape and she thinks he'll use it. She offers to take care of it. She'll provide Nick with a lethal dose of drugs and his death will look like an accident.

At the estate, Nick's gone and so is the judge's Corvette. Mark pleads for more time but Hardcastle calls it in to Harper. The ceremony is only a few hours away. Mark still thinks Damion will be there.

At the marina, Jeannine meets Nick. He tells her he has to be at the ceremony. She tells him it's dangerous. Nick is feeling the pangs of drug withdrawal but he's still determined. He gives the tape to Jeannine for safekeeping. She hands him the drugs.

At Kello's office, Rutledge tells Joey everything will be okay. He's bought Nick off. Kello, looking grimly satisfied, agrees that it's all under control. He pulls out a gun.

At the museum, the crowd is gathering for the ceremony. Nick's nowhere in sight and Mark is losing hope. Kello arrives. Hardcastle confronts him and asks about the connections between him, Jeannine and Damion. Kello claims to know nothing.

After the guys walk away, Jeannine approaches Kello. He tells her it's all just speculation and there's nothing to worry about.

Sitting in the 'Vette, Nick reaches for the supply of drugs Jeannine provided. The radio is on and the newscast announces that Warren Rutledge's body has been found, shot. Nick, appearing grief-stricken, tosses down the drugs and screeches off.

The ceremony has commenced. The Jazzmasters are playing. Harper arrives and tells Mark about Rutledge's murder. He also tells him that Rutledge was Damion's brother. A moment later Nick pulls up in the 'Vette and heads for the podium. He addresses the startled audience, using his trademark sixties DJ style. Nick accepts the blame for taking payola and accuses Kello of giving it, and of killing Danny Phillips. Then he attacks Kello, who pushes him away and draws a gun.

Kello bolts, pursued by Mark and Frank. Mark knocks him into a reflecting pool and Frank arrests him. Nick goes to Jeannine. The judge and Mark approach this touching scene. Hardcastle shows Damion the newspaper photo of Jeannine and Kello. He stares at it in shock, then tells Hardcastle the tape is in Jeannine's purse.

In the epilogue, the guys visit Damion at his new job. He's now the mid-morning DJ at an L.A. radio station. He's in a drug rehab program. As they step out the door, Nick punches up the next song. He announces that it's a special request from a friend, Mark McCormick. It's the Jazzmaster's stirring demo tape rendition of "When the Saints Go Marching In".

The Context

It's a plot that hearkens back to the second season episode, "Pennies from a Dead Man's Eyes". Mark recognizes an old performer, who's now laboring in obscurity under an alias. The man's former associates want him to stay retired, and one of them wants to make it permanent.

This time though, it's much more personal. The drop-out is a hero of McCormick's, and one who had a direct impact on his life. We get some back story touching on Mark's mysterious and misspent youth, and yet another insight into the effect that Sonny's abandonment had on him.

In this episode Mark's been off in Palm Springs (something to do with racing, according to the script), then he tools over to Las Vegas, and finally, on a whim, down to Lost Springs (it must have been nice to finally have the Coyote back). His only commitment appears to be his promise to run the sound equipment for the Jazzmasters' practice session.

Once again Mark is the source of the case, and Milt only grumbles a little before pitching in. There are no dire threats from him, stemming from McCormick's visit to the Lost Springs lock-up, and no major difficulty getting him out.

It all seems to point to a change in Mark's situation. The most obvious one is that he's no longer a parolee. His three years would have been up sometime in March, going by the dates given in "Rolling Thunder" and placing the episodes in an approximate relation to real time.

This one picks up the tone hinted at in "Poker Night". Mark now has a social life of his own, and he comes and goes with no supervision.

And while cases still come to Gull's Way with astonishing frequency, Hardcastle isn't digging into the files and coming up with new projects the way he did in first season episodes such as "The Black Widow" and "Flying Down to Rio". The newer crop of incidents stem from garage sales, poker games, and museum dedications.

The writer, Tom Blomquist, called this episode a "change-up", and said he enjoyed the chance to explore a new aspect of the character. As he put it, it was "an opportunity to 'peel the onion' and get to a character's deeper levels." It's the kind of thing that can only come after the characters are established and there's something to change *from*.

It would have been interesting to see the avenues this series would have explored, had it run for a fourth season. Episodes like this hint at what might have been the direction of development in a show in which the characters and their relationship were evolving.

The Trivia

The songs Damion plays, in order of appearance, are: Don McLean's "American Pie", Marvin Gaye's "I Heard It Through the Grape Vine", and The Beatles' "Hey Jude". In the epilogue he played Sonny Curtis' "I Fought the Law", with a dedication to bad guy Joey Kello.

KKSB, the station Damion is working for in Arizona, are currently the call letters for an oldies station in Santa Barbara.

In the scene on the pier between Nick and Rutledge, the ship in the background is the Queen Mary, permanently docked in Long Beach.

The establishing shot of Kate's office building is the County Hall of Justice, at 210 Temple Street in Los Angeles.

The "Pioneers of Music Hall of Fame" exteriors were shot at the Mark Taper Forum, a 745-seat theater which opened in 1967 and is part of the Los Angeles Music Center. At minute 42:12, the Jacques Lipchitz sculpture, *Peace on Earth* (said to be the most photographed piece of public art in L.A.) is seen over Mark's right shoulder. The Dorothy Chandler Pavilion is directly behind that.

Having not made any appearances since season one, the judge's 'Vette returns for one last drive in the hands of Nick Damion, though it's gone from a manual transmission to an automatic.

In the epilogue, the station decal on the control board Nick's sitting by is for KCED, the same station call letters featured in the episode "Games People Play".

Memorable Quotes

Damion: Don McLean—the classic "American Pie". So why isn't this guy on the charts today, huh? Where are the Buddy Hollys, the Presleys, the Dylans? They're all gone, people, and you know why? You can't put that music in the elevators.

McCormick: You're not making this any easier. I'd like to help you.
Damion: Yeah, how? You know a friendly judge?
McCormick: Well, that's a matter of opinion.

Hardcastle: That's better than the chair I got in my den.
Damion: Well, hey, Judge, that's show business. You ain't the midnight prince of rock and roll, you know.
McCormick: Yeah, but his connections are unlimited. Now, because you enrolled in that drug rehabilitation program, he was able to get you off with probation. But for the next two months at least, you're gonna have to be content with being the mid-*morning* prince of rock and roll.

Chip Off the Ol' Milt – premiered May 5, 1986

Written by	Carol Mendelsohn and
	Marianne Clarkson
Directed by	Les Sheldon

Cast

Billie Bird	Mimi LeGrand
Walter Brooke	Kenneth Malcolm
John Ashton	Leonard Porter
Camila Ashland	Myrtle
Frank Hamilton	Bob Franklin
Joe Santos	Frank Harper
Victoria Young Keith	the dance instructor
Dub Taylor	Willie Kagin
James Lashly	Leroy, the nephew
Barbara Mealy	
Beaumont Bruestle	The man in the dance class
Lenore Woodward	Mrs. Cudahy (in the dance class)
Phyllis Erlich	the secretary
Tony Montero	the man in a t-shirt

Cast Notes

Billie Bird got her start in vaudeville in 1916. Her screen career began with the 1921 film *The Grass Widowers*. She died in 2002.

Walter Brooke also appeared as a guest star in two other Brian Keith series, *Archer* and *Family Affair*. He played the role of Mr. McGuire in the movie *The Graduate*, and gave Benjamin the famous single word of advice—"plastics". This episode of *Hardcastle and McCormick* was his last television appearance. He died in August of 1986.

John Ashton was Detective Sergeant John Taggart in the movie *Beverly Hills Cop* and its sequel.

Victoria Young, Brian Keith's wife, who was Rosie in the records department in "Did You See the One That Got Away?", reappears as the dance instructor in the opening scene.

Dub Taylor was credited with over 225 film and TV roles. He appeared with Brian Keith in an episode of the 1960 series *The Westerner* and again when Keith reprised that role in the 1991 movie *The Gambler Returns: the Luck of the Draw*. He died in 1994.

Tony Montero is also credited as the "So-so head of Stu" in the 1997 movie *8 Heads in a Duffle Bag*.

Lenore Woodward was a columnist for the *Pasadena Star News* and the first runner up in the 1984 contest to find an "official" Little Old Lady from Pasadena—conducted by Dr. Donald Altfeld, the creator of the 1964 hit single. Ms. Woodward eventually took over the role from the retiring champion and made public appearances at such events as the Worlds Finals of Drag Racing, until her retirement from the gig in 1987.

The Details

At the Sunset Acres Retirement home, a new resident, Bob Franklin, is getting the welcoming spiel from director Leonard Porter. After listing the amenities, he asks Bob to sign a few papers. Mr. Franklin is not pleased. He's also not "Bob", except to his friends, and he's not signing any papers until he's read them first.

In a night school classroom, McCormick, looking very dapper in a dark suit, is giving a dramatic closing argument in a civil case. As he takes his seat, his professor, Kenneth Malcolm, compliments his enthusiasm and says he'll be a fine attorney.

After class, Mark asks him if he was serious. Malcolm says he was. He talks about what makes a good lawyer and mentions Hardcastle. He asks Mark what the state of his parole is. Mark says it's finished, though neither of them has said anything and he doesn't know if the judge even realizes it. He hopes Hardcastle doesn't think he's sponging off him. Malcolm tells him that he could round out his legal education working as a paralegal. There's an opening at his firm. It would be a full-time position.

In the judge's study, a colorful character named Willie Kagin is closing a deal with Milt. He's selling the judge his repossession business and heading down to Florida. He warns Hardcastle that he won't like the repo biz very much. Hardcastle tells him it's really for Mark ("a graduation present"), and they'll switch it over to car repairs as soon as the current jobs are done. He muses about

Mark's parole being up and thinks he's probably eager to be off and independent.

Kagin, leaving, meets Mark in the doorway a moment later and gives him some prudent but baffling advice about knives and guns. McCormick, looking puzzled, enters the study. There's an awkward moment, and then Mark says they need to talk. They're barely sitting when both blurt out, simultaneously, that his parole is up. More fumbling occurs. Hardcastle says they need to think about McCormick's future. Mark assures him he has, and announces that he's been offered a paralegal job by Kenneth Malcolm.

Hardcastle looks stunned. He asks when it happened. Mark fudges slightly, saying "today". The law school class isn't mentioned. Hardcastle hems and haws a bit, but says it's a good offer, and maybe McCormick could even consider law school someday. Mark hems and haws and says yeah, he might.

Hardcastle finally says go for it. Mark turns hesitant, saying maybe he's not ready. Hardcastle pooh-poohs that. He says there must be a lot of things McCormick wants to do but hasn't had a chance at. He says the hours at his new job will be long and McCormick ought to get a place closer to the office. Mark looks slightly disappointed and asks if he has time to pack.

It's daytime, and out on the front drive Mark is putting a box into the Coyote, which is already crammed full. He tells Hardcastle he'll be back for the rest when he finds an apartment. They say good bye and McCormick even gives the judge a hug, which is shrugged off. Mark climbs in the Coyote and drives away.

At Malcolm, Hughes, and DeWitt, Mr. Malcolm shows Mark the layout. He's given an office and a Rolodex. His first assignment is to go out to Sunset Acres and pick up the personal effects of one of Malcolm's deceased clients.

At the repo office, Hardcastle is meeting Leroy, Willie's seedy nephew ("He sort of came with the place").

In a room at Sunset Acres, the walls are decorated with old black and white showbiz photographs. A box is sitting on the bed. A silver-haired woman sits quietly in a chair. She pours a glass of champagne and lifts it in farewell to her

departed friend, Elsie. At a knock on the door she pulls herself together and quips that the visitor had better be good looking and six feet tall.

It's Mark and he enters hesitantly, hoping he's not disturbing anyone. He is, but it's in a good way. Mimi LeGrande lights up as she offers him a seat and a glass of champagne.

She and Elsie were partners. Mimi talks about her career on the stage and screen and shows Mark pictures from her scrapbook. Before they part, she asks Mark to open a checking account for her so that she will be able to send flowers for Elsie's grave every month. Mark says he'd be honored.

Later that day, in the law office, Mark reports a strange occurrence. He tells Malcolm that when he took Mimi's fifty dollars to the bank, they told him that she already had an account with over a hundred and fifty thousand dollars in it. Malcolm is reassuring. He says Mimi's income is managed by the firm and her investments have done well. He intimates that Mimi doesn't pay much attention to such things.

That evening, at the retirement home, Porter and Malcolm discuss recent developments. Malcolm assures him that McCormick accepted his explanation. Porter says there's still Bob Franklin to deal with. Malcolm tells Porter they don't need Franklin's money. Porter says it's not just a matter of one person; Franklin is a trouble-maker and is riling up the others.

Malcolm says he'll talk to the man. He says the arrangement has worked so far with no one getting hurt. He wants to keep it that way.

In a motel room, Mark is studying while a John Wayne movie plays on the TV. He's distracted by a familiar move in a bar brawl scene. Back at the estate, the judge is watching the same movie. He's eating popcorn.

Mark gives up on the studying. He mutters wistfully about popcorn. The judge grumbles that he's made too much popcorn again. He figures McCormick's out with his friends.

On a simultaneous impulse, each reaches for his phone and dials. They both get the busy signal.

The next day, a delightfully chipper Mimi LeGrande assures Mark that if she had money in the bank she'd know about it. She seems to be in complete possession of her faculties. Mark tells her he'll look into it. He gives her his phone and beeper numbers, and then also gives her Hardcastle's address and phone number, in case of emergency.

At Frank's office, it's lunchtime. He's having his calls held for fifteen whole minutes. Across the desk from him is Hardcastle, who's apparently been hanging around a lot. Frank offers to have Claudia start making Milt his own sandwich. He encourages him to give Mark a call. Hardcastle is reluctant. He thinks Mark has his own life now.

The next day it's Mark who's interrupting Frank's sandwich. Harper's had enough. He offers Mark twenty cents and tells him to call Hardcastle. Mark says he'll just stop by Gull's Way, instead. Frank tells him Milt won't be there. He says he's down at "Hardcastle's Repo and Repair".

Mark finds him behind the desk in the ramshackle office. Hardcastle explains his newfound interest in auto repair. Leroy saunters in, demanding the night off. Mark says he'll fill in for Leroy. When the judge steps out for a moment, Leroy makes an unauthorized withdrawal from the cash box. Mark pulls him up sharply and threatens him. The money goes back where it belongs.

At Sunset Acres, Mimi is introducing her new roommate, Myrtle, to Bob Franklin. He talks about forming a complaint committee. Mr. Porter approaches and asks Bob to drop by his office after lunch.

In Porter's office, Franklin meets Malcolm. Mimi walks by, hearing the discussion becoming heated. She pops in and claims that she and Franklin have a tennis date. After they leave, Malcolm still isn't worried, but Porter is.

At a hot dog stand, Mark tells the judge Mimi's story. Hardcastle remembers her fondly from the movies. He says he'll look into it but he thinks Malcolm is probably right about the situation. The conversation segues to Leroy and the repo shop and from there to an argument about Hardcastle's original motivations. Mark says he's doing fine on his own.

Later that evening at Sunset Acres, Bob Franklin, heading out of the shower, turns and encounters an intruder. He says to the unseen figure that he's figured out the scam. He lifts his arms to fend off an attack.

That same night, Hardcastle is trying to hotwire a car as Mark watches impatiently. Mark takes over and does it efficiently, but his beeper goes off in mid-repossession. He doesn't know how to shut it off. Chaos escalates as he returns to the truck and then collides with Hardcastle, who's backing up the repossessed car. By now the former owner is aware and they are chased off with a shotgun.

Back at the repo office, Mark finally answers his page. It's Mimi and she's frightened. Bob's dead and she thinks he was murdered. Mark promises he'll help. Hardcastle is fussing about the damage to the repossessed car. Mark tells him he's going to Sunset Acres to check things out. Hardcastle, still grumbling, goes along.

At the retirement home, Mimi tells them about Bob Franklin's lethal shower accident. He was the only one who had refused to sign over his power of attorney to Malcolm, Hughes, and Dewitt. In her room, she introduces them to Myrtle, who seems nonplussed and says Bob was a troublemaker. Mimi tells them that she'd shown Bob her mail, with her many unsolicited credit card applications. He'd told her she must have money she didn't know about and Malcolm and Porter were up to something.

As they leave, Mark still can't figure out what's going on. The judge suspects that Malcolm is using the power of attorney authority to roll over accounts of dead residents into other residents' accounts before the deaths are reported, sheltering the capital and taking the income.

Later that night, at Frank's house, they ask for subpoenas on the retirement home residents' financial records. Frank points out that it's Mark's employers who are managing things there. Mark says he's probably out of a job. Hardcastle's reassurance that he can get other employment quickly degenerates into an argument.

The next day, at the law office, Malcolm asks the secretary if McCormick has been in. The secretary says he asked for the Sunset Acres file, read it, and left.

Malcolm meets with Porter, who chastises him for letting McCormick get so close to the information. He says it will take a few hours to transfer the money to overseas accounts. He also says he'll do something about Mimi.

That night, in her room at the retirement home, Mimi refuses when the night nurse offers a sleeping pill. The nurse is harried. She tells Mimi that rumors are flying. Porter is in his office with his lawyer packing up to leave. Mimi takes the dose and the nurse leaves. Mimi quickly spits the pill out and then confronts Myrtle, who admits she told Porter about the judge and McCormick's visit. She was afraid that if something happened to Sunset Acres, she'd have nowhere to go. Mimi says she's going to find Judge Hardcastle and get his help.

That same night, Mark and the judge are strolling down a dark residential street. Mark reports the results of his search of the files—the residents have no families. Their accounts are controlled by Malcolm. Hardcastle says as soon as

they've done their car repossession chore, they'll take the information to Harper. They reach the address they were given (by Leroy) but can't find the right car. Their search is interrupted by a very pro-active neighborhood watch group.

In the lock-up, Mark rails at Leroy's stupidity. He sent them to the wrong street. Mark holds Hardcastle responsible. The judge quietly agrees, taking the wind out of Mark's rant. He confesses he bought the repo place for McCormick. Mark is stunned. He questions why the judge would do something like that for him. The judge evades the issue and Mark finally confesses that he didn't just walk into the law firm and snag a job—he's been taking night classes in law school for months. Hardcastle looks quietly pleased, then says he never doubted McCormick's abili-

ties. He figured the repo place was only a stepping stone to bigger things, maybe even the wherewithal to go to law school. Mark nervously interrupts him, and they're soon back to bickering. Mark says he wasn't planning on just walking out when his parole was up. The parole was never what kept him there in the first place. He stayed, and put up with it all, because he's the best friend Hardcastle will ever have. Again the judge quietly agrees. Mark is shocked into silence.

He doesn't have much more time to ruminate on his latest incarceration before Frank arrives, looking beleaguered, to have them released.

Returning to the estate, the guys find Mimi waiting on the front porch. Frank, having just arrived home, gets a call from the judge, who wants him to meet them at Sunset Acres to prevent Malcolm and Porter from skipping out.

At the retirement home, Malcolm and Porter discuss their arrangements. As they head for the door, they find the way is blocked by a group of residents, led by Myrtle. Police sirens are heard. Porter panics and runs, tripped by a well-placed wheelchair. Mark enters with Hardcastle and Mimi. He sees Malcolm and, when his professor turns and walks away, Mark follows him.

In a dead-end corridor Malcolm stands, silently distraught. Mark approaches; the judge stays a little ways back. Mark asks Malcolm if he hired him because he was stupid, or would look the other way. Malcolm says he offered him the job for the reasons he originally stated.

In the epilogue, in the front drive at the estate, Mark is unloading his things while Hardcastle reads a letter aloud. It's from Mimi and she's happily settled into a new retirement home. Mark has a standing invitation for champagne.

McCormick ponders selling the Coyote. With the money, he could attend law school full time. Hardcastle offers him a proposition—a game of one-on-one; if Mark wins, the judge will foot his whole law school bill.

It's a hard-fought game that comes down to two free-throws for Hardcastle, who manages to miss twice. Mark sinks a final basket to win the wager. He tells the judge he can still get out of it. Hardcastle says he never welshed on a bet in his life, and he's bet some long shots. Mark claims to have been the longest. Hardcastle smilingly agrees.

The Context

In the face of impending cancellation, the series went out in grand style. We discover that Mark's parole is up, but neither one of them seems to be in a hurry to do anything about it. Through a determined lack of communication, the two guys end up at cross purposes, each one not wanting to impose on the other.

This is Mark's second run at a "grown-up job". He finally gets the Rolodex he'd been pining for, and even Hardcastle can't fault his new employer, a prestigious law firm.

But Mark's finally got it right. It's not fame, fortune, or the accoutrements of success that are important. When things start looking hinky, he can't turn away and ignore the evidence. He has to help Mimi, even though it's going to cost him his coveted job.

Hardcastle's attempt to set up a business for Mark is touchingly awkward. Here's the man who once classified McCormick as not college material (in "Third Down and Twenty to Life") almost tripping over himself trying to alter course once he hears the news of his enrollment in law school.

The denouement in the jail cell is a perfect bookend to the jailhouse scene in "Rolling Thunder". They're still a couple of guys who can barely say two words to each other without falling into an argument, but they're now, self-admittedly, also the best of friends.

In the end—honest but unemployed—Mark once again considers selling the Coyote. This time though, it's not to get the down-payment for a more grown-up car, but so that he can go to law school full time and finish sooner. He says he has something to contribute, a delightful reversal of the notion that success is measured by what you've acquired. And, once again, Hardcastle makes a gesture (this time disguised as a wager) that would be far more typical from a father to a son—an offer to pay for his law school tuition.

The final scene is another wonderful reprise from the pilot episode, in which a basketball game planted the first seeds of grudging respect between the two men. We see, one last time, that nothing (and everything) has changed.

The Trivia

The movie being watched in Mark's motel room and Hardcastle's study is the 1947 classic *Angel and the Badman* which starred John Wayne as Quirt Evans and featured Lee Dixon as his friend, Randy McCall. The barroom brawl they are watching occurs sixty-nine minutes into the movie.

Through most of this episode (except for the epilogue) Hardcastle is wearing a baseball cap with an insignia that reads "Special Weapons Man" with the acronyms LASD and SEB below that. This is the insignia of the Los Angeles County Sheriff's Special Enforcement Bureau. Established in 1968, it is one of the nation's first and most respected SWAT organizations.

Memorable Quotes

Mimi: (as McCormick knocks) Well, you'd better be good-looking and six feet tall.
McCormick: Hi.
Mimi: I wasn't expecting the Sheik of Araby.
McCormick: Ah, I hope I'm not disturbing you.
Mimi: Oh, I haven't been disturbed this good since Count Evermonde showed up in my dressing room in Pittsburgh with a diamond bracelet.
McCormick: Well, I could come back.
Mimi: They all say that…but they never do.

Hardcastle: (referring to Leroy) What's the matter, are you jealous of this…?
McCormick: Jealous? Jealous of what? You think I can't get along without you? You really bug me. Here I invite you out to lunch, as an equal. But all you can think about is I'm a kid—still a kid to you. Even if I've got a great suit, responsibilities, a job, a Rolodex, a parking space. I've even got a beeper!
Hardcastle: You have mustard on your tie.
McCormick: I like mustard on my tie.

Hardcastle: Listen, I don't waste three years of my valuable time on a loser.
McCormick: Why, I think that's one of the nicest things you've ever said to me.
Hardcastle: Don't let it go to your head. I just meant you're well-trained.
McCormick: Like a monkey?
Hardcastle: Don't get defensive.
McCormick: Every time I disagree with you, I'm defensive.
Hardcastle: Every time you disagree with me, you're wrong.

Chapter 3
Behind the Scenes
Creators, producers, directors, and writers

Making a television series is a group effort. Even Stephen J. Cannell's studio, a relatively intimate operation, had a staff of over four hundred at the outset of 1983. The effort, though, begins with the one thing—a script, usually the product of one, or perhaps two people.

Cannell himself had spent his first five years out of college investing nearly every free moment in honing his skills as a writer, while working full time in his father's business. Breaking into television wasn't easy. He sold a couple of scripts to *Mission: Impossible* and *Ironside*. His big opportunity finally came as a last minute assignment—a replacement for an *Adam-12* script which had been rejected by the network. The show's producer, Herb Saunders, was a friend of Cannell's. There were already other writers who'd been scrambling to come up with something since the Monday before. Cannell didn't get word until Thursday, and had a narrative proposal ready by the following day. He was sent home with a request for a final script by nine a.m. on Monday. He knew it wouldn't be a problem; it was what he'd been doing all along. He was the only one of the prospective writers with a script finished by the deadline.

Two days later, he was offered a job as story editor for the series. From there he moved into close association with Mark VII's partner, Universal, and its large and fruitful television division. By way of yet another two-day deadline (this time for the show *Jigsaw*) he met Roy Huggins, the former producer of one of the favorite shows of Cannell's youth, *Maverick*. This time his ability to produce a script under pressure led to an offer to become a producer.

Eventually his credits at Universal included *Toma, Baretta, City of Angels, Black Sheep Squadron, The Duke, Stone,* and *Richie Brockleman, Private Eye.* But his best remembered effort from that era was most certainly *The Rockford Files,* which he co-created with Huggins. Cannell both produced and wrote for the critically acclaimed series, and its success established him as a creative force to be reckoned with.

In the beginning, though, he was a writer, and almost everything he did in his career path seemed to be guided by that lodestone. To be a writer in television is to put your work at the mercy of others. Will it even be considered and, worse yet, if it is accepted, what will *they* do to it?

The solution is clear. In order to maintain control, the writer must become one of them—the producer, the executive producer—as high up in the hierarchy as is necessary, while still reserving enough time to write. But if you aren't going to forsake your roots and become yet another studio executive, it helps to be a fast writer—or a very determined one.

By all accounts, Stephen J. Cannell is both. Determination is a given, knowing that he was dealt a hand that included dyslexia along with the desire to be a storyteller. It seems an unlikely combination, except for the fact that in script-writing, words on paper are merely a temporary storage unit; the end result is what matters. It may be that a man who is tuned to the spoken word, to the *meter* of conversation, already has an ace in the hole that more than compensates for the challenge of the mechanics.

In an interview in 2004, Cannell told a story of how he helped his future wife compose a high school term paper. Using her research, he dictated final copy to her, going for, as he put it, "an erudite textbook style." He succeeded too well. She was threatened with expulsion for what was suspected as a direct borrowing from a book. As the man says, "I have a good ear."[1]

James Garner put it this way, "Steve has a feel. He gets a character in a mood, gets in it with a character, starts writing, and it just comes out."[2] Tom Blomquist, who was a contract writer and later producer for Cannell Studios, said his boss could turn out a script in four days, and that was *while* juggling his duties as studio head.

The process of gaining control that began with writer-producer status at Universal culminated in the founding of Cannell's own production company in 1979. The quirky and fondly remembered *Tenspeed and Brownshoe* was the first of his independent efforts. Critics liked it but it never found its audience, and its departure from the schedule (after only fourteen episodes) left Cannell's production company in peril.

The Greatest American Hero followed, debuting on March 18, 1981 and surviving for forty-four episodes. Though very different from *Tenspeed,* the two series had two commonalities; both were character-driven and both could be classified as comedy-dramas. In the second series, the main character's derring-do was a gentle parody of the superhero genre, just as *Tenspeed* had been a whimsical take on the hardboiled detective.

But as *The Greatest American Hero*'s run drew to a close in early 1983, there was no certainty that Cannell's studio would survive it. He needed a solid hit.

On January 30, 1983, riding the coattails of the Superbowl, *The A-Team* premiered with a solid 26.6 rating. Moving to its regular slot on Monday evenings, over the next month it sustained weekly ratings above twenty points, beating CBS *Happy Days* and *Laverne and Shirley* handily.

No one was more surprised than Cannell himself. He later explained that he'd intended the series as a comedy, an upending of the action hero tradition. Given his previous experience with turning genre conventions on their heads, it was understandable that he might have expected the critics to like it and the audiences to be lukewarm, at best.

But it's hard to argue with success, no matter what the cost in critical esteem, especially when you have a payroll to meet. While the critics sharpened their knives, and bewailed the decline in Cannell's *oeuvre*, *The A-Team* kept the bills paid and became an eighties cultural phenomenon, complete with tag lines and a break-out star in Mr. T (as B.A. Baracus).

There are several unmistakable trends in this series that would carry over into Cannell's next project. *The A-Team* was, above all, an action show. Critics called it violent, but it was primarily action detached from consequence. You would see, by some estimates, over forty "violent" acts in a single episode, but rarely did anyone die, or even get seriously injured. It was in this series that Cannell's writers developed the classic "walk away shot", in which the audience would see that the passengers (good and bad guys alike) of a crumpled vehicle were mostly okay.

Another theme (one which had previously been used by Cannell to good effect in *The Rockford Files*) was "the crime they didn't commit". His heroes in *The A-Team* had been falsely imprisoned. While they stayed on the run for four seasons, in the fifth they came to work for the military, through a liaison, with the carrot of an eventual pardon dangling before them.

Action, humor, and good guys who operated on the lam, and who ran into adventure wherever they went—Cannell had unexpectedly caught lightning in a bottle. He also had some breathing room, and networks eager for him to replicate his success.

Now that he had one hit, and hoped soon to be managing more, a division of labor was required. This meshed well with Cannell's second intent, to develop other writers and writer-producers. The pattern was set with Patrick Hasburgh, who had written for *The Greatest American Hero* and *The A-Team*. He knew his way around both Cannell's kind of action-comedy *and* his more character-driven work.

Hasburgh calls himself a ski-bum. He also had an interest in race cars—the perfect background for an action writer. Better still, he shared Cannell's liking for the father-son theme which had surfaced in *Rockford*. A buddy relationship that spanned a generation would do in a pinch, as seen in *The Greatest American Hero*, and better yet if the buddies were trying *not* to be buddies, at least at first.

The co-creation pattern, with Cannell pairing off with another writer-producer to write a pilot episode, would be the system that allowed him to have as many as six series in production at one time, while still turning out scripts of his own. In the case of *Hardcastle and McCormick*, six episodes were written by Cannell while eighteen came from Hasburgh, not counting their teaming for the pilot. Together they accounted for forty percent of the show's writing.

Cannell's and Hasburgh's episodes were often responsible for elaboration on the back story, as in the reappearance of Mark's failed prototype in "Goin' Nowhere Fast", and the exploration of Milt's real motivations for taking in a Tonto in "She Ain't Deep but She Sure Runs Fast". The father-son theme was also a frequent part of the subtext, particularly for Hasburgh, as seen most explicitly in "Ties My Father Sold Me". This theme wasn't always restricted to the title characters, but also surfaced among the people they dealt with, as in "The Boxer", and "The Game You Learn from Your Father".

Of the remainder of the episodes, twelve were written by Lawrence Hertzog, who was also on board as a series producer, and later co-executive producer. In a 1999 interview, when asked about the collaborative nature of television production, he said, "It's critical to find people (particularly directors) who 'get it'. Without that—we're looking at a car wreck—a salvage job."[3]

There was no question that Hertzog "got" the humor and character-driven nature of *Hardcastle and McCormick*. His episodes often poked fun at the life of a TV hero. He managed to get Mark behind the wheel of a Studebaker in two separate episodes ("Really Neat Cars and Guys with a Sense of Humor" and "Hardcastle, Hardcastle, Hardcastle, and McCormick"). There was almost invariably a running gag in his scripts—the party of the century coming back to haunt Mark in "You Would Cry, Too, If It Happened to You", the hazards of visiting the bathroom in "Something's Going On On This Train", or the slow, step-wise, destruction of the Coyote in "When I Look Back On all the Things".

He was also capable of highlighting aspects of the buddy relationship, from the flat-out statement "that's what friends are for" in "You Don't Hear the One That Gets You", to the low-grade conflict in "There Goes the Neighborhood", to the head-on collision in "Duet for Two Wind Instruments". At the same time, he created memorable one-time characters such as Arvin Lee and Melissa Kantwell ("You Don't Hear the One That Gets You").

Of the remaining twenty-five scripts, five were written by Marianne Clarkson, who also co-authored a sixth episode with Carol Mendelsohn. Clarkson was a staff writer for the series. Mendelsohn functioned as story editor in the last half of the third season and authored two additional episodes.

Mendelsohn had gotten her start as a free-lance writer, creating scripts for *Fame*. Knowing she had no agent, one of her fellow writers for that show put her in touch with someone who also happened to represent Larry Hertzog. From this chance encounter, she was soon drafted as a staff writer for Cannell Productions.

She recollected her first day on the job: "Just to make sure I got to work on time the first day, I did a dry run over the weekend. That Monday, I arrived at the Cannell offices at 8:30 (well, maybe a little before). I was alone in the

Rosemary Clooney and Daniel Hugh Kelly on set. Courtesy Les Sheldon.

building for at least an hour. That's when I learned there are many more late nights than early mornings. For the record, Stephen Cannell was at home writing since the crack of dawn, something I tried in vain to emulate."

Long hours were an essential part of television work in those days. It was not unusual for scripts to go through five or more revisions. Mendelsohn remembers being only one of two writers in the company who owned a computer. "When we would issue page changes, every assistant in the building would have to start typing and the process would take all day and all night."

Her enthusiasm for the job won her the script assignment for "If You Could See What I See. "We were watching dailies down in the screening room at Cannell, when Patrick Hasburgh announced we didn't have a 'next' script, did anyone think they could write one in a two and a half days. I raised my hand. Again, eager."

In keeping with Cannell's focus on scripts, he tended to put writing talent on retainer. Tom Blomquist was another such contract writer. He'd begun his career as a production assistant, at one time working for Orson Welles. What he wanted to do was write. His break came through yet another curious coincidence in the small world that is Hollywood. Roger Young, the man who directed the pilot episode of the series (who was a friend of Blomquist's) mentioned him to Hasburgh as a prospective script writer. By coincidence, Les Sheldon, another member of Cannell's staff, also knew Blomquist, and thought his style would be a good fit for the show.

After the second mention, Hasburgh's attention had been caught. Blomquist was summoned. He pitched the idea which became "School for Scandal". Blomquist was honored to have a Cannell favorite, Robert Culp, cast as Hardcastle's nemesis, Arthur Farnell. He remembers being invited to watch the dailies as the episode was shot, and the thrill of seeing his words come to life.

While that script was still in revision, he received a second assignment. Beginning with the idea of Mark back in a prison setting, at a point where that would be an uncomfortable fresh experience—that story became "Scared Stiff".

After this second script, he moved on to a new Cannell series, *Riptide*, where he became story editor and producer. The Cannell operation was not so large, though, that he lost touch with the other series. His *Riptide* office was still only down the hall from the *Hardcastle and McCormick* team and production staff from both those two shows and *The A-Team* often lunched together.

In early February, 1986, Hasburgh asked him to write yet another script for the show that had been his entry to Cannell Productions. This time it was an opportunity to "peel back some layers of the onion" and look deeper into the characters—the sort of story that can only be done after a series is more estab-lished. Blomquist came up with "The Day the Music Died", which touches on McCormick's teen years, and one of his fallen heroes.

Among the other series writers were Shel Willens ("The Georgia Street Motors"), who had been associated with Cannell projects going back ten years, to their days at Universal, and David Ross ("Brother, Can You Spare a Crime") who went on to write thirty-two episodes of *Murder She Wrote*, and was one of the story editors for that series.

Alan Cassidy wrote the episode "Hardcastle for Mayor". As assistant pro-ducer, his duties included a myriad of finishing touches—getting inset shot material and stock footage, but he also put in a cameo appearance as a garage mechanic ("When I Look Back On All the Things").

Other Cannell contract writers who crossed back and forth between series included Steven Katz. In addition to the five scripts he wrote for *Hardcastle and McCormick*, he also did ten episodes for *The A-Team*, and was story editor for *Hunter*.

Steven L. Sears and Burt Pearl were a duo who also wrote for several Cannell shows. They'd met while working at Womphoppers, a restaurant which used to stand adjacent to the Universal Studios tour. From wait-staff to collaborators, they broke into the script-writing business together. Sears found an agent who was willing to lend his letterhead in exchange for a percentage. They were interested in writing for *Riptide*. They submitted two sample scripts (*Magnum* and *Simon and Simon*). On the strength of those, they were invited in for a story conference.

After pitching some ideas, they were sent home to work on three. To this they added one more, and on a second meeting this was the story they were told to develop. After a third meeting (and instructions to take the story to script form) Sears asked if that meant they'd been hired. The story editor looked at him in surprise and told them that had already happened two meetings earlier. In Sears' words, "to show you how naive we were to all this, when we left, Burt asked me how much we were being paid for writing this script. I told him I didn't know, but I imagined it to be at least $500. I was only slightly off. Scripts at that time for one hour network prime time were going for $15,000."

He and Pearl called it "Cannell Camp", and, like many of the other young writers on contract, they got to know all the producers, moving between series as the need arose. Their opportunity to write a *Hardcastle and McCormick* script came at the end of the season, when there wasn't much work needed for *Riptide*. Hasburgh invited them to do an episode for his show. They met with him and Larry Hertzog…"The pitch meeting being very friendly and casual. Patrick had many, many stories in his head and a lot of anecdotes about his life. Larry was much more focused on keeping to the pitches but was also friendly and humorous."

The story that emerged was "Conventional Warfare". Sears called it "right on the mark as far as the kind of complicated cross-purpose story that Burt and I enjoyed writing. It reminded us of a classic theatre farce." He says Pearl wrote Hardcastle's acceptance speech, which he practices endlessly and to humorous effect. When Burt got to the word "penultimate", it was Sears who wasn't sure what he meant, and supplied McCormick's rejoinder: "It's a great word, Judge. I *never* heard of it before, but it's a great word. Look, don't you think you're getting ahead of yourself here? I mean it *is* just a nomination."

Writer-producers were only one set of hyphenates at Cannell's studio. Les Sheldon, who joined the series as a producer shortly after the pilot, began his television career as an apprentice film editor. From that start he moved into the role of assistant director on series like *Wild Wild West*, and *Mission: Impossible* and in movies such as *The Man Who Loved Cat Dancing* and *Le Mans*, as well as features with Elvis Presley and Sidney Poitier.

In 1983, Sheldon was under contract with Universal and already a strong admirer of Stephen Cannell. "I was a huge fan," he said, "but he didn't know me. My agent, Lew Weitzman, called and told me they were working on a show about a judge and a race car driver. He said, 'This is perfect for you.' He told Stephen I might be available. I went over to Paramount, where the Cannell offices were. Jo Swerling and Patrick Hasburgh were there as well as Stephen. We talked. Afterwards Swerling met me outside and said, 'Why don't we grab a sandwich?' We went down to the commissary and, a half-hour later, when the check came, he said, 'By the way, we want you on the show.' Steve was my hero, but I still had a year on my contract with Universal."

His agent called Robert Harris, then President of Universal Television, who agreed it was a wonderful opportunity. Sheldon was released from his contract to take up a position at Cannell's company. There was a verbal promise to return, once this project was done (he did, eventually going back to Universal to work on *SeaQuest DSV*). "That's how I met Steve," Sheldon concludes. "He was a wonderful, down-to-earth guy. He took me and so many people under his wing."

As a producer for *Hardcastle and McCormick,* Sheldon was responsible for bringing in several of the series' directors. Just as it's not possible for a single writer to keep pace with the demands of a weekly series, directors require at least a week of preparation time and a shooting schedule of about six days. They are sometimes involved in post production as well. As a result, a series requires at least three directors, and most often many more.

Hardcastle and McCormick had twenty-nine, including Les Sheldon himself, who made his directorial debut with "Undercover McCormick". For his "first time out of the box" Sheldon remembers having a stellar cast to work with. In addition to Kelly and Keith, there was Dennis Farina, a former Chicago cop who was able to exude a totally convincing mobster persona. The guest stars also included James Cromwell, a theater actor who received an Oscar nomination for his role in the movie *Babe*.

Sheldon remembers one element of Cromwell's performance in particular: "I got him in a crouch, against the side of a building at midnight and kept moving in with the camera and kept pushing. He was a very methodical actor, from the theater. I was purposely trying to keep him off balance—a take, another take, and another take. I kept pushing him, asking for more. He gave it. He got himself into that state of fear and confusion. He was brilliant."

There were occasional specialty directors, like Charles Picerni, who had an extensive background in stunt work and directed "Faster Heart". Richard Colla, who had considerable made-for-TV movie experience, handled "The Long Ago Girl" with its period flashbacks. As Sheldon put it, "He came in, got it done beautifully, and stayed on a very difficult schedule. In those days we were shooting those episodes in six, maybe seven days. I think Richard actually did that one in six days. It was enormous; we had a hundred extras down in Union Station, all in period costume, and Richard Colla pulled it off."

Another director with a reputation for efficiency was Bruce Kessler. He is credited with seven episodes. Sheldon says he "hit the ground running. He was very fast, but he knew when to go in there and capture the little moments between Brian and Danny."

A different sort of expertise was required from Kim Manners. Among the six episodes he directed was the charming "Hardcastle, Hardcastle, Hardcastle, and McCormick", which featured Mildred Natwick, a seasoned TV pro, and the more theater-oriented Mary Martin. The series staff was delighted to nab her for a rare television appearance. Sheldon said, "She loved Brian, and she thought Danny was adorable. Danny is an absolute gentleman to everyone—the people he works with, the people he meets—a professional and an artist, but always a gentleman. And Mary just fell in love with him, because to her he was a throwback to the old days when theatrical people treated each other with courtesy and respect."

In television production, a master shot is made of an entire scene, sometimes five or more pages. Then the director goes back in, breaking the scene down and shooting individual actors in takes known as "coverage". The final sequence is edited together from the two. Experienced TV actors are accustomed to working with relatively little rehearsal time for each master.

Sheldon recounts the filming of the kitchen scene from that episode: "I remember Kim Manners went into a master shot—it was a very long scene with Mary and Mildred. They were supposed to be talking and baking things. He realized that Mary was a theater actor, not used to dialogue on camera, but rather weeks of rehearsal. Mildred was a film actor. She would feed Mary a line here and there, and Mary would either forget to move on a line, or she'd move, and forget the line. It was so charming. Mildred would throw her the line under her breath and Mary would say, 'Oh, yes, that's right, and what I meant to say was—' It was so funny, and so wonderful to watch. But Mary was a total pro. She wasn't going to quit until someone told her to. And finally at the end of the scene, Kim said 'Cut' and he said 'Damn, I gotta tell you, that was the best master I've ever seen in my life. Print that, we're going in for coverage.' God bless him; his care and sensitivity put a big smile on her face. Kim was just terrific."

Ron Satlof was another directorial favorite of Sheldon's. He is credited with five episodes beginning with the first season episode, "Killer B's", which featured Buddy Ebsen. "Stunt casting" is often a result of network suggestions. In this case, it came from Peter Roth, then an executive at ABC. Sheldon was delighted. He'd been an apprentice film editor twenty years earlier with Ebsen's hit show, *The Beverly Hillbillies*.

Satlof handled the dynamics of the unusual episode and made the most of the chemistry between two old pros, Ebsen and Keith. On his fourth outing with the series, he tackled the pivotal episode "Ties My Father Sold Me".

Casting was again a key element, with Hasburgh's script calling for McCormick's father to be flawed, yet charming. The actor would also have to convincingly play a singer. Sheldon suggested Steve Lawrence, whose musical career had also included a turn on Broadway in *What Makes Sammy Run?*

As down-on-his-luck lounge singer Sonny Daye, Sheldon says Lawrence "painted the character like he paints songs," while Satlof "really guided those scenes; he staged them so well, and so simply. Danny stepped up to the plate. You could see what was going on between those two guys, how Steve became comfortable in the character because of Danny. Those scenes were impeccable. They just flowed. They were one-take scenes."

Kelly, Keith, and Lawrence during filming. Photo courtesy Les Sheldon.

In addition to the producers, writers, and directors, and the multitude of talented actors and actresses who worked together to produce the series, there were hundreds more crew people, both in production and post production. Again Les Sheldon summed it up: "Every morning you'd show up on the set, there'd always be sixty-five to eighty people there...always someone to learn from. It was important to know what every person on that set could do and how well they could do it—what they were capable of. The team effort."

And what they were capable of was turning a script—in a matter of three short weeks—into an hour of entertainment, ready for broadcast.

1.   Interview with Stephen J. Cannell for the Archive of American Television, conducted by Stephen J. Abramson, June 24, 2004
2.   Thompson, Robert J. *Adventures on Prime Time*. p. 68
3.   O'Shea, Tara "Lawrence Hertzog, Executive Producer" www.ljconstantine.com/nikita/larry_interview.html

Chapter 4
The Usual Suspects
Cops, judges, family, and friends

The Lieutenants

Amateur fictional detectives operate outside the usual constraints imposed on professional members of the criminal justice system. This is an advantage sometimes, especially for the looser cannons, such as Mark McCormick, who hardly ever leave home without a set of lock picks. But it is a disadvantage as well. The most complete set of private files can't compete with the records kept by the police.

A smart amateur has a mutually beneficial working relationship with one or more members of the police department. A really lucky one, like Milt Hardcastle, has a whole stable of good friends (even when pursuing investigations out of town) who are more or less willing to do him a good turn in exchange for a chance at an arrest.

Fingerprint checking, running license plates, a little time on the computer, are all routine. Sometimes the requests run a little steeper—the address of a suspect, and the opportunity to visit him at home ("Hardcastle Goes to Washington") or even in the hospital ("Hardcastle for Mayor").

While in Los Angeles, the choice of departmental liaison was initially Carlton or Stanton. Carlton also seemed to be someone the judge hung out with ("Man in a Glass House" and "Crystal Duck"). Neither man was particularly distinctive, and in one script ("Black Widow") Carlton was named and Stanton substituted for the filming. There was also out-of-town back-up in Riverside and in Washington, D.C.

In the first season, only seven episodes included police cooperation of this kind. Stanton had one scene of good cop/bad cop in "The Black Widow" and Carlton got to wax indignant in the bookstore in "Man in a Glass House", but for the most part these guys were just there to run the plates and put the handcuffs on.

In the second season, a more definite pattern was seen. Out of twenty-two episodes, fifteen involved a friendly cop. "Outlaw Champion" introduced Lieutenant Mike Delaney. He returned eight more times that season. There was also one appearance by Captain Switzer in "Never My Love", an episode that also featured Delaney. Lieutenant Bill Giles, who had appeared once in season one ("Whistler's Pride") was seen in four more episodes ("Hate the Picture, Love the Frame", "What's So Funny?", "The Long Ago Girl", and "Surprise on Seagull Beach").

Delaney was the most distinctive of the pack. He got to rescue Hardcastle once ("You and the Horse You Rode in On") and seemed more involved in the cases as they unfolded. He occasionally appeared aggravated at Hardcastle's requests ("There Goes the Neighborhood"). Giles, on the other hand, was very much of the Carlton/Stanton mold, though he did get to reluctantly arrest Hardcastle on one memorable occasion ("Hate the Picture, Love the Frame").

Two-thirds of the way through season three, in "Hardcastle, Hardcastle, Hardcastle and McCormick", the guys took their troubles to yet another lieutenant. Frank Harper—rumpled, put-upon and by no means cheerful—walked into the middle of the case and immediately rose above the level of plot device. He'd still run the plates, but he'd usually grouse about it. We didn't need to be told he'd known Hardcastle for years; it was obvious. Although he appeared in only one more episode that season, Harper was eventually established as the primary "friend in the department".

In the third season he appeared in eleven episodes and was twice mentioned as the guy Hardcastle was calling to get information from. He offered sage counsel to Milt ("Games People Play"), and sympathy to Mark ("Strangle Hold"). We found out that the judge hadn't stopped talking to him about Sonny Daye since he and Mark had gotten back from Atlantic City a year and a half earlier ("McCormick's Bar and Grill"), and Frank showed up as part of Hardcastle's regular poker group ("Poker Night"). He rapidly became one of the guys, even sharing the unfortunate distinction of being shot—*twice*—in the course of the series ("Poker Night" and "In the Eye of the Beholder").

In the end, Frank's office is where the guys went when they were trying to find their bearings ("Chip Off the Ol' Milt") and he was the one who told them, in exasperation, that they were friends and ought to start acting like it. He was part Dutch uncle, part unwilling co-conspirator, and always more than a liaison.

While Hardcastle was generally revered by the local cops, and even got a standing ovation in one squad room ("Man in a Glass House"), dealing with the federal authorities was another matter. The FBI obstructed him in "Did You See the One that Got Away?" and hauled him in for questioning twice ("There Goes the Neighborhood" and "When I Look Back On All the Things"). Mark also ran afoul of the State Department in "Mirage a Trois". At least once, though, Hardcastle was able to get an extraordinary amount of cooperation from the feds ("Ties My Father Sold Me").

Here, in order of appearance, are the men who portrayed Hardcastle's mostly helpful cop friends:

Robert Hooks played **Lieutenant Kelly Carlton** in "Man in a Glass House" and "Crystal Duck" (in the basketball scene). His theater career began with a role in the first Broadway run of *A Raisin in the Sun*. He founded two theater companies, the New York's Group Theatre Workshop and Washington, D.C.'s Black Repertory Company. He was the co-founder of a third group, the Negro Ensemble Company (which helped launch the careers of Samuel L. Jackson, Denzel Washington, and many others).

He made the transition to television in 1963, with a guest spot on the Emmy Award-winning series *East Side/West Side*. He played a police detective. In 1967, he was cast as Detective Jeff Ward, in the series *N.Y.P.D.* In addition to that groundbreaking regular role, Hooks has over eighty other television and movie credits, spanning forty years.

Arthur Burghardt played **Lieutenant Stanton** in "Black Widow" and "Prince of Fat City". Ten years younger than Hooks, Burghardt began his screen career with a role in the 1976 film *Network*. From there he went on to a continuing role as Dr. Jack Scott in the daytime series *One Life to Live*. Though he's made many guest appearances on TV, he's best known for his voice work. He was Destro in the *G.I. Joe* series and Devastator in *The Transformers*.

He was the only *Hardcastle and McCormick* lieutenant who had a chance to really cut loose, unleashing his inner bad cop to sweat some information out of a henchman in "The Black Widow". A little knuckle-cracking, a little growling, and the bad guy gave it all up.

Howard Witt played one-shot Riverside lieutenant **Bill Jenkins** in "Hotshoes". Witt has had guest roles in many TV series including *Hill Street Blues* and *Law & Order*. He received a Tony Award for his role as Charley in the 1999 revival of *Death of a Salesman*, and reprised the role in the 2000 made-for-TV movie.

Ed Bernard played **Lieutenant Bill Giles** in five episodes ("Whistler's Pride", "Hate the Picture, Love the Frame", "What's So Funny?", "The Long Ago Girl", and "Surprise on Seagull Beach"). He had previously played Detective Joe Styles in *Police Story*, a role that carried over to become a regular in the 1974 series *Police Woman*.

Jack Rader played the very helpful **Detective Thomas** in "Mr. Hardcastle Goes to Washington". A character actor with a familiar face, he appeared in over seventy movies and TV shows including, alas, the 1978 *Star Wars Holiday Special* as an Imperial Guard Officer.

Doug McClure played **Detective Jeff Hamilton** in "School for Scandal". Perhaps best known for his role as Trampas in the TV series *The Virginian*, McClure also appeared in the 1972 made-for-TV movie *The Judge and Jake Wyler*, in which he played an ex-con working for a retired lady judge. He, along with Brian Keith and many other former western stars, had a role in the 1991 movie, *The Gambler Returns: The Luck of the Draw*. He died in 1995.

John Hancock played **Lieutenant Mike Delaney** in eight season two episodes ("Outlaw Champion", "D-Day", "Never My Love", "Whatever Happened to Guts?", "You and the Horse You Rode in On", "One of the Girls from Accounting", "It Coulda Been Worse, She Coulda Been a Welder", "Pennies from a Dead Man's Eyes", "There Goes the Neighborhood", and "Angie's Choice"). He was yet another *Hardcastle and McCormick* cast member who also appeared (along with Brian Keith)

in the 1984 pilot episode of *Murder She Wrote*. He played the recurring role as Judge Armand in *L.A. Law* and, at the time of his death in 1992, he was appearing as a regular in a series called *Love & War*.

Harvey Vernon played **Captain Switzer** in the episode "Never My Love". Vernon had guest roles in *The Rockford Files*, and *Riptide*. He also appeared (along with Daniel Hugh Kelly) in the 1987 film *Someone to Watch Over Me*. He died in 1996.

Joe Santos played **Lieutenant Frank Harper** in thirteen episodes during seasons two and three ("Hardcastle, Hardcastle, Hardcastle, and McCormick", "Undercover McCormick", "Do Not Go Gentle", "Games People Play", "Strangle Hold", "Duet for Two Wind Instruments", "If You Could See What I See", "Round Up the Old Gang", "McCormick's Bar and Grill", "Poker Night", "Eye of the Beholder", "The Day the Music Died", and "Chip Off the Ol' Milt").

After a series of roles in lesser films, Brooklyn-born actor Joe Santos was forty when he landed a part as a detective in the 1971 film *Panic in Needle Park*. In 1973 he had another cop role, this time in the award-winning Joseph Wambaugh miniseries *The Blue Knight*. That same year he appeared in an episode of the series *Toma* ("The Oberon Contract") which had been written and produced by Stephen J. Cannell.

He was tapped by Cannell for a role in the made-for-TV movie *The Rockford Files: Backlash of the Hunter*, appearing as Detective Dennis Becker. He stayed on in the role for five years and a hundred episodes of the Rockford television series.

As Lieutenant Frank Harper, Santos dropped into the second season of *Hardcastle and McCormick* with an air of having been there all along. It might have been his credentials as Rockford's beleaguered police liaison, a role Santos seemed born to play, but there was an instant feeling that Harper and Hardcastle went back a long ways.

After two appearances in the second season, he returned in the sixth episode of the third season. He appeared ten more times, including a capstone performance in "Chip Off the Ol' Milt".

Santos went on to appear as Police Lieutenant Nolan in five episodes of *Magnum, P.I.*, as well as recreating his role as Detective Becker in eight *The Rockford Files* movies in the 1990s. His onscreen cop persona was the basis for a guest appearance as himself in the short-lived 1993 comedy series *Bakersfield P.D.* In that episode the local police immediately recognized him as Rockford's cop buddy.

Most recently, though, he played Angelo Garepe, former consigliere to crime boss Carmine Lupertazzi in the TV series *The Sopranos*. He appeared in seven episodes in the 2004 season before Garepe fell victim to a hit.

Reni Santoni played another out-of-town police colleague, **Sergeant John Thomas** in "You're Sixteen, You're Beautiful, and You're His". Like Robert Hooks, one of Santoni's first TV roles was a guest spot on the series *East Side/West Side*. Santoni had started his career as a comedy writer but viewers are more likely to recognize him as Harry Callahan's partner, Inspector Chico Gonzalez in the 1971 film *Dirty Harry*.

Dan Lauria played **Lieutenant Adkins**, one of the few unhelpful (but not crooked) cops. He appeared in the episode "Conventional Warfare". He's best known as Jack Arnold from *The Wonder Years*, but has made well over one hundred other TV and movie appearances.

Richard Kuss was a one man good cop/bad cop, playing the hardnosed and corrupt **Captain Don Filapiano** in season one's "The Black Widow", and then returning as the hardnosed but honest **Lieutenant Lou Donovan** (a guy who even puts up with McCormick's feet on his desk) in season three's "Hardcastle for Mayor". Kuss also had guest roles in two other Cannell shows, *The A-Team* and *Stingray*.

The Judges

All evidence to the contrary, Milt Hardcastle was an *ex*-judge, but he never lacked for friends on the bench when he needed a quick warrant or a little legal aid. At the end of the pilot episode he's on the phone in a Las Vegas casino, leaving a message for "Judge Robinson", a local guy, apparently, and one who could be tapped to get "the writs filed right away". In Barb Johnson's words, "He knows everybody; he's kind of a judicial celebrity."

Most of the time, the guys on the bench were just names, like the usually indecisive Judge Hightower in "Man in a Glass House" whose decision to stay home from the opera saved Hardcastle from burglary charges. Some, however, like Judge Benson in "Goin' Nowhere Fast", would put in a personal appearance to bail out their old colleague and even provide a little background information.

A few judges were just faces up on the bench. In "Once Again With Vigor-ish" it was the Honorable William Robinson (different jurisdiction) presiding over superior court twelve for *both* of Mr. Kelly's trials.

There were an astonishing number of bad guys among Hardcastle's old fraternity. The worst offenders were the vigilante mob in "The Georgia Street Motors". Judge Emmett Parnell and his partners in crime, Cadigan and Stern, were basically serial killers. On a slightly lesser note, the ersatz Judge Calvin Moreland was guilty of identity theft, and then succumbed to blackmail from the mob. Judge Bryan in "Prince of Fat City" was also in league with a hit man, and willing to see murder done to hide his previous crimes.

On the other side, sometimes a judge was the last honest man in town, as in "The Homecoming" where justice of the peace Daniel J. Stuber was killed to prevent him from issuing the warrant Hardcastle needed. In "Flying Down to Rio" it was Judge Ramirez who counseled McCormick on the harsh realities of the law in that Caribbean nation.

There were times, too, when judges were just people, foibles and all. Winslow K. Gault, in "The Crystal Duck", with his taxidermied tiger and cranky tem-perament, was one. Judge Dremmond, retired to become a TV celebrity, referred to his fellow jurists as "stiffs"—especially the unseen Judge Jessup.

Hardcastle didn't always think too highly of other judges, either, though he tried to put a good spin on it from time to time, at least in front of McCormick, with comments like "Judges are important people around here" ("Once Again with Vigorish"). How could he have been surprised that the kid didn't take him seriously when he also grumbled that Gault had overturned six of his decisions? Neither did he have much good to say about his fellow Supreme Court nominees in "Mr. Hardcastle Goes to Washington". Maggie Williams was "an old battleship", and Judge Blackstone played polo three times a week. In "Conventional Warfare", Bucky O'Neill, his major competition for the lifetime achievement award, had spent "about half his time in Tahiti" (not to mention being involved with the mob), while the rest of the crowd at the judge's convention seemed to be channeling their inner frat boys.

There were two judges who were apparently high in Hardcastle's esteem. Shelia Mooney in "Brother, Can You Spare a Crime?" was "somebody special" with whom Hardcastle had been trying to get a date. In "Poker Night", Mattie Groves seemed to be a much closer friend, though with no romantic inclinations.

None of the judges were recurring characters (as much as we might have liked to see Mattie again). After all, this was an action show, and for the most part the job was done when the handcuffs went on.

The Relatives

Members of Hardcastle's extended family were a rich source of complications for him. Warren Wyngate, his niece, was the one who seemed closest to him in temperament—stubborn and implacable when she perceived her cause as just. In "It Coulda Been Worse, She Coulda been a Welder" she even had the temerity to depose her uncle, and then ask him for a ride home.

Like all the rest of Hardcastle's family, Warren accepted Mark (even though she rather casually described him as "the guy who cleans the pool"). They'd even gone out to a movie together—and didn't get in until seven in the morning. Both Mark and Warren offered to do it again, if only to provide the judge with some needed distraction, though when Warren did come on strong, half in jest, Mark wasn't really all that keen about riling "Uncle Miltie". More than that, though, he pointed out to her that she was a typical Hardcastle, and every conversation with her was an argument waiting to happen.

The judge's aunts, May and Zora, ("Hardcastle, Hardcastle, Hardcastle, and McCormick") shared a different family trait—incessant curiosity and a highly-tuned inclination toward suspecting that mischief is afoot. In Hardcastle's opinion, they were obsessed, or even a bit potty. *He* was certainly never that way. It also seemed to annoy him that his aunts doted on Mark, and Mark was gently tolerant of them.

Didi Drylinger wasn't a blood relative, only a sister-in-law, so it's harder to explain her Hardcastle-like tendency toward investigation. She'd never met Mark before, but almost immediately assured him that she was "safe", being family. An odd way of putting it, but clearly a sign that she accepted him, whatever the heck he was.

There was evidence in the scripts that Didi had been intended as a continuing character. She appears in an early draft of "Outlaw Champion", living at the estate and responsible for the *frou-frou* coffee that Hardcastle despised in the final version. Of course that episode eventually aired *before* "D-Day", and she had been taken out of the cast, with some of her lines given to the guys.

Gerald, Hardcastle's younger brother, was a classic black sheep, a rogue who managed to stay just this side of unlikable. Once again, Mark was far more tolerant, maybe in part because Gerald drove the judge nuts, but also because he couldn't seem to imagine someone not liking his own brother. As Mark put it (in "Brother, Can You Spare a Crime"), "I may be an only child, but I understand the importance of family."

If he did, it was understanding won despite an absence of personal experience. Not only was McCormick an only child, but his mother was apparently also dead (though when, and how, were never explained). There was an uncle, mentioned in passing (in "Whistler's Pride") who bequeathed him a sport coat and a bottle cap collection. It's possible there were others. In "Strangle Hold" Mark says no one ever came to visit him in San Quentin, "not even my family", which seems to imply that there were a few left, though too distant to bother with him.

There was certainly one person who met that description. It took a private detective and a black bag job to hunt him down, and even then he was tough to keep track of. Variously known as Tommy Ray, Micky Thompson, and Tommy Knight in his earlier career as a safecracker, Mark's father had been out of touch with his son for twenty-five years. His most recent reincarnation was as Sonny Daye, lounge singer and distant associate of East Coast mobster Tommy Sales. Where Sonny went, trouble was never far behind. Like Hardcastle and his kin, Sonny and Mark had family traits; both were glib talkers with an unusual gift for getting into locked places.

Sonny was the only family member of either man who made a second appearance. He ducked out the first time, but returned in the season three episode "McCormick's Bar and Grill" after experiencing a rare moment of personal insight—he wanted to leave a legacy behind. Sonny turned out to be a little more complex than just the charming but self-centered heel that we met in "Ties My Father Sold Me". He had a few small sparks of honor left, or maybe it was something he picked up from his son.

The Housekeepers

The mysterious Sarah Wicks, who looked like a fixture at Gull's Way ("I'm in charge around here," she said in the pilot episode), was an odd mixture of deference and steel spine. She invariably addressed Hardcastle as "Your Honor", and she brooked no criticism of him from Mark or others. Her loyalty was unshakable, but she also didn't hesitate to speak her opinion, even defending Mark against the occasional premature assumption of guilt by the judge ("The Crystal Duck").

Around criminals, she was utterly self-possessed and fearless and would speak her mind ("Man in a Glass House" and "Goin' Nowhere Fast"). Toward Mark, her attitude was initially prickly, but gradually became more tolerant. She at least worried that if he was injured, he wouldn't be available for his chores ("Hotshoes").

Sarah disappeared from the cast without a trace after six appearances in the first eleven episodes. Her first absence came in the fifth regular episode, "The Black Widow", when the kitchen and table-waiting duties for Mark's big date fell to Hardcastle.

There was never again regular household help. In the second season episode "D-Day", it's Hardcastle who is armed with mop and bucket, and is called "Attila the Homemaker" by Mark. In "There Goes the Neighborhood", the judge tells Lieutenant Delaney that if the housekeeper hadn't arrived that morning, he and Mark would still be tied up, but by season three, they're back to cleaning up after themselves. In "If You Could See What I See", Mark hires Millie Denton to be their live-in housekeeper, but she only lasts a few weeks.

There was a gardener, seen only once (in "You Would Cry, Too, if It Happened to You") and various pool guys, who were often suspect ("D-Day" and "There Goes the Neighborhood"), but, for the most part, Mark was in charge of skimming, trimming, clipping, painting, unclogging pipes, puttying windows, fixing lamps, and weeding the garden. It's a miracle he had any time left to go after the bad guys.

The Friends

The most common sources of case material, by far, were old friends. For Hardcastle, it was old sports chums, twice ("The Homecoming" and "Round Up the Old Gang"). For Mark it was a whole constellation of former associates, from prison buddies ("The Crystal Duck", "The Boxer", and "Duet for Two Wind Instruments"), to old girlfriends ("Never My Love", "Strangle Hold", "Faster Heart", and "When I Look Back On All the Things"), an ex-racing colleague ("Outlaw Champion") and school friends ("The Yankee Clipper").

But, curiously, there was no continuity in the friendship department. Mark often refers to the friend-of-the-week as someone he'd been very close to, but at the same time nobody (except Katie, from "Strangle Hold") ever visited him in prison. The Johnsons (Flip and daughter Barbara), would seem to be the best bets for close friendship with Mark. He knew them from his racing days. He was close enough to both of them to risk re-imprisonment to help Barbara, and to receive the gift of Flip's prototype car, and yet Barb is never again seen or mentioned.

Hardcastle has monthly dinners with Sandy Knight ("The Birthday Present"), someone Mark can barely stand. Mark goes and hangs out with the Fosters, while Milt is off fishing ("The Career Breaker"). Who are they? How does he know them? Another mystery.

In the end, it's about the friendship between Milt and Mark, and with forty-five minutes a week to get everything said and done, there was really no time for other continuing relationships. The better guest stars made it work, dropping in out of nowhere and looking like they'd been just off-screen all along.

Chapter 5
Modus Operandi
Themes, methods, trends, and the Hardcastle worldview

No other form of entertainment (except perhaps improv theater) demands so much from its creators, in such a short time, as the one-hour dramatic format on television. The viewing audience basically expects the equivalent of twenty-two movies, produced in the space of about eight months, each one with its plot and character development crammed into less than half the viewing time of an ordinary motion picture. We demand characters who will catch and hold our interest, and who must be thrown into conflict week after relentless week (even year after year), yet emerge still recognizable.

The very thing which is a burden to series television (its need to produce and sustain likable characters across sixty or more hours of programming, telling their weekly story in forty-seven minutes) is also its salvation. If the characters are consistently written and performed, the audience comes to know them, and care about them and their fate, a degree of understanding that telegraphs a great deal of information that would otherwise have to be spelled out.

For Stephen J. Cannell, the goal was to marry character and plot. He believes in the three act play—act one being the delineation of the problem, act two being the hero's response, and the antagonist's countermoves, leading often to the temporary stymieing or peril of the hero, and act three holding the resolution. Through all of this, aspects of the character are revealed, though every scene should also forward the story.[1]

The end result, for *Hardcastle and McCormick*, was a deft mix of comfortably recognizable behaviors and actions—things the audience could reasonably expect—punctuated by the occasional "change-up" event which revealed some deeper aspect of the characters, or some reason why they behave the way they do.

Before we can appreciate those moments of character-enlargement, it might help to look at the underlying nature of the series and its two protagonists (and how their behaviors sometimes belied their words). From there we can see the way that the creators, writers, and actors developed them into something other than an endlessly repeating forty-eight minute loop.

Crime and Criminals

The premise of the series was good overcoming evil or, as Milton C. Hardcastle put it, "You've got your legal and your illegal". ("Mr. Hardcastle Goes to Washington") While there was occasionally a secret villain, usually the perpetrator was known to the viewer from very near the start. Even Milt and Mark often knew who they were going after.

Criminal activity was invariably high-stakes. Of the approximately 123 criminal acts that occurred over the course of the series, sixty-three (about 51%) were murders. The most common mechanism was by shooting, which accounted for twenty-three of the homicides. Interestingly, the second most common cause of death was "unknown"—a body simply lying somewhere with no obvious signs of how it had met its end. This is in keeping with the relatively non-graphic nature of the show.

As might be expected, car crashes were the third most common mechanism of murder, and were responsible for eight deaths, but despite accounting for 12.6% of the murders, relatively few of the ninety-four car crashes ended in fatalities. Significantly, all the fatal crashes were the result of bad guy-instigated chases. If Mark, Milt, or the cops were driving the pursuit vehicle, the pursued always walked (or crawled) out. No one even got carted off on a stretcher.

The remainder of the murders was a motley collection, ranging from death by bio-warfare agents ("There Goes the Neighborhood") to electrocution ("Games

People Play"). What was never seen in any significant quantity was blood. Even the starker death scenes were often presented in a less-graphic manner, such as the hanging corpse of the guard in "Scared Stiff", seen only as a grim shadow cast on a wall. Other deaths were never seen at all, just a moment of shocked surprise as the victim was attacked, and then a quick cutaway ("Whatever Happened to Guts?" and "Chip Off the Ol' Milt").

Another principle that tended to mitigate the impact of the murders was the frequency of bad guy on bad guy crime, which accounted for over half the victims. Milt pointed out in "Conventional Warfare", "Killing's killing…It doesn't become moral because you don't like the intended victim." The viewers, though, might tend to agree with McCormick that, while Hardcastle's principle is a good one, the end result is, "the world's down one bad guy."

There were twenty-eight strictly innocent victims in the course of the three seasons. The pilot had two deaths by car crash. After that, it would be seventeen more episodes (all the way to the first part of "The Homecoming") before another wholly innocent party would die in yet another crash. On both these occasions there was little time available for the audience to establish any rapport with the deceased. With Flip Johnson, it was Mark's reaction to the news that created a sense of grief. In the case of Bucky Miller's demise, followed by Hardcastle's suspected death ("The Homecoming"), it was Bucky's daughter and Mark sharing their mutual losses that brought the deaths into focus.

By comparison, the other two deaths in "The Homecoming" were closer to plot devices, as was the one in "Really Neat Cars and Guys With a Sense of Humor", though perhaps more shocking because of its incongruity—a man shot by his bride at the outset of his joyful honeymoon night. Most perfunctory of all is the corpse at the beginning of "Scared Stiff"—we don't know his name, why or how he was murdered, or what had caused him to be a target.

The second season didn't have its first innocent victim until episode five, in "Never My Love", with the death of the semi-honest political advisor. The next episode ("Whatever Happened to Guts?") brought two deaths. The second one was non-graphic but still a Hitchcock-like shocker, with two false threats followed by an unexpected third attack. This was also the first woman to die.

Six more episodes passed and then "Too Rich and Too Thin" had the murder of a friend of Hardcastle's. The death was initially thought to have been from natural causes, but even as that version started to unravel, there was more determination than grief from the judge. It fell to the man's law partner, in the epilogue, to express measured sorrow.

The next four episodes had one innocent victim each. "What's So Funny?" was perhaps the grimmest, with a man forced to jump to his death from the top of his hotel. Once again there was a cut-away, but the terror of the victim beforehand, and Mark's reaction shot, told it all.

In "Hardcastle, Hardcastle, Hardcastle, and McCormick", we weren't introduced to the victim. In keeping with the rules of a "cozy" mystery, his death was a puzzle to be solved. It's only later in the episode that we saw that one act of violence leads to another, in an inexorable chain of events that consumes the perpetrators.

"The Long Ago Girl" and "You Don't Hear the One That Gets You" present two problems in record-keeping. In the first, the victim falls to his death in the opening credits. Was he a party to the murderer's embezzlement scheme or an innocent victim? We'll give him the benefit of the doubt, though we never had a chance to work up any sympathy for him and don't even know what he looked like. In the latter episode, a guard is shot during the opening bank robbery. Innocent, yes, but is he dead or merely wounded? The script said injured, but the reaction of the teller, and the demands of foreshadowing, plus the Cannell technique of the cut-away, suggests that the ante was upped between script and screen.

The last of season two's innocent victims was the rookie cop in "Undercover McCormick". This was another death from unknown causes, as well as another friend of Hardcastle's, though not one he'd kept in touch with. Again the judge's response was to seek justice, with no strong emotional reaction.

The third season was the most lethal of all, with twelve innocent victims. It may be argued that the first two (the probable poachers in "She Ain't Deep but She Sure Runs Fast") don't entirely deserve the appellation of "innocent", but we've still got ten others.

Two more died in "Something's Going On On this Train". Again, it's an episode that is shaped as a mystery, but the second victim, a woman, was given one wordless scene in which she established her fundamental loneliness so well that she can't be entirely typed as a plot device.

"Games People Play" brought death to a third female victim. It's a scene reminiscent of the one in "Whatever Happened to Guts?", in which the station employee is stalked and murdered because of what she knows.

The fourth and last woman to die was Katie, Mark's friend in "Strangle Hold". This time McCormick is a witness to the death and, just as in "Rolling Thunder", it's his reaction that elicits our sympathy for a character who had very little time to establish herself. His emotions at the death of this friend (just as in "Rolling Thunder", with Flip's death, and with the suspected deaths of friends in "The Homecoming" and "Never My Love") stand in contrast to Hardcastle's cooler, almost withdrawn demeanor in the same situation, though both men take the same practical actions.

The two deaths in "You're Sixteen, You're Beautiful, and You're His" created a mostly abstract sense of injustice. Even though we briefly meet the second victim, his nephew didn't exhibit much feeling of loss.

In "If You Could See What I See" it's yet another friend of Milt's, a fellow lawyer, and the death takes place before the opening credits. This was the fifth friend he'd lost through violence in three years and, once again, he looks solemn at the graveside and then gets to work. Only one episode later he lost friend number six— a city councilman. This time the victim established his own sympathy in a little gem of a scene in which we see him chatting with his secretary, and then on the phone to his family. It's only a few moments, but enough for us to understand who he is, and why he most certainly doesn't deserve to be brutally assassinated.

In "Poker Night", the death of the shop owner near the beginning (as in "You Don't Hear the One That Gets You") created foreshadowing, showing us that the men who will soon descend on Gull's Way are ruthless. With that purpose served, the point was also made, a little further along, that the victim was a person, a guy who was just running a business and trying to get by, but also someone the main characters had met and liked. The whole episode starkly underlined the unpredictable suddenness with which violence can intrude on ordinary events.

The series ended with one last innocent victim. This was Bob, the crusty new member of the retirement home in "Chip Off the Ol' Milt". While not exactly sympathetic, he was most definitely right in his suspicions. His passing provoked a testy comment from his recent acquaintance, Mimi, who said it most certainly couldn't have been an accident because he'd had years of experience taking showers—hardly a moment of deep mourning. It's all in keeping with the focus of that coda episode, which was on Mark and Milt, and their awkward adjustment to moving forward.

In comparison to the sixty-three murders, innocent and not-so-innocent victims alike, there were also eight justifiable homicides: six by gun, one by bow and arrow, and one fall. The police were responsible for one death ("You Don't Hear the One That Gets You"). Two deaths were caused by other characters, both times in the defense of others ("She Ain't Deep but She Sure Runs Fast" and "One of the Girls From Accounting"). Milt shot and killed two people, both times a professional assassin who was about to shoot Mark ("Faster Heart" and "Hardcastle, Hardcastle, Hardcastle, and McCormick"). Mark shot one ("The Birthday Present"), and had one man—a crazed murderer—fall to his death in the course of trying to subdue him in a fight ("Games People Play"). This last death is only implied, and seems to run contrary to the script.

Murder is usually a secondary crime in *Hardcastle and McCormick*, being used at least twenty-eight times to conceal another crime, most often a crime committed for monetary gain. Only twelve times was murder an act of revenge, anger, or passion.

The second most common criminal endeavor in this series was kidnapping, again usually as a secondary crime (to conceal a previous act or control the actions of another, rather than for monetary gain). Of the nineteen kidnappings, Mark was the victim four times ("The Black Widow", "School for Scandal", "Ties My Father Sold Me", and "Surprise on Seagull Beach"). Hardcastle was also kidnapped four times ("Hotshoes", "Mr. Hardcastle Goes to Washington", "You and the Horse You Rode in On", and "Round Up the Old Gang").

Theft accounted for another fifteen criminal acts. Mostly it was big ticket items and theft rings: cars, yachts, and jewels. Information theft occurred once and Hardcastle was the victim.

Organized crime figured prominently in the series, with general mob activity being the main crime seven times, and mobsters or hit men making up 15% of the perpetrators of crime (not counting henchmen). Career criminals in general (including loan sharks, mobsters, convicts, and teenage gangs) made up a solid 33% of the miscreants.

Interestingly, the most common evil-doers after mobsters were members of law enforcement, with 8.5% of the bad guys having started out wearing badges. Add to this prison guards, wardens, judges, parole officers, lawyers, ex-members of the CIA, mayors, other elected officials, and a retired army officer, and we account for nearly 23% of the perpetrators.

The remainder of the criminals were scattered among many professions, with CEOs and businessmen leading the pack (a combined total of 13%). The only other significant concentration was among sports figures, at slightly less than 3% of the total. Actors and producers together made up yet another 3%. People in the music business also accounted for 3% of the bad guys.

As might be expected, with so many businessmen behaving badly, the estimated income levels of the offenders was skewed toward the higher classes. Nearly 90% of the bad guys qualified as middle class or better. 67% were *upper* middle class or above, and fully 30% would have to be classified as wealthy. Among the mere 10% who were below middle class, only two were blue collar workers. Half of that underclass group consisted of failed criminals, mostly still incarcerated.

Men and Women

There were no regular female cast members of *Hardcastle and McCormick* with the exception of Sarah Wicks, the housekeeper who, after making a strong showing in the pilot, appeared in only four more episodes. Hardcastle was widowed, and seemed not particularly in pursuit of further female companionship, though he was often the subject of admiring women, sometimes to his chagrin ("The Homecoming", "Never My Love", "It Coulda Been Worse, She Coulda Been a Welder", and "Something's Going On On This Train"). On occasion Mark nudged him in the direction of a suitable lady friend ("Flying Down to Rio"), even coaching a little from the wings ("Long Ago Girl").

In "Brother, Can You Spare a Crime?", Hardcastle announced to his brother, Gerald, that he was having someone over who was "special". Though it appeared

to be a first date, the venue was Gull's Way and it was dinner for four, with Mark and Gerald in attendance—hardly a romantic interlude.

One serious fling of Hardcastle's came to light during the series. His unrequited romance with his wartime sweetheart, Jane Bigelow, led him to look her up after the purported death of her husband in "The Long Ago Girl". But even with nothing now standing in their way, the two seemed to be content to leave their relationship in the past, at least until Chip Meadows' trial is concluded.

By comparison, Mark's pursuit of the fair sex was relentless, though the results were uneven. Left waiting in any outer office, he would generally make a pass at the secretary ("Rolling Thunder", "Did You See the One That Got Away") unless he was too nervous, in which case the secretary would make a pass at him ("You and the Horse You Rode in On"). Sometimes it seemed as if he were just staying in practice, with no real interest in the object of his attention ("It Coulda Been Worse, She Coulda been a Welder", twice—a co-ed *and* Hardcastle's niece). He flat-out admitted to having gone through an adolescent dating phase, long after he'd left adolescence behind ("The Career Breaker"), but had the good sense to recognize jail-bait when he saw it ("You're Sixteen, You're Beautiful, and You're His" and "When I Look Back On All the Things").

Sometimes he romanced women in the line of duty ("The Black Widow", "Killer B's", "School for Scandal", and "What's So Funny"). In those cases, it was usually a tight competition as to whether he'd get his nose or his heart broken first. On one occasion he put devotion to duty *way* above personal safety, taking Ali Casir all the way to the altar (but not quite to the "I do's") in "Mirage a Trois".

Mark's previous track record with women was rockier still. Of course he lost his Porsche—and his freedom—in a breakup with his girlfriend, Melinda Marshall ("Rolling Thunder", "When I Look Back On All the Things", and many, *many* references in-between), but he'd also been dumped by at least one earlier woman ("Never My Love") and both deceived and dumped by another ("Faster Heart"). Despite these unfortunate experiences, he was mostly willing to lend a hand when a former girlfriend was in trouble.

It was his own assessment that his magnetic attraction to willowy blonds with cobalt blue eyes was not getting him anywhere ("One of the Girls from Accounting"), and he sometimes disparaged his luck with women ("The Birthday Present"), but he had his moments, blond and otherwise ("The Long Ago Girl" and "Poker Night"). As for serious romantic entanglements—always a risky proposition in series TV—he had Christy Miller in "The Homecoming", a rather interesting attraction (particularly since we discover that Hardcastle had formerly romanced Christy's mother) intensified by the proximity of death.

Kathy Kasternack, the aforementioned accountant, was an even stranger match-up, being neither willowy, nor blonde. It was this encounter that got the attention of one group of experts on television content, who said "the script...opts for equality over chivalry."[2] It certainly did, leaving Kasternack the task of dispatching the bad guy with a shotgun moments before he would have killed McCormick. In the epilogue, though, there was a return to a level of chivalry not often seen in this series, as Mark shows up on Kathy's doorstep, flowers in hand, determined to proceed slowly and carefully with this one.

In addition to romances, there were female friends for McCormick. Flip Johnson's daughter, Barbara, was the first, and his willingness to help her out seemed mostly free of romantic possibilities. The second was Kate Murphy, who also seemed to be more friend than potential lover. Mark by no means limited his attention to younger women, flirting outrageously with Hardcastle's fellow jurist, Mattie Groves in "Poker Night".

There *was* one thing that could get Hardcastle's heart pumping (besides a good chase ending in a recital of the Miranda warning) and that was a little competition from his sidekick in *l'affaires de coeur*. The issue came up twice, first in "Once Again With Vigorish" when the judge learns he missed the boat years earlier with his former law clerk, Pamela Peterson, and seems annoyed by the idea that Mark might now sweep her off her feet.

Later that season (in "Really Neat Cars and Guys With a Sense of Humor") it happens again, when the guys infiltrate a corrupt dating service and the judge submits a little falsified data. It's in the interests of justice, of course, but the stack of date requests his overture generates has the side benefit of tweaking McCormick's ego.

That's only the first of two times when one of the guys goes for the "I'm a producer" gambit as a pick-up line. The other is at the A-list party in "If You Could See What I See", though Mark doesn't have time to act on his impulse before he's shot down. Mark's overtures lean toward the extravagant, ranging from "I'm a concert promoter" ("The Black Widow"), to "I write songs for Barry Manilow" ("Goin' Nowhere Fast"), to "Yeah, that's my car" ("Third Down and Twenty to Life"). The overall effect seems to be underwhelming, and the impression is that women are sometimes savvy, but often shallow (and many are also apparently blind). Mark bemoans the fact that he has to trot out his astrological sign to start a conversation ("One of the Girls from Accounting").

Of course Hardcastle assures him that things were different in his day. He offers dating advice, both solicited and unsolicited ("Once Again with Vigorish" and "One of the Girls From Accounting").

Shallow though they may sometimes be, women aren't generally dangerous in this series. In the sixty-five episodes, women were in charge of the evil-doing only twice ("Really Neat Cars and Guys with a Sense of Humor" and "Whatever Happened to Guts?") and one of those was the completely unhinged other personality of Dr. Stephanie Gary. On another eleven occasions, a woman was partnered with a man, including some very conniving ladies in "The Black Widow", "The Career Breaker", "You Don't Hear the One That Gets You" and "The Day the Music Died". In the remaining forty-three episodes, the villains were men, with minor female accomplices, if any.

Getting the Job Done

In "Rolling Thunder", Hardcastle briefly explains his reasoning for taking Mark on as his fast gun. "It takes one t'catch one" is his motto. The suggestion is that he intends to put Mark's criminal talents, such as they are, to work for him, despite his frequent and ardent polemics about the straight and narrow and one false step being the road to anarchy.

For a guy who sticks to the rules (even the Miranda must be read off the card) and knows the perils of technicalities, Hardcastle fell in with the scamming

side of the operation with a fair amount of alacrity. He was the *faux* stunt double in "Killer B's", Mr. Milton in "Strangle Hold", the guy from editorial in "The Long Ago Girl", and the Reverend Hardcastle in "Duet for Two Wind Instruments".

Still, Mark was the head of that department. Even his employer, usually tightfisted with a compliment, admitted he was a "facile liar" ("The Career Breaker"). In the course of the sixty-five episodes, Mark pulled twenty-three line-of-duty scams that involved lying about who or what he was. He portrayed everything from a psychopath ("Mr.Hardcastle Goes to Washington"), to a doctor ("Faster Heart"), to a cop ("Undercover McCormick"). His routines often involved elaborate props (a cast with built-in gun in "The Career Breaker") and even documentation such as resumes or IDs ("Too Rich and Too Thin" and "Duet for Two Wind Instruments"), but sometimes he required nothing more than a cigarette and a change of attitude ("Strangle Hold"). There was also the occasional clock-tampering incident ("Rolling Thunder" and "Whistler's Pride").

About the only person he had trouble pulling one over on was Hardcastle, though he tried valiantly on two occasions ("Crystal Duck" and "You Would Cry, Too, if It Happened to You") and succeeded briefly once ("Goin' Nowhere Fast"). The only secret he successfully concealed for any length of time from the judge was his entry into law school, which he claimed to have been attending for six months when he finally confessed all in "Chip Off the Ol' Milt".

But scamming can only get you so far. Sometimes the evidence you need is in someone else's file cabinet. That ought to have been Mark's department, too, since Hardcastle claimed to disapprove of breaking and entering, but the judge was at least an accomplice on eleven occasions (ten times with Mark, and once with Mark's father). He went solo three additional times.

Mark did twenty-three unauthorized entries, including twice into government buildings ("Ties My Father Sold Me" and "Hardcastle for Mayor"). His

standing policy seemed to be to ask for forgiveness rather than permission, or to even just pretend the evidence had arrived with the morning paper ("The Long Ago Girl").

He also appropriated fifteen wheeled vehicles over the three year run, starting with the Coyote itself, and including a motorcycle, an Excalibur full of heroin, several trucks, and a bus (and not including his unsuccessful return to the repo trade in "Chip Off the Ol' Milt"). Again Hardcastle said he disapproved, but was a party to the activity six times.

Jailbreaks were a specialty of Mark's. Sometimes this meant a straight-up plan with a helicopter and a bag of cash ("Flying Down to Rio"), and sometimes it involved subterfuge, plaster of Paris, and chewing gum ("The Career Breaker").

Guns were Hardcastle's area of expertise; he was an ex-cop and had an extensive collection. There was even a rifle out on display on his desk ("Prince of Fat City", et al.). He kept another stash of weapons in a storage area near the pool ("Goin' Nowhere Fast") and had a holster under his judicial robes. His favorite pieces had names, like members of the family—Henry ("The Crystal Duck") and Millie ("The Birthday Present"). But his weapon of choice for chasing bad guys off the estate was a shotgun ("Rolling Thunder", "Prince of Fat City", and "The Birthday Present"). In the final season, he sometimes substituted a pistol in each hand, wild west-style ("In The Eye of the Beholder" and "When I Look Back On All the Things").

Mark, who as a parolee wasn't supposed to be handing firearms at all, still wound up holding one on thirty-eight occasions, starting with the morning after his arrival at Gull's Way, when he leveled a gun at some kidnappers. He was a good shot with a large caliber handgun ("Goin' Nowhere Fast"), but he seemed a bit erratic ("Undercover McCormick" and "The Long Ago Girl"). He fired a weapon on eleven occasions in the course of three years, twice being target practice. He shot (reluctantly) and killed one man, Weed Randall, in "The Birthday Present" to prevent Randall from killing a police officer.

By contrast, Hardcastle, in addition to sometimes wearing a holstered weapon, had one in his hand approximately sixty-nine times, and fired a gun on forty-five occasions. As was previously noted, he killed two professional hit men with no apparent hesitation or compunction ("Faster Heart" and "Hardcastle, Hardcastle, Hardcastle, and McCormick").

From time to time, the firepower escalated. Nazis brought in Schmeissers ("Surprise on Seagull Beach"), and domestic bad guys peddled automatic weapons by the crateful ("Flying Down to Rio" and "Hate the Picture, Love the

Frame"). One of the neighbors even had an M-16 ("There Goes the Neighbor-hood"). Always resourceful, Mark and Milt seemed to be able to pick up and fire whatever was at hand. In one episode it was a rocket launcher from the arsenal of some rogue cops and they took out an unoccupied car very thoroughly ("One of the Girls from Accounting").

But when it came to guns, no matter who got to fire them, Mark was stuck with cleaning them ("If You Could See What I See").

Time Off for Good Behavior

Mark sometimes referred to himself as "a slave" ("Rolling Thunder", "Goin' Nowhere Fast", and "You and the Horse You Rode in On") but there were a fair number of leisure opportunities for both guys. No one ever seemed to go in the pool, except once (Nicky, in "Angie's Choice") but they were seen playing bas-ketball twelve times. Popcorn with TV was popular, as were squabbles over the remote. They even watched television during meals ("Mr. Hardcastle Goes to Washington" and "Do Not Go Gentle"). Mark had a stereo system that was loud enough to get him a ticket for being a public nuisance ("Another Round of That Old Song"), and left his tapes in the truck ("If You Could See What I See").

Right from the beginning, Hardcastle often dragged Mark along to social occasions such as poker games ("The Crystal Duck"), dinner parties ("School for Scandal"), and his class reunion ("The Homecoming"). It wasn't that he didn't trust him enough to leave him at home. That was an option all along, too, though Mark didn't always stay where he was put ("Mr. Hardcastle Goes to Washington"). There were times when Mark relished being left behind—at least until things got out of hand ("You Would Cry, Too, If It Happened to You"). But increasingly, in the second and third seasons, Mark went where Milt went because that's what buddies do—hang out together.

Buddies or not, it was Mark's moral obligation to do a certain amount of kvetching on these jaunts, even before the inevitable downward spiral into mayhem that was the typical result of Hardcastle's travel plans ("She Ain't Deep but She Sure Runs Fast" and "Conven-tional Warfare"). Once in a while they were even Mark's excursions and Hardcastle's turn to kvetch ("Ties My Father Sold Me"), though both guys seemed to know when something was important to the other, and could even dredge up a kind word or two in a moment of success ("The Homecoming" and "You Don't Hear the One That Gets You").

Mark's racing career had been put on hold after Flip's death in "Rolling Thunder", but he still apparently had connections, and kept his Trans Am racing license up-to-date ("Hotshoes"). He raced three times professionally in the three years of the series ("Hotshoes", "Faster Heart", and "You Don't Hear the One That Gets You"). He was sabotaged once and won twice. Despite Hardcastle's general disapproval of the hazards and expense of racing, he backed Mark in his bid to beat Sidewinder Sammy O'Connell in a drag racing grudge match ("Faster Heart").

Mark also appeared to be attending night school during his years at Gull's Way ("The Long Ago Girl"). This was in spite of his protestations that he wasn't a college kind of guy ("Third Down and Twenty to Life").

Long Shots

Mark and Milt shared a deep interest in wagering, along with a liking for nearly every sport. In addition to playing basketball, and the occasional game of touch football out in the yard ("Third Down and Twenty to Life"), they followed professional basketball and football (and wagered on both) and had strong opinions about boxing ("The Boxer").

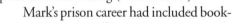

Mark's prison career had included book-making ("Scared Stiff"), and wagers around Gull's Way weren't limited to sports. Pulses were bet on avidly, with six actual incidents (wins were split evenly), and three more challenges going unanswered. Other sources for gentlemanly wagers

included who could get a door painted faster ("Whistler's Pride") and whether or not Mark could get accepted as a game show contestant ("Games People Play"). For both men, the trait seemed to be familial. Hardcastle's younger brother and Mark's father were both inveterate gamblers.

It was only too appropriate that the series should end with a bet, for very high stakes, followed by an extended metaphor for wagering, with Mark as the longest shot of all.

Sartorial Considerations

According to Mark, the judge dressed "like a referee in a girls hockey match" ("Rolling Thunder"). Actually, the grubby sneakers, shorts and Hawaiian shirt combo gave way fairly quickly to Hardcastle's humorous T-shirt era (season one) and then settled into some less extreme clothing. Hawaiian shirts were an occasional recurring leitmotif, especially when packing for judges' conventions. It took extreme provocation for the judge to put on a tie, and very little excuse for him to take it off ("Mr. Hardcastle Goes to Washington").

Mark was hardly in a position of moral authority when it came to clothing. He routinely got his outfits off the floor, and wore them if they passed the sniff test ("The Crystal Duck" and "The Birthday Present"). He wore suits when necessary, but shared Hardcastle's tendency to jettison the fancy dress when provoked ("You and the Horse You Rode in On"). His most distinctive outfit was his racing gear—a white jumpsuit with red stripes on the sleeves. The Nomax™ underwear got a little airtime, too ("Hotshoes").

Both men wore hats. Hardcastle favored a Yankees cap, alternating with one for the L.A. Dodgers, and, in season three, a cap from the fictional California Stars. He also had a cowboy hat, a golf cap, and a Homburg for fancy occasions.

Mark's hat-gear went through stages, with the E-Street Band cap dominating the second season, and a Toronto Blue Jays cap making an appearance right about when that team had beat Hardcastle's beloved Yankees by two games in the American League Eastern Division. While the E-Street hat was Danny Kelly's own touch, reflecting his New Jersey roots and friendship with the band members, he says the Blue Jays cap was just something he found lying around his trailer.

Mark also had a helmet, which he managed to crack in "Hotshoes". He said replacing it was going to cost him five hundred dollars.

Nicknames and Taglines

Although the scripts frequently had the two men on a first name basis, the actors mostly stuck to addressing each other by the characters' last names. For Hardcastle, this was occasionally converted to "Hardcase". Nearly everyone called him that, cops and bad guys alike. The term was heard thirty-eight times in the three year run, most often spoken directly to the man's face. Only on twenty of those occasions was Mark the one saying it (ten times in season one, six in season two, and four in season three). The person who bandied it the most frequently was crusty old-time robber Henry Willard, who said it seven times.

The other term of endearment that McCormick occasionally trotted out to describe the judge was "donkey", but this tapered off quickly, with ten instances in season one, and only one in season two. In the third season, for variety, it was "jackass" and "mule".

The series' most memorable tag line was, of course, "Now you're cookin'!" which was uttered nineteen times in the three seasons. Mark even said it three times, but the other sixteen times were by Hardcastle (including the final line of dialog in the last episode).

Heroes and Icons

Hardcastle was straightforward about his heroes. He owned Lone Ranger comic books, and even left them out in plain sight in his chambers. Mark seized on this, imposing his own instant pop psychology on the situation. Curiously, though, he painted himself into the mythology right from the start. If Hardcastle was the Lone Ranger, then he must be Tonto. There are sixteen Lone Ranger references in season one. It seems a very short step from joking about it, to accepting it as shorthand for their relationship and work.

Only a few episodes into season two, Mark was the one trying to persuade Hardcastle that "the work we do is important" ("Whatever Happened to Guts?"). By that point, the nicknames are hardly gibes anymore. Now when Mark wants to give the judge a hard time, he ups the ante to "Superman" ("D-Day" and "There Goes the Neighborhood"), or "The Justice League" ("Hate the Picture, Love the Frame"). In the third season there are only six Lone Ranger references versus nine to other super heroes, spread all over the board from Superman and Batman to the Green Lantern and Green Hornet. The Cisco Kid and Pancho even get a mention, with Mark suggesting that he and Hardcastle might want to trade places and let the judge be the sidekick for a while ("Strangle Hold").

Change and Character Development

From episode to episode, the exigencies of that week's plot had to take precedent. If the story was designed to put Melinda Marshall and Mark on a collision course and the subtext was about wanting "a grownup car", then Mark would consider sacrificing the Coyote without a backward glance.

Mark and Milt both varied from tongue-tied to astonishingly articulate, according to the necessities of the situation. Mark would alternately trip over flower pots and drop into a high security building with the aplomb of an experienced cat burglar. Hardcastle would mispronounce the word "regatta", and half-stutter his answers to the Washington press corps, but was able to take command of a court room or give a considered opinion on a particular year's vintage of an obscure wine.

It helped that both actors were good at physical comedy and absolutely willing to engage in moments of absurdity. It was, nearly always, a comedy-action show. For all that (or perhaps because of it) the moments of drama stood out in high relief. Mark's anger at being harassed by his old nemesis Hardcastle at the beginning of "Rolling Thunder", and his grief upon hearing of Flip's death a few scenes later, both set a benchmark that indicated the creators were reserving room at the top for some dramatic range, and the actors were not going to have to stretch to reach it when it was called for.

The early episodes, written by the two creators, allowed the characters to move quickly toward a working relationship, and even some grudging affection, though they wouldn't yet admit to it. A basketball game ("Rolling Thunder"), Mark finding out that Hardcastle had lost his only child years earlier ("Man in a Glass House"), a wallet found and returned ("Goin' Nowhere Fast"), Mark discovering the basis for the judge's animosity toward a police captain ("The Black Widow")—all are points on a scatter chart, rather than a distinct line. It trends toward friendship, without proceeding at a steady or predictable march.

The end of the first season saw the facts well-established. In "The Homecoming" Mark eulogizes the presumed-dead Hardcastle in a way that might sound insulting coming from anyone but him. But he's clearly just a guy trying to hold it all together—already having sworn that he'll do whatever he must to avenge the man, no matter what the cost.

In season two, more back-story is revealed. Mark finds his father, and, in the gulf between expectations and reality, we see that Hardcastle is more than just a buddy. Mark even hints, in his disappointment, that the judge would make a better father than Sonny. Hardcastle edges back from the notion, even scoffs at it, while unconsciously doing everything a father would do.

Hasburgh extended this idea a few episodes later. The problem with having a father is that he treats you like a kid. Mark starts to mutter about wanting to be a grownup—another theme that would carry through to the end of the series.

Another Cannell episode, late in the second season, further highlighted the change that had occurred. On the surface, the two still bicker. It's a continuous test of wills. But when Hardcastle is shot, Mark is deeply shaken. He becomes a different person—grim, angry, determined, but still working (mostly) within the Hardcastle rules.

In the third season, Hasburgh added new layers to the judge's character. For the first time, Hardcastle confesses that he might have had some ulterior motives in hijacking Mark's life. In some ways, this character has come further than McCormick. Mark merely had to stop hating the man who sent him to prison. Hardcastle had to learn how to express feelings that he'd kept securely locked away for a long time.

A few episodes later, in the crucible of terminal illness (only imagined, but every bit as effective as the real thing) many truths are revealed. Hardcastle, who has blood kin of various sorts, makes Mark his legatee. This time it's McCormick who shies back, as though if he accepts the one possibility, he is accepting Hardcastle's death as well. He's no more reconciled to that than he was a year earlier. In the end, the issue recedes to merely hypothetical, but now that it's all been unfolded and examined, it can hardly be expected to fit back in the little box again.

Through the third season, the feeling of partnership grows. More situations stem from Mark's friends and activities. It doesn't take a psychic to recognize that he's "another son" to Hardcastle. He's still delivering his little polemics on adulthood—how he and the judge are stuck in a loop, drinking Pinky Fizz, eating cookies, and chasing bad guys. At the same time, there are more trousers, fewer jeans, night school, a visit to friends while the judge goes fishing, a weekend trip to Catalina (almost), and lots of sideways references to the law and lawyers. Meanwhile, though there are plenty of misadventures, they're hardly ever the result of opening the file drawers anymore.

There's one last digression when Sonny shows up again. This time Mark can hardly be bothered with the man. It takes some heavy leaning from an equally concerned Hardcastle before he'll even listen to what Sonny has to say. It's only a temporary distraction. Even the new, improved Sonny Daye is only able to hang around for so long and now Mark understands and even expects that. This time there may even be some mutual relief when the man finally departs.

But Mark's parole is up. He's living in limbo and his schedule seems to be mostly his own. In the final episode, two people who aren't all that good at talking about the important stuff at long last get around to the truth. Mark, a guy who said he wasn't college material, has been sneaking off to attend law school. It's not the Rolodex and the grownup car that matter anymore.

1.   Cannell, interview with Abramson for the Archive of American Television. June 23, 2004 part nine
2.   S. Robert Licher, et al. *Prime Time—How TV Portrays American Culture,* p. 139

Chapter 6
The Other Star of the Show
The Coyote(s), specs and trivia

As Howard the mechanic once said, "Girls and cars, cars and girls". But this is an eighties action show we're talking about here, so you've got to expect a certain amount of both. And since *Hardcastle and McCormick* never quite gave in to the Love Interest of the Week syndrome, the testosterone had to be mostly satisfied in the form of cars.

Enter the Coyote. When you've got bad guys to catch and an ex-race car driver to help catch them, it's almost a given that you'd need a snazzy, souped-up car to do the chasing. And the Coyote certainly filled the bill. It was the very antithesis of what Mark is looking for toward the end of season three: small, eye-catching, and very definitely red. But in the television landscape of the day, the competition came in the form of *Knight Rider*'s KITT, *The Dukes of Hazzard*'s General Lee, and even a GMC van in Cannell's own *The A-Team*. Nondescript wasn't going to be acceptable. Depending on who you talk to, the Coyote either was or was not a character in the show, but there's no denying it was integral to the look and feel, the advertising, and occasionally even the plot.

Beginning with "Rolling Thunder" we see that the car is going to play an important part in the lives of these characters. McCormick is impressed with the car on the strength of blueprints alone, but the first time he actually sees the Coyote, he has to take a minute—even in the midst of a burglary—to admire its

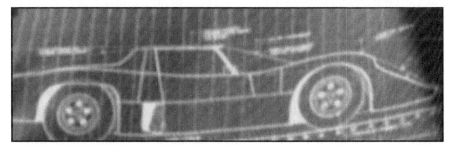

McLaren body style hero car. Photo courtesy David Dines.

beauty. It won't be long until he's putting it through its paces, reveling in the car's speed and agility, and taking a willing audience along for the ride.

When a show created by a couple of guys—one of them a confirmed *car guy*— needs an automobile for a little derring-do, it can't be too surprising that the prototype they had in mind was a unique car built by a racing legend. The McLaren M6GT was built by driver/designer Bruce McLaren, and was originally intended to be raced on the Can-Am circuit. There were certification problems, however, and McLaren determined to make the car into a world-class road car. Tragically, McLaren was killed in a race less than a year after creating the original M6, so only three were ever built. Like the Coyote to follow, the car would never completely fulfill its designer's dreams.

The car was far from forgotten, though, and more than a decade later would serve as the basis for the season one Coyote. Designer Mike Fennel, of Mike Fennel Restorations, was brought in to give his own artistic renderings of the car, and his choices and alterations turned in to what the producers had in mind for the Coyote. Fennel would ultimately build three cars—and many other fiberglass bodies—for "Rolling Thunder". He worked with the show through the pilot, then left his creation in the hands of others.

That's where Mario Sciortino and Unique Movie Cars came in. Good friends with Mike Fennel, Sciortino got the call when Mike was ready to leave the Coyote behind. His company has long been in the business of providing cars to film and television productions, beginning with *The Waltons* back in 1972. At the time *Hardcastle and McCormick* found themselves in need of someone to take the reins on their automotive endeavors, Sciortino had already set up cars for films such as *Smokey and the Bandit*, and *The Cannonball Run*, and done television work for many series, including *Charlie's Angels*, *The Fall Guy*, and *The A-Team*, so he certainly had the credentials to pick up where Fennel left off.

The three cars used for filming had separate and distinct purposes; one for chases, one for jumps and other stunts, and one for interior shots with the actors.

The interior car—also known as the hero or beauty car—was used primarily by the first unit, but the others were the domain of second unit, under the direction of Gary Combs. And while on screen the Coyote is everything it's cracked up to be— a fast ride seemingly custom-made for taking out the criminals, and every guy's dream when you slide behind the wheel—getting that dream machine on film could be a different thing altogether. While the McLaren had a list of technical specifications to highlight its racing pedigree, all underscored with a Chevrolet V8, the production Coyote was essentially a kit car, with a fiberglass body riding on whichever chassis was needed for a particular shot, powered by a small Volkswagen engine. Though cast and crew chalked up working with the car as all part of a day's work, none of them used words like "fast", "sleek", or "impressive" to describe it.

Reliable didn't make the list, either. First unit spent far less time working with the car, and Les Sheldon wouldn't have it any other way, for a couple of reasons. First, as he points out, the show was never intended to be a race car show. They were trying to make "a special show", about relationships, about characters, and the Coyote was merely a backdrop.

But second, with the car being essentially a prop, designed for something other than reliably moving people from one place to the next, using the Coyote in principal shooting could be problematic. Sheldon relates that any scene taking place in the car would automatically add half an hour to the production time, allowing for on-the-spot maintenance and the like. As such, that scene choice would only be made if a good fit for the actual story. Far easier to have the Coyote waiting in the background, "walk and talk" the actors up to it or even into it, and then cut the scene there. And, whenever possible, use the judge's pickup instead.

Second unit didn't have it quite so easy, though, as their job was to bring the Coyote to life. And with almost a hundred chases and more than a dozen jumps, they certainly succeeded.

As the primary action vehicle, the chase car could be the subject of a lot of attention, and Gary Combs was the guy responsible for making sure the attention was positive. Underneath this fiberglass body, though, was a frame that stunt driver Gary Hymes had cobbled together into a configuration of unusual metal pieces and misaligned pedals that Combs called "awful". It was so unlike any other car that only Hymes could drive it, and no one else even really wanted to try, and that's the way the chases got filmed.

The jump car was physically different, primarily due to the suspension necessary to survive the jumps. The engine didn't matter in this car since it didn't have much actual driving to do, but the frame was pitched higher, the springs were stiffer, and it was equipped with double and triple shock absorbers to help keep it in one piece. Of course, that caused a noticeable difference in ground clearance; the chase car—like the hero car—was low to the ground, whereas the jumper was significantly higher. Side by side, the difference is immediately identifiable, but as Combs says, "You only ever see the jump car in the air, so no one could tell".

Season 2 jump car and Season 1 hero car. Photo courtesy David Dines/Suzanne Forgo.

But even with the admitted technical problems with the car ("sometimes we just towed it to the starting point instead of driving it"), and even though time could sometimes be lost to patching up the fiberglass before the next shot, Sheldon says Combs and his unit never once failed to come through. "They were geniuses," he says. "They delivered the footage every time, on time, though that car gave them nothing but trouble."

Combs agrees that there were technical problems, but that's why second unit was equipped with a mechanic and body guys; it comes with the territory. Sciortino agrees. He says the production companies always say the same thing: "We're not going to hurt the car; we're not going to wreck it", though he estimates that ninety percent of the time they do. He says at the end of the day's filming, he'd just take a truck out and pick up the pieces and put them back together again.

But Combs did worry about operating with only one chase car that only one guy knew how to drive. He spent a lot of time trying to explain that if anything ever happened to the car or to Hymes, production was going to be up a creek. Building a second car could solve both problems. But costs outweighed concerns and they continued through the first season.

But toward the end of that first year, Combs' point was finally made. During a stunt, Hymes lost control of the car and smashed it into a light pole. No one was hurt, but the Coyote "came apart like a two dollar suitcase. We put it back together with some red tape and got through the day, but it cost us two hours." At last, the studio agreed to get him a second car.

That's when the DeLorean—the car used throughout the second and third seasons—came into the picture. Viewers might not have been able to tell the difference between the three cars used during season one (though that is debatable), but they were unlikely to miss the change from the McLaren style to the DeLorean. No one seems sure why that particular car was chosen rather than build a replica of the existing Coyote. Sheldon says maybe the car was given to them, and transportation coordinator Jim Sharp agrees that product placement was alive and well, even in the eighties. (He can still tell you that he used American Racing wheels and BF Goodrich tires.) But by 1984, the DeLorean Motor Company had already hit bankruptcy and closed its doors, so no deals were being made on their behalf. But Sciortino echoes the thought that two DeLorean DMC-12s were gifted to the studio, though whether specifically intended for *Hardcastle and McCormick*, who's to say? But since Combs was looking for something more durable and reliable, the stainless steel construction had to be seen as a definite improvement, and there's no denying some resemblance to the original Coyote, which had to be taken into consideration, so the new Coyote was born.

The DeLorean might've had the necessary basic size and shape to begin with, but it could hardly be used as is. Sciortino had to remove the body and essentially build it from scratch. The existing back end and windshield were both cut off and redesigned to suit their purposes. And the top had to be cut out T-top style, both to allow extra head room and to make the style more consistent with the season one car. The end result was a new car with at least a minor similarity to the original that could be put into production with no concerns. As Jim Sharp says, "Those sorts of changes happen in TV a lot. Unless someone's just a huge fan, they're probably not going to say anything or maybe even notice." He admits, though, that people did notice, though it was not a negative issue for the show. And, perhaps most important, the company had the new car it needed.

In addition to more stability and reliability for the second unit, the DeLorean was bigger, more comfortable, and a much more suitable vehicle for the interior shots than what first unit had been using. Not only did it provide a more accommodating personal workspace for the cast, it made filming more practical. As Sharp says, "Those kit cars didn't even have an interior; it was all just fiberglass and bare metal inside. We had to use mock-ups for the interior shots. But the DeLorean was a real car; the gauges worked and everything."

DeLorean body jump car. Photo courtesy David Dines.

Not that the new car solved everything. Even though second season was already showing a decline in chases, jumps, and such, both Sciortino and Combs recall that making sure the *Hardcastle and McCormick* stunts kept up with the competition could take its toll on the vehicle, and keeping everything in one piece was always a challenge. Sciortino laments that sometimes it could get to the point where "it just explodes the cars". As such, in the ongoing quest to have duplicate vehicles, Combs recalls they had built yet another car in third season, pieced together from whatever they had on hand. As he describes it, it was "part Ford, part Chevy, and part everything else, but still not a very good car."

Just don't tell that to the fans. While the show may never have been *about* the Coyote, the car certainly had a following. The Coyote showed up in publicity shots and on t-shirts, and plastic replicas and model kits could be found in toy stores. The car was even featured in a 1986 issue of *Hot Rodder Magazine*. Even now you can find the occasional fan conversation debating the relative merits of the McLaren body versus the DeLorean, or whether the Coyote could outrun KITT. And some of the prop cars have survived, making their way into the society of free enterprise and ultimately landing in the hands of fans and collectors.

One such fan is Robert Quast, who is in possession of one of the DeLorean beauty cars, which still has its camera mounts. He treasures the car and displays it proudly on the lot of his limousine rental business in Iowa. And even though it's technically for sale, Quast vows never to part with it.

Another fan with his own piece of television history is Brian Bell, living in New Jersey. Ten at the time the show premiered, he thought the Coyote was the "coolest car that had ever been made", and decided then he was going to have one someday. He had settled for die-cast and plastic models until one day in 2008 he saw a listing on eBay. His wife, Tammy, didn't initially share his enthusiasm with the find, but before the auction had closed, they had decided it was a once in a lifetime opportunity, and he placed a bid. He and Tammy are now the proud owners of the season one hero car.

Bell is pleased that he can trace the history of the car since the time of the show. Immediately following cancellation, it was on tour with car customizer George Barris and other famous cars, including KITT, the A-Team van, and the Batmobile. Then, in approximately 1987, the car was sold to its first private owner, and disappeared from public view. But in 1991, the Coyote was sold to a new owner and again became accessible to the public as she displayed it in her automotive museum. Fan and car collector David Dines purchased the Coyote in 2007 for his collection, the Hollywood Car Café, though he sold it to another collector later that year. The new owner then listed it on auction a few months later, and Bell finally acquired his childhood dream.

Bell reports that Dines was responsible for what restoration has been done, and though it sat idle for many years before Dines ever tried to get it running again, he says it's not in bad shape. As he puts it, "There are things it could use; it

Brian and Tammy Bell with their "Best of Show" Coyote.

needs tiny odds and ends. It's mostly the original paint, and there are tiny cracks in the fiberglass, but from six feet away, it looks perfect." Others must agree; at a local car show in June, 2008 Bell and his Coyote walked away with Best of Show.

The debate for Bell now is whether to maintain as much originality as possible with the car, or to try and correct the flaws in the fiberglass and paint. But whichever he chooses, Bell says the car will absolutely be kept essentially intact to honor its heritage from the show.

One of the other show cars was also recently up for auction on eBay. Current owner Scott Velvet had offered a second season DeLorean stunt car for sale. As mentioned earlier, the number of jumps was on a drastic decline by second season, and this particular car had the honor of performing the final Coyote jump filmed in the series, seen in "The Birthday Present".

Following the completion of the series, the jump car was still in possession of Mario Sciortino. He ultimately sold it to the Disney MGM Studio in Florida, where it was displayed on a back lot tour, just waiting for the attentive fan to recognize it. Recognize it someone did, and a fan purchased it from the studio, rescuing it from its slowly decaying end. Then the car was sold to the same museum that housed the season one Coyote. David Dines bought them both in 2007.

While in Dines' possession, he performed an off-body restoration, and Velvet says he did "quite well". Though Velvet says he was and is a fan of the show, he's in the business of buying and selling movie cars, so he tries not to get too attached to any of them. But though he's committed to the business model that caused him to offer the Coyote for sale, he admits that "ten years from now, this will probably be one of those cars that I wish I'd never sold". And he speaks highly of the vehicle he's trying to sell: "This is a highly recognizable, iconic artifact from the television era before CGI, in a time when car chases were king. I believe this show and this car will be around for years after I'm gone for others to view and enjoy."

Thanks to the fact that the Coyotes are now in the hands of fans who view them as cars, rather than mere props, we are able to have some technical specifications that the film crew are not able to provide.

Of his car, Velvet says, "The car is basically a dune buggy with a sports car body attached. It was equipped with the latest in VW technology (circa 1970s-1980s), a large high-performance VW type III engine, dual carbs, off-road shocks, and tube chassis."

And for anyone who might be thinking about recreating a Coyote, Brian Bell has the necessary details.

1983 Cody Coyote

Manufacturer	Mike Fennel
	(for Stephen J. Cannell Productions)
Use	Principal Photography, Season 1

Molds based on McLaren M6 GT

Body Material	Fiberglass
Frame Type	Volkswagen with custom tube frames
Wheelbase	94.5 inches
Length	163 inches
Width	75 inches
Height	41 inches
Ground Clearance	6 inches max, 3 ½ floor pan (seat buckets)
Curb Weight	Approximated to 1900 pounds
Suspension	Modified VW and custom
Brakes	Manual Drum
Steering	Manual
Clutch	Hydraulic Assisted
Engine	1835cc, high-output modified, flat 4 cylinder, carbureted
Horsepower	150 + (estimated)
Exhaust	Custom
Transmission/Transaxle	VW 4-speed and transaxle
Wheels/Tires (Front)	Deep-dish, Centerline 15 inch rims. B F Goodrich P265/50 R15
Wheels/Tires (Rear)	Deep-dish, Centerline 15 inch rims. B F Goodrich P295/50 R15
Interior	Black vinyl bucket seats/dash and black carpeting
Gauges	VDO
Steering Wheel	Vilhem B. Haan

But those who have been lucky enough to own the actual cars used in the filming of the show are not the only fans trying to put their very own Coyote in the garage. Commercially produced kit cars of the day, Manta Montages were also modeled on the McLaren M6GT, and fans of the show have purchased Mantas and had them painted in the Coyote color scheme. They can be found on internet message boards dedicated to both *Hardcastle and McCormick* and Manta cars alike. And, like the show vehicles, they are also occasionally offered on eBay. At the time of this writing, there is a self-described "tribute car" listed, with an asking price of $59,900. Mario Sciortino is astounded, indicating that the total budget for each of their cars was about $12,500. Even allowing for inflation, you ought to be able to build a Coyote for less than thirty thousand…if you could find a body to start with, of course. Manta Cars closed for business in 1986.

But back in 1987, with both the show and Manta still a recent memory, the cars were a bit easier to find. Carole Manny, a fan of the show since the beginning, remembers her attempt to purchase a Coyote of her own. Describing her younger self, she says, "I was a 23-year-old woman with the brain of a 17-year-old boy, at least on the subject of cars", and she was sure if she just read enough car magazines, she could find someone who would sell her a Coyote. And it turns out she was right. An owner had a car listed in *Kit Car Magazine* for $12,500, and Carole was more than willing to go into debt at her local bank. After scraping together enough cash for a flight from Chicago to Seattle, she went to see the car of her dreams. And, though the headlights weren't quite right, and the red paint job was missing the necessary white trim, she was hooked.

Though she returned home promising to "think about it", she knew she fully intended to buy the car. Bargaining with the owner to install headlight covers like the show car, she agreed to his terms of payment up front, though it ultimately took repeated phone calls, hints of legal action, and eight months before the car would finally make it to Denver, the agreed upon delivery site.

Upon receiving the car, Carole noticed that the almost-new BF Goodrich tires that had been on the car in Seattle had been replaced with a set that was practically bare, though, without pictures, she knew she had no recourse for that. What she didn't know (as there had been no test drive in Seattle), was that the transmission was finicky, and it was an open question on whether or not it would shift into first gear. Making her way back to Illinois, she also discovered that the car was no longer fit for night driving, since when the headlights were refitted after installing the requested covers they were not properly aligned and did not illuminate the road. After an overnight stay at a motel, she set out for home again, only to have the car die completely about an hour short of her final destination. A clogged fuel pump was the diagnosis, but the car had to be towed home and never ran again while she owned it.

But though her Coyote experience was a fiasco from start to finish, and though she ultimately had to sell the car for a loss, she finds the silver lining to the situation. "It made me realize that I could get just about anything I wanted to get, if I wanted it badly enough and tried hard enough. Nothing has happened since to make me change my mind about that…So a little embarrassing, but in retrospect I'm glad that at that age I gained the confidence to go after what I want. It's a lesson that has worked for me ever since."

Not a bad lesson, and all because of a show that was never intended to be about the car.

Chapter 7
"Play It For As Long As It Holds"
Action sequences, stunts, and the people who created them

Though Stephen Cannell is a firm believer in the character-driven plot, *Hardcastle and McCormick* was conceived as an action show as well. Most scripts included at least one "director's sequence" in which the writer would give a brief description of a period of dialog-free activity, usually a chase, and end it with the immortal license for mayhem: "play it for as long as it holds". Cannell's studio had a dedicated team of stunt and special effects people who were kept fully occupied during that era, providing on-screen mayhem for *The A-Team, Riptide,* and *Hunter,* as well as *Hardcastle.*

Some second unit personnel were shared between these four series but each show had its own stunt coordinator/second unit director. For all but the pilot episode of *Hardcastle and McCormick* (in which Jim Arnett did stunt coordination), it was Gary Combs—a second generation Hollywood stunt man whose father, Del, had gotten his start in the silent movie era. Combs' assistant director, through most of the three-year run, was Robert Del Valle.

Combs' son, Gil, was also part of the team, alternating with Gary Hymes as Daniel Hugh Kelly's stunt double, as well as handling car stunts. For Brian Keith, the double was veteran stunt man Chuck Hicks for most of the three-season run. Providing explosions and other special effects was Terry Frazee, also the second generation of his family to explore the art of blowing things up.

Frazee's father had developed some of the techniques used in the special effects business and from him came the adage that—impressions to the contrary—less is better in the pyrotechnical business. Frazee used a wide range of things to produce explosive mayhem: black powder, chemicals, even plastic explosives, but the idea was to have the action happen as slowly as possible, so that the audience could *see* it. In terms of explosions, even slow is fast.

401

Frazee's other jobs included constructing many of the objects that were being destroyed. Trucks, buildings, boats—all had to be manufactured to explode, or be rammed through, safely and effectively. Balsa was a frequent component.

Both Frazee and Combs did research and development. One of the most common stunts, especially in the auto-centric world of *Hardcastle and McCormick*, was the car rollover. The typical way in which this stunt was achieved was by using an explosive charge to shoot a large pole from the underside of the vehicle into the pavement at a critical moment, adding enough upward force to start the roll.

The pole, of course, was a heavy, high-speed projectile which could behave unpredictably, including the occasional rollover in which the charge failed to go off, leaving a wrecked and still potentially explosive vehicle. Combs wanted something safer. Frazee designed an "air cannon", based on Combs' impression that, at the moment when a car is thrown into a skid on a turn, it wouldn't take all that much force to lift it. The blast of air, combined with the simultaneous explosive flattening of the two tires on the downward side, was often enough to create the effect.

When more lift was needed, for aerial corkscrews, and flips, a pipe ramp was employed. This device was simple and effective: a pipe placed at an upward angle and designed to be driven onto at sufficient speed to get the vehicle temporarily airborne. As Bob Del Valle put it: "What it is is what it sounds like—a big piece of pipe anchored to the ground that goes up at maybe forty-five degrees. It's hidden from view of the camera. The car rides up on it at maybe fifty miles an hour, and it will flip the car over. If you drive straight up on it, you're screwed—the car's not going to flip; it isn't going to do what you want at all. It's going to go up and come straight down."

"Jarring," is how Gary Combs described that.

The driver aimed to catch the pipe to the left or right of center, depending on which way he wanted the car to turn ("driver up" or "driver down" in stunt parlance). There were a lot of precautions, Del Valle recollects. "They had to put a roll cage in, and take the gas tank out and use a fuel cell. When the bad guy's car

turns over you'll see the roll cage. More often than not, those cars were driven. The driver wears a helmet, which is painted black. They have padding on, under the wardrobe. The passenger, if needed, is a dummy."

It was not without risk, even with extreme care to detail. A stuntman would earn $2500 for a pipe ramp flip. But, despite the inherent risks, Combs only remembers one stunt that resulted

in a knock-out. He occasionally used a dummy (affectionately dubbed "Rodney", short for Rodney Dangerfield), for head-on collisions and other stunts deemed too hazardous.

Through the course of three seasons, Combs and his team filmed one hundred and eleven chases, and about ninety-four crashes (from time to time, some of the more spectacular chase and crash sequences were reused). They developed a system to maximize their efficiency. Because the second unit was shared with other series, each episode's main action sequences usually had to be filmed in one day.

As Del Valle tells it: "What we would do is get the beginning of the chase out of the way, and then the next thing we did was set up and film the wreck. And the wreck, we knew, would always take us about three hours. That meant placing the seven cameras, getting the driver set up in the wreck car, and the car ready with the pipe ramp in position. All that would take us until about lunch. And then after lunch we would spend the rest of the day getting as many shots as we had time for. You knew the second half of your day was the middle part of the chase. Whatever you got was good, and even if you didn't get something, you still had your story told."

Combs recalls that unless the storyline called for something specific—say, a particular jump, or a necessary rollover—the chase sequences were pretty much left to him. The script would essentially say "chase ensues", and then he and his team would go to work. But though he liked the freedom, he says it took a while before he learned exactly what the producers were looking for. One of the first things he discovered, though, was that Cannell liked the action coming to the camera; going away wasn't exciting. So they learned how to bring the Coyote racing toward the camera and screeching right into the viewers' living rooms.

The mechanics of camera placement were designed for maximum efficiency. Combs would pick an intersection, get the cameras set up, then shoot the vehicles coming toward, or heading away from that point in four different directions. This allowed for a greater variety of footage with minimum camera movement.

"Lock-off" cameras were often used in crash scenes. As Del Valle said, "You simply put a camera there, often in a crash housing, in a spot that is very dynamic, but too dangerous to put a person. Maybe you think the car is going to crash on top of it, which is always exciting."

Though first and second units rarely did their work in the same time and place, their results had to mesh. No matter which unit shot first, the first unit's footage of the main characters driving out of frame had to match the second unit for costumes and vehicles. For the Coyote, it was a transition from the "hero car" to one of the stunt vehicles—with an occasional lapse between the Delorean and McLaren designs, especially when older jump footage was used, as in "Faster Heart".

Bad guy cars, often doomed, were arranged by the transportation coordinator. They were usually purchased in sets of two or three, permitting one to be destroyed before lunch, while the others were preserved for the afternoon's filming. Having two of any vehicle available simplified matters greatly, allowing for camera mounts to be changed while filming continued, and reducing the risk that filming would grind to a halt if repairs had be made.

Matching costumes was nowhere near as expensive, but occasionally tricky, as Del Valle relates. "We would go to the wardrobe department and get our stunt doubles the same outfits that Danny and Brian were wearing. I'd traditionally go to the set and make sure we had that all coordinated. One time, I remember watching the chase that Monday night's broadcast. I see Danny and Brian run out of frame, climb in the car, and drive off. Then the stunt guys do their driving and the wreck happens and the Brian and Danny doubles grab the bad guy and run out of frame. One of them was wearing jeans. When first unit picked up, he came back into the frame wearing khakis. Wrong wardrobe, and we didn't see it until the episode aired. The wardrobe guy came up to me the next day and said, 'Bobby, what happened?' I usually brought Polaroids."

In the midst of all the details, there was also a certain style to be maintained in *Hardcastle and McCormick* roadway mayhem. One part was the rule, as Del Valle summed it up, "that the good guys could never put the public at jeopardy in a car chase. The bad guys could, but not Hardcastle or McCormick. That's not the perception that you want to give the audience, that the heroes are cavalier."

Also, despite the extent of the action, the emphasis was never supposed to be on real violence. Out of the ninety-four car crashes, only five resulted in fatalities (with six deaths), and all of those were caused by bad guys. The more frequent outcome by far (and universal when the good guys were doing the chasing) was survival with minimum cosmetic damage to the people involved, usually documented in a shot of the bad guys exiting their vehicle more-or-less under their own power, or the sidelined cops waving their buddies onward to continue the chase. In the words of Bob Del Valle, "You could have the most horrendous car wrecks, but the bad guys always stumbled out, brushed themselves off, and went to jail."

Beyond the general approach to the chase stunts, certain sequences stand out over the years and deserve special attention. Some were unusually complicated, some just looked that way.

In the first season episode "The Homecoming", a spectacular stunt involved crashing a police vehicle off a cliff into a reservoir. The sequence was critical to the plot of the two-part episode and was described in detail in the script. Gary Combs had the perfect location in mind, a cliff up at Indian Dunes that would more than adequately meet the script's requirements for a fifty-foot drop. Unfortunately, there was no reservoir, only a small creek below. This deficiency was overcome by the use of a temporary dam, which created enough surface of shallow standing water.

This was a stunt that would have called for the use of Rodney, except that in that sequence the purported passenger, Judge Hardcastle, is unconscious and not in sight. Either way, the car had to be released at the top of a slope and then roll off the cliff. It sounds simple, letting gravity do the work, but the point of departure was critical, since there were people down below waiting to film the crash and the path leading down to the cliff's edge was not smooth.

Del Valle tells the story: "We actually had to get a big tractor, and grade slope. There was a particular guy who was really good at doing this stuff, and the company used him for all of this. But you couldn't just take a tractor on that slope, because it was such a steep grade. You didn't want to let that tractor get away, and all of a sudden *it* goes over the cliff. So, he got a big huge honking tractor, and parked it at the top of that road. That didn't move. And to that he attached a smaller tractor, and with that he went up and down the road. He did that and the road was fine, all graded. The car was brought up and the special effects guys rigged it. The cameras were all down below. On action, they released the car. It had a motor, but it had been drained and the tank was out of it. They let it roll and of course it hit the water like it was concrete. Once the shot was over, we let the water drain out and the car was pulled out with a tractor. The car was just flattened. But it was really cool, really nifty." Mission accomplished.

In the second season episode, "D-Day", the bad guy makes a run for it in a stolen power boat. The sequence called for the escaping felon to be tackled and pulled into the water by McCormick, after which the runaway boat would crash explosively through a structure on a pier. The Long Beach Fire Department requested a report on what explosives would be used. Frazee and Combs obliged and got their approval after a demonstration of Frazee's "less is more" technique in a Long Beach parking lot.

The structure was built, along with an underwater device to help get the boat airborne. This would be the nautical version of a pipe ramp stunt. The result was spectacular enough to make it into the credits of later episodes.

Some stunts look like they ought to be more complicated than they actually are. In the episode "Did You See the One That Got Away?" the Coyote is menaced by several eighteen-wheel trucks. It appears to make a nail-bitingly tight diversion under one of the larger vehicles, pacing it for some distance before turning sharply left, leaving both the threat and the highway behind.

It's not easy, Combs says, but it's doable, with skilled drivers in both vehicles. In this case it was Gary Hymes in the car. Del Valle explains how they managed it: "You start doing things at quarter speed rehearsals, then half speed, and you just see how it goes. You might start with the truck going ten miles an hour, then slide the car in there. The car matches the speed of the truck—it's easier to do that. The guy driving the truck just has to be very careful to hold a steady speed. You gradually work your speed up, and then you play your cameras for the most dynamic shots. There are some secrets: if a chase is shot perpendicular to the vehicles, they appear to be moving up to twice as fast as they're actually going. It's all that background whizzing past."

Del Valle remarked on one of the other advantages of having a group of shows that were all stunt intensive. "The thing about Cannell Productions is that you had a core group of stunt guys—men and women who were really top drawer. They were the best around. Gil Combs and Gary Hymes—Gary McClarty was one of the best stunt truck drivers around. They knew what the heck they were doing, and they knew and trusted one another."

But mostly, Combs and Del Valle agreed, to do *that* particular stunt you need two things, "a very low car and a very high trailer."

The third season saw a marked drop-off in car stunts for what may have been a combination of reasons. Foremost is the idea that there are only so many ways to crash a car. Combs and his colleagues had explored the art form pretty thoroughly, and by season two had already branched out to include boats ("D-Day" and "Surprise on Seagull Beach").

Season three, which started off with the whitewater raft chases of "She Ain't Deep but She Sure Runs Fast" (further described in Chapter Nine), moved on to the quirky murder-mystery episode "Something's Going On On this Train", which involved an elaborate car/train chase sequence.

The studio rented a train and crew, and used a piece of track near Valencia. A sequence in which a stunt double portraying McCormick paralleled the train in a squad car was made more difficult by the poor condition of the road alongside the track. It was a case for "undercranking", in which the standard camera speed of twenty-four frames per second is slowed to twenty-two, allowing for an eventual ten percent increase in apparent speed when the film is projected back at normal speed.

Del Valle reports that working with trains has one advantage over boats: "At least outside a train you have something to stand on." But just as with the nautical chases, it takes a lot of time to back up for a second take.

The bottom line on *Hardcastle and McCormick* is that it was an action-oriented show in the pre-CGI era. With no computer generated effects to fall back on, without the use of miniatures, the second unit crew worked at breathtaking speed, with fixed resources, to produce what was needed. Combs and his crew came through, producing memorable stunts which have stood the test of time.

Chapter 8
Another Round of That Old Song
The music! The montages!

It started with a dispute over some sand. That's how Stephen Cannell and Mike Post both remember it. Cannell recollects that he was down in his family's house at Newport Beach. Post says his brother and he were staying in the lower rent district, a couple blocks inland, and had come out early that morning to stake a claim to a spot on the beach for a family get-together later that day. They messed with Steve's stuff.

The way Cannell tells it, he looked out his window and spotted them moving things around. An argument ensued. Post, not one to back down even when the other guy has five or six inches on him, was ready to fight. Common sense (or his even larger brother) prevailed. Later that day, when the testosterone had dissipated and both guys had their families out on the beach, introductions and apologies were made. Post discovered Cannell was a TV writer, and Cannell found out that Post was in the record-producing business and had just won a Grammy for his work on Mason William's hit single "Classical Gas".

Mike Post had been born and raised in California, spending his teen years in Burbank. He became a professional musician while still in high school, making fifteen dollars a night playing gigs at clubs like Mama's down on Pico Street. He toured with Frankie and the Jesters, and played back-up for recordings by Sonny and Cher. He recognized early on that he preferred the studio atmosphere to live performance and almost as soon as he'd gotten settled as a studio musician, he realized he wanted to be "the guy who said how it should be played." [1]

He segued into arranging, and from there into producing, in an effort to maintain some control over the final output. It's a path that sounds very reminiscent of Cannell's own.

But the two men might have remained just beach acquaintances. Post's career was gearing up. "Classical Gas" had led to a call from Andy Williams. Though he wasn't all that eager to immerse himself in the medium of televi-

sion—the speakers were too small and the sound was mono—he did two years as musical director for Williams' show and had the opportunity to work with guest performers like Ray Charles.

Meanwhile Cannell was starting to do his own producing over at Universal. His first show, *Toma*, was a gritty series about an urban cop. He needed that kind of music. He wanted Post.

More "itty-bitty speakers"—Mike almost demurred. Fortunately he didn't. He discovered he could compose soundtracks faster than he could write English. He'd met a guy named Pete Carpenter—a generation older and with a background as an arranger for television. Their exchange of ideas slid seamlessly into a partnership. Post estimates that together they scored over 1800 hours of programming.

Fans remember theme music—the harmonica riff that kicks in right after the famous opening telephone message of *The Rockford Files*, the piano chords, gently syncopated, that evoke an almost Pavlovian memory of *Hill Street Blues*—but Post calls that "the tip of the iceberg." It's scoring that is the real task—receiving a finished edit of an episode and creating the "art on art" that highlights the emotions and actions of the story. At the height of their partnership with Cannell's company, Post and Carpenter were scoring as many as ten shows a week, an astonishing pace.

He called the process "very efficient"—"Go to the studio, look at the film, go home, get the cue sheets from the editors." One man played and the other wrote, switching back and forth. "There was no time to go to meetings." In those days the scorer had to remember the images that went with the cues, recreating the mood of what he had seen at least a day or two earlier.

In addition to scoring, there were other duties that fell on the team's shoulders. Pete Carpenter, who was a jazz trombonist, taught Brian Keith the moves for that instrument for episodes featuring Hardcastle's Dixieland band. Moves were all Keith had to master; his trombone was muted.

And of course there was the theme music. Post had received his second Grammy for the opening theme from *The Rockford Files*. He had a number one hit with "Believe It or Not"—the theme from *The Greatest American Hero*. For that he'd teamed with lyricist Stephen Geyer, and together they'd produced a song that was a perfect metaphor for the show. For *The A-Team*, on the other hand, Post did a mock-stirring instrumental piece, with lots of brass to reflect the larger-than-life quality of its ex-military heroes and their over-the-top exploits.

For *Hardcastle and McCormick*, it was to be another song, but this time an edgy, up-tempo piece that perfectly suited the double meaning of its title, "Drive". Sung by David Morgan, Geyer's lyrics go for an extended metaphor: "push it to the floor", "a hard road", "keep it in gear", "the straight and narrow", and move from there, after a brief instrumental bridge, into a second

motif that puts two characters in counterpoint to each other. It's "slow motion man" vs. "high flying heart"—the whole concept of the series in forty bars. Under that is the sound of electric guitars, and over it a series of images—changing through the seasons as more material became available, but always heavy on the Coyote, being driven hard and fast, and ending on a freeze-frame and a reverberating electric guitar chord.

Post calls the whole process of theme writing the effort to make "a one-minute hit record." When you factor in the visuals of the opening credits, it really becomes a one-minute music video. The viewing audience imprints on it, and comes to expect it every week.

Most shows only get one good theme song. *Hardcastle and McCormick* had two. In the second season, with the show shifting gears and starting to emphasize the friendship of its two title characters, Post and Geyer provided a new opening theme. "Back to Back" premiered in the episode "Outlaw Champion". Gone were the darker, slightly threatening elements of "Drive". In their place were more relaxed lyrics set to an upbeat tune and accompanied by more humorous visuals. While "Back to Back" still talked about "two strangers in dangerous times", it immediately acknowledged that they were doing their shooting "straight from the heart". No more stern cautions about hard roads and nobody caring. These protagonists might be "over their heads" but they were always "in it together".

There were, in fact, two versions of "Back to Back". Version one was used eight times. Sung by Joey Scarbury, with backup vocals entering on the chorus, it was upbeat and brassy. Version two (occasionally referred to by some fans as "extra twangy") was heard four times, beginning with the episode "Ties My Father Sold Me", followed by "D-Day" and "Never My Love". It then was shelved until "Pennies from a Dead Man's Eyes", perhaps a coincidence, or maybe an intentional paring with an episode that had a country music theme. This version did have more of a country feel to it. The back-up singers were gone and the energy level was lower.

Neither version survived much past midseason. With the thirteenth episode of season two, there was a permanent shift back to the original theme music. With it came a refresher course in the show's premise in the form of the courthouse steps scene and voiceover introduction, again at the top of the opening credits for all but one of the last ten season two episodes ("The Birthday Present" was the exception).

Fans still debate the relative merits of the two themes, with a significant minority believing that the lyrics and tone of "Back to Back" fit the evolving series well. But mostly everyone agrees that "Drive" captured the essence of the premise and many were glad to see it return.

Along with its extensive original scoring, the series used a number of popular songs either occurring incidentally in scenes, or as part of montages. Season one had a Joey Scarbury cover of Paul Simon's "The Boxer" in the episode of the same name. This song, with its references to the seamier side of pugilism, was the perfect counterpoint to Kid Calico's first, untroubled, training scene. Eleven more episodes passed before "The Homecoming" used "On the Sunny Side of the Street", a depression-era song that set the tone for the Clarence of Hardcastle's childhood, a town that no longer really existed.

In "Really Neat Cars and Guys with a Sense of Humor" Neil Diamond's "I Am I Said" is heard as the triumphant anthem of guys who overcome the Studebaker Effect and somehow (against all odds) end up with the girl.

Season two's second episode, "Ties My Father Sold Me", introduced the viewers to Mark's father, lounge singer Sonny Daye. Steve Lawrence's performance of "Strangers in the Night" conveyed the perfect sense of world-weary sadness that we'd expect from a down-on-his-luck guy who'd walked out on his family and never formed any lasting commitments.

In "Never My Love", an episode that has unrequited love as its subplot, we hear the title song played in a flashback scene. It's a song with a special meaning for Mark and Cyndy (or at least for Mark). It's used as part of the plot—the means by which he is able to verify that the mystery caller is really her—and it crops up again in the epilogue.

The seventh episode of season two works in the then *au courant* Bangles' single "The Hero Takes a Fall". The hero has also apparently taken to MTV, which had premiered only three years earlier, in late summer of 1981. The episode also used the Silhouettes' 1957 R&B hit, "Get a Job", to highlight Mark's dogged determination to do just that. Sometimes a montage is just what's needed to show a rapid decline in expectations.

One episode later, Mark's looking for love rather than work, and the task is almost as daunting. "To All the Girls I've Loved Before" plays in the opening, as the camera pans wistfully over a collection of photographs—all beauties, and apparently all strikeouts.

With "It Could Have Been Worse, She Could Have Been a Welder", we're hit with a record three musical interludes, all contemporary rock hits with a backbeat you can't lose and no other apparent significance for the plot.

Two episodes later, another professional singer crossed over to guest on the show. Larry Gatlin brought his own material with him. In a clever bit of retrofitting, one of Gatlin's own hits, the 1976 Grammy Award winning "Broken Lady", is woven into the story, with its lyrics attributed to McCormick. In a charming subplot, Hardcastle discovers the lyrics, pokes a little fun at them, then eventually, and unbeknownst to Mark, hands them over to country singer "Jesse Wingo" (played by Gatlin) to be set to music.

Six episodes after that, it's gospel favorite "I'll Fly Away" that sets the mood for "You Don't Hear the One That Gets You", along with Juice Newton's title song. The final four shows of the season each have songs used as part of their incidental music. In "Surprise on Seagull Beach", it's the all-purpose "Miles from Nowhere", which returns in season three as well. In "Undercover McCormick", it's the edgy "Burning Down the House" that provides the background music for the equally edgy cop party scene. "The Game You Learn From Your Father" has John Fogerty's "Centerfield". "Angie's Choice", following the now-established pattern, uses Judy Collins' "Born to the Breed."

Season three continued the trend, with eleven of the episodes featuring songs. The season opener, "She Ain't Deep but She Sure Runs Fast", included a recap of "Miles from Nowhere"—remarkably suited to this episode's storyline—and uses Creedence Clearwater Revival's eminently appropriate "Run Through the Jungle" to underline the nature of the ba1ckwoods chase. In "Faster Heart", the drag racing environment was well-served by the pop hit "The Heat is On", heard several times during the show.

The season's third episode, "The Yankee Clipper", again featured a montage—the delivery and burial of the title character's "body" accompanied by the all-too-appropriate "You're Still the Same". In "The Career Breaker", Mark's preparations to break the judge out of jail were done to the tune of "Lean on Me", another evocative choice.

Using "The Sloop John B." as the two men set off on what was supposed to be Hardcastle's last fling, in "Do Not Go Gentle", was a more whimsical choice, but it helped achieve a light tone that showed, without words, that the judge had come to grips with his supposed terminal diagnosis. "Hardcastle for Mayor" had a true montage, combining scenes from earlier episodes along with historic footage of political campaigns, all in black and white newsreel style set to a depression-era rendition of "Happy Days are Here Again".

"You're Sixteen, You're Beautiful, and You're His" had two musical interludes. One used the mood-setting "Will the Wolf Survive" to encapsulate the sense of desperation among illegal immigrants, but it was the completely unexpected "I Think It's Gonna Rain Today" (sung with heart-breaking purity by one of the contestants in the otherwise nearly talentless beauty contest) that was a poignant overlay on what might otherwise have been just a necessary bit of plot furtherance.

Three episodes in season three used pop songs to accompany characters driving somewhere. "Mirage a Trois" blasted a bouncy, bubbly pop tune over the car radio to escort a dyed-in-the-wool Valley Girl to her appointment with destiny (and Mark). In "Duet for Two Wind Instruments", Mark drives off in a huff (and the Coyote) after a major disagreement with Hardcastle. The breezy and utterly contrary "You've Got to Have Friends" reassures the audience that the break-up will be both amusing and temporary. By contrast, in "McCormick's Bar and Grill", Sonny Daye's drive from Las Vegas to Los Angeles is accompanied by Cat Stevens' pensive ballad "Father and Son", pointing through the dark night toward a potentially rocky reunion between him and Mark.

The penultimate episode of the series was set in the music industry—this time rock and roll, payola, and murder. "I Heard It Through the Grapevine" is played as Mark tries to triangulate the source of his flash from the past, and that quintessential song about American rock and roll, "American Pie", provides additional atmosphere during the show.

But throughout all three seasons, it was Post's and Carpenter's distinctive original score material that provided the backbone of the music for this series. Les Sheldon called Post "a true storyteller and an absolute genius. He and Carpenter were a very important part of that show."

There is no clearer example than the episode "Undercover McCormick". Sheldon, seeking a *film noir* atmosphere, got decidedly atmospheric music even for the scenes shot in broad daylight. In the opening sequence, a jarring, reverberating chord is the harbinger of a character's death during what looks like a routine police stop. The same music returns, threatening peril for Hardcastle a few scenes later, when he, too, is flagged over by a cop.

Augmenting this minute attention to mood, an astonishing variety was another hallmark of Post's and Carpenter's work for this series. This was just as true for the original score as it was for the musical borrowings listed above. "Pennies From a Dead Man's Eyes" contrasted country with Hardcastle's beloved Dixieland. "Too Rich and Too Thin" had a crisp classical string quartet in counterpoint to murder. "The Long Ago Girl" used big band to evoke a sense of nostalgia for a thirty-years-past love affair.

Original scores weren't limited to instrumental pieces, either. In addition to the two themes, there were original songs like "Wings of My Heart" ("The Homecoming"), "Two Bad Seeds" ("You Don't Hear the One That Gets You"), "The Game Goes On" (originally written for an episode of *The Greatest American Hero* and reprised in "The Game You Learn From Your Father"), and "Somebody Stole My Dream" ("Do Not Go Gentle") that were every bit as memorable as the hit tunes that studded the series.

It was the merest chance encounter that brought Stephen Cannell and Mike Post together and led Post into the business of scoring television programs, but it's abundantly evident that television in general, and *Hardcastle and*

McCormick in particular, benefited immensely from the teamwork of Post and Carpenter, and from the talented musicians and singers that Cannell assembled for his projects. It's a pleasant surprise that the soundtracks, despite being packed with hits whose rights are still in the possession of a multitude of artists, were preserved intact in the current Canadian release of the series on DVD.

1.   Most of the stories and quotes in this chapter are taken from an interview done by Stephen J. Abramson for the Archive of American Television in 2005.

Chapter 9
"Seven Acres of Topiary Trees and Grecian Fountains"
On Set and On Location

In the revision of the pilot script dated February 28, 1983, in scene ninety-seven, our intrepid heroes arrive at Hardcastle's home. The creators of the series described it thus: "EXT. HUGE PASEDENA (sic) ESTATE—NIGHT. It sits on a knoll, surrounded by grass and bordered by a huge brick wall and wrought iron gates. This is a seven acre spread. On the gate is a gold plaque lettered in black which says, GULL'S WAY."

Though the decision to use the real Gull's Way property, located in Malibu, was apparently made months before shooting started, there remains evidence of an earlier incarnation of Hardcastle's home base. In scene ninety-nine, an error was preserved. Mark says, "Here you are, living at Knoll House, seven acres of topiary trees and Grecian Fountains, yet you run around dressed like a referee at a girls' hockey match." The line was eventually updated in the filming.

The real life Gull's Way, which was used extensively for exteriors, was ideally suited for the show's concept. In the context of the back story, it became part of Hardcastle's deceased wife's inheritance. Its oceanfront location allowed for great visuals, including a particularly stunning vista out over the pool and across the ocean toward Santa Monica. The two separate structures allowed for flexibility in the staging, and the grounds were both attractive, and the scene of frequent mayhem.

Gull's Way had been one of Malibu's most utilized TV and movie locations. In addition to *Hardcastle and McCormick* it can also be spotted in the series *Perry Mason, Dark Shadows*, and *Murder She Wrote*. It's been estimated that over one hundred movies, TV series, and commercials have used it as a backdrop.

The name of the estate came from a poem titled "Sea Fever" by Great Britain's former Poet Laureate, John Masefield. The first couplet of the third verse reads, "I must go down to the seas again, to the vagrant gypsy life, To the gull's way and the whale's way where the wind's like a whetted knife." (Fans of

417

Star Trek will recognize another line from the same poem, "And all I ask is a tall ship and a star to steer her by," quoted on several occasions by Captain Kirk.)

With all of its cinematic history, and the timeless quality of the main house and grounds, the estate gives an impression of considerable age. In fact, the property was undeveloped before it was purchased from the Marblehead Land Company in 1943 by Erving and Louella "Billie" Ulrich. The original parcel consisted of six acres and sold for $10,000 (about $126,000 in 2008 dollars).

At that time there was no Pacific Coast Highway. Route 1, the Roosevelt Highway, ran along the base of the bluff. There were no utilities at the property on Latigo Point, and virtually no neighbors. The vegetation was brown turf and weeds. Erving, known to his friends as "Rick", was an inveterate builder. He and his wife initially had a trailer on the site, and stayed in it for weekend visits.

When the Ulrichs first moved to Malibu, the threat of war hung over the coast. The U.S. Army conducted patrols in the area immediately after the bombing of Pearl Harbor, and by 1942, the U.S. Coast Guard had established eight stations along the Malibu shoreline. For the next two years, there were coast watchers on duty, alert for the anticipated enemy invasion.

During this same period, civilian building was at a low ebb, with many materials diverted into the war effort. It wasn't until after the war's end that the Ulrichs were able to construct the first permanent dwelling on their property. That house was finished in 1947 and became their primary residence at Gull's Way for the next twenty-four years. About 1800 square feet of living space designed in the Norman style, it would eventually become the guesthouse (known as the gatehouse to fans of the series). The Ulrichs were especially pleased that the structure boasted two bathrooms.

The "'47 House" was at first the Ulrichs' retreat from their home in Santa Monica, where they owned and managed a trailer park. They were soon living in Malibu full time. Mrs. Ulrich was an enthusiastic gardener and this devotion, paired with her husband's passion for building, created extensive landscaping, a greenhouse, and a pool, as well as the often-filmed Freedom Fountain. The original trailer eventually evolved into a cottage with the addition of a shingled roof and siding.

In 1971 they completed the main house, which was patterned after a postcard picture of the House of the Seven Gables. This 6,000 square foot, three-story home used recycled materials for some of its structural elements, including trusses that were salvaged from the demise of the Pacific Ocean Park in Santa Monica, and rocks washed up on their Malibu beach after storms. Uniquely, despite its size, it only had one bedroom.

The wrought iron gate was designed by Mr. Ulrich and created by the Culver Iron Works. A second wooden gate, formerly located on the grounds, was constructed for the Jerry Lewis movie It's Only Money, which was filmed at Gull's Way in 1961.

The gate at Gull's Way Estate as seen in the 1980s. Photo courtesy Heidi Jaeger.

The exteriors of the estate figured prominently in many episodes of *Hardcastle and McCormick*, beginning with Mark's astonishment at the palatial nature of his new digs in "Rolling Thunder". The security was spotty at the Hardcastle version of Gull's Way. Despite the early appearance of an electronic alarm system ("The Crystal Duck"), bad guys made frequent appearances, with intentions ranging from kidnapping ("Rolling Thunder", "Black Widow", "Prince of Fat City", "Seagull Beach", "Angie's Choice") and attempted murder ("Goin' Nowhere Fast", "Really Neat Cars", "D-Day", "The Birthday Present", "Mirage a Trois", "Poker Night") to general mayhem ("When I Look Back" and "In the Eye of the Beholder"). The estate was the target of burglars three times ("The Crystal Duck", "You Would Cry, Too", and "There Goes the Neighborhood") and a horse-napping once ("Whistler's Pride").

The Gull's Way interior scenes were all shot on a sound stage. The discrepancies between the layout of the main house and the constructed sets can be best noted in the episode "D-Day" when Hardcastle is seen looking out through the front window of the house from what ought to be his den, but which appears to be a formal living room, complete with chandelier.

Also, since the interior and the exterior shots were filmed many miles— and often several days—apart, special attention had to be paid to ensure continuity. Sometimes, though, things still slipped through, such as one of the early scenes of "The Birthday Present". When Sandy Knight pulls up in the drive of

The real interior of the main house. Photo courtesy Heidi Jaeger.

Gull's Way, he's carrying a gold-topped bottle of champagne. But when he presents the bottle to Hardcastle in the den, it's become a bottle of red wine. Of course, usually, the transition between the real outside property and the inside stage was seamless, and the illusion was preserved.

In the real Gull's Way main house, the area to the right of the front door was a parlor, with a large, natural rock fireplace in the outer wall and a grand piano. Portraits of Mr. and Mrs. Ulrich hung alongside the hearth. The estate was the scene of numerous social and charitable events during the Ulrichs' time there. The Fourth of July, Billie Ulrich's birthday, was celebrated with fireworks.

The set which was used to portray the interior of the "'47 House" is also a very loose interpretation of the original. The main room of the guest house does have a cathedral ceiling, a stone fireplace, and a stairway which makes a ninety-degree turn to follow the wall up to a second floor sleeping area. But the actual room is far smaller than the set, and is located to the right of the front door. At the top of the stairs there is a doorway, leading to a bedroom. Back on the first floor, to the left of the entryway, the area of the house that abuts onto the basketball backboard was formerly a garage, and is now another bedroom.

The strongest impression one gets from the estate is of its quirky charm as a world apart from the bustle outside. A window placed in a sheltering wall permits a view of the ocean beyond. The glass is a former automobile windshield. A mural made from Malibu tiles has one tile placed intentionally wrong,

The real interior of the "gate" house, looking from the balcony.

in the Italian tradition. One spot, known as "The Point", with its three-sided overlook of the ocean, was Mrs. Ulrich's favorite retreat—a combination of astonishing view and intimate reading spot. Heidi Jaeger, the current manager of the property, said the setting "encourages contemplative thought."

As Daniel Hugh Kelly put it, "Hey, I'm from Jersey—out in Los Angeles, driving through Malibu Canyon to the set, and I'd think, my God, this is incredibly beautiful. I can't imagine, going to work here; it's like a dream. And when you arrived at Gull's Way itself—it was simply extraordinarily beautiful."

The Ulrichs' longstanding relationship with the TV and film industry, and the income they obtained from it, allowed them to enlarge the estate to its current eleven and a half acres. Mrs. Ulrich said she didn't watch much TV or go to the movies very often, but she got along very well with her guests. Kelly called her "a sweet, classy lady—on Friday nights, I would stay, if we had finished early, and sit and have a glass of champagne with her. She loved company as much as the champagne.

As far back as 1972, the Ulrichs, who had no children, made efforts to conserve the property. After the death of her husband in 1988, Billie arranged for Pepperdine to manage the estate as a "life trust", allowing her to continue to live there until her death in 1997 at the age of 96. The intention was for the University to eventually convert the facility into a conference center.

Mr. and Mrs. Ulrich, circa 1970s, on the steps of the main house.
Photo courtesy Heidi Jaeger.

Those plans foundered on the zoning concerns of the City of Malibu. Pepperdine was compelled to place the estate on the market in 2002 with an asking price of fifteen million dollars. The furnishings alone garnered $40,000 for scholarship funds. The money generated by the estate's eventual return to private ownership was used to create a conference center elsewhere on Pepperdine's campus.

Although the property remains readily recognizable to fans of *Hardcastle and McCormick*, there have been some necessary alterations in recent years. The pool was thought to be contributing to land shift below the estate. It was removed, and a retaining wall was created, in a thus-far successful attempt to stabilize the bluff. The original arched entryway was also removed, and is in the process of being replaced. Fine white stone has been substituted for the former red-paved driveways.

In the center of the main drive, the Freedom Fountain, originally built and dedicated by the Ulrichs in 1953, was recently refurbished. It still bears its plaque of dedication to WWII veteran, Richard Swanson. Throughout the grounds, white roses flourish, while to the east of the main house, a more densely planted area of multicolored roses and lavender evoke a sense of a formal garden in the remaking. The current owners continue the efforts of renewal and preservation and the estate shows every sign of becoming a lasting part of Malibu history.

The Freedom Fountain, now fully restored and operational.

While the Gull's Way estate stood in for the exteriors of its namesake on the series, the interiors were constructed on a soundstage in Culver City. *Hardcastle and McCormick* sets occupied stage D at 8660 Hayden Place, which had been converted from a former warehouse. Within this structure were the regular sets— the familiar "interiors" of the main house and gatehouse. A separate swing stage, at the same location, allowed for the construction of larger temporary sets.

Cynthia Shannon, editor of a *Hardcastle and McCormick* letter 'zine, re- members taking a tour of stage D back in March of 1986. "The Day the Music Died" was being filmed and a small casino set was being used for a scene in which Mark makes a brief phone call back to the estate from Las Vegas. It might seem expensive to construct something for such a short scene, but the realities of location shooting dictated sets whenever possible.

Some specialized settings were easier handled as location shoots. In the episode "Do Not Go Gentle", an entire day's shooting took place at Central Receiving Hospital, located at 1401 Sixth Street. L.A.'s receiving hospital sys- tem began in the early 1900s and, along with the fire department ambulance service, provided a way of caring for trauma patients, especially injured police and firemen. Robert Kennedy was taken to that facility after being shot at the Ambassador Hotel in 1968, but by 1985 the hospital was closed, superseded by Good Samaritan Hospital, which was across the street. It was then a perfect setting for both exterior establishing shots, and the hallways, offices, and patient

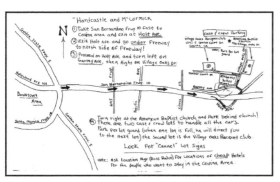

Hand drawn map which was included with the location
shooting schedule for "Conventional Warfare".

rooms of a medical facility.
Following a full day of
shooting at that location,
the first unit decamped to
Marina Del Rey for two
additional days of mixed interiors and exteriors, with
that location standing in for
both itself, the Newport
bank, and the Newport
water shots used in the final part of the episode.

For "You're Sixteen, You're Beautiful, and You're His", the crew headed
north, to Agoura and its high school, which stood in for the border town. For
"Conventional Warfare", the town of Covina (about thirty miles east of Culver
City) along with a liberal sprinkling of establishing shots of stock footage, substituted for the more distant Palm Springs. Interestingly, though the filming was
taking place at an Embassy Suites, the shooting schedule directs crew members
to inquire with the location manager for the availability of "cheap hotels".

More distant locations were relatively rare. Palm trees are visible in both
the "Atlantic City" and "Washington, D.C." exterior sequences, and Indian Dunes
substituted for rural Arkansas.

One thing that could not be duplicated close at hand was the white water river
needed for "She Ain't Deep but She Sure Runs Fast". The first unit was sent to the
American River, near Sacramento, while second unit director, Gary Combs, and his
assistant director, Bob Del Valle, headed up to the Klamath River, near the Oregon-
California border. Using a special crew of whitewater specialists, they filmed the
action shots of a chase sequence involving two river rafts. The stretch of the Klamath
below the J.C. Boyle Dam has several sections of grade IV rapids, as well as spectacular scenery, but it's subject to the vagaries of the water flow through the dam's
spillways. Del Valle recollects that they could only film in the morning, when the
spillways were open, allowing enough volume downstream to produce rapids. Of
course it was necessary to haul the rafts back up to the starting point for each take. As
he ruefully put it, "It's not like backing up a car." As a consequence, the shoot took
two to three times as long as an ordinary episode's second unit work.

Race tracks were another specialty location used frequently in the series. The
pilot episode had locations shots set at Saugus Speedway. This one-third-mile oval
track was originally built in the 1920s as a rodeo venue. Hoot Gibson purchased it in
1930 and it was soon being featured in motion pictures.

After a brief use for open wheel racing prior to the Second World War, it
hosted midget cars, stock cars, and truck racing from the 1950s to 1995. Both
NASCAR and USAC events were held there in the 1980s. The distinctive red and

white boards that form the perimeter of the track can be seen
in Mark's practice sequence in
"Rolling Thunder" and in the
track scene in "Killer B's". It was
also used for the after-hours
match between McCormick and
E.J. Corlette in "Outlaw Champion". Since its closure to racing
in 1995, Saugus has become a spe-

cialty event facility, with twice weekly swap-meets and frequent car shows. It is still
available as a rental facility for movie and TV productions.

For the episode "Hot Shoes", a longer track was needed. Riverside International Speedway, in Riverside, California, had been designed as a multiple length
track with a 2.62 mile NASCAR configuration that featured nine turns. It acquired a reputation as a dangerous course when its first fatality occurred on the
opening weekend of racing in September of 1957. Its 180-degree Turn 9 was lethal
to brakes and eventually revised. The lap record for that course was 118.484 miles
per hour, set in 1988 by Ricky Rudd. The track was a favorite with TV and movie
producers, and had been used in episodes of *The Rockford Files*, *Simon and Simon*,
and *Knight Rider*. It closed in 1989 to make way for a shopping mall.

Waterfront scenes featured prominently in several episodes. In addition to
Marina Del Rey, which was used in "Do Not Go Gentle", Long Beach was the
backdrop for several episodes ("D-Day" and "The Day the Music Died").

Seagull Beach (the supposed stretch of coast directly below the estate and the
site where Hardcastle had originally proposed to his wife) was seen in several episodes
and featured prominently in one. While the Gull's Way estate currently has access to
the beach at the foot of one section of its rocky bluff, it also sits above a row of newer
houses, built directly on the shoreline. When a walk on the beach or some surfing
action were integral to the plot ("Do Not Go Gentle", "Surprise on Seagull Beach"
"Strangle Hold", and "There Goes the Neighborhood") the open vistas and rocky

backdrop of Point Dume were
used instead.

Just down the coast
from Point Dume is a well-
known private beach, Paradise Cove. Used for many
years as the location where
Jim Rockford's trailer was
parked in *The Rockford Files*,
as well as for dozens of other
movies and TV productions,

this beach cove was seen in several episodes of *Hardcastle and McCormick*. It was the backdrop for the final game of "chicken" in "Goin' Nowhere Fast" and its pier was used in "The Long Ago Girl".

Cemeteries were seen in six episodes of the series ("Rolling Thunder", "School for Scandal", "Never My Love", "Too Rich and Too Thin", "The Yankee Clipper", and "If You Could See What I See"). Of these, the most recognizable are the mausoleum shots, which were done at what was then Hollywood Memorial Park, conveniently located adjacent to Paramount Studios. Under new management since 1998, the renamed "Hollywood Forever Cemetery" emphasizes its cinematic connections—after all, it is the last resting place of Cecil B. DeMille and many other movie luminaries. The management offers guided tours and it is the home to a series of outdoor film screenings twice a month, hosted by the Cinespia, a non-profit film society.

In addition to these locations there were dozens of others, usually taking up several days of each episode's filming, and presenting a never-ending logistical challenge to the crew. It was a challenge for Daniel Hugh Kelly as well. He recollects that, despite those detailed daily shooting notes, "I didn't know L.A., especially how big the county was. I would look at maps and how to get to locations, and invariably would underestimate the time required to get to the location, so I was late a lot. Very unprofessional. And Brian, may he rest in peace, God bless him, he never once complained about it to me. He never said anything; he never displayed an attitude about it. And since then, since *Hardcastle*, I've became very aware about being prompt on the set, following his example."

Gull's Way, 2008.

Chapter 10
May 5, 1986
How it ended, and life after cancellation

In its third and final season, *Hardcastle and McCormick* was paired with *Monday Night Football* on the ABC schedule. Following a summer of preemptions by *Monday Night Baseball* and preseason football games, and the irregular ending times of the games, the series was hard to find. Its ratings suffered accordingly (see Appendix A).

By midseason the feeling of cancellation was in the air. Though it was by no means official, everyone on the set was aware that the series was on the bubble. In an act of unwarranted optimism, Daniel Hugh Kelly had invested in a trailer, to make the long hours spent on location easier.

"I bought a trailer and rented it back to the company and—as usual with my business acumen—it was bad timing, because by the time they built this and delivered it from Indiana, it was apparent to all of us that it was extremely unlikely that the show was going to be renewed for the fourth year. So, the day that they delivered it to the set, this huge trailer, everybody knew the show was going down, and the entire crew broke out singing 'Trailers for sale or rent'. I was laughing my butt off at that. We had a great crew."

The final six episodes show a departure from the series trademark car chases and stunts. The last car crash came in "Brother, Can You Spare a Crime", which broadcast on February 10, 1986.

Second unit assistant director Bob Del Valle remembers one reason for the shift. "The last part of the third season, Hap Weyman, our beloved production manager for the series, passed away. He was the sweetest man in the world. I don't think the company wanted to bring someone new in at that point." But in addition to that loss, he spoke of other reasons for the decreasing reliance on action sequences.

"If they knew that was the end after that season, then between the network and the studio they would probably have made a concerted decision, 'This is it, six or seven more episodes to go, we're going to try and scale some of our costs down.' And sometimes they'll look at the season as a whole 'Are we over budget so far?' Coming to the end, there might have been a decision to control the costs, maybe to make up for the big bus chase ["Duet for Two Wind Instruments", which had broadcast in December of 1985]. Sometimes what you'll do is say, 'Okay, we're going to blow a lot of money on a few big chases, but we know that by the end of the season we'll need to come in on our overall budget. You may blow your budget on episodes that air at certain times of the year. Shows that aired in November and February, the sweeps periods, those would be a little more jam-packed with action."

Of course by May, 1986, the final sweeps month of the season, the series was down to its last episode, "Chip Off the Ol' Milt". Written by Carol Mendelsohn and Marianne Clarkson, it was an exceptionally graceful coda. Fans generally agree that if the show had to end, it was nice to have it go out on a high note, and with style. In Mendelsohn's words, "We wanted to give the audience closure."

Carol Mendelsohn, who was also story editor during that period, described the waning days of the series. "During the later half of season three, Larry Hertzog was writing and producing *Stingray*. Patrick Hasburgh was also doing a pilot. Which left Marianne, myself, and Stephen Katz on staff, and of course Les Sheldon who was running the show. There were several unproduced scripts that had been bought from non-staff writers over the life of the series. We were instructed to rewrite them, and turn them into a fitting end to the series. The finale was totally original and nurtured the whole way by Les Sheldon, who also directed it."

Sheldon remembers it distinctly, even twenty-two years later. "The whole episode was memorable. The scene at the beginning, where Danny's studying to be a lawyer. He and I had discussed it quite a bit, how much histrionics to use.

Director Les Sheldon, Daniel Hugh Kelly, and Assistant Director J.J. Candrella, on the set of "Chip Off the Ol' Milt". Photo courtesy Les Sheldon.

Les Sheldon, Brian Keith, and Billie Bird on location at the Motion Picture Home for the filming of "Chip Off the Ol' Milt." Courtesy Les Sheldon.

We worked it out. And now it was a question of staging it right, so I could capture it all. I used a moving camera with the cameraman being pulled in a wheelchair, because I didn't want to do it in cuts. We were in a real office building, about eight stories up with windows everywhere. I'd made the decision, 'We're going to do this in one, and here's how I'd like to play it.' Instead of standing there and giving that speech, I had him walk around the entire classroom. He was on camera the entire time. You see the reflections of everyone else. I did it to put the focus on performance. Danny was just brilliant. Normally when you make a decision like that, you're taking a chance, because the performance might not hold up. You might be doing something interesting with the camera but the performance doesn't work. But Danny was so riveting; you didn't even know the camera was there. It couldn't have worked better."

Much of the location shooting for that episode was done at the Motion Picture Home in Woodland Hills. William Campbell, the then-director of the facility, gave the series crew full access. In the script, the retirement home is called Sunset Acres and after its scurrilous manager is arrested, the heroine, Mimi LeGrande, happily moves to the Motion Picture Home, to safely enjoy her golden years.

For Sheldon, that location shoot was especially memorable. "My father, who's since passed away, was one of the founding members of the Directors Guild. He had friends at the home, and used to visit them frequently. He came to visit me there while we were shooting. That was the only time he ever saw me direct. I'll always be grateful that we were able to share that day together."

Billie Bird, who played the aging but feisty Mimi, had the history to back up her performance. Her acting career had begun in 1916, at the age of eight, when she was discovered in an orphanage by a group of traveling performers. Just as "Mimi" gently eulogized her friend and former stage partner in the episode,

Billie had teamed with another young actress to become "The King Sisters". They toured successfully on the King-Orpheum circuit for years. Billie advanced from there to light opera. But no aspect of the performing arts was left unexplored on her journey to seasoned character roles. She even spent a period in burlesque, in the late 1940's, and had perfected her striptease skills.

In 1986, at the age of 78, she danced a memorable soft shoe, to the tune of "Tea for Two". Out on the landscaped grounds of the retirement home, Sheldon placed the camera at a distance, with foreground objects. "It was a complex shot. Steve Bridge was the camera operator. He got it in one."

To set the mood, for that scene and the others set in the retirement community, Sheldon was looking for music with a historic feel. "I knew I wanted 'forties'. I went to Mike Post, whose musical genius is unsurpassed. Mike said 'Go talk to Pete, that's where he's from'. I talked to him at night while we were shooting, told him what I wanted. Pete Carpenter, who was Mike Post's partner, wrote all the original period music in the score."

This episode is one of only two in the series to use music other than the theme for the closing credits. "Tea for Two" makes a return there—a hint of heartfelt nostalgia for the passing of a series, but also the perfect humorous touch.

As the shooting came to a close, the critical scenes between the two leads were being filmed. The relationship between the two characters, perpetually left undiscussed except under duress, was finally being brought into high relief. One particular scene, set in the living room of Lieutenant Harper's house, begins with a compliment, and nearly ends in an argument. Sheldon said, "I wanted to play it simply. I didn't want the staging to interfere. I put the camera on these two wonderful artists and let the audience watch them reflect the magic of the relationship they had created. When they were satisfied that it had been captured we walked away."

But everything must come to an end. In the shooting sequence, the last scene filmed was, coincidentally, one of the most pivotal. Set in a holding cell, Mark and Milt finally have a discussion about friendship. For Sheldon, coming at the end of three years of commitment to the series, and culminating in the fourteen days it takes to prep and film an episode, the final "cut" was a catharsis.

"It was really hard, from my heart … the jail cell scene, the last one shot, it hit me very hard. At the end of a shoot, particularly—you're exhausted. The scene was over, everyone had left. I went in and sat down in the cell. I cried. The family that had given me so much joy and support, and countless opportunities, was moving on to share their gifts with other shows. That's how it was for me."

For fans, the word came later. Liz Tucker caught a note in an Atlanta newspaper column, in which a TV reporter complained that lesser shows had been spared while this one had gotten the ax. Others remember watching *Entertainment Tonight* on Monday, May 12, a week after "Chip Off the Ol' Milt" was broadcast. The list of ABC programs returning that fall was announced. *Hardcastle and McCormick* wasn't on it.

Cynthia Shannon was a California fan who had started a letter 'zine called *Now Yer Cookin'* in the second season. Her attempts to unite fans by collecting their letters about the episodes and characters, and getting this feedback to the show's staff, had given her contacts in the Cannell organization. She had been aware for a while that the show was perched precariously in the ratings, but in those days—when putting out the word meant nothing more high-tech than a typewriter, a paste-up job, an industrial copy machine, and the U.S. Postal Service—getting support organized was hard work. She'd placed an ad in *USA Today* and had spoken a few times with Charlotte Clay, then in charge of public relations for Cannell Productions.

As a result of this, when Brian Keith had made an appearance that spring on the San Francisco TV talk show, *People Are Talking*, to promote the renewal of the show, Cynthia and another fan were invited to attend. They'd sat front and center in the audience, and then had a moment on camera to pitch the renewal campaign.

But the numbers were in and the bubble hadn't held. By the time the fifth issue of *Now Yer Cookin'* was sent out (in early summer), though the campaign to get a change of heart from the network was still underway, the devoted fans were in deep mourning. In that issue, Shannon talked about the final episode in a way that evokes the director's own feelings: "What made me sad watching "Chip" besides it being the last show? The atmosphere…reminded me of a graduation. One part of your life is over and another one starting and, oh, isn't it hard to let go even though you know it is inevitable and probably for the best? … The feeling of finality was so intense; I could have sworn I heard a door slam somewhere."

For others, the final impact came later. Daniel Hugh Kelly said, "You get so involved in doing a scene properly that you forget that, yes, this is the last time I'll be working on this. And then, this is very strange, four or five years ago I was asked to guest star on *Las Vegas*. I flew out from New York. They gave me the address for the location where they shoot in Culver City, and I drove over. I was following the route they had given me on the call sheet and I kept thinking, 'This is weird. Where the hell is this place?' And finally I'm looking down the street and I think—oh my God, they're shooting it where we used to shoot *Hardcastle*.

"It was formerly a big clothing warehouse, and Stephen Cannell had converted it to a studio—it had terrible acoustics with a metal roof—and that's where we shot most of our interiors. Now, *Las Vegas* had built the whole casino set. I walked in, not having been there in twenty years or so, and *that's* when it got emotional. I walked over to the exact spot where I knew Brian's desk had been, in his 'study'. It was pretty hard. Weird, you know—over there was where McCormick's guesthouse was, over there was where Brian would sit and tell stories. But now the crew was entirely different, the actors, everything. That's where we shot that last scene, the 'jail' in the studio there, in Culver City."

Television can be a very ephemeral art form. Even as the show was being cancelled, its cast and crew were already moving on to new projects. For Brian Keith it was two made-for-TV movies, *The B.R.A.T. Patrol*, (in which he costarred with Tim Thomerson, who played Duke McQuire in the episode "The Game You Learn from Your Father") and *The Alamo: Thirteen Days to Glory* in which he portrayed Colonel Davy Crockett. This was followed by a role in the feature film, *Death Before Dishonor*. The following year he settled into another TV series, *The Pursuit of Happiness*.

Daniel Hugh Kelly had a role in the Emmy award nominated miniseries, *Nutcracker: Money, Madness and Murder*, as well as the feature film, *Nowhere to Hide*, and the made-for-TV movie, *Night of Courage*. He, too, had a new series the following year, the light-hearted family comedy *I Married Dora*.

Stephen J. Cannell, his flock of talented writers and producers, and his nonpareil technical crew, were in full creative bloom in the mid to late eighties. Cannell created the edgy series *Stingray* which premiered that spring, after a made-for-TV movie the previous year. Richard Colla (of "The Long Ago Girl") directed the pilot, Alan Cassidy was associate producer, and Gary Hymes moved into second unit directorship. Larry Hertzog transferred over later as executive producer, and Tom Blomquist as producer.

The following year Cannell and Hasburgh created *21 Jumpstreet* as a flag-ship series for the new Fox Network, while *Wiseguy* (costarring Jonathan Banks, and with Les Sheldon on board as co-executive producer, with additional direct-ing credits) explored new territory with multi-episode story arcs.

But there were forces at work in the eighties that would have far-reaching effects on television. Cable services, which had offered only a scant dozen or so channels in 1983, now typically provided thirty-five or more, including an ex-panding array of premium channels. An article in the April 14, 1986 issue of *Fortune* was titled "Culture Shock Rattles the TV Networks". The author, Tho-mas Moore, pointed out that "Of the three networks, ABC seemed to have the most problems adjusting to the environment of the Eighties. Independent sta-tions and cable TV have been stealing viewers from the big three, cutting the nation's prime time audience from 85% in 1980, to 73% last year."

In a description that sounds like it might have been lifted directly from the script of "Games People Play", Moore described the new corporate culture at the networks, "In the brave new post-takeover world, life is changing disturbingly for those who prospered there in the past. Professional managers with little or no broadcasting experience are replacing some of the clubby, freewheeling types who grew up with the networks. Declining growth in advertising revenues, and debt taken on to finance takeovers and defend against them, are forcing the networks to pay closer attention to costs. CBS and ABC in particular are tightening financial controls ... the networks continue to infuriate Hollywood producers by paying less and less of what it costs to make programs."

During the same period, another innovation of that era was catching hold. With the steepest acquisition curve of any consumer electronic device since television itself, the VCR (owned by fewer than 5% of American families in

1983) was now in over one-third of U.S. households. That percentage would continue to skyrocket, reaching 75% by 1991.

This development had little impact on *Hardcastle and McCormick* in first run. Subscribers to Shannon's letter 'zine talked mostly about catching the show in summer reruns and one correspondent, Rowena Warner, wrote wistfully, "This is the first time I've ever wished that I owned a VCR. Someday, maybe."[1] But at least one other writer mentioned "subsequent viewings" of an episode, in a way that suggests ardent fans were well represented in the rising tide of VCR ownership. Another fan, Marilyn Hay, recollected making and keeping such recordings. "From the first viewing of an episode, I taped the show and saved those tapes, replaying them until they all wore out." Other fans acquired copies when the show was released to syndication in 1987. It continued in second run in some markets for a decade, but as recently as 2005, with the series no longer on any U.S. network, sharing those old tapes, sometimes lovingly transferred to DVD, was the only way to see the show.

All this changed in February of 2006, when Toronto-based VEI acquired the Canadian distribution rights and released the pilot and season one in a five-disc set. Tapping the larger North American market, the set went briefly to number one in DVD sales on Amazon.ca. Even a viewer unfamiliar with the show gave it a positive review. Gord Lacey of *TV Shows on DVD.com* caught on right away: "I was very impressed with this show, and I enjoyed it a lot more than I thought I would. I figured this would be another "the car is the star" type show, but it's not at all. Sure, they drive the Coyote a lot, but it factors into the series about as much as Magnum's Ferrari does in *Magnum, P.I.*; not a whole lot. I liked the banter between Hardcastle and McCormick, and it was fun to watch their relationship mature over the season."[2]

As another indicator of demand, the boxed set was originally priced at $20.30 Canadian. The price rose, steadily, while the item was in stock and currently, with the set temporarily out of issue, a used copy is priced at $65.99 Canadian.[3] VEI followed up with a release of the season two boxed set in August, 2006, and season three in September, 2007. Both are still available in Canada and on the internet via Amazon.ca and Amazon.com.

An earlier generation of fans waited patiently for the rerun of their favorite episode, hoping it wouldn't be preempted in the doldrums of August by a pre-season football game. They labored over typewriters and copy machines to share their thoughts and opinions about the series.

Nowadays a fan of the show can watch a pristine, uncut version of "Rolling Thunder", on DVD, just as it appeared on September 18, 1983. The devotees gather in cyberspace in two active groups, the GullsWay list at Yahoo groups (tv.groups.yahoo.com/group/GullsWay/) and the message board of www.hardcastleandmccormick.tv. The resulting discussions are detailed and wide ranging, and the authors of this volume are grateful for the invaluable input those fans have made to this book.

Other fan sites include Michelle Furnas' Hardcastle and McCormick directory (www.fortunecity.com/lavender/poitier/1005/id6.htm). In addition, there is a complete listing of episodes, airdates and brief plot summaries at The HTK TV Site, (www.htktv.com/hardmc.htm), and a page devoted to the show at Kevin Burton Smith's very thorough "The Thrilling Detective Web Site" (www.thrillingdetective.com). Of course there are *Hardcastle and McCormick* entries at www.IMDb.com and Wikipedia.

The Coyote is not without it own fans, and gets top billing at www.angelfire.com/tv2/coyote/. The Coyote still comes up for discussion at Delorean sites, such as at DMCTalk.com (www.dmctalk.com/showthread.php?t=619).

Meanwhile, despite having been gone from primetime television for over twenty years, *Hardcastle and McCormick* continues to leave an imprint on the often shifting sands of popular culture and memory. That grass-roots arbiter of American needs, eBay, on one particular day, offered up twenty items to the search term "Hardcastle and McCormick", including a replica California license plate with the imprint "Coyote X" and a t-shirt bearing the phrase "I'd rather be watching Hardcastle and McCormick".

Of course there's a market for that.

1.   *Now Yer Cookin'* issue 5, Summer, 1986. p. 15.
2.   TVshowsonDVD.com, "Canadians get lucky on this one" Lacey, Gord. February 10, 2006.
3.   Amazon.ca listing on July 21, 2008

Epilogue
Where Are They Now?

Television is a cooperative activity, demanding the efforts of hundreds of skilled people. In production staff, cast, and crew, *Hardcastle and McCormick* benefited from the talents of some of the best. In the past twenty-two years, they've gone on to make their marks elsewhere. Some are no longer with us, but all gave us the gift of their creativity, passion, and humor through their work on this series.

Stephen J. Cannell produced ten more television series, as well as many feature-length projects. He is also a prolific and successful novelist, with nineteen books to date and is the writer-producer for a film, now in pre-production, based on his series *The A-Team*.

Patrick Hasburgh went on to produce *21 Jump Street* and *SeaQuest DSV*. He also wrote and directed the film, *Aspen Extreme*, and most recently turned his writing talents to a novel, *Aspen Pulp*. Patrick now lives in British Columbia. He still skis.

Brian Keith starred in three more TV series after *Hardcastle and McCormick* as well having numerous guest roles, and appearances in several feature films. His last role was in the movie *Rough Riders*. He died in 1997 at age 75, and in 2008 he received a posthumous star on the Hollywood Walk of Fame.

Daniel Hugh Kelly has appeared in three additional series since *Hardcastle and McCormick*, including *Second Noah* and *Ponderosa*, along with numerous movie and guest star roles and a lead role in the Broadway revival of "Cat on a Hot Tin Roof".

Les Sheldon continues to produce and direct. Among his numerous credits are *SeaQuest DSV*, *Seventh Heaven*, *Charmed*, and *Dawson's Creek*. He is married to actress Patricia Harty.

Jo Swerling worked as a supervising producer on many later Cannell series, as well as several television movies. He still works with Cannell Studios.

Robert Del Valle has most recently been credited as producer and unit production manager for the series *Six Feet Under*. His book, *The One Hour Drama: Producing Episodic Television* is available from Silman-James Press.

Lawrence J. Hertzog had a successful career as a writer and producer until his untimely death in 2008. He was perhaps best known for *Nowhere Man*, and his last series was *Painkiller Jane*, on the SciFi Channel in 2007.

Joe Santos has had a long and varied career as a character actor and appeared in several *Rockford Files* television movies. He guest-starred in several feature films, and most recently appeared in *The Sopranos* as Angelo Garepe.

Tom Szollosi's television scriptwriting led him to the script editor position on *Hardcastle and McCormick* (with Richard Christian Matheson). He continued writing scripts, for Cannell series and others, and is now also a producer.

Steven Sears began his career as a scriptwriter with an episode of *Riptide*. He wrote for more than a dozen series, then became a producer, mostly notably for the long-running series *Xena: Warrior Princess*.

Carol Mendelsohn was the story editor for Cannell's series, *Stingray*. Her most recent career path has been as indefatigable writer and executive producer for three of TV's biggest current hits: *CSI*, *CSI: Miami*, and *CSI: N.Y.*

Joe Candrella continues to work as a director. Some of his most notable series are *Star Trek: Deep Space Nine*, *Star Trek: Voyager*, *Seventh Heaven*, and, most recently, *The Secret Life of an American Teenager*.

Richard Christian Matheson, son of a screen writer and novelist, has followed in his father's footsteps. In addition to many television scripts, he has penned several stories, mostly in the horror and supernatural genres.

Tom Blomquist got his script-writing career started on *Hardcastle and McCormick* and went on to write many scripts for other Cannell shows, as well as several others. He now teaches writing at C.S.U.—Long Beach.

Gary Combs passed on his expertise in stunt coordination to his son, Gil, making three generations of Combses in that profession. They have developed stunts for several recent major motion pictures, including *Mission: Impossible II* and *The Bourne Ultimatum*.

Terry Frazee was also the middle member of a three-generation tradition. After a long career, capped by the original *Pirates of the Caribbean* film, he has retired and his son, Donald, now carries on the Frazee special effects heritage.

Ratings for Hardcastle & McCormick in the First Run, 1983-1986

(Ratings numbers referred to are from the Nielsen ratings service, with each point representing one percent of all households with televisions. Quotes are from the series Hardcastle and McCormick.*)*

Season One

> "*Thirty share, top show for women eighteen to forty and men over fifty-five. Mark tells me you're a fan.*" Patrick Burke to Milton Hardcastle, scene 33, "The Yankee Clipper"

The series premiered on September, 18, 1983, in the 9 p.m. time slot (Eastern Time) on ABC. Its competition was *The Jeffersons*, on CBS, and a special on NBC. In **week two**, it continued against *The Jeffersons* and the second hour of the Emmy Awards, beating both. In **week three** it moved one hour earlier, to the 8 p.m. slot, encountering *Alice* and *One Day at a Time* on CBS, and *Knight Rider* on NBC. It placed first again, but by only three-tenths of a point over *Knight Rider*.

In **week four** it slipped slightly, landing in third place against a two point lead by *Knight Rider*. In **week five** the race ended in a dead heat—one-tenth of a point difference and both a point ahead of *Alice*, but losing to *One Day at a Time* in the second half hour. In the **sixth week**, *Hardcastle and McCormick* beat all competitors by nearly two points with the episode *Killer B's*. In **week seven**, it came in a distant third to a miniseries called *Chiefs*, losing by nine points, though it maintained its own share.

There was a one week hiatus, in which it was preempted by a movie, *The Day After*, which garnered an astronomical forty-six percent of households. It returned in **week nine**, beating *Knight Rider* by over one and a half points.

However, that week *Sixty Minutes* had its start time pushed back by a football game and had an overall rating of 26.4, overlapping with the first half hour of *Hardcastle and McCormick.*

On December 4, the **tenth week** and ninth episode, "Flying Down to Rio" beat *Knight Rider* by two points and *One Day at a Time* by two-tenths of a point. In **week eleven**, it lost by just over seven points to a Frank Sinatra special, and by almost three points to *Knight Rider.* It placed third in its slot the next two weeks while in reruns during the holiday season.

In **week fourteen**, on January 1, 1984, it placed first, beating a rerun of *Knight Rider* by just under two points, and in a virtual tie with *Alice* and *One Day at a Time.* A week later it lost by a point to *Alice,* and a half point to *Knight Rider.* In **week sixteen**, it was in the middle position of a one point spread between the three shows. No ratings are available for **week seventeen** (the episode "School for Scandal").

On February 5, 1984, the **nineteenth week**, it came in first again, with the episode "The Georgia Street Motors", leading *Knight Rider* by half a point, and the series premier of *Four Seasons* by over two and a half points.

The next two weeks were pre-empted by the Winter Olympics, which lost in both weeks to *Knight Rider.* The twenty-second week was a movie pre-emption on all three channels.

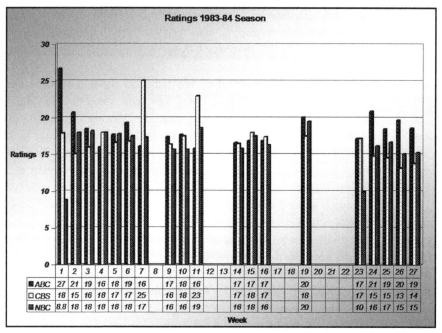

	1	2	3	4	5	6	7	8	9	10	11	12	13	14	15	16	17	18	19	20	21	22	23	24	25	26	27
■ABC	27	21	19	16	18	19	16		17	18	16			17	17	17			20				17	21	19	20	19
□CBS	18	15	16	18	17	17	25		16	18	23			17	18	17			18				17	15	15	13	14
■NBC	8.8	18	18	18	18	18	17		16	16	19			16	18	16			20				10	16	17	15	15

Graph 1: *Hardcastle and McCormick* season 1.
The overall cancellation threshold based on ratings that year was 15.1-15.5

In the **twenty-third week**, a month after its last airing, *Hardcastle and McCormick* was moved back to the 9 p.m. slot, tying with *The Jeffersons* and beating a special on NBC by over seven points. The program which had moved into the 8 p.m. slot was *Ripley's Believe It or Not*. It lost to *Knight Rider* by six points. In the **twenty-fourth week**, *Hardcastle and McCormick* moved back to 8 p.m. and hit its highest rating since the second week at 20.9 with the part one of "The Homecoming". It beat a *Knight Rider* rerun by seven-tenths of a point and a new episode of *Maggie Briggs* by over six points. The following week, the second half of that episode received a rating of 18.5, beating another *Knight Rider* repeat by nearly two points and *Domestic Life* by four points.

In the **last two weeks** of the regular season, *Hardcastle and McCormick* again beat *Knight Rider* (which was still in reruns) by 4.5 points, and 3.3 points.

Season Two

> *"Look, Jay, all this show needs is a little more time to find its audience."*
> – Producer to the Station Executive, scene 2, "Games People Play"

The series returned for its sophomore year on Sunday, September 30, 1984, again in the 8 p.m. time slot. It scored a rating of 14.8, losing to a two-part *Knight Rider* season premier by four points. More significantly, however, was the identical four point loss to the two-hour pilot of the series *Murder, She Wrote*, which, ironically, included Brian Keith in its guest cast.

In **week two**, *Murder, She Wrote* increased its lead to nearly 6.5 points over *Hardcastle and McCormick*, which continued to flounder in third place. In **week three**, the gap narrowed slightly but both the other shows beat *Hardcastle and McCormick* by five points. In **week four**, *Knight Rider* lagged back, only beating *Hardcastle and McCormick* by 1.3 points, but *Murder, She Wrote* continued its strong showing with a 4.4 point lead.

In the **fifth week**, *Hardcastle and McCormick* was moved to the 10 p.m. slot, and beat *Trapper John, M.D.* by two points while losing by a half point to the NBC movie. In the 8 p.m. slot, *Murder, She Wrote* lost by three points to a movie on ABC. The following week, *Hardcastle and McCormick* was back at 8 p.m. and lost by five points to *Murder* and over three points to *Knight Rider*.

Pushed to 10 p.m. again, in the **seventh week**, *Hardcastle and McCormick* tied a Johnny Carson special and beat *Trapper John* by 1.4 points. In **week eight**, it was back to 8 p.m., and a near-tie with *Knight Rider*, but a scathing 13.5 point loss to a Kenny Rodgers/Dolly Parton Christmas special.

The following week, still at 8 p.m., *Hardcastle and McCormick* lost by 8.4 points to *Murder* and nine-tenths of a point to *Knight Rider*. Its rating had been under 14 percent for two weeks straight.

After a two-week holiday hiatus, *Hardcastle and McCormick* returned, now on Monday night. Against *Scarecrow and Mrs. King*, it lost by only three-tenths of a point, while beating the Orange Bowl Parade by a tenth of a percent.

In the **thirteenth week**, it lost to *Scarecrow* by three points and beat NBC's *TV Bloopers and Practical Jokes* by 1.6 points. The following week, *Hardcastle and McCormick* and *Bloopers* were a tenth of a point apart with *Scarecrow* ahead by only 1.2. *Hardcastle and McCormick* had been at a rating of 17.6 for two weeks running. In the **fifteenth week** it surged ahead to 21.5 percent—the first time above 20 that season. The episode was "What's So Funny?" It beat the CBS movie by six points and *Bloopers* by 2.2.

On February 4, 1985, *Hardcastle and McCormick* and *Scarecrow* both lost to *Bloopers*. The following week brought another three point loss for *Hardcastle and McCormick*, with the other two programs nearly tied for first. In the **eighteenth week**, *Hardcastle and McCormick* and *Scarecrow* virtually tied, both beating *Bloopers* by 3.5 points. A week after that, they again tied, but *Bloopers* now had a lead of 3.6 points.

In **week twenty**, *Hardcastle and McCormick* lost by nearly three points to *Bloopers,* and 2.5 to *Scarecrow.* In the **twenty-first week**, it lost by three-tenths to *Scarecrow* and 3.5 to *Bloopers.* A week later it beat *Bloopers* by four-tenths and lost to *Scarecrow* by eight-tenths.

After a pre-empted week, *Hardcastle and McCormick* returned on April 1, beating *Scarecrow* by three-tenths, and losing to *Bloopers* by 1.1.

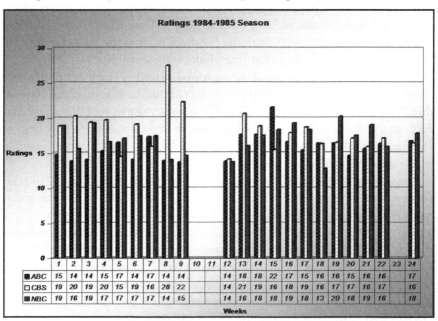

Graph 2. *Hardcastle and McCormick* season two. The first nine weeks are on the Sunday schedule against CBS's *Murder, She Wrote* (the Rogers/Parton Christmas special is the outlier in week eight). Week five and seven were in the 9 p.m. time slot. The second part is on the Monday schedule, against *Scarecrow and Mrs. King* (CBS) and *TV Bloopers and Practical* Jokes (NBC). The overall threshold for cancellation that year was 11.2-14.2.

The Second Season Summer Hiatus

Staying in the Monday, 8 p.m. slot, *Hardcastle and McCormick* began repeats on April 8, 1985. In the first seven weeks it maintained a respectable 13.2 average percent despite competition from new episodes of *Bloopers* and *Scarecrow*, several specials, and a heavyweight boxing match.

On June 3, a six week pre-emption began with Monday Night Baseball. When *Hardcastle and McCormick* returned for one week, on July 15, it had only a 9.3 rating. After that came another two weeks of baseball, then a return for three weeks, averaging 10.9. Two weeks of football preemptions followed.

The last two weeks of the summer brought the lowest ratings yet, averaging a 10 rating while paired with *Monday Night Football*.

Season Three

> *"One month, get the ratings up or you're off the air."* Station executive to producer, scene 2, "Games People Play".

On September 23, 1985, *Hardcastle and McCormick* returned for its third and final season. It now becomes difficult to assess exactly what the competition was. In the Eastern Time Zone, the program led off the schedule at 8 p.m., with football following at nine. In the Central Zone, the relationship was the same, but starting at 7 p.m. In the Mountain and Pacific Zones, football preceded *Hardcastle and McCormick*, with the start of each episode subject to the vagaries of overtimes. In order to watch it, first you had to find it. In this setting, over the next 12 weeks, *Hardcastle and McCormick* averaged a 14.1 rating and ranked below *Scarecrow and Mrs. King* uniformly, and *Bloopers* eight times (though, in fact, it often didn't appear opposite them at all).

After a holiday hiatus of two weeks, *Hardcastle and McCormick* returned on January 13, paired with the *Monday Night Movie*. It took two weeks to regain a foothold and a rating above 15. On February 3, it rose to 16.1 with the episode "When I Look Back On All the Things", and beat *Bloopers* by 1.5 points, but lost by 5.4 to *Katie and Allie*. Over the next two weeks, it stayed above 15, but still came in third. The following week it slipped slightly to 14.6, again against *Katie and Allie* with 19.7, and the movie *Annie* with 19.3.

On March 3 it hit a new first-run low, with the episode "Poker Night" receiving a rating of only 11.2. That night *Scarecrow* scored a 16.6 rating and a new program, *You Again?*, snapped up a 19.8 percent.

Two weeks later, the episode "In the Eye of the Beholder" pushed back above 14, but was still in third place against a strong *Katie and Allie*. From there it was a slight decline to 13.9 the following week, then a four week hiatus, followed by the final episode, "Chip Off the Ol' Milt", which only managed to beat a rerun of *Scarecrow* by three-tenths of a point with a rating of 12.6.

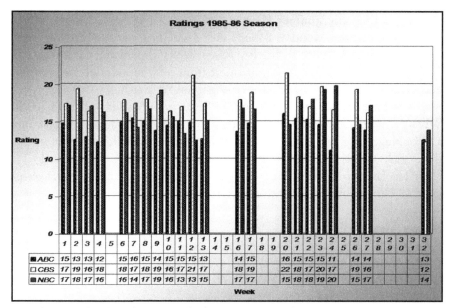

Graph 3: *Hardcastle and McCormick*, season three. The first 13 weeks have it airing in tandem with *Monday Night Football*, leading to variable show times. The data reflects the Eastern Time Zone match-ups. The cancellation threshold that year was 12.6-14.8.

Factors in the Decline and Fall of a Prime Time Show

Citing low ratings as the cause for a program's cancellation is a lot like writing "cardio-pulmonary arrest" on a death certificate. It's usually true, but hardly informative.

The ratings profile for *Hardcastle and McCormick* is interesting. It made an exceptionally good showing in its first weeks, and as late as March of 1984 was considered "a strong contender".[1] It placed first in its time slot about half the time that first year, and logged a reliable 19 rating over the entire first run season. The average rating for renewed series in 1983-84 was 17.2. The threshold range for cancellation was 15.1.[2] Although it was by no means a runaway hit, it had a very decent margin of safety.

Interestingly, it did reasonably well in competition with another car-oriented show—*Knight Rider*, probably because, with its emphasis on the relationship between the two lead characters, it managed to attract something other than just the car-focused demographic.

The second season began soft. The pilot for *Murder She Wrote* did not make as strong a showing as *Hardcastle and McCormick* had the previous September, but it did hold its own against two first-run shows of established series. And this "cozy", closed mystery continued to perform well, leaving the two action shows to split the rest of the audience.

In the face of *Murder's* steadily rising numbers, *Hardcastle and McCormick* was repeatedly shifted on the Monday schedule. This was possibly better than staying in the 8 p.m. slot and being run over by the juggernaut that was Jessica Fletcher, but it was a harbinger of what was to come.

In the first half of the season, in eight appearances opposite *Murder, She Wrote*, *Hardcastle and McCormick* averaged only a 14.2 rating. In its two airings away from that spot, it jumped to a 16.2 average. The overall rating for the first half of the season was 14.6, putting it squarely in the kill-zone.

In the second half of the season, the move to Monday nights raised the half-season average rating to 16.8—lower than season one but still safe. The overall yearly rating was 15.7—survivable, but hardly secure.

But Monday night was not the safe haven it appeared, even in the second season. While *Hardcastle and McCormick* did passably well against *Scarecrow and Mrs. King* (a character-driven romantic/action show), a third contender in that time slot was pointing the way to the inexorable future.

The other side of ratings, in the broadcast television equation, is cost. The average production cost of an hour of prime time television rose dramatically in the 1980s. It was estimated at $661,058/hour in 1983-84, and $725,151/hour in 1984-85. [3] *Hardcastle and McCormick,* with its second unit director, action sequences, and elaborate car stunts, would have been by no means below average in this regard. *TV Bloopers and Practical Jokes,* on the other hand, was a foretaste of the shift to cheaper, reality programs, using outtakes from other shows to ease the budget and allowing for a greater number of non-repeats. It's understandably annoying for network executives to see the competitor getting higher ratings with less outlay.

On *Hardcastle and McCormick*'s side, however, was yet another mid-1980s phenomenon. With the broadening of the media market, and the increased availability of cable and satellite access, the overall share going to network shows was dropping. On September 25, 1983, the percentage of households tuned to the big three networks during *Hardcastle and McCormick*'s slot was 56.9, a year later it was 51.6, and a year after that, 49.4—a good representation of overall trends in viewership. The average series rating on the national networks had dropped from 15.1 to 14.4 in those three years. By necessity, the cancellation threshold dropped as well. The fall was most dramatic in 1984-85, when it ranged between 11.2 to 14.2. This stabilized a little the following year, when average ratings rose to 14.8 and the cancellation threshold came up to between 12.6 and 14.8. [4]

In the summer of 1985 (having ducked the bullet, and even gathered some steam in its final four regular season episodes), *Hardcastle and McCormick* fell prey to the dark side of the Monday night schedule. Doing fairly well (by second run standards) in the first seven weeks of the off-season, it was then preempted by baseball. When it finally returned, six weeks later, it had lost one third of its audience. It's not a surprise that the network had no qualms about replacing it again for two weeks. Over the course of the summer it appeared on the schedule only thirteen times. While *Scarecrow* and *Bloopers* maintained their viewership, the rare sightings of *Hardcastle and McCormick* doomed any chance of it holding its ground.

This wasn't the final straw, though. That came in September, when the baseball season made way for *Monday Night Football.* Although it won its slot only three times in twelve outings (the last three games of the regular season), night time football's average rating was 19.6. With those numbers at stake, anything else on ABC's schedule on Monday night would be a sacrificial lamb.

Cannell had once called the Friday night slot "the Stephen J. Cannell memorial time period" for the number of times his programs had fallen to CBS blockbusters *Dallas* and *Falcon Crest.*[5] This, however, was a different sort of demise, losing to the 500-pound gorilla on your own network. Viewers couldn't be certain what time the show would appear in zones where it came on after the game.

With an average rating of 14.1 during the football season, *Hardcastle and McCormick* was back on the bubble, and sinking fast. Meanwhile, *Scarecrow and Mrs. King* had stabilized at 17.7 and *Bloopers* was holding its own. Though ratings improved after the football season ended (and the program's start time again became fixed), it was too little and too late. Occasional encounters with the very strong *Kate & Allie* were only the final nails in the coffin.

Whether cause or effect, the show's retreat from chases and crashes (culminating in the entirely automotive-free episode "Poker Night") also coincided with a final ratings drop. In the second half-season, *Hardcastle and McCormick* had an average rating of 14.2. Whatever savings might have accrued by trimming jumps, rollovers and crashes, it wasn't enough to save a series that had descended, relentlessly, below the threshold of cancellation.

1.   Waters, Harry F. and Janet Huck "The Merchant of Mayhem", Newsweek , March 12, 1984. p. 91

2.   Atkin, David and Barry Litman, "The Cancellation of Prime-Time Networks Programs: Changing Responses to Costs, Revenues, and New Technologies". A paper presented August, 1986 to the Association for Education in Journalism and Mass Communications. p. 34.

3.   ibid. p. 34.

4.   ibid. p. 34.

5.   Thompson, Robert J. *Adventures in Prime Time* (Praeger: New York, 1990) p. 26.

All ratings taken from: www.trivialtv.blogspot.com/2007_06_01_archive.html, and gathered by Nielsen Media Research.

Appendix B
Episode Titles
English, German, and French

What's in a name? Maybe nothing, but sometimes it makes all the difference. Fans in the U.S. may know the episode titles by heart, but would they be able to pick out their favorites based on the titles translated from other countries? While in German and Italian the series title remained essentially unchanged, in France the series was known as *Le Juge et le Pilote*. In Spain it was *Dos Contra el Crimen* (Two Against Crime). In Sweden it was called *Sista utvägen*, and in Finland *Viimeinen keino*, both of which translate roughly to "The Last Resort".

Original Title	German Title	German Translation	French Titles	French Translation
Rolling Thunder	Der Coyote	The Coyote	Le monstre d'acier	The Steel Monster
Man in a Glass House	Wer selbst im Glashaus sitzt	Who sits in the Glass House alone	Sans intention de nuire	Without Intention to Harm
Goin' Nowhere Fast	Flucht ins Nichts	Escape into Nothing	Je ne sais pas où je vais, mais j'y vais	I Don't know Where I Go, but I Go
The Crystal Duck	Die Kristall-Ente	The Crystal Duck	Le canard de cristal	The Crystal Duck
Hotshoes	Heiße Spur	Hot Scent	La course infernale	The Hellish Race
Once Again with Vigorish	McCormick alias Slattery	McCormick alias Slattery	Le convoi de tous les dangers	The Convoy of all Dangers
Killer B's	Sein letzter Film	His last Movie	Silence, on tourne	Silence, (Cameras) Rolling
The Boxer	Kid Calico, der Boxer	Kid Calico, the Boxer	Le boxeur	The Boxer
The Black Widow	Die schwarze Witwe	The Black Widow	La veuve noire	The Black Widow
The Prince of Fat City	Ein Basketball spielt Schicksal	A Basketball plays Fate	Chef de gang	Leader of the Gang
Flying Down to Rio	Abenteuer in San Rio	Adventure in San Rio	Vacances à San Rio Blanco	Vacation in San Rio Blanco
The Georgia Street Motors	Henker der Straße	Executioners of the Road	Les motards justiciers	The Vengeful Motorcyclists

447

Original Title	German Title	German Translation	French Titles	French Translation
Third Down and Twenty Years to Life	Neues Opfer im Longren-Fall	New Victim in the Longren Case	Révision d'un procès	A Lawsut Appealed
Just Another Round of That Old Song	Der Ton macht die Musik	"The Note makes the Music"	La chasse au trésor	The Treasure Hunt
School for Scandal	Schule für Diebe	School for Thieves	L'école du crime	The Crime Schoo l
Whistler's Pride	Ein geschenkter Gaul	A Gift Horse	La course truquée	The Fixed Race
The Homecoming	Highway des Todes	Highway of Death	Les vieux copains/La chasse à l'homme	The Old Companions/The Manhunt
Mr. Hardcastle Goes to Washington	Gefährliche Tage in Washington	Dangerous Days in Washington	M. le juge va à Washington	The Judge Goes to Washington
Did You See the One That Got Away	Unheimliches Computerspiel	A Scary Computer Game	Celui qui n'existait pas	That Which Doesn't Exist
Scared Stiff	Meuterei in Block A	Mutiny in Block A	Traitement de choc	Shock Treatment
Really Neat Cars and Guys with a Sense of Humor	So eine Art Kontakt-Service	Some Kind of Contact Service	Une histoire de voiture	A Story of the Car
Never My Love	Cindys Begräbnis	Cindy's Funeral	Jamais mon amour	Never My Love
D-Day	Sauber ist besser als tot	Clean is Better than Dead	Le jour J	The French term for the Allied invasion of Normandy
Ties My Father Sold Me	Die Angst, Vater zu sein	The Fear of being a Father	On ne choisit pas son père	You Can't Choose your Father
Pennies From a Dead Man's Eyes	Ein Toter soll nicht singen	A dead Man shouldn't sing	Le mort qui chantait encore	The Dead that Sang Again
My Girlfriend's Back and There's Gonna be Trouble	Never produced			
Outlaw Champion	Der gekaufte Pokal	The Bought Cup	Le champion hors-la-loi	The Outlaw Champion
It Coulda Been Worse ... She Coulda Been a Welder	Jeder hat eine Vergangenheit	Everybody has a Past	Le juge et l'étudiante	The Judge and the Student
Whatever Happened to Guts	Mein Herz gehört nur Daddy	My Heart belongs only to Daddy	Bonjour monsieur le juge	Hello, Judge
You Would Cry, Too, If It Happened to You	Einmal Hawaii und zurück	(Once) Hawaii and Return	Une fête qui déménage	A Moveable Feast
Hate the Picture ... Love the Frame	Kaution für den Richter	Bail for the Judge	Joyeux Noël, M. le juge	Merry Christmas, Judge
You and the Horse You Rode in On	Wasserfilter – sonderbar	Water Filters – Strange	Une proposition alléchante	An Enchanting Proposition

Original Title	German Title	German Translation	French Titles	French Translation
One of the Girls From Accounting	Mach es oder laß es!	Do it or leave it!	Une comptable trop curieuse	A Too Curious Accountant
Too Rich and Too Thin	Die zwölf Arten des Dr. Death	The Twelve Ways of Doctor Death	Trop riche pour maigrir	Too Much Wealth to Lose
Surprise On Seagull Beach	Strand der Vergangenheit	Beach of the Past	Ce trésor	The Treasure
There Goes the Neighborhood	Die Spitze des Eisbergs	The Tip of the Iceberg		
Angie's Choice	Angie hat keine andere Wahl	Angie has no other choice	Le choix d'Angie	Angie's Choice
What's So Funny ..?	Pamela und die Komiker	Pamela and the Comedians	Drôle d'histoire	Funny Story
Hardcastle, Hardcastle, Hardcastle and McCormick	Hardcastle, Anverwandte und McCormick	Hardcastle, Relatives and McCormick	Les deux vieilles dames mènent l'enquête	The Two Old Ladies Investigate
The Long Ago Girl	Freundin aus alten Tagen	Girlfriend from the old days	Amour de jeunesse	Young Love
Undercover McCormick	Mark McCormick - Streifenpolizist	Patrolman Mark McCormick	Dans la peau d'un flic	In the Skin of a Cop
You Don't Hear the One That Gets You	Melissas Rechnung geht nicht auf	Melissa's plan didn't work out		
The Game You Learn From Your Father	Nicht ich bin es gewesen	It wasn't me!	Une leçon de courage	A Lesson in Courage
The Birthday Present	Ein Geburtstagsgeschenk für den Richter	A Birthday Present for the Judge	Joyeux anniversaire	Happy Birthday
McCormick's Bar and Grill	McCormicks Bar und Grill	McCormick's Bar and Grill	Le beau cadeau	A Lovely Gift
Mirage a Trois	Kleiner Irrtum, große Wirkung	Small Mistake, Big Effect	Erreur sur la personne	Mistaken Identity
Conventional Warfare	Im Kriegszustand	At War	Une convention pas très conventionnelle	An Unconventional Convention
Games People Play	Die Millionen-Dollar-Frage	The Million Dollar Question	Faites vos jeux	Make Your Play
She Ain't Deep, But She Sure Runs Fast	Terror in Oregon	Terror in Oregon	La vie au grand air	The Outdoors Life
Something's Going On On This Train	Mord im Chicago-Express	Murder on the Chicago Express	Il se passe quelque chose dans le train	Something's Happening on the Train
Faster Hearts	Ein fast perfektes Paar	An almost perfect couple	À toute vitesse	At Any Speed
Hardcastle for Mayor	Der Todeskandidat	The doomed Man	L'élection	The Election

Original Title	German Title	German Translation	French Titles	French Translation
The Career Breaker	Milt und Mark auf der Flucht	Milt and Mark on the Run	Pêche en eaux troubles	Fish out of Troubled Water
Duet for Two Wind Instruments	Ende gut, nicht alles gut	Not all is well that ends well	Le juge se brouille avec son pilote	The Judge is Embroiled with the Racecar Driver
The Yankee Clipper	Eine kostspielige Beerdigung	An expensive Funeral	Éternelle amitié	Friends Forever
Strangle Hold	Damen-Catch und Mädchenhandel	Women Wrestling and White Slavery	Triste sort	Sad Fate
Do Not Go Gentle	Bitte nicht freundlich	Don't be so kind	Grand départ	Grand Exit
Brother Can You Spare a Crime	Rivalen, Brüder und ein Mord	Rivals, Brothers and a Murder	Des promesses, toujours des promesses	Promises, Always Promises
You're Sixteen, You're Beautiful and You're His	Die ihr Leben verkaufen	Those who sell their Lives	La frontière de l'espoir	The Frontier of Hope
If You Could See What I See	Ich sehe was, was Du nicht siehst	I see something that you don't see	Visions prémonitoires	Premonitions
Poker Night	Pokernacht in Malibu	Poker Night in Malibu	Poker mouvementé	Poker Action
When I Look Back On All the Things	Wirf keinen Blick zurück	Don't look back	Quand je repense à tout ça!	When I Reconsider it All!
Love and Pain and All That Stuff	Never produced			
Round Up the Old Gang	Alle für einen - Einer für alle	All for one and one for all	Les retrouvailles	The Reunion
The Day the Music Dies	Die Stimme aus dem Äther	A Voice out of the Ether	Le prince du rock'n roll	The Prince of Rock and Roll
In the Eye of the Beholder	Eine irre Geschichte	A crazy Story	Légendes d'Irlande	Irish Legends
A Chip Off the Ol' Milt	Rätsel im Seniorenheim	Mystery of the Retirement Home	McCormick joue les juristes	McCormick Plays the Lawyers

Appendix C
"Love and Pain and All That Stuff"
An unproduced script from
Hardcastle and McCormick

Late in the third season, staff writer and story editor Carol Mendelsohn was involved in organizing the final series of scripts. One that she wrote was never filmed, though it lasted through one revision and was even assigned a script number. Mendelsohn says, simply, that Brian Keith didn't want a relationship for Hardcastle.

It certainly has that, going far further than "The Long Ago Girl" in the direction of establishing a romantic situation for one of the main characters. Now, thanks to Ms. Mendelsohn and Cannell Productions, a copy of this script is available. It's a fascinating look at the days of television writing before computers, and a look down one of the roads not taken by the series.

(All errors are original.)

HARCASTLE AND McCORMICK
"LOVE AND PAIN AND ALL THAT STUFF"
by Carol Mendelsohn

A STEPHEN J. CANNELL PRODUCTION

January 17, 1986 (F.R.)
Rev. January 27, 1986 (Limited Run)

CAST

MILTON C. HARDCASTLE
MARK McCORMICK

LT. FRANK HARPER

KAY PHILLIPS
DAVID VINCENT
WYLIE CROWDER
ART McGOWAN
MATT ARNOLD
WAITER
SALESMAN
APARTMENT MANAGER
RECEPTIONIST
P.A. ANNOUNCER
TICKET AGENT

SETS:

INT.
GULL'S WAY
        /FOYER
        /HARDCASTLE'S BEDROOM
        /GUEST ROOM
        /KITCHEN
        /HARDCASTLE'S DEN
RESTAURANT
LE MONTI'S JEWELRY STORE
SAN FRANSISCO
        /OFFICE IN MANSION
        /AIRPORT TERMINAL
CORVETTE
KAY PHILLIPS' APARTMENT
BOUTIQUE
LT. FRANK HARPER'S OFFICE
N.D. SEDAN
L.A. AIRPORT
        /TERMINAL
        /SECURITY CHECK POINT
        /GATE AREA

EXT.
GULL'S WAY
        /BASKETBALL COURT
        /PATIO
        /GATEHOUSE
        /GARAGE
        /BEACH
        /DRIVEWAY

THEATRE
LE MONTI'S JEWELRY STORE
SAN FRANSISCO
        /STREETS (STOCK)
        /MANSION
        /INTERNATIONAL AIRPORT
GARDE NRESTAURANT
L.A. AIRPORT
KAY PHILLIPS' APARTMENT BUILDING
KAY PHILLIPS' APARTMENT

ACT ONE

FADE IN:

CLOSE ON – A BASKETBALL

…we watch as it's dribbled toward the basket… the ballhandler (we don't see his face yet) pretends he's in the NBA… changing the direction of his dribble… changing speeds… holding the non-existent guards off with his free arm… he drives for the basket… pivots… shoots… as we…

WIDEN TO REVEAL – EXT. GULL'S WAY – BASKETBALL COURT – DAY

And McCormick as he sinks a beauty… then fields the ball, turns around and sees…

HIS POV – HARDCASTLE

As he makes his way past the court to the Pickup.

ANGLE – McCORMICK AND HARDCASTLE

As McCormick calls out to him… and Hardcastle keeps moving toward the Pickup.

                    McCORMICK
        Hey, Judge, how about a little two-man cut throat?…A dollar a point…
        Play to twenty… have to win by two.

                    HARDCASTLE
        Some other time, kiddo. See ya'.

And as Hardcastle continues toward the Pickup…

McCORMICK

I'll let you take it out first.

HARDCASTLE

Some other time.

And McCormick shrugs... and turns... and hooks a shoot that caroms off the backboard... as we...

SMASH CUT TO

STOCK FOOTAGE. – A BASKETBALL

As it caroms off the backboard and into the basket... and we HEAR the ROARING CHEERS of a crowd... as we...

CUT TO

STOCK FOOTAGE – AN NBA BASKETBALL GAME

And as the crowd goes wild the CAMERA MOVES in on...

ANGLE – HARDCASTLE AND KAY PHILLIPS

On their feet and cheering along with the other sports fans... Kay looks over at Hardcastle and smiles... he smiles back... and we...

DISSOLVE TO

CLOSE ON – HARDCASTLE

And we HEAR water running in a sink and Hardcastle WHISTLING... and we see Hardcastle lean into the bathroom mirror covered with a single white strip of shaving foam... and as he draws a razor down his cheek...

ANGLE – McCORMICK

As he steps into the doorway of the bathroom and we see his reflection in the mirror... he's holding two tickets in his hand

McCORMICK

What do you think these are?

HARDCASTLE

Two tickets to Hawaii.

> McCORMICK
>
> Better... Two fifth row... center ice tickets to tonight's hockey game.

> HARDCASTLE
>
> (unenthusiastic)
> Terrific.

> McCORMICK
>
> Terrific. It's fantastic. Judge, we've been talkin' about this game
> for weeks.

And as Hardcastle wipes his face with a towel and applies a dose of aftershave...

> HARDCASTLE
>
> Listen, why don't you call up what's her name and invite her...
> y'know... that Disney character.

> McCORMICK
>
> Bambi... And she's not crazy about sports where the players are miss-
> ing their front teeth... but if you can't make it... I'll give her a call...
> (just looks at Hardcastle a beat; and then)
> Judge, are you alright?

> HARDCASTLE
>
> Me... fine, kiddo... just fine.

And as Hardcastle starts WHISTLING and sweeps past McCormick on his way out
the door...

OMITTED

EXT. THEATER – NIGHT

As Hardcastle and Kay exit a performance of something very "New York" and very
"not Hardcastle"... we can just glimpse the quick, nervous look Kay throws over her
shoulder... then she looks back at Hardcastle and smiles... Hardcastle puts a
protective arm around her and steers her through the crowd... as we...

DISSOLVE TO

INT. GULL'S WAY – FOYER – NIGHT

It's dark... we SEE the headlights of a car sweep through the glass window in the
front door... we HEAR a car engine killed... we HEAR the SOUND of a key in the
lock... and the door swings open... and as Hardcastle enters... we HEAR

                      McCORMICK
You mind telling me where you've been?

And the overhead lights CLICKS on… and we see McCormick parked on the
stairs… and Hardcastle reacts.

                      HARDCASTLE
    McCormick… what are you doin' up?

                      McCORMICK
    I'm waiting for you… It's four o'clock in the morning… where
    have you been?

                      HARDCASTLE
    I've been out.

                      McCORMICK
    No kidding… Out <u>where</u>?

                      HARDCASTLE
    Just out… And what're you gettin' so upset about?

                      McCORMICK
    I'm not upset… Y'know you could've called… You had me worried.

                      HARDCASTLE
    Well, you can stop worryin'… I'm home. And I'm tired… so
    goodnight.

And Hardcastle steps over McCormick… climbs the stairs to his bedroom… and as he
switches off the light at the top of the stairs, leaving McCormick in the dark… and we…

                                              SMASH CUT TO

CLOSE ON – A CANDLE

As it's being lit… and we…

                                                      CUT TO

INT. RESTAURANT – NIGHT

And Hardcastle and Kay dining at a candle-lit corner table. …Hardcastle smiles,
starts to take a bite out of his meal… looks up to find Kay staring at him… and as she
reaches out and squeezes his hand… we…

DISSOLVE TO

EXT. GULL'S WAY – DAY – PATIO AREA

As Hardcastle, lost in thought, pours himself a cup of coffee… the coffee spills over the rim of the cup onto the saucer before he realizes what's happened… and he stops pouring… and McCormick REACHES INTO FRAME and wipes off the saucer with a cloth… then shoots Hardcastle a look.

                    HARDCASTLE
          (defensive)
          Somethin's wrong with the coffee pot.

                    McCORMICK
          Give me a break… you've been spilling coffee, whistling Dixie,
          and shaving twice a day for the last six weeks.
          (a big grin)
          …What's her name?

                    HARDCASTLE
          What are you talkin' about?

                    McCORMICK
          The woman who put the dent in your cologne budget… C'mon,
          Judge… man-to-man… Who have you been seeing?

                    HARDCASTLE
          Seein'?…Who said I was seein' anybody.

And we…

DISSOLVE TO:

INT. HARDCASTLE'S KITCHEN – DAY

And we HEAR all the normal kitchen sounds… coffee PERKING… Bacon SIZZLING… Egg timer TICKING… and we see McCormick drinking juice, eating cereal, reading the newspaper… and Kay, wearing Hardcastle's bath robe, pushes in through the door and enters… and McCormick without looking up, assumes it's Hardcastle…

                    McCORMICK
          …It's about time you got up… Listen, Judge… if you need a car
          today… take the corvette… I'm gonna work on the truck… needs
          new sparks… new filters… Okay?

And as McCormick turns around expecting to see Hardcastle... sees Kay... then looks all around the kitchen...

                          McCORMICK
        Is this 1 Pacific Coast Highway, Malibu?

                              KAY
        I think so.

                          McCORMICK
        Milton C. Hardcastle's house?

                              KAY
        Definitely.

McCormick nods... and then...

                          McCORMICK
        Can I help you?

ANGLE – HARDCASTLE

... as he enters... WHISTLING...

                          HARDCASTLE
        Mornin'... You two introduce yourselves?

                              KAY
        Not yet...

                          HARDCASTLE
        (making introductions)
        Well, Kay... this is Mark McCormick... Mark... meet Kay Phillips.

... and Kay crosses over... and shakes hands with McCormick...

                              KAY
        Nice to meet you, Mark.

                          McCORMICK
        Hi.

And McCormick just continues to alternate stares between Hardcastle and Kay. Kay pours two cups of coffee. Hardcastle crosses over to the stove, turns off the frying pan.

HARDCASTLE
(to Kay)
What can I get you?…Bacon?…Eggs?…French toast?

And as Kay hands one of the cups of coffee to Hardcastle, she takes a sip from the other.

KAY
Just coffee, thanks.

And McCormick continues to stare at Kay and the bathrobe… and Kay looks down.

KAY
Guess I better get dressed. I don't want to be late for work.

HARDCASTLE
Kay works at a boutique in Santa Monica… Y'know it's amazing
how much she knows about women's clothing.

McCORMICK
Amazing.

KAY
Actually, I've only had the job a couple of months and I'd hate to lose it.

HARDCASTLE
Don't worry… I'll get you there in plenty of time.

KAY
(to McCormick)
The corvette, right?

And as Hardcastle shoots Kay a puzzled look.

McCORMICK
(to Hardcastle)
Yeah… I thought I'd do some work on the pickup today…

HARDCASTLE
No problem.

Kay looks over at the stove and the bacon and we sense that, at the moment, the
thought of food is disagreeable.

KAY
I'll just be a couple minutes… nice meeting you, Mark.

McCORMICK

Same here.

McCormick watches as Kay exits. Then he gets up, crosses over to the door, listens to make sure she's gone, then turns back to Hardcastle.

McCORMICK

Why didn't you tell me we were having company?...Do you know how embarrassing it is to have a stranger walk into the kitchen wearing <u>your</u> robe?

HARDCASTLE

Gee, I don't know... I only know what it's like to have Bambi paradin' around in <u>your</u> t-shirt...and that red head from Santa Barbara shadow boxin' in the buff on the front lawn...

McCORMICK

April happens to be very spiritual and into Eastern meditation philosophies... besides, that's different.

HARDCASTLE

Different how?

McCORMICK

...Y'know... I'm thirty-two... and you're... you're a judge. You have a position in the community.

HARDCASTLE

Listen, kiddo, just 'cause I'm a couple years older than you doesn't mean I gotta live like a monk.

McCORMICK

Okay, but just don't do it in front of the neighbors.

HARDCASTLE

Y'know, a lot of women find mature men very attractive.

McCORMICK

I know. Bambi's crazy about George Burns.

HARDCASTLE

And you want to know why women are attracted to mature men?...Because mature men never push... they let a relationship develop... take things slowly.

                    McCORMICK
They have to.
(off Hardcastle's look)
No offense.

                    HARDCASTLE
This I can do without. I'm gonna go see if Kay's ready.

And as Hardcastle starts out the door—

                    McCORMICK

Judge...

And as Hardcastle turns back to face McCormick—

                    HARDCASTLE

Yeah?

                    McCORMICK
Is it serious between you two?

                    HARDCASTLE
Me and Kay? Nah... We've only known each other for six weeks...
How serious could it be?

And we:

                                              SMASH CUT TO

CLOSE ON – DIAMOND ENGAGEMENT RINGS

On a velvet tray... inside a glass display case.

SALESMAN (V.O.)
...an excellent choice... Mr. Hardcastle... a gift that will last forever...

And the CAMERA TILTS UP TO...

ANGLE- HARDCASTLE

Standing over the case... smiling... signing a charge receipt...

                    HARDCASTLE
I want it wrapped up real special...

WIDEN TO INCLUDE – INT. LE MONTI'S JEWELRY STORE – DAY

Everything about this place spells expensive... maybe there's even a waiter serving champagne... the SALESMAN hands a credit card back to Hardcastle... takes the signed receipt and...

                    SALESMAN
        I'll see to it... I'll just be a minute...

And as the Salesman picks up a small jewelry box from the counter and starts to leave.

                    HARDCASTLE
        Thanks.

And as Hardcastle smiles at the departing Salesman...

                                        CUT TO

EXT. LE MONTI'S JEWELRY STORE – DAY

And McCormick with his nose pressed up against the glass... and as we see Hardcastle look out at the street and catch McCormick spying...

ANGLE – McCORMICK

As he quickly begins to backpedal... past the VALET PARKING ATTENDANT... slowly making his way to the curb and the parked corvette...

ANGLE – HARDCASTLE

As seen through the jewelry store window... the Salesman hand him a gift-wrapped box... neither too small nor too large to be an engagement ring... and Hardcastle exits the store to the street and a waiting McCormick...

                    McCORMICK
        I've been standing out here for an hour.
        (Re: attendant)
        That guy thinks I'm too cheap to park the car... How come you
        wouldn't let me go in there with you?

                    HARDCASTLE
        There're some things a man has to do alone, McCormick.

                    McCORMICK
        Well, going off to war comes to mind... not shopping in the most
        expensive jewelry store in Beverly Hills.

HARDCASTLE
You really think this is the best store in town?

McCORMICK
Judge, if this store was any more exclusive, you'd have to take a blood test to shop here.

HARDCASTLE
(defensive)
What do you mean by that?

McCORMICK
Nothing. Don't get so defensive.
(re: box)
What'd you buy?

HARDCASTLE
A little something for Kay.

McCORMICK
A little something for her neck? ... no... the box is too small...
Her wrist?
(Hardcastle doesn't respond)
... Not her finger... Judge...

HARDCASTLE
I'm not gonna tell you, McCormick... so you might as well get in the car.

And as Hardcastle and McCormick start to get in the car.

McCORMICK
Don't you think you're moving a little too fast?...I mean, you hardly know Kay. What happened to the mature approach... taking things slow... George Burns would let a relationship like this develop.

HARDCASTLE
I'm just helpin' things along.
Now willya get in the car?

McCORMICK
Have you met her parents yet, Judge?

HARDCASTLE
Just get in the car.

And as they get in the care, we

                                                                    CUT TO

EXT. SAN FRANCISCO – DAY – ESTABLISHING – STOCK

And we HEAR classical music on a stereo… and we…

                                                                    CUT TO

EXT. MANSION IN SAN FRANCISCO – DAY – STOCK

The best section of town… the best house on the block… and we HEAR the
MUSIC abruptly stop as the needle scratches across the surface of the record…

                          VINCENT (V.O.)
        I'm paying you for results, Wylie… and all I'm getting is jerked
        around…and we…

                                                                    CUT TO

INT. OFFICE IN MANSION – DAY

ON the swinging arm of the stereo… and we WIDEN TO DAVID VINCENT, the
owner of the mansion and Chairman of the Board of Vincent Shipping Lines.
Vincent is in his late-forties, well-dressed, with the grace that comes with education,
money and breeding. He looks pissed as WYLIE CROWDER puts a fresh stick of
chewing gum in his mouth…

                             VINCENT
        …the woman didn't vanish off the face of the earth.

                             CROWDER
        Look, Mr. Vincent… I already checked and double-checked the
        airlines, trains, buses, rental car agencies… no Blair McKenzie
        checked out of San Francisco in the last two months.

                             VINCENT
        You moron… she's a very smart lady… too smart to use her own
        name.

                             CROWDER
        I know that… and I'm checkin' under aliases… showin' her pic-
        ture around… but that takes time.

VINCENT

Time… Wylie, I don't have time… I have the FBI, DEA, not to mention the police department breathing down my neck… and if they connect me to Carlyle's murder, I've bought myself a one-way ticket to San Quentin.

CROWDER

How're they gonna connect you to the murder without the McKenzie dame's testimony?

VINCENT

They're not… which means they must be looking for her, too.

CROWDER

We'll find her… She's gonna slip up…

VINCENT

Slip up or no slip up… the important thing is to find her first… Did you check with the medical association?

CROWDER

Yeah… their records still show she left San Francisco General eight weeks ago… and she's no longer in active practice.

VINCENT

She must be running scared to give up her practice… y'know, she worked her way through college then med school… she was five years into her surgical practice before she paid off the last of her student loans.

And Vincent Crosses over to his antique desk… and we…

INSERT – A PICTURE FRAME

As Vincent picks it up off the desk… looks at it…takes a moment… this is hard for him…

VINCENT

She's one helluva doctor… One beautiful lady.
(beat)
Look, she's gotta be somewhere… She's gotta have a life and a job and friends… Now, I want you to find her… and then… I want you to kill her.

And we come over Vincent's shoulder and move in on a photograph of Vincent and Blair in happier times… revealing Blair to be Kay Phillips… and we…

CUT TO

CLOSE ON – KAY

As she turns around… throws a look over her shoulder.

WIDEN TO INCLUDE – EXT. CLOTHING BOUTIQUE – DAY

And we PICK UP Hardcastle and Kay who have just exited the store and are headed down the street… And Hardcastle observes Kay looking over her shoulder.

HARDCASTLE
> Y'know, I noticed you're always doin' that.

And as Kay turns back to face Hardcastle.

KAY
> I'm sorry. What did you say?

HARDCASTLE
> I said you're always doin' that… lookin' over your shoulder… (joking) Who're you afraid you're gonna see… an old boyfriend… an ex-husband?

And Kay doesn't respond.

HARDCASTLE
> Maybe a not so ex-husband?

KAY
> Don't be silly, Milt… You're the only man in my life… I guess it's a bad habit I developed being on my own for so many years… I even check the closets and under the bed before I go to sleep.

And as Hardcastle takes her arm and they continue down the street.

HARDCASTLE
> I hadn't noticed.

And we:

CUT TO

EXT. GARDEN RESTAURANT – DAY

As a WAITER hovers over Hardcastle who is seated across the table from Kay.

WAITER

Can I get you folks anything else?

HARDCASTLE

A check'll be fine.

And as the waiter leaves a check for Hardcastle—

WAITER

Whenever you're ready, I'll take the money up.

And the waiter moves off. Hardcastle looks at Kay. Reaches into his pocket. Fishes out the gift-wrapped box. Sets it down on the table in front of her.

HARDCASTLE

This is for you.

KAY

It's not my birthday or anything.

And as she hesitates…

HARDCASTLE

I know that… but it's a lot more fun buying presents when they're unexpected… and it's no big deal… Go ahead and open it.

KAY

Alright… And thank you.

HARDCASTLE

You're not supposed to thank me until after you open it… who knows. Maybe you won't like it… Y'know, I don't have a whole lot of experience with presents… criminals maybe, but not presents.

And Kay smiles faintly at Hardcastle… this is really affecting her. She opens the gift wrapping. We sense her worry this is an engagement ring.

INSERT – A JEWELRY BOX

As it's unwrapped. And Kay opens it to reveal a gold watch.

RESUME – KAY AND HARDCASLTE

As she reacts…

KAY

It's beautiful... I don't know what to say.

HARDCASTLE

Yeah... well, you don't have to say anything. You could try it on though.

KAY
Okay.

And Kay's all thumbs as she tries to remove the watch from the box.

HARDCASTLE

Here... let me help you with it.

And as Hardcastle removes the watch from the case, unlatches the band, puts it around Kay's wrist...

HARDCASTLE

Looks pretty good... doesn't it?

And as Kay starts to cry...

HARDCASTLE

Look, Kay, don't cry... if you don't like it... we can take it back... get you somethin' you like.

KAY

(fighting her tears)
Like it... Milt, I love it.

HARDCASTLE

Yeah, well, maybe it's a little too personal... maybe a bowling ball or a toaster oven would've been better.

KAY

It's perfect... really. I don't know why I can't stop crying.

And Hardcastle hands her a handkerchief.

HARDCASTLE

Well, you better stop it... what are people gonna think?

KAY

Right...

And she wipes away her tears. Looks up at Hardcastle. He smiles. And she makes a decision.

                         KAY
        Milt… there's something I need to tell you.

                      HARDCASTLE
        As long as you stop crying… I'll listen to anything.

                         KAY
        I want you to know that I won't blame you if… after you hear
        what I have to say… you get up and walk out… take the watch
        back… never want to buy me a bowling ball.

                      HARDCASTLE
        Kay, listen… Havin' been a cop… a lawyer… a judge… I've heard
        everything there is to hear, and more than once… so I'm not gonna
        take the watch back or get up and leave you… 'cause I don't shock
        that easily… so, what is it you want to tell me?

                         KAY
        (a beat)
        Milt… I'm pregnant.

And Hardcastle doesn't respond.

                         KAY
        I'm going to have a baby.

                      HARDCASTLE
        Ah… are you… a baby… hell…
        (smiles)
        Are you sure it's yours?

                         KAY
        Yes, I am.

And as Hardcastle gets up.

                      HARDCASTLE
        Oh my God.

                         KAY
        I don't expect you to take responsibility for it.

HARDCASTLE

Here… why don't you pay the check.

And Kay watches as Hardcastle walks out past the waiter.
And we:

FADE OUT

END OF ACT ONE

ACT TWO

FADE IN.

OMIT

EXT. STREETS – DAY – SERIES OF SHOTS

Hardcastle in the pickup – thinking things over. We build a MONTAGE as
Hardcastle drives by maybe a park with children playing… a school… a toy store…
then we HEAR a DOORBELL RING, and we:

DISSOLVE TO

EXT. KAY'S APARTMENT – THE FRONT DOOR – DAY

This is one of those typical California courtyard-type apartment buildings. Maybe
there's a swimming pool in the center. Hardcastle stands at the door to Kay's ground
floor apartment. He rings the bell again. A beat. Kay opens the door.

KAY

(genuine surprise)
Milt.

HARDCASTLE

I've been thinking things over… and I think it's great about the
baby… just great.

KAY

I think we need to talk.

And as Hardcastle pumps up a smile, we:

CUT TO

INT. KAY'S APARTMENT – DAY

Hardcastle is pacing nervously back and forth in front of Kay who's seated on the sofa.

                              KAY
         I can't marry you.

                          HARDCASTLE
         I want to do the right thing here… I want to take care of you and
         the baby… now I know I may not be the handsomest guy around.

                              KAY
         You're very attractive.

                          HARDCASTLE
         …and I can be a little gruff at times…

                              KAY
         The baby isn't your responsibility.

                          HARDCASTLE
         …and I like to have things my own way…

                              KAY
         This is crazy.

                          HARDCASTLE
         …but we get along pretty well… I had a great time at the basket-
         ball game even though the Lakers lost… and that new wave adap-
         tation of the Trojan Women play you took me to… I didn't fall
         asleep until the second act.

                              KAY
         It won't work.

                          HARDCASTLE
         Sure it will.

                              KAY
         You don't know anything about me.

                          HARDCASTLE
         You're a Golden State Warriors fan… You love hamburgers… hate
         hot dogs… Your favorite movie is "The Turning Point"… as a kid
         you never made your bed…

                              KAY
        Milt, I've done some things I'm not proud of.

                          HARDCASTLE
        So you married a sailor once. I'll tell you… one time… in France…
        I met this woman… I still get embarrassed when I think about it.

                              KAY
        It'd be a mistake to rush into anything.

                          HARDCASTLE
        I don't think the baby's going to wait for a long courtship… the
        best bet is a long marriage.

                              KAY
        I don't think I can marry you.

                          HARDCASTLE
        You'll change your mind.

And off Kay's look of frustration and resistance, we:

                                                                    CUT TO

CLOSE ON – McCORMICK

His face painted with shock.

                        HARDCASTLE (V.O.)
        I thought you'd be happy for me and Kay.

WIDEN TO INCLUDE – EXT. GULL'S WAY – GARAGE – DAY

And McCormick caught in mid clean-up by Hardcastle. And as McCormick puts
down a box.

                          McCORMICK
        I am… I just don't know what to say… it's all so sudden.

                          HARDCASTLE
        You could say you'll be the baby's godfather.

                          McCORMICK
        (a beat)
        I'm touched, Judge… really… I've never been a godfather before…

                    HARDCASTLE
Then you'll do it?

                    McCORMICK
Sure... It'd be an honor.

And as Hardcastle smiles.

                    McCORMICK
Look, I don't know how to say this exactly... I don't want you to
think I'm not happy for you... but two days ago you told me it
wasn't serious between you and Kay.

                    HARDCASTLE
Two days ago I didn't know I was going to be a father.

                    McCORMICK
Y'know, you've got nine months... Maybe you shouldn't rush into
anything... You and Kay haven't known each other that long.

                    HARDCASTLE
Long enough. And Kay's a lot of fun. I like her.

                    McCORMICK
Yeah, but do you love her?

                    HARDCASTLE
She's gonna have a baby and we're gonna get married... and that's
that. So why don't you go back to doin' whatever it was you were
doin', 'cause I got a lot of things to do... startin' with plannin' an
engagement party.

And as Hardcastle exits, McCormick picks up a box, holds it a beat, then sets it
down, sits down on top of it. And as we play his look... we HEAR the sounds of
AIRPLANES taking off and landing.

                                                            CUT TO

STOCK FOOTAGE – EXT. SAN FRANSISCO INTERNATIONAL AIRPORT –
DAY

To establish.

INT. DEPARTURE TERMINAL – DAY

And the CAMERA PANS from the TWA ticket counter to a row of telephone booths and MOVES IN ON...

ANGLE – CROWDER

On the phone... chewing gum... a picture of Kay in one hand...

> CROWDER
> One of the ticket agents recognized her from her picture...

INTERCUT – INT. VINCENT'S MANSION – ON VINCENT

> VINCENT
> Does he remember when he saw her?

> CROWDER
> It had to be the first week in December... 'cause, get this, he invited her to the ballet... thought she looked like a patron of the arts.

> VINCENT
> (wistful)
> The man has an eye. Blair adored the ballet... Once, when Baryshnikov was in town... she made me sit through the ballet three nights in a row... then dragged me to a Sunday matinee of "Fire Bird"... That was very special.

> CROWDER
> Whatever you say, Mr. Vincent... Look, I'm gonna check the dates on the ballet.

> VINCENT
> Right...
> (snaps back)
> Does the agent remember where she was headed?

> CROWDER
> L.A.... only she didn't use her real name... told him her name way Kay somethin'... now it's gonna be expensive... but he's gonna get us a copy of the flight manifest.

> VINCENT
> Run down the name... I'm running out of time.

RESUME CROWDER

As he takes a wad of gum out of his mouth and sticks it under the ledge of the phone booth…

                    CROWDER
        I'll call you when I get to L.A.

And as he hangs up the phone and starts toward the ticket counter… we close in on a poster of L.A. showing the deep blue Pacific Ocean… and the sand… and the surf… and we…

                                                CUT TO

EXT. GULL'S WAY – THE BEACH – DAY

And the sand… and the surf… and McCormick hurling stones into the ocean.

                    HARDCASTLE (V.O.)
        What are you doin' down here?

And we:

                                            DISSOLVE TO

OMIT

ANGLE – HARDCASTLE

As he walks over to McCormick who doesn't turn around.

                    HARDCASTLE
        I told you Kay was on her way over… I want you two to spend
        some time together.

And McCormick hurls another stone into the water, then turns to Hardcastle.

                    McCORMICK
        I'm sorry, but I can't take this. You've spent the last couple of days
        acting like the social director on a cruise ship… McCormick, why
        don't you and Kay go to the market… kiddo, why don't you and
        Kay watch T.V.

                    HARDCASTLE
        She's gonna be part of our lives… you better get used to it.

                    McCORMICK
        What do you know about her?

HARDCASTLE

I know all I need to know.

McCORMICK

That she's having your baby.

HARDCASTLE

I know, that may not mean much to someone of your generation, but I was brought up to take responsibility.

McCORMICK

I'm all for taking responsibility... doing the honorable thing... but...
(spits it out)
Alright, I gotta say it... Judge, how do you know it's your baby?

HARDCASTLE
(pissed)
What do you mean... how do I know?

McCORMICK

Well, maybe Kay just told you she was pregnant.

HARDCASTLE

She's not that kind of lady, McCormick

McCORMICK

You just met her. How do you know what she's like?

And as Hardcastle and McCormick move closer to each other... squaring off...

HARDCASTLE

Because we're not talkin' about on of your beach bunny pick-ups... we're talkin' about a refined, educated, mature woman.

McCORMICK

Who probably knows a good thing when she sees it... Milton C. Hardcastle... eligible bachelor... retired jurist... millionaire.

HARDCASTLE

She's not after my money if that's what you're thinkin'.

McCORMICK

Think about it, Judge... before you walk down the aisle with a gold digger.

And as Hardcastle lunges at McCormick, grabs him by the collar...

ANGLE – KAY

As she races up.

> KAY
>
> Stop it!

ANGLE TO INCLUDE HARDCASTLE AND McCORMICK

And they start to back off... eyes glaring... and as Hardcastle smoothes down McCormick's collar, and McCormick pulls away.

> HARDCASTLE
> Kay... It's not what you think. We were just horsin' around.

> KAY
> I heard everything... Mark, you don't have to worry about the Judge marrying me... I'm leaving.

And as Kay starts to turn and leave.

> HARDCASTLE
> Like hell you are.
> (to McCormick)
> See what you started? Now apologize.

> KAY
> I think you should listen to Mark...

A beat as McCormick looks at Kay... trying to size her up... then looks at Hardcastle who's looking at her, too.

> McCORMICK
> Look, Kay, I apologize. Sometimes my Irish temper gets the better of me.

> KAY
> You don't need to apologize.

> McCORMICK
> No, Hardcastle's right. You're not going anywhere...We never sent an expectant mother out into the cold and we're not about to start.

And as Hardcastle and McCormick exchange a look, we:

DISSOLVE TO

CLOSE ON – ICE CUBES

As they're tossed into a glass by a BARTENDER. And we HEAR the sounds of party chatter in the b.g. And we…

WIDEN TO INCLUDE – INT. HARDCASTLE'S DEN – NIGHT

And a formal party in full swing. There are lawyers and judges and other Hardcastle cronies present. And a buffet table. And WAITERS passing drinks and hors d'oeuvres.

ANGLE – McCORMICK, KAY AND FRANK HARPER

In the middle of the room. McCormick's mind is still working overtime trying to figure Kay out.

>   HARPER
>   Have you and Milt set a date?

>   KAY
>   Well, we're not officially engaged.

>   McCORMICK
>   (smiling)
>   Not yet anyway.

>   HARPER
>   But Milt told me this was an engagement party.

>   KAY
>   (hedging)
>   You know how Milt is. Always two steps ahead of everyone.

And Harper looks puzzled.

>   McCORMICK
>   What Kay means is… their plans are still kind of indefinite.

>   HARPER
>   I see… well, don't wait too long to pin him down. Hardcastle's a
>   great catch.

McCormick and Kay trade looks. And Harper looks over at the buffet table.

>   HARPER
>   Think I'll help myself to a few more hors d'oeuvres… Have you
>   tried the rumaki? They're terrific… Get either of you anything?

                          KAY

No thanks.

And McCormick shakes his head. Looks over at Kay. And as Harper smiles and
moves off.

                          KAY

(to McCormick)
Thank you.

                      McCORMICK

For what?

                          KAY

For making an awkward situation less awkward.

                      McCORMICK
                          (nods)
I'm only looking out for Hardcastle.

                          KAY

He's lucky to have a friend like you.

                      McCORMICK

Yeah, he is… and as his friend, I'll do anything to make sure he
doesn't get hurt.

And Hardcastle walks over.

                      HARDCASTLE

Glad to see you two getting' along so well…
(to McCormick)
You don't mind if I steal Kay away for a minute?

                      McCORMICK

No, I think we finished our conversation.

Kay and McCormick exchange a look. Then, Hardcastle steers her across the room
and out the door. McCormick waits a beat. Then, as Harper approaches:

                       HARPER

Mark, you should really try one of these rumaki's…

                      McCORMICK

Later, Frank.

And McCormick sets down his drink and follows Hardcastle.

CUT TO

EXT. GULL'S WAY – PATIO – NIGHT

TRACK with Hardcastle and Kay as they exit the house.

> KAY
> Milt, we have to talk… and what about your guests?

> HARDCASTLE
> They can take care of themselves… c'mon.

And as Hardcastle leads Kay out toward the pool.

ANGLE – PHOTOGRAPHIC EQUIPMENT

On the patio table. CAMERA TILTS UP to MATT ARNOLD, the photographer, waiting. And as Hardcastle hustles Kay over.

> MATT
> Judge, we're going to have to hurry this up. I gotta be back in Beverly Hills to cover some rock video awards banquet.

> HARDCASTLE

Ready whenever you are.

> KAY
> Ready for what?

> HARDCASTLE
> To have our picture taken.

Matt picks up his camera… adjusts the lens… and we can't help but notice McCormick, in the B.G., watching.

> KAY
> (panicked)
> I take a terrible picture.

> HARDCASTLE
> Someone as pretty as you has to be photogenic.

                    MATT
Not to worry… everybody looks great in my stills… I happen to
be a prize-winning photojournalist… thanks to the Judge and some
"stories" he sent my way.

                  HARDCASTLE
And that's why you're gonna make sure this picture makes the papers.

                    KAY
I can't have my picture in the paper.

                    MATT
(to HC)
I can't promise front page.

                  HARDCASTLE
Try the Society page.

                    MATT
Maybe "Metro."

                  HARDCASTLE
You owe me… Besides, this is only the second time I ever met
somebody I'm really proud of.

Hardcastle looks at Kay. Matt focuses the lens. And as Kay struggles to move away.

                    KAY
No.

And Hardcastle puts his arm around her.

                    MATT
Say happily ever after…

And Matt takes the picture of Hardcastle and Kay.

ANGLE – McCORMICK

Watching as the FLASH POPS… And we:

                                        SMASH CUT TO

CLOSE ON – A PHOTOGRAPH OF HARDCASTLE AND KAY

On the "society" page of a Los Angeles newspaper. And the CAMERA PULLS BACK TO REVEAL that we are:

INT. VINCENT'S MANSION – DAY

And Vincent lowers the paper.

> VINCENT (re: photo)
> Photographs never did you justice.

And as he tosses the newspaper on the desk, we:

SMASH CUT TO

CLOSE ON – A COPY OF THE SAME NEWSPAPER

On the seat of the corvette.

PULL BACK TO INCLUDE – INT. CORVETTE – DAY

And McCormick on stake-out detail outside Kay's apartment. At that exact moment he looks up to discover:

ANGLE – KAY

As she steps out of her apartment, crosses the courtyard to her car, gets in, switches on the engine, backs out of the driveway and drives off.

RESUME – McCORMICK

He gets out and heads toward the building.

OMIT

EXT. – KAY'S APARTMENT

McCormick moves to the front door, picks the lock and opens the door.

INT. KAY'S APARTMENT

McCormick enters and looks around. There's a sofa, table, couple of chairs. And a bookshelf with a couple of medical texts, novels, magazines. And as McCormick crosses to the bedroom door.

OMIT

INT. – BEDROOM

McCormick moves in and opens the closet.

POV – THE CLOSET

Clothes… price tags hanging from some of the sleeves… and several brand new pairs of shoes.

RESUME – McCormick

As he crosses over to the desk. Rummages through the drawers and pulls out an official looking document… a medical license.

> McCORMICK
> (re: license)
> A medical license?…Dr. Blair McKenzie… Surgeon… San Francisco General… That's strange.

McCormick pockets the license. Tries to slide the drawer shut… it sticks… he gives it an extra shove… rattles the ashtray that's sitting on top of the desk… and for the first time McCormick focuses on…

CLOSE ON – THE ASH TRAY

And two cigar butts.

RESUME – McCORMICK

As he makes the inevitable conclusion…Kay is entertaining a man other than Hardcastle. And we:

                                                    CUT TO

OMIT

EXT BOUTIQUE – DAY

To establish.

> STORE MANAGER (V.O.)
> Kay's not on the floor… but I could check the stock room.

INT. BOUTIQUE – DAY

Strictly top dollar. A high class clientele. And McCormick standing at the counter with the STORE MANAGER.

                              McCORMICK
        I'd appreciate that, thanks.

And as the Manager's about to start away.

ANGLE – ART McGOWAN

As he muscles his way around McCormick and steps up to the counter. He's smoking
a cigar.

                              McGOWAN
        (to MC)
        Excuse me... I'm looking for Kay Phillips.

And at that instant, McGowan looks over and sees:

HIS POV – KAY

As she steps out of the stock room.

RESUME SCENE

McCormick quickly ducks behind a rack of dresses. And as McGowan crosses over
to Kay.

                              McGOWAN
        (to Manager)
        I see her... thanks.

McCORMICK'S POV – KAY AND McGOWAN

As he takes her arm. And they exchange a few words. Kay nods.

ANOTHER ANGLE

As McGowan follows Kay over to the counter. She steps behind it, reaches down,
pulls out her purse, then:

                              KAY
        (to Manager)
        I'm going to lunch.

And as the Manager looks around for McCormick.

MANAGER
There was someone asking for you... I don't see him now... I guess it wasn't important.

KAY
I'll see you later then.

And as Kay and McGowan exit...

ANGLE – A CUSTOMER

With an armload of dresses. She WIPES CAMERA to REVEAL –

NEW ANGLE – McCORMICK

Peering out through a rack of evening dresses. His look says it all... Kay's a two-timing golddigger. McCormick plays the beat, then:

OMIT

FADE OUT

END OF ACT TWO

ACT THREE

FADE IN:

EXT. GULLS WAY – DAY

To establish.

McCORMICK (V.O.)
What more do I have to do to convince you... I got the evidence.

INT. HARDCASTLE'S DEN – DAY

And Hardcastle and McCormick in mid-argument.

HARDCASTLE
What you've got is a lot of explainin' to do.

McCORMICK
Me? Kay's the one who needs to do the explaining starting with... who's Dr. Blair McKenzie? Who's this guy she's been seeing?

HARDCASTLE

One call to Frank Harper and I could have you arrested for breaking and entering.

McCORMICK

I know what you're doing... Denying the facts... Transferring your anger from Kay to me... I'm not taking it personally.

HARDCASTLE

You're worried I'm gonna turn your bedroom into a nursery.

McCORMICK

Is that what you think?

HARDCASTLE

Yeah... I think you're worried you're gonna lose this cushy life you got goin' for yourself.

McCORMICK

You call this cushy?! Cleaning garages, waxing cars, trimming hedges, getting shot at every other day... Let me tell you... life'd be a hell of a lot easier in the French Foreign Legion.

HARDCASTLE

In case you hadn't noticed, this isn't a prison and I'm no warden... so you're free to take a hike.

McCORMICK

Well, you could've fooled me.

HARDCASTLE

You want my permission?...you got it... and your walking papers.

McCORMICK

Fine.

HARDCASTLE

Fine.

A beat as McCormick looks at Hardcastle, tries to cool down, then:

McCORMICK

I'm telling you, Judge, it's not your baby.

HARDCASTLE

And I'm tellin' you... I want you out of this house.

                    McCORMICK
Well, hallelujah… I've been looking for a way out of this inden-
tured servitude since the day I got here.

And McCormick starts to leave.

                    HARDCASTLE
I'm gonna inventory every item in the gatehouse… and if anything's
missin'…

McCormick stops just before the door and turns to Hardcastle.

                    McCORMICK
(insulted)
Hey, Hardcase, I lived with you for three years… I thought by
now you at least trusted me with the furniture.

ANGLE – KAY

As she enters carrying two glasses of lemonade.

                    KAY
I made some lemonade.

And as Kay hands a glass to McCormick and he throws Hardcastle a cold look.

                    McCORMICK
You don't mind, do you?…if I swipe it, you can always have me
arrested for grand theft glass.

Whereupon McCormick heels around and exits. Kay looks at Hardcastle. We HEAR
the FRONT DOOR SLAM. Hardcastle turns away. And as Kay crosses over to him.

                    KAY
What's going on?

                    HARDCASTLE
It doesn't concern you.

Hardcastle takes the glad from Kay.

                    KAY
I think it does.

Hardcastle slams the glass down on the desk next to the medical license. And Kay
sees the license and reacts.

HARDCASTLE

McCormick has no business prying into my life. And he oughta know that.

KAY

What about my life?

HARDCASTLE

It's the same thing.

KAY

Milt, I could never forgive myself if I thought a misplaced sense of loyalty made you chose me over your best friend.

HARDCASTLE

That's not why I'm doin' it.

KAY

You have this wonderfully old-fashioned sense of what's right... of honor and integrity.

HARDCASTLE

This has nothing to do with integrity.

KAY

It has everything to do with integrity.

And we play the moment, then:

CUT TO

EXT. THE GATEHOUSE

We PICK UP McCormick carrying a suitcase. He makes his way over to the corvette, tosses the bag in, gets in, guns the engine and SCREAMS out of the driveway.

EXT. HIGHWAY

As the corvette explodes out of the driveway and onto the highway PAST CAMERA

INT. CORVETTE – MOVING

As McCormick jams up the volume on the radio. Grips the steering wheel in anger.

INT. INTERSECTION

As the corvette approaches. Suddenly McCormick cranks a vicious left hand turn, traversing three traffic lanes and heads off in a different direction.

CUT TO

CLOSE ON – THE LEMONADE GLASS

As McCormick sets it down on Harper's desk.

                    HARPER (V.O.)
          You want me to do what whit this glass?

WIDEN TO INCLUDE – INT. HARPER'S OFFICE

And Frank Harper seated a this desk. Across the desk is McCormick and we can see that he's on a short fuse.

                    McCORMICK
          Look, it's very simple… Kay's fingerprints are on the glass. All you
          have to do is run them through your files.
          (a bit tentative)
          And maybe the FBI files.

                    HARPER
          I thought you only needed a blood test to get a marriage license.

                    McCORMICK
          I'm asking this as a favor. If not for me… then for Hardcastle.

                    HARPER
          Did Milt put you up to this?

                    McCORMICK
          No… he doesn't know anything about it… and I'd like to keep it
          that way.

                    HARPER
          (rising)
          I don't get it. I only talked to the woman for a coupla' minutes the
          other night at the party, but she seemed like a nice person.

                    McCormick
          Just run the prints.

HARPER
(a beat)
Okay. Okay. And if I come up with anything... which I'm sure I
won't... I'll give you a call.

McCORMICK
(shrugs)
I better call you.

HARPER
Why? Is there somethin' wrong with your phone?

McCORMICK
Yeah... I don't have one.

And as Harper and McCormick exchange a look, we:

CUT TO

OMIT

INT./EXT. THE CORVETTE – NIGHT

Parked in some out-of-the-way place. And McCormick, covered with a jacket, asleep
in the driver's seat. And as he stirs...

CUT TO

INT. HARDCASTLE'S DEN – NIGHT

It takes a beat for our eyes to adjust to the dark, then we can make out Hardcastle
seated behind his desk. He hesitates, then opens the top drawer, pulls out the
medical license. He stares at it a moment, then quickly replaces it, closes the drawer.
We play the moment, then:

DISSOLVE TO

STOCK – EXT. AIRPORT (LAX) – DAY

To establish.

P.A. ANNOUNCER
Arriving passengers on TWA Flight 103 from San Francisco...
proceed to the Baggage Claim Area... Carrousel Three.

INT. GATE AREA

Where we see a few tourists, businessmen, airline personnel. And we PICK UP Vincent and Crowder as they move through the terminal.

> VINCENT
> What did you find out about this Milton Hardcastle?

> CROWDER
> He's everything you're not.

> VINCENT
> What's that supposed to mean?

> CROWDER
> Strictly legit. Ex-cop. Retired Judge. Pillar of the community. God's gift to law enforcement.

> VINCENT
> I wonder if he knows anything?

> CROWDER
> Why take any chances? I bill by the day… it won't cost you.

Vincent gives Crowder a hard look… for all his underworld dealings, it still offends something deep in Vincent to have to deal with low-lifes like Wylie Crowder.

> VINCENT
> Let's stick to the plan… You do your job, then meet me at Blair's apartment and we'll clean the place out.

And as they move off past a phone booth, we:

CUT TO

OMIT

INT. HARPER'S OFFICE – DAY

Harper on the phone. He's holding a very official looking government I.D. card. And as a hand REACHES INTO FRAME and flecks the ashes from a cigar into an ashtray.

> HARPER
> That's right… Inspector Art McGowan.
> (listens; then)
> San Francisco office… fifteen years… no, that's all I need to know…
> thanks.

Harper hangs up the phone. The CAMERA PANS TO REVEAL McGowan standing next to the desk.

> HARPER
>
> Well, you check out.

And as Harper hands the I.D. card back to him.

> HARPER
>
> Just doin' my job.

> McGOWAN
>
> (smiles)
> You said you were a friend of Mr. McCormick's.

> HARPER
>
> That's right. And when I said I'd run the prints for him, the last thing I expected was a visit from the F.B.I.

> McGOWAN
>
> Well, your friend has stumbled into the middle of a federal narcotics investigation.

> HARPER
>
> What's Kay Phillips'... I mean Blair McKenzie's involvement?

> McGOWAN
>
> A year ago she became involved with a guy named David Vincent... an eligible, well-to-do San Francisco businessman... owner of a major shipping line.

> HARPER
>
> And...

> McGOWAN
>
> And it turns out, Mr. Vincent is using his company to import pure Columbian flake... we're talking major league... $20 million deals every coupla months.

> HARPER
>
> Was she in on it?

> McGOWAN
>
> No and he wanted it that way... but then he slipped up... iced his partner in the shipping company... one of our agents... in

front of her... well, she freaked... ran to the police... they called us... we all wanted a piece of Vincent.

> HARPER

And she took off.

> McGOWAN

Couldn't take the heat... The DEA and the Bureau were pushin' for protective custody and a new identity after the trial, but all she wanted was to get back to her medical practice.

> HARPER
> (rising)

Did you know she's engaged to be married?

> McGOWAN

Read about it in the paper... frankly, we'd lost her trail until we saw that photo of her and her fiancé.

> HARPER

Milt Hardcastle

> McGOWAN

Right... We've had her under surveillance since then... made contact once or twice... were waitin' for Vincent to make his next move.

> HARPER

Well, before he makes it... don't you think we oughta fill Hardcastle in... Kay and he could be in a lot danger.

> McGOWAN

No can do. My orders are to sit back and wait for Vincent show his hand.

And as Harper heads for the door.

> HARPER

You do whatever you want... I'm gonna fill Milt in on what's goin' down.

And as McGowan picks up the phone.

> McGOWAN

One call Lieutenant... that's all it'll take to stop you dead in the water.

And Harper heels around. McGowan hangs up the phone.

> McGOWAN
> This is my ballgame… we play by my rules.

And off Harper's look of frustration, we:

                                                        CUT TO

EXT. GULL'S WAY – THE BEACH – DAY

As Hardcastle and Kay walk along the sand. She looks at him a beat then:

> KAY
> I'm leaving. Leaving L.A.

We sense that Hardcastle half-expected this.

> HARDCASTLE
> If you're sure that's what you want… I can't stop you.

> KAY
> I'm sure.

And Hardcastle stops walking. Turns toward the ocean. A beat, then Kay moves over to him.

> HARDCASTLE
> I want to pay for the baby.

> KAY
> (with difficulty)
> The baby has nothing to do with you, Milt.

And Hardcastle takes a beat to digest this… but we sense that he's known it for some time.

> HARDCASTLE
> (a look)
> You're not just sayin' that to let me off the hook… are you?

> KAY
> I only wish I was.

And Hardcastle slides his hands deep into his pockets and walks away. Kay follows.

EXT. GULLS WAY – ON CROWDER

As he moves across the lawn. He's carrying a rifle.

EXT. THE GATEHOUSE – ON McCORMICK

As he exits with a couple of boxes and moves toward the driveway and the corvette.

ANGLE – CROWDER

As he looks down and sees:

ANGLE – HARDCASTLE AND KAY

As they make their way back toward the house.

ANGLE – McCORMICK

As he shoves the boxes into the car. He takes one last look around and in the B.G. sees:

HIS POV – CROWDER

Moving into position.

ANGLE – McCORMICK

As he moves forward to investigate.

OMIT

ANGLE – CROWDER

He waits for the perfect moment.

ANGLE – McCORMICK

As he sees Crowder take aim.

> McCORMICK
> Hey! What do you think you're doing?!

And McCormick takes off. Crowder tries to get a shot off... he's just about to fire... McCormick tackles him from behind... and the gun goes off.

ANGLE – HARDCASTLE AND KAY

And Hardcastle's hit... and he goes down... and Kay reacts.

ANOTHER ANGLE

As Crowder lands a punch and takes off to his feet, looks after Crowder, then looks down at the beach.

HIS POV – HARDCASTLE

Lying in the sand.

ANGLE – McCORMICK

As he rushes down the side of the hill to the beach.

EXT. THE BEACH

As McCormick hot foots it over to Hardcastle who is now sitting up. Kay has taken his handkerchief, made a tourniquet for his arm.

> McCORMICK
> Judge... Judge... Are you alright?

> HARDCASTLE
> I'm fine... The guy was a lousy shot... Well, don't just stand there... call the police.

> McCORMICK
> First, I'm calling a doctor.

> KAY
> You don't need to call a doctor.

> McCORMICK
> He needs medical attention.

> KAY
> He has medical attention... I'm a doctor.

And as Hardcastle and McCormick react.

> KAY
> (to HC)
> I think it's time I told you about my past... and this time you have no choice... you have to listen.

Play the moment, then:

FADE OUT

END OF ACT THREE

ACT FOUR

FADE IN:

INT. HARDCASTLE'S DEN – DAY

Hardcastle's arm is bandaged. He's sitting in a chair. Kay is pacing in front of him.

KAY

I was introduced to David at a hospital benefit dinner... we were raising money for the new surgical wing... he's always been a major contributor.

And she looks at Hardcastle, gets no reaction, continues.

KAY

He called me up the next day... we started dating... everything was really good... until that damn night.
(beat)
I had a patient scheduled for a by-pass... she developed a secondary infection... I couldn't operate... so I went home early.
(a look to Hardcastle; then)
I heard loud voices coming from the den... David and his partner had been arguing for weeks, he wouldn't tell me why...

And Kay exchanges a look with Hardcastle.

KAY

I went to the door... looked in...oh my God... I saw David shoot Carlyle.

HARDCASTLE

Did you go to the police?

KAY

I had no choice... I'd witnessed a murder... but it all got so complicated... David's partner turned out to be an undercover police officer... and, Milt, you know what it's like when an officer gets killed... it's like the whole force goes out of its mind... and I was at the center of all that insanity.

HARDCASTLE

Is that why you ran?

And Kay moves over to Hardcastle... kneels down next to his chair.

KAY

I don't know... I guess I was scared... I thought being a surgeon meant I could handle anything... What's two federal agencies and a police department pressuring me into a witness protection program?

HARDCASTLE

Probably unconstitutional.

KAY

Oh, they were willing to have me testify without their protection, but that scared the hell out of me, too... I was getting death threats sometimes two, three times a day.
(beat)
... But you know what really got to me, the way they kept looking at me... like I was a criminal.

HARDCASTLE

Cops have a tendency to do that.

KAY

And you know the rest... I left San Francisco... and Blair McKenzie... tried to start a new life...
(a look to HC)
I tried to tell you.

HARDCASTLE

(a beat)
You didn't try hard enough.

And Hardcastle gets up and exits the room.

CUT TO

EXT. GULLS WAY – PATIO

McCormick's looking down at the ocean. And Hardcastle walks over to him. They exchange a look... neither knows what to say. Finally:

McCORMICK

How's the arm?

> HARDCASTLE

Bullet just nicked me... don't feel a thing.

> McCORMICK

You were lucky.

> HARDCASTLE

Yeah.
(beat)
Thanks.

> McCORMICK

For what?...If I was in better shape I'd have tackled the guy before the got the shot off.

> HARDCASTLE

No... You were right... It's not my baby.

And McCormick looks at Hardcastle and senses his disappointment.

> McCORMICK

Hey, Judge, a guy your age can always have another baby.

> HARDCASTLE

Sure... but y'know, I've been thinkin'... and the way I see it... I got my hands full with just you.

Play the moment, then:

ANGLE – HARPER AND McGOWAN

As they cross the patio towards Hardcastle and McCormick.

> HARPER

Milt, I got here as soon as I could... you okay?

> HARDCASTLE

Yeah.

NEW ANGLE

As McCormick reacts to McGowan.

> McCORMICK

Judge, that's him... that's the guy.

                        HARDCASTLE
What?

                         McCORMICK
That's the guy Kay's having the affair with.

Hardcastle looks at McCormick, then:

                        HARDCASTLE
(to Harper; re: McGowan)
Who is this?

                          HARPER
Sorry.
(making introductions)
Milt Hardcastle... Mark McCormick meet Agent McGowan of
the Federal Bureau of Investigations.

And as Hardcastle and McGowan shake hands.

                         McCORMICK
She's having an affair with a fed...

                          McGOWAN
Look, I'm not having an affair with the woman... I'm just doin'
my job.

                        HARDCASTLE
(re: MC)
See, wiseguy... you'll have to excuse him, he's suspicious of everyone.

                         McCORMICK
Am I the only one that doesn't know what's going on?

                          McGOWAN
I'll be glad to fill you in, but first, I'd like to see Blair... ah, Kay.

                        HARDCASTLE
She's in the house... I'll show you the way.

And as Hardcastle starts toward the house.

                                                    CUT TO

INT. HARDCASTLE'S DEN – DAY

Harper and McGowan standing in the middle of the room. In the B.G. we PICK UP Hardcastle as he moves down the stairs. He is about to head into the den when McCormick enters from the kitchen.

> McCORMICK
>> She's not in the kitchen.

> HARDCASTLE
>> Not upstairs either.

And as they move into the den.

> HARDCASTLE
>> It looks like she took off.

> HARPER
>> She would've been a lot safer here.

> HARDCASTLE
>> (angry)
>> Don't you think I know that.

> McCORMICK
>> She probably went back to her apartment.

And as McGowan picks up the phone and offers it to Hardcastle.

> McGOWAN
>> Give her a call... Tell her we're coming over.

And as Hardcastle puts the receiver down.

> HARDCASTLE
>> Let's get something straight... the only thing we're gonna do is find Kay... not pressure her into doin' something she doesn't want to do.

> McGOWAN
>> Harper tells me you were a cop... so you understand... we need her testimony to nail Vincent... to shut down one of the major drug syndicates in the country.

> HARDCASTLE
>> Every person has their limit.

> McGOWAN
>
> That's Miss McKenzie's problem.

> HARDCASTLE
>
> I'm makin' it my problem... And we're wastin' time.

> HARPER
>
> Why don't we head over to her apartment... You can call her from the car.

> HARDCASTLE
>
> Let's go.

And as Hardcastle and Harper head out the door, McCormick eases up to McGowan.

> McCORMICK
>
> (re: HC)
> Step on his toes and Hardcastle's got a funny way of saying ouch.

And we play the beat, then:

CUT TO

EXT. N.D. SEDAN – MOVING

As Kay swings into the parking lot of her building. She gets out and moves toward her apartment.

OMIT

EXT. KAY'S APARTMENT

As she walks to the door. And we HEAR the PHONE RINGING. She unlocks the door and steps into:

INT. KAY'S APARTMENT

And she crosses over to the phone, starts to answer it, changes her mind, turns around and comes face-to face with:

ANGLE – VINCENT

And Vincent flashes a smile.

> VINCENT
>
> It's good to see you, Blair.

                              KAY

David...

                            VINCENT

You're looking well... I missed you.

                              KAY

What do you want?

                            VINCENT

I think you know.

And Vincent throws a look over at the bedroom door and we:

ANGLE – CROWDER

As he steps out of the bedroom. Levels a gun at Kay.

ANOTHER ANGLE

As Kay looks from Crowder to Vincent. And maybe she instinctively puts a hand
over her belly... shielding her baby.

                              KAY

David, please... just leave me alone.

                            VINCENT

I wish it was that simple... but you're holding the ace. (beat)
Remember that weekend we spent in Carmel? At the Sea Side
Inn. I can't stop thinking about it.

                              KAY

Me, too.

                            VINCENT

You're only saying that because Wylie here has a gun pointed at you.

                              KAY

No.

                            VINCENT

Don't lie to me Kay... it's beneath you... I read the papers... I
know all about your engagement to that Judge... If you hadn't
fallen in love... I might never have found you.
(to Crowder)
Let's go.

And as Crowder crosses over to Kay and takes her arm.

                    VINCENT
        I want you to know Blair... I'm sorry.

And Kay resists as Crowder pushes her towards the door. And we:

                                              CUT TO

OMIT

EXT. KAY'S APARTMENT

As Crowder, a gun on Kay, starts leading her out. Vincent follows. Silent signals pass between Crowder and Vincent conveying there's no one in sight. They head for an N.D. Sedan parked in the parking lot.

ANOTHER ANGLE

And we see Harper's car pull into the parking lot. The men pile out. McCormick looks over and sees Kay being led to a car.

                    McCORMICK
        Judge.

And as Hardcastle reacts and starts for Kay, McGowan draws his weapon.

                    McGOWAN
        (to Vincent)
        Hold it! FBI!

ANGLE – VINCENT AND CROWDER

As they react. Crowder throws Kay toward Vincent, levels his gun and gets off a good five rounds of artillery exploding the windshield of Harper's car.

OMIT

A SERIES OF SHOTS – DIRECTOR'S SEQUENCE

As McCormick grabs Hardcastle and drags him down behind another car. Harper crouches down behind his car and draws his weapon. McGowan returns the fire. Crowder takes a slug in the shoulder and goes down. And as McGowan rises and starts toward Vincent.

                    McGOWAN
        It's over Vincent... Let her go.

ANGLE – VINCENT

As he pulls a gun, grabs Kay and points it at her.

> VINCENT
> She's my insurance out of here.

ANGLE – McGOWAN

As he takes aim… appears ready to take Vincent out. And Hardcastle puts a restraining hand on him… might even be ready to strike out at him.

> HARDCASTLE
> You're startin' to get on my nerves.

> McGOWAN
> You're interfering with a federal officer in the line of duty.

And as McCormick moves over.

> HARDCASTLE
> So sue me…
> (to McCormick)
> Watch this guy for me, McCormick.

And as Hardcastle starts to walk toward Kay and Vincent… his arms raised… and Harper crosses over to McCormick.

> McCORMICK
> (to McGowan)
> I told you not to step on his toes.

ANGLE – KAY AND VINCENT

As Hardcastle approaches.

> HARDCASTLE
> Put the gun down and let her go.

> VINCENT
> Give me one good reason why I should.

> HARDCASTLE
> She's pregnant.

                            VINCENT
        (laughing)
        That's a good one.

                            HARDCASTLE
        I'm tellin' you the truth, Vincent. She's having your baby.

And as Vincent looks at Kay and she looks at Hardcastle.

                            VINCENT
        What's he talking about?

                            KAY
        It's true.

                            HARDCASTLE
        You gotta admit that's a pretty good reason to give yourself up.
        (edges still closer)
        Y'know, when I thought it was mine... somethin' changed... I
        would've done anything for that kid... I don't know... maybe a
        man always thinks he can live again through his children... have a
        better life... not make the same mistakes...
        (beat)
        I know what I'd do if I were in your shoes... Give yourself a sec-
        ond chance, Vincent... let her go.

ANGLE – VINCENT

As he takes a beat to consider, then lowers his gun and releases Kay. And as Harper
and McGowan move over and take Crowder and him into custody.

NEW ANGLE

McCormick watches as Kay slowly walks over to Hardcastle. And as she throws her
arms around him and hugs him, we:

OMIT

                                                            FADE OUT

                        END OF ACT FOUR

                            TAG

OMIT

EXT. AIRPORT – DAY

To establish.

OMIT

INT. GATE AREA

As Hardcastle hands a boarding pass and a huge stack of magazines to Kay. Kay smiles.

> KAY
> San Francisco's only an hour-and-a-half flight. I can't possibly read all this.

> HARDCASTLE
> I didn't want you to get bored… Besides, the company's not gonna be all that great.

HIS POV – McGOWAN

Standing with McCormick nearby.

RESUME SCENE

> KAY
> Inspector McGowan's only doing his job.

> HARDCASTLE
> Yeah, well, don't let him bully you into anything.

> KAY
> I know what I have to do now.

> HARDCASTLE
> Testify against Vincent.

> KAY
> Take responsibility for my life… Do what you would do if you were in my place.

> HARDCASTLE
> You never know what another person's gonna do.

> KAY
> Well, in your case, I think I can be 99 and 9/10's percent sure.

NEW ANGLE

As McGowan approaches.

> McGOWAN
>
>   It's time to go.

And as McGowan shakes hands with Hardcastle.

> McGOWAN
> Thanks for all your help, Hardcastle.

> HARDCASTLE
> Yeah... You take good care of her.

> McGOWAN
>
>   You got my word.

And McGowan looks at Kay, then moves off a discreet distance.

> KAY
>   I guess this is goodbye.

> HARDCASTLE
>   Guess so.

And Kay kisses Hardcastle.

> KAY
> Thank you for everything... and I'm sorry.

> HARDCASTLE
> (smiles)
> You must've seen that stupid movie a few years back... you re-
> member what they said.

> KAY
> Yeah... and it was a stupid movie.

Kay smiles at Hardcastle, then crosses over to McGowan. And as they head through
the door past the TICKET AGENT... down the ramp... and disappear.

ANGLE – McCORMICK

As he moves alongside Hardcastle who's watching Kay go. Finally, they exchange a look, then turn around and start to exit. And as McCormick puts a consoling hand on Hardcastle's shoulder, we:

OMIT

FREEZE FRAME

THE END

Odds and Ends

We have just a few things lying around, so we thought we'd share before the fire marshals come calling.

Press release issued for premiere. Notice McCormick is called "Skip" according to Paramount.

511

Unfortunately, Mark's identity problems didn't stop there; pre-production was a difficult time for the ex-race car driver turned thief.

Very early publicity picture, apparently before the wardrobe department got word it was Hardcastle and McCormick.

But with the help of a marker pen, eventually they got it right.

Back in 1984, fan Mac Patterson was on vacation in California and had the opportunity to watch a day of location filming. The day he visited, "One of the Girls from Accounting" was in production. He snapped a few photos to immortalize the day.

Brian Keith arrives on location, accompanied by his wife, Victoria.

Daniel Hugh Kelly crosses the street from his dressing room.

Kelly walking with crew members; stunt double Gary Hymes can be seen in the background.

SUNDAY

Hardcastle and McCormick

Milton C. Hardcastle (Brian Keith) is not your typical retired judge. When he was on the bench, his judicial robe covered a gaudy Hawaiian shirt, running shorts and grubby tennis shoes. He often shoots baskets at night and has a resting pulse rate of 64—not bad for a man of 65. But don't let all that stuff fool you. "Hardcase," as he's called, is an ex-judge with a mission. He may be off the bench, but he intends to go on dispensing justice, frontier-style—to all those cocaine dealers, mob killers and slimeballs who got off on a technicality, as when a careless cop forgot to read someone his rights. In this series Hardcase will team up with a good-looking, smart-mouth ex-con ("I figure it takes one to catch one") who's also a racing driver, Mark "Skid" McCormick (Daniel-Hugh Kelly). "Skid" Mark—get it? So, is America ready for a cross between *The Lone Ranger* and *The Dukes of Hazzard*? Could be. On the other hand, you have the right to remain silent. . . ABC. *Pictured (l.-r.): Daniel-Hugh Kelly, Brian Keith.*

The week prior to the show's premiere, *TV Guide* featured a short preview column.

38   TV GUIDE SEPTEMBER 10, 1983

TV Guide also featured Hardcastle and McCormick on its cover, including this Canadian edition. Cover courtesy of *TV Guide*, Canada.

And on a regular basis, we could count on the television listings to include a dose of intriguing art work to lure us toward the week's episode.

"Man in a Glass House"

"Prince of Fat City"

"One of the Girls from Accounting"

FEBRUARY 4, 1985
PROGRAM CHART IS ON A-68

22 28 31 67 WP3 WILD, WILD
WORLD OF ANIMALS
Information on the mental processes
of dolphins and whales is drawn from
comments by scientists and whalers.
25 SALE OF THE CENTURY—Game
32 EVENING EXCHANGE
—Discussion
65 CAROL BURNETT AND FRIENDS
—Comedy
Jim Nabors is the guest. In a sketch, a
soldier (Tim Conway) declines a medal

Monday
7:30 PM
from his king and queen (Carol, Har-
vey Korman), insisting he'd rather
have a pony.
53 54 VIRGINIA LEGISLATURE
CNN CROSSFIRE
—Buchanan/Braden
ESM COLLEGE BASKETBALL
REPORT
HBO FRAGGLE ROCK—Children
Boober travels to the Cave of the
Shadows to collect plants.
NIK DANGERMOUSE—Cartoon

"Hardcastle, Hardcastle,
Hardcastle, and McCormick"

Daniel Hugh Kelly on location during "Duet for Two Wind Instruments" and "Hotshoes". Photos courtesy Les Sheldon.

The fictional address of Gull's Way migrated north slowly during the three years of the series. Originally, Hardcastle's estate was supposed to be the entirely invented "Knoll House", in land-locked Pasadena. By "The Black Widow", Gull's Way was said to be in Santa Monica. Eventually it was "101 PCH, Malibu", though in one episode ("Yankee Clipper") a letter arrived addressed merely "Gull's Way, Pacific Coast Highway, Malibu, California".

On two occasions, though ("Hate the Picture, Love the Frame" and "Too Rich and Too Thin"), and with noticeably different handwriting, insert shots revealed the real location of the Lone Ranger's hideout:

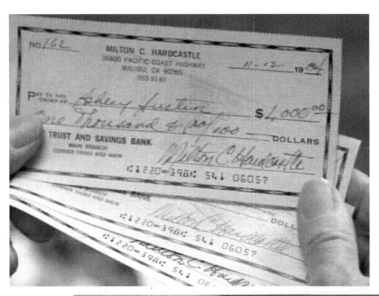

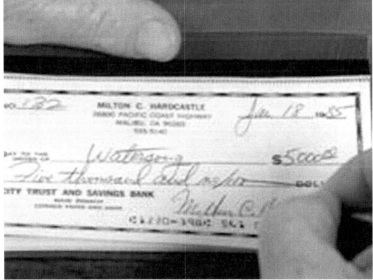

Call sheet for October 22, 1985, "Conventional Warfare".

Test Your Knowledge of *Hardcastle and McCormick*

No, we didn't mention there'd be a quiz. It's all right though, "they mark on a curve now" (and if you know which episode that comes from, you should do just fine).*

1.   In which episode did the judge's old truck finally expire? (one point)

2.   Name three of the people McCormick knew as fellow inmates. (one point each name)

3.   What was Hardcastle's nickname when he played college basketball? (two points)

4.   List one of Sonny Daye's previous names. (one point for each of three)

5.   What is the title of Joe Cadillac's book? (one point)

6.   What is the tune played on the music boxes in "Whatever Happened to Guts"? (one point)

7.   What animals are the poachers hunting when discovered by Taylor Walsh in "She Ain't Deep but She Sure Runs Fast"? (one point)

8.   Name the two comedy clubs in "What's So Funny?" (one point each)

9.   What is the name of the game show in "Games People Play"? (one point)

10. What brand of rum does Hardcastle give to bailiff Charlie Masaryk in "Poker Night"? (one point)

11. Name seven different types of conveyance used in the chase scenes (no, you can't use different models of cars). (one point each for six and five bonus points for the really unusual one)

12. In which episodes do we see Mark wearing a towel? (two points for the first one, chronologically, and four for the second)

---

* "Relax, they mark on a curve now." Milt to Mark in "Third Down and Twenty to Life". If you got that, it's worth another half-point.

13. Where is McCormick headed on his free weekend in "Mirage a Trois"? (one point)

14. What drink does Aggie Wainwright suggest that the judge try? (one point)

15. What item does Mark go out to buy in "Hate the Picture, Love the Frame"? (one point)

16. What are the names of the two adorable tots in "Angie's Choice"? (one half point each)

17. What law firm does McCormick work for as a paralegal? (one point)

18. What is the Black Widow's real name? (one point)

19. What name does Kathy Kasternack joke that she will adopt to have a little more glamour? (two points)

20. In the restaurant in "Do Not Go Gentle", what dish do the guys have? (one point)

21. In "Rolling Thunder", what fish does Sarah say the judge likes? (one point)

22. How does Mark want his steak tartare cooked? (one point)

23. What stuffed animal do we see in "The Crystal Duck"? (one point)

24. What is Kiki Cutter's husband's nickname? (one point, plus a bonus point available)

25. When Mark tosses his watch into David Waverly's aquarium, what else does he drop in? (one point)

26. Name any three ingredients in the macrobiotic dish in "Mr. Hardcastle Goes to Washington." (one point for each, plus two bonus points for each extra ingredient you remember)

27. What streamside snack does McCormick have in "The Careerbreaker"? (one point)

28. In "Eye of the Beholder", what is the name/title of the leprechaun leader? (one point)

29. In "Too Rich and Too Thin", what professional baseball team does Mark claim he played for? (two points)

30. A passenger dies from arsenic poisoning in "Something's Going On On This Train". How is the arsenic administered to him? (one point)

31. What is the name of the street gang in "Prince of Fat City"? (one point)

32. What garnish for champagne is shown in "If You Could See What I See"? (one point)

33. In which three episodes did Victoria Young make an appearance? (one point for each episode, a bonus point for each of her characters' name/title in each episode)

34. What liquid refreshment do the aunts order at the airport? (one point)

35. In his tall tale in "Surprise on Seagull Beach", what is McCormick's surfing buddy's name? (one point)

36. In the very first scene of "Rolling Thunder", what do we see Mark drinking? (one point)

37. What does Hardcastle name his yacht? (one point)

38. What is the judge's niece's last name? (one point)

39. Name three people other than McCormick who have driven the Coyote. (two points each)

40. Notes for what test are scribbled on Mark's arm in "Third Down and Twenty Years to Life"? (one point)

41. Dennis Franz guest-stars in which two episodes? (one point each)

42. What Army rank did the judge hold in World War II? (one point)

43. What famous sports announcer appears as himself in "The Boxer"? (one point)

44. What song is sung by a contestant in "You're 16, You're Beautiful, and You're His"? (one point)

45. Which musical instrument does Hardcastle play? (one point)

46. Which instruments does McCormick play in "Too Rich and Too Thin"? (one point for each of three)

47. Where is the judge shot? (one point, plus a bonus half-point available)

48. In "Pennies from a Dead Man's Eyes", what is the name of the record company? (one point)

49. In which episodes does the judge wear a satin basketball jacket and what two teams are represented? (one point for each episode and one for each team named)

50. What is the name of Arthur Farnell's girlfriend? (one point)

51. How does Chip Meadows supposedly die? (one point)

52. Kenneth Mars plays what two characters? (one point each)

53. Name the three places in which Hardcastle has attended a judges' convention. (one point each)

ANSWERS:

1. "Hotshoes".

2. Your choices include: Teddy Hollins, Buddy Denton, Randy Hopke, Weed Randall, Fix Henderson, Pops Witherspoon. (Five bonus points for remembering Arnie de la Rosa from "Scared Stiff".)

3. "Stumpy" Hardcastle.

4. Tommy Knight, Tommy Raye, or Micky Thompson.

5. *Without Sin.*

6. "My Heart Belongs to Daddy".

7. Bighorn sheep.

8. The Grin Bin and the Laugh Factory.

9. "One Million Dollar Trivia Master".

10. El Papagayo.

11. Jet ski, bus, boat, truck, car, motorcycle, helicopter, horse. Award yourself one point for each of the first six and five bonus points for remembering the horse.

12. "Once Again with Vigorish" and "Georgia Street Motors" (yep, he grabbed a towel on the way out to augment the sheet).

13. Catalina Island.

14. A San Rio colada.

15. An angel for the treetop.

16. There were no adorable tots in "Angie's Choice", but the kids were named Nicky and Lindsey Bloom.

17. Malcolm, Hughes and Dewitt.

18. Tina Grey.

19. Kathy Kastenberger.

20. Hot roast duck salad.

21. Halibut

22. Medium.

23. Judge Gault's tiger.

24. Sammy O'Connell is known as "Sidewinder"; take an extra point if you also remembered "Slammin' Sammy".

25. The keys to his rental car.

26. Soy beans, wild rice, seaweed, tofu, bean sprouts.

27. Peanut butter and crackers.

28. Cluracan.

29. Tokyo Giants.

30. It's injected into an éclair.

31. The Hub City Cobras.

32. A strawberry.

33. "Did You See the One That Got Away?", "You Would Cry, Too", and "Chip Off the Ol' Milt". Her name was Rosie Carlucci in the first two, and she was an aerobics dance instructor in "Chip".

34. Rye, straight up, ginger back.

35. "Long Board" Larry Morgan.

36. White wine.

37. The Fury.

38. Warren's last name is Wyngate.

39. Howard Kaye in "Really Neat Cars", Bill Bauer in "The Yankee Clipper", and the judge himself.

40. American History.

41. "There Goes the Neighborhood" and "Did You See the One that Got Away".

42. Captain.

43. Chick Hearn.

44. "I Think It's Gonna Rain Today".

45. Trombone.

46. Tambourine, kazoo, drums.

47. The heart, more specifically the right ventricle. Half a point extra if you also answered, "in the courtroom".

48. Jadestone Records.

49. In "The Birthday Present", it's the Lakers, and for "In the Eye of the Beholder", it's the Celtics.

50. Trish.

51. A fall from a mountain.

52. Burt Schneider, investigator, in "Too Rich and Too Thin" and Gerald Hardcastle, brother, in "Brother, Can You Spare a Crime".

53. Atlantic City, mentioned in "Ties My Father Sold Me", Hawaii, in "You Would Cry, Too, If It Happened to You", Palm Springs, in "Conventional Warfare".

Ratings

0 – 25 points: You've just begun to enjoy the episodes and are look-
                   ing forward to watching them again.

26 – 50 points: Two or three times through has made you familiar
                   with them and you're ready to start right back at the
                   beginning.

51 – 75 points: You're an expert on Mark and the judge and a dedi-
                   cated fan.

76 – 101 points: Seriously, you need to get a life!

Index

CPSIA information can be obtained at www.ICGtesting.com
Printed in the USA
LVOW010738120613

338190LV00013B/785/P